MY
ZOMBIE
BODY

by dudley c gould

TURNER PUBLISHING COMPANY

Also by dudley c gould:

History Cast in Metal

Copyright © 1976, Cast Metals Institute
Library of Congress Catalog Card No. 76-4193

TURNER PUBLISHING COMPANY

Library of Congress Catalog Card No. 98-89377

ISBN: 978-1-68162-309-2

Printed in the United States of America. Additional copies may be
purchased directly from the publisher. Limited Edition.

TABLE OF CONTENTS

DEDICATION

To Kitty and forty years that were.

PREFACE

I was advised by two publishers not to bother to write this book. "Nobody wants to hear about the Korean War." And Ernest Hemingway should not have written about WWI. This work is no more about the Korean War than *Farewell To Arms* was about the war to end all wars. They are both about what happened to men at war — *You Tremble Body* about a rifle platoon leader and his defenseless wife.

Why should a war be forgotten that, by the presence of my old American infantry division, continues to guarantee the peace of Asia? It's not forgotten by America's fighting men — the war that wounded 103,000 American soldiers, lost 7000 prisoners of war, half of them in torturous and miserable deaths, 8177 still missing in action and 54,246 killed outright, compared to the very well-remembered, well–advertised war that followed in Vietnam, that drew American civilians to their TV sets, that lasted six years longer than the Korean War with only 4,000 more killed. Counting buddies of mine, our foreign battalions, ROKS and enemy civilians, some 4,000,000 died in South and North Korea.

Korea was particularly hard on infantrymen, 11,800 howitzer rounds one night by the 38th Field Artillery Battalion on one small area in an eleven-hour TOT, time on target; and the longest linear ground combat ever endured, twice as long as in either world war, leaving some of us engaged in firing positions somewhere across the 150-mile front until fatigues gave in to the moldy rot of bunkers.

The Korean War is forgotten because it was only five years after the largest, most costly war in history and, for a frightful year after our entire Pacific Navy was sunk at Pearl Harbor, a seemingly unwinnable war. Who, having lived through that trying period, can forget how emotionally drained, how involved everyone was, dragged right into your home, hundreds of deaths on newspaper pages daily, strict rationing, buying war bonds, saving grease from your frying pan, tinfoil from gum wrappers.

Following that impossible-to-forget war by only a few years occurred a tank-led blitzkrieg invasion on an otherwise quiet Sunday morning into the southern half of a small politically divided country in Asia. One must not ever forget this war still going on, especially when the aggressor still threatens with the fifth largest Army in the world, with short supply routes, brought up-to-date with the latest armament, most probably nuclear.

Korea was already forgotten when the highly publicized, bitterly denounced Vietnam War took over the news. When the Korean War broke out less than a fourth of Americans had television. Eighty percent had sets during the dragged–out Vietnam War, bringing the fury of combat into living rooms everywhere by the latest broadcasting news device. Of even greater sustained fear and interest, brought right to the homefront, was the stealthy terror of the up-and-down Cold War with constant threats of worldwide destruction, individual gas masks, backyard bomb shelters, Soviet missiles ninety miles from Miami, intercontinental ballistic missiles prepared to blast the Nation's Capitol. Korea? What's that?

What follows is not about nations at war. It is a down-to-earth rifle platoon leader's journal, faction, fact and fiction, fiction only in the minor shuffling of places and happenings that occurred; use of pseudonyms for some officers and the consolidation of a few sergeants to shorten the narrative while covering more action and enhancing readability. Facts are facts and they come forth uncontrived, only by the angle of delivery, sometimes altered a little. Except for composites for readability, I need not substitute pseudonyms for enlisted men I knew who served magnificently, at times maligned, some I have renewed acquaintance with over the telephone after all these years. I apologize for the confusion it might cause other ancient buddies, but for narrative pace, it has to be shortened and simplified.

This rifle platoon leader, me, began this journal in 1952 while memory was still exciting but put it away for what I felt was need for collaboration. In truth I had not been able to settle my troubled mind nor had I learned to write. That was half a century ago when I decided this must not be a one-sided, impersonal account as others of infantry combat I've read. For instance, it was embarrassing and seemingly conceited to state, as I found myself doing, even though justified by enormous pride, that I took Fool's Mountain (Hill 1179) on the Punchbowl in the south of North Korea. Although no other officer can boast of having been there that day, artillery and Air softened the objective to the extent that the press nicknamed it the Five-million Dollar Hill, before my men and I overran it.

Having since 1994 located survivors of that uphill battle, nameless they need no longer be. Together we conquered 1179 on the Punchbowl, and another one even more difficult.

Pride it rightfully is, for this platoon leader, dudley c gould, had the responsibility as acting company commander to line up attackers to make the assault; direct supporting artillery, mortars, heavy machine guns, recoilless rifles, large and small, whatever could be thrown against it, positioning himself close behind the lead platoon where I could inspire and control upward progress and momentum and assess continually the whole ever moving operation, stopping occasionally to humor the battalion commander trying to follow us with his powerful BC, battalion commander's scope.

On this particular attack on Hill 1179, alias Taeusan, Gateway to the Orient, on the early morning of 29 July 1951 Korean time, in desperation I doubled and wrapped a bright red air panel around my helmet and tied it with commo wire for there was some confusion as to whether or not we would be getting an air strike whether we wanted one or not. In May 1952, it was my word alone that this unusual event occurred, but since 1994 men who recall my bright red hat are resurrected by name.

Already a member of the 450th Bomb Squadron Association with a year's training and adventures as a B26 B tailgunner at the beginning of World WAR II, commissioned in the Queen of Battles later in the ETO, European Theater of Operations, assigned to the Yankee Division, in 1994 I discovered by accident the Second Division Association and its Korean War Veterans Alliance with a roster of survivors. Although WWII vets like me are dropped every printing or so, others, via telephone-tracking computer were being located. Only then, when I contacted more than a dozen buddies who shared memories of combat with me was I confident to sit again at a typewriter and arrange what we all recalled, as accurately as we can after half a century of forgetting.

Some veterans were of no help since they spent the intervening years trying to forget; others had little to relate because they had simply outlived their memories. A minority, like me, nurtured memories over time with great pride and retained good, often vivid, memories of the bulk of what transpired.

Example of the former: John W Glisson, Andrews, South Carolina, who packed a SCR (Signal Corps Radio) 300 in February 1951 for F Company at Hoengsong, being overrun by chinks in the terrible cold; later, hit bad on Heartbreak, spent time in the 278th US Army Osaka General Hospital before being reassigned to artillery. John got out of the Army just as soon as the duration allowed and went to work for the International Paper Company until retiring in 1988. He told me how anxiously he examines each new *Morning Report* survivor roster from the Korean War Alliance, searching for a name he can recall. So far, he says he's sad not to recognize any of the buddies he suffered so much with and would I mind, when contacting Fox Company men of 1951, ask if any remember Johnny Glisson who packed the company 300. I don't remember Johnny myself but I was in Fox a very short while and the only company radioman I remember there was killed early one morning with Captain Poston.

The survivor list grew slowly and also shrank as I was forced to commiserate with new widows, learning sorrowfully of buddies during the dying years of sixties and seventies succumbing to cancer, strokes, or overtired hearts, pining to hear from comrades in arms. We, all of us hoary veterans near to life's ending, are being reacquainted with Death, who once needed no introduction.

At least two buddies died at Audy Murphy VA Hospital unknown to me, although only a few miles from where I live. I cry for them belatedly, in vain and apologize over and over. We just didn't know how near we were to one another and so reachable. None of us knew how to find the sequence of numbers that could bring us together again.

"How Johnny would have loved to hear your voice," Mrs Warnock of Kansas City remarked one painful night over the phone. "I wish you'd called a month sooner, before Johnny's stroke; he often talked about you, Lieutenant Gould.... I'm so awfully sorry."

"No, I'm so sorry, Mrs. Warnock."

I was in much better shape in 1994 than 1952 to write this chronicle, for I am retired from the Army and after fifteen years as publications editor of a large Chicago-based technical society, retired on Social Security. I am a widower hermit with enough physical disability to keep me in a wheelchair researching and writing memoirs of my days in combat and early American military histories.

With living buddies to jiggle my memory and back me up, I pulled out the yellowing copy of the 1952 draft and banged away at a substantiated journal on a more modern typewriter, spending hours and hours on the telephone, which, though costly, is cheap research for such a book as this.

I served in Fox, George and Love companies of the 38th, Rock of the Marne, and was P&A, pioneer and ammunition, platoon leader at Third Battalion headquarters, in all but Love Company briefly, and, without adding or subtracting facts, for continuity and smoother reading, I merge G into L Company as it pertains to my journal; for instance, Master Sergeant Karl Eppler, my platoon guide of the Banzi Third Platoon of G Company during the May Massacre, by composite, remains the contrived platoon sergeant of the Third Platoon of Love. The name Banzai Third, incidentally, pertains to the Third Platoon of G Company.

Forty-five years erodes lots of memory and there were bound to be polite misunderstandings. Example: A Bobby Estes of Magolin, California, retired Air Force E-8, fellow Korean War Veterans Alliance member, tells me that he was acting platoon leader of the Third Platoon of Love while I led Love Company to take 1179. We argued back and forth a bit and gave up. I don't doubt Bobby's word but do not recall him. We are even—he doesn't remember me though I led the company that bloody day. His is among many episodes I evidently did forget, for such is the cursed memory loss in the passing of half a century. Then, too, my attention the day of that great battle was directed elsewhere than on my old platoon.

I am lucky to work closely with wonderful guys from all over the country who, knowing full well the odds were that they had a good chance of ending up in one of the large American military cemeteries in Korea decided in their honor they would put up a noble performance en route, and I have been blessed to reclaim friendship with two of my platoon medics over there, one being, before he was promoted to SFC and moved up to battalion, survivor Bill Maddox of North Little Rock, Arkansas; and one of my best riflemen, Bill Miller, retired truck driver of Clarence, Oklahoma. Also on the survivor *Morning Report*, among others, is West Pointer, formerly US Navy in World War II, then infantry lieutenant, John Fox, retired colonel, loving life and teaching college at Trenton, New Jersey. He inadvertently helped save my life with his evasion and escape lecture, although he has no reason to remember me. And there is Tom M Miller, Oakmont, Pennsylvania, no relation to Bill, a brave young private who earned a Silver Star the hard way as only enlisted men did.

There to exchange happy greetings over the phone was former SP4 Myles Carlson, lucky of luckies, my last medic. Doc recalls one of our living nightmares during the monsoon when, after the machine gunner's bunker caved in, I pushed broken ribs into his lungs—gurgling, bloody foam from his nostrils—as I used the old form of artificial respiration trying to resuscitate him, laid out on his stomach on the litter in the rain near my bunker. I'll never forget that crime, particularly since Myles warned me against it. No consolation, but Ich's neck was broken anyway, which I would have noticed had there been more light. Surely, it seems some days, given the prolonged tragedies we survived, too many of us are here to answer the morning report.

At thirty-one, a recalled reservist, I was the oldest in my company to climb mountains, dodge enemy fire, and rove the line with my platoon sergeant nights and days and it has been near half a century since I led the Third Platoon, Love Company, and Love Company itself, 38th Infantry Regiment, US Second, Second to None (Indianhead) Infantry Division, X Corps, US Eighth Army, Korea (EUSAK), United Nations Command, good guys, determined volunteers of the Regular Army, recalled Reserve, National Guardsmen and unhappy, sacrificing draftees, lined up over hills, mountains and valleys against those who 'statesmen' under Washington's domes warned were bad.

We did find them a bit touchy, bad as we were bad, taught to kill and never yield, men of a so-called yellow complexion, initially innocent as were we when we arrived, my men and I, enlisted, drafted or recalled against our wishes; forced like us to become hardened murderers. Respecting, not hating enemy, just wary of each other's moves.

So dramatic were the days of *YOU TREMBLE BODY* there's no need to exaggerate. In any event, there is enough unintended disinformation in the pages of our official blue-bound history book to fulfill that need for fiction wherein our battalion was concerned, printed in Japan, the *SECOND TO NONE HISTORY OF THE US ARMY SECOND DIVISION 1950-51* in Korea, especially quotes from X Corps concerning the numbers we were supposed to have killed with small arms.

Certainly the rear echelon statisticians who came up with the figure 547 enemy KIA, killed in action, on H 1243 weren't there at any time before or after. Unless an air strike caught them along a road at night, we seldom saw enemy dead. Although we sometimes, reluctantly left behind our dead in withdrawing from an objective, the chinks and gooks seldom did, even facing machine gun fire, for it was Communist commissars' orders, which we reserved for our wounded, holding life more sacred than losing others recovering already dead.

Nor was bayoneting and killing prisoners our wont, as it was at times with our pagan enemies, which you heard at lying bars at home, haunts of dishonorable rear echelon wretches. Although we always sought to get them before they got us, once POW they were no longer enemy. We saluted our prisoners as real men do real men, not as juniors do superiors for they never wore their ranks, but shared fear with us and dodged fire even as we did and were manly in optimum, demonstrable ways.

Some old-timers wanted replacements to think they were calloused, desensitized to death; personally, I continued to be shocked every time at life's most violent ending, the absolute appalling, instantaneous difference between life and death in the same man's face drained of blood. In two wars I never became inured to or felt at ease in the presence of combat's horrible crimes. Facing uncomfortably the hideous frozen smirk of a guy lying broken on the ground, I would glance quickly for a fast identification and more quickly look away and start talking about something else and was never one to coldly examine a corpse, especially a guy I knew. He died there for me; let him be, is there no dignity? To me, cadavers I was forced to look at in civilian life, our neighbor Mr Easton and my mother, were cruel caricatures; horrible interruptions to living. But, strangely, there also seems a certain quiet comfort in the death of old ones, an unquestionable necessity in death's termination, when led that way by the determined life span of man. Most who die peaceful deaths get there on their own.

Most field grade officers I served were somewhat older and crossed over the river some time ago. I've been able to contact two. One I knew very casually as Lieutenant Colonel Edward L Rowny, 38th regiment exec, now of Alexandria, Virginia, who once sent me a personal note of congratulation telling me what a good platoon leader I was as he stepped in to endorse my Silver Star. I was greeted on the phone by a butler: "Good evening, sir. This is the residence of Ambassador, retired Lieutenant General Edward L Rowny. Who may I say is calling?"

Rowny and I talked stiff-legged very briefly, an ambassador to a former lieutenant, after he lied how good it was to hear from an 'old comrade in arms.' As far as I can remember, Rowny never carried arms. He always seemed, since Lieutenant General Almond sent him down from X Corps for combat on his record, to have been only diplomatic. After about three minutes on both calls, he cut me off, apologizing for being so preoccupied. I could tell he hadn't recalled me at all, nor made any effort to.

As for combat buddies, I spent more than half an hour at a time on the phone with terrific sixty- and seventy-year-old PFCS and sergeants. We'd suffered combat together on the wild ridges and held it in common to reminisce, trying almost desperately to be young again. "Well, Bill, enjoyed our chat, be hearing from me."

"Say, lieutenant, how about Woody? Remember him?"

"I'll say I do. I'm putting him in *You Tremble*."

"And don't forget that ball-busting climb from the Pia-ri Valley."

"Sh-e-e-it, who could?"

Meshed with my personal rifle platoon leader's journal are pertinent excerpts passed along from the official history of the Second Division to give it backbone, but which, among other things, ommissively perpetuates the lie that our battalion of the 38th was withdrawn before 15 May 1951 from our outpost-patrol base, even though it's a depressing fact chinks overran us. I should know, I was forced to play dead on that tragic knob as buddies in two companies were viciously gunned down after surrendering. If an order to withdraw ever was sent, it got no further than battalion. The cruel fact is that although both battalion and company headquarters pulled back the three miles to the MLR without loss, we were left in the open, a long nail on a sore thumb.

Infantry combat is a rapid series of still pictures strung together, one etched cruelly in the memory of former rifleman Joe Layne, retired truck driver of Coalmont, Tennessee. On 29 August 1951, a perimeter guard on Fool's Mountain on the Punchbowl, he and his holemate were wounded by a gook hand grenade just after dawn, he in the guts, his buddy in the chest. Lying there bleeding internally, Joe has no memory of being placed on a litter. The last he recalls is holding his buddy's hand in the slowly growing light, patting the back of it, assuring him as he himself drifted in and out of consciousness, that everything would be all right, until the hand grew cool and stiff.

Buddy of ours, Master Sergeant Elmer L Falconburg of Jerome, Idaho, communications chief at Headquarters Company, third Battalion, was taken by chinks near Hoengsong, along with thirty or so comrades, all of whom the chinks released and herded south. For two nights they were corralled under a threatening machine gun and on the third day reached the US Marines. Elmer could never figure out why such good treatment, enemy guiding and guarding their march some forty miles to freedom, finally standing on a knoll above them gesturing where their friends would be found.

Contrast this with the experiences of Corporal Bernard Goldman, radioman, of Milwaukie, Oregon, taken with about thirty Love Company men the same frozen day near Hoengsong, lined up along a gully by a chink colonel, a graduate of the University of Washington he bragged, who solved his prisoner burden in a different way, telling them in perfect English, "I am sorry, men, we do not have food or men to guard you, so we will shoot every other one of you." Whereupon, the man on either side of Bernard was shot in the face with a captured US Army forty-five pistol, reloaded as the executioner strode down the ranks. Weak, frightened, half-starved, half-frozen survivors, Bernie and his remaining buddies were deserted the following day by their reluctant captor, withdrawing in a hurry at the clank, clank of our tanks.

Combat was like that—and many other things.

Most of my fellow officers and sergeants have passed on but not only did I take notes of phone conversations with twenty-seven survivors, I mailed drafts of *YOU TREMBLE* to buddies who shared combat and the in-between-times with me; who made suggestions and corrections to keep this story especially true and complete. They were Karl Eppler of Venice, Florida, retired procurement officer of Chrysler Corporation, my former platoon sergeant; Myles Carlson, my last platoon medic, retired school teacher at Joliet, Illinois; Conely Clarke, author and gentleman farmer from Hickory, South Carolina, whose POW experiences, *JOURNEY THROUGH SHADOW*, were so controversial and true, written right after POWs got home, he had to publish it on his own. From his moment of capture to release, it is far and away the best unpurged account I have read of the adventures of POWs anywhere.

Another reviewer is John Pater who fought King Company while I fought Love, relieving one another on the Punchbowl through several important attacks. John was invalided out of the service in '51 after being sorely wounded. He is now 83, living in pain south of me at Weslaca, Texas. I hope he lives to read this.

Friends and relatives of those young warriors who served the Indianhead unto death in faraway Korea, those long, frightful days and ever-watchful nights, so cruelly shortened, work hard to understand that they remain spiritually alive in an energy linked to the great power of cosmoses; physically, in atoms here and there and everywhere part of the divine force that sends worlds whirling through black-velvet space, stars zipping across our lefts and our rights; brilliant lights through our dark age of mankind, living things on our tiny earth, bound to atomic nuclei, producing vast new sets of catapulting quantum-jumping particles, forms of matter never registered, never sensed, made of yet more fundamental particles than we know of, and have departed from here to everywhere with their souls; gone forever, echoing forever and ever away, soldiers who live forever—returned to loved ones.

In the midst of life we are in death.
St Notker Baloulus, the Stammerer, d. 901.

dudley c gould, Silver Star, Soldier's Medal, Bronze Star, Purple Heart, Emeritus; yes, coined to honor retired Roman soldiers, purloined by college professors.

San Antonio
1999

1
YOU TREMBLE BODY

"You would tremble more if you knew where I am going to take you."
– Henri de Navarre, on the eve of the battle of Ivny, 1590.

I first heard tell of Korea while having my 1938 Ford pickup filled at Hap's Shell station about nine in the morning, Sunday, 25 June 1950. Korea was a pain in the ass from the beginning. That afternoon, Kitty, her stepfather and I got arguing over a few beers whether Korea was in Taiwan or Formosa, and she won the bet that it was a peninsula on the Asiatic mainland. Who would've thought it. Later, over in Korea, one of my runners told me he was puzzled too. "I done heard of diarrhea, pyorrhea, and my sister had that gonorrhea, but what's this thing called Korea?" Or, as our regimental Catholic chaplain explained: "When God created the world he had to have some place to put the anus."

As a reserve infantryman, I should have been concerned but instead I believed President Truman, that the border crossing was just a matter of policing—nothing to fret about. Now, half a century later, confronting my typewriter, I must return to Korea daily, vividly recalling mountain trails we slogged over, fatigue that grew and grew upon us like disease, days hard to supply, little to eat, morning mists and heavy fogs through warming spring and summer monsoon rains; living outdoors, always exposed to Nature's raw weather; wild, deep valleys that hid us in cool shadows until the sun was perpendicular. Interspersed with memories of this are violent actions that come to mind of their own will.

Some recollections of days long past were clear; often, however, reluctantly and unfinished until I got on the phone with living buddies and together rehashed some savage attack we withstood, which of our buddies lost that time, recalled with them terrors of darkness, sudden fluttering blue flashes of burp guns, of penetrators of bodies of guys we knew, in contorted positions, some half buried, inert as the earth thrown up with them and now I'll tell you how they died in torn fatigues, bloodied, or sleeping off morphine on litters outside busy aid stations waiting for triage, which in the May Massacre was too often too late. Blood everywhere, bodies penetrated, punctured, torn to pieces and defiled—red blood glittering in sunlight and black pools drying, gluing buddies to canvas litters. Enemy blood, yes! Blood of ours, with which we reckoned success or failure.

I recall with a strong sense of guilt and often uplift, those with whom I shared persistent infernos. Foremost was the outstanding John Pater, tall, handsome and so reckless and brave as to be known throughout the battalion as a brave man among brave men; enlisted leader of King Company in two attacks on prominences of the Punchbowl. Twice he passed through my company into the attack and then in support right behind, as at times we found ourselves bossing men of the other's company, leap-frogging, unbeatable, under mild curses and orders from our battalion commander, former 101st Airborne commissioned in the field after the Battle of the Bulge, Patton-style fighter, Lieutenant Colonel David Duncan (a pseudonym two-man composite), juggernauting along those highland hells.

Pater, my buddy, lives about 100 miles to the south and passed through here two summers ago from the Audy Murphy VA Hospital ten miles from my house, where he had the last piece of shrapnel removed from his spine and two vertebrae fused. He has lived with iron and used iron, but one little piece made his life painful since being invalided out of service. Now, although he says he must always suffer some reminder of the North Korean mountains, he sports an electric shock packet on his belt to help take his mind off it. "At least, they say it'll help keep me off drugs."

There were days when combat stayed away and let the sun shine on us, followed by discouraging monsoon rains—July through September—in season and surrealism, in and out, none in focus, bits and pieces of weather, whether you're conscious or unconscious, worn on and beneath the skin always part of—because you are always in or under it. Glimpses often closely related to me alone, that fly away and return but never faces. I have no lingering image of a single face of my soldiers, anywhere or anytime. What has happened to all the faces of the wonderful guys with whom we restrained death, guys we shared great dangers with? I remember idiosyncrasies and peculiarities, outstanding occurrences, tall, short, red face, etc., but how faces appeared has to be studied in hindsight and aided. Of all those who return in haphazard memory, closest is my wife Kitty, dead now fifteen years, and I have to turn to a photograph to remember how she looked. The deepest warm spot within me is my mother, who left me seventy-three years ago, for she was the beginning of memories, sometimes even this late coming near enough to the surface of reality to bring tears to my eyes. I wept loudly for her in my very early years; in youth and middle age hardly at all out loud. Now in old age, I cry more often again, inside for short periods, especially when my mind returns to Korea; drowning my eyes, as my brother drowned in lake water many years ago, and, on rare occasions, cry, sigh really, silently at the relentless approach of my own demise, as wet eyelashes speckle inside my glasses.

During mid-life, when agonizing at times about the wonderful young men we lost in Korea, reminiscing while having a few, my wife swore my bladder was connected to my tear ducts. But whenever I'd seek pardon for such soupy behavior, she'd interrupt, "Never apologize for tenderness; that's your best quality, Dud. I love you for that."

Although I treasure the great excitement of combat, the hurtful brotherhood of pain, as do daredevil skymen free to sail the sky today, like a bitter draftee I hungered for the day of my release from the Army, one way or another. Yet, when it came down to making a living while studying to research and write military history and being RIF'd, reduction in force, I elected to remain in uniform, a sergeant first class. What civilian work with a month's annual vacation would allow my mind the peace to turn to my writing every day after retreat?

I can easily recall idiosyncrasies of my commanders from division down. My first battalion commander, for a few weeks, Lieutenant Colonel James H Skeldon, 36, West Point 1937, had a hare lip which he tried without success to hide behind a contorted moustache. Naturally, as we respected and liked the heroic man, we called him Bugs Bunny. Later in his career I understand he had the lip repaired. SLAM Marshall, in his exciting *THE RIVER AND THE GAUNTLET,* describes Colonel Skeldon, "... as rugged a fighter as to be found in the Army." Skeldon retired a lieutenant general and lives with his lovely wife in San Francisco. When I last interviewed him over the phone, at 81, he allowed, "I hardly ever think about those days anymore."

As soon as Bugs Bunny rotated, his temporary replacement ordered that no man could wear a moustache in his battalion; what he had against moustaches we never learned. Sounded like the old peacetime Army.

"Officers too, sir?" I asked, facing him with my red, waxed handlebars.

"Well ..." he murmured, "I'd rather you wouldn't. Be discreet and don't flaunt it."

Handlebars are hard not to flaunt.

The next day the leader of my first squad, J C Rodriguez, came to me crying that the major was destroying the only thing he had to be proud of: the big black moustache he was born with.

"Is it all right for men who have always worn moustaches to keep them, maybe if they cut them shorter?" I asked the major.

His face flushed in anger. "Dammit, Lieutenant Gould, you've gone too far. Better get rid of yours too."

I stormed back to my tent and without worrying about consequences, believing it a matter of constitutional rights, shaved off the left half of my slick handlebars and went around as conspicuous as possible wearing the other half. Two days later I was sent to audition for a liaison job at division and shaved it.

I remember well the constant rain, especially the steady monsoon that began at two-thirty the morning of 15 July 1951. I lost $10 when a company officers' houseboy, Shorty, bet it would stop raining at noon on the 15th of September. Even though I was no longer in the kitchen trains, Shorty hunted me down for payment. I have never been able to figure out how he predicted the weather so closely but did find that Koreans are a naturally talented people. Hand them a musical instrument and they play it; hand them the company barber kit and they cut your hair for cigarettes or PX, post exchange, candy.

Much later when I took over Love Company, Smilcy, our combat interpreter, who never smiled and was cruel, going out of his way to stomp on little red frogs that emerged during a rain, graduate of the University of Seoul, history major, told me something that I doubt anyone in the Second Division knew. I know I didn't. The 38th Infantry Regiment was mustered at the New York State Fairgrounds at Syracuse in 1917 from a cadre of personnel from the 30th Infantry. Both regiments, 30th and a 38th, of militiamen fought poorly at Blandensburg, Maryland in the comic opera War of 1812. The 38th was assigned to the Third Division in December 1917, where it earned the proud name, Rock of the Marne, but not until 1939 did it become part of the Second Division. As a regiment of the Third, it took part in the French Campaign of 1918 at Chateau Thierry on the Marne River in July where it broke up a large German attack, noted in the regimental shield by broken chevrons denoting a rock, and it and the Third Division share the motto 'Rock of the Marne' which shield the Third Division today wears for its shoulder patch and the 38th Infantry regimental insignia on its shoulder tabs.

The Second Division was brigaded with the First Marine Division in France in WW I even as in Smiley's country it served in X Corps with the US First Marine Division. How did Smiley know all this? He read it somewhere, for he was an avid student of military history. "Did you know that Korea used the first ironclad ship in the 1500s to beat off a Japanese invasion?"

"No, Smiley, but then I don't know any Asiatic history. Hell, I didn't even know where you guys were when this thing started."

"Perhaps you are studying it even now, sir."

*   *   *

I attended a shortened officers' candidate school, a sixty-day infantry field ordeal quartered in Napoleon's old artillery school at Fountainbleau thirty-five kilometers south of Paris in the Barbizon Forest. There was a shortage of weapon instructors and being a veteran of the Royal Canadian Infantry with a Soldier's Medal (pulling four British fliers away from their crashed Lancaster on our base after a fire aboard made them abort a mission), and with two years college, which in those days was a definite plus, I was made a temporary assistant instructor and delegated to school troops to instruct weapons for the duration of that training period. I then turned down an offer to join the school permanently with a promotion to staff sergeant and had taken enough of the course to be commissioned with my class.

Like any real man, I had a craving for combat. WAACs were serving in the Third Air Division and in Italy and my mental health required that I become a combat veteran and prove myself. A real man is a man inside, in wartime avoiding the soft safety of the rear echelon. He wants to use the muscles he's endowed with; be an active, healthy, struggling animal rather than rely on brainpower sitting at a desk. He must act, not just think, do what comes naturally, not just write on paper. Combat soldiers, fire-

MILITARY TRAINING CERTIFICATE

Citizens' Military Training Camps

4

men, policemen, professional athletes, daredevils are alike in this regard. I identified closely with them and grew fearful that the war would be over before I was acclaimed without question, a man, with a combat infantryman's blue and silver badge to prove it. Crimus, hadn't I volunteered for CMTC, ROTC in '37 and '38, the Royal Canadian Infantry, 1940, paratrooper jump school, ski troops, glider pilot training, and wasn't I a graduate of the second class, Tyndal Field, US Army Air Force Gunnery School, flown a year's hard training in a bomber crew without experiencing combat, although the saying for our 322d Bomber Group was "One a Day in Tampa Bay"? Was I all talk and no action?

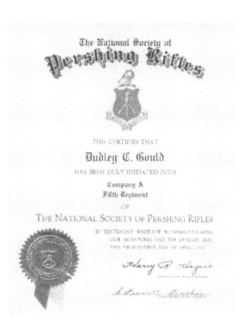

The National Society of Pershing Rifles

THIS CERTIFIES THAT

Dudley C. Gould

HAS BEEN DULY INITIATED INTO

Company A
Fifth Regiment

OF

THE NATIONAL SOCIETY OF PERSHING RIFLES

How the spirit of my childhood friend, Jimmy Lynch, despised me. I remember both of us in uniform—hot shit!—having a few laying elbows on the Woodruff Hotel bar in the late summer of 1940 and all the admiring stares we got from everyone, and several pretty girls we knew, Jimmy a brand new second lieutenant of Engineers from Clarkson College ROTC, north of Watertown, where he worked his way through with a scholarship. He ranked me but they looked longer at me in my khaki shorts, wrap leggings and proud Glengarry parade cap with black tails. American men didn't wear shorts or fancy hats in those days. How proud we were to represent Watertown in the upcoming war. Cocky? Jim and Dud, hot shit! Dud and Jim, warriors. I stole a rowboat on the St Regis Indian reservation Canadian side to row across the St Lawrence on a long weekend pass and despite the strong current landed only a mile north of where I was headed and hitch-hiked home. Fuck the Neutrality Act. We were ROTC warriors, both honorary members of the Pershing Rifles, ready to combat wicked dictators around the world. We schemed that one and only night as we drank to each other for me to get a transfer to the Governor General's Footguards, then serving in Hong Kong, and, already with orders for the Philippines, Jimmy would get a leave and catch a tramp steamer to Hong Kong for a wild night or two; find out for ourselves if Chinese girls were built crossways.

> *"Every man thinks meanly of himself for not having been a soldier."*
> —Samuel Johnson (1709 84)

Across the road, Gordon Barr, a year ahead of Jimmy and me at Watertown High, was gone from home long before Pearl Harbor and we never heard from him. At the end of the war in the Pacific, our quiet neighborhood learned that Jimmy, survivor of the Bataan Death March had, according to a telegram from the War De-

Born two years after the WWI Armistice, I found patriotism still flourishing in kindergarten.

partment, died of malnutrition—starvation, damn it!—in a prison camp in Japan. Divorced from Jimmy's alcoholic father, the news left his lonely mother forever in shock; gone forever her sole protector for the three years left.

Yes, dammit anyway! It's always damn japs and krauts to me, heartless destroyers of the happy, peaceful, simple, sunny summer life that was in our land; so many laughs and jokes and songs, touring big bands and swing and boogie woogie and big bonfires on campus before games in the fall that will never be again, and later North Korean Communists—gooks and their buddies the chinks—cruel torturers, murderers, not soldiers; inhuman beasts in uniform, fuck them all, krauts, japs, gooks and chinks all guilty of hundreds of thousands of barbaric, evil, unmilitary deaths, assassinations really, all against the Geneva Convention. And were we ever politely Americans to the enemies in the lands we occupied? Hell no, never, always Yanks. "Yanks, go home." Would that we had never been forced from our homes. Jimmy, a bright young guy, would be a retired, pot-bellied chemist now. With the depression still on, he had a job offer soon as he graduated, but the Army graduated him first.

Gordon, son of a hardworking railroad worker and a crippled mother, was last seen by a wingman trying to make a high pass in the light air of the Himalayas in an overloaded C-47. Good God, will these neighbor guys, wherever they are, ever forgive me, gutless slacker? Was I man or just a big mouth? I was, for multiple reasons, driven to prove my worth, if only to the memory of Uncle Art, my mother's older brother, gassed and unsung hero machine-gunned in the Argonne in WW I.

"Dud, don't ever ask Uncle Art about the war, it's too painful."

And I was that considerate and respectful of Uncle Art to his dying day and not until I saw beaucoup combat myself did I know it was a damn lie; it's never too painful to talk about dramatic experiences. Uncle Art would have wanted to unload and as a hero worshiper I might have learned a few things

No matter how many times 90-day-wonders have been razzed by soldiers for being greenhorns, triple it for us 60-day OCS grads with no administration, military law, supply, or food service, all emphasis outdoors where infantrymen live, on physically surviving and leading in combat. The first class from our hurriedly-assembled school saw a little combat but by the time our second class reached the front, it was all but over in Europe.

I was assigned to the 104th of the 26th Yankee Division, Massachusetts National Guard. In 1635, my Puritan forefather, Ezra Gould, fought Pequots with a borrowed arquebus in the 5th Massachusetts Bay militia, forerunner of the 104th Infantry, the oldest regiment in the US Army. By the time I joined the Yankee Division, the YD, however, there were so many southern replacements they called it the Yeah Dixies. The 104th had a special combat team, three 2-ton supply trucks with

.50 caliber machine guns mounted over the cab on ring mounts, three armored jeeps from Recon Company at Regiment with single 50's on post mounts in the middle, followed by six ten-ton quartermaster trailers for POWs rat-racing twenty miles ahead of the main body down the dusty road in the Sudentenland headed hellbent toward the Ruskies.

Having failed to experience combat, ironically after volunteering for it all, my superego gave me a severe lashing and kept it up until I saw action in Korea. Man, did I make up for it.

*   *   *

As a reserve infantry officer I did nothing until December 1949 when I was told by letter in so many words to shit or get off the pot. Commit myself; if I didn't attend weekly classes, take extension courses to bring myself up-to-date on Infantry matters. I was working second shift at a foundry in Syracuse then, building a house part-time and subscribed first to a military justice correspondence course, for which, because of absolute lack of interest, I was graded unsatisfactory.

While Congress preached isolationism, "Let Britain fight the war, she started it," I hated that bastard Hitler so that in May 1940 I upped in the Royal Canadian Infantry and here I am in the Stormont, Dundas, Glengerry, home for a weekend despite the International Neutrality Act.

There were months when I did nothing to satisfy my obligations, neither took courses from Fort Benning or attended classes at the Syracuse Army Reserve Center, and I was threatened with expulsion which failed to motivate me; after all, Army efforts and plans for us Reserves were dulled by peace, and for reasons favorable to the US Army expulsion never came about. Kitty took a very mild interest in my tenuous association with the Army and considered it a waste of time.

"All those bad things you told me, didn't you get enough of the Army?"

As the war, excuse me, Police Action, in Korea progressed unsatisfactorily for our side, I attended eight weekly classes in a row. Per diem pay wasn't high enough to attract many below master sergeant and almost all of us were low-ranking officers and master sergeants. Some would come at seven in the evening, sign in for the pay, sip a coffee and take off with a couple doughnuts provided generously by our Regular Army instructor. He must have read Ben Franklin's autobiography where he advised a harried young preacher that to get his militia unit to attend divine services, withhold the rum ration until after prayers. Our instructor thereupon started withholding his coffee and doughnuts and signing the official attendance roster until after classes.

Paid reserve meetings were supposed to last two hours one night a week but usually broke up or faded away after an hour. Most field grade officers, working or potential politicos, were businessmen or local leaders, as for instance Lieutenant Colonel Persons, AFL union boss. Most supported rather large bellies that made it awkward to appear in uniform any more, as our Regular Army man, Major Fryer, begged us to do at meetings. "Act like soldiers," he whined. In their tight uniforms were minor businessmen and petty executives, officious and self-important shopowners, insurance salesmen, attorneys, and a couple of bank employees. Only two of them wore combat infantryman's badges. There were two aside from me who hadn't gone soft in civilian life, who engaged in physical work and were therefore considered unsuccessful civilians, unpromotable officers.

I trained some weeks and then did not for several months. Beginning in 1950, those of us whose MOS, military occupational specialty, was 1542, infantry unit commander, began soon to receive a letter a week from the First Army Reserve Center, 90 Church Street, New York, telling us how badly we were needed in Korea and, with the Puson perimeter only thirty-five miles from that seaport, would we please apply for active duty. While most pooh-poohed it I reminded myself—

> Here dead we lie because we did not chose
> To live and shame the land from which we sprung.
> Life, to be sure, is nothing much to lose;
> *But young men think it is, and we were young.*
> —A E Houseman.

Perhaps my opportunity to prove manhood was approaching, to acquire the tremendous thrill I suspected combat was. Wearing a genuine combat infantry badge, I could face any man at any station in life. My foundry job, like several jobs I worked at the five years since the end of World War II, was merely fill-in while I learned to write well enough to sell, but foundry labor, itself, attracted me originally because, like infantry combat, it's a manly job, more dangerous than the average, hence more important to my ego and more thrilling.

Only a few Americans worried about how the Police Action, alias Korean Conflict, was going in southern Korea as the Eighth Army was pushed down to the Naktong river just north of Pusan, but as the news

Lt. J. D. Lynch, 25, Dies in Jap Prison

Succumbed to Malnutrition Last Feb. 5 in Camp on Honshu Island

Lieut. Jas. D. Lynch

Jimmy and I had chemistry labs in our cellars when we were fifteen. We jimmied a rear door one night at the High School lab and stole equipment. It was thrilling and we worried weeks about it. We got sick one afternoon on one of his dad's big cigars.

8

Hastily arranged Officers Candidate School at Fountainbleau, Barbizon Forest, 34K south of Paris in Napoleon's old artillery barracks and school.

became darker, my interest in training increased. In this regard I volunteered for summer training camp at Camp (now fort) Drum and struck up a friendship with a gung-ho paratrooper, Lieutenant Johnny O'Brian. We met at a local bar the second night in training camp and before the two weeks were over, after a lot of drinking, singing, carousing and derring-do, announced to each other that when we got home, although we had never discussed it with our wives, we'd volunteer for recall. Like me, Johnny was bypassed by combat in World War II and knew, as I did, the internal anguish of a real man who undersells himself.

Every night I knew it was wrong not to drive the seven miles to my in-laws in Watertown to be with my wife and baby, but each night I was compelled as though hypnotized to go drinking with Johnny and several young infantrymen at the Deferiet Hotel. Derring do, just as it says, daring to do, even if only at a bar tossing a few. The two young ones were infantry sergeants as yet only partly challenged to prove themselves.

I got to my in-laws in Watertown just one night in the two-week camp and caught hell from Kitty for not being there before. "I get lonely for you," she accused me. I lied we had important night training—stuff like night patrols, you know. Would she believe I was responding to a serious challenge of manhood? Being a woman, I think not. To make matters worse, we went bar hopping with one of her girl friends whose boy friend, Al, got banged up pretty bad at Anzio, Italy. He never rubbed it in me, but he limped noticeably and it was very embarrassing not to have my own battle tattle. What could I say? I flew for a year in a bomber, was a damn fly boy never shot at, although we lost ten seven-man crews in training and transit to England.

It's wrong to blame my conscious mind for my obsession (I think you could call it) to prove my manhood. The drive was hidden much deeper and frankly it's only in old age that I recall or talk about it so casually as a real form of mental anguish, a bona fide psychological drive or worry.

In his cups one night, Johnny confessed that, although he had made his share of peacetime jumps and wore the parachutist badge proudly, as indeed I wore my aerial gunner's wings, he was worried, as I was, and wondered to himself if he was truly, well, what they call brave. 'Could really take it,' was the common expression. I, for one, knew I was no coward. Scared shitless, I earned my Soldier's Medal, but in and out fast and was I really willing to die, actually die helping those Limeys from their burning Lancaster? Were we real men? Once Johnny learned that I thought of sending in my application for active duty, he raised his glass and swore that he'd do the same as soon as he had talked it over with his wife, whom he described as even more combative than both of us. "As a matter of fact, in an unfair fight she...."

I got only one letter from O'Brian in reply to two of mine from Korea. He was sad to say his Irish politician uncle got him appointed the youngest member of the Bronx County Draft Board, and, "you see, Dud, I can't get away."

As I struggled to make a home of the unpainted walls and second-hand furniture of our house, I reacted to what had, without me really knowing it, become my hope for a return to what I tried to accomplish in WW II, and so, in response to weekly pleas by the Army Reserve I broke down a week after returning from summer camp and wrote a letter volunteering to return to active duty.

With my first application, I took Major Fryer's advice and began looking for a buyer for our house.

"You'll get orders any day, lieutenant. They need you Reserve guys bad over there."

"Don't I know. I get letters from 90 Church Street and Benning all the time, and look how the Chinese shot through Seoul. They might drive us off the peninsula."

"Sell our home, you crazy?" Kitty cried. "Sell our home after all that separation and scrimping and hard work; you're out of your head."

When she found out why sell so soon, she broke out sobbing and turned away. "You've changed since summer camp," she sobbed, "and you and that paratrooper from New York, but I never dreamed in my worst nightmare you'd do anything like this. Not without saying a thing to me; without thinking of Dickie and me, what we'd think. You must have gone crazy. One minute you loved us and the very next you want to get away from us. Don't you love Dickie and me?"

She paused, sobbing, wiping tears on the back of her arm. "Dudley, I don't understand why you prefer the Army to us and your home; didn't you get enough in the Army killing all them people?"

"It wasn't that bad," I confessed. "I laid it on a little, actually I didn't get to kill very many," which was a little less of a lie. "As to preferring the Army and the guys, you're a woman and wouldn't understand."

It was hard to sell our house, having sent to California for our plans, although it seemed everyone was out looking. I made the mistake of building one of the first poured-concrete-base houses in the area, although I had been advised not to by my neighbor, former builder himself, the old guy who sold me my lot. Since no bank in the Syracuse area in 1947 would mortgage a house at the time without a cellar, I'd have to find a buyer with the cash. Kitty and I worried and argued bitterly and panicked and not until I got my orders in December to report did I return to an earlier would-be buyer and take a licking, throwing in all my tools, brand new Servil gas-operated refrigerator, and furniture, such as it was. Our buyers were each on the rebound and the woman insisted I accept as part of the settlement her $100 former engagement ring, a quarter caret affair that my wife refused to use and would soon lose. I was never able to afford one.

The few months we lived there we spent many happy hours sucking beer, planning landscaping and an additional room for our baby boy and after I gave notice at the foundry, banked the $8000 check for paid-in-full, handed over the deed to the lot and crowded in with in-laws at Watertown until we could find a small house or apartment we could afford, which wasn't much on a lieutenant's pay. We called the place we lost Heartbreak House, which didn't shelter us long enough to be called a home.

Not only that, it took years to enjoy what little we made for we felt sorry for Kitty's stepfather and loaned him over $6000 at four percent interest to pay off his own home and save on extra payments. After all, Kitty convinced me, we'd have to live with them until we found a decent apartment in Watertown and I went off in the Army.

Kitty's real father was a hard-working heavy drinker who never missed a day in the pulp yard of the nearby St Regis Paper Mill where he landed me a temporary job handling a pickaroon maneuvering two by four foot frozen hemlock logs from boxcars to conveyor belts to the debarking pond and onto huge hard rubber tumble barrel belts.

Her stepfather had been a staff sergeant in the Fifth Field Artillery in the twenties and mid-thirties at Madison Barracks as motor sergeant and her mother, imbued with the unjus-

Unhappy vet of the big war; Soldiers Medal and Canadian Volunteer Medal, tail gunners wings and crossed rifles without a combat infantryman's badge.

tified bias of the people of that day and age, refused to marry him until he quit the Army. Bud did this reluctantly with eighteen years service; after all, soldiers were bums. In 1945 a law was passed allowing retirement from the Services after twenty years instead of thirty, and through the years I knew them, I witnessed more than one drunken argument—"if I hadn't listened to old know-it-all. Just two more years!"

I never heard from two applications for recall to active duty, although I twice drove the 400 miles to 90 Church Street, New York City, First Army US Army Reserve Center. Both times I appealed to the same colonel, an adjutant general, who avowed that my trips were unnecessary and since 'they need you badly' my orders would arrive any day. Tell that to a man who has sold his house, quit his job, dropped out of his Reserve training unit, crowded in temporarily with in-laws and waited two months. I asked him to check his files again and as he and I both raised our voices he stood up behind his desk threatening to have me recalled and court martialed, and, like everyone who felt sinned against in those days, I threatened to call 'my good friend,' the columnist Walter Winchell. The colonel calmed down and so did I, and, like most good, well-meaning men after a foolish argument, parted friends.

"Too bad you can't call me to active duty; that's all I want."

"You're something else, Lieutenant Gould. Give 'em hell."

Having dropped out of an organized Reserve unit when I moved to Watertown, my orders arrived in December recalling me involuntarily to active duty to report to Fort Lawton in late January, 1951. Over a few Carling Black Labels, my father-in-law and I had a friendly argument over where in hell was Fort Lawton. In all his Army time he swore he'd never heard of it. Kitty willingly stayed out of it this time; there was no bet anyway, but I thought it was somewhere in Kansas and he said, 'No, that's Leavenworth," and I reminded him, "There can be more than one fort in a state." Rechecking my orders, I realized it was in the state of Washington outside Seattle.

So far, I hadn't interested a literary agent or a publisher with my several pieces of colonial American military history, and wouldn't for many years, but among the rewards for my extensive, enjoyable research—readings—was a kinship with First Lieutenant Ulysses Grant, ten years in grade, through his wonderful, readable Memoirs. Being forced to resign his commission on his first and only command at Fort Humboldt, California, because of a drinking problem, performing menial jobs for his father at Galena, Illinois, trying to feed his family, after an unsuccessful attempt to

---

501 Davidson Street
Watertown, New York
11 December 1950

Colonel E.A.Cooney
Chief New York Military District
90 Church Street
New York, N.Y.

Dear Sir:

About 25 September, I made application for EAD pursuant to an Army letter I received placing my MOS number, 1542, in a critical category. Having been advised by my unit instructor in Syracuse, N.Y. that I would have fast action on my application, I seized an opportunity to sell my unfinished home and through necessity, quit my job to settle my affairs.

Due to the apartment situation in Syracuse, I was forced to come to Watertown and live with relatives, only then while talking with Lt. Colonel Garner did I learn that I had wasted a month because I had been in an active Reserve T/O and E up until the time I left Syracuse. I received orders to report for a physical on 30 October but have heard nothing since.

I have been refused employment repeatedly because my application for EAD is pending and my financial situation is becoming unbearable. If it is impossible to have my orders soon, I would appreciate it very much if I could receive at least a rejection in order that I might obtain civilian employment.

Yours truly,

Dudley C. Gould
Dudley C. Gould
1st Lt. Inf. USAR
1651 (Tng) P.O. Bldg.,
Watertown, New York

My letter, using a borrowed rather dirty typewriter, the second of five pleas desperately trying for an answer to my request for EAD, extended active duty. I was recalled in January, denying me the privilege and honor of volunteering, because I dropped out of the active reserve after selling my newly built house. Our heartbreak house Kitty and I called it.

sell real estate while living with in-laws at St Louis, and as the Civil War broke out, penniless, writing to the Army headquarters in Cincinnati to a fellow veteran of the Mexican War, Major General George McClellan, for active duty .

"Having been educated at public expense..." he began, suggesting he could handle a regiment this time. Hearing nothing, he applied again and without an answer reentered the Regular Army by accident as a governor appointed militiaman volunteer via his successful disciplining of a riotous Illinois division. He brooded for years about those applications to return to active duty and while President had Army leaders take an active interest in finding out what happened. The second application never surfaced, the first was found tucked into the deep recess of a pigeonhole in a roll-top Army desk.

One more minor comparison between Lieutenant Grant and Lieutenant Gould was that we were both better infantrymen in the field than in rear echelon, who, in our old age, sat down to write memoirs; his, poor fellow, at the tender age of 63, fifteen years younger than me, during the agony of terminal throat cancer at Saratoga, only sixty-five years earlier a hundred miles east of Watertown.

*   *   *

The night I left, my hometown was undergoing one of its worst blizzards, going back to the cold winters of the late twenties and early thirties when coal and baggage was still delivered by horse and sleigh. I got covered with snow going to the cab, me and my old WW II B-4 bag.

While waiting for the late New York Central Empire Express headed west to Buffalo, Kitty and I sat on her mother's davenport listening to the late night radio, kissing, hugging and feeling each other, and when her folks went upstairs, at one point we tore off a piece and swore undying allegiance to each other as I formally charged her with the responsibility of missing me.

"We can get along without you," I was informed.

Then she started automatically crying and blaming me for wanting to go, volunteering without talking it over and deserting her and our eleven-month-old son. I explained what could I do. I was recalled involuntarily and we argued a little and then kissed and made up and then argued some more and, half polluted on vodka collins, kissed and made up and tore off another piece.

The cab wasn't due until 0200 and I finally talked Kitty to bed and sat there sucking fags, feeling sad and awfully sorry for myself. 'Off to the wars,' ran through my mind less and less dramatic each time. What a lonely, awful way to be off to the wars, no brass band at all. I'm risking my life for this whole country and does anyone care? No one gives a hoot whether I live or die; look how quiet it is out there... a damn blizzard. Crimus, nobody even knows I'm going.

Then I scolded myself. What to hell you complaining about? Isn't this what you ordered? You sure did. You had to see if you could take it, so don't give us that horseshit about dying for the country. If you get it, that is get hit, get killed maybe, don't forget you did it to yourself, old numero uno. And, damn it, here's the damn cab right on time.... Well, so long everyone I know. My father and stepmother? Shit, what do they care.

"Good bye Watertown, I'm off to revenge Jimmy and Gordon, only this time a different set of yellow bastards. So long Uncle Art, I won't let you down.

*　　*　　*

At Lawton we turned in our luggage and civilian clothes and drew infantry field garb and as our bags were secured by metal tape and locked in storage, we said good bye to civilization. Here we go to the war in Korea. We, a class of thirty-five recalled Reservists collected at Fort Lawton, Seattle for processing and re-fresher infantry training at nearby Fort Lewis prior to shipping to Korea. The group included a Signal Corps captain who amazed us with tales of bouncing radio waves from cloud formations behind jap lines in China, a Baptist captain chaplain who borrowed ordnance brass before hitting a neighborhood bar every night and a fat doctor pediatrician from Washington, DC we nicknamed Cannonball, whose short legs the permanent party used to set an agonizing pace on our marches to the rifle range, rather than have him fall back embarrassed every time. There was also a first lieutenant of Infantry named Logan who ended up with me in the same regiment in Korea. He was a farmer and lay preacher so we had little in common but Lieutenant Logan was to become a hero in a rather unique way, refusing to be corrupted by his battalion commander.

During a five-day delay after finishing the course, waiting for an Army troop ship, we were marched into a large room at post headquarters and handed a docu-ment to read and sign. It was the first loyalty certificate I'd heard of since the very first one foisted by the nine-man Congress at York on the wretched, starving, half-naked survivors of Valley Forge, including badly crippled Major General Benedict Arnold, who took it as one other personal insult by the inept Congress.

Cannonball, whose hard-earned practice was just beginning to grow, stood up and asked the West Pointer in charge why we, obviously on our way to Korea, were treated this way. The permanent party captain apologized but allowed he didn't know anything about the certificate. Another, an ordnance major, remained seated demanding, "How about you, captain, signed one?" Rather taken aback, the captain admitted that no permanent party had to sign. Stymied, my fellow officers grumbled and discussed it in small groups and, in the end, signed the damn thing.

One side of the form asked me if I ever belonged to any of dozens of listed organizations declared subversive by the US Attorney General. When? When could I? I joined CMTC and ROTC in 1937, '38 and the Royal Canadian Infantry in 1940 and after Pearl Harbor was allowed a convenient medical discharge to enlist in the US Army at Fort Niagara, New York where I was shanghaied into the US Army Air Force.

While brooding over my prior service and Kitty's bitterness at my applying for active duty—"running away to be a hero" and the ineptness of the damn Reserves, after everyone else turned in his, I handed over my certificate.

"Lieutenant, you forgot to sign this."

After a short argument, the captain ordered me to accompany him to the post S2, intelligence, a major. In short order I was threatened with a general court martial.

"I'm no lawyer," I told them, "but I don't think you have any grounds."

It was beyond reason to believe that a man who served an Army at war two years before we were in it, to fight the same enemy, now on his way to serve his own country again in another war, who had volunteered for Army Reserve training, should be insulted this way.

"I want to talk with the Judge Advocate," I told them.

When they advised me that I had no right to do that, I suggested that I get in contact with 'my friend,' the most powerful columnist in the Nation, Walter Winchell, who specialized in attacking this type of government bullying.

The S2 quickly hit upon what seemed a face-saving deal, offering to let me sign a statement that remains in my permanent 201 file today in retirement. After Korea, disregarding my refusal and arrogant accusation, for the convenience of the Army, I was given Top Secret clearance to work on classified materials. So much for our security system at the time when common ordinary training manuals were categorized Restricted.

In the block that asks for 'status being considered,' the form applied to men coming on active duty, permanent party officers already on active duty didn't have to sign.

On arriving at the end of the line in Korea, I was assigned to Fox Company, 38th Infantry, US Second Infantry Division, West Pointer Captain Poston commanding and two weeks later I was transferred to G Company, then short of officers. We were in division reserve training and for reasons unknown, I was selected over nominated officers from the two sister regiments for duty at division forward as liaison officer to the Seventh Division headquarters, thirty kilometers on our right where I had a few interesting experiences. This important security job with my unsigned loyalty certificate in my records made me presume someone merely wanted me out of a combat position, probably because of my age; kick me upstairs as it were.

I wrote Kitty I had the war knocked, which I did for nine days until the Seventh, the Hour Glass Division, headed out overnight for the west to block for the US Marines after the breakthrough of the defenses of British Commonwealth 27th Brigade on their west. Then the Fifth ROKs pulled west to guard our flank and a KMAG, Korean Military Advisory Group—what they themselves called Kiss My Ass Goodbye—captain took over my liaison job.

My job was to worm my way up to the Seventh's huge plastic situation overlay maps in the war room tent showing the fighting front fifty miles east and west, a smaller map for intelligence incidents, and make my own scaled-down overlay of pertinent information, showing positions of all known units, Chinese, ROK and American. When map changes were being made, I stood back out of the way and watched and listened. All-in-all, what with the drive each way over a back road, it was a tough job.

Driving my jeep back to the Second Division late one afternoon, I ended up somehow in a convoy of a battery of the big tractor-drawn pieces of the 555th, all-black 155mm artillery who lost their guns twice in furious combats. With the enormous weight and vibrations on the makeshift Korean back road, they not only threw dirt clods high into the air but such a thick cloud of red dust I was hardly able to see the taillight of the piece in front of me, none of it if I dropped back over ten feet. I know this fact all too well for I scared the hell out of myself once by dropping back too far leaving nothing but a cloud to follow. The huge artillery tractor drivers' seats were five feet higher than me in my jeep, my windshield covered over with red dust and I was forced to peek around it, which, even with road goggles, was hard on the eyes. And I had to drive with one hand, wiping my goggles with the other.

The dirt road was newly rough-graded by Army engineers and like so many in wild Korea, a cliff on one side and a drop-off to a small river on the other. Our convoy rattled along at 55 mph, headlights and taillights on, twisting and sometimes turning rather suddenly and had one of the black drivers slowed a bit too much, he'd lose his bearings and go off the road, either into the drainage ditch on our right or through the air way down to the river. Had he suddenly exceeded 55 mph, the huge tractor following might have lost the sole guidance of his taillights and would at the first unpredictable bend have shot into the air out over the river far below on the left.

Somewhere along that fearful ride I heard a loud bang underneath my jeep and assumed I hit a small road mine which, at such speed, I rationalized, spread the blast out mainly behind me. Anyway, that was the mental vision I had. The race went on about four miles and when we finally slowed, the monsters pulled to the side of a valley road. I stopped on the shoulder about a quarter of a mile ahead of the first vehicle, shut off my engine and shook uncontrollably on the steering wheel for a good five minutes. Brother Dante had no worse a ride in hell.

Headquarters motor pool captain threatened to have money held from my pay to replace the oil pan ripped entirely off, caused by a boulder, not the mine I was trying to tell him about. He must have discussed the accident with some of his prize drivers for it was never mentioned again.

Another day, about a mile from the turnoff to the Second Division forward command post, I entered a wide ford, shallow except in the very middle. The three or four days I made the trip I'd been lucky enough to draft one supply truck or another, that is, get in close enough to his rear to ride through the more shallow water produced by his wake. This time, I went charging alone over the ford until my foot, with all the distracting bumpity bumping, slipped off the accelerator and stalled the engine smack in the middle with water running over the top of my seat. I sat there for two hours while one truck after another, about six, bypassed me, saluting sarcastically. Finally, a 2-ton pulled in front and its driver jumped down, sloshing through the water to run a large hook over my front bumper and pull me to freedom. I couldn't thank him enough. He explained I had to run the ford at a steady rate to keep the water blown out of the exhaust pipe and first disconnect the fan belt. (After Korea the M38 jeep was built with a snorkel to prevent water blocking the exhaust.)

I was half an hour late for the general's briefing, still obviously wet from the waist down, and caught angry looks from Lieutenant Colonel Foster, my G2 boss.

Object of my liaison trips was to keep Major General Clark Ruffner, division commander of the Second, informed daily of the situation, operations and intelligence, and all major plans to his right flank. I was part of the 1800 hour briefing by his staff. Neither division was engaged with enemy and the most exciting matters to report were sightings of Chinese line crossers, spies and saboteurs disguised in the white garb of Korean civilians. Once I was handed a button for Colonel Foster, which enemy agents in Korean garb sewed certain places to authenticate one another.

War began for me with the Chinese buildup after I returned from my liaison job and was reassigned to Love Company, Third battalion of the 38th Regiment. Some readers may recall the first step of the enemy's Fifth Phase to recapture Seoul and cut off United Nations troops. Seoul was saved but the eastern flank of Eighth Army's line across Korea was forced to pull back. Roll with the punch, they liked to say.

Only for the days when I was liaison to the Seventh Division did I glimpse the big picture, otherwise every setback or success to our division plans was a total surprise, as it was to my buddies. To strengthen my personal account and support it with an official chronology, I will quote now and then from our division official, blue- bound history book, from July 1950 to October 1951, printed in Japan in November 1951, referred to from here on as the Blue Book, my corrections or comments in brackets—

General James A Van Fleet assumed command of the Eighth Army on 13 April, relieving Lieutenant General Matthew B Ridgway who had gone to Tokyo to become Supreme Commander of Allied Powers, following the dismissal of General Douglas MacArthur by President Truman.

Preparation and occupation of the Noname Line was complete on 30 April. The Third, Blue Battalion, of the 38th, in order to keep contact with the enemy, moved forward of the line and set up an advance patrol base [my battalion three miles in front of the MLR, main line of resistance] with L and K companies reporting minor contacts during that time. To the west of the Second Division sector, were strong spearheads of communist buildup areas, particularly in the Iron Triangle. The 9th and 23rd continued training and girding themselves for the test which seemed imminent. Preparation of defenses on the Noname Line began on 27 April as the 38th Infantry moved into position. And, although pressure against the entire front began slacking off on the 27th all nontactical equipment impedimenta was sent south. Division artillery moved up into new positions from which it could mass its fires anywhere in front of the new defensive line.

The 23rd Regiment commenced its withdrawal on 28 April together with the elements of Task force Zebra, passing through the 38th Infantry which had its First, Second and Dutch battalions on the Noname Line with the third battalion in reserve. The 9th moving from Corps and Division reserve went forward to the 38th.

Further knowledge of enemy movements was limited as haze and smoke from grass fires continued to obscure the vision of air observers. Division liaison pilots, ranging far behind enemy lines in their thin metal-covered L-19 Piper Cubs had little to report.

April closed with the Division digging into position to meet whatever new moves might be brewing under screening smog which blanketed movements of the enemy lurking, still powerful, in the north.

The Division front on the night of 13 May was manned, from left to right, by the 9th Infantry, two battalions of the 38th Infantry and Task Force Zebra. [Our battalion still on outpost three miles ahead of this line.] The 23rd Infantry designated as Corps Reserve, had its French Battalion at Hangye as Division Reserve, prepared to counterattack anywhere in the Division sector. The second Battalion was with Task Force Zebra, having relieved the French Battalion on 12 May.

Patrols continued throughout the 14th with stiff resistance encountered in the vicinity of Hill 699. Air observers, late in the afternoon of the 14th, reported masses of enemy troops moving southeastward along a trail between Nae yongni and Saojti-ri, headed for the Second Division positions. Immediately the entire 503d Artillery Battalion, two batteries of the 196th and one battery of the 38th Field Artillery Battalion were shifted to cover the area and opened fire with heavy concentrations.

The CCF, Chinese Communist Forces, a peasant Army of illiterates, a *jen hai,* human sea, endless columns of earth-brown, cotton, padded-quilt figures turning back from their overall unsuccessful attacks were spotted dog-trotting on mountain valley roads north and east of Seoul out of range of heavy artillery, headed our way, leaving thousands of dead, gunned down from the air, poorly concealed in hastily scraped graves on the fast-warming hill and mountain sides. The grim joke went the rounds: "A worried chink top general, Lin Piao, head of the Fourth Field Army's eighteen divisions, reported to Mao Tse-tung, 'We lost 5000 men today, a regiment and a half.' 'And how many Americans were killed?' Mao asked. 'Five hundred,' was the reply. This went on several weeks, every day thousands of chinks killed to a few hundred Americans, until the end of the month when the figure for their dead was 50,000 to 1800 Americans. 'Good,' smiled Mao, 'soon no more Americans.'"

Our Second Division claimed to have inflicted 37,750 casualties on the enemy by May 21, while understating our own losses at 900. Such claims were accepted uncritically by the eye-to-Congress Pentagon. At a military briefing of ambassadors of those nations with forces in Korea, the Pentagon officially put enemy losses for the three-day period May 17 to May 20 at 67,800, of which, the Pentagon briefer stated, 36,000 were killed and 31,800 wounded. This proportion is impossible, close to one-to-one, when the average in the bitterest close-in combat through history is seldom more than one-killed-to-four-wounded, as was the extremely bitter battle on Bunker Hill.

The Blue Book—

The 20th and 27th Armies of Ninth Army Group of a 400,000-man Chinese Communist Fourth Field Army shifted eastward from positions west of Chunchon in the early days of May, moving well-indoctrinated yellow men from the wide plains of China, heavily laden, obedient animals on two legs. Three more powerful armies, the 12th, 15th and 60th of the Third CCF Army Group poured into newly captured Chorwan as weary GIs watched from afar wormlike columns crawling fast through mountain valleys; long lines of dilapidated trucks captured from Chiang Chek's Army and lately Americans in Korea, and supplies on bicycles and the backs of hairy Mongolian ponies. Repeated airings of the Peking radio bragged that this time the Indianheads would be annihilated, even as the Gloucesters. Political leaders, lower echelon commissars, peddled alongside those pushing burdened bicycles, haranguing, telling of great victories soon to come, warning them to conserve their light rations of dried corn, fried flour cakes, kaoliang and rice; hardening their resolves with lies of upcoming fleets of airplanes, masses of tanks soon to support their drive.

Our men, 'the good guys,' dug in along the crest of a great rugged hill mass separated by the Hongchon and Soyang rivers; part of the left flank, with trails low down level enough to introduce tanks. The First Battalion of the 38th occupied part of the left flank, extending about two miles to the Second Battalion anchored on Hill 809. Battalion outpost bases were established on salient positions ahead of the MLR to push combat patrols ten miles north to the Soyang river. When I returned to the 38th and was assigned to Love Company, our Third Battalion was pulling this outpost duty, with a platoon from each company alternating daily combat patrols. From

8 May on, the chinks showed increasingly more reluctance to withdraw and disperse as we called in heavy long-range artillery and air strikes to blast their underwater bridges. By 10 May the buildup increased dramatically and they resisted our combat patrols aggressively. Air reported much greater enemy traffic. Chink patrols behind our lines were numerous and dangerous and there came to us a sudden flow of terrified white-clad civilian refugees, intermingled with white-clad line crossers.

From this time on to the bitter end of my service in Korea, in our rugged, isolated, roadless terrains, all equipment, tools, barbed wire, mines, commo wire, etc., along with weapons, ammunition, C rations and water, had to be backpacked or A-framed up often very slippery and dangerous foot paths from hills into mountains over half a mile high.

Blue Book states—

Harried intelligence officers at every level struggled to piece together the puzzle which faced them. Curling east and south through the rugged hills and mountains air reported a great buildup and Peking radio increased its boasts to wipe out the Indianheads. Feverish preparations were made to place the Division into positions from which to absorb the coming attack. The 155 mm 96th Field Artillery battalion was put in direct support of the Division and operation plans at all levels based on every conceivable emergency. A special Roger Line was established 4000 yards forward of the constantly improving Noname Line of Eighth Army. The 9th made company-size attacks from the Roger Line and, meeting practically no resistance, occupied Hill 899 five miles from Chunchon.

Old timers worried we'd be clobbered good this time, harder even than at Kunuri where the Second Division took 5000 casualties and had to be pulled behind Army reserve areas and rebuilt. That was November 1950 after chinks first appeared in North Korea. Intelligence told us that this time there were twice as many. Night reconnaissance planes, crisscrossing X Corps's front, flying low, returned film that revealed traffic of heavy wheeled vehicles, many taken from UN positions, particularly ROKs, whereas last November supplies of forward units were almost all carried on bicycle trailers or Mongolian ponies. Air was unable to pierce the heavy morning fogs and mists covering deep valleys that the sun wouldn't light until high noon. After the fogs lifted, Chinese fired smoke pots, lit grass fires and repaired low bombed-out bridges overnight.

In mid-May there was thrown at Eighth Army the heaviest assault of the war, 762,000 infantry and artillery, 551,000 chinks, 211,000 gooks—96,000 chinks against the 38th and our French and Dutch Battalions alone. Unknown to us, the 15th division of the Fourth CCF Field Army was to make a frontal assault on our battalion outpost. We wouldn't have worried had we known, for we had every right to assume we'd pull back and indeed it was made known that our outpost, with no more patrolling to do, would soon be pulled in as had all outposts west of us with the massive enemy thrust rolling our way.

The Blue Book continues—

The Chinese decided to open a wide breech in Noname Line stretching across the Korean neck and the 60th Army would pass through in column and fan out to the flanks in a thundering assault, hammering with its 12th Army—twelve full-strength infantry divisions screaming out of the night in a concentrated move to annihilate the Indianheads. Following them were 4th, 35th, 44th, 181st, 80th and 81st divisions. After it was over, dead from the Chinese 29th, 179th, 180th and 79th divisions were also identified.

By 0230 hours, 15 May 1951, reckless attacks by the enemy overwhelmed positions of Love and King companies of the 38th Infantry, a regiment of the US Army Second Infantry Division, X Corps, Eighth US Army of the United Nations Command in Korea (EUSAK). [Unmentioned was the fact that we were on an outpost three miles in front of the MLR.] As dusk began to settle, the tempo of the battle sharpened as reports from across the front revealed increasingly numerous clashes and focused attention on the worsening situation to the east where units of the Fifth ROKs were falling back.

The daylight hours of 15 May saw all the usual signs of impending enemy attack, including an increased number of enemy agents trying to slip through the lines. Air patrols reported more bridge construction, and enemy probing attacks grew more numerous. Van Fleet's command made ready to stand firm. The night of 15-16 May, Communists launched a preliminary attack against the Fifth ROK Division on the Second Division's right flank. An enemy force, trying to infiltrate between Task Force Zebra and the 38th Regiment, walked directly into the blocking positions of the Ivanhoe Security Force. And, although the determined Chinese pressed their attack until daylight, they were forced to withdraw and were observed moving into the village of Hachon which was immediately subjected to a heavy artillery concentration.

The attack in the ROK sector was launched at 0300 hours on the 15th and continued throughout the day. By 1800 hours, the entire ROK front was under heavy attack and all units were forced from their positions. Withdrawing south of the Inje-Hongchon road, ROKs laid bare the entire east flank of the Second Division, and as this threat developed, contact patrols from the 38th Infantry and Task Force Zebra, reaching out after beating off attacks of the previous night, quickly encountered enemy groups, withdrew and called for artillery to break up the concentrations they had discovered.

By nightfall of the 15th it was apparent the long-expected offensive had begun. Later intelligence reports revealed the full extent of the assault. Three Chinese Armies rolled forward in the Second Division zone. The 12th aimed to penetrate the ROK positions on the right then turned in behind the Indianhead Division and enveloped the right flank. The 15th Chinese Army was to make the frontal assault then split and move onto the flanks while the 60th CCF Army passed through in a column of divisions.

On 15 May 1951, the day we were overrun, hauling heavy loads of ammo both ways, it was our platoon's turn to try to keep chinks from finishing an underwater bridge over the shallow Soyang-gang (Soyang river) where I had my first taste of abject fear.

Combat, I found, is a shock every time, never to become more familiar than an unexpected ice cold shower. A battle, combatants working hard to kill one another, is always routine hysteria evoked by sheer terror and threat of harm and death causing bodily malfunction. It begins with complete surprise no matter how long before you knew it was coming. Terror to your entire person, fatal to your faltering ego, your little entirety; no way to prepare for such emotional commotion, what Karl von Clausewitz called realm of confusion. Suddenly, too late, you discover there is no preparation for this debilitating horror, the strange, ugly, all-powerful sensations. You stand, if your rubbery legs will allow, or crouch shaking, seeming naked there in a faraway land; the why escapes you, feeling you have to do with what you were trained all your young years not to do, piss or shit your pants, crawl into a hole and hide, scream and throw away your rifle that attracts them to you and run like hell for the safety of the rear, behind the tanks and artillery, way back down the main supply road somewhere where the big tents are.

Suddenly you are alone with no way to understand what is the powerful paralyzing happening or do nothing but call God, whose main job now is serving you; none but Him to listen as you beg for your life; nothing but keep calling on God. God help me! No appeal to anyone lower will help. Obviously your platoon leader is not up to it. It takes a god to get you out of this terrible thing. Call for god, if you have one and if you are Agnostic like me, appeal to your lucky stars or some all-powerful force as yet undisclosed. Then when you're actually penetrated by a bullet or hunk of shrapnel, skip God and yell for your on-hand savior, the platoon medic. MEDIC! MEDIC! God's sake, DOC, save me! Stop my blood!

Soon as this ripping electricity you never suspected existed has torn and shocked your body, somehow you must remind yourself you are *the* rifle platoon leader on whom others depend, supposedly their leader because they are even less prepared than you who has studied all about it at infantry OCS. Everything but how to control fear reaction.

"C'mon guys, c'mon, let's go!" Run that ugly gauntlet of debilitating fear, let's go! Safeties off, one in the chamber, let's get 'em. "Get 'em. Careful they don't get you first."

Approaching our objective, our platoon was caught by a machine gun in an open field away from cover. We hit the dirt; that is, laid down as low as possible and every time one of us made a visible move, the gunner let loose, sweeping back and forth to cut the weeds above our heads. You could reach up your helmet and scoop it full of bullets. Good for us the gunner couldn't lower his muzzle and swerve down to our level.

After his first engagement defending Fort Necessity in the Pennsylvania wilderness hearing musket balls whizzing overhead, young George Washington was quoted in the London *Gentlemen's Magazine* saying, "There is something charming about the sound," upon reading which, George II, last British king in combat, sneered, "He wouldn't have thought so had he heard very many."

It is proper to say an overhead bullet either whizzes or whines because this word is from Old English *hwinan,* to whiz, as an arrow whizzes or whines overhead; sound of a more modern object passing swiftly through the air.

My body trembled helplessly, anticipating a blow from what whizzed and whined over my head, a sudden brilliant flash to end me. I froze as low to the ground as I could, learning what an earthworm does, understanding for the first time the protection and comfort Mother Earth offers the desperate; hugging her without moving any of me up an eighth of an inch; unable even to think of giving orders, praying without thought as, I confess, properly frightened Agnostics do from habit acquired in childhood, unless born an Agnostic, that Sergeant Ulriche would emerge as our leader, which, of course, he actually would have to be until I learned to control my fear reaction and get some combat under my belt.

Fully frightened, the guys hugged the bottom of what scant declination each had, some old-timers turning low down accusingly on elbows to appraise me. When my brain was able to work, it was to express my helplessness over and over to myself with the phrase, 'What to do? What to do?' Not until I sensed the guys were thoroughly disgusted with their new officer could I force control over my automatic violent fear reaction with Ulriche's help as he shouted from a hundred yards behind, testing me, "What you want us to do?"

God, what a joy hearing his confident, commanding voice.

"Hell, man, you're the veteran. What *do* we do?"

"Yeah, Lieutenant, but I ain't in charge." Then having established supremacy, he went on, "Now if I was you, with that there radio, I'd get some artillery. If I'm not mistaken, we got 155s on call that can reach past us. Have them throw over a few. Give the underwater bridge azimuth, concentration one zero, first and then FO (forward observer) it back, bring it in twenty-five increments at a time. Have them throw a few and walk them back toward us, and while the chinks are busy we'll bug out."

"Git some good news on that thing of yours," he ordered our radioman.

Hearing Sergeant Ulriche, the guys relaxed, cat-calling around to their buddies, discharging the energy that stunned them, dammed up by fear.

Half an hour later, being registered correctly, 155mm shells came overhead like hot, deep-treaded rubber tires of heavily-loaded 18-wheelers purring 80 mph on a

Stop to check bleeding on way to aid station.

midsummer, tar-bubbling macadam midday roadway and, like Sergeant Ulriche said the machine gun quieted and we chogeed out of there. I mean we slid away low and got up staying low, running back, motored; our equipment jingle-jangling like junk men. Running dogfaces, scared shitless, an ungainly sight to see, holding rifles tightly to a high port, everything bouncing from the waist up, reaching one hand to hold a side of their helmets lest they bounce out of the chin straps.

Assembling in a hollow behind a grove of pine trees, I felt wonderful,

Hip wound bouncing on buddies' shoulders on way to aid station maybe miles away. Black soldiers of a segregated battalion of our sister regiment the Manchu 9th Inf.

completely self-controlled, primarily, I believe, by the exercise and, refreshed, I was cleansed of fear; born again. I stood shouting hackneyed orders, first to one and then another squad leader—"What to hell you guys think this is, a picnic? Shape up and get ready to move back. Right, Sergeant Ulriche?"

Jesus, what a powerful, brave, clean feeling. A thoroughly baptized man! Damn it, mister, I made it. I'm still alive, by God. I'm still alive. I behaved! Hand me my combat infantry badge.

While returning up the valley floor, chinks followed on a ridge and we got into a real hot scrape. One guy caught a fragment and the medic's tag—Private Perkins— who was carried immediately toward the rear with what we all prayed was a stateside wound; hopefully no bone to cripple him but maybe a large enough nerve in the hip to get him home.

For the first time I watched with interest and admiration an enlisted physician, nurse and specialist in many branches of medicine; in fact, our sole medical salvation, at work. First he assured the frightened young private that he was in good, experienced hands (Doc was all of sixteen) and would have no difficulty living through it and then went quickly to work to stop the bleeding. He directed Perkins to drop his fatigue pants and underwear bottoms and worked on two large pressure bandages applied under two-inch-wide adhesive tape to absorb the blood and dam the bleeding long enough to thicken and coagulate... no place to apply a tourniquet. No man in our platoon but Doc could have done it right. Doc Lynch was able to determine that no artery was hit although from the pain exhibited he believed Perkins's right pelvis was penetrated. Asking again how painful it was, Doc stabbed him with a little plastic, morphine ampule and helped him pull up his bloody shorts and fatigue pants, staying close to him all the way back, stopping occasionally to check for dripping blood, keeping up a running query—how Perkins felt, was he dizzy, more pain, less pain, etc.

It takes twenty minutes before morphine stops pain. Pity the chinks who, even for those lucky enough to have glass vials of raw, waxlike opium, would take an hour for the pain-deadening effect of opium is due to morphine, only ten percent of its bulk.

Blood flowing away must be stopped or the biggest cause of death in combat, irreversible shock from loss of blood pressure and circulation, will collapse too many small blood vessels; with sufficient pressure no longer coming from the heart pump, blood seeps back into the major arteries and unless pressure is soon reestablished, the smaller vessels cannot be reinflated or expanded and the average guy of about 170 pounds will die if he loses fifteen pints of blood unless given an IV (intravenous infusion) of a saline solution to inflate minor blood vessels. When Doc got Perkins to the aid station, the surgeon shot him with a syringe of penicillin and gave him a transfusion of whole blood.

If Doc wasn't smooth, fast and very capable, the guy's blood pressure was apt to drop below 80, diastolic upper count, when he loses consciousness, his pulse flutters, he breathes rapidly, shallowly, his temperature falls away fast, lips turn blue, jaw drops, skin turns a pale blue-green-yellow, and the sweat of death lies over him. God, how I learned to hate that cheap, certain way of dying.

We spent over an hour without luck trying to get an air strike on the underwater bridge. On the return we caught up to Perkins and three of his squad and Doc Lynch taking turns carrying him on their backs. They could make a chair from two rifles and a buttoned fatigue jacket but because his wound was on his ass, it was better to ride belly to back. It was good that he was lighter than most. Don't ask me why we never took a litter. Perhaps psychologically a bad omen. I packed Perkins about half a mile myself and the rest of the platoon took turns without having to be named.

This day the chinks were especially mean and didn't disengage at the big hill coming in. My platoon sergeant and I, Master Sergeant Onis L Ulriche, took rear guard, prodding stragglers, the few times necessary, for the chinks were a pack of wolves 500 yards back on a ridgeline taking pot shots, throwing captured 60mm mortar shells, getting a couple almost to us. They'd tossed the tripods and base plates to sit down with the tube between their legs, estimating range by raising or lowering it, pointing it on-line-target, dropping in rounds one after the other. They had a lot of our ammo.

For a few miles hauling Perkins, a little blood dripped on the back of our legs although the wound was mostly clotted. My over-tired brain played tricks on me, or I daydreamed, that we should have gutted Perkins as we did deer in the deep woods before dragging them out. I tried to squelch this ugly comparison but was too fatigued to control my thoughts. You bleed pretty bad in the ass, but every two or three miles our medic, Doc Lynch, helped ease him down to check the heavy bandage the adhesive tape was keeping tight. Until we got Perkins to the aid station, stopping the blood and easing his pain was all he could do.

The sun was dropping of its own weight behind a mountain miles and miles west of us when the tail end of the platoon hand-over-handed up knotted ropes on the bare, steep rise to the top; with ropes under his armpits, we pulled Perkins on his stomach. It was an 800-yard, 30-degree descent down the back side to the litter jeep dismount point where Doc Lynch snapped on high above Perkins a gravity feeding I V saline bag, and then made the shaky four-mile ride to battalion aid station.

There was a listening post run by battalion about 100 yards lower than our ridge, down a wooded finger, likely avenue of approach leading north from Love and King Company. Being on the enemy side behind a hill mass, radios couldn't read. I was told by our company commander, First Lieutenant I B Foney (pseudonym), to get a squad over to man the listening post. I was told to get a squad down to the listening post and didn't have to lead them like I did after trying to change Foney's mind.

"My guys are plain pooped," I argued. "We just came in from Soyang and there's plenty of battalion headquarters never seen a patrol. How about Major Wilkes's personal shotgun guard? It's not legal anyway, and how about reconnaissance sitting on their ass at regiment all the time. What're they paid for?"

"Want to tell Major Wilkes it's illegal? And stop crying over those guys; you don't have to go so why worry?"

True, I didn't have to go there. It was Sergeant Dorn's turn, his second tour. But why, I thought, couldn't I ever win an argument with Foney? He was a Reserve like me, manager of a Safeway grocery store in Chicago, bucking for promotion and a commission in the Regulars.

Returning from the listening post, I checked the yellow strand of wire, the right one of the four various-colored wires strung by previous units on this outpost. We'd say they could get through our tactical barbed wire but not our commo wires.

I was bushed and once the sun was down, chilly in my sweaty fatigues. I flopped into my hole. If I took off my boots to massage my feet I'd perk up some but the rest of me ached so I decided to forget it. Redoing the laces would be a chore. A rock stuck in my back. It had projected there from the side of the hole since my runner, J J, and I and our medic dug our CP, command post, two days before. We'd been away much of that time.

Beat up though I was, I couldn't fall asleep; some guys whose tense voices I couldn't identify were yakity-yaking a few yards toward the ridge trail above. It wouldn't have been so bad if I could have made out something they were saying, even the topic, for that matter. I rested, an OD (olive drab) wool Army blanket doubled about my shoulders, ears ringing from fatigue, eyes so dry they scratched when I blinked, irritable from lack of a good sleep for two days and nights, chain-smoking, trying to disregard what they were talking about—more arguing than anything. I asked J J lying half upright against a tree near our hole, "find out who's yappin' up there."

"Sergeant Miller, sir, company commo, and some new guy on their way to check the line to Dorn. Nobody's heard from them."

Sergeant E-5 Chuck Dorn, leader of the third squad, had the listening post end of a battery-operated EE-8 field phone line directly through our position to company and the Battalion S-3. Starting at dark the listening post was supposed to call in a situation report every half hour like night watchmen in a spooky factory.

Our battalion was especially vulnerable for we were the most advanced outpost patrol base across Eighth Army front, in fact by that night, the 15th of May, although we didn't know it at the time, the only outpost remaining. The Marines to our left pulled in theirs on 13 May as waves of chinks approached and, I learned much later, tragically much too late, ours was supposed to be in also.

Logically, and from common sense, one should withdraw a battalion from an unnecessary outpost patrol base three miles ahead of the main line of resistance when exposed to the great peril of being surrounded. Withdrawal, when it came, however, did not occur in response to an order, but in complete disorder, deserted after Lieutenant Foney and Major Wilkes and his staff sneaked away to the MLR, ending in a terrible bugout of frightened riflemen, every man for himself, hysterical.

Again, from the official Division Blue Book history—

A special Roger Line was established by the Second Division 4000 yards forward of the constantly improving Noname Line, and from it the 38th Infantry sent patrols which met little resistance from enemy groups who seemed prone to turn and flee at the approach of the friendly force.

On the 15th the 38th Infantry stemmed repeated attacks early in the night with the Third Battalion coming under the brunt of the enemy effort together with a Company which clung to its positions atop Hill 1051, a main anchor on the Noname Line. Through the darkness, the confident enemy masses broke their endless columns against the positions of the 38th with L and K Companies [note: no mention made of being on an outpost] fighting to hold their positions. Artillery, crashing into the ground forward of the lines, took a terrific toll of the attackers while other hundreds died in the mine fields checkered with barbed wire. The groans of the wounded, screams of the attackers and the blast of bugles mingled with the clattering roar of battle as waves of Chinese pushed against the lines.

Searchlights were turned on by the Second Engineers to illuminate the battle area and aid the defenders in locating and slaughtering onrushing Chinese.

By 2030 hours, 15 May, bloody, reckless attacks by the Chinese had overwhelmed the positions of K and L Companies of the 38th Infantry and the entire Third Battalion was under extreme pressure and ordered to pull back. [Orders which my platoon never received.]

This combat operation description contains a blatant omission. I would very much like to know who in our history section was ordered to cover for the commanders from Major General Clark Ruffner on down. Or, possibly, the order to withdraw did come down and our Major Wilkes did not receive it because he was already bugging and out of contact. Whatever, a similar military disgrace inspired Britain's poet laureate, Alfred Lord Tennyson to pen the *Charge of the Light Brigade*—

> 'Forward the Light Brigade!'
> Was there a man dismay'd?
> Not tho' the soldiers knew
> Some one had blunder'd.
>
> Theirs not to make reply,
> Theirs not to reason why,
> Theirs but to do and die.
> Into the valley of Death
> Rode the six hundred.

Someone blundered on our sad night of May 15, 1951. On our own hill of death ninety-seven years after the ill fated Light Brigade were left two rifle companies on outpost three miles ahead of the main line of resistance as on, on, on, ever on that screaming hill of death they died.

If such withdrawal orders were indeed ever issued, it was too late for our dead and dying. Apparently battalion headquarters and Love Company CPs withdrew soon after dark some time before our platoons were bloodied and surrounded.

What the American Press called the May Massacre began in late April with the annihilation of the Gloucester Battalion of the 27th British Brigade beyond our First Marines to our left. Many of their men were found shot in the neck after surrendering, hands raised above them as they fell, 1000 casualties in all; thirty-nine reached friendly lines and 830 became POWs.

In 1759, the Duke of Gloucester's 28th Foot, its Slashers Battalion, stormed Quebec for General Wolfe; its Sphinx Battalion battered Napoleon on the Nile and in 1951 in Korea its heroic commander, Lieutenant Colonel S P Carne remained with his wounded to be with them in prison or worse.

Battalions from other old reliable British regiments served alongside us in Korea, some that fought in the American War for Independence, as The Royal Scots, King's Own Scottish Borderers, the famed Black Watch, first royal Scotch highlanders that were designated Royal and served in the British forces over thirty years in the American wilderness, and the Sutherland Highlanders. Two rarely bestowed Victoria Crosses, highest British award for gallantry, were made posthumously in Korea to private soldiers.

Not long before Sergeant Ulriche and I brought back the platoon from the Soyang river, X Corps Intelligence phoned a scrambled message classified top secret for morale that enemy forces in excess of 200,000 were bouncing rapidly across the Corps, penetrating where they could, raising hell with the rear, killing and taking no prisoners, building for a massive breakthrough.

Suddenly sharp whistles came one after another over our platoon's sound-powered phone, First Squad leader Sergeant J C Rodriguez whistling loudly for attention—whistle! "CP?"... whistle! "CP?"... whistle! "CP? Damn it, somebody answer!"

"Lieutenant Gould here."

"J C, lieutenant. There's something fishy out there!"

"What do you mean, fishy?"

"Better come up, sir, there's lots of lights or something and funny noises from the hills we was at today."

As I started up to the ridgeline to the combat positions facing chinks, I passed the two wiremen who kept me awake and told Sergeant Miller to get down there and check the wire to Dorn. Neither Miller nor his young assistant said anything.

J C Rodriguez was standing beside his hole pointing north, "See 'em, those weird lights I was telling you about. Look, look up there!"

About ten miles due north, straight across a large valley on a hillside finger parallel to our outpost, piercing the darkness were irregular lines of lights twinkling in the twilight. They made the Korean mountain wilderness seem heavily overrun. As I stared, a light on the far left blinked out and then another and another and hundreds of them from left to right with increased rapidity; then they came on again, or maybe chinks, someone suggested, holding lights, turning their backs to us in rotation. It continued so fast you couldn't begin to count all that went on and off, on-and-off, on-and-off, on-and-off, on-and-off, on-and-off; on-and-off like thousands of busy fireflies. There wasn't any counting or even estimating how many; the whole mountainside blinked on and off and gave you the jitters.

"God Almighty!" someone swore. "Look at all them. What're they up to?"

I shuddered.

"What do you think they're doing?" someone asked.

There were no guesses.

"They must be crazy doing that. What do you think, lieutenant?"

"Beats me," I said. "Never heard tell of anything like this." It made me more than a little uneasy. Some trick they've read in the Bible; I thought. What kind of psychological warfare was that?

"Listen!" J C continued, holding a cupped hand to his ear.

We cocked our heads listening. Whenever an evening breeze came from the north up toward the Soyang where all the strange lights were, we heard fragments of sounds wavering in and out—sounds being torn apart by the wind.

"Chinks blowing bugles," J C concluded.

"Listen to them drums," someone said. "Just listen."

I looked sideways both ways. Eight or ten of my guys were out of their holes to see what the confab was about.

"Hey, you guys, get some shuteye," I told them. "Keep the racket down, we're trying to hear."

I listened carefully and heard screaming, broken and fragmented, wavering to us in and out and high-pitched gibberish and occasionally clanging of cymbals. Our veteran platoon sergeant, Master Sergeant Ulriche, came up and after listening a second, swore, "Dammit! We're getting it tonight!"

"Those instruments," he told us, "are looted from bands they overran."

Sergeant Rodriguez and I stared at him.

"What're all them lights for?" Rodriguez asked.

"Dunno; they had them at Kunu-ri last November after they got in Korea. We saw and heard them our last night at Kunu-ri—rice paper lanterns running all over the hills on either side of us blowing bugles and after we saw them, they got closer and we couldn't get out fast enough. Line crossers blew the only bridge on the road south and everyone and the officers stood around talking in low voices waiting for orders, and turned out it was too long. Even nurses in a MASH hospital were taken there at Kunu-ri. I took out remnants of four platoons and we hid in a gully until the shooting died down and the bugles and horns and I'll tell you, we bugged! I'm telling you, nobody, but nobody, could've done better and lived to tell about it and I led guys cross country to a ROK outfit. They didn't bother ROKs then; they was after the Indianheads."

"What are they, flashlights?" someone asked and quickly answered, "Hell no, they're too soft."

"I heard they was rice paper lanterns," Ulriche told him. "They even had Halloween racket makers; those wooden things on a handle we used to whirl in the air."

My guys and I reflected for a time, looking through the gloaming past the valley toward the strange lights wavering and blinking on and off, on-and-off, listening to the night wind blow down snatches of sounds of yelling and bugle calls and cymbals, as if the horde of chinks were celebrating. Not really bugle calls, sort of urgent, sustained ta-ta! ta-ta! Most of the chinks couldn't play bugles; they just blew into them as hard as they could, trying to sing at the same time like a kazoo. After listening a bit more, I skuddled down to the platoon CP and cranked my EE-8 magneto phone to Dorn and company and battalion all the way back at the jeep dismount point. The field first SFC Roy Martin answered.

"I'm trying to raise Sergeant Dorn," I told him.

"Hang on, lieutenant, the lieutenant's on with S3; wants to talk to you."

"Anyone heard from Dorn?" I asked.

"That's what S3's asking. Not since their second call after dark. Miller's on his way laying new wire. Battalion was supposed to send their own wire team this time, it's their listening post, but you know battalion, they shoved it on us…. Just a minute, hang on, lieutenant. I've got to raise the other platoons."

When we were all on conference call, Foney told us to be on the ball because eight chinks heavily armed, dressed in white Korean civilian clothes, were killed an hour earlier all the way back at regiment forward. "Don't tell your men, keep that poop to yourselves and third platoon!" he said, catching me before I could hang up, "make sure those wiremen get to the listening post; it's critical, we could get hit any time in the next five hours. Battalion's on my ass; haven't heard from your man Dorn or the wiremen in over an hour. They've been told to carry a spare phone. Bastards, that's battalion's baby, not mine."

I heard the wiremen still yakking near our hole. They weren't arguing anymore; reassuring each other how dangerous it was. I called them down and told them what the CO said and in the sternest command voice I could muster, ordered them to get crackin'. They stood to me silent, heads hanging.

"Sir," Sergeant Miller pleaded in a low, respectful voice, "It's awful dark down that saddle, can't see your dick."

"The Chinese moon'll be up soon."

"That's what we know, that's when they hit."

"Christ!" the young wireman swore, "they got the nerve. Got good wiremen at battalion sitting on their asses all the time. What do they ever do but run wire to regiment where it's safe. Dorn and his guys must be sound asleep down there or a thumb screw's loose on their battery or something."

Sergeant Miller joined in. "We should've buried our wire. But lieutenant, there ain't been mortar or artillery or nothing along that trail. Nothing wrong except they're not on the ball. You know how pooped your guys are."

"Yeah," reflected the young one, "unless some chinks cut the line or let 'em have it."

"If there was even one shot we'd heard it," I rationalized.

Miller, quickly, "I know there's other ways," and he and the wireman gave each other anxious stares and shook their heads.

A single airplane came over fast headed north toward the strange lights. It was unusual to hear a plane after dark, except the chink's Washing Machine Charlie routinely trying to reconnoiter in the dark, and this was an entirely different sound, a prop job, definitely a bomber. The wiremen and I were quiet, searching the night sky, trying to follow the path of the sound back up to the source. It sounded to me like a medium twin-engine prop job.

"Probably one of them black Douglas B26 Invaders running no lights," I said. For a moment I thought of my training back in 1942 when I flew the tail of a B26 B

A B-26 Douglas Invader, black for night work, not the B26 Marauder in the tail end of which I flew in 1942. The Marauder had four-bladed props.

Marauder bomber at night without lights, the pilot's windshield covered with purple plastic so the pilot and copilot wouldn't be blinded, at 6000 feet as a target to train searchlight crews of the antiaircraft battalions in central Florida.

"Wish I was up there," the young wireman mumbled.

The EE-8 rang angrily. It rang twice and twice more, all three rifle platoons and weapons platoon, another conference call.

"First Platoon," Lieutenant Hollingsworth acknowledged.

A long pause.

"Is there a second platoon?" Foney asked sarcastically.

"Second Platoon, sir," Second Lieutenant Fred Hurtz, a New York City ROTC officer, answered a little unconvincingly. His platoon sergeant was killed three days before.

"Third Platoon here," I checked in.

"Fourth Platoon, sir," Master Sergeant Billson answered.

"This is Lieutenant Foney. Listen good. Battalion says there's a big buildup this side of the Soyang-gang and we should get hit some time after false dawn. They're ahead of schedule and will have their moon nearly full. They've got infiltrators everywhere. Two cooks were killed outside their mess tent all the way back to division forward just two hours ago; they were after General Ruffner. According to Air they're pouring over that damn underwater bridge. Gould, you were supposed to knock it out." I shivered at all the bad news. A pause, "Gould, you got air strikes. How come you didn't knock it out? By the way, did Miller get off?"

He didn't wait for answers; Baker company behind us on the MLR, the Noname Line, was reporting on the radio that mines began detonating the hard way within shadows left by the sinking sun. Then our outpost mines, the few we were allowed, began exploding one after another. We counted twenty of the thirty Second Division Engineers planted for us. (See Second Division History Blue Book, p 79, "of hundreds dying in Second Division mine fields.") We had argued with the engineer master sergeant who laid and mapped our field just two days before that with the very likely avenue of approach up the finger between us and King Company, we needed four times as many. Sergeant Ulriche and I did our best to get him to plant at least a dozen more and Ulriche had insisted we needed fifty-five gallon drums of fugasse and primer cord to wrap around trees down the saddle, to say nothing of barbed wire.

"We aren't in fighting positions," Foney reminded us, defending the engineer sergeant. "Don't even have clear fields of fire, nor covered bunkers so we can call for air bursts." Fact was, we were not even supposed to be exposed to an enemy. He was suspected of being the strong, silent type because he was smart enough to keep quiet most of the time. I knew him as a sneaky asskisser; silent, all right, about to take his CP back to the rear without us.

We were informed that the mines we heard popping one after another were detonated by volunteer Chinese National soldiers of Chiang Kai-shek who, after volunteering, were allowed to select one of three styles of caskets displayed back at their division rear and were promised to be classed and treated as loyal, reliable communist soldiers if they survived. With no time to probe for the mines, they walked steadily upright on the trails to clear safe approaches; every explosion a dead or badly wounded chink.

As near as I can reconstruct it from eyewitnesses, this is about the time the Company CP began pulling back.

There was a loud, sharp cracking explosion in the air to the north. It came from the valley a few miles south of the Soyang river where the chink buildup was behind the row of lights.

"What in hell was that?" J J asked loudly.

"That bomber got hit," Doc Lynch offered.

"No," Sergeant Ulriche corrected, "that's butterfly bombs. Whole package explodes after it leaves the bomber and scatters little cans all over. They lie dormant until you pick one up; blow off hands, not kill."

He returned to his hole on the right.

"Christ," Foney swore, "a million chinks and all Air has is one lousy load of tin cans."

I handed the phone to J J Jenkins, and turned to Sergeant Miller standing outside the hole.

"What was that?" Sergeant Miller asked, "bomber blow up? Lieutenant," he paused before going on in a humble low voice, "would you send just two guys like this? Plain crazy for just two down there. Couldn't you talk the lieutenant out of it? It's battalion's job and Dorn can take care of himself. There ain't a better fighter in the company, you know that. Would've heard if something bad happened."

The young wireman sounded off. "I wouldn't mind going so much, personally, if there was about six of us at least. At least six, maybe a dozen. We need a BAR, (Browning automatic rifle) and some rifles, you know that, lieutenant. We're only commo, not supposed to be fighting like riflemen. Right? That's not our MOS." He paused, listening for an answer that didn't come. "Look, we got pea shooters," he said, raising his voice, holding out his single-shot M1 carbine.

"What can I do?" I asked. "You're making too much of this whole thing. You'd been back if you hadn't balked so long. There's nothing between here and there can hurt you. I know, I came back from there a couple hours ago and the wire was okay. I double-checked coming back. I'd notice if it was cut; now calm down."

"That's just it, the wire *was* okay," the young wireman said. "Me and Sergeant Miller heard they caught a squad of line crossers south of regiment just yesterday.

Them chinks got suicide squads. They ain't scared to go no place. Probably cut the wire after you passed. Wonder they didn't jump you and that's probably what happened to Dorn and his men later."

Suddenly he burst out, "Hell with it! Miller, let's chogee and get it over with!"

They started for the ridge trail. I watched for a few minutes without saying anything, worrying about how pooped I was and started to pick up the EE-8 to ring Foney then threw the receiver into the dirt. "Sh-e-ee-it!" I lay back as fatigue made a heavy attack on me and had nodded off good when Miller and the young wireman came scuttling down to my hole, Miller hissing fearfully, "Lieutenant! Lieutenant! He can't order us down there alone. Damn it, that's suicide down that saddle path, just two of us with pea shooters."

The excited young wireman exclaimed, "That's right, sir. Gonzales heard them jabbering down there. Lieutenant, you ought to talk to your guys down the ridge, they're plain scared. Gonzales heard chinks arguing. We're walking right into them."

I was worried. If Speedy heard something, it wasn't just nerves. For all his surliness he was an *ichibon* fighter, *numero uno*. I went to Gonzales' hole.

"I was going to call you," Gonzales hissed at me. "Did those guys tell you there's *takuson* chinks down the saddle path? Flashed a light; them crazy hombres got flashlights."

They can have anything they overrun, I told myself.

Suddenly all hell broke loose at Baker Company about three miles southwest on the main line behind us; a rash of rapid popping small arms. We heard the sharp snappy thwaps of hand grenades and hollow thu-umps, thu-umps and muffled crunch of 60 and 81mm mortars and the even, steady rat-tat-tat of a Browning 30 caliber machine gun through the cool mountain air, each weapon identified by its characteristic sound. Russian burp guns reached rapid crescendos instantaneously—heavy canvas ripping, r-r-r-r-r-ept! Salvo after salvo and a number of deep w-o-o-oumpts of Russian 120 mortars in battery and then high velocity 76mm SP, self-propelled artillery ka-pow! ka-pow! terrific velocity like kraut 88s, and our familiar 105 and 155mm howitzer and long tom cannons replying, while parachute artillery flares lighted the night sky so brightly for miles around you could read a newspaper as everyone describes it. Zipping dots, little balls of burning yellow-orange thirty calibre machine gun bullets strung outward like fiery beads, one burning every fifth round tracing the way to targets, occasionally bouncing off rocks, dancing straight lines high into the air. I lay on my stomach peering down the steep, dark saddle path and heard dead branches snapping and other accidental sounds of movement, even over the distracting noises of the firefight behind us—excited, high-pitched jabbering in a sing-song rhythm, a chink argument or heated discussion. Trip flares closer to our position began popping high into the air, especially in front of King Company on the left flank of our outpost and red chink attack flares giving the trees below a fiery glow and the soft crackling and white smoke in darkness of random grass and brush fires.

I took the wiremen back to my CP and got Foney on the EE-8. "I don't think you ought to send just two wiremen down that path. We need a combat patrol at least, maybe some of the reserve platoon. They hear chinks down that saddle. I heard them too, and they're pretty sure of themselves."

Foney, obviously fighting to control his voice, scared as were all of us and angry at losing control, talked too fast in a shrill voice. "Goddammit, Gould! Get on the ball. Hasn't that wire been checked? I just told battalion it was! Regiment's getting into it now and the reserve platoon is on its way to help King Company. It might be too late for anything. Your men know the escape route. Stop crying over those characters. I've had enough trouble with Miller; tell that coward if he doesn't get cracking and hightail it to the listening post with new wire, I'll see he gets a court-martial. What're you so worried about anyway, letting them eightballs scare you? You don't have to go."

No, I didn't have to go, they're his own company wiremen, I slammed the phone at its leather case swearing to myself, "And you sonofabitch, he's not a coward!"

"What did the commander say?" Sergeant Miller asked.

"Never mind what he said. Listen, you guys are getting on my nerves. You belong to company headquarters and you got your orders direct from the company commander to get over with new wire. I'm not telling you anymore. I'm ordering you, understand? Get chogeeing ... now ... NOW!"

I sounded mad and I was, at that bastard Foney. Ordering two defenseless guys to certain death. Nobody's getting wire down to that listening post. Dorn must've been jumped, gagged and cautioned to be quiet. Sh-e-e-it! Nobody's helping him now.

Both wiremen glared angrily at each other and me. They didn't say a word, just gave me dirty looks in the dark and then the young wireman slung the wire reel on his back with Miller's help and hitched over his left shoulder the strap of his single-shot carbine, the weapon most support troops were armed with. The young soldier had the issue M1 carbine with fifteen-round magazines instead of an M2 with automatic selector switch, single shot or automatic, and a number of thirty-round banana magazines taped together upside down for fast recharging.

"Jesus!" the young wireman swore, pleading hopelessly. "If asshole thinks for one friggin' minute I'm yellow, he's full of shit! It's plain suicide, that's all, but if you order me to go, I'll goddamn go, all right. Won't we, Miller. Lieutenant, you and asshole divvy up my Medal of Honor; hope you're goddamn proud."

"Who's ordering you to go?" I asked. "Let's get one thing straight. You're not my concern; all I'm doing is passing along orders as I'm told to do. It's not my idea; you heard me talk to the guy."

"He's all right," Sergeant Miller told the young wireman. "The lieutenant's okay. It's that chickenshit Foney; he's a first class prick. He's buckin' for captain, won't say shit if he had a mouthful; not to battalion. Probably even volunteered to run battalion's wire. Who's ever heard of asshole being anywhere there's chinks?" After a long pause, "Well, as the man says, when you got to go, ya gotta' go. So long lieutenant, you tried."

The wiremen moved slowly, reeling out the new wire, heads down, up towards the saplings to Gonzales's hole; certain they were being fed to a monster, the private bending slightly under his load. When they were almost dissolved by darkness, I caught up. "Hold a minute," I growled and took a man apiece from the first three holes. They hitched but hurried after us with their standard five grenades, double bandoliers and rifles with bayonets fixed. One, a PFC Philip Funaro, pleaded he lost part of his M1 in his dark hole trying to clean it. No time to argue, I took his holemate instead, whose name I don't recall. He pleaded he was scared, but came on anyway.

"How come I get it?" he complained. "Nothing wrong with Funaro but he's a coward. Lieutenant, you picked him first, give him my rifle. Honest, sir, I've been trembling half an hour. Can't get control of me."

There was no time then to consult a conscience like the one nagging ever since. I salute that nameless young hero, and, I suppose to relieve the pressure of my guilt, still must believe that Funaro's holemate was taken POW and survives. I hope he will read this and help me feel better. I'll try to make it up to him but of course he won't be a kid anymore.

I stopped at Gonzales' hole and got J J on the sound-powered platoon phone at our CP to tell him that I was heading toward the battalion listening post to check Dorn and for him to call Sergeants Ulriche and Karl Eppler, our guide, if they heard shooting toward the listening post, warn company and right away take the platoon out the evacuation trail we rehearsed.

"I haven't received word," I told J J, "from anyone but we're sure we're infiltrated and now company won't answer their phone or the 536, walkie-talkie. Whatever happens at the listening post, we'll try to cut sharp left to get to either the company or battalion CP. Quick, questions?"

"I tried to raise Ulriche," J J told me, "but I think the bulk of the platoon has already gotten out. Good luck, sir, I'll wait for you."

"No," I shouted, "get out _now_!"

Except for company headquarters, down the jeep trail, our platoon escape route was the best on the outpost.

No matter what happened, Master Sergeant Ulriche, RA 35968263, was much better qualified than me. He earned two Purple Hearts and a Silver Star at Guadalcanal and was commissioned in the field fighting japs. It was he who knew of what he talked who named our third platoon banzai. In 1948 he resigned in lieu of a court-martial for slugging a drunken rear echelon bird colonel for pinching his wife's butt at an officers' club and was allowed to enlist as a master sergeant. In Korea he was awarded a cluster to his Silver Star leading remnants of several companies out of Kunu-ri. Colonel Coughlin, regimental commander, desperate for officers he could trust, twice asked him to accept another field commission, guaranteeing he would make first lieutenant within a month. This was again discussed by Major General Clark Ruffner who personally presented the cluster to Ulriche's Silver Star, assuring him that Lieutenant General Almond, CO of X Corps, would make it automatic. Ulriche, however, remained bitter that the colonel who insulted his wife was not even reprimanded. If he wasn't good enough for a peacetime officers' club, he'd remain with the guys.

Everyone on the outpost listened in dread to the firefights behind him on the MLR moving relentlessly company to company up the line, from Baker to Charley. At the close sounds of battle, with voices yelling, chink and American, more and more audible under great stress, I shuddered from the base of my spine, vibrating between my shoulder blades, short hairs standing on my neck as I shivered and shook.

"Geezus crise!" a rifleman muttered.

"Oh my God!" another prayed.

"Hell's here," I told myself, "we'll be dead."

When our makeshift patrol arrived at Gonzales' hole, he said, "They're down there all right; anybody hear anything from Dorn and his men? There's movement at the bottom of the saddle, lieutenant. It sure ain't Dorn."

Suddenly a hot firefight blazed in King Company on our outpost. Bullets snipped in low overhead; those headed straight at you made loud crack sounds. Two riflemen tried to squirm into Gonzales' hole, others flattened and slid on their bellies over the ground like snakes to get behind a large tree stump. Sandy Opoulus, King Company's new CO, commanding officer, was heard yelling through the black air, "Watch it! Watch it! Dammit, watch it! They want us out of ammo."

Other GI voices joined with Sandy's and King's fire lessened; not so burp guns and screaming chinks building to a fury. We searched the hill trail under the daylight of chandelier flares, four tiers of magnesium candles from an eight-inch cannon swinging back and forth high above us, as busy little men in padded earth-colored clothes trod toward us searching King for a spot to break through. It was recorded in the Blue Book—

The 38th Infantry stemmed repeated attacks early in the night with the First Battalion on H 1051 coming under the brunt of the enemy effort together with Charlie Company which clung to its positions. Through the darkness the confident enemy masses broke their endless columns against the positions of the 38th with Baker Company fighting to hold its positions.

This took place three miles behind us on the MLR. According to our Blue Book, our outpost had been withdrawn prior to 15th of May mass attack. Not true, it was never withdrawn, brutally overrun and scattered and the more phoning I did in my research for this journal, the more I heard of men deserted wholesale by their companies and battalions, not privates bugging out but majors and light colonels fleeing in jeeps to avoid chinks, and, in our case, a Major Wilkes and Lieutenant Foney deserting hundreds of faithful, obedient enlisted men and a few lieutenants; left helpless, but for the little ammo each owned, tragically to face individually the loss of their place on this earth.

One, Sergeant Jerry Sperbeck of Utica, New York, with whom I was to recruit for three years, was positioned in another division at twilight by his weapons platoon leader with a 57mm recoilless rifle at an intersection to try to hold back the enemy and his company left without contacting him; the next man he saw, in the dim light of dawn, was a quilted stranger motioning him to leave his weapon and surrender. Jerry was lucky to survive two years of Death Camp 5, Pucktong on the Yalu, where, in his three-year captivity, he helped bury hundreds of buddies with no funeral service or word of pity or kindness, no covering or casket, half naked in unmarked graves on a barren hillside. Poor guys, I often feel for them, cast into a cold, cruel wilderness, stripped of basic humanity, among vicious, evil savages—chinks and gooks, like the dirty, slant-eye japs who killed Jimmy. Fuck them all, the whole damn Orient.

2

DON'T WORRY HONEY

The rifleman fights without promise of either reward or relief. Behind every river there's another hill—and behind that hill, another river. After weeks or months in the line, only a wound can offer him the comfort of safety, shelter, and a bed. Those who are left to fight, fight on, evading death but knowing that with each day of evasion they have exhausted one more chance for survival. Sooner or later, unless victory comes, this chase must end on the litter or in the grave.

– General Omar Bradley

I led our impromptu wire patrol past a thin roll of concertina barbed wire, whispering hoarsely to step over a trip wire I pointed to, and to pass the warning back, stepping high, as a brilliant rising Chinese moon freed itself of witch's arms, the bare branches of leafless saplings.

Once I stopped, demanding to know what in hell I was doing. Who ordered me here? How'd I get suckered into this crazy thing? Company's responsible for commo I explained to myself but the guys down there on the listening post are mine.

A terrible silence hung over the listening post and vicinity. Aside from one partly concealed rifle, the circular trench emplacement was empty. There were no bodies nor signs of struggle and it seemed evident that the six men had been surprised before they could get off a shot. Years later, Conley Clarke told me he thinks he remembers the name Charles Dorn written in charcoal on the wall of one of the prison camps he passed through, but despite our most strenuous efforts researching this book, searches by computer and telephone, I have been unable to locate Sergeant Dorn. VA could tell me only he was dropped KIA after carried MIA for a year. They had no record of his imprisonment.

I learned it was not unusual for small units to disappear this way. General Marshall, in his THE RIVER AND THE GAUNTLET has Lieutenant Robert H Rivet at Kunu-ri radioing the Second Battalion 38th that a force of an estimated 2000 chinks was coming against his platoon from the east.

Lieutenant Colonel Skeldon asked, "What are you going to do about it, Bob?"

Rivet answered, "I will take them under fire as soon as they get close enough."

This was the last Colonel Skeldon or anyone heard of Lieutenant Rivet or any of his men; their fate unknown to this day.

I tried to raise company and battalion on Dorn's EE-8 to no avail and after a few rings to my CP heard J J's voice.

"Lieutenant?" he said. "Get back fast! Company and Battalion pulled out. Chinks are overrunning King Company, headed our way. A King Company guy is here with me says there're thousands."

Red and white flares rose from the valleys around us; undoubtedly Chinese for their white flares had a reddish cast.

"Can't get back; we're cut off," I told J J. "Raise Ulriche again and Eppler and have them take the platoon back our withdrawal route."

"No need, sir, Ulriche's gone and Eppler called ten minutes ago to tell me to let you know they would make it okay and you to take care of yourself."

"Good luck, J J. I'm ordering you *now*, stop fooling around; take off *now*, we're going to try to take a shortcut to company CP and on out the jeep trail. Good luck, buddy."

J J made it out alone minutes before the entire outpost was surrounded. The following is from a letter from my platoon guide at the time, Sergeant Karl Eppler—

> I'll never forget the reassuring sound of King's 30-cal. machine guns and how I held my breath for them to continue. The Chinese hit our company in at least four separate attacks, all of which were repulsed, while our unit sat and waited. I heard noise in front of my position and several land mines were detonated, but I never saw anything or fired a shot.
>
> Somewhere around midnight I was told by J J that Lieutenant Gould was on his way to check on Dorn and the Third Platoon was to leave its position and withdraw. Knowing the trail and location of the flares, I was point man. We had to walk through an open field, down a hill, and then up the next hill toward King's position. I remember every time an artillery flare went off illuminating us we drew small arms fire from the top of the hill. At the time I didn't know if this was friendly fire or not.
>
> As I approached the bottom of our hill and started up the next, I met two GIs from King Company running down saying their position had been overrun and we should get the hell out of there. I started back to report this to you when it really hit the fan.... Chinese had come in behind us as we pulled out and were now shooting up the people behind me very seriously. I couldn't tell our people from theirs, but as I had been point, I was not directly engaged.

A sadness overcomes me to recall that hour; a strange bitterness, a deep hurt that never left me. The world was coming to an end that night and for a second I was five again losing my mother. "Mommy, mommy," I pleaded, "mommy don't let it happen," and just as suddenly I was returned to the present and dropped the phone and scrambled out of the listening post trench to get the guys going, only to discover they'd taken off while I was on the phone. Which way I never learned. A burp gun fluttered its short blue flame a few feet down the ridge. I headed away,

The night I returned from the Third Station battalions of artillery lighted the valley at Inje, throwing shells for a night attack by the Third Division and the 187 Airborne Regiment.

south, down a wild brush-covered finger without a trail and in a few minutes came across Sergeant Miller, desperately pawing at someone's fatigue top, popping buttons trying to find where the man was hit. I grabbed the guy squirming sideways right and left and held him to ease Miller's job as the wounded man rolled his eyes, frothed at the mouth and convulsed. The flare light disclosed a large goiter about the size of a billiard ball growing on his throat. Then I realized I was holding Miller's young assistant. "You and asshole divvy up my Medal of Honor...."

Bullets were zipping in close to us and I ordered Sergeant Miller to drop his man before we were hit and follow me as I bolted down the wild finger.

Later, Miller told me he disregarded my orders and stayed with his young assistant a few more minutes before taking off after me. Like J J, he miraculously escaped by the same route I took, only with stamina enough not to have to drop as I did and play dead but make it through, apparently not far behind J J. He must have passed close to where I was to end up.

Sergeant Miller's fingers felt some slippery blood and a small puckered hole behind each ear where a bullet passed, evidently from a burp gun at close range, unable to find much blood, our battalion surgeon explained because his man bled internally. I asked if I could have saved his life by cutting open the goiter to relieve pressure but the major didn't think so.

During our long reserve in June, Sergeant Miller and I were called to the battalion adjutant's office to sign sworn statements that we saw his assistant, so-and-so (I can't recall his name) dead at such-and-such a place. I swore, assuming his death because of the large internal bleeding and Miller believed he was gone before he left in haste. Otherwise, the kid would have to be carried MIA,

missing in action, for a year. This way it was KIA, killed in action, allowing his next of kin to receive his GI insurance and begin a closure. As soon as the territory in which he fell was retaken, as it was two days later by US Marines, a search would be made to recover his remains which, in his case, I doubt were ever found without dogs and I don't recall there being any canines in the Second Division.

Although by necessity sometimes left lying where they fell zeroed in, our dead were treated with more respect than in any previous war, beginning in the War for Independence when corpses of soldiers after a battle were stripped of clothing for sale and reuse and naked bodies assembled and lowered together in mass graves, or buried individually beside rough roads they'd been traveling. Only when they died near their homes were their bodies turned over to relatives and friends fully clothed to be interred in local graveyards. The morning after Lexington, mothers sent their sons searching for fathers and older brothers. British dead were buried in graves earmarked for Massachusetts' 5000 slaves. After the battle of Monmouth, reacting to accusations of insubordination, Major General Charles Lee, retired British officer, second in command to George Washington, angrily belittled the General by com-

plaining that while he was risking his life in battle, Washington "had nothing to do but disrobe the dead."

In the world wars, bodies were pushed into mattress covers, in Korea black rubber body bags that today are nylon with plastic liners and carrying loops, two at either end and two in the middle, in case of a heavy body. After being shipped to an Army mortuary in Japan in body bags for embalming, they were returned and buried in cemeteries at Pusan, Seoul, some at Taegu, and when, after the war, remains were requested by next of kin in writing, were shipped home in all-metal transfer

Crew prepares to fire a 105mm howitzer M2A1.

canisters and into brown Army-issue metal caskets. Those not claimed remained in Korea until sometime after the war when they were reburied, as was Ernie Pyle after WWII, in American soil in the National Cemetery on a hilltop in Hawaii. UN Forces dead, other than Americans, not requested and sent home, remain in Korea in cemeteries tended by the United Nations.

I fled crashing down the brushy finger and with no hope of holding off the horde, tossed my heavy helmet, discarded my carbine and pistol belt and chogeed, a badly frightened animal, in the direction of the jeep dismount point and trail leading to the MLR. Burp guns and grenades sounded everywhere in front, behind and to the sides, and hard-blown crude bugle blasts, screaming chinks shouting to one another and American voices in great alarm issuing violent, agonized curses and desperate pleas. "SARGE! SARGE! WHERE ARE YOU? LIEUTENANT! LIEUTENANT, HELP ME. I'M HIT BAD! MEDIC! MEDIC! PLEASE, PLEASE, SOMEONE PLEASE! And among it all, calm, hardly audible resignations, "Oh, my God. My God. My God, this is it," and for all I ever found out, they were talking directly.

A diabolic fury in a small area of a Korean ridgeline, our underworld above ground, its own terror equal to when Hercules hurled boulders, Spartacus defied Rome, Attila swept across Europe and General Benedict Arnold spurred his charger hell bent into the German nobleman Breyman's redoubt at Saratoga. God only knows what unsung heroes went straight to soldier's heaven that horrible night.

As I reached a dry creek bed at the foot of the finger, short of the company CP, our 105s began landing rapid fire on the ridge above three minutes apart. Then as stragglers radioed in more accurate information to the guns, they dropped round after round in three-gun salvos without letup into an impact area behind me, sometimes burning barrels, joined by the heavies, 155mm howitzers, and later, those throaty monsters, eight-inchers, 203.28mm, the largest cannon in Korea in 1951, before the 240mm and 280mm atomic cannons President Eisenhower sent over to end the war.

Suspicious of the open jeep trail, I ran up the east side of the small valley, which in more peaceful surroundings one might call a glen, and as I climbed desperately, suddenly my legs simply gave out, dropping me flat on my stomach unable to move, completely exhausted, aching all over and gasping like a stricken asthmatic with a raw throat. Scared shitless was the only expression close to describing it, understood only by those of us who have literally had shit scared out of us. I remembered an evasion and escape lecture several weeks ago and decided I'd have to try playing dead. There was no alternative but one form or another of suicide.

Two weeks earlier, during a short reserve, young First Lieutenant John Fox, mentioned in the preface, gave the battalion an escape and evasion lecture (after the war, changed to evasion and escape, the preferred order), ending it with the advice: "If everything else fails, don't hesitate to pretend you're dead."

Gunner pulling the lanyard of a 155mm M41 carriage howitzer, self-propelled.

I approached him after the class to express my doubts. "C'mon, Fox, don't tell me you've got the nerve to just lie there with them all around and pretend you're dead. Crimus!"

Fox, who doesn't recall me at all, was aware that at one time about then he went around the compa-

M26 tank hulled down to fire its 76mm cannon in direct support.

nies giving all kinds of lectures. I remember him as a bright, young-looking guy, he tells me he was only twenty-six, out of West Point that year, who took time to show me in the manual where it was written, making no effort to defend the advice.

"Don't know, Gould, never met anyone who's gone through it."

Except for rare, slowly-brought-about sideways peeks, everything I experienced from that moment until the next afternoon came either through my ears or sixth sense, intuition, which I had no means of verifying but trusted unquestionably. Chinks came suddenly then and dug shallow foxholes about thirty feet on either side as I hugged mother earth as close as possible and strained with my lips to suppress noisy gasping as much as I could, but continued to puff along like a run-away steam engine making a hill. By then the Triple Nickel, Heavy Artillery Battalion who gave me the hellacious ride, and Wyoming National Guard powerful eight-inch 'persuaders' were tearing up the rocks and bushes around me. The only thing that saved my Chinese neighbors and me was the fact that we were in a depression on the hillside. Shrapnel, miniature sirens, whirred overhead. The Blue Book explained—

As night fell in the vicinity of Hill 699 on 15 May air observers reported masses of enemy headed for the Second Division. Immediately the entire 555th and 503d Field Artillery, two batteries of the 196th, X Corps' 155s, and one battery of the 38th's 105mm field artillery were shifted to cover the area and opened fire with heavy concentrations with the kind of monumental artillery support which helped to create the so-called ammunition shortage that later was the subject of public debate and a Congressional investigation in the United States. All UN artillery units were firing the 'Van Fleet load,' five times larger than the ammunition allowance previously in use. The Van Fleet load, together with a shortage of motor transport and the difficulties of supply inherent in mountain warfare, was largely responsible for the much-publicized shortage.

41

Van Fleet authorized Almond's 105mm howitzers to fire 250 rounds per gun per day. Maintaining that rate required twenty heavy ordnance truckloads of artillery ammo per hour, but managed only twelve until Van Fleet directed his G-4 to do so and he did by daybreak the following morning.

As I lay there in great trepidation, I must have heard every one of the 11,800 rounds, the 38th Field Artillery's record, that landed behind me in an area slightly larger than a football field. I later learned that this was an all-time world record for an eleven-hour period for 105 howitzers, but because of the nearness and the massing of men in earlier wars, perhaps less lethal and frightening than fighting man-to-man with swords or the short range of muskets. We and the chinks never sought to fight man-to-man, for modern combatants plan on doing major damage with long-range artillery and Air. Only when mistakes are made is there close combat, as not being pulled in from off that damn knob of an outpost when there was no longer patrolling to do, that sort of mistake bringing man-facing-man. Otherwise, when outmaneuvered or outnumbered, threatened by superior firepower and mass attack, we simply "pulled back to strengthen our line" and at times, as during the May Massacre, pulled back to draw the enemy further from his supply base, an old tactic of Genghis the Khan.

Tanks of regimental tank company and the division's 72d Tank Battalion were employed in direct fire missions. Together with other available supporting weapons, 200 artillery pieces were brought to bear on the Second Division front, much of it directed at me. In addition were the quad fifty caliber revolving four-gun mounts of the 82d antiaircraft battalion half tracks which could be hulled down and lowered in the rear to fire like long-range mortars over a ridge.

I gagged quietly many times and almost puked from cordite fumes settling into our depression. One descending 155mm flare swung so violently in such a wide arc it caught its parachute on fire and came down sizzling loudly. Chinks to my right yelled warnings before it landed, I guessed about fifty yards away, and started a small brush fire which they extinguished.

I lay there still for hours with nothing to defend me but a grenade from which I'd pulled the cotter pin, when I don't recall. It remained in the grip of my tightly closed fingers of my right hand for about seventeen hours, most of which time I was not conscious, but the grenade remained locked in my right hand. I crawled the fingers of my left hand forward under my head and using neck muscles to press my head down on my left hand to give it weight, dug a hole in soft woods dirt to hide the grenade and

155mm self-propelled cannon of the 9th Inf. Golden Dragon sister regiment.

my right hand under my head. I slowly pulled up my right leg in an awkward position as I imagined a dead man might appear and then remembered I had written down the code, HOT CARBINE, for the grids on our 1:50,000 combat maps, one through ten, H being numeral one, O two, T three and so on, and very slowly worked it with my left hand out of my inner jacket pocket to wad it and push it under the grenade in my hidden right hand. Even slight movements were risky and I felt enormously proud of myself.

At one point I made up a joke, "the next war I'm invited to, I'm hiring a stunt man like they do for John Wayne and those other big movie heroes."

In the record-breaking cannonading that followed, VT and proximity shells burst in the air to send large hunks of shrapnel thudding into the ground around me and once during the long night, one chink cried out in pain. "Good," I thought, "hit him again." Countless light and heavy artillery flares swung back and forth in the sky, which I clearly experienced through half buried, closed eyelids but mainly through their sizzling noises as they descended. A number were chandelier flares exposing all about me, throwing long, dark, shaking shadows of trees and boulders as they swayed back and forth above, sizzling loudly. I was further lighted by the full Chinese moon and I learned later a C-47 Firefly made several passes dropping huge parachute flares whose wide canopies allowed fifteen minutes of brilliant 1,000,000 K candlepower turning night into day. I heard it passing over but had no inkling what it was doing, hoping whatever it was it wouldn't bomb me.

I sensed from a rustling sound and an angry exclamation in Chinese from what was apparently a leader, that a scavenger was scooting over to me. In my fear fantasy I seemed to actually see the soldier as he quickly yanked the watch from my limp, exposed left wrist without changing my position. I thanked my lucky stars I wore a loose expansion bracelet. The scavenger's leader hissed at him and the man hesitated as he gave me a push with one foot meaning to roll me over, I suppose, for my wallet. My body was halfway up and I had to use poorly responsive muscles to cause it to drop slowly back. I didn't worry about the whiteness of my face for I'd smeared it well with black woods dirt and it was half buried. His squad leader spoke in an authoritative voice and the looter replied a few rapid words in Chinese, and returned. I felt confident then that I was doing a good job of pretending.

I tried to think of ideas to make me look more like a dead man. Unfortunately, a rock pressed against my bladder and I had to piss badly for several hours and tried constantly to put it out of mind. A frightened young man ran down the rocks of the dry creek bed below yelling, "Sarge, sarge, you said you'd wait. Where are you? You didn't let me know. They got Bob. Bob's dead, sarge…. Hey, sarge, where are you guys?" Chinks jabbered and answered b-r-r-r-rpt! b-r-r-r-rpt! to his cry, and he was heard no longer. I learned that the vanguard sweeping through us were ordered not to take prisoners, they didn't have the wherewithal to feed or guard us.

I had to piss so badly tears came to my eyes. The night air grew chilly as I agonized about having to take a piss with no hope of relief. I had to go so badly my bladder ached. I considered digging a hole down there for it but knew there would be too many movements of my body to a watchful chink.

An authoritative loud voice sounded off below and behind me, evidently on a radio, distracting me momentarily: "Hey, you guys, for Christ's sake lift the damn stuff. You're killing us. This is Lieutenant Baker. I repeat, Bill Baker. Lift the damn artillery. It's smack on top of us. Lift the stuff; the chinks have gone; you're killing your own men. Lift the stuff!"

Damn traitor, I thought.

As though it quit me with the theft of my watch, I lost all understanding of time. Soon the need to piss was my total concern; tears dropped from my eyes; never had I disregarded the need so long and suddenly I chuckled quietly to myself: "Here in your own graveyard afraid to piss your pants," and so let it go. Letting it go out of control wasn't that easy and it shut off automatically several times, not consciously for fear of making a mess, but because I'd been trained long ago not to pee my pants. The hot liquid flowed unpleasantly around the upper parts of my thighs and made me uncomfortable, dirty and guilty and as the temperature cooled, more uncomfortable because of it.

I began to catalog the pains, fears and miseries that beset me inside and out and I lay in constant dread of the curious chink's return the night of my baptismal of fire. I felt a terrible pity for the deserted young man they murdered down behind me. Even in war, how can they be so callous? Or are they hop heads? Doc Lynch, our medic, once showed me a little glass vial of waxlike lumps some of their riflemen carried. Just knowing they had opium gave us the willies, feeding rumors that this is why they are so wild when they attack and scream and yell, forgetting we did the same. They were fanatic little devils, as our 9th Infantry, sister regiment, the Manchus, found out during the Boxer Rebellion.

At what I guessed from the lessened intensity or angle of the Chinese moon whose light I sensed was about four-thirty in the morning, I raised my head slowly, deciding I couldn't take fear any longer, there'd be no happy end no matter what and I was convinced the chinks were there to stay; why extend myself for their ultimate pleasure? If this is where I'm supposed to die, so be it; I will fear no longer. No reason to hang on miserably in the short time left, better die a soldier than prolong what would most certainly be my life's end when the light of day came.

The thought of being POW frightened me even in civilian life and I know I could never survive it, any more than I could visualize without dread being a sailor drowning at sea or an airman falling from the sky, an old familiar fear. I fretted that the sun would be up in a couple of hours and they'd see me for sure and the guy who got my watch, or one of his buddies, would roll me all the way over for my wallet and see the grenade in my hand and finish me off, lying there entirely helpless—hopelessly helpless. Better the end be my doing.

I was conscious of that grenade for the first time all night and tried to remember if I'd pulled the ring. Something told me to be careful in case I had. Fingers that held it were unable to stretch to an open position. All this time I held down the spring handle mainly by the weight of my head resting on my tight hand grip and now felt nothing in that hand. I could sense that my cocked leg was asleep, also without the usual prickling feeling; certainly, I thought, my right hand was past prickling. I would flex the muscles in my legs from the inside and get blood flowing and work all my muscles from inside without outward movement, working them from inside to get blood circulating, smear dirt again ever so slowly over my head and face for more camouflage, crawl slowly to get close as possible to the bastards on my right, then jump up, toss the grenade in the middle and scramble on hands and knees to the ridge trail above. Should the shock be enough, I might possibly make it. Fortunately, the Chinese moon had set behind the ridge, flares were no longer falling and the shadows were dark in our little woods.

My legs balked at such unexpected duty. Let's break them in more slowly, I told myself. By knowledge garnered by my ears I knew that chinks were passing intermittently all night in groups along the ridge about forty feet above and I'd be damn lucky not to get it before I made ten feet. Nevertheless, call it a death wish if you will, I decided to go and was flexing muscles internally preparing to move when Kitty, a bold, glowing vision in color, came floating, a shimmering icon as I'd seen of Jesus along country roadsides in Czechoslovakia in WWII. Just head and shoulders. My face buried, I saw her through the top of my head.

I married Kitty three weeks after returning from four years away from home, not counting two years Canadian Army time, a year bomber training in Florida without a pass long enough to get home by the fastest train, and three years to the day in 1945 in Africa, England and Europe. At the ripe age of twenty-six, I imagined my hair was falling out (my father was partially bald at twenty), I was fast becoming an old man; I must get married while I had a chance to attract someone pretty. The longer overseas the more I yearned for American women. Sex over there, few and far between, was too often unsatisfying.

On sight, Kitty was the one and only for me. She was nineteen, high spirited like no girl I'd seen overseas, at odds with her mother and stepfather and as eager as I to marry someone and start a family. Besides, she often told me, I was her hero, the most manly guy she'd ever met and an officer. Aside from all practical reasons, we were hopelessly in love, head-over-heels in a hurry in less than a week.

We eloped wearing fifty-dollar wedding rings. Only her mother and stepfather, sister and brother-in-law, stood with us, my father having disowned me in so many words for at least the second time, "running off like a damn fool to join the Canadian Army, getting married instead of returning to college now it's free."

Kitty came down to me as an icon that troubled night, her hair worn down to her shoulders as she appeared our first week together, after which she had it cut shorter and always wore it very becomingly up in back.

Through the top of my head I watched her floating down from the ridge, so realistic I worried the chinks would shoot her. She shimmered slowly below me out of 'sight' and after I believed her gone, stroked the back of my head tenderly and said soothingly: "Don't worry, honey, everything will be all right," and vanished, or melted away.

I immediately fell into what I can describe only as a coma—somehow initially revisiting the horrible reality of the week of my mother's death when I was five. I cried hard that terrible time her casket was wheeled into our parlor, before my father told me sentimentality was wrong, weakening the mind, leaving it more vulnerable to pain. He told me that sentimentality is not felt by lower animals nor hard-working, honest, primitive people, who, in their miserable lives, face death young and frequently and do not have the luxury to dream while awake; not those busy with constant grief and danger, but when I tried to act blasé about her death it wouldn't work. Later he explained he was so rough with me (today, tough love) to prepare me for her death. I recall, however, after I'd gone to bed that night he kissed me and told me she was gone and not to cry and every night for a week from the big bedroom came my father's heart-wrenching sobs of self-pity.

I was not ready for her death from her old adversary tuberculosis. Not science, intelligence, learning, experience, nor religion, can prepare one for such a nightmare of grief. Even forewarned, nobody can be ready for this shock; no lecture, no religion, no prepared consolation, none but bitter, numbing, first-hand shock leading to absolute despair. With no history of death in your mind, it's the worst shock there is. No matter when, it stuns you. We feel and try terribly hard but never understand. We know death for the first time when it puts its hand upon the one we love.

Death of loved ones is unreasonable—impossible to explain. Soothing words of philosophy, theology or plain common sense are but bla-bla-bla. As love is the most creative force, it's abrupt loss is the most destructive.

> *She's dead; when thou know'st this*
> *Thou know'st how dry a cinder is.*
> – John Donne

> *One can no more look steadily at death than at the sun.*
> – Francois Duc de la Rochefoucauld (1603-80)

A single person gone from me, my mother, emptied the whole world. Why did I have to live on? Her lying dead above me in her casket in the parlor with the dead, dead flowers; how horribly I remember shuddering with the world suddenly gone cold. Sobbing uncontrollable spasms, gulping for air, agonizing cries for my father to bring her back, as from a far corner of my bedroom I began in a whimper, ending in fatigue, wailing like a beaten dog begging and for years I *was* an abandoned puppy, running head down a lonesome road at dusk, always at dusk, nowhere, her death left me so inferior.

I woke from my coma, or whatever, as suddenly as it came, sometime in the afternoon. My ears told me I was alone and I slowly, cautiously lifted my head to make certain with my eyes. The chinks were gone all right and I learned later that even before first light this crack assault unit and many thousands of their swarm had dogtrotted east to cave in the Fifth ROKs. I stood slowly, looking around and, listening carefully, with my movable hand massaged my right thigh and leg, which at first collapsed as I put weight to them, and drew myself up again favoring that side, stumbling uphill until the leg and thigh finally worked.

On the ridgetop a few yards overlooking my platoon's withdrawal route, I saw a large lump of fatigues on a litter, an image I'll never be free of. Another soldier, half sitting, slumped forward on the ground beside the man on the litter. In one agonizing flash, my spirit cried out, "God make them alive." For a long moment I stood staring transfixed at the pitiful scene; a badly wounded man, perhaps bleeding his life away and by now certainly dead, being carried on a litter by a wounded man now slumped and also apparently dead, or would soon be that way, and I thought of another soldier, missing, who obviously left his buddies at the collapse of the other carrier, took off running to save himself.

It was too far to be sure but I believed, because my platoon among others must have passed this way, that at least I might be able to identify these guys. As I turned to go over to check if there was life left in either of them, I was shot at by a small chink patrol coming up the trail behind. I took off, crazed, a wild thing, down across a winter highland wheat field toward the jeep trail, hurling myself through the air like a drunken acrobat, down a plowed hillside, each leap forward landing me many feet down the steep slope. I did not count the times I was shot at until I was able to slide to my right into a bushy gully and get behind rock formations.

When I got down to the jeep trail, I could hear them jabbering somewhere above me but at no time did I see them. I ran pell mell into my second wind and loped easily, thanking my legs for saving me, three miles to the MLR. As I approached M Company's barbed wire concertina rolls across the jeep trail, I was shot at by a trigger-happy guy who was immediately admonished, "Don't shoot, he might be GI." I had a short crewcut, about half an inch and with wood dirt smeared over my face and head must have resembled a wild man. I yelled the only thing that came to mind: "It's me! Don't shoot, it's me! It's me! It's me!" A soldier came forward to separate the concertina as another man yelled, "Is there a pin in that grenade? Get rid of that grenade!" For the first time in hours I was aware of it in my seemingly frozen right hand. I saw the ring was gone and all I had to do to arm it was to let go of the handle. I tried to get my fingers to open by themselves to throw it in the stream that ran to the right of the trail but they refused to move and I twisted my whole torso facing away from the stream to move my entire right arm and shoulder back, keeping it straight at the elbow as far as it could go through an arc and like a discus thrower swung the grenade sideways, centrifugal force taking the heavy grenade from my fingers through the air into a pool of the stream that flowed by the jeep trail. As guys manning the roadblock scurried for cover, I stood watching it blow up a small geyser.

Safe among my own, I began to quiver all over and laugh uncontrollably, and shudder deeply, then suddenly sob loudly, pitifully, like a badly hurt child, changing back and forth that way, laughing and crying, my emotions gone wild—laughing and crying, laughing and crying and sobbing. Captain George Brownell, a big guy, put his arm around my shoulder and escorted me to his jeep, saying all the while, "C'mon, buddy. Now c'mon, buddy, you're out of it now, buddy. Get hold of yourself, lieutenant. C'mon now." To a sergeant staring at me, "He's hysterical, out of control."

I was the last man to get off the outpost alive and Brownell drove me six miles to the door of the large squad tent that was the 38th regimental forward CP and war room, and ushered me inside to be debriefed by General Ruffner, Colonel Coughlin and two full birds from X Corps. After answering several questions and blabbing the little I knew of interest to them, and being escorted away by a major, I recalled the traitor in the middle of the night trying to lift our artillery. Ruffner had his back to me talking to the colonels as I rushed back, grabbed his shoulder and spun him around. He was built solid, an all-American lineman at VMI, Virginia Military Institute. Fortunately, my anxiety was quite obvious.

"Baker's turned traitor," I told him. "Lieutenant Baker, Bill Baker, kept yelling over the radio, 'lift the artillery ... lift the artillery!'"

General Ruffner gave a cold stare and ordered me to get hold of myself. "Calm down, lieutenant. We've checked that out. There was no Lieutenant Baker up there but they've got plenty of intelligence officers educated in the States. Had a Lieutenant Baker's tags."

Other escapees had been debriefed before me and the Baker incident noted.

Remembering how I, at some risk of being seen to move, had protected our top secret map coordinate code, I explained proudly how I risked my life burying it. "They'd never learn our secret code from me." The general was annoyed rather than pleased and reminding me, "*Gould,* those codes are changed every day," and gave a hand sign for the major to move me out.

Ruffner made a searching second look as I turned, glancing at my still wet pants, perhaps recalling the fact that, for a short while the previous month, I gave part of his daily briefing, perhaps linking my piss wet pants then with how wet they were after that incident at the ford sitting in my stalled jeep. If he did, he failed to acknowledge it. I was just as happy that the general chose not to recognize me, for late one dark, rainy afternoon, relieving myself before the briefing, daydreaming about how important I was associating with the brass, in turning quickly, shaking off the drops, I bumped smack into him. I was using what, unbeknown to me, was the commanding general's private piss tube, an empty 155mm cardboard shell container slanted into the ground with small stones and a sprinkle of lime around the base. Next morning, Lieutenant Colonel Foster warned the enlisted staff as he stared over at me, that someone illegally used the general's private pissoir, almost knocked him down.

Lower ranks I passed by at regiment seemed properly awed and I overheard an observant PFC say respectfully, "That's the last guy to escape from the outpost!"

I was anxious to reach Love company and find out if the rest of my guys made it. Again the man prone on the litter and the pathetic shape of the one half-sitting beside the litter revisited me, as it has many times over the years. Was either of them alive; could I have saved one? Of course not, but my conscience was never reasonable.

I was escorted to the transient officers' mess tent where I gulped down what the mess sergeant handed me on a tray, and leaned over outside and violently released it. On the way to where they said Love was, I spied a form I recognized from the rear, chubby Father Carl Carrol (having left the priesthood, now married and living in Roswell, Georgia), one of our regimental chaplains. He was stepping his way carefully flat rock to flat rock over a makeshift ford and, splashing through the foot-deep stream, I grabbed his elbow and blurted: "Boy, have I got religion now."

He turned trying to recognize me, which he never had any reason to do.

"Good," he said. "I'm holding a special mass in half an hour, although most have already left."

"Oh, no," I told him, "I'm Agnostic."

I hadn't attended church or Sunday School willingly since my mother died. When I was little, my mother had me kneel by my bed every night to recite after her—

> Now I lay me down to sleep,
> I pray the Lord my soul to keep.
> If I should die before I wake,
> I pray the Lord my soul to take.

... and bless mommy and daddy and grandma and grandpa Gould and grandma and grandpa Weideman and uncles Art, Herbie, George and Leo and aunts Greta, Helen and Bertha and great aunt Nelli who's up in heaven now, God bless her soul, and the Reverend Doctor Stokes, and the poor Italian kids on the Sand Flats less fortunate than me ..." and when my mother learned of destitute people anywhere, she included them in my monotonous supplication. I particularly remember blessing starving Chinese.

The simple quatrain, now I lay me down to sleep, was supposed to make me feel protected but not being able to understand how, it backfired; meaning for me that the Lord, whoever he or that thing was, would sneak in some night when my mother wasn't there and take my soul, whatever that was, which I guessed amounted to killing me in my sleep. Later, I learned that this quatrain came from a New England primer of the days when little boys did die more often in their sleep. I never understood the ditty, only that some thing called the Lord, or God, or Jehovah, or whatever, might sneak up the back stairs and steal my essence, which, I concluded from the seriousness of my having to kneel, I couldn't live without.

> *There is only one religion, though*
> *There are a hundred versions of it.*
> – George Bernard Shaw

Does combat require all to be religious? I think not. Toward the beginning of World War II someone quoted an Army chaplain on Bataan, coining the expression: "There are no atheists in foxholes." A frightened, emotionally excited populace, superstitious, their lives seriously threatened and accustomed to believing in the supernatural; needing God's help desperately to keep from losing the war, read that bit of Readers Digest milk-and-honey about Atheists and gulped it down. I'll admit scared soldiers pray all right when Nature lets them down, that's all their mothers and fathers know to teach them, pray, that is, beg, and demand prompt service, relief from mysterious pressures. Their fathers never explained why prayers from such a disparate demand are not answered, leaving it up to me, an Agnostic.

> *There is no death, there's only me.*
> – André Malraux

When dying suddenly in combat, like someone hit by a car, one hasn't energy or time to waste crying out anything more than *medic, my God.* Nor conjure up calculated pathetic looks; unthinking, thoroughly frightened cornered animals like I once saw in the face of a wounded doe, silently pleading please don't kill me. Deer don't know God, not that we know of, but in our hunting days in Korea the name of God bursts forth as a hard, vindicative curse or threat, rather than a pious supplication or proper noun.

Most of my guys died not begging or soliciting any supernatural thing, but hurling their last dire expletives at our enemy, bottled-up fear suddenly released to anger. God was mentioned alright. "Goddammit! Goddamn chinks! Oh, my God, I've had it!" God is the most anguished verbal expression associated with the most violent surprise that you can ever get, the strongest expletive intended as such in our limited infantry combat vocabulary, limited at the final moment to the greatest mystery of all, God, whose great power remains a supposition to the very end. Where are you God? God, stop sliding around up there and hear me! You got to listen to me! I need you badly, God. Now! Now! Catch me, I'm falling to Hell!

The sudden realization to young men crouching near the end of their lives on a dark ridge facing heartless reality, shocked by the violent death of buddies, fearful that they are going to be killed, is a hell of a demoralizing blow to their egos, not an indication of religious neglect. They might answer this fierce, frightening realization with a very short, desperate prayer of sorts, but one's pending, premature death is contrary to things one was taught to believe in church, besides, they are too young to die. "Who, me? Not me, I just prayed." They immediately find that doesn't work. It may have once got them a shiny new bicycle should their parents overhear them praying, but they need something more bulletproof than prayers to cover their trembling bodies, something to comfort their minds, like the sweet warmth from memories of family dependencies and affections, thoughts of home, itself a religion much more powerful than any supposedly revealed or organized.

My dog tags read A, Agnostic, not atheist. I capitalize Agnostic, although it is not an organized belief and has no illusions. The closest I ever came to what could be an Agnostic manifesto is—

> A winter seagull
> in its life has no home
> in its death no grave.
> – Kato Shuson.

I have said I am Agnostic since Philosophy 101 at Syracuse University in 1937, my freshman year, confirmed by James Thurber's observation, "Sixty minutes of thinking of any kind is bound to lead to confusion and unhappiness." Sometimes I wish I was amenable to the purely spiritual, for I learned the very hard way that only man's spirit, his soul, can outlive war and the other treacheries of life. Would I could be a steadfastly devout believer of any religion, able to concentrate on any abstract such as Christianity, but unfortunately, like the English preacher, poet-mystic John Donne, I am too easily distracted—

> I throw myself down in my chamber and I call in and invite God and his angels thither, and when they are there, I neglect God and his angels for the noise of a fly, for the rattling of a coach, for the whining of a door.

On the broad scale, death itself is beyond doubt or criticism for it is every bit as essential as life; without its steady pressures little conscious effort would be made and to intelligent people life would become an endless bore. Pity poor Cartaphilus the Wandering Jew, against whom immortal life was imposed as the heaviest penalty—

> Whoever has lived long enough to find out what life is knows how deep a debt of gratitude we owe to Adam, the first great benefactor of our race. He brought death into the world.
> – Mark Twain.

Some of us more philosophical who, with our sophistic presence of mind when hard hit, yell out the real root of life and death—SHIT! Hear me foul excrement that was us, leftovers of living, the ugly remainders we shed each day and one day, embalmed or not, will be.

I discovered in the Land of the Morning Calm that in the beginning we were created, just like Genesis says, indeed from dirt, and from that day on every day of our dirty, useless lives get rubbed in it and eventually give up struggling and become one big glob of it; shit, our organic discharge, the stinking conversion of us, the part of her my little calico cat, Tweety, is so disgusted with she carefully buries.

*   *   *

Again, from the Blue Book—

After darkness fell on the night of 15-16 May, an estimated twenty-one Chinese divisions, flanked by three North Korean divisions in the west and six in the east, struck down the center of the peninsula against X Corps and the ROK III Corps in the Naep'yong-ni-No-dong area. To the right was the US Second Division, with the ROK Fifth and Seventh Divisions on its right, and the ROK III Corps to their right. Chinese units crossed the Pukhan River west of Chunchon, and on 16 May other units struck hard against the ROK Fifth and Seventh Divisions. The patrol base regiment [only us terrified survivors] fell back to Noname Line, and by 1930 hours of 16 May the two ROK divisions were heavily engaged along a twenty-mile front in the vicinity of Hangye-ri, a village ten miles northeast of Inje. The two divisions held their ground for a time, then fell back, disorganized and broken.

On the left [west] shoulder of the enemy salient, the Second Division, including the French and Dutch Battalions, withstood resolute enemy attacks until 18 May, and then, together with the First Marine Division, moved right to fill the gap left by the two ROK divisions. IX Corps extended its front to the right to cover the area left by the Second Division and the marines. Van Fleet raced the 15th RCT [regimental combat team] of the US Third Division from Seoul to bolster the west face of the salient, and sent the Seventh and 65th Infantry [Puerto Rican Regiment, Third Division], to blocking positions at the southernmost part of the penetration.

The swarming columns of Chinese and North Koreans soon almost surrounded the Second Division, pushing against its front, right, and rear. The Chinese even blocked the Second's main supply route, but a coordinated attack by the 9th Infantry driving northward, and the 23d and 38th Infantry Regiments attacking southward along with their French and Dutch contingents, regained control of the route.

The Second Division stood fast and punished the enemy heavily.

I had Kitty send me a book made of blank pages for a diary or note taking and to jot down highlights of my experiences. I hoped never again to suffer so terrorizing a time as when I was forced to play dead, my second taste of infantry combat, so awfully alone going through it. I wrote about it in this blank book and it became a sort of handbook of fear and how to try to react to and control it.

Was ever a civilian ordered in to fight made aware of what total fear would do to his mind and body? If fear was mentioned at all, it was the disgraceful motivation of a coward. And did any Army official ever tell him what made him a coward and what a hero? Hell no, all left to chance in the most terrifying seconds of his life.

Combat fear is often totally disorganizing and demands the best of esprit de corps and training to counteract, which Marines advertise they have in abundance. What they find at last, however, is that it is more basic and necessary to know the awful truth beforehand than to simply be told you're invincible. Percentagewise, more Marines and airborne cracked up in combat than Army draftees, combat stress being equal. I saw that. The young Marine is fed horseshit about being invincible and tough and when he actually gets mortared or machine-gunned, he's stunned. This wasn't supposed to bother a Marine. Draftees are ordinary, not tough guys like him. Just the opposite happened to my draftees, they weren't ever told they were tough guys and all the time felt picked on and incapable of real combat, which was a job for professionals, Marines, tankers and paratroopers, who gloried in it. When they got mortared the first time or worked up close under artillery preparation and didn't get killed, my men were elated.

"My God," I've heard them say many times when baptized by fire, "My God, I'm still here. I ain't dead. I ain't touched…. I can take it; goddamn, don't nobody call me damn draftee no more. I'm a combat veteran." Everyone I talked to, replacements like me, agreed that it would have been helpful had someone let them know in advance what would happen to them physically and mentally when the shit hit the fan and found them mentally alone. All volunteered that it made it impossible to maintain full control since no one knew what would and should happen within himself or how long it should and would last. They were never prewarned how damn scary that first fright was, utterly debilitating, how so suddenly in a stunning flash all your blood got redistributed, mixed with adrenalin.

The sudden shock of a burp gun fired by a hidden infiltrator in the dead of night is arguably the worst, makes those who have heard it before have an instantaneous, uncontrollable recognition, the prime signal for fear reaction, for the sound is a peculiarly rapid, tearing, ripping sound that automatically affects your need to shit as the similar, suddenly bloodless, sphincter muscles around your asshole and your mouth react to loss of blood and your bladder suddenly is too full, and cause you to babble like an idiot when you mean to give firm orders. One must wait a few minutes to regain at least a part control of the rushing blood flow that by then is strumming violently across his temples.

I reviewed what was done and said, especially by me, before and after the over-running of our outpost. The first mistake I made was tip-toeing around the holes whispering, asking if anyone had spotted anything and were they all right. I learned later from J J that Sergeant Ulriche said I was spooking the guys. "Christ, you don't talk to men as though they was scared kids."

When we had a chance during the long June reserve, Sergeant Eppler and I drew up what we called a fear course for newcomers. S3, a regular Army captain who made the rank in combat in WWII, thought it was a pretty sensitive subject and wondered, too, that the Army spent no time on it, never even mentioned it, and though he didn't want to mess with it, he'd refer us to the division shrink, whose business he figured it was if anyone's in the Army.

The shrink turned out to be a New Yorker, like our Fred Hurtz, one of the few Jews I met in Korea; another was a Second Division chaplain, Sternberg, who insisted on being called rabbi rather than major.

Still another was a fighting fool you wouldn't suspect was Jewish. I mean he didn't have any of that citified finesse, overt, self-advertising superior intelligence sort of careful awareness of the proper suit and necktie vs the ordinariness of the average slob of a physical guy in a workman's jacket and cap advertising one beer or another. I became acquainted with Master Sergeant Herb Cohen of G Company, 23d Infantry when I sat by him on the hillside during a movie, one he'd missed in his battalion area four days earlier. He turned out to be a real sharp, intelligent guy; why he was making a career of the Army I never found out, it's so unJewish, although I suspected it had something to do with a woman, the motivation the Foreign Legionnaires were supposed to have. Was it coincidence the *Legion Etranger* battalion was working with his regiment? A graduate of New York City University with a psychology major, Cohen intended to get to a medical school to be a psychiatrist. He warned me to steer clear of the Division Mental Health Officer. "He's a regular Army medical *service* officer, not physician, appointed to Mental Health and, psychologywise, rather ignorant.

"You were scared," Cohen told me, "that's why you sneaked so quietly around your men who were in their holes hiding like rabbits. They added your obvious reaction to fear as proof of their own and it scared them more. You did spook them. You figured if you're very quiet and don't make any noise, they won't be mad at you but will go after someone who's shooting at them. First, you get hit by the fear stimulus that gets your mind and body working against each other too fast and the adrenalin pours into your blood stream and makes it flood everything, pressuring your brain, and without proper mental control, lets your action muscles take over, moves which can't be logical with no sane advice from that brain. Blood pounds over your temples getting to the arm and leg muscles so you can get the hell out of there. When a fear stimulus hits a rabbit, it either freezes or bugs out; even a lion bugs when scared by an unexpected threat.

"Man, of all animals, subjects himself to the unnatural situation wherein he allows himself to be hunted down and killed and has to stay put and fight back, not avoid and hide from whatever threatens him. If a stranger went after you with a gun on a street back home, you'd haul ass, right; that's the nature of us healthy animals. You tell me you played dead—the rabbit again—but it wasn't your choice. You tell me you dropped in your tracks from exhaustion and were unable to move. You had no alternative and before you got your breath, they were digging in on either side. All in all, lieutenant, you're damn lucky."

"Telling me?"

"Did you ever feel like you had to suddenly take a shit or a piss when the stuff hits the fan? Well, that's because your blood is moving so fast to supply energy to your action muscles it leaves your less important muscles, bladder and sphincter muscles that control your asshole and your lips without strength. Undertakers will tell you that any shit left in a man when he dies will drop out automatically because there's no blood-energy to control muscles that normally pinch off shit and piss. You not only have to shit and take a piss, but can't talk or think straight for the same reason. The big scare sends the blood to your arms and legs for sudden action and as it pulses like a torrent over your temples going from one side of your head to the other, your brain is stunned. Be careful what you do when you're that scared; first get control of your blood flow; stop and breath deep and shout and think aggressive rather than retire and die timid and afraid. You have the advantage that they haven't locked on to you yet, so try to build up a firepower in their direction before they spot exactly where you are... only your firepower will discourage them, not your silence."

Fred Hurtz, Second Platoon, suggested that we humans, especially Westerners, have unnatural fear, artificial fear, that other animals whose brains are free from worry aren't burdened with, fear of failure and death and we have no reason to fear death either unless we have no belief in the soul, which is the real us. Way too much attention is given to our fragile, short-lived physical bodies which we know very well are transitory. Fear of the transformation of one's body to shit—or clay—is no reason to fear the extinction of us, the real us, souls.

Prepare for change, taught Buddha the Enlightened One. Prepare for change, for all life and all things in the universe are always changing. With deeply ingrained ignorance and fear passed along from the Dark Ages of Christianity, Westerners make dying seem dreadful when there's no need because no one has ever returned to tell us what it is like. It could be good as easily as it might be bad. This abnormal fear of death began with early Christian teachers who, while extolling the desirability of Heaven sought to reduce suicide by teaching the fear of death. If we knew that to die was a pleasure or to remain in that nothing state called sleep, the suicide rate would be appalling. We should try to understand death beforehand, Fred told me. Embrace it honestly.

> Death is either annihilation with no consciousness at all or it is a migration of unseen, unknowable essence from one place to another. If there is no consciousness but only dreamless sleep, death can be a marvelous gain . . . to be afraid of death is another form of thinking one is wise when one is not; it is to think that one knows what he does not know. No one knows in regard to death whether it is not really the greatest blessing that can happen to man; but people dread it as though they were certain it is the greatest evil; and this ignorance which thinks it knows what it does not know, must surely be ignorance most culpable....
>
> – Socrates.

> Death is nothing so terrible; the common opinion about death, that it is terrible, is the terrible thing.
>
> – Epictitus, Greek Stoic philosopher slave.

I put everything together and told the division shrink how it would help new men especially prepare themselves for shit to hit the fan and maybe there wouldn't be so many crackups who hugged the bottom of their holes or bugged out. He acted aloof, unfriendly and mysterious like shrinks are trained to do, and failed to ask me anything, but did accept my notes. I was told a week later by the S3 that the shrink suggested I stick to platoon-leading; he knew his job and didn't need amateur help.

> Men fear death as children do the dark; and as that natural fear in children is increased with tales, so is the other.
>
> – Francis Bacon (1561-1625).

"I'm no psychologist," I told the major, "but I damn well have been scared a few times. If you go out with us one time, maybe you'd know what it's like; know what should be known beforehand."

Maybe the shrink felt I was ridiculing him, daring him to go on patrol with us, men are defensive that way. I'm sure he knew a lot of psychology, mostly theory. I'm also certain that if he went on patrol and we got hit, he'd want to start a fear course if only for himself. It would save him a lot of work if he could stop the wondering what fear is and start letting guys in on the secret so they might know what to expect, more importantly, not to let reacting to fear control him but to regain control of himself and take over.

Like most rear echelons, he was an asshole. His sergeant, however, a draftee psychology student, sympathized with what we were trying to do and let Sergeant Eppler and I thumb through some books. One I had already read in my military history researches after WWII was the six-volume study by Harvard psychologist Professor Edwin Garrigues Boring, in 1942 made brigadier general by President Roosevelt, called STUDIES IN SOCIAL PSYCHOLOGY IN WORLD WAR TWO, in which hundreds of infantrymen were interviewed before and after combat. Over varying periods and extremes of exposure to fear, fatigue, and bad or indifferent leadership, it concluded that at the end of six months, a combat infantryman's efficiency dropped off abruptly to the point that the average was a liability to himself and his unit.

Dr Boring's team isolated the important variables of infantry combat leading to combat fatigue or breakdown, an infantryman's inability to control himself. Listed, not necessarily in order of occurrence or importance, the factors that materially and vitally affected him are—

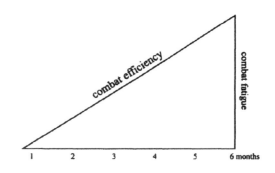

Almost every man has a breaking point, eventually ending in one or another form of combat fatigue.

terrain
climate
supply, adequacy
leadership, competency
medical attention
tactics
enemy morale
communication
local attack
success of action
anticipated duration of action;
anticipated length of war
general attack; defense against
local counterattack

training, adequacy to prepare an individual
type and intensity of enemy resistance
intensity and duration of fire
defense against largescale attack
raid or reconnaissance in force
weapons used
casualties incurred
unit's mission
replacements, adequacy
prospects for success in ensuing mission
type and numbers of supporting or cooperating
fires
ensuing mission
support from home

R & R, rest and rehabilitation, began in the ETO toward the end of WWII, with five-day passes to Paris and early April 1951, a rotation policy was announced in Korea whereby various points for rotation were given each month, depending on how near one was to combat: four for a man in a combat unit, three for direct support, and two for rear echelons. He needed thirty-six to qualify for rotation.

Units of the division left Fort Lawton at Seattle in three troop ships in early July 1950 and in May 1951 began losing old timers to rotation, guys who came over with the Second Division in the anxious call to stem the tide.

One poll in STUDIES IN SOCIAL PSYCHOLOGY asked what would you recommend for guys who crack up in combat. Surprisingly, at that time, WWII, with even greater ignorance of the effects of fear, 77 out of 100 combat veterans answered they should be treated as sick men. Only six said they should be treated as cowards and punished. Fifteen thought they should be treated in some other way and two had no opinion. As to the symptoms of violent combat fear, all pertaining to the flow of blood—

84% experienced a violent pounding of the heart	49% felt weak or faint
69% felt a sinking feeling in the stomach	45% felt stiffness
61% shook and trembled all over	27% vomited
55% felt sick to the stomach	21% lost control of their bowels
and 10% urinated in pants.	

And no doubt there were plenty of combinations, including guys like me who invariably, when surprised by fear, felt a looseness of the asshole.

"It's not so much for me," I told the shrink, "I've been through it. How about new guys? They deserve better than what happened to us. I know now what's coming and how to get control but how about new guys?"

"If it's so important," the shrink answered, "Washington would've done something."

So much for our all-knowing, friendly, division psychiatrist.

I thought back to a number of things I did wrong with the screaming, bugling chinks arriving so fearfully—damn blinking lights up toward the Soyang river and musical instruments made to sound aggressive and Sergeant Dorn's plight, and back to the little training I had in WWII—two security patrols I led 'supposedly' as a shavetail in the Yankee Division in the last week of war in the ETO where I'd been elbow-to-elbow with some pretty tough men who fought from Moncourt Woods, France, through Nurenberg, Munich, Passau, to Prague and survived. They liked me enough to wise me up with personal battle-tattle, probably because I was a shavetail in the two weeks I was with them, never got fired on and had no opportunity to earn a combat infantryman's badge. Shavetail, for second lieutenant, incidentally is from the custom in the old Army to shave the tails of new, untrained mules for easy identification.

*   *   *

The combat men of Love company had left the kitchen train by the time I arrived. None of the rear echelon, supply, morning report clerks who jotted me down MIA, mess personnel, etc. acted as though they didn't recognized me. Grapevine preceded me from regiment that I was back alive and I wondered what sort of a virus made people unable to recognize a former acquaintance merely because of a rumor that he might be out of favor. Crimus, for no reason I was made to feel like a rogue elephant cast out of the herd. "Hey, guys," I wanted to demand, "No trial, questioning, nothing? I deserve a medal if anything."

I felt like Ulysses after all I'd been through when I reported to the company CP, exec officer Lieutenant Roy Carse and he gave me the cold shoulder.

"What's wrong with everyone?" I demanded.

"Everyone knows," Carse said.

"Knows what?"

"You bugged out. Lucky you don't get a court-martial."

Roy Carse was one of the very few friends I made in Korea. He was a year older than me, a cop from Maplewood, New Jersey. Most of the company didn't know it, but Roy was a rifle platoon leader in Love Company, 38th in WWII from the landing on D Day plus one, through the Bulge where he got hit in the leg. He volunteered to waive a disability pension to return to combat if he could be in the same unit. His offer was accepted and processed that way and although he didn't suspect it a hold in his personnel records at Division saw to it that he wouldn't be in combat again. Perhaps because of two Purple Hearts.

Everyone who knew Roy liked him. In the summer of 1952, back on the force he and Rosie stopped at our apartment on their way to a vacation in the Thousand Islands and stayed overnight. The following year Kitty and I were supposed to get together with them for a two-weeks vacation in the Adirondacks but best laid plans, etc. Rosie told me that Roy died a very painful death from cancer in 1988.

Lieutenant Foney's first words were, "Gould, you'll have a chance to explain your actions."

"Accusing me of bugging?"

"I didn't say you bugged; said you've got explaining to do."

"Lookit, Goddammit, I may be junior in grade around here but if there's anyone to be blamed for anything, it's you sending two poorly armed guys down that path after you learned chinks were all over the place."

"I didn't know anything for sure."

"You still don't; I warned you and did you have any reason to think it was safe.... You know, Foney, I'm a recalled Reservist like you but without a chance of becoming RA no matter how hard I try, and frankly, I don't give a shit what I say. You think you're John Wayne just because you're tall and grunt short answers because you don't have a damn thing to say that's worth listening to."

"Keep that up, Gould, you'll get your court martial. I'm company commander and don't forget it."

"I hear you put yourself in for the DSC that X Corps is handing out to each company on our outpost. True?"

"None of your business."

"I'd like to read the citation... for pulling your phone and radio without notifying the platoons and being right on Wilkes' ass getting off the outpost? C'mon, Foney, let's see the citation. Poston and Opoulus put in real heroes who died on their machine guns—Sergeants Erasmo G Lopez and Robert K Imrie."

Foney and I had a whizzer of a personality conflict. I was honest, forward, talkative and friendly; medium height and all. He was the so-called strong-silent type, about 6'2". I have in mind several examples of why he had to be smart enough to keep his mouth shut, but since John Knight (Colonel retired, San Jose, California) told me that Foney died several years after the war from a rare form of sleeping sickness, of all things picked up in Korea, I'll refrain from relating them, even though I don't use his real name.

After I received my RIF (reduction in force) dear John in June 1954, I drove with a major acquaintance from headquarters First Army to the Infantry Career Branch in the Pentagon and requested my records. One puts in a signed written request, is seated in a special reading room and waits for his personnel 201 file to be brought to him. At the time, and for years after, the Army was the only military service where a rating officer was not required to call the rated officer in and explain the rating. We called it the gestapo report. I was infuriated. Foney described my miraculous escape on the night of the 15th of May as having taken off in panic, discarding my carbine, helmet and belt, deserting my men: "while other platoon leaders led their men down the evacuation routes in good order." He was right in saying I discarded my steel helmet and carbine but a damn liar about deserting my men. It was he who deserted all of us. I also learned that Sergeant Ulriche had been willing to testify to my deserting the men until he learned the whole story from J J with an explanation of my actions—sticking my neck out for two of Foney's wiremen following his orders.

The major and I discussed my efficiency report on the return to Governors Island.

"This has to be reviewed by your battalion commander, charges made by your company commander, what did you say their names were?"

"Foney and Wilkes."

"Yes, well, those charges should have drawn an automatic court martial, desertion in face of an armed enemy, at least an investigation for a general court martial which used to carry a death sentence and is still good for a few years in Leavenworth."

"Wish I'd seen the lying report, I'd have demanded a court martial to clear my name."

"Your company commander realized that and decided to do it behind your back where, evidently with the silent concurrence of your battalion commander, it would survive and would end up with your being tossed out at the first RIF."

"Shit, major, I gave them a hell of a lot more reasons than that."

When I first got home I didn't want to stay in the Army and when a query came out for us Reserves to indicate our retention desires in categories one to five, I signed one, meaning that I desired to stay in the Army no longer than the mandatory one year. I figured I could sell some of my history articles by then and be on my way. And there's the college thing; after the Korean War they didn't contemplate needing dogfaces like me. What they wanted was every officer, even Infantry, to have a college degree and if you wanted to make captain, better get a masters. Over 20,000 of us footslogging company grade Infantry officers without college degrees, regardless of valor decorations, got it on the RIF of '54 when there were as many thousand other jobs in other branches we could easily be trained to do. As a matter of fact, while awaiting my discharge, they detailed me to help ordnance at Fort Dix, New Jersey and I spent time inventorying ammo bunkers for which I didn't get a bit of training or even a fair warning. They gave me a list of what serial numbers and lots they wanted to record and an ordnance sergeant to make the actual count.

The third day a Hercules Powder truck backed up to unload at the eagle (bunker) I was inventorying. The driver got out with a bunch of paperwork and receipts I was to sign and as he talked he followed me to the entrance. Craning his neck studying what was visible he swore, "Goddammit, lieutenant, know what you've got there?"

"A bunch of explosives."

"Where's your felt slippers?"

"What for?"

"Are you kiddin'?"

"Why?"

"Did they give you any training, lieutenant? You're sporting cross rifles; you're Infantry, yes?"

The driver could see I was serious and shook his head and gave a couple of 'I-don't-believe-it' whistles.

"Lieutenant, I'm turning around tip-toeing away from that poor man's atom bomb and seeing the colonel," meaning the post ordnance officer. "I wouldn't set foot in there for a million bucks; no felt slippers to prevent sparks; primer cord, caps, old boxes of dynamite turning amorphous about to leak nitroglycerine, all in the same bunker. When that happens, a fart can set it off. I ain't never seen such a dangerous mess!"

I laid down the inventory clip board, warned the sergeant to come out, shut the heavy door, told the sergeant where I was headed and hopped into my car to return to Governors Island, dropping him off at the NCO Club. Nor did I ever hear from the ordnance colonel. I was hoping I would; real business for 'my friend' Walter Winchell.

But to return to Roy, who, along with Freddy Hurtz, became my only real buddy among the officers, I mention Conley Clarke and John Fox and a few more, but in Korea they were at best passing acquaintances.

"My God," I swore at Carse. "After what's happened to me, what's wrong with everyone? I've been thorough hell and you guys think I bugged?"

"C'mon, Gould. Sergeant Ulriche says you took off to save your skin without telling anyone... but never mind the talk, get something to fight with and we'll see you catch up to company. Lieutenant Foney will have something to say later. Right now we got a fight coming."

I was a pariah without knowing why, but like Carse said, we had a fight coming and pooped as I was, I was part of it. The supply sergeant gave me a surprisingly warm greeting.

"Hi, Lieutenant Gould. See you made it; a guy's got to watch out for himself. I know just how you feel. I was cut off from the guys of my rifle platoon at Kunu-ri. Lucky to be alive. Don't worry, sir. They'll come around."

"What do you mean, come around?"

"You know, lieutenant; they'll get over it."

"Never mind the talk," I told him. "Get me outfitted."

I gathered that the supply sergeant didn't appreciate my aloofness, as though I owed him a little more friendliness because we had some failing in common. He handed me an old steel helmet someone had been driving pickets with, an M1 rifle with a chipped stock and a frayed pistol belt with a battered canteen.

"Out of ammo belts and carbines," he said, handing me the one-bandage medical pouch and one bandolier of M1 clips. I was too tired to argue but found the chance a week or so later to tell him off and was able to sign out an issue watch, along with an illuminated dial wrist compass. "Sergeant Ulriche has your platoon binoculars," I was told.

"Honest, lieutenant, you weren't the only one threw away equipment. I haven't had the opportunity to resupply. You're lucky I had this stuff to turn in."

The motor pool sergeant jeeped me five miles down a bumpy road parallel to what had been the front, now penetrated in several places to where Love Company was chogeeing along bent over, either sad or real tired or perhaps both. Sergeant Ulriche grunted acknowledgment as I fell in behind him leaving him at the head of the Banzai Third Platoon and I said hi to several others I was glad to see, but it was a long march following a frightening night for survivors and nobody was talkative or glad to see me, glad or anything. I was ignored except by J J Jenkins who saw me get out of the jeep and came running up.

"Lieutenant! Boy am I glad to see *you*! I heard we lost Dorn and his guys along with that wire patrol you made up. Speedy Gonzales made it out okay although nicked in the left arm. He'll be back in a few days."

I was the only one not hauling a pack which was just as well because I was too pooped to carry one anyway, or talk. I'd gone through every type of fear and worry known to infantrymen, plus great energy lost escaping and running three miles to the MLR, fast as I could without stopping, later tossing my cookies, as well as two almost sleepless nights on the patrol base outpost, but, bushed though I was, I was happy to discover how well the platoon made out without me.

We were on a twenty-mile forced route march to the northeast where chinks caved in the Fifth ROKs. All available trucks in X Corps were dispatched to move ammunition and the US Third Infantry Division's 15th Infantry over to back up our old positions, even as ten-ton trailers were borrowed from Eighth Army Quartermaster to haul ammo from the docks at Inchon. Hiking relentlessly along, I asked J J why Sergeant Ulriche and Lieutenant Carse thought I'd bugged and he said he didn't rightly know. He told the platoon sergeant how I was drawn away trying to help the wiremen. Sergeant Ulriche seemed to prefer to believe I was a coward and deserter, I think, simply because I'd not cleared with him personally as if he was still the platoon leader. I was hoofing in my place beside him but too pooped to explain and he never even glanced my way and it grew dark.

Before he died, I'm happy to say my platoon sergeant and I got to talk it over and he apologized for jumping to conclusions not knowing the real sequence of events. I was right worrying about Dorn and his men but I didn't have to guard those wiremen. He told me accusingly that wasn't my job and we didn't have to lose the three guys I ordered along on wire patrol. There was no reason they had to get it and custom was, he explained, not to pick riflemen on my own; first ask squad leaders for volunteers.

All I had to do was follow back out the withdrawal route with the platoon altogether, particularly with Master Sergeant Onis L Ulriche. They made it out, even as he led out the scattered men at Kunu-ri. I let him know I made a mistake and was sorry and Sergeant Ulriche finally told me, begrudgingly it seemed, that it was a fine thing I'd tried to do, but next time take care of our own men and don't risk them in such a hairy enterprise. If they needed help, it was Foney's job.

"But he…" I started to explain to myself, but we were bushed and it was over and another battle maybe worse down the way.

I heard from grapevine on the march how my first company commander in Korea, Captain Edmund D Poston of Fox Company was killed. He believed that everything was to be done by the book. He didn't know how to deal with real men or stand on his own. The April day in reserve when I reported he motioned me out of the arctic tent and said he wanted to show me something. He had me sling my carbine and climb with him up a nearby ridge toward deserted chink holes, moving right along, trying, I think, to see how much endurance I had. On two occasions he stopped abruptly and drew a forty-five from a holster on either hip and aimed them at the holes. The first time I didn't know whether to shit or wind a watch and came around rather clumsily, with my carbine pointed to where he thought the target might be.

He was killed and took recalled Reserve Lieutenant Andy Austin and about ten guys with him simply because, as his field first told me, when he could get no radio contact with anyone for permission to pull out of a draw in which they continued to take plunging fire from two sides, as veteran Lieutenant Austin, field commissioned in the Texas National Guard at the Rapido River crossing in WWII, begged Poston to make his own decision to pull back. The field first sergeant took out the survivors the minute after Poston and Andy got it. I was surprised to learn the captain won a Silver Star for that botched up action, but then, he was a West Pointer and it was posthumous and his bosses liked him.

The main reason I wasn't killed with Poston and Austin was, of course, I'd been transferred to G Company, then short of officers. In Fox in short order I learned how nice a guy Andy was. He was two years older and beginning to break into the clear with an insurance agency in San Antonio. His second daughter, Jennie, was born the day he went up the gangplank of the Army transport *Patrick*.

We marched wearily, faced away from the new rising Chinese moon, until 2200 hours when we quit the main road and headed due east down a mere pathway. Much later during a ten minute break at a road junction and an artillery aid station, *I* showed them my swollen left thumb, infected from a cut on a C ration can the day before, the very day we were overrun. A medical sergeant gave me a shot of something and a little glass vial of Benzedrine something or other which he warned me to use sparingly—tiny hard white pills.

"Maybe they'll keep you going," he said.

We went another four or five miles up a different trail and mounted a small steep foothill of about 500 meters. Almost to the top we started digging holes and waited. It began to pour and turn cold—mid-May in the South Korean east central mountains—and I ached all over. Stupid, I forgot to draw a blanket and poncho and the supply sergeant hadn't volunteered them. I was never so conscious of my age. Knuckles of my right hand were blue holding the rifle sling and I transferred the piece to my left shoulder and got my left knuckles blue; the scab over the infected thumb, whitened in the cold rain, softened and the Band Aid loosened and slipped off. That thumb continued bothering me, throbbing and jumping. I tried to force my teeth from chattering. Counting out three of the little pills, I remember thinking, "You'll need a dozen next time," but thought better of it. J J eyed me a bit, then reached under his poncho pointing to his blanket covering his shoulders, motioning that I could borrow it. I thanked him, but declined. I was already soaking wet. My lower teeth beat against uppers in noisy percussion like what would one day be called rock 'n roll. I played a game making rhythms from otherwise uncontrollable shivering and shaking, managing a staccato Clementine. I was about as miserable as animals get and for the first hour I sucked in my breath every ten minutes or so and held it as I tried to make myself stop shivering, my teeth from chattering.

We backtracked down to a valley and marched and at about 2400 stopped for a long rest and I bent down and put frozen hands in my crotch tight under my balls until I got tired bending and then tight under each arm pit, and then alternatingly under my balls again, which heaters were my only sources of warmth. I told Sergeant Ulriche to take over the platoon. He grumbled something. We both knew that I joined his platoon, officerless for the past four months, and it was very unnecessary to tell him anything. I went through the formality anyway, too pooped to argue with myself. If anything happened, I told him, I'd be out of it; do my best to take care of myself.

A secret voice within me jumped up and down clapping hands whispering: "Boy, oh boy, are we ever lucky; we've got it good this time. We're no good to anyone anymore; when a surgeon sees us in the morning we'll be evacuated all the way to the States." I had wished shamelessly since my first patrol that, like most guys I knew on the job, I'd soon get a stateside wound; now I was contracting pneumonia, or worse, hopefully ambulatory so I could still otherwise get around.

I shivered badly through the night not knowing whether I was getting any sleep or not. I must have, for in the morning, as the sun exploded over the eastern mountains, things around me steamed, including me, and I blew hard and hawked yellow-green stuff up from my chest, which became much less tight—I took deep breaths without hurting and the swelling and throbbing had subsided in my thumb. The medic's shot was a winner.

To the dismay of the little voice that assured me we'd be evacuated, instead of quitting I began to feel I had the making of some heroic rifle platoon leader all right; could really take it. Crimus, in the past few days; I'd taken more than a young George Patton or, further back and better yet, Napoleon. Napoleon Gould standing on the banks of the Neman, or maybe, to be patriotic, twenty-one-year-old George Washington trudging knee deep through cold west Pennsylvania swamps in that miserable winter weather, warning young French Lieutenant Jumonville to get his ass off British colonial property.

From our division Blue Book—

By early morning of 18 May, the situation in the sector of the 38th Infantry had become critical with many of the units fighting Chinese on all sides. The First Battalion of the 38th was in particularly dangerous shape with the main enemy penetration between A and B companies [where friend Conley was taken away POW]. It was evident that help would have to be provided, so, at first light the Second Battalion of the 9th shifted eastward behind the 38th and attacked northeastward while the Third Battalion of the 9th launched a drive to the north. The purpose was to seal off the enemy who had succeeded in bursting through the lines.

As there was no reserve available to the 23rd, the Division commander attached the strongest company remaining in the Third Battalion of the 38th to the 23rd as reserve, it was Item Company, then composed of one officer and 94 enlisted men. The enemy hurled fresh waves of troops at the modified Noname line shortly after midnight on 19 May. The fire of battle raged for 90 minutes with the Third Battalions of both the 9th and 38th bearing the brunt of the attack.

By 1030 hours, 18 May, communications were reestablished with the First and Third Battalion of the 38th and arrangements made to air-drop urgently needed supplies to the units that had been cut off. Both battalions had suffered heavy casualties and were extremely short of ammunition and rations.

That night, the first night after being overrun, we hit it lucky and found no chinks. We passed a warm day in sunshine and took a hot meal from insulated marmite cans brought to us by Carse in a Love Company jeep trailer. Having been informed of my plight over the radio, Lieutenant Carse saw that I got with poncho and blanket, a field jacket (a bit too large), an M2 carbine with thirty-round magazines joined by adhesive tapes, carbine knife (bayonet) and an entrenching tool.

I listened to battle tattle of some of the guys, especially Sergeant E-5 Raymond Roundtree, who, as Lawrence 'Pop' Miller's assistant replacing Dorn's lost Third Squad. Pop, back to sergeant E-5, on his way up again to E-6, which stripe he lost in April for telling off a rear echelon officer, and Tree, with us by mistake, the first Negro assigned to the 38th until August when all segregated Negro combat units in Korea were disbanded and many more assigned to the 38th Infantry. Tree had a great sense of humor, so typical of his race, greeting us in the Banzai Third as he reported in with a grin: "Here's yo token nigger."

Late in the day trucks came to pick us up. I rode in the cab of one containing half of what was left of the Banzai Third, Ulriche in the other cab. It was an all-colored trucking company of the Transportation Corps (despite the Truman Executive Order) and my driver chattered like the proverbial monkey—"I'se sure glad I wasn't with youse guys. Man, I heerd youse clobbered bad. I mean bad bad." I dropped off half asleep half daydreaming, in which this time I threw my grenade to kill the chinks and busted through and rescued the man slumped beside the litter. Unfortunately the guy on the litter was dead, bled to death as I presumed but I packed his buddy on my shoulders for he had a chance and he turned out to be the great hero, Master Sergeant Ulriche, former first lieutenant, two Silver Stars and Purple Hearts, veteran of Guadacanal and Kunu-ri, North Korea. He kept telling me, "Let me down Dud, can't make it with me, let me down, get out yourself."

"Nothing doing, sarge, it's both of us or none."

I stumbled with him on my shoulders and he was a couple inches taller than me, to the MLR and a movie cameraman took our picture and got a shot of me easing Sergeant Ulriche down on a litter carried by two medics with red crosses on their helmets, as they wore only in World War II before japs and krauts used them as aiming stakes. A well-lighted photo showed my sweaty face, dirty beard and firm jaw. Man, it would be in all the papers and the Watertown Times, me covered with blood, beaten, staggering through a mine field in spite of everyone yelling to set him down and save yourself. And Ulriche would have a young, beautiful sister and....

"Say, lieutenant," the driver was saying, staring straight ahead, "I could have spark plug trouble. Nobody's got to know and we could wait until daylight and make sure where we're at."

I tried to return to my satisfying daydream but he broke the rhythm and he squirmed at the disgusted look on my face, knowing he'd said something wrong he began to talk more rapidly to cover up.

"I mean this old bus ain't been acting so good lately.... Wouldn't be like bugging, we'd stay here and catch up early tomorrow. I wouldn't do a thing like that on purpose but probably them plugs ain't so hot anyway. You can never tell with everyone driving these wrecks. Chinks all over; a convoy got ambushed just two nights ago. Man, they's waiting for us every place." A long pause and, "Suh, we'll keep on chogeeing just as you say, suh, and see what happens. I don't like the looks of this road; too many places they can jump you."

"What'd you say?" I asked. "I was thinking."

The driver seemed relieved that I had not been listening. "Nothing, suh, just wondering."

Motoring along we passed small bands of ROK soldiers strolling along, deserters of the Fifth ROK Division which unit also bugged out at Wonju in February 1951, exposing an American flank to be overrun. They were silent, guilt-ridden, smiling nervously, too broadly. Some very few wore bandages and other few limped, all hurrying south unarmed toward safety, smirking with what seemed luminous smiles in the darkness. We Americans stared back in disgust.

"Your goddamn country we're fighting for," a soldier called out in the dark.

"Hey, Kim," another called. "Where you go, Pusan? Suck a hatchi."

Matthew B Ridgway, commanding general, Eighth Army—

I drove out north of Seoul and into a dismaying spectacle. ROK soldiers by truckloads were streaming south, without order, without arms, without leaders, in full retreat. Some came on foot or in commandeered vehicles of every sort. They had just one aim—to get as far away from the Chinese as possible. They had thrown their rifles and pistols away and had abandoned all artillery, mortars, machine guns, every crew-served weapon.

And on one of his visits to Korea after the second fall of Seoul, General MacArthur complained of the mass desertion of ROK units; "I haven't seen a wounded man yet."

Officerwise, the Republic of Korea Army was at the stage ours was at the beginning of the Civil War. I don't mean our very small professional Regular Army, but the regiments quickly fabricated from states' militia. American colonels of militia regiments were wealthy, politically well-connected men, as were those in equivalent slots in the South Korean Army. Most were of the opinion that all they had to do was appear in the rear on the morn of battle in full uniform and order their troops to assault. And little Kim did; he crawled up those slopes and died. Night was different; there were no officers in their holes like with us, they were strangers to darkness. We forced the chinks and gooks to move about only under cover of darkness to become and remain well coordinated night fighters Like the battalion and a half of the 9th, the blacks, whose white officers slept well back down the friendly side of the ridge, Kim was alone and afraid of spirits of darkness, easily spooked and run off.

In the June reserve I was detailed to advise the 23d ROK Regiment for a week at the ROK Third FTC, field training camp, at Yangu, set up by X Corps to train and inspect ROKs. I took the newly promoted Master Sergeant Eppler with me in a borrowed jeep. We found the regimental commander, a large man with high cheek bones, more Mongolian than Chinese and not at all Korean, who have finer features. We discovered him to have been a former major in the North Korean Army, before that, like many North Koreans, a mercenary two years in Manchuria in WWII in the Japanese Imperial Marines. His big project while we were there was to cut firewood, which his soldiers were doing rather than train. The regularly assigned KMAG captain pointed disgustedly at a training schedule in Korean and English on their bulletin board. Fire wood? In June? Why, yes, it was trucked to Seoul a hundred miles away to be sold, profits ostensibly for the enlisted men's mess, actually split among the officers. KMAG could only advise, never order.

X Corps Ordnance was inspecting weapons when we arrived. Lying in one row were about ten M1s with a Korean-made sign, THESE RIFLES OF COR-RUPTED BORE. Little Kim would be cleaning his rifle when a patch came off in the barrel and no amount of pushing with his ramrod could dislodge it so he took a round and blew it out, each barrel 'corrupted' the same, a big bulge or rupture in the barrel where the patch had been. Lucky that none of them were killed.

On a makeshift table made of saplings were four .30 caliber Browning machine guns, all of which had their barrels welded, carbonized to the front bronze bushing. Seems KMAG told Kim how to take apart and clean everything but that critical front barrel bushing through which the steel barrel slid back and forth for stability during firing.

Each of their 105mm artillery brass shell casings was polished to a mirror and little Kim was a number-one soldier when let in on the secrets of warfare American style, even with shit hitting the fan when backed by a trained officer.

The Chinese moon popped up as the convoy made a sharp turn off the MSR, main supply route, and pulled up in the middle of a large treeless valley. Hopping down, the guys lined a ditch, then hurriedly zipped up their flies to go looking for buddies. Lifetimes were about to shorten, and they sought to fraternize with guys among them they felt comfortable with before they, too, were gone forever. No one mentioned that, but all felt the need for close association. Me? No one but J J and Sergeant Roundtree looked my way. Five Negro drivers made a tight, intimate group, joking and laughingly slapping one another on the back, stabbing playfully at one another, kidding because this or that individual had been hard to overtake motoring down the undeveloped oxen roads as they lifted off what was left of the Second Battalion the night before.

"Woo-heee! man! I'se seen folks move, man. You was movin'. Hear what I say, man, you was long gone."

"Say I was skeered? Sh-e-e-et, man, I ain't the onliest one," laughing and rolling his eyes. "Ain't nothin' slow about Jesse, man. You ain't the onliest one."

God, I thought, guys like that can't ever be lonely.

French Legionnaires were grouped loosely at the truck dismount point waiting for a ride, talking in low voices in broken English with survivors of King Company. Around the corner 105s fired frantically answering trouble in the hills to our right front. Nearby a battery of their big cousins, 155mm long toms, longer barrels than ordinary howitzers, sent out volleys and after the initial smoke blows behind their shells large blue-white smoke rings floated up lazily from their barrels high into the clear air through moonlight. As each smoke ring dissipated, wisps of residual blue smoke, seemingly an afterthought, came up lazily from the barrels for night breezes to whisk away—bad-ass Wild West gunfighters puffing to clear powder smoke from the barrels of eight-ton six shooters.

A crowd of ROKs, fully equipped, uniformed in fatigues like us—from a little distance the same as us—bustled and jabbered, gesticulating excitedly in clusters of two and three, as an American KMAG advisor, a major, pushed through trying to get them to assemble. "Hey!" he shouted at his ROK lieutenant interpreter. "Let's get some organization around here. Line them up!"

"Them ROKs bugging out on us?" a voice demanded.

"What's it to you?" came the angry reply.

Mike Company, battalion's heavy weapons, was seating 81mm mortar base plates for tubes over to the left. In the center of activity nearer to the road a hamlet of primitive huts thatched with bundles of aged rice straw rested behind light green, double-walled arctic tents for battalion staff officers and across from Mike Company CTC (civilian transportation corps) laborers were boiling huge fire-blackened pots of daikons (elongated white radishes) and rice.

A KMAG captain, on the defensive for the misbehavior of his ROK unit, demanded somewhat aggressively of Lieutenant Fred Hurtz: "What unit you with?" Fred told him "Second Platoon, Love of the 38th" the officer asked, "Where's the rest?" When told, "This is all that's left," the captain shut his eyes hard and turned away.

The Chinese moon was straight up when Foney caught up to us in his jeep. Peering nervously at his watch, he demanded of no one in particular: "Why hasn't the company fallen in?" Spotting me, he ordered, "Gould, get on the ball; fall them in."

"All right," I yelled. "The company commander wants you to fall in. Let's get on the ball."

After Love fell in, First Sergeant, Master Sergeant, James B Luther, RA16230326, marched us out to the road and up a valley leading to where more artillery was firing. A zig-zag file of French Foreign Legionnaires passed us boot-sloshing, headed to the dismount point we just left. A strange meeting of Caucasians in that Asian wilderness. It seemed obvious they were quitting the fight, while we were being committed. Private First Class Kiezlowsky, Ski, whose first name was Spudacus, whatever that is, sounded off: "Hey, Frenchy, no chinks that way."

"They're lovers not fighters," snapped another.

"Yeah, frogs are funny people," Private Funaro sounded off for them to hear. "Fight with their feet, fuck with their face."

"Shut up!" Sergeant Ulriche snarled.

Bringing up the rear of the weary French column were five Legionnaires shrouded, motionless on litters.

A few miles north we watched red flares sailing high along on low sky winds, and tracers bouncing off Hill 442, small seemingly redhot balls, as units of the 23rd Infantry attacked, and across a narrow valley was H 710 where the French Battalion had been repulsed after forty casualties. The fatigued silent Legionnaire company that passed us had gone back to retrieve the last of its dead. Seeing us headed for their old objective, a small group of 23rd's walking wounded waiting for ambulances or litter jeeps cheered us on in low, subdued voices, offering what little ammunition they were carrying away, holding out grenades and taking off over their helmets olive drab cloth bandoliers, drab necklaces of M1 clips.

We route-marched at ease, in spooky moonlight, beat up and silent, behind a handful of headquarter's platoon and First Sergeant Luther. Next came the Fourth, weapons platoon, led by Master Sergeant Darrow Billson; then our Third Platoon, Sergeant Ulriche and me; the Second Platoon, ROTC Second Lieutenant Fred Hurtz, a nice guy, very intelligent but a sheltered city-bred young man; a bit naive about nonintellectual ways, the only Jew I got to know personally; and the young battle-field-commissioned Second Lieutenant Dale Hollingsworth with the First Platoon. I got really close to Fred, as with no one before; for my money he was one of us; whatever was obviously Jewish, that irritated gentiles, he left at home.

Beaten though we were, and in this condition like every platoon across the line, looking around I felt we were still a good match for chinks. Or maybe it was only my confidence growing for some reason. I hadn't actually killed anyone yet but I'd been shot at enough to call myself veteran, earned a combat infantryman's badge of honor. At last I was an unmistaken machismo man not to be trifled with. As we marched along I checked our strength. Aside from the small arms we packed on us were the real powerful weapons: 57mm recoilless rifles that replaced the WWII 57mm cannon company at regiment and the old one-pounder, 37mm cannon company at battalion. The 3.5-inch hand-held rocket launcher replacing the WWII 2.5-inch bazooka, and there were 60mm mortars of company weapons platoon and the 81 mortars of weapons company at battalion, with the 4.2-inch chemical mortar company at regiment, so-called in WWI designed for throwing poison gas shells, same caliber as the Russian 120mm mortar. Light 30 caliber machine guns carried for rifle platoons in company trailers and the heavies, water-cooled for steady overhead firing were in Mike, battalion heavy weapons company carriers.

Ammunition for all was hauled behind the column in battalion's 3/4-ton P&A trucks, pioneer and ammunition, weapon carriers, or in company quarter-ton jeep trailers. On our long marches guys with truly handicapping afflictions, still-draining nonvital wounds, rode in weapons carriers or jeep trailers as they could find room.

By the time I got to Korea, chinks, with all the American stuff they'd captured, especially out West and North, weaponwise were as well armed as we were, and we all knew only too well they had something that we could not count on—an avowed necessity to die before their ever-present commissars who very vehemently declared at every opportunity the obvious lie that they all were happy volunteers defending their homeland. Compare those persistent, narrow-minded assholes with a rather easy-going platoon leader like me. After Ulriche left, I seldom ordered my guys around. Chink writers may have boasted of their soldiers' willingness to die but, aside from those Nationals who stepped on mines, I never heard of one going that far, nor any chronicler of modern military history being able to say he was told by a chink he was *willing* to die. I've been close enough to enough Chinese soldiers to think otherwise. I suggest that they are no more weary of life than we; though we were all guilty, one way or another, of being there to die—a long way from being willing. Trained to obey like animals performing in a circus maybe, but sealed in one-way kamikazes, no!

I felt much closer to my guys, even the hero of two wars, former First Lieutenant Onis L Ulriche. I decided that in the next battle that seemed about to happen, I'd take over and show everyone how brave *I* really was, that is, granted the circumstances were right. Of course, I could never supplant Sergeant Ulriche in the eyes of the guys and I wouldn't want to; he'd already proven so much to them. In the first place, I tended to be a little round-shouldered and only five feet, eight and a half inches, although I could bench press 140 and was as wiry as they come. Much as I pined to be a professional writer, I had always to do hard physical labor for a living.

Slogging along, it hurt to realize I'd never see the platoon together again. Dorn and his six-man squad and three from Pop Miller's gone forever. One thing for sure, I'd never be separated from the guys again. I couldn't understand how they might think I deserted them looking out for my own hide by the very hazardous path I took if nothing else. Seemed obvious to me, and mentioned once to J J that if anything, I should get a medal. After all, nobody ordered me to do such a dangerous thing. I was an asshole. If it happened to some photogenic Limey leftenant, they'd call it noble, no greater love and all that, not that Love wasn't involved—a pun or something.

At the least I guess I should have let Sergeant Ulriche know where I was going because I felt so sorry for those wiremen but it was kind of spontaneous. I never decided anything; just got sucked along. He probably would have talked me out of it as suicidal, which is a hell of a lot different than heroic. At least J J and Gonzales knew the truth.

As a combat veteran, at last I sensed an opportunity to be a winner. If only I could survive long enough. "Boy," I thought, "we're the Banzai Third all right." Company, battalion and regiment were all out of my perspective. Of the combined effort, all that mattered was our platoon. I'd get them to like me as they do Sergeant Ulriche, at least show me some respect. I'd stick out my neck on purpose and do something foolishly reckless to prove how brave I was; maybe Onis would get to like me, or grow to respect me. How to do that I decided was to rush right into things without worrying what could happen to me; maybe knock off fifteen or twenty chinks. I'd need a BAR for that, and maybe yank a burp gun from one of them and turn it around.

As we continued our slow climb up a valley, I couldn't believe my eyes. There up ahead were chinks, silhouetted against distant flares, on the skyline about two miles to our left front where, I estimated, the French had been. My eyesight seemed superior to everyone's, for on several other occasions I spotted chinks or gooks before others did. Some might not think it a manly thing to do, look all over like that all the time. Maybe I was more apprehensive, or worried, or concerned as a leader; or, hell, let's be frank, more scared than most. I tried to get the message passed up the file ahead of me but nobody would repeat it and my message died a few men away so I hightailed it up the rocky trail pushing guys out of the way when necessary to reach Lieutenant Foney, practically shouting for him to stop and have a good look. When I got to him, military decorum, hell, I grabbed his left arm to turn him around and pointed to where I saw chinks as their legs showed in the flare light, snipping dots under the lowest branches of pine trees, more visible as they crouched over to run across a clearing to the next group of trees. Hundreds of busy ants flanking us.

Foney halted the column and finally after making out the chinks called for his radio and soon we were ordered to retrace our steps to battalion headquarters. I returned to the platoon and fell in in the lead with Sergeant Ulriche feeling important. Someone was rewarded for listening to me. Probably saved battalion headquarters.

We retraced our steps and took the left turn in a fork in the foothill trail, wading a small river grown uncomfortably deep from spring rains. Cold water came to my knees, the footing was difficult and later clammy water sloshing and squishing inside our boots for miles made our toes sore where they rubbed against wet leather despite our socks.

"Man," Pop said in a low voice, "seems I washed dishes with them feet; toenails limber as rubber."

Our eyes focused on H 710, in plain view from a slightly different angle this time. We stopped for a ten-minute break, filling canteens, supposedly after dropping in a little Halazone pill of tasteless water purifier that supplanted the strongly flavored chlorine tablets of WWII. Few ever used them, subconsciously, I suppose, preferring to get sick enough to be sent home; at least back to the rear for a while, like a self-inflicted wound.

We gathered in small bunches, speculating about the heavy firefight we heard going on to our left in the black of night lit here and there by magnesium flares, crisscrossed by tracers. Although they were used by us for tracing lines to targets, correcting sightings, the enemy never used anything to give a fix on their starting points, nor willie peter (wp, white phosphorus) hand grenades or 60mm mortar shells, unless taken from us. Holly, Sergeant Billson, Hurtz, Sergeant Ulriche and I were called by Foney who pointed to his map lit by his flashlight, at one hill, 442, one in a group of foothills between us and H 710 and told us we were ordered to fortify it and remain there until further notice. Sergeant Ulriche still had our platoon map without inviting me to share it.

We began to climb a finger leading to 442. Someone grouched, "Look, it's 0100 already," and I looked in vain at my left wrist for confirmation. A couple of guys pooped out on the first ascent, up the last of what seemed to be a perpendicular climb. Our soaking wet boots seemed made of limber lead and all that drew us along was the persistence of the lead man and the necessity to maintain the regulation five yards apart. "Keep up. Keep up," we nagged one another. "Don't bunch up." "Crimus," I muttered. "Don't lag."

Carbine strapped cater-corner over my back, I learned to remove my steel helmet, piss pot, carrying it under one arm to relieve my neck muscles or held by the brim, swinging it low to my side back and forth steadily as a pendulum to keep me moving at an even pace. I learned to walk sideways flat-footed up steep inclines, to stomp my feet down heavily, digging with the sharp outside of the soles of my boot at an angle, followed by a stomping out with the inside of my other foot for better traction. Sometimes we moved on hands and knees and, when we stood did so slowly, experimentally, leaning forward to prevent ourselves from being pulled backward. It was impossible always to resist the sliding down pull unaided, and we searched ahead as we climbed for large rocks or shrubs, or even better, low-growing gnarled mountain trees to cling to or brace our feet against. At rest our bodies had to work against gravity.

Starting up each time I carried myself low, zig-zagging like the others back and forth on the trail up the slopes. It was better to move steadily, deliberately, planting your feet heavily on their sides stomping one foot after the other; better to take plenty of two-minute breaks than fewer longer ones… get you out of rhythm.

Foney called so many halts and lit his map so often we got the impression we might be on the wrong finger. Good or bad, one had to trust his superior. After coming down on the other side, we soon found ourselves climbing up from another saddle.

"Crimus," I thought.

"Will someone make up his friggin' mind?" one complained behind me.

"Who's in charge of this mob?" another groaned loudly.

Funaro added his bit, "Suck a hatchi.

Others snickered, "S-s-h-h-e-e-it!"

"We're trying to confuse enemies," Sergeant Roundtree explained.

Suddenly, two, three, four, up to six three-round vollies of friendly 105 artillery exploded proximity shells fifteen feet in the air just beyond the company command group and lead rifle platoon, luckily catching our platoon on the protecting side of a gully. We 'heard' each other yell my God only by seeing open-mouth, strained expressions as chunks of meteors, hunks of almost red-hot shrapnel showered down, crackling and sizzling on the damp ground, zinging through trees and bushes, dropping leaves of one tree like heavy hail. Proximity are shells, still a top secret to the end of WWII, in the nose of which a tiny radar reckons the distance to objects exploding at a preset footage from any solid object to get an airburst that would reach men cowering in the bottom of their holes. VT, variable time, shells, are fuze timers set by artillerymen also for air bursts, in which the time in flight to a target would be known and a nose fuze set to explode after a certain time in the air so many feet above.

Guys slid downhill on their bellies, propelling themselves pushing off with their hands; others dropped their rifles, stood panic-stricken with arms over their faces as though to ward off the cutting steel fragments, and ran stumbling into one another. Our company lost two KIA and three WIA, one critically. The Banzai Third was spared.

"Gawd!" someone growled. "My gawd, this is awful!"

I was left shuddering with hunched shoulders as a weird feeling came over me. What was this strange primeval dread I felt? Surely, something that wasn't supposed to happen to civilized men. 'Friendly' fire they always admitted was a sorry accident and yet it happened on and off in all wars. Obviously not intentional, although chinks were known to have overrun artillery batteries and turned cannon on us. To me there was no explanation; no excuse at all. It was a sinister thing with deeper meaning of self-destruction, assisted suicide of a strange sort. But I had no time to dwell on the feeling other than record the impression.

The US government has always softpeddled, even denied, the occurrence of short rounds killing friendly troops as late as the Desert War, but its existence cannot be denied as the following note in Training Bulletin 2, 14 March 1952, Office of Chief Army Field Forces, Fort Monroe, Virginia dispensed to all US Army infantry units down to company, proves—

> It was observed on numerous occasions that frontline commanders hesitated to call for close artillery support because of a frequently justified fear of short rounds. It is important that constant attention be directed to elimination of faulty range estimation and firing techniques. They can spell the difference between an easy victory and a costly defeat (Comd Rept - 2d Inf Div - May 1951)

The faulty sighting was corrected and the next salvo went sailing high over us to the hill we faced. We were called to order again.

"Okay, fall in; on the ball; let's chogee."

"It's all over men. Second platoon here, fall in on me," I heard Fred Hurtz yell.

"Okay," I yelled. "Third platoon on me."

Instead, they sought Master Sergeant Ulriche. By sheer luck alone, none of our platoon was hurt.

Foney started us up 442 again from a different finger with a much easier-going trail. We bent forward, once more climbing until we reached the summit unopposed. Straight ahead, lighted by the full Chinese moon, was H 710, chinks swarming all over it. Thousands.

"Crazy," Tree moaned. "All them enemies crawlin' 'round."

"Plain suicide!" someone insisted. "They'll pick us off like flies."

We were allowed to mill around our peak as freely as the chinks and guys soon became more curious than frightened; the first time I observed enemy without being shot at, or so I hoped. I borrowed the platoon binoculars from Sergeant Ulriche and focused to see what I thought was an officer, some kind of honcho because he had binoculars too and was watching me. Most probably captured from us. After a bit, both let our binoculars drop on their straps to our chests and then, disappointed with what little we could see without them, put them to our eyes and observed one another once more. I wondered about him; was he as amazed as I was at this harmless sport?

Our excuse for avoiding making an attack, I learned later, was lack of artillery preparation and air support, it being night. What, I wondered, was their excuse? Certainly they could have clobbered us. Their ammo, of course, was much more difficult to replace than ours.

I had to shit urgently. I asked myself why, since I'd eaten so little the past four days. Pissing my pants and now having to go to the bathroom at a time like this, I scolded, should have gone before you left this afternoon. Like the stone pressing against my bladder, I couldn't put it off forever. Going behind a large boulder, I dropped my fatigue pants and shorts and let it drop. Fortunately it was hard in one piece for there was no ass wipe in the helmet given me. Prefolded tissues come with Cs and normally I'd have a few leaves in my upper fatigue jacket pocket or, most often under my helmet liner.

When I came back from the bushes, a private next to me was shivering as though cold, not that it was exactly mild.

"Sir," he asked hoarsely, "Goin' to make us go up there?"

"Expect so," I answered and to myself, "somebody do something, do something —get us out of here."

Then, as though the private's God took pity on him and me, battalion radioed that they couldn't get artillery so we should hold up until plans were made. How rumor starts, I don't know, but it went around that we were not going further, probably that whole night. Rumor or not, we were ordered to take over old chink holes and make them deep enough. We knew chinks had been there recently from the strong odor of garlic. It was difficult scratching and trying to shovel the stony earth with little collapsible entrenching tools. What we needed were pick axes. We had a few and D handle engineer shovels as well, in jeep trailer number four, not enough to go very far.

Once again I realized how damn pooped I was. J J sensed it and offered, "Just sit there, Lieutenant, I'll dig us a CP and you take it easy. I know what you've been through."

I thought this was the nicest thing anyone said to me since I got to the asshole of the world. As he chopped at the hard dirt, he sang low and soft, "O'ver the mountain, o-ver the see-ah-ee. Bring back... oh bring back... oh bring back my baby to me. O-o-over the-e wide ocean, o-v-er the s-e-e-a... bring back my bonnie to me."

Fog that rose from the ground on rainless nights effused moonlight in great empty expanses of valleys, swirling around below hilltops of that eerie world of hills and mountains as the flickering light of flares in our small portion of a great battlefield showed down, reflected from black night clouds. Our position on 442 was quite low for the average Korean hill in the east central mountain spine, and fog and mists of the night reached up from valleys almost to us. Far west an angry storm flashed and sounded. Valleys were bottomless, only surrounding hilltops visible, stepping stones across an endless fluffy white river, marked by chink red attack flares, huge blobs of blood thrown into the sky.

Under each misty hole or valley we worried were ghastly secrets, battalions of enemies lining up to get at us.

At about 0330 tracers drew our eyes to two firefights progressing at levels lower even than 442; one, we worried, from the direction of our battalion command post. Fog obscured the red tracers from one anxious machine gun that sent ricocheting rounds long distances through the free air above the white screen, burning brightly; at other times striking the ground near their starting points, angling into the night air in rapid red streaks, little burning balls bouncing off boulders, disappearing, burning out to mere wisps high above. Here and there from other valleys came red chink signal flares from captured Very pistols and, from an engagement miles to our west, chandelier flares swinging back and forth delivered high above by our heavy artillery. The chink light bursts we wanted to see were green Very flares that signaled retreat—pull back from an objective.

Company CP was under an overhanging rock shelf out of sight of chinks as the yellow horde stopped digging to watch the rest of us and, as though by tacit agreement and being out of easy small arms range, neither side fired a shot until one asshole from the First Platoon turned loose his automatic rifle. The chinks scurried for cover and a sergeant down the line roared, "Can it! Damn it, can it! Dumb sonofabitch want to fan things up? We ain't lookin' for medals, pinhead!"

Rain water still dripped from the rocks an hour later when bugles and flares came against the forward, northern, part of our loose company perimeter, a sharp reply to the pinhead BAR hero. No warning shots, no warning at all, and there was Death spread out wholesale once more, going down the ranks flipping coins—squat Mongolian death makers and taller, less high cheek bones and lighter colored death-dealers from the ricelands of China in their winter quilted jackets, rapidly penetrating between two of our platoons. Sergeant Ulriche quickly had the guys in a tight, self-supporting, criss-crossing fire plan and the Banzai Third, spitting out a hateful volley at one chink effort was left alone, although our position was sprayed overhead and an occasional shell from a captured 60mm mortar fell not far away.

A kid from one of the other platoons with a jammed automatic rifle scrambled panicky into the hole with Sergeant Ulriche who worked out a separated cartridge case with his pocket knife like the proverbial thorn in the lion's paw and sent him rearmed back to his platoon. Before the furious attack was over, which it was as suddenly as it began, three guys lay bloodied and limp in the first platoon, five altogether, high price for such a brief attack and withdrawal, and seven wounded. Afterward, guys scooted from hole to hole, checking on buddies, drying off, congratulating one another on a questionable victory, thankful the chinks disengaged. Our platoon was alerted by Pop Miller, his squad leader, to look for Ski.

"Missing all right, upstairs," one said.

"Might know it would be Ski," another piped up.

It became one of the platoon jokes how Ski, in the midst of the action jumped up and followed the guy with the jammed BAR back to his hole and, deciding to stay put until the fight was over, fell sound asleep.

Our brief, bloody engagement that night was lost in bigger, more tragic battles as splintered, stubborn companies, battalions and regiments of the US Second Infantry Division, the Indianheads, took on the many enemy units let into our rear by the wide breech opened in the Fifth ROK Division. Loss of the good men in Love Company was painful but little compared to some units as together we halted the last of the Chinese offensive starting them in a grand retreat north across the 38th Parallel.

Sad news over the SCR 300 back-pack company to battalion radio, from 38th Regimental Tank Company, our battalion CP was overrun and, among others, replacement battalion executive Captain Tracey marched off POW. Grapevine was that Colonel Coughlin was furious when he learned of Tracey's fate. Not just that he was a likeable young officer, but the fact that Major Wilkes, battalion commander, remained safe in the kitchen trains and let his executive go forward. Such procedure was unheard of, unexplainable and outrageous and should have resulted in Wilkes immediate removal. The fact that Tracey, a fellow West Pointer new to Korea, eagerly volunteered was no excuse.

Foney headed us hurriedly downhill. As we neared the valley where battalion set up headquarters, two of our regimental tanks came roaring ingloriously from out a side valley—whipped elephants shaking their big butts taking evasive actions—running from trouble, making gruff, mechanical growling noises, shifting, gear-meshing, pouring it on, spewing black puffs of diesel smoke. We discovered why when a strange, startling new sound made us pull our heads deep under our helmets and down under our collars—chinks halfway down a neighboring finger throwing low velocity shells at the tanks from a 75mm recoilless rifle captured from the heavy weapons company of a ROK regiment.

L B Bounds of Fort Worth, commo officer, fellow member of our Korean War Alliance, was taken prisoner on a short mission to aid Company A, First Battalion nearby on Wilkes's order and ended up a long-term companion of our buddy Conley Clarke in several Chinese POW camps. Ask *him* about Major Wilkes, despised by practically every officer who served under him.

This confirmed that they *were* enemy I spotted sneaking down the ridge to our left and that's a better reason that our attack on 710 never came off. My platoon was put out to scout and as daylight prevailed, we had plenty sightings of chinks on ridges around us. Our heavy artillery landed on a long finger to our right front on the white-clothed chink scouts disguised as Korean civilians who overran battalion headquarters and slunk off the skyline headed north with prisoners. I saw chinks on a hill ahead of us pointing our way excitedly and as our mountain domain was lighted by the sun, we located six sets of identifying air panels, four laid down by the enemy correctly to conform to the day's secret code to protect them from air strikes, yellow shank, red-topped design pointing north.

We returned to where we left battalion before midnight at a crossroad. I sauntered over to a group of officers where Captain Brownell was explaining what happened. He greeted me, "Hi Gould, doin' better?" Set up with his heavy weapons company across from battalion's forward CP, he witnessed what went on by gunflashes when the CP was clobbered. "Just an hour after King, the last rifle company left, chinks came through our Civilian Transportation Corps across from where our heavy machine guns were sand bagged. Like a streak of shit through the dark they were, well rehearsed, screaming, 'Don't shoot! CTC, don't shoot!' Them little bastards had regular CTC shoulder patches pinned to their white civilian sleeves and had been taught those two words in English. "Don't shoot!" When we opened up we had to kill CTC as well. We got a few chinks and eight CTCs killed and a number wounded.

"Lieutenant Carr, motor pool officer, came over with the outfit, did his best to line up jeeps to pull them out when a burp gunner caught him low at close range shattering his shin bones. When he stumbled down, another bastard walked over and shot him in the head. So many things happened, I can't remember all. It was dark, of course, and I was busy as a cat covering shit on a hot tin roof. It was mass confusion. Not the chinks; they'd been trained as a raiding party to hit us. Seemed only a second before they were gone, taking about ten of our guys, including the new exec, Captain Tracey. With the Fifth ROKs collapsed, they were taking POWs again.

"Molinsky, you know Molinsky, the new supply officer. He dropped into a hole with wireman Sergeant Kramer and pretended he was dead. Kramer was hit already and unconscious and a goddamn chink heard him groan and worked a barrel into his mouth and pulled the trigger. Molinsky said he liked to shit his pants. Then that dirty little cocksucker stepped on Molinsky's stomach, bent down and grabbed both their wristwatches.

"With the exception of Molinsky, all officers on the battalion staff were killed, badly wounded or led off POW. Captain Marcy, Battalion Surgeon, got it from a grenade as he was examining a guy. Others said they could never find his body and it was likely he was led off POW."

Tankers reported to regiment that King Company and Item, too, then assigned to the 23d, had been wiped out to a man. We knew it wasn't quite that bad; the further to the rear, the more absurd worries. Less confident than we dogfaces of their strength, they had doom on their minds always. Those not directly involved always expect the worst, fear more than us warriors, and we found that our sister company, Item, had not been engaged at all that night due to sudden rains and shortage of artillery ammo which precluded them from attacking. Besides, she had less than a hundred survivors.

We grabbed a quick breakfast of C Sixes. In reserve we got B rations—three hot meals at regular stateside times, 0700, 1200 and 1730 after daily retreat when we stood to lower and salute the national flag that flew over us in reserve. Old Glory to infantrymen. There was never a special time to eat in a combat situation; whenever we felt the urge and had rations.

Out of sight down the long valley parallel and to our left, an early-morning air strike by South African F-51s (formerly P-51) made repeated passes. Although the target was out of our sight, we could see

Morrison Field, West Palm Beach, waiting for trucks to take us to our bomber, January 1943, under secret orders to fly the southern route across the South Atlantic to Africa and England.

Roberts Field, Liberia, January 1943. The chief tried to sell me the fifteen-year-old girl on the right.

they were Mustangs as they zoomed up fast into the open sky after dropping their loads, on the first pass five-inch HVAR rockets, second napalm, and final four fifty-caliber machine guns each. I thought they zoomed up into the air away from the targets dangerously sharp and warned them, "Level off! Level off!" I don't know how to fly a kite but then I got the feel of maneuvering a plane while risking my life in the wing-heavy B26 B, redlined for 360s and less than 150mph landing, for fear of winging over. Our young pilots that year, 1942, at MacDill Field, called our kite 'The Flying Prostitute, no visible means of support.'

I mused about my year, released from the Royal Canadian Infantry after Pearl Harbor on a convenient medical discharge—athlete's foot, 'One a Day in Tampa Bay,' and the ten crews we lost, for there were few survivors at our low training level, and two down flying the southern way, Brazil, Ascension Island (a 1900 mile hop) and Accra on the Gold Coast (now Ghana). I considered the extremes, my wasted training to war in the sky in the 450th Bomb Squadron, 322d Bomb Group, and now fulfilling my desire for combat, my first choice, on and in the ground; flying backward at great speeds through the air with twin fifties solenoid-fired by thumb buttons with 1500 rounds running on tracks down each side of the aft bomb bay and, grunting heavily, pack animal under lethal loads. It wouldn't take a fighter pilot millions of dollars and a smorgasbord of instruments to fly a rifle platoon. No, but it takes guts, with more sustained, tested stamina, not minutes at a time, but hours, night and day for days and days and fearful nights after fearful nights. Both required a lot of luck. Infantry is much more simple than piloting a complicated bomber, after all, infantry comes from Italian *infante*—boy. It's boy this and boy that and boy stand behind, but when it's fighting to be done, down and dirty, muddy and bloody, it's boy on the line, ask Rudyard Kipling.

Time is a big factor when comparing pilot with rifle platoon leader, for a flyboy is over and done in cleanliness and comparatively little fatigue measured in hours at the most, while a rifle platoon leader's work is in many ways evermore fatiguing, through all the lights and darks of time and wet and dry weather, sweaty, bearded and dirty, warm and damp cold without letup, always under the weather. A fighter pilot rides off alone while a platoon leader has as many as forty lives to direct and account for. A pilot has millions of dollars of machine to care for but what about a rifle platoon leader's priceless charge?

Other air strikes came from Shooting Stars, F-80 jets, and F-86 Sabre jets but most jets often flew over targets too fast to be very effective. The Marine Corsair, F4Ws, a prop job, on the other hand, had ground support down to a T. Normally they supported the First, Fifth and Seventh Marine regiments of the First Marine Division and knew well how foot slogging dogfaces wanted the ridges worked. It angered and frustrated us to watch the high-speed jets zip in after chinks, who early on, spotting Mosquito Air circling waiting for fighter bombers, ran over the ridge to hide behind rocks below to avoid all three terrible passes. Marine Corsairs, on the other hand, lowered their big flaps to slowly rake both sides of the ridgetop; first a plane on, say, the right just off the ridge with rockets, his mate following, slanting to the left just off the ridgeline from whence the chinks had vanished, and the flight of usually four planes would alternate this way through rockets, machine gun and napalm running chinks back and forth.

Although no platoon leader was in on the secret, movement orders arrived from regiment for us to proceed to Hongchon for hasty reorganization, absorb newcomer replacements and supplies. More than bloodied, we were half drained. The battalions would be shuttled in the order White, Red and Blue, second, first and third, we to do the most hoofing, the last to ride out alive.

Our dead were rolled in pup tent halves, ponchos, blankets or slid into black reusable rubber body bags if and when we had them. Regimental graves registration wouldn't be on the scene for several days, if the Noname Line was reestablished. However, three officers of the battalion staff and the sergeant major were rolled up and taken out on a battalion headquarters 2_-ton truck with the badly wounded to the nearest helicopter pad.

Regiment assumed battalion forward headquarter's work and radioed for an ambulance and three machine-gun-toting armored reconnaissance jeeps from regimental Recon platoon for guard while retrieving and assembling the dead. Name, rank and serial number of KIAs, WIAs, and MIAs were radioed as soon as possible to their company headquarters clerks where they'd be noted on the morning report. Thus an official record was kept of what goes on personnelwise every day of the war. Through them division knew its real tactical strength; how deployable its units in that sector.

Bodies were usually gathered by Korean labor teams of graves registration and delivered in the backs of trucks, or, if only a few, in a jeep trailer, weapons carrier or ambulance to one of four platoons of two companies of the 23d Graves Registration Group. The 148th Graves Registration Company headquarters was at Wonju, the 293d at Seoul. When up to strength, each platoon had thirty men, including my contact for this journal, Corporal Lynn Hahn of Whitehall, Michigan, trained for the grisly job at the Fort Lee, Virginia Quartermaster Graves Registration School where he was taught such deadly, earnest business as handling bodies and proper maintenance of soldiers' graves.

With transportation engaged in supporting fighting all over the map, moving priority supplies, food, water, ammo and troops to engage the enemy, units had to recover their dead as best they could and pile them at crossroads for Graves Registration recovery teams to collect and ship to the large Army mortuary in Japan for embalming before returning to the fast expanding American cemetery near Seoul or one of the other American cemeteries.

Where we failed to hold ground or lost it for days, enemy were depended upon to bury our guys, at least put them under and out of sight. Once that land was retaken, if it was, they were supposed to be located using campaign maps to pinpoint where bodies had to be left and might have been buried. None of the Grave Registration people in a division is formally quartermaster-trained to recover and handle dead and none but cemetery workers allowed to bury our dead. A reported 8600 or more remains will never be recovered, a fact not publicized until the nationwide protests of gold star mothers of the Vietnam War.

Those of us not burdened with dead and wounded pushed through a small river and over a dirt road, jostling, shouting back and forth until we were worked by First Sergeant Luther into a presentable column of twos on opposite shoulders of the roads, on trails single file in proper position in relation to organization and we hoofed it a couple more miles.

"Hey, lieutenant, how you doin'?" some rifleman shouted.

I tried to smile. I'd hardly slept three days and nights and occasionally quivered in spasms from fatigue. I stumbled a lot because my muscles seemed to be becoming flaccid, rubbery, harder to control, which worried me.

"Yah, lieutenant, what you think of Korea now?" an old-timer shouted.

"Yeah," was all I could answer rather weakly.

Rumor matured that we were headed for division reserve for, with the outpost tragedy, we were widely acclaimed a badly mauled battalion. Man oh man, anywhere there were no chinks would be home. We laughed at nothing, using our hands for emphasis as we filed into a large assembly area of dry rice paddies, and one guy ran over to waiting tanks to give an iron hulk a big kiss.

"Baby, baby, am I glad to see you."

"Yeah?" he was warned from the open hatch. "Not when chinks are on us."

Guys ran around stowing what was allowed on company trailers. "Load up! Load up!" a tank sergeant mimicked. "You heard the boss man, chogee! What outfit's that?"

"Mushroom Company," Pop Miller answered. "Fed bullshit and kept in the dark!"

Lieutenant Carse led a convoy of company jeeps with trailers and Lieutenant Foney did something seldom seen—he smiled broadly. "Let's get at it," he shouted. "Let's go now. Fall in." So saying, he mounted the lead jeep and turned the company back over to First Sergeant Luther who had already quietly fallen us in.

We were charged with a strange electricity, alert and expectant. We heard we were going all the way back to Pusan; one of the guard divisions on its way from Japan would take our place and the way things were, we'd probably hoof it.

The 40th California National Guard and the Oklahoma Thunderbirds 45th, were both federalized and sent to Korea. Two more National Guard divisions, the 28th Pennsylvania 'Bucket of Blood,' and the 43d Connecticut, Rhode Island and Vermont, were brought on active duty in general reserve and then committed to West Germany to strengthening NATO and discouraging Soviets from jumping in.

Replacements for active duty with the Regular Army were drawn at random from Reserves, unsuspecting guys like me not active in units and from the standby federalized National Guard units, backing us up in Korea. After chinks entered, the 31st Alabama and Mississippi, the 37th Ohio, the 44th Illinois and the 49th Minnesota and North Dakota National Guards entered federal service on a standby basis.

My last medic, Doc Carlson, Joliet, Illinois, was transferred to the active Regular Army from the 44th. Some 244,300 Reserve officers and men were called on active duty to join the 43,000 Reserve officers already on active duty when the war began.

"Where's John Wayne?" someone suggested.

"Fuck Wayne."

"Forty-eight, forty-nine, fifty!" my guys shouted in unison. "Fuck Wayne!"

"Yah," I told them. "That'll be the day." I glanced around for appreciation and felt just a little warmer.

A tanker said he heard we were slated for some prison island off the south coast where gooks were rioting . . . Koje-do Island. "What?" Sergeant Burris asked unbelievingly. "Rioting? Prisoners? Mow the bastards down. Don't play with them."

"Forty-eight, forty-nine, fifty, s-o-o-me s-h-e-e-e—it! Mow 'em down!"

"That'll be the day," I joined in. Several of the guys gave me a cold stare and I realized I was pushing for acceptance maybe a little too fast. It wasn't quite time to be a spokesman.

"Hey, foot sloggers!" a tanker called. "What's that, sick call?" His buddies snickered.

"You tell 'em horseshit, you been on the road," Private Funaro yelled back.

"Fuck you! Got any friends? Fuck 'em. They got friends, fuck 'em too."

"Y-a-h," Ski sounded off. "You tell 'em Kotex, you been up against it," looking around laughing heartily because he knew what Kotex was.

"Twenty years in the cavalry, ain't stepped in horseshit yet," added a tanker master sergeant.

Funaro again with the familiar widespread Eighth Army threat, "Suck a hatchi!"

We fell in to march as far as we could to meet trucks returning for us. Drivers on QM heavy-duty trucks got as little sleep as we did. Time was saved this way by marching for we released hard-run valuable trucks to haul emergency ammo and supply runs during the hectic May Massacre. Besides, time saved could be used to move some other beat-up unit some other place. Along with what was left of battalion forward, we dragged our feet on down the weird Korean mountain valley road, sand-dancing, stomp-shuffling, wearing down the soles of combat boots; as Kipling com plained: "boots! boots! sloggin', movin' up and down again, there's no discharge in the war." Different war, same problem, Rudyard..

Behind survivors of battalion headquarters the little group of two depleted rifle companies moved out tediously, battle weary, leather slings slapping against hard-used rifles stocks. Happy to leave death behind, the guys began to shout, "When this bloody war is over we will all enlist again... like so much shit we will... like so much shit we will."

I tried to interest them in several ditties we sang in the Canadian infantry, who did a lot more singing, as "You are my sunshine, my only sunshine, you make me happy when skies are gray, please don't take my sunshine away." And one I was able at one time to sing in French Canadian: "*Adieu, attend moi j'esperer, de vous j'pensera souvent. Cette pour la payee, j'risque mon vie*"... something like that; ten years is a long time to remember something you hardly understood the first time. Anyway, the guys had their own favorite songs of the war we just won to relieve tedium, like *Roll Out the Barrel*, which I think was Australian.

Leaving, we passed where battalion CP had been where the dead were piled conveniently for Graves Registration, passed silently as our eyes went to them humbly, sorrowfully, deeply appreciative, hurting like we were them.

"There's Captain Allen," his S-2 clerk, a corporal, said in a low voice. "Bye, sir," handing out a sweeping salute. Allen, already stiffened, was easy to spot, tall and thin; wrapped tight in a poncho tied with commo wire like a rolled-up, misshapen rug.

"Good day for murder," someone observed wryly, meaning, I guessed, that the sky threatened another rain. Lifting his head, heavy with fatigue, swinging his battered steel helmet to his side and rear, J J began: "Over the moun-tain . . . ov-er the see-ah-ee, oh ma baa-bee-ee come back to mee-ah-ee. Oh honey, bring back my bonnie to me."

"What's that mean?" he was asked.

"Scotch, where mom's from."

"Where's them damn trucks!" came an empty demand.

Changing shoulders frequently, the guys decided neither would do, that old M1 was too heavy no matter where you slung it—nine pounds grown to about fifty. For short time relief, many laid them casually over their forearms, like dirty, bearded deer hunters or grabbed them by the small of their stocks, swinging them along their thighs front to rear, back and forth as we often did our piss pots for pendulum thrust momentum.

We infantrymen, whom Western Indians called 'walk-a-heaps,' trudged ten miles more. Me? I counted footsteps one to a hundred, starting over again and again and again, one to a hundred, one to a hundred, etc, etc, etc, but despite good intentions lost count of how many hundreds by the time a halt was called. Sweat, rain and water of the fords last night softened the blisters on my feet and mashed them into weeping sores. Fatigue silenced songs except a soft, lonely, lament from Tree, whose throaty, very Negro voice, was soothing as a lullaby: "Is I blue… Is I blue… Tell everyone 'round de place, I is blue… Is I blue…," taken over twenty feet up ahead by J J's perpetual wail: "O-ver the moun-tain, o-ver the sea, o-ver the moun-tain all the way." Just as we all felt ourselves soft and whimsical, purified by physical weakness and were falling asleep marching, some asshole of the First Platoon assailed our reveries with the shouted vulgar Marine chant: "If I die on the Russian front, bury me in a Russian cunt!"

"Yah," someone sneered among laughter, "beats this shit!"

We were awake a few more miles until hiking along I fell into a trance, sleep-walking. Some oldtime soldiers, CMTC instructors of the First Division at Plattsburgh in the summer of '37, told me it's possible to fall sound asleep marching, especially when you've been run hard and have made over ten miles already. I used to think they were full of shit.

Old infantry combat vet, Teddy Roosevelt, his last year as President, 1909, issued an executive order that all infantry field grade officers be tested by making a twenty-mile march in twelve hours, all cavalry thirty miles mounted or be discharged, and President Kennedy did something similar while he was in office, ordering that all officers, including generals, perform daily PT, physical training.

Thinking no longer about all the bodies I'd seen and would certainly see, and dead chinks, not neatly piled but tossed in heaps to be bulldozed under, and having to attack or be attacked by those persistent little guys and possibly, very possibly, getting it this time—I mean getting it, killed, like the young wireman and Captain Allen and others. "My God! there's too much exposure time, too many ways of getting it."

During our first ten-minute break, worrying that blood poisoning might set in in my infected thumb, I faced away and pissed on it. It smarted some, which gave me confidence and I did it on the march whenever I had to go. I read somewhere, Lawrence of Arabia I think, that piss was a good disinfectant, but the thumb continued to swell and throb worse than ever. Adding to my discomfort, my asshole both smarted from sweat and itched from hemorrhoids beginning to protrude, rubbed almost raw from chaffing. My athlete's foot squished when I walked. It's possible in such a situation, your thighs rubbing your sweaty crotch up and down hundreds and hundreds of times to have knots tied in your pubic hairs.

It seemed that each time we had just collapsed the break was over. A wave of grumbling aroused us. "Hit the road!" I noticed grenades, bandoliers of M1 clips, and other equipment, even bayonets left lying each time we moved.

One gripped, "Here we go already."

Private Philip Funaro was still lying down. His squad leader, Pop Miller, yelled from up the road, "C'mon, Funaro, catch up! Cut a chogee!"

"Can't go no farther," Funaro whined. "Lung's paining me."

"That's not all going to pain you," Pop threatened, walking backward slowly.

Tree, Pop's assistant squad leader, snickered. "Sh-e-e-eit!" and several joined in: "Sh-e-e-eit!" "Sh-e-e-eit!"

"Nobody can make me go," Funaro threatened. "I ain't RA; I never signed up for this horseshit. I got rights to see a lawyer."

"Lawyer?" Pop laughed loudly, "There ain't no law around here! This is the wild, Wild West, man" Everyone snickered sharply, "Shit!"

"Them's guardhouse lawyers; ain't no guardhouse here," someone explained.

"Nobody asked you how you got here," Pop said, "now chogee."

"How about it, lieutenant, can I wait for the ambulance?"

"They tell me the ambulance is full."

Pop was secretly angered, I am convinced, less by Funaro's appealing directly to me than at my taking three of his men as guards to Dorn's post without consulting him; learning that I let that liar off the detail by his phoney stripped rifle trick without consulting him infuriated Pop. Reaching down without warning, he pulled the helmet from Funaro's head, slapping him three or four times across his face, whack, whack, whack, with the flat front and back of his hand, grabbed him by a shoulder and one-handed him up the road toward his place in line, bending down on the march, scooping up Funaro's helmet and bowling it after him.

"Pick that up, you sonofabitch and chogee! Hear me, *motor!*"

Bushed as I was, I could sympathize a little with Private Funaro, but Pop had his tough job to do.

Even right after the long march was over I couldn't remember a single particular about a whole long stretch of that wild valley road. I do remember passing our march leader, company first sergeant, Sergeant Luther, almost forty-four, his back leaning on a large boulder, face buried in his hands. Sergeant Pater of King was thirty-six or thirty-seven, too damn old for a prize fighter or pro football lineman and what Pater was doing. I thought, "I'm thirty-one; he's much too old for this sort of thing," and, I asked Luther in passing, "Where's your field first, Sergeant Martin, old timer?"

He tossed me a hand. "Don't worry, sir, they're sending a weapons carrier for us old farts."

There must have been a squad of stragglers, one of whom, thanks to Pop, was not the city boy, Private Funaro.

I wondered where was the age cutoff. One did not have to serve overseas in WWII if over thirty-eight. In the US Army prior to the Civil War officers could serve until they dropped, some seventy and even in the case of higher grade, in low eighties. They mounted a horse or walked, although General-in-Chief Winfield Scott, hero of the War of 1812 and the Mexican and Seminole Wars, eighty when he died at the end of the Civil War, was carried by four soldiers from place to place in a sedan chair. Although eased out of command, it was his Anaconda Plan that won the war.

We overtook and passed Item Company guys miles behind their order of march, arguing bitterly.

"I told you for the last time, pick it up."

"I packed it the last five miles; it's his turn again, he knows damn well."

The man referred to whined, "But, sarge, I got an awful stitch in my side."

The sergeant roared, "I ain't fooling no more! One of you shoulder that goddamn machine gun or I'm personally kicking the shit out of you both!"

"Okay, sarge," the man with the stitch said, lifting the heavy metal load. "I've got a bad hernia. I know you're going to be sorry."

I could sympathize with that guy with the stitch in his side, though, of course, his sergeant had his job to do. I told the sergeant as I passed it was none of my business but our first sergeant had just fallen out and they'd radioed for a special weapons carrier.

I wondered could a draftee or someone like me, recalled Reservist, ever be a professional soldier? That is, could we be that impersonal and cold?

I could feel us grow more sullen in our hiking, 120 beat guys left of a rifle company of 400 strung out loosely along a winding hilly valley road; two files of wobbly guys. We marched, no, walked, no, slogged along through dark, daybreak and fifteen miles into sunlight, thoughts submerged in silence, as sweat stains under our straps and behind our belts grew larger and darker.

"Where's them damn nigger trucks?" some loudmouth up front with a heavy southern accent demanded after an hour more of silence.

"Yeah," he was answered loudly in good humor by our self-proclaimed 'token nigger,' Sergeant Raymond Roundtree. "Where's niggers when you need 'em?"

Most everyone who knew Tree laughed sardonically.

"Tell 'em, Tree!"

I daydreamed I stood before the Division Provost Marshal threatening him, "Court-martial me, sir, but don't make me go back to that platoon. I'm not cut out for this sort of thing. I'm too old, I worry too much and I'm more sensitive than others. Most of them are kids who deserve better than me," and I tried to explain to the Army police chief how Sergeant Ulriche earned a field commission and Silver Star at Guadacanal and at Kunu-ri and how could I ever live up to that?

"That's well and good," the major sympathized," but he won't be around to father them forever... he's four on the battalion rotation roster."

I switched off that daydream which had nowhere to go that I could see, and when every bit of energy was gone, I had to make meanness do. "That old bastard sun, high over that mountain. Fuck the old bastard sun! Hear? Fuck you, Chinese sun!"

Finally, we arrived at the junction of a small road leading into what was our regimental assembly area. Red Battalion trucked by on its way out to reserve. I B Foney stood up in his jeep yelling at us, "Love over here. Let's shape up there; you act like you're going to a funeral. Get on the ball now, heads and eyes off the ground, shoulders back, chin in. Pick up the step. You're marching at attention now. Hup!

Two! Three!... Hup! Two! Three! Let's show these people Love Company. Straighten your shoulders, Lieutenant Gould, get your men in step. Hup! Two! Three!"

"Sh-e-e-et!" I thought. "You wouldn't dare talk to Sergeant Ulriche like that. You bastard had a ride all the way; bury *you* in a Russian cunt and ain't nothin' permanently wrong with my shoulders."

We got relief from the old sun all right; it darkened and without warning clouds swirled low and rained us hard. What harm had we ever done that yellow jerk, Korean rain god? We milled about into the valley bowl, hunched over under ponchos, talking in low voices, wondering collectively what, if anything, we'd accomplished the last couple days. Guys with sweaty blankets doubled around their shoulders covered with ponchos squatted around sputtering fires or sat on upturned helmets to keep their rears dry.

The sharp rims cut off circulation around our butts and standing to massage them was all that kept many of us from falling asleep. Every once in a while a GI on the outside of a fire went into nearby bushes and returned with an offering of wood. Having earned the privilege, he remained near the fickle heat until a new offering pushed through the circle. Stale wood smoke was our brand of perfume.

Some guys sitting on upturned helmets when the rain let up took off their boots and sticky socks to massage their aching, itching feet. Areas of the toes on my left foot were in bad shape, white from sweat and water, bloody from athletes' foot. I put a sock over a trigger finger and rubbed the area, so sensual I worked up fresh blood before forcing myself to stop. Damn, do I have to die to get rid of this burning, itchy bastard? Despite a month in the Rideau Convalescent Home, Ottawa, it kept returning.

I sucked my infected thumb. It was coming along slowly except at one end which cracked open as it tried to heal over. Later, our battalion surgeon lanced the thing and released some pus. I told him about my athlete's feet and piles and how tight my chest was, hawking globs up from a bad post nasal drip, especially right after I awoke.

"Nothing unusual for smokers," he warned, shooting me with penicillin. In WWII they'd have to hand you some APCs, Army aspirin.

The guys murmured about all their troubles with the Chinese Fourth Field Army. I still hesitated to butt right in and offer opinions, even though I was beginning to have a few. Generally speaking, we were two groups, those who talked of rotation and the rest of us. I was too tired anyway, so much so that I was way beyond even extraordinary tired feelings. My ears hummed like rural telephone wires I remembered as a kid and my eyes burned intolerably sore, scratching like sandpaper when I blinked; all of me overly sensitive. My bladder burned to be relieved, but when I tried to go, not a drop would fall. I was unreasonably bugged by mumbled conversations fifty yards away and several times my overworked eyes saw chinks again moving through trees of a nearby murky skyline.

"Man," Sergeant Karl Eppler, fellow vet of WWII, sighed, seated cross-legged under a wide, black umbrella he'd latched onto in the ruins of one Korean farm house or another. "If this ain't the hardest war I ever fought."

It might have been humorous but I was too pooped to respond.

Rain! Rain! Rain! Drifts of cutting rain started blowing again down the valley to make a complete mess of the slowly diminishing light. Thinking it much later than it really was, I was surprised when someone remarked how dark for five o'clock.

"Seventeen-hundred?" someone said unbelievingly. "We been here all day!"

Service Company trucks returned from hauling the Red Battalion to shuttle us the rest of the way and carried us in the dark of an off-and-on rain over a rickety Bailey bridge at Upchon and south over a washboard road for another hour until we reached Hongsong directly north of Hoengsong where the guys found their packs, those the chinks didn't have, lined up, pitched pup tents and were handed metal mess trays like in the field in the States as back in our kitchen trains we got a hot late supper of chicken pot pies almost like a stateside garrison A ration. Guys went back for thirds. All I could handle was sleep.

After breakfast most headed for a quartermaster shower point tent as hot as the meal. They put personal belongings in OD colored cloth bags, dropped handkerchiefs, underwear, socks and fatigues in piles, set boots down under the bags and ran en masse, dog tags swinging along with another thing, under the hot showers naked as their mothers made them—oh, my God, that wonderful hot water, made for us by Quartermaster, toweling off with good, rough towels; receiving brand new handkerchiefs, underwear, socks and steam-sterilized fatigues.

We stayed in that level valley of dried rice paddies three and a half days and the first day I zipped my sleeping bag to my chin, curled up facing the wall of our officers' arctic tent and slept twelve straight hours while J J covered for me, explaining to Foney all we'd gone through on the outpost such a short time ago.

Replacements poured in by the dozens the second day and when I woke up, Sergeant Ulriche and I ladled them out to squads, run skimpy for too long. Dorn and his men were replaced by eight guys and Pop Miller, who'd been acting squad leader, with Tree as assistant. One replacement from Mississippi convinced Sergeant Ulriche he was so much better than 'niggers' he'd have to be reassigned. "That guy should have been drafted before he got so mixed up," Ulriche swore. "He's got one helluva' lot to learn," and proceeded to play him up for a swap to Hollingsworth where his platoon guide, Zigerfoose, in two weeks had him on charges for stealing a money belt and headed back to the division stockade for a fair trial and, after serving six months in the stockade at division, reassignment somewhere other than Love of the 38th. Word was the belt was a plant to nail the bigot.

Our PX rations arrived, free candy, lifesavers and lifesavers and lifesavers UTA, up the ass, candles, cigarettes, toothpaste, writing pads and envelopes, etc., along with paid-for items like pocket books, watches, shortwave, longrange overseas radios that could get San Francisco when high clouds were right and, of course, our own Armed Forces Radio Far East network, and cameras guys ordered and paid for in advance. Some ordered by guys since killed or evacuated disappeared mysteriously, making for furtively happy supply sergeants and other headquarters scums. The majority, however had been willed to buddies prior to going back on line.

Working on our fear course, Sergeant Eppler and I recorded our experiences, and worked out a system of our own for when shit hit the fan, particularly late at night. We'd stay in our holes near the center of the platoon and begin by getting control of ourselves, harness some of that wild energy upsetting our bodies, shouting things such as "play it cool! ... play it cool!" and with the guys, neutralizing their sudden fear reactions, shouting back as we scooted along to opposite ends of our positions: "Hey, Jerry, you guys all right? ... Bud, how are you and Ed? C'mon, get some talk going. Be alert! Make sure there's one in the chamber and the safety's off."

Like a successful football team thinking and working hard together, the more so, the greater our morale. Could that be getting on the ball?

3

TASK FORCE JOKE

All are but parts of a stupendous whole,
Whose body Nature is and God the soul.
– Alexander Pope

March orders disrupted our repose as early on the morning of the fourth day of rest we struck tents, made legionnaire rolls of blanket and pup tent halves to strap to our packs containing private possessions, cameras, radios, cherished letters, spare candy bars, toilet articles, pocket book or two; everything we owned tagged with our names by platoon in a mound behind the supply tent and filing over to the trucks, loaded in the silent aftermath of a well-enjoyed slumber—we all, we fierce warriors, all condemned, all of us—guilty without evidence or proof, sentenced to die we knew not exactly when.

We left the dregs of a big hot breakfast, coffee, cereal and reconstituted milk, bacon and powdered eggs, toast and jam and the friendly atmosphere of our cozy kitchen train smelling like home (mainly the hot food) through a drizzly, low-hanging mist. Oh, smell it, man! Say good bye again to civilization!

An hour later, winding up an old, unused oxen trail, we passed two fire-blackened hulks of tanks rusting there since January, displaying the heroic fatal acts of unsung chink peasants, two dead Sherman M24s, brightly painted tiger faces on the forward slopes, on the side of which holes burned neatly through eleven inches of armor steel by otherwise poorly-equipped big game hunters, individual champions of the Orient with captured 3.5-inch rocket launchers.

We didn't stop grinding and shifting gears, straining, revving, engine-snorting, diesel fuming, spewing, combined driving effort until three in the afternoon. We dismounted (a term held over from when horses were the mounts to come down from) as rain approached solid water, dissolving mud we splashed slowly over until we circled into a perimeter on a valley floor and squatted under individual shelters of our ponchos. Word passed along for each platoon to send three men to the Company CP, offerings to climb a nearby hill and set up a listening post, flank security for a newly organized battalion headquarters. J J and our soon-to-rotate hot-to-trot medic, Doc Lynch, dug our platoon CP hole on higher ground while I went with Sergeant Ulriche, checking squad leaders, helping settle new guys, trying to answer questions.

By now, I was a bona fide oldtimer to all replacements, with combat under my belt, having been shot at more times than could be counted. I looked like I'd been there a year, that weatherbeaten look. One had to be a real oldtimer to make it the other way around, shooting more than being shot at. Despite being in Korea less than two months, and all the off-and-on cloudy spring weather, I was tanned from being constantly outdoors, getting so thin my normally well-padded hip bones had little natural cushion, forcing me to be more fussy about working a hole to fit me just right, like that girl they tested for princess, sneaking a dried pea under her mattress. I was by now not only a regulation dogface infantryman, digging like a dog, squirming around in tight circles to fit a lie-down place just so, stopping to paw away imaginary stones, tree roots, peas, or whatever, before flopping to do some serious resting. Other less delicate guys I've witnessed just fell into their holes and slept. Since leaving Watertown, I'd lost twenty pounds, mostly my ass.

At 0530, dripping wet and chilly, we were lined up in tight formation to answer roll call. Released, we each scooped up a C6 box with three little tin can meals, one can for each meal of the day, chopped fruit for desert, cigarettes and ass wipes, and saddled up again to continue motoring to the east, as near as I could tell, where chinks had busted through the 7th ROK Infantry. We stopped four times for piss calls, although whenever a guy had to go bad, he'd stick it over the sides or, better yet, the tailgate. Pity the guy who let it go up wind.

At last the trucks zigzagged up a steep mountain road that our engineers carved out, sinking two-foot thick logs into angled holes they drilled somehow in the hard rock cliff for cribbing, and cementing them in; such skillful road engineering no Army in history ever heard of. Once we were held up half an hour while drivers up front ever-so-carefully winched the right rear wheel of a heavily loaded 2-ton truck back onto the narrow road from a drop off of hundreds of

A road several hundred feet above a valley carved from a mountainside by the U.S. Army Engineers who always amazed us.

Army engineers under poncos plan how best to blow down more of the mountain to fill the hole washed out by the monsoon.

feet, and, coming down from one high pass, we watched in awe swirling vapors of cold mountain winds circling and twisting and, higher up, storming in earnest to clean themselves of cruddy clouds.

We descended the newly engineered road, covering a long wilderness track in third low gear, a narrow, treacherous trail over which nothing but engineer vehicles had rolled, cautiously; the outer wheels of six-wheeled 'six-by' heavy supply trucks skimming carefully, breathtakingly along the rim of one great drop off after another, passengers walking well behind, the driver, a demonstrating hero, riding with open door, ready to jump, moving slowly in lowest gear, concentrating his eyes, for the life of him, fixed on the edge of the drainage ditch cliff side or on the forward edge of the drop off hidden by the body of his truck. I'll never forget our mad, dangerous ride on those desolate manmade mountain wilderness trails. It was a long, dangerous struggle by itself which everyone talked about for days and like me still clearly recall; another time our engineers were real heroes. We pulled to the side after coming down to a valley and, it being dark early, again drew rations for the coming day from a jeep trailer and slept under or on the truck, drivers and officers, and, of course, Sergeant Ulriche, still an active platoon leader.

The next day was, for me, the red letter, unforgettable, 23d of May, 1951. About five miles farther on we pulled into a large rice paddy, unflooded that year because of the war. As the sun came out to welcome us, officers and platoon sergeants walked to a briefing by the G3 of X Corps laying the groundwork for a coordinated drive to push back the overextended chinks. It was given by a white-haired bird colonel, a crisp old Army pro who must have been in his late 50s.

Our acting battalion CO, Major Wilkes, had been sent down from X Corps staff to our battalion, not to benefit troops by his combat leadership for sure, but because he was a West Pointer who required command following his staff job to be eased upstairs to light colonel. He was older than me even and while I was huffing it around from Passau into the Sudetenland, he fought a desk in the Pentagon, world's largest office building. As an assistant G3 of Almond's X Corps, he was being favored with a combat command he knew nothing about. Later his former boss, the G3 colonel in overall charge who briefed us, failed to mount the hill himself to see that the support part of his five-paragraph field order was implemented, and failed to see his protegee, Major Wilkes, in a hole back down the ridge sucking on a bottle.

The colonel stood before us and read off a classic five-paragraph field order, as taught, I understand, to ROTC college graduates at the Infantry School at Fort Benning, Columbus, Georgia. What we hard-working combat recalled Reservists with a two-week refresher course termed Benning School for Boys.

"Your battalion under your leader, Major Wallace W Wilkes," he began, pointing to the guy who was presumed to lead the attack, and went on almost tediously to point out where everything we needed would be—"Ammo supply at the dismount point; medical evac through the 15th Infantry's collecting station here," pointing to the 1:50,000 map, copies of which we all read from. Sergeant Ulriche let me read from his. No need was omitted but explained in detail how we would fulfill it. According to the colonel, we had priority on Fifth Air Force Air support and an assortment of artillery that was, or soon would be, in position to give us battalions of preparatory fire, including the Wyoming National Guard's long-barrel eight-inchers on whose tractor bumper were the unit's insignia, black silhouettes of cowboys riding bucking broncos, whose shell impacts I dreaded most while playing dead, and we had the Triple Nickels again, the all-black 155mm unit mentioned earlier.

At battalion level, Major Wilkes, we were told, could, in addition to artillery and Air, call for 4.2 chemical mortars from Heavy Mortar Company at regiment and his own 81mms and 75mm recoilless rifles, heavy, water-cooled machine guns and our own company light machine guns.

"Your battalion is the left flank attacking force of Task Force Yoke, with Eighth Army priority. A ROK regiment is already in position at your jumpoff ready to sweep up to your objective once it is taken and set up for counterattack. An entire tank battalion, the 72d of Second Division, will come down the valley in sight of your objective to work the target point blank. All fires are on call and all that stands between you and victory is a battalion of demoralized, poorly equipped Chinese, short of ammo, at this minute ready to desert."

All were elated, relieved for a time from normal apprehensions. Man, this is class, I thought, the way we should be committed; a five-paragraph field order clear and as inclusive as you can get. Man, have we got firepower and support. I pity those chinks up there with all that artillery and Air. After all that shit, all we have to do is walk up and take it and let ROKs prepare the defense.

"Any questions?" the colonel demanded, giving a stern look around to preclude any. "All right, soldiers, move out!" We saluted and he pivoted around like I'd never seen before except in a movie.

Another thunder storm was brewing. Someone asked, "Is it like this every day of the war?"

An oldtimer replied, "Wait for the monsoon."

"What in hell is *mon soon,* or whatever you call it?"

"You'll see."

While all units reported successes in their sectors, the 38th Infantry left Corps Reserve and moved north to Sokpyokkol on the Division right flank where it went into blocking positions. As it came onto line, its Third and Dutch battalions reverted to its control.

At 0800 hours on 23 May, the Second Division initiated its aggressive offensive, one of the most remarkable and spectacular of the war. For six days, the Division had fought a determined enemy, giving ground slowly while inflicting casualties estimated at 10,000 for each day of the Chinese offensive. Throughout the period, the Division had maintained its tactical unity and freedom of maneuver. Now it turned and drove against the desperately tired enemy who no longer had the numerical strength or supplies to continue the pressure. The heroic stand of the previous days and the sudden reversal of tactics embodied in the new offensive marked one of the most dramatic achievements of the Korean War.

The attack moved out on schedule against light resistance. Both the 9th and 38th Regiments secured their first-day objectives [lie]. The 187th A/B RCT, [airborne regimental combat team] making the main thrust, battled stiff resistance as it advanced along poor roads, ringed with enemy-dominated peaks.

A hastily-organized assault group, Task Force Yoke, commenced a limited northward drive to keep the enemy forces off-balance while the counter offensive was being racked up. Composed of the 3d Bn, 38th Inf; 72d Tk Bn (-)[minus a unit or more]; a platoon from the 38th Inf Tank Co; a battery of division field artillery and a tactical air control party, the mobile force moved northwest from Pungam-ni toward Habae-jae.

To the west, along the familiar Hongchon-Inje road, the 187th A/B RCT passed northward thru the lines of the 23rd picking up B Company of the 72d and securing the high ground around Hangye by nightfall thereby permitting the 23rd to fall back to an assembly area in the vicinity of Hongchon to prepare for its part in the coming counter-offensive.

And as Task Force Yoke and the 187th sent twin-pronged drives short distances northward, the 9th Infantry, operating between the two forces, jumped-off for two objectives—Hill 592 and Tappung-ni, former road-block area. With the First Battalion on the left and the Third Battalion on the right, the Hill was secure by nightfall and the regiment buttoned up for the hours of darkness.

Love and King, with Item, the most beat up, still assigned to the 23d, climbed a narrow trail for three hours without stopping longer than five minutes at a time. Despairing replacements wondered what they had gotten into and some fagged out, offering weak little smiles for consideration and consolation. After we hand-counted their loads, they were constantly ordered to go back and recover grenades and whatnot. Losing Government property is a court martial offense they were reminded, to say nothing of weakening us all. Thinking only of dying from utter fatigue, they were astonished the following day to discover what grit they really had to fall back on; this necessity for exercising your grit, a prime combat lesson learned.

Around noon we reached a high point on the ridge where lead scouts of King Company lay sprawled behind rocks and knobs of earth and small mountain trees. South Korean soldiers were there, helmets and shoulders covered with wilted grass and twigs, cutting fresh camouflage with bayonets so dull they were having a hard time. "Look, Kim," Sergeant Burris said, motioning them to come closer as he made a single swipe with his bayonet to cut off a twig the size of his finger, then thumbed the blade cautiously from one side. Pointing to one of their bayonets, he said with exaggerated disgust, "ROKs no hucking good!" Like many North American Indians once did, they had difficulty pronouncing the letters *f* and *l*.

Sighting us Americans, many ROKs ran with unusual enthusiasm up to their emplacements and fired wildly hundreds of rounds at a bush-covered ridge to their immediate front. An angry KMAG sergeant tried to stop them, introducing them to some choice English. A few of our riflemen crawled up to peek at the enemy, picking out places where ROKS dug in and one show-off, new to combat, went walking back and forth exposing himself on a short section of ridge top. Guys gave him cat calls for his trouble: "My he-e-ero!" a sergeant imitated a woman's voice appealingly and then roared: "Get your fuzzy ass down!"

"I didn't mean nothing," the replacement pouted, a little proudly, crawling down. "Just wanted to see what it's going to be like. They wasn't comin' anywhere near."

"Stand there another minute you'd find out." As though to demonstrate, a high-powered Russian sniper rifle round landed where the showoff had been, anticipating his reappearance.

The chinks had excellent fire discipline and, aside from their almost playful sniper round, wasted no ammunition taking pot shots. After all, I thought, look at the thousands of miles and the way they have to carry it ultimately on their backs. Still, had they been at a greater distance I could have better understood their restraint but those aggravating chinks were only 400 yards away as a crow might fly, straight across a saddle. I thought hopefully that maybe as the colonel said they were short of ammo and not anxious to fan things up. Pity things couldn't work out so there didn't have to be a fight. I wished I knew Chinese like Captain Brownell, old China hand from the Marines. I'd holler over and come to some kind of an agreement. I wished hard that Brownell was with us. I heard he talked friendly to chink POWs. "Okay," I'd say, "when I count three throw away our rifles and get the hell out of here."

Instead, the order was passed up for King Company to move out. "Tell King to haul ass!" was what we passed along for King to lead out on the attack, over to our right a bit. The lead squad of the first platoon of King took off right away but reaching the bottom of the saddle directly under the chinks, ROKs, suddenly brave after facing the enemy overnight without assaulting, fired so closely to the front men of King they balked. From the ridge to our right in King Company came Sandy Opolous's replacement, Captain Toth, mad as hell, "What they trying to do, kill us!"

While the attacking squad dribbled back to the bottom of the saddle without orders, its aggressiveness gone, the acting battalion S3 (on loan from the 72d tanks) ran around in a tizzy hunting for the Korean military advisor and his interpreter. "Tell your people to cut that shit! Tell them to mask their fires! Where's KMAG? Where's KMAG?" he stewed.

"Dammit, Lee," the KMAG captain ordered his interpreter angrily, "Do you want to try again to take that hill? You been here since yesterday. You want to have to go it alone again? Then tell them to cut out that shit!"

"That not shit, sore," the Korean officer answered gravely, not knowing about American idioms.

"Dammit, you know what I mean."

"Yes, sore!" he smiled with big teeth, saluting twice.

One or two artillery batteries slipped HE, high explosive, shells over the chink hill on their way to another objective, directed by a little L-19 observation plane. From the height he was cruising, we surmised he was about to rotate. Loafing on the friendly side of the ridge, curious guys peeking over the top of the ROK positions started snip-

Artillery air spotter searching rugged peaks and valleys for enemy. The enemy were disciplined not to fire to disclose their position.

ing at a cocky chink believed to be an officer. Not over a football field away, he stood, arms folded, looking us over coolly, it seemed utterly disdainful. More and more guys crawled up to investigate, some old veterans. I wondered if he was their answer to the rookie exposing himself on our side. Answering a challenge, maybe?

"Hey, guys!" Sergeant Eppler yelled, waving his furled black umbrella. "We got a turkey shoot."

Lieutenant Hurtz and I left Foney with King Company commander and the assistant acting battalion S3 in the security of an overhanging rock ledge and climbed up cautiously to keep watch on it. This was the last I saw the acting S3. Soon half of Love was lying along the ridgetop firing at will. Once dirty smoke thrown up by a bursting ROK 57mm recoilless hid the solitary enemy. "Hot dog, they got him!" Ski yelled, jumping up and down. "Give that man a Kewpie doll." Settling smoke disclosed the officer on the same spot, arms still calmly folded.

"Didn't hit him any!" Ski accused, imitating a woman's voice.

Word passed along to hold fire and after a moment of silence, when the chink was sure we'd ceased our futile efforts, he knelt down and sneaked out of sight. Sonofabitch! Gave us the willies; were we all that lousy shots?

As the KMAG officer finished his pow-wow with the offending ROKs, King's field first sergeant, Master Sergeant Pater, guided a very young-looking ROTC officer and his platoon reluctantly over the ridge down through the bushes of a faint path to the bottom of the saddle, stirring up a hornet's nest of enemy fire. Pater harangued the leader who seemed to be a teenager and returned. Twenty minutes later we could pick out individuals of that platoon coming briefly into sight between bushes, climbing rapidly cover-to-cover like animated puppets, one foolhardy rifleman a full twenty feet in the lead, an inspired hero or just ignorant of basic military science.

Chinks poked their heads up over their trenches behind chopped brush camouflage, running back and forth, chattering like squirrels in strange sing-song. Now and then an arm came over the top to throw a tiny object down toward the guys of King Company crawling up from the saddle, followed by a weak-sounding ka-rumpt! of distant potato masher grenades, with a two-foot-high black dust cloud on the ground near the miniature soldiers crawling their way to the top. Suddenly a rash of cheering broke out among King's men; then ceased as suddenly, and when it began again was sporadic and less confident. Twenty minutes later, word came filtering up with the first walking wounded that the platoon guide, an oldtimer and two of his men lay in their blood on the hill. Shocked, the remainder slipped and slid slowly down to the bottom of the saddle to crowd behind boulders with their young ROTC officer. Intermediate bugouts, I call them.

Another rifle platoon of King Company, led by an acting platoon leader, a sergeant first class, was immediately committed full front against the objective, but fired half-heartedly and only one squad managed to crawl up more than a quarter way, on level with the frightening dead of that platoon then sank down to join those among the large boulders. I listened to a thoroughly frightened shavetail over the 536 radio. "But, but ... but, ... sir, we can't, sir.... Can't go no farther, sir ... pinned down, sir. Three guys dead; they must be dead, they're lying there. No, no, sir. We can't."

Wilkes was nowhere to be found and it took about ten minutes to raise Lieutenant Foney. Some of us wondered aloud about the preparatory fire we were promised, but left it up to our commanders, whose responsibility it was.

"Where are you?" I demanded.

"Never mind," he said, "get ready to relieve King Company."

"Where are you?" I asked again. "Can you see what's going on?"

Foney was described to me after it was over, moving slowly on the friendly side, ears cocked, ridiculous, hunched over beside men walking upright, eyes peering back and forth as though looking for someone, occasionally peeking over the ridge top to the enemy hill.

I discovered later that in his five months in Korea, by luck and good maneuvering this was the closest he'd been to the enemy. While Foney and I talked, Lieutenant

Dale Gordon Hollingsworth almost ran by me ahead of his faithful platoon sergeant, former Filipino scout, Master Sergeant Quaid (phonetic), and the rest of his platoon by about ten feet. I was surprised and yelled "Good luck" after Holly, looking straight ahead, a fixed stare on his face, his mind seemed too preoccupied to acknowledge. I read about this heroic guy after returning from Korea, in Major General S L A Marshall's book, THE RIVER AND THE GAUNTLET, whose book, MEN AGAINST FIRE, was one of the mandatory readings I enjoyed while in the Reserves. SLAM, as he once asked me over the phone to call him, wrote about the heroic acts of three men I met after I got to Korea. He described our Holly "baby-face, thick-lens glasses, about twenty, smallish, talked quietly ... a Guthrie, Iowa farm boy." After two

Brave little Holly, field commissioned, Silver Star and Purple Heart with cluster, died from a broken heart.

91

days and nights at the Kunu-ri trap last November he was one of the few leaders left to the company, field commissioned when they got back to South Korea. The others Marshall was impressed by were Lieutenant John Fox, whose lecture helped save my life and who is now writing his own book, and Corporal Edsel Turner, of L Company, RA35545252, wounded quite badly and frostbitten at Hoengsong 12 Feb '51, who died hard of cancer several years ago at Kalamazoo. His wife and I deplored the fact that I didn't find their telephone number sooner. She was elated and proud, she told me, to learn of his exceptional heroism.

"I know he had that medal, that cross, but he was so quiet about Korea, he never told us things like that."

Holly was a very bright, brave young second lieutenant whom everyone liked. Three days before trucking out for Task Force Yoke after mailcall Holly came into the officers' arctic tent, was quiet for a time and threw a one-page penciled letter and four colored films on his cot, blurting: "Want to see something good?" He picked up the letter and forced it on Foney; giving the photos to me. The letter was from the girl he married a week before embarking for Korea. She was doing a strip tease and named the neighbor who took the pictures. If Holly needed any more evidence, just say so and she'd send it. She wanted a quickie divorce to marry the neighbor and if the pictures weren't enough, she'd send more. Did he think she was nobody, waiting patiently while he got all the glory? The last photo showed her naked on the couch, her legs apart. No words were said for a few minutes while we read and stared and Holly retrieved the pictures from Foney who spent too long studying them.

"Dirty bitch," Foney said.

I put my hand on Holly's shoulder and told him how sorry we were. He started to sob, then suddenly stopped and shook his head.

"Why'd she do it, Dud? What's wrong with this crazy world? Oh my god, it's all over."

Holly didn't say a word to anyone except his platoon sergeant during the few days he had left. Like my Kitty, his wife blamed his being away in Korea on a desire to be "a big heee-ro . . . didn't you think how lonely I'd be?"

The Third Division unit that finally took the hill found Holly and his faithful former Filipino scout a few feet apart, riddled with bullets from one of the Maxim machine guns.

I called General Marshall in June '52, at his editorial position with the Detroit News, because of the good things he had to say of Holly in his book and his first words were: "My god, what a terrible thing. I thought he was such an outstanding little man. My god, what a nasty thing." As an afterthought, "I hope she didn't get his $10,000 insurance." I learned that Foney called the division JAG officer to try to cancel it but never found out how it came out, presumably negatively.

Lieutenant Foney called on the walkie-talkie where we were huddled on the enemy side in a small gully, asking for Sergeant Ulriche. "Why?" I interrupted. "I'm platoon leader; what you want with Ulriche? He's talking with a buddy in the second platoon."

"Okay, Gould. I'm used to dealing with Sergeant Ulriche."

"I understand," I replied, "but I've ordered him to stay back with Doc Lynch at the rear. Dammit, Sergeant Ulriche is number four in the whole battalion rotation roster, should be back at the Rotation Center with some of the guys he came over with from Fort Lewis. Besides, I've got to take over sooner or later."

"Well, okay," Foney answered. "If you're sure you can swing it, follow Holly and give him all the support you can."

My talking with the company commander seemed the signal for everyone to watch me—everyone of the Banzai Third watched me—disdainfully, I felt, certainly critically. I'll show 'em, but as I stood, I fumbled and dropped my carbine twice when I called the platoon together, stammered and stuttered. I was embarrassed to show uncontrolled fear, not the fear Sergeant Eppler and I'd been training for that you can fight down by shouting, threatened by immediate action of an enemy, but the purely mental kind, blood that didn't race around your body but stayed in your head to make you stutter and say strange things. Something like being at a podium under spot lights to give a speech you hadn't prepared for. Shouting wouldn't help a bit but would sound funny.

"Where's Sergeant Ulriche?" someone demanded.

"He's staying back; I'm in charge now; he's going to rotate."

I'd never done anything so crazy and dangerous in my life, try to take a hill from someone who wanted desperately to keep it. Not many sane people do and tell about it. This for which I am named rifle platoon leader, fully trained, ready to go on command, now compelled professionally to do without further preparation. No, my frightened friend, no more time for training, reading instructions or field manuals, only this threatening heroism on order that scares you so. Oh god, what a crazy thing to do.

Then, after a few full breaths, with everyone staring critically at me, I sounded off tough as I could manage, "You're acting platoon sergeant now Sergeant Eppler. Sergeant Ulriche will stay to the rear with Doc, and Sergeant Roderiguez's squad is leading out. I believe it's his turn and then the second squad with Sergeant Miller. C'mon, Banzai Third, let's chogee!"

Talking firmly now, I'd prove I had the right to call myself Banzai.

"Sergeant Ulriche!" I yelled over my shoulder, catching sight of him returning from the second platoon. "And you, Specialist Lynch, I'm ordering you both to stay in the rear."

Moving out first, I planned to work right behind Speedy Gonzales, assistant squad leader of the First Squad. Sergeant Ulriche always put a squad ahead of him as protection so he could lead without being pinned down. As we moved from the bottom of the saddle, I had already stopped shaking uncontrollably—just by moving—no longer felt helplessly frightened. Cautious now, in charge, studying the situation like any predator, hunched like a hunting lion in as low a profile as possible, ready to spring; completely in charge, on top of things, alert to what could happen to hurt us. I found it the best way to go into a fight after yelling off the fear pressure; in charge of things; wade right in with eyes open; judging both the front and sides—front where the enemy is, sideways for my men. Scared, alert and determined to kill!

Suddenly, why was I physically leading? I turned and yelled for Rodriguez to bring his men up and explained to him where I intended to be. Rodriguez demanded only that I be in close proximity, not in safety far away. We'd do it together, like the gang at home in Laredo he used to run with together, always together. He'd be damned proud to lead out in front of the lieutenant, long as the lieutenant kept pace. And right here and now I want to say Mexican Americans have been the backbone of our infantry combat in every war since WWI. I'd very much like to learn what was the percentage of American Indians and Mexican-Americans in the infantry to big city and suburban Anglos in combat both with US Marines and US Army, especially the Marines, compared to the percentage of well-off young male Anglos in the general populace. No coincidence that no sons of pink-finger bankers or suck-ass politicians were there with us. Men only. The Marines needed only a few; we needed more.

Bullets from three old Maxim machine guns zipped overhead. All at once I realized how naked we were, we should have had all sorts of preparation the colonel promised—air strikes, heavy artillery, mortars of 60 and 81mm, light and heavy machine guns, recoilless rifles—everything that bird colonel promised—and here we were, a skinny rifle platoon, a few days after being overrun, banzaiing with bare hands. Where were our vaunted leaders, Wilkes in charge of it all? Even one company commander? Three rifle platoons preceded me—the college kid, the SFC from King Company and Holly's. I suddenly realized to take a hill like this we first of all needed heavy preparation and then, like we did so many times later, move fast and build a momentum and go right over the top yelling our lungs out.

I came fast to understand that close combat is never smooth, seldom beginning in an orderly surge of men altogether like in movies, and once it begins, always behind a spiritual leader of some sort, of whatever rank, it proceeds haphazardly from individual or small groups, twos and threes, well-trained fire teams formed around BARs darting now forward, inspired by natural leaders, inspiring others, now individu ally falling behind boulders or trees, out of breath, reloading, panting for air or demoralized and overcome by fear reaction and then regaining control rushing upward again, encouraging, urging all to join the intoxicating melee. And always, an individual in angry denunciation of his personal anxiety who inspires forward movement at the end funneled down to a nobody dogface, an enlisted or officer platoon leader yelling his lungs off.

Right behind him are the wonderful, courageous, temporarily crazy ten or twelve dependables to give body to the assault. This time there was no preparation, no Air, no artillery, no overhead machine gun of our own; no support at all and the absence and silence of Lieutenant Foney, supposedly our company commander, whose commitment the attack was by tradition, not a mere rifle platoon leader's task.

The company commander and commanders above carry the responsibility to plan the action and supply, observe, direct and command. The rifle platoon leader is just that, leader who leads his riflemen to carry out the commander's wishes. I never could prove where Foney, the acting S3 and Wilkes were when we got pinned down but nobody, I mean none of them, got us support or preparatory fire as customary. I would have liked to testify to where I found Major Wilkes.

There was no battalion OP, observation post, established from which to watch our progress and give orders, nor was there communication from Love or King Company commanders. Those already committed, the two rifle platoons of King and Holly's men (where is Holly I wondered) were lying safe behind what cover they found at the bottom of the saddle, maybe one-fourth way up, the little momentum was what J C Rodriguez, Speedy Gonzales and I were able to whip up by screaming threats. I glanced back over my shoulder and was happy to find the second and third squads moving with Speedy and me. I like to think that Burris and Pop Miller were inspired to see me ahead of them. "C'mon," I shouted. "Get the bastards! Banzai! Banzai!"

I scurried, crouching, running like a crab or a crippled man from boulder to boulder sidewards or up, tree to tree, tuned to the jabbering of excited chinks above. With energy I never had before, I pushed myself smack into the hottest center of the hill, without scouts, for we were now all of us front men, pushing up fast through thinning bushes, yelling over my shoulder, getting the guys to follow me without thinking. "C'mon, Banzai! Let's get them! C'mon, keep your ass down and chogee. Get 'em on the run."

I have thought since that day how I must have sounded like a seasoned veteran; in order to survive, combatants must be scared as they come, harnessing the high energy adrenalin loosed by fear to yell and inspire your guys over the top, like no yells from athletes, it's no game observed by peaceful civilians; your life and the trusting lives of your men are at stake and you put your entire being, hope for future, into it.

Heavy, unaimed chink fire cracked and zipped threateningly overhead. Pinned down in their trench by fear of our fire, heads down, chinks held rifles and burp guns over the edge above their heads, trying to point the muzzles down at us. As long as we kept firing low, they'd be afraid of the zip-zip and crack-crack we were throwing at them. We crawled and pulled ourselves on our stomachs up to what I call the grenade line, until suddenly one of Speedy's best riflemen straightened up just a bit too much and was suddenly jerked upright to go reeling backward with a curse cut off abruptly, hit hard in the liver, heart or lungs or a heavy bone—"Oh g-a ..." All he got off was the surprised, angry, "Oh g-a ..." arms and legs out of control, flailing, wild arms and uncontrolled legs propelled by gravity as he fell with momentum down the steep slope, dropped with whirling extremities, crashing into a guy crouching below as his bright red blood sprayed wantonly away, reflecting sunlight with every involuntary move. His body crashed through a clump of low bushes, grunting loudly as air in his lungs was forced out, his chest banging heavily on boulders, slumping at last, a sickening sight lying still like I once saw an old overworked horse fall in harness, pulling a heavy scoop digging a cellar.

As long as we menaced them, if only with sounds of anger and small arms, they stayed down holding burp guns and rifles over the parapets, fired without aiming or being able to fire low enough to hit us without exposing themselves, but the picture of the dead man flying through the air stopped us in our tracks.

For the first time my men and a few of Holly "on the grenade line were aware of King Company's leaderless men cowering behind boulders and bushes behind us. With their organized fire we could've rumbled over the top.

"Get up here you sonsofbitches," Sergeant Eppler yelled at King's men and their ROTC officer. "This ain't no private war." Peering down the saddle out of the corner of one eye I saw Private Funaro and several others scurry behind cover back with the demoralized guys of King. I counted only eight of Love Company and two from King on the grenade line. Looking behind me, I yelled: "You heard the sergeant. Keep your ass down and get up here and fight. What're you afraid of?" They knew well what they were afraid of, our attack momentum, which we never really established, was gone.

We were caught in a dangerous stall. On my left Corporal Ichimura dropped his machine gun into a groove of a boulder, useless without the bipod carried by an assistant, and tried to charge it to no avail without the stability needed. As he yanked on the charging handle, the barrel skidded to the right across the flat top of the boulder. He called angrily for his assistant, the only time I heard a Nisei use foul language. As I continued to yell for guys to join us, a series of rapid single shots went off beside me, an M1 carbine fast as the guy could pull the trigger. It was our sixteen-year-old platoon medic, Doc Lynch. He paid me no attention until I reached over and tugged on the little canvas bag flung over his back. "Damn it, Doc, back where you belong. We might need you."

We were beginning to dodge potato masher grenades with wood handles. I tried to think what was best to do but could only shiver and stutter and smell a strange antiseptic odor I have smelled at several very dangerous times in my life. For example, once when I was almost clobbered by a taxi as I stepped off a curb in New York City. The chinks stopped jabbering in subdued voices as they did while we came caterwauling up at them and now the most timid yelled loudly individually with inflections that could only be insults. Ski behind me answered, "Up your gigi with a rough wire brush!"

Karl, Pop, Edsel, and Burris all yelled, as we had in our little amateur fear course decided was best to do. "C'mon you yellow cunts! Eee-dee-waa [come here]! We got something for you! Come and get it!" and other strong curses.

"C'mon, you guys," I turned and shouted below me. "You heard 'em. Let's chogee…. Get the lead out; we got 'em on the run! Move! Move up! Damn it, get the fire going and they won't stick their heads up."

"Dunee! Dunee! Dunee!" a voice yelled, which I learned later was a Chinese dialect for 'fuck you,' certainly appropriate for the occasion but which never caught on nor replaced familiar English threats. I never found out who yelled it and by some strange fluke, although it must have originated above us, it seemed to come from behind; a chink ventriloquist?

Eppler looked at me in amazement. I'd worked myself up to such a pitch of enthusiasm I was standing in plain sight, unmindful of bullets. The guys told me later they thought I'd lost my marbles.

"Get your fire up. On the move!" I yelled. The chinks lowered their voices again, fearful of the sounds of rising morale. "Banzai!" I screamed. "Banzai the bastards!" Swinging my carbine with fixed bayonet over my head, I yelled, "Banzai the bastards!" I know banzai was a jap yell in WWII (meaning may we live ten thousand years) and there must have been at least one chink up there who recognized what meaning it once had for them. Captain Brownell told me how chinks feared Japanese more than us and have been known to use banzai themselves as an expletive, similar to a North China yell, *wan-sui,* a cry I remember but whose meaning escapes me.

The chinks scooted back and forth above us, agitated pixies, busily firing three slow Maxim machine guns well over our heads, unable to depress down the steep slope. They were of pre-WWI vintage obtained as were burp guns from Russia, as captured Springfield rifles were from America via Chinese Nationals. The heavy cast-iron wheels and armor plate were well dug in and with flash hiders and smokeless powder, difficult to spot. We picked them up one at a time by catching sight of the flutter of leaves and camouflage twigs and the slow, measured chug chug chug sound they made.

I yelled a warning to the guys and tried to point them out, and, out of ammo, four 30-round banana magazines emptied, I went so far as to stand again and heave a rock in the direction of the gun in the center. "Let 'em have it right back of where that rock landed. C'mon, guys, work your way up and toss a grenade." Chain reaction kept me going, but the majority, uninspired, feeling only guilt and fear, overpowered by their own vulnerability, were unimpressed and lost enthusiasm as they figured the odds.

J J handed me our 536 radio, Lieutenant Foney who, I realized, had to be on the enemy side of the ridge facing us for his radio to read. "C'mon, Gould, you're doin' good! That's it, right on up there! Atta' boy!"

"How about some of that stuff they promised," I demanded. "Where's Air and artillery, tanks and mortars? For Christ sake, Foney, where's our own weapons platoon?" I practically threw the radio back to J J. What did Foney know about taking a hill?

Soon I was all alone yelling. The morale had sunk so low it seemed time for someone to play the hero. Since no one in the platoon was shackled with that job, it dawned on me I must appoint myself. Damn, I thought, strangely pleased with the assignment, I'll have to show them. I had been so very active the past half hour and my survival instinct was so refreshed in the persistent excitement another flash of adrenalin swept over me; all of a sudden it seemed onesided and I told myself, "after all, they're hiding, not us."

"Watch me!" I yelled, facing dramatically from left to right. "Keep your other eye on them chinks and keep them pinned down." Pulling the pin from a fragmentation grenade, I scooted low uphill. Ten yards from the chink trench, slapping myself against a thin tree, I slid down it to my knees and threw the heavy hunk of metal up with all my might. I had the terrible impression of it hitting a thin sapling, bounced back, rolling, smoking and sizzling right at me.

"Crimus!" I yelled, standing up, back to the enemy, scampering down the hill, invisible bullets cutting the air above me with incredible zip-zapping sounds. "One could end it all."

Tripping over a rock, which fortunately lowered me as a target and probably saved me, I rolled over and over without losing speed until I reached the depression I started from. I instinctively tucked my head under my arm while the dangerous thing went off three feet above my helmet. Plowing into the ground, lying half submerged in loose mountain dirt, the grenade fragments sprayed up rather than down toward me. Because of many fragments arranged to break away, the hand fragmentation grenade was named after Spanish *granada*, pomegranate; lit seedy apple.

Few soldiers listened to the fearful nearness of the high nervous whine of metal fragments as I did for hours during my night of terror, one-night stand on the night of the 15th of May, and lived to tell about it and I came suddenly to my senses. "Crimus!" I shuddered, raising the front of the heavy helmet from over my eyes. "Don't push your luck, you could have been killed. What a crazy thing to do." Crazy, yes, but not unlike a furious moment in a strenuous game—glorious, an aggressive act I'd succumb to several more times on my Korean tour.

Fortunately, the chinks had few frag grenades, some Russian antitank grenades, short wooden-handle affairs about the size and appearance of toilet plungers, kraut panzerfusses captured by the Russians that weren't made for antipersonnel and wouldn't detonate unless hit on the fuse end squarely in a rock (or tank as they were designed to do). Mostly they used chink-made potato mashers, small imitations of kraut wooden-handled grenades with a small explosive charge in thin, metal containers, similar in size and thickness to six-ounce tomato juice cans.

Quiet and sober then, I watched Sergeant Eppler out of the corner of one eye handle a potato masher grenade like a hot potato, picking it up by its wooden handle and dropping it twice in a row, and, unbelievably, a third time, fumbling for it frantically as it exploded behind or beneath him in a small cloud of smoke and dust. Until then we had no idea how weak they were.

"Goddammit!" I thought. "There goes Karl."

His body cleared the ground by an inch and plopped back, dropping his rifle. Seconds later, over the shock of it, he sat up, popeyed, fingers scrambling around his back and sides, rummaging under his fatigue jacket for blood. Convinced at last that he was untouched, he exclaimed, "Shit!" One would give a lot for a legitimate stateside wound.

Seconds later it happened to me, making the left side of my chest black and blue and sore for several days. The cans were too thin to fragmatize and for the most part simply flared back to their junctions with the wood handle.

Dirty tan sleeves popped into the air above us as the chinks' morale returned higher than before; heavy salvoes of grenades got closer and closer as they rose from their knees to take aim. We became contemptuous but watchful of this danger. There were but two choices as a grenade landed near by—pick it up by its handle and toss it downhill, or roll away and cover your head and chest. Within the time allotted by short fuses, throwing them back up was out of the question. In each case it had to be a snap judgement, either cover from it or toss it downhill. I was right ninety-five percent of the time to toss them away and it annoyed me to think one was ready to explode while I lay there facing away, cowering, shivering from fear.

Sergeant Eppler or I, one of us or maybe both, started yelling as we tossed chink grenades down away from us, "Here's one from me, you yellow bastards; get up here and help us."

All too often, when they saw one landing close, so menacing, the guys, afraid they might miss and have no time to duck, ducked away from the confrontation and allowed the grenade to have its way.

"Crimus," I fumed to myself. "If you'd the guts to pick it right up, you wouldn't be cringing like a damn fool." Once I turned away and covered my face with my hands, safe under my steel pot it seemed, it was too late to change my mind. Being delayed, most we tossed exploded in the air.

About every twentieth grenade was a dangerous frag. A guy to my left caught a fragment and skidded downhill yelling, "Oh God, oh God!" a quivering layer of blood over the side of his face, fresh liquid sheen of scarlet. Doc Lynch dropped his carbine and like a frantic mother scooted after him over a low rock ledge. The wounded rifleman came back to us three weeks later with pink facial scars.

Impressions were how we decided whether we were dead or alive; impressions one after another in rapid succession, one an extremely accurate ROK machine gun from overhead behind us preventing chinks from standing to lower fire to finish us off. One impression of two of King's men came to me later, firing angrily up at the bushes, yelling, "Stick up your heads, you bastards." Someone, Pop Miller, I believe, urged a King Company rifleman to edge up closer to the enemy, get a fire going at any place he saw leaves fluttering, "they're all the same, all good targets," and one of my guys yanking desperately at the jammed cocking lever of his M1, making a strange whimpering sound for being so scared and defenseless.

After I ran out of ammo, I tried to raise either the company commander or battalion, on my 536 walkie-talkie, although seldom used by battalion, "anyone send backup in a hurry; land some preparatory fire on the chinks, bring us ammo, shoot some outfit through us, or give us permission to withdraw." From the growing silence at my sides, I realized other guys were running out of ammo and some were sliding on their stomachs down hill, as, with nothing with which to fire, well they should. I knew when there was no answer to my 536 calls that Foney had gone back to the safe friendly side and must have taken his radio and King's Captain Toth with him since we were all on the same channel. Where, I stewed to myself, was all that five-paragraph field order preparation, especially the third paragraph—supporting troops? Where was Fifth Air Force and Eighth Army artillery and all those tanks? And where was Love's 60mm mortar?

Hearing our momentum falter, chinks started lowering their fire; with no higher echelon radio than a 536 that wouldn't reach over the hill where we assumed the company commanders were, we were on our own. The battalion commander hadn't been seen or heard from since the Colonel's briefing and I sent J J, stunned by a grenade, back to the rear to get permission to withdraw. "Hurry!" I ordered. "Hurry!" Meanwhile, out of contact with superiors was all the permission I needed to use my own judgement. I wouldn't make the same mistake as Captain Poston and just as I was about to tell the guys in a normal voice to pull back carefully down the hill, a young kid, loud mouth new runner from battalion charged with giving me the message in person, shouted from below, "Hey, you guys. They want you off the hill; we're pulling back."

"Let's go-o-o!" a King Company man shouted hysterically. A badly frightened replacement of Holly's platoon faced around, dropped his rifle and started pell-mell down the hill. Breath stopped in my throat and my heart held its beat. Grabbing my empty carbine I chased after the panicked guy until close enough to prick him in the shoulder with my bayonet. He came to a skidding halt as I wheeled to face three more, insane with fear. I held my carbine bayonet up at them until they saw the look on my face and stopped, staring in surprise and disappointment at being held up. Take any book on infantry tactics, Clausiwitz, Baron de Jomini, or Mao, you'll read retreat is the most difficult combat maneuver to control at any echelon. The men looked at me and then turned to look up where the chinks were chattering.

"Okay, now," I told them calmly. "*You* reach up and get your rifle. Okay, you see, easy does it. See, you're all right. Now take your rifles and come down firing back if you can. Toss their grenades away. Let Ich's machine gun down first and that BAR. C'mon, steady does it."

We leapfrogged backward that way down to the bottom of the saddle, those with ammo fired to keep chinks from lowering their fire on us. King Company's hideouts preceded us without instructions, in fact, they hugged like big birds, as two of Mike Company's heavy water-cooled machine guns finally got in the act, pouring red-hot shit on the chink line overhead in unison with the gung ho ROK gun, keeping the chinks down so they dared not aim at us. Eppler, a sergeant from King Company, Tony Burris, and I fanned out to inspect the hill. We confirmed that two of our five known dead were indeed dead and left there and three earlier dragged away by King Company's platoon medics, and Doc had done such a good job evacuating the wounded there was no one to haul for I was so occupied I completely forgot Holly from the word go. With the enemy menace so near and aggressive, we made no effort to bring off the two dead, nor, of course, had reason to inspect the hill left or right above the grenade line.

As Eppler and I walked carefully backwards watching the chinks' position above, we came across a chubby, pale-face King replacement sitting head between his knees sobbing softly. I saw no medic tag and asked where he got it.

"I can't move, sir. I can't move. I'm tired right out. Let them get me, sir. I can't go no further."

There was no reason for a medic's tag and Pop Miller taught me not to let guys fag out like that. Teach them to find their grit; force them to try. Instinctively, I jabbed at him hard with my bayonet but not intending to actually stick him, as though I hated him, bawling him out: "Now get off your ass and chogee. I'm not leaving you here and I am sure as shit not staying with you. In a minute those bastards will push their machine guns forward, lower them and sweep the living shit out of this place. Now move! Hear me? Move!" The surprised replacement, frightened by the bayonet wounding as I threatened another, jumped to his feet and scrambled ahead of me over the ridge to the friendly side.

There was no officer on either side of the ridge, nor could I raise Lieutenant Foney or Captain Toth on the 536, nor was there any sign of a battalion observation post. Uncommitted guys from both companies were goofing off on the ridge trail in front of the ROKs in their holes, stretched out on the enemy side watching the show, chink heads popping up and down, paying no heed to Maxim machine gun bullets cracking away, sniping like angry bees well over their heads.

I once asked Sergeant Eppler if, through all this activity we were engaged in, he recalled seeing any other officer. Negative except Totten and Foney one time each, and getting together this journal I asked Sergeant Eppler to jot down his impressions of that day—

Dud,

Let me write of my recollections of May 23. The first thing that comes to mind is how ill-prepared I felt our platoon was when it jumped off that morning. We had lost heavily since before the May 15 debacle and were now almost 50% replacements whose names we barely knew and whose knowledge and training were doubtful. I never felt any of our replacements had adequate training, especially those from reserve or guard units. Brave, maybe, but trained? NO! I also recall we had little or no artillery preparation. We did succeed in closing within grenade range (theirs—one does not throw grenades uphill). But didn't have the firepower to go to the top. As I indicated, I got tossed around pretty good by a grenade and as my legs hurt, really thought I was wounded. I think I got the SOB that threw the grenade as I saw where it came from and drew a sight on the opening and waited. In a few seconds a face appeared for a moment and I fired. No more grenades were thrown from that position.

When the order came to pull back, I was much relieved to realize I could walk without difficulty as I was convinced I was wounded. When we pulled back and dug in, I was very disappointed when I couldn't find a wound.

I vividly remember your wound and seeing a very small amount of blood appear. Initially you made almost no reaction. It didn't appear to have caused much pain, but everyone, including yourself, was concerned as to the consequences of the wound. You initially moved very cautiously but once you realized you could move, assured us you could evacuate yourself and left for the aid station. I don't believe our unit saw any further action that day.

So much for May 23. It feels good to write it down for someone who understands.

Thanks,
s/s Karl Eppler

No one but me and Eppler seemed aware of the great danger we faced. "C'mon," I yelled. "Get off the ridge you guys. You're silhouetted. Get over to the friendly side."

W-a-opt! I was slammed by an axe, one ton per square inch, my head was shook forward and as my helmet and liner went flying. I was driven to my knees before managing to stumble several steps forward to get my balance and straighten up. I donned my cotton fatigue cap. Many years later seat belts were designed for less force. My neck and a streak across my back burned white hot for a split second. I was furious, thinking I'd been accidentally hit by one of the guys. "Who did that? Who's the dumb bastard?" I yelled.

Sergeant Eppler, directly behind me a bit lower, heard the same sharp crack of the bullet headed straight at us and knew immediately what happened. "Medic! Medic! Doc, over here!" he yelled.

"See! See, what did we tell you!" I yelled. "See, you're sitting ducks! Now clear the ridgeline. Move!"

"Lieutenant Gould's got it!" Burris yelled, proudly it seemed, and an anonymous surgeon with buck sergeant stripes addressed himself confidentially to Doc Lynch: "Got it in the back, he'll be paralyzed!"

"Shut your face!" I told him. "I need a swig of water and someone light me a butt; can't you see I'm hit?" I remember thinking that's what they'd do for John Wayne. I kept hearing: "He'll be paralyzed," and worried the more that I could feel nothing from where I suspected the wound was. What was happening?

Doc studied two spots, the small, slowly spreading blood where the slug went in my neck and, lower down across my back, a slightly larger, faster-spreading blood stain on my fatigue jacket. He acted pleased and I called him on it. "No," he said. "I'm just happy to see that

Master Sergeant Karl Eppler safe in reserve down from the mountains. Smile, damn it!

the damn bullet came out." He opened his little aid kit and slipped off my fatigue top. J J offered me his remaining water and someone handed me a cigarette. "Gee, lieutenant, that's awful," he said, lighting me up.

I didn't agree it was so awful; after the initial shock and sudden flash of burning along the path of the bullet, I never felt a thing nor have I ever since. It was only the memory that bothered me from then on, a heavy speed slugging me; power of a sudden ax blow. Pain was an imagination; the reality feeling nothing to this day.

"My," Doc clucked like a contented hen, "sit on that boulder, sir."

"What's that mean?" I demanded. "*My*?"

"You're lucky, that's all; it could've got your spine."

"What's that like?"

"You'd know, be dead or couldn't move some part of you, or all."

Crimus, I thought, hit my spine so bad I can't feel anything. I was ready to agree wholeheartedly with the guy who said I'd be paralyzed. He, alone, was honest enough to tell the truth. Whatever the lack of pain was in worst wounds, I had it good. But, hell, I was standing there feeling nothing; I didn't keel over, what about that fact?

At long last Doc reached his hands around my head from the front, snipped the top of my undershirt with surgical scissors and ripped the undershirt most of the remaining way, letting it fall below my armpits, placing a 4x4 Carlisle bandage over the bottom hole that was bleeding slowly. I started to move.

"Wait a bit," Doc said, rummaging through his aid kit. "There's a littler hole on your neck there," and he put a large Band-Aid over the small, puckered entry hole.

Basically it was me and Doc Lynch, my sole caretaker, on-hand savior, entirely at his mercy, his to help me live or let me die.

For many years thereafter, I told people I was hit by a burp gun, but have recently been corrected by my platoon guide at the time, Clarence Karl Eppler, who has studied enemy weapons. Standing right behind me and listening to the cracking sound of it, he says that it was a sharp-pointed Russian 303 armor-piercing sniper bullet which, because of its sharp point and extreme speed, made a much cleaner wound than a burp gun. At the distance from which it must have been fired, Karl explained a burp gun would have made the sound of a lot of bullets rather than a single 'crack' and have torn a nasty hole, probably cutting the spinal cord. I shuddered to think of it.

Doc Lynch, with life or death in his hands, was about five nine, a little taller than me, ruddy cheeks, a Nebraska farm boy whose sharp city relative altered his birth certificate to seventeen and appeared as his father when enlisting. It was okay for his father or mother to sign for him to join the Army at seventeen but our gung-ho buddy, our sweetheart of a medic, fifteen then, was hot to trot. A man prematurely, he was a quiet, very modest young man, chock full of an urge for adventure, who rode bulls and broncos in local rodeos at fourteen.

With his little canvas aid kit and surprising tenderness submerged under his aggressive masculinity, Doc had plugged fifty dangerous bleedings and set a few bones in his very valuable year in Korea. And, yes, closed the lids on more than a few accusing eyes.

I suddenly felt beaten and terribly tired, yearning for another drink of water, entranced by the gentle medic's fussing over me, deluding myself for the time being that it was all a dream. Then as suddenly I was very important, very much as though

I just paid my debt to the entire world, cleansed myself of all guilt and obligations forever. Having been sentenced to a long, dreary internment, at last I made the big sacrifice to spring me loose, free, free at last, free for good. I would never owe anyone, any institution, never be nagged and driven to prove myself ever again, anything ever again. I've had the bullet of self-importance through my back, fully delivering me from doubt; once carrying the clinging oppression of inborn debts to society, I freed myself in defense of our great nation, paid my debt to society; don't call on me no more.

While Doc filled out the cardboard evacuation ticket, DOD AGO, Department of Defense, Adjutant Generals Office, Form 8-26 Emergency Medical Tag, I tried cautiously to feel the extent of the wound, a definite pain or ache. "Crimus," I brooded, "I'll settle for an itch—anything."

"What's this place we're at?" Doc asked.

"Habae-chae," I said, annoyed at the technicality of Doc's having to fill out an evacuation form. "The nearest village anyway."

Doc wrote Habae-chae with his stub of a pencil and 1300 hours, 23 May 1951 for the time I was wounded. For the location of the wound he scribbled neck, even though the bullet had passed out lower down across the back, and signed his name and number, noting that I wasn't given morphine.

"Does it hurt, lieutenant?"

"I wouldn't say it hurt."

"Got plenty of morphine, say the word, one's yours."

"Wait till I feel something."

I began to worry, particularly because I couldn't feel anything except the outside of my left side and chest becoming quite sore. I thought, "maybe I should take a morphine for what the damn grenade did," but then I became anxious by the numbness, wondering if I had an important nerve shot up; better not numb it any more with morphine. I wished I could feel some little pain just to let me know I was all right back there. Doc tied the strings of the evacuation tag to the top button of my fatigue jacket and slipped the jacket back over my ripped undershirt carefully, although, I thought, there didn't seem to be any need to be careful.

I suddenly realized how free I was. Damn it all, 'free as a bird' was to me more than a saying. Being wounded in the service of one's country the most beautiful fulfillment of responsibilities. Bled for our country—what a ring to it.

We Reserves were recalled to active duty for seventeen months, subject to extension, told to pass a year of that in Korea. With my MOS, 1542, infantry unit commander, we had but five choices of avoiding the terrors of combat: refuse to go, get too ill to fight, get a branch transfer and any other MOS, or be killed, missing, and, next to putting in a full tour, I had the best—being wounded; that dreaded category, one if not the easiest in my case, bullet through the flesh of the neck and back, I guessed hitting no major nerve, blood vessel or bone, not that I could feel.

In a random second, I'd paid my way honestly through all social levels the hard way, beyond question and on the immediate local level, no more fretting about right to lead the guys. Instantly, I became an undisputed authority on combat, no more worry about ammunition, chop chop, what's next, or anything. I was free now to go to an aid station and have others worry about me, little as it would be. As for Master Sergeant Ulriche, he can rest on his laurels now until he rotates. I'm in charge and don't nobody forget it.

I turned and yelled, "Sergeant Ulriche, take over."

There was no answer and I yelled once more. "Sergeant Ulriche, I'm leaving. You're it."

In retrospect, it never occurred to me that although I remember Holly's men on the extreme left, I have no memory of Holly pulling back or any recollection at all of Sergeant Ulriche.

I turned to Sergeant Eppler and asked about our platoon sergeant and Karl shook his head and told me he hadn't seen Sergeant Ulriche since we took off in attack. "'Till Sergeant Ulriche shows up," I told him, "You're in charge."

Doc assured me two wounded were on their way down with an armed escort, one wounded in an arm, no bone, the other something like Perkins in the fat of the flesh of the ass went on a litter carried by two CTCs along with two ambulatory WIAs from King Company, and an armed King sergeant with a persistent stomach pain, like appendicitis, down the long winding mountain trail to where litter jeeps were waiting to take them to the 15th Infantry collecting point aid station of the Third Division which made a wild 100-mile ride in less than twenty-four hours from the Seoul front to block behind us.

I presented Doc with my M2 carbine with the scarce bell-shape muzzle flash hider and heavy pistol belt with first aid bandage, ammo pouch, empty canteens and bayonet scabbard. The bayonet was still on my carbine in place of the flash hider. Suddenly, though wonderfully free, I was small and all alone, withdrawing within myself, no longer responsible for a thing, my worries were all private, my only desire to get away to absolute safety as soon as possible. Escape, yes; escape forever from dangerous situations.

"Well," I said, "tell Sergeant Ulriche what happened to me. You guys did a terrific job and I'll be seeing you, I guess. I better be going now. Take care of each other."

"Take it easy, Lieutenant Gould."

There had been a short discussion before between myself, Doc Lynch and Sergeant Eppler about how every time a man got hit, three or four others, some he knew only by sight, were more than eager to see that he got to the rear. Such solicitude was another way of bugging out. I waved my would-be companions away and started down, beginning to worry about the wound I could not feel or see and which I wanted to know the extent of.

A few hundred yards down the ridge, I found a small party of officers and sergeants taking a break. Two CTC carriers had been toting a large radio which I recognized as an Angry-9, AN/PRC-9, long-range for aerial support. It was owned by X Corps and there were two Corps FOs, forward observers, who should have gotten us Air and heavy artillery support, as promised by the colonel who briefed us so eloquently. Ranking man was a captain with a 'flash-bang' outfit from Eighth Army, able to triangulate incoming fire by calculating backward the inverted legs of a V in both sight and sound, not needed on our attack since rearguard chink units left to fight us were not supported by artillery which they hustled north to save.

"Where the hell you guys been?" I demanded, facing the captain. "Where were you when we needed you?"

"It's all over?" he asked. "You got the hill?"

"No, the hill got us."

"We're damn sorry, lieutenant. Nobody told us you were pushing off so early. We understood the attack was slated for afternoon. We heard you'd laid on an Air strike first; you know how slow they are."

Seems the colonel hadn't waited for them to attend the briefing and I found out what the Blue Book meant by "a hastily organized task force." We referred bitterly to the operation thereafter as Task Force Joke. The damn colonel or somebody should have been cashiered. Some good guys got killed because it broke down, despite his detailed briefing. The shadowy character Major Wilkes should've been court-martialed for not even showing.

A hundred yards more down the hill I came upon the bastard, our new battalion commander, Major Wallace W Wilkes and Captain Jones, his S2. I surprised myself at how authoritative and bold I became after wounding, which made me tower above all those not wounded. Further, I was a recalled Reserve who everyone knew had no intention of making a career of the Army. The hell with ratings! Our tour by law was just long enough to fight the war for the Regulars while they worked at bettering their careers. It infuriated me, not so much because Wilkes was hiding out, but neither his SCR 536 nor 300 radio was on nor had he any phone lines. How could they call for artillery or Air, or hear my plea for permission to withdraw? I noticed a half full bottle of Jack Daniels Black Label beside Wilkes.

"You bastards!" I yelled. "Where the fuck's our fire? What're you doing hiding out? At least get up where you can see what's going on."

The captain jumped to his feet, leaning forward to read my name tag. "Who the hell you think you are, you sonofabitch, talking to a major that way. You the Lieutenant Gould the major tells me Lieutenant Foney told him bugged on his men at the outpost?"

"What do you know about an outpost? None of you were ever up there. Why didn't you inform the companies you were pulling your wire and turning off your radio?"

"Shut up, lieutenant!" Jones yelled. "We're going to bring you up on charges."

Wilkes glared a little, content to leave it to the captain.

Court martial me for cursing a shirker? Go ahead; who of us closing with the enemy on those ridges was afraid of a court martial? She-e-e-it! That's a friendly game—way back, comfortable where everything's normal and nobody gets hurt—hot meals, compared to what we go through.

Wilkes noticed me eyeing his bottle and slid it behind him as his S2 continued to threaten. I stood glaring until, finally, as I took off, they began to gear up slowly so as not to seem in a hurry toward where the action had been.

Pushing my way around large rock outcroppings, rehashing my brief moment of glory—not the wounding but chastising those cowards—I kept my neck and back stiff, visualizing my spinal cord as white wrapping twine partially severed. If I was the least bit careless, it would fray against a splintered vertebrae and cut the rest of the way through God, would anyone find me in time on this lonesome mountain trail?

It grew very muggy as far away to the west, the sick, angry sky spit lightning toward us, coughing heavy rolls of thunder.

I must hurry out of the mountain before the rains return; before it gets slippery; before night falls on me stumbling. I wished I had let one of those volunteers run guard for me. Anxiously scanning the lowering sky for the first signs of trouble, I replayed with uncanny vividness memories of my playing dead on the outpost.

"Crimus," I fretted. "I was lucky Kitty visiting me. Who'll believe it? Let a shrink figure that one out. It was her, no doubt it was Kitty, alive. Crimus, she could've got killed or do you suppose she was a ghost of some kind? Something I've never read about."

Back down the ridge I could still hear occasional bullets from the maxims high above fanned wide apart, wailing lonesomely way above me over the scrub oaks and twisted mountain pines and I worried that someone was engaging them again, or do you suppose the ROKs were giving it another try. No, I concluded, just a machine gun duel with those gung ho gunners of Mike Company.

There was a small man beside the trail, about my age, certainly older than most PFCs; thirty or so, without a rifle or a belt, an earlier derelict of King Company's defeat, sitting under a huge overhanging rock, listening intently to the steady chugging away of slow maxim fire. He seemed to be counting bullets and gave the impression from the intent way he searched the air that he worried because he could hardly see them.

"Where'd you get it?" I asked, feeling need for company on the way. There was no answer.

"All right?" I asked more loudly.

"Huh?" the numbed man asked, looking slowly in my direction.

"I asked where'd you get it."

"Oh," he whimpered, "they finally got me."

"Well, where?"

The badly-frightened man neglected to answer, or he still hadn't really heard the question; his face fixed into the sky, eyes glassy, dreamlike.

"C'mon now, where'd you get it?"

With that, the derelict turned, still staring vacantly, and pulled up his right trouser leg tenderly, careful that the cloth didn't rub against skin. On his knee was dried blood over a scratch.

"Nothing wrong with you," I told him angrily, looking closely at the scratch and then at the man's lapel to be sure he was wearing no evacuation tag. "Get back to your platoon before you're in trouble."

"Oh," the hopeless man complained with a self-piteous look, "I couldn't do that, you don't know how bad it hurts."

The man's eyes were much too large. Not knowing what more to say, I left him sitting by the trail in a widening pool of self-pity. How could a PFC his age still be in uniform?

A mile down the ridgeline I stepped aside for ROKs bent over by large rice straw bags of rice on their backs and heads. They saw the lack of helmet or weapon on this American and the evacuation tag on his lapel and made toothy grins of approval, proud and respectful as combat men, especially, are of wounded. One ROK stopped, balanced his load on his bent-over shoulders, put the palms of his hands together on his forehead, and, facing me, bowed several times, saluted, then faced away and when his courtesies were finished, pointed first to the just visible bloody Band Aid and then to the enemy hill. Easing down his bag of rice, he grinned broadly, made zip-zip bullet noises, jabbing his right index finger through the air pointing imaginary bullets at my neck, smiling more broadly yet with two gold-capped front teeth.

"Numero uno," he giggled. "GIs number one, joto. Chink, number hucking ten."

The guttural way he said 'fucking' made me smile.

"Number one. Ichiban uno," the ROK reassured me. Encouraged by my smile, he laughed uproariously, shaking his head up and down vigorously, apparently telling himself one helluva' a joke.

I straightened and in doing so spread back my shoulders slowly, carefully. At last I had something good strangers might relate to, a Purple Heart for all my troubles, true as a thousand dollar gold piece; take one look at it on my lapel they'll know automatically what for, like Senator Dole I thought as I wrote this and don't forget he's our buddy too, a rifle platoon leader. But crimus, how bad he got it.

"Here, you darn monkey," I told the ROK. "Have a cigarette."

There were treacherous slides where our battalion stomped steps with the edges of their boots into the mud of short, steep climbs. Great quantities of ammunition were scattered along the trail; must have been from the ROKs, mortar shells, metal boxes of machine gun ammunition, bandoliers of M1 clips, and especially frag grenades. An empty ten-man chogee train could have been sent up and loaded on the way. Hell, I thought, we didn't need them anyway.

King, Love and heavy machine gun crews of Mike had so ruined the trail I was forced at times to stumble uncertainly through the rocks and brush off the path holding my neck rigid as possible.

I left the low rounded foothill late in the afternoon and, peering anxiously back over my shoulder, saw the Chinese hill half hidden under a mass of swirling black clouds centered where mountains meshed into a purple sky and man, it was raining bad. I stumble-walked to the fork of the peaceful valley road where medics and drivers from forward battalion aid station of the 15th Infantry of the Third, Rock of the Marne Division, sat beside double-decker litter jeeps heating C's, looking up from time to time at the long winding mountain trail for their work to arrive—us dirty, dejected, weary, bloodied men coming like as not stumbling individually from that hill, smiling secretly, proud as peacocks. "I've got my wound! My ticket out," for a while, anyway.

"How they doing up there?" one asked. "They take it?"

"No," I answered, "it's all over. We got kicked off. Far as I know, I'm the last wounded."

"We seen ya' startin' down that last rise," a driver of an unlittered jeep remarked. "Gotta' wait for two more walking. Any right behind you, sir?"

"Didn't see any. We pulled off the objective, so I doubt it." Boy, oh boy, I thought, wait 'til everyone in Watertown learns what I've been through. Nobody from Watertown's been wounded way out here. Jimmy, Gordon, Uncle Art, this is for you! We're buddies now, me and you, know what it's all about now.

"You guys should've been up there," I told the driver. "Boy, were we ever close to those chinks. Crimus, they must've had seven machine guns. I wouldn't wait for no more from this fight, I think I was the last to get it."

The driver was silent thinking, and then, anxious for shelter and a hot meal, waved me onto the front seat. "You say you're the last?"

"We've been out of it hours now," I told him.

"Let's chogee, sir."

Important, dramatic and novel as my observations were to me, the driver appeared to listen only while he waited impatiently to change the subject. Wounding was normal, carrying wounded was what mattered.

"Awful lonely road, he mumbled. "Hope you guys didn't bypass no chinks."

Just him and me together spoke our minds to ourselves.

"I'll bet they had a thousand grenades," I went on absentmindedly. "You should've seen us banzaiing up there."

"Listen to this old wreck," the driver replied. "They got new jeeps in Japan where they don't need them and we get old wrecks. I hear we're getting new ones. Sure hope it's true."

Waiting for solace that never came, I ventured, "Funny, I can't feel a thing." I cautiously reached back and touched the Band Aid. "Wonder just how bad it is. Can you tell if it's still bleeding?" I asked the driver, trying to expose that side of my neck. To myself, "Suppose the nerves are dead and that's why it's so numb?"

Thinking I had his attention, I repeated myself.

"Can't see it's bleeding no more, lieutenant.... I'll shit you not, sir, one day the ass end's dropping clean out of this wreck and they'll have to give me a new one. You'd think with us fighting their war rear echelons would be more considerate."

Rear echelon? I guessed it was relative to where you worked.

The trip of the self-concerned was about five miles and, rounding the last bend, the driver pointed to the 15th Infantry Regimental Collection Station, a large squad tent. I hoped there would be a war correspondent and a photographer. I'd remind them that one of my heroes, Audy Murphy, went through this 15th Collecting Station on three occasions in World War II. It would make good copy to go along with my story. Where's that good-looking Maggie Higgins, correspondent you see in Stars and Stripes? Wait 'til Kitty, my father-in-law and the folks in Watertown, hear how I was wounded in action. I visualized big headlines "IN DEFENSE OF HIS COUNTRY." Funny, it was that way, for his country, and God, too, always when I was a kid.

An evacuation helicopter, whirlybird H-13, circling blades around and around and up noisily to whisk off head and chest wounds—at a distance a large plastic bubble between two litters lifting itself. It was the first chopper I'd ever seen. In a few minutes another pushed itself into the air, two full covered baskets hanging below the fuselage, aerial litters or coffins, depending sometimes on how fast they were. Slipping awkwardly sideways, tilted unnaturally to one side as it flew low above the valley road, it seemed that a fat man rode in one and a skinny guy in the other. Indeed, if an H-13 had one wounded only to haul, someone or a weight had to ride in the other basket to equalize the load.

We pulled over behind an ambulance from another battle somewhere unloading and a captain-surgeon met us and made a quickie triage. "You there, you there, and, Sergeant Queen, this man *now*," and, sorting the last litter case, turned to me, pulling up my jacket to check the bandage and Band Aid.

"How'd you get that bruise?" he asked, looking it over professionally, and when I told him grenade, he asked, "One of our concussion ones?"

"No sir, one of their own; ours would have killed me."

"I don't understand, lieutenant, a frag would have done a lot of damage."

"No sir, a potato masher, a small can of explosive."

"How's it feel?" he demanded, glancing hurriedly at the ticket, poking near the exit point, taking a quick look before staring blankly into my eyes for reaction.

"Okay, I guess, okay."

"Guess?" the surgeon snapped. "Take off the jacket."

"Does this hurt?" he asked removing Band Aid and bandage, impatient to find something, while pushing between the two holes from top to bottom and before I had time to answer, poked harder, on the spine.

"Ouch!"

With no further questions, he scribbled, 'missile in back,' on back of the evacuation tag, waved to one of the enlisted medics to rebandage me and turned to survey ambulatory wounded who stood behind the tent smoking, talking quietly about their big battles and how, when and where they'd been hit. They were from about ten different companies, not one but me from Love.

I was among the least damaged ambulatory and was told, rather coolly, I thought, to wait outside for the next crackerbox ambulance. Four lay on blood-smeared litters outside the door, frightening, pasty-pain faces who no longer grimaced or reflected pain, the last of time for those brave soldiers; shot full of morphine, forever avoided by medics, slowly passing beyond all miseries without wasting anyone's time, waiting patiently for Graves Registration.

"Bring that head wound over here!" a blood-splattered surgeon ordered crisply.

Wounds were his job, not people.

Dusk spread rapidly through the muggy air. Lighting another cigarette, I had to shit. Either I'd been too preoccupied or was constipated, but I hadn't shit in two days. I think it was two days, maybe three. Searching my way through the growing darkness, I found a long canvas screen strung near the collecting station to form a box about 20x20 feet, open at the top, around six upright poles. Assuming it was a large latrine, I went to the entrance in the rear. Inside, about thirty dried blood cadavers, many hurt bad or mangled, dead soldiers, including ROKs and a couple chinks no longer enemy, clothed in white, line crossers, piled three high, heads and feet alternating. Four Negro soldiers lay together on one stack beside ROKs as though they died separate from whites. One, drained of blood was ashen, seemingly turning white. I wondered if they had been segregated before or by some racist medic after death, or was it just an accident they ended up so tight together? There beside their stack of horror was a captain, perhaps to be the bottom of a new pile, officers only.

A sergeant from Graves Registration, 15th Infantry, supervised Korean laborers sliding board-stiff bodies into black human remains pouches. As I watched in horror, a large private's stiffened arm, outstretched as though signaling was dislocated at the shoulder and brought down to his side in order to fit into the rubber bag. As something broke, it made a hideous crack, not loud, just hideous. One little rifleman with a frozen smile, eyes protruding, body bent at the waist, sat up in a grotesque position of a puppet made up to be surprised as two Korean workers relaxed their grip on him for a moment to guide the opening over his legs. He was straightened at the waist without noise.

Another Korean behind the sergeant held a flashlight for a clerk filling out personal effects forms on a clipboard; identifying objects brought out of the dead men's pockets, Korean laborers placing them in individual tagged olive drab cloth property bags.

"Get this one here," the sergeant said, "and we'll call it a day."

"Hey, lieutenant, sir, strangers are not allowed in the morgue."

I hardly heard him, so sensitive was I of the grounded dead. "Sergeant," I told him, "I'm no stranger, I'm one of them." I felt I was with them in a trance, a purgatory in which combat soldiers are held until they finally fall to the real hell. Night was falling heavy on us hiding environment until we were united in that macabre scene and silent voices were telling me, "We're gone, gone, gone away, lieutenant, want to join? Come, buddy, good bye; honey, I'm with my buddies forever. Gone, gone, gone far, far away, gone into the Land of the Morning Calm."

I bent close to a gangly young master sergeant and saw that he and his new companions had been used hard, dead the hard way, faces and fatigues caked with dried brown mud and blackened blood; wide-open eyes of some staring unbelievingly at their ending. "Is this really it, sir?" They seemed to say, "We finally worn-out dead men gone forever? This is how, stacked here? This is it?" Pity, I thought, such young men meet their Maker dirty like this.

They died dropped like a rock or falling and stumbling forward or thrown backward by the force of a hard flung blow, on their faces facing enemy, or flipped up or down; left behind by their buddies forced to evacuate fast; spent shell casings, their lively load emptied, dropped carelessly in bushes off the trail. If you stared back at them you sensed they were no longer them that breathed steadily and sometimes yelled or laughed and joked and cursed or said hello; no, all those left for a very few others to see were still, frozen images. Here and there in stacks of the dead a guy more cared for, rolled carefully in an Army blanket, poncho or shelter half bound with commo wire like tall, thin Major Allen his guys took care of prior to meeting his black rubber bag.

As I stepped aside for the Graves Registration party to leave the stacking place, the sergeant asked kindly, "Looking for anyone in particular, Lieutenant? I got a list here."

"No thank you, I appreciate that."

Ten of us less seriously wounded were locked in a crackerbox (square-built Army ambulance with large red cross on its sides) from the outside by a young PFC medic who rode shotgun beside the driver with a puny little single-shot carbine to protect us—guarding a stage coach of invalids through Indian country with a BB gun. One of the less handicapped guys sidled back to the only exit, the rear door, and tried unsuccessfully to open it. "Dammit!" he said. Come what may, we were trapped.

Darkness found us zig-zagging up a steep mountain road on high brights to light the way as far forward as possible, one wounded from a nearby artillery battery warned us that chinks were everywhere. When he left the battery, their 105s were firing north, south, east and west and two MPs patrolling this same winding road two nights before were taken POW, their burnt jeep found at one sharp turn behind a large log dropped across the way.

We wounded were too excited to be alive to nap despite a string of hectic days and the monotony of winding slowly back and forth up the hill, that and the excitement of wounding. We were from different units; each related when questioned how, when and how bad his wound. We were the more important the worse it was. One guy's tag said 'missile in chest.' Another guy with a painfully shattered forearm in a tight sling groaned whenever the ambulance hit a large bump, but broken arms were ordinary, too stateside to hold interest. Another, a young pimple-faced rifleman, sick to his stomach from an unintended extra shot of morphine and utter fatigue, puked green slime between his legs on the floor, apologizing profusely as any drunk. The first medic to treat him had forgotten to place the empty morphine ampule in a buttonhole to let other medics know one had already been given.

When asked where I got it, I pointed to my neck and back, telling them the doctor said I was lucky it went all the way through. Seems everyone but the chest wound lit cigarettes and, despite a small ventilation fan up front, the air fouled and burned our eyes. At first everyone talked all at once and then all together grew quiet, each overcome by fatigues of several natures, screening thoughts of how thankful he was for getting this far, and the overall unique pride and excitement of being wounded, as though we were acquiring something of commercial value, joined an exclusive brotherhood, going so far as to feel sorry for those never wounded in combat. As our crackerbox ground back and forth up the hill, we sat bent over or slumped right or left against buddies, which we wounded strangers all were automatically, lost in thought and daydreams; blank, weary expressions on dirty, bewhiskered faces. Now and then, out of the corner of my eyes in the dim glow of two overhead dome lights, I watched a guy smile to himself and I knew just why; a combination of being damn glad to be out of it for a while and the thought, so important an accomplishment to a combat infantryman, I ain't dead or near to it yet and I'm in for the Military Order of the Purple Heart. When I get back home people will know automatically from the little purple and white pin on my lapel what a hero I am." And, not last, I'm looking forward to pretty nurses, white sheets, lengthy sleeps; softness, kindness, all kinds of cleanliness, niceness and sweet thoughts, warmth, sympathy, hot food—maybe baked pies or chocolate cakes—indoors away from that unpredictable sky; comfort and again being among innocent ones who've never been ordered to kill or even taught how. Are there pretty nurses this far away? Oh yes, oh yes! one way or another they're all pretty, even in combat boots, above which is all soft and warm and desirable, just to say hello to and look at and daydream about screwing. Hear the comforting melody of their laughter; a wonderful cure just being near and smelling them going by.

As the ambulance settled in low gear up the grinding zig-zag mountain road, in between battle-tattle, we all pitied a young PFC staring straight ahead, wearing large Band Aids over small blood smears on each cheek. I, and others, I learned later, were convinced the poor guy had his teeth badly shattered and his tongue as well, and, for one, I figured he'd never be able to talk right again and would be on liquids the rest of his life. How'd you like to lose your tongue? Among all wounds he was number one in my book, above the sergeant with a missile in chest which, with the proper equipment and technique, could easily be removed.

We reached the summit at last, worrying all the way that infiltrating chinks would finish us off, and when the driver slammed into high and we began to roll freely downhill, the kid with the bad mouth we all thought must be so painful, unmoving as it was all the hour-long climb, shook his head and enunciated clearly, "Boy, am I glad that's over." I felt like choking him and a sergeant growled, "Why you sonofabitch!" I thought of all the pity wasted on him. When he saw our angry stares, he quickly apologized for not having the troubles we feared. The bullet passed from one side to the other clean through his mouth, cheek to cheek, without hitting tongue or teeth as he yelled to a buddy.

This was the first of a number of close calls I saw or heard about. A corporal of King Company, for instance, whose case was well discussed and discussed among medics all over the regiment, hit in the front of the throat, passed through and came out the neck, missing spine and everything vital. A replacement captain of the same company later, during the monsoon, on the Punchbowl in brand new fatigues and untanned, was climbing to take over from Master Sergeant Pater. He carried $40,000 in South Korean currency, August pay for the troops, and was hit in the flesh of his right leg and helped back down by two CTC carriers. After the seven-hour descent in the cold monsoon rain he collapsed at the aid station and, despite all the battalion surgeon tried, could not be revived—dead, I learned, from irreversible shock. His musette bag with the money was never found.

We remounted our box on wheels after a piss stop and motored as fast as traffic and man-size potholes would allow down a much-traveled valley road with one of the guys up front giving a play-by-play account of what he saw in the darkness peeking through the small window behind the driver. A steady stream of vehicle lights lit the twisting road all the way to Hoengsong. Big powerful trucks from ordnance ammo dumps, shifting gears, revving up, ten-ton trailers, huge rubber-tired bulldozers on lowboys in a hurry to make a supply road somewhere, and many six-bys full of white-faced, wide-eyed, superstitious, prayerful replacements speeding north, relating dire misinformation back and forth; empty trucks returning for another load and several crackerboxes like ours speeding south toward serenity, full of wholesale misery. Once our small world stopped abruptly, throwing us onto one another from front to rear as our driver tooted and set off a loud tank siren.

"Get that goddamn Mack to the side. Can't you see we're wounded?" our young shotgun hollered in a thin voice.

"Want to haul them youself?" boomed a large black sergeant standing one foot on the running board to assess the situation ahead. Don't nobody tell him they don't cry up there for them big shells.

Pretty soon we felt ourselves turning onto a side road. Tired of my own desperate, somewhat enforced, therefore artificial and obviously unofficial opinion, I lapsed into a senseless series of frustrating semiplan or loose daydreams, progressing haphazardly along between short periods of somewhat intelligent or rational worry. Proud as I was of my wound, I resented not having it worse, one of those million-dollar ones that got you stateside. Or did I really? Really? Wasn't I getting a little hooked like a gambler on the unpredictable thrills of infantry combat now that my survival chances seemed better? On the other hand, "Crimus, some of those could cripple you for life and get worser and worser as you got older. Look how crippled with rheumatism and disfigured Uncle Art was from scars from old wounds from the Argonne and his bad knee." My little wound was nothing, but was legal and would have to do.

Come about midnight we corkscrewed into a broad valley with a partially illuminated air strip. We could hear diesel generators humming away. We slowed down and parked and our shotgun guard unlocked us and, stiff and somewhat sore from the long bumpy ride, we got out and pissed and were led into the receiving tent of a field hospital. Two chest wounds from another ambulance who hadn't been air evacuated from the 15th Infantry Collecting Station were well covered and belted down in litter baskets, one on each side of an H-13 big-bubble helicopter and flown to the Air Force evacuation field some twenty miles south over another mountain. The only chopper we had in the Army in Korea in 1951 was the H-13 and few there were. Mean while, Marines had the larger, lifting H-19s and were experimenting relieving men on listening posts and hauling heavy equipment.

We were experiencing what the Press labeled the May Massacre and triage selected a few more guys to go south immediately. We ambulatory, those able to walk, dozed on freshly washed litters until dawn to climb into an old Army C-47. Ten badly wounded chinks were carried aboard and strapped down on litters in the aisle. We studied our adversaries, the first most of us had seen up close. About that time, my buddy Conley Clarke, *JOURNEY THROUGH SHADOW,* who hadn't the opportunity to play dead, marching north nights with starved buddies dropped along the hidden ways, never seen again, was knowing chinks better than one ever wanted to. I thought what underfed, pathetic little buggers they were. I stared particularly hard at one little chink under five feet who seemed chinless. What a lousy deal, I thought, to be killed by a jerk like that. As time went by on my tour in Korea, I saw many, many more chinks, dead or POW, and remember many quite tall but never heavy and filled out, like too many were on our side. Six footers with large, high cheek bones, I learned, were likely to be Mongols or Manchurians.

We had a short flight over two low mountains just barely visible in the light of dawn below us and on to an Air Force field where they loaded us into a white Constellation with large red crosses on its sides in case they met enemy Air this far south. Ambulatory sat in bucket seats facing the aisle; layers of litters slung above us. After takeoff, the guy immediately above bled all over my collar and right shoulder, the side of my own little wound. I called for a nurse and stood out of the way while she worked frantically to stop his bleeding. Damn it, standing in the aisle watching her work so efficiently only a foot away, I fell in love with the back side of that wonderful young Air Force nurse, her pants stretched tight over her lovely butt while reaching for the guy. Angel, that's what she was, flying in the air, a damn angel. How I'd like to get her between some sheets.

Landing at the K-9 airport outside Pusan at daybreak, the more serious were again whisked away, either to one of the several Army General hospitals in Japan, such as Tokyo or Osaka General, after a long wait, in large white school buses converted to run to the Third and Tenth Station hospitals on railroad tracks to avoid bumpy roads and traffic. It was the height of the

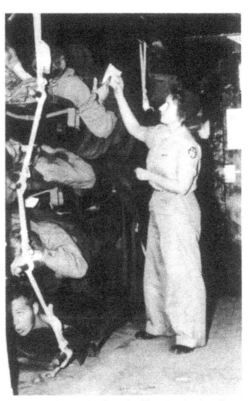

Our sweetheart checking buddies in the Air Force Constellation air ambulance.

May Massacre and all medical facilities were working day and night until medics were forced to medicate one another for fatigue and lack of sleep. One MASH handled 700 wounded in seventy-two hours.

POWs were counted by thousands and there must have been at least 400 litters of their seriously wounded lying near a hanger on the ground at the airport. They were being treated, for the most part, by Korean physicians and enlisted assistants, Air Force male nurses and master sergeants, who, for the immediate work they did were as skilled as any doctor, treating them every bit as well as we, if a little slower. Lightly wounded POWs were cared for by the medical detachments of those that captured them and at division stockades by Korean UN doctors. POW doctors were seldom seen since Chinese physicians were never forward of division.

We ambulatory got out and formed rough ranks under the big Constellation; it seemed awfully big to a wounded man standing under its broad wings. We had a roll call and Air Force medics checked our evacuation tags to match them with our dog tags. We were then released to wait around for one of the big white ambulance buses

COMBAT NURSE
by Mary E. Hill Arthur
Army Nurse, WWII

I will not fail you, fall or crumble
At the sight and smell and touch of blood
Open cavities or missing limb or mind
I will not cry when you have to die
I wrap wounds, medicate, inject
And hold your hand
To let you know I understand
I will change you, turn you like a baby
Call the OD and Chaplin on the double
Stay after hours to help write to your true love
If it be your struggle is over, it is your last fight
I will gently close your eyes and
Prepare you for your next flight
As your young weary soul takes wing
Into the subtle shadows
Of this cold unending pain-filled night
I must not crumble, I must not cry,
That would not do at all
I keep hearing yet another frantic call
And though at times it seems
My fluttering heart may faint, I know that
Someone needs my cool hand, needs my clear head
So Lord help me keep my wits together
Keep my heart rhythm steady, keep it strong
Lest my senses fail me and I fall
I cannot crumble, I will not cry
No, that would not do at all

Time to relax and clean up. One Mash tent hospital in the Second Division area treated seven hundred wounded in one week of the May Massacre.

114

to take us into Pusan and certain cases to the large white Danish hospital ship, the *Jutlandia*, docked in the harbor, later to be relieved by the big US Navy ship, *Hope,* painted white also with its own large red cross midway on both sides.

A bunch of sight-seeing airmen and a few officers apparently too diffident or embarrassed to look us face-to-face, drifted by gawking at chink POWs. Most prominent was a tall, handsome, mustached Hollywood-type lieutenant colonel and two captains in leather jackets taking pictures. We assumed they were pilots off duty and resented the way they pushed into our group, carefully ignoring us, looking right by us to get closeups of the chinks, not saying a thing or being friendly. They invited our hostility and one of our guys said, "Ain't we cute! Pin wings on me ma, I'm a bird."

The Air Force group pretended they didn't hear him and the colonel, face against a soft fluffy fur collar, with a voice calculated to sound macho, snapping his camera at a little bandaged chink at my feet said, to impress his captain friends, "Don't look so tough now, do they."

I could see the wounded dogfaces behind me didn't like it any better than I did and, although usually I don't think of the right thing to say until too long after, this time I was proud of myself. "Where the fuck *you* seen them before?"

The wounded around me let out guffaws and the colonel glared at me but said nothing. I noticed that one of his captains covered his mouth and snickered quietly. Instinctively, I took the cigarette out of my mouth and put it into the mouth of a wounded teenage chink. He gave back a weak smile.

Knowing I did this for his benefit, the colonel snapped, "Lieutenant, you can be court martialed for giving aid and comfort to an enemy."

"He's no enemy. He's a wounded dogface like us. Now get the fuck out of here, this is Army business."

The colonel did the only thing he could: demanded my name and unit.

"Lieutenant Gould," I told him proudly, "Second Infantry Division, Love Company, 38th. Come up and see me sometime, we'll climb some mountains."

The GIs let out another big laugh which made me feel important for having twice said the right thing at the right time.

This strange clash with the pilot bothered me off and on for some time, until a psychologist acquaintance took a stab at it. "What happened," he surmised, "was that you two big egos met in a very dramatic spot that excited you both. There you were, a messed up, dirty, blood-covered, somewhat pathetic hero of the ground war, surrounded by the enemy you wounded, all thrust on the pilot's home territory, the land he left behind each day to face his heroic job, not knowing whether he would ever return. It was as though you two proud studs faced off in a combat of your own. This is my territory, man, bow to me, I'm the hero here, thought the colonel; address and salute me because I rank you and I'll return your salute and be friendly and we'll chat and ask about your wounding and the territory you hail from. No, colonel, I'm the wounded hero, address me first with a pretty smile and ask me how I feel, sympathize and ask how bad was ground combat and maybe I'll ask a little about your job."

Three ambulances backed up and picked up the more seriously wounded chinks as we ambulatory sauntered on foot across the field, along with a growing crowd of curious off-duty airmen who made no bones that they were our fan club. We entered a temporary shelter, a bare Quonset hut. Wounded prisoners, guarded by five armed air policemen, were parked unceremoniously in the sun which even so early in the morning this far south was becoming quite warm.

"How is it up there?" one of the guards asked politely.

"See for yourself," he was told from the doorway. "This ain't no private war."

The airman snickered self-consciously.

"Anyone bring a burp gun?" one asked. "Get you fifty bucks."

"Naw," a rifleman drawled. "They was hanging on 'em."

The Army guys laughed as walking wounded, which most were, filed in out of the sun to flop on straw-filled mattresses lining the walls. I sat next to a grizzled master sergeant on a bench by the front door near the prisoners. He eyed my bloody shoulder so long I think he wanted to ask about it. My sore thumb was slowly healing but had cracked open again when I hit it on something and a little blood oozed out. In the excitement of battle and my real wound, I'd forgotten it completely. My bullet wound didn't hurt at all but that darn thumb was sore as anything. I sucked on it brooding and my goddamn athlete's foot was itching bad and my bruised side hurt when I moved sideways.

From a gaily decorated Red Cross airmen's club next door came the plaintive strains of Patti Page singing the *Tennessee Waltz* over and over by homesick youngsters. "I was waltzing with my darling to the Tennessee Waltz when an old friend I happened to meet." How I'd like to get my hands on her.

"Crimus," I thought. "That's sad." I'd never been to Tennessee but it made me wonder if anyone really cared what happened to me and the rest of us. God almighty, that's so sad it hurts; reminds me of songs in WWII that gripped us hard: 'Heard they crowded the floor ... Don't get around much anymore' ... 'I'll walk alone' ... 'The last time I saw Paris' ... that brought you closer to any girl you dated, as though you were a potential combatant so long as you were in a uniform; misery could happen to you and they better be nice when they have the chance. Oh how I used to daydream in WWII of a real hero's welcome; being helped off the train at Watertown by the porter, one sleeve pinned shut, Purple Heart with two clusters, and the light blue ribbon with small white stars, Medal of Honor, and women to lay, no damn Frank Sinatra bobby-sockers, big-breasted, sexy, mature women who had real nipples that tightened when you sucked and knew how to fondle a cock.

One of the prisoners moaned. An older, wizened POW consoled him. The young chink moaned again, louder, making a languid, supplication with one hand. The master sergeant, named Comifort, an ex-Marine, old China hand like our Captain Brownell, whom he'd heard tell of, talked softly to the chink in his own dialect. The pitiful young man who'd been napalmed and had that smell made a weak smile and waved a limp forefinger of his right hand half an inch up and down above the heavy bandaging and God, how stunned I was, hating the pilot who did that, oozing tears in my eyes, wishing I too could say hello, good luck young fellow, I'm sorry.

"He says he's going to heaven soon and join his buddies who burned up," Comifort told me, and "an older wounded POW, a commissar, warned him against talking like that."

Commissars often allowed themselves to be captured so they could continue to lie to the POWs, proving to me that they didn't believe their own crap about us torturing and bayonetting chinks as the damn japs did as part of their training, and their charges were all made up. They would lead the mutinies at Koje-do prison island.

I was more tired than I'd ever been in civilian life, but at the same time, wildly excited. I was awfully proud to be in the company of such terrific guys and dammit, I mean chinks as well as Yanks; we who handled guns were alike; just being unlucky enough to be wounded somehow seemed heroic. How many Americans except after the greatest battles in American history have been with so many wounded battle-tested guys in one place? Friends with their foes side-by-side together temporarily joined honorably by war? Chink or Yank, Union or Confederate, by God, none of us had anything to prove the rest of our lives. I'll admit it's a pity this sort of thing has to come about through war, but wars happen because of a greater misery, bastards like the dictator Kim Il Sung. Sitting there quietly, the plaintive music in the background, I was suddenly very tired again and with all the excitement and danger and little rest in the past week, I fell asleep soundly and once again had to watch the ravaged refugee families at the big intersection fleeing gooks. God what a pitiful mess, tiny babies bound tightly to the breasts of thoroughly fatigued mothers and grandmothers with their own or other papooses strapped to their bent backs with huge loads on their heads, or, too often, discarded in shallow graves of the dry, hard roadsides, mangled remains of human bodies scattered promiscuously along mountain roads.

Pitiful little kids, age of my own little boy, toddling to keep up made old and worn so soon, with snot from perpetual head colds dripping from their pink little noses, and old mamasons, their men killed or driven off to serve the gooks. No stoic or Spartan was ever greater, more steeled. And the heart-wrenching, chirpy, little sobs those little, wrinkled, bent over old ladies gave us for meager handouts and, standing feet together at attention, bending sharply down and up to us from all their great personal sadness: "Thank you, American soldier. Thank you. Thank you for your food and medicine. Thank you. But why, American soldier, you bring this ugly war on our peaceful mountains?"

"Okay, old mamason, give me time we'll put an end to your miseries."

"Why," I asked of myself, "Don't gook soldiers realize what liars their commissars are? Can't they see which way their poor people are fleeing?"

"Lieutenant? Lieutenant Gould, coffee and doughnuts?"

"What? ... Who? ... What's up? ... Time to move on? ... I was just thinking. Why, yes, are the guys getting coffee too?"

"Some back for seconds. They didn't want us to wake you."

"How did you know my name? I don't know anyone down here."

"Why, Sergeant Comifort said he'd met you a little before."

Several wounded chink prisoners smiled and conversed with Sergeant Comifort as a small crowd of our walking wounded gathered to listen. We sensed hostile thoughts and fear between us wounded guys disappearing from both sides. What a difference communication makes. All of us should know some kind words in Chinese.

"What did you tell them? I asked Sergeant Comifort.

"I said we're sorry about the damn napalm, it wasn't our idea of combat."

"Ask them how fast them burp guns," one asked.

"About 900," the sergeant answered without hesitation.

A faceless young private asked through his bandages, "Hey, sarge, ask 'em why they wanted to start a war."

"It was gooks," someone offered.

At 1100 the Red Cross woman returned with a couple of airmen volunteers with more trays of doughnuts. We made sure to thank her.

"Any of you men would like to," she cooed, "come to the Club. We'd l-o-o-ve to have you."

Four or five privates accepted her invitation but the others were too conscious of the contrast; tanned brown by the weather, hard and thin, wearing prominent evacuation tags, blood-stained, filthy fatigues, OD stretch-bandage head dressings, arm slings, or hobbling on crutches, most of us patches of blackened blood —Spirit of '76 multiplied, in dirty fatigues.

"Well," the Red Cross woman continued, "you boys are more than welcome, you know. We'd l-o-o-ve to have you, deserve it after what you've been through."

As she left, an Air Force major walked by, civilian type, fuzzy, fur-collared flying jacket casually draped over his arm.

"Hi, Joe," she waved.

"How's things?" he purred, carefully ignoring me and the sergeant.

"Sh-e-e-it!" Comifort sneered.

"Sh-e-e-it!" I repeated, looking over at the sergeant. "See that flyboy?"

Brought me back to Cornwall Barracks, Ontario, Canada, in 1940, and what we did to RCAF blokes at local taverns, with their fancy blue uniforms associated with the violent air war going on over England and all the girls going for the blue rather than the old olive drab oversize tam-o-shanters disdained as 'cow flops.' They wore albatrosses on the coat buttons and we called them the 'bloody pigeons.'

For the rest of our stopover at K-9 airport, we wounded sat or laid on rice straw mattresses in the Nissen hut, listening through walls to the heart-rending *Tennessee Waltz.* Hear it a thousand times, you still sympathize. A substantial box lunch was served around noon and several Air Force doctors came out at 1300 with enlisted medics and several trays of supplies to check wounds, still triaging looking for head or chest bandages. The excitement and novelty had worn off. I wished that I hurt or the dandy flyboy would come back to give Comifort and me a hard time.

"Jam it up your ass!" I'd tell him. "Got any friends, jam it up their's!" The guys would get a kick out of that.

At 1500 our turn in the steady influx of WIA came and the big white bus on train wheels took a load of us into Pusan and the Third Station Hospital.

It was a fluke of luck my getting as far down as Pusan. Compared to most wounds I saw, mine was very petty. Years later, in my column in *Army Times,* I pro posed three orders of the Purple Heart. General Washington first devised it, strictly for valor, only four of which, of cloth, were given out toward the end of the War for Independence. They were not for wounds; everyone got wounded.

In the Forgotten War, an eighth of all soldiers in a rifle platoon were wounded. The nick I got would be of the lowest rank and no one would get one for a barbed wire scratch as one I know of, a blowhard Lieutenant Tasker Haines (pseudonym). Only the highest, for being killed or very badly torn up, would be pure gold and have a profile of Washington in a green enameled wreath. The other two would be ordinary-looking, one a little more precious than the other.

As General SLAM Marshall complained in a letter to me, the whole system of awards and decorations needed revising: the Purple Heart, highest for the likes of Senator Dole to a widow or a mother. It should ever be a sacred symbol and never given so wrongfully as when rear-echelon Hollywood soldier President Reagan awarded one to a Department of Army civilian and an Air Force female who got scratched in a German gasthaus by flying glass from a terrorist's bomb during a refugee Turk protest against Germans. She had no business in the quarrel or being in the way. But then pretty boy actor Reagan also awarded the nation's highest civilian decoration to Frank Sinatra; remember in WWII how we GIs hated his guts, avoiding the draft with a scarred ear drum which didn't slow him down singing to underage Bobby Sockers. Remember when we guys came home he had to hire bodyguards?

All my mother's brother, Uncle Art, gassed and machine gunned in the Argonne in 1918, got for the short while left in uniform, most of which he spent in Walter Reed, was the ability to wear a gold thread wound stripe on his left sleeve below the elbow, unrecognized by most. For a small sniper bullet in the back that did no harm but cauterized the wound as it passed between two vertebrae, I was in the hospital three days, walking around, going down to watch the movies. For this time out of combat I'd be willing to pay somebody , contrasted with the great pain, despair and fear in his life and years in hospitals as Senator Bob Dole, fellow rifle platoon leader.

I have talked with many guys who ended up at the Third or Tenth Station who, without exception, have nothing but high praise for them. When I got to the Third, the so-called May Massacre had been going on for about two weeks, beginning as chinks overran the Glousters, our Second Division and the Fifth and Seventh ROKs. Doctors, nurses and attendants were practically out on their feet, as much as seventy-two straight hours without more than an occasional catnap, some leaning against a wall between jobs.

The light colonel in charge of the receiving ward triage motioned to me out of ten or twelve standing just inside the door. I hesitated, not believing it was me he wanted and he waved again harder, raised his voice across the large room: "Right here, lieutenant, don't be modest." It then dawned on me that what interested him was the great amount of blood splattered over one shoulder and in front by the guy hemorrhaging above me on the Constellation.

"No," I said soon as I reached him. "That's someone else's blood."

"Well, let me check while I've got you."

He had me remove my fatigue top and slashed my torn undershirt away, raise my arms and twist my torso in a number of awkward positions.

"That was fortunate," he told himself aloud.

"Why?" I asked suspiciously. "What happened? What is it?"

Ignoring me the colonel called over a captain and the two inspected my neck and back without Band Aid and bandage, using Latin words, pressing with their fingers, shaking their heads knowingly from time to time. The bullet, a .30 caliber, curved somehow or torqued through the muscles of my neck and back to pass safely between the projections of two vertebrae. Being Agnostic, I thanked my lucky stars.

"Hurt anything?" I wanted to know.

Looking at me the colonel answered, "Real close!"

"Crimus," I thought, "I could be dead already."

According to the colonel's chart, which went with me to a large company grade officers' open ward, I was "white male, First Lieutenant Dudley C Gould, 160 pounds, five feet eight inches, thirty-one, blood type O, agnostic, married, recalled Reservist. Aside from a minor gunshot wound, in good health. Temperature and heart rate normal." The nurse scolded me when I insisted I was five feet, eight-and-a-*half*. She wouldn't change anything for half an inch, she told me. Nearly out on her feet from fatigue, her speech was slurred and she looked at me with heavy eyelids, all of which I mistook for her being sexy, coming on to me.

"I can show you I got more than eight-and-a-half-inches," I told her.

"That so?" she told me, walking away.

The company grade officers' ward was full. One of the ward boys told me that every time a big push was made up north, officers with doctor friends came flocking in with all sorts of medical problems that, in most cases, had been pending for some time. Many were accepted, not through normal receiving channels, but by orders from the front office from other than practicing physicians.

The long process of evacuation and passing through echelons of medics dulled the original excitement of being wounded and for a day or two I was almost morose as hardly a sound was heard in the large open company-grade officers' ward except for an occasional suppressed cough or the pages of a paperback novel turning at intervals; now and then an easy-going conversation in low voices. Even those who rested all morning took long siestas after lunch. When my initial two day off-and-on recoup sleep was over, I lay on my sterile white metal hospital cot staring at the white ceiling, designed squares in stamped thin-gage metal repeated from one side to the other, thinking seriously of all the bullets that passed me by until that one hit, I got thinking about all the comfortable safe living back home I was missing and I confess I was so occupied with my own problems and worries I seldom thought of Kitty or Dickie, our little boy. I was surprised later that Kitty had no such compelling diversions as beset me all the time. Afternoons, she'd tell me were worst; at night there were programs on the radio to give her unceasing worries a little rest.

I was ordered to soak my wounds in both places with four-by-four compresses of hot water in gauze three times a day. In those days I was flexible enough to reach back there but even so I did it only three times. Potassium permanganate foot baths were prescribed for my athletes' foot, which afflicted me on and off since high school gym classes. Embarrassingly enough, it was the technical excuse for my medical discharge from the Royal Canadian Army on a tacit understanding with the friendly doctor representing me on the medical board that I would enlist in the US Army right across the border at Fort Niagara. It was just weeks after the big shock of the jap attack on the Pearl Harbor Naval Base, and Americans who wore USA on their left shoulders were being given the options of refusing overseas shipments. It became a common cause and most of us preferred fighting for our own country.

There was far more concern about that persistent fungus infection, whatever it was, than my honorable, unnoteworthy neck wound and nothing said or done about my black and blue side and chest. Perhaps it was because the wound had, like John Wayne's wounds, healed overnight. Athletes' foot continued to be a big problem until fairly recently when a dermatologist at the USAF Wilford Hall Medical Center in San Antonio prescribed *griseofulvin* in pill form to clear it up for good. For thirty some years it had always been treated from the outside.

Once in mid-morning and again before supper, a tall, mannish woman nurse, warhorse, Kitty would call her lovingly, in Army boots clomped in carrying a wooden tray of assorted hypodermic needles, pill bottles, bandage materials, and miniature bottles of serums.

"Okay, buster, expose it!" she'd command, and I'd roll over on my stomach on the bed and modestly pull down the back of my pajama bottoms. She'd give me a hard slap on my pink upturned ass with her fingertips and simultaneously jab the needle in all the way.

"Ouch!" But I never felt a thing.

"Like that, honey?" she'd smile.

I became convinced she was out to get me and one time became so rattled I sneaked out of the ward before she arrived. That sadistic woman returned after lights out to give me a stab. I was told she always hunted down deserters.

"You men are babies."

After two days of rest, we lightly wounded sat on the edges of our cots amazing one another with original battle-tattle. "Yeah. You should have been with us." Adding them up it was a terribly gory, hopeless war. And then we tired of combat stories and sat for hours thinking or daydreaming and maybe some were praying. Of course, I had the athletes' foot to rub as well.

The most important quality time was 1400 when we filed down to the big hall to catch a movie. One lieutenant, a West Pointer in the Signal Corps, spent his spare time groaning for the nurses' benefit, when everyone knew he'd broken his arm playing volleyball. Hurting or not, in each of the three days I was there he beat everyone to the movie.

Some went down to see what the PX offered, but I was short of cash and wasn't there long enough to be that bored. One we felt really sorry for was a 6'3" black Transportation Corps captain having his piles taken care of lying on his belly over a form to take the pressure off his ass where his hemorrhoids had been.

The third day I was allowed out on pass in my hospital pajamas, bathrobe and slippers to call my wife from the Korean Overseas Telephone Center near the Pusan train station. I used the last money I had doing it and as it was they kindly stretched our time a little. The come-and-go static on our line was unnerving and frustrating.

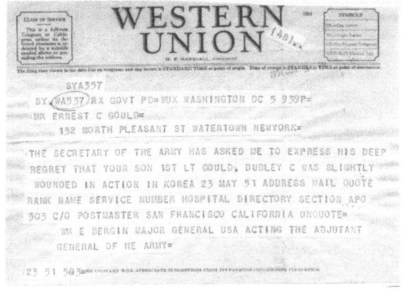

Many of us listed our fathers to be notified in case of death or wounding so he could break it to our wives more gently, but of course I informed Kitty by telephone.

The Pacific overseas radio was having sunspot troubles so they let me talk only after promising not to blame the Korean Overseas Office. Our voices kept trailing off suddenly to nothing or into an eerie screech and we had to keep repeating ourselves, during which Kitty sobbed. All I can compare it with was my father's first radio in the late twenties, a Crosley, which would resort to crazy e-e-e-ouw, e-owow-eeee phantom static noises. I told Kitty I had just a little nick and a telegram would arrive from the Department of Army and not to worry that I was wounded all over again.

After I'd been back home a while, a friend told me the phone company might reimburse me. My local Bell telephone company contacted San Francisco where the taped call was replayed and sure enough, I was sent a check for $31.00.

I heard that some of our people were in the *Jutlandia,* the white Danish Hospital ship. I walked up the gangplank and was welcomed aboard and, looking at a list, found in English what stateroom I would find a First Lieutenant Alexander Opoulus. What a break! Everyone at battalion wondered how he was doing, if he was still alive. Sandy's dad was a Greek immigrant who was a silent partner in a large Ford Agency in Mt Kisco, New York. We were fellow platoon leaders in F Company Second Battalion when I first arrived and a week or so before we went on outpost he took command of King, which company was clobbered more than Love. I kidded him about the white crib he was in with side bars to keep him from falling out, one foot in traction guyed up high, his Achilles heel slashed by a stray grenade frag, definitely a million-dollar stateside wound; in fact, a medical discharge wound.

Under flare light, I heard and watched Sandy's company being overrun while trying to evacuate and heard him yelling for them to conserve their ammo. His radioman was killed by a chink frag grenade, bits of which caught Lieutenant Opoulus in one heel and simultaneously several small shards in his head. The superficial scalp wounds saved his life for they knocked him unconscious and since one bleeds copiously from there, chinks passing by on the trail seeing him in the dark under the flares bathed in blood must have thought him dead and though one took his wedding ring, wristwatch and wallet, left him alive.

I tell everyone who will listen about Sandy, for even though I was with him only a few days, he made a deep impression. At seventeen, Sandy was arguably the youngest man commissioned in the Infantry in WWII, machine gunned in Italy fighting German rearguard action and invalided out with a forty percent medical pension. In 1950, like any red blooded man, motivated for action as were some of us, he waived his forty percent disability pension and volunteered to return to active duty with an almost unnoticeable limp. Four of us platoon leaders, at the time in F Company, celebrated our April officers' liquor ration in one very short reserve. We ended searching for a song we all knew and let loose with the *Wiffenpoof Song,* although none of us had been anywhere near Yale. I was a would-be writer scratching out a living laboring in a foundry; Sandy, son of a successful immigrant car salesman, was in college, Chuck Kariva, son of a Pennsylvania coal miner, and Lieutenant Austin who was beginning his insurance agency business. At the end of *Little Brown Jug,* Sandy pulled over an empty grenade box, mounted it and in mock serious soapbox style, began reciting Kipling's *IF.* Yes, we were quite happily drunk. We had great fears to face full on which, with the Chinese Army approaching, were immediate, and we stumbled along repeating line after spoken line, repeating the solemn pledge. Sentimental as we all were that memorable night of the war, we requested Sandy give us encores.

When I got back from Korea, I met Sandy by accident going into the officers' club at Fort Dix and we tied on a load and had a big spaghetti dinner and sobered up. I learned he waited to be released to VA per instruction of a medical board and would use a cane and at times be on crutches the rest of his life. Sandy broke my old heart again when he died in great pain from lung cancer and complications in November 1995 in an upstairs hospice bedroom at his home in Charleston, South Carolina three days after I managed to find him. Charlie Heath at Korean War Alliance headquarters located Sandy through a computer telephone search.

As Sandy and I joked around there on the *Jutlandia,* a corporal draftsman from the S3 section of battalion HQ looking for buddies saw me through Sandy's open door and, apologizing for intruding, came in to talk with us.

"Are you going back to battalion, lieutenant?" he asked me. "Sir, a couple of guys and I want someone to prefer charges against Major Wilkes and Captain Jones. While you guys were trying to take the hill, they were drunk, arguing which was most worthy of rotating first. I was transferred down with Major Wilkes from X Corps where he and the captain was buddies. Both should be court martialed. I've seen them plastered more than once."

"Yeah," I told Sandy, "I passed them hiding out on the trail."

"I know, lieutenant," the corporal said. "I was there and heard you bawl them out and after you left they sobered up fast and we moved up toward where the fighting had been. I left for the rotation center next day."

"I don't know anything about Army law," I told the corporal, "but I can't do it alone. Are you and your friends willing to testify?"

"Sorry," he said, "we'll be boarding in two days."

Had I any legal know-how, I was told later, I might have gotten a sworn deposition.

When I finally got back to battalion, I found morale so bad under Wilkes that: while we were trying to banzai those three machine guns, battalion headquarters and people at the kitchen trains rifled our personal packs, stole cameras and radios and drank up the beer ration which came in just after we left. We found letters and other personal stuff scattered over rifled packs.

Our Blue Book, page 136, has this little to say of my wounding, 23 May in early afternoon—

A hastily organized assault group, Task Force Yoke, commenced a limited northward drive to keep the enemy forces off-balance while the counter offensive was being racked up. Composed of the 3d Bn. 38th Inf; 72d Tk Bn (2); a platoon from the 38th Inf Tank Co; a battery of Division Field Artillery and a tactical air control party, the mobile force moved northwest from Pungam-ni toward Habae-jae.

And so was our sad story told in the limited edition of our official history book for 1950 and 1951, one short paragraph for no one but professional warriors to read. Nothing was said of two rifle companies weakened from being overrun on an outpost and further debilitated with green replacements to care for. Evidently no one in our history section at division rear knew about what an abortion our so-called attack was, especially the failure of leadership at any echelon higher than platoon. What burned me most was in skipping over this futile effort no mention was made of the good, courageous men we left there.

4

RETURN OF THE WOUNDED

If some people died and others did not,
death would indeed be a terrible injustice.
— Jean de La Bruverd

No one admits knowing how our regimental commander, Colonel John Coughlin, got the nickname Bloody Boots. His unofficial publicity man, TI&E, troop information and education officer, Lieutenant Charley Heath, retired light colonel, secretary/ treasurer of the Korean War Veterans Alliance, Olympia, Washington, US Second Infantry Division Association, denies starting it by describing his leader in the May Massacre as "wading through pools of Chinese blood. However, someone printed that in our inhouse regimental mimeographed publication, *The Warrior,* normally a TI&E function. I quote again from the Blue Book—

> This latest flurry brought to a close the most notable period of the Second Division's actions in the campaign. It brought forth, for the first time, a powerful counterattack which followed on the heels of one of the most spectacular defensive stands of the war. It was a counterattack which not only killed thousands of enemy troops, caught completely off-balance, but proved that the Second Division could absorb the pounding of overwhelming numbers of enemy forces only to turn and cut them to ribbons. In the 20-day period preceding the conclusion of the final attack the Indianhead Division had killed more than 65,000 enemy soldiers, the cream of the armies of Red China.

Judging from Love, King, Item and other companies I knew of in our vicinity, to make such a great slaughter, the rest of the division must have gone off like a million-dollar fireworks. Me and my guys? Busy as we were on the outpost-patrol base and Task Force Joke, I never saw a chink or gook close up dead or alive in the wild except peeking over a parapet until I returned from the Third Station and joined the guys working for the Dutch battalion near Inje, where plenty of the poor, hard-working little rice farmer draftees were caught by our state-of-the-art, million dollar fighter bombers, on the roads in broad daylight and the unChristian one-sided technology napalm.

Again from our official Blue Book—

It was a major defeat for Chinese and North Korean forces. Their ranks were decimated, entire divisions rendered useless. They had flung themselves in an all-out attempt to annihilate the Second Division and had failed under the merciless pounding of hundreds of thousands of rounds of artillery, tons of bombs and millions of rounds of small arms ammunition thrown at them by the determined, steadfast and victorious men of the Second Division.

On 5 June, the Division began its movement into reserve in the vicinity of Hongchon and by 11 June the move was complete. The relief from combat was utilized for the needed training and reorganization accompanied by corps command inspections of all the units. It was to be the longest non-combat period enjoyed by the Division since its arrival in Korea and it was the unanimous opinion of all that no division deserved it more.

As the first year of the Korean conflict came to an end, the United Nations could look back on their accomplishments with considerable satisfaction. South Korea had been cleared of the invading enemy, and the UN forces, after receiving and delivering severe batterings, had pushed north of the 38th parallel and successfully executed the missions that were within their power to accomplish. Thus, when on Sunday evening, 23 June 1951, in New York City, Jacob Malik, Deputy Foreign Commissar of the Union of Soviet Socialist Republics and his country's delegate to the United Nations, proposed cease-fire discussions between the participants in the Korean conflict, his proposal, while it may have been made for the convenience of the Chinese, came at a fortunate time for the Eighth Army.

Enemy casualties for the last half of May, Eighth Army headquarters reported, included 17,000 counted dead and 17,000 prisoners of war. Its own casualties for the entire month numbered 33,770. South Koreans lost the most; American losses totaled 743 dead, 4218 wounded, 572 missing, and 6738 nonbattle casualties, most of which were caused by disease.

Time Magazine reported 28 May 1951—

The Second Division historian wrote that the second Division alone had "killed more than 65,000 enemy soldiers, the cream of the Armies of Red China ... the 23rd Infantry claimed inflicting over 13,000 casualties of which 2200 were counted...." There was little evidence to support these claims. General Ridgway asked for an end to such guesses ordering that claims henceforth be limited to counting enemy dead and prisoners.

Early in the afternoon of the fourth day at the Third Station I reported downstairs to supply to trade in pajamas, slippers and maroon robe for new socks, underwear, fatigues, fatigue jacket with my Indianhead patch sewed on, and cap, and checked out my boots with a property tag. Freshly laundered fatigues and jacket felt good again. I couldn't wait to get in harness, resupplied with hunting paraphernalia at company; field pack with entrenching tool in canvas case, poncho and blanket, area map, and on my web belt canteen, first aid pouch, bayonet, carbine ammo; binoculars around my neck and on my left wrist with my Army watch a wrist compass, and secreted about my pack or upper body pockets, at least one box of C rations.

With some hours to spare before catching the next train north, while strolling among the many tables in a flourishing black market, I noticed olive-drab cotton US Army-issue socks. All I could draw through our supply were heavy wool ones and I needed light cotton to keep from causing my toes to sweat, encouraging my athlete's foot.

I picked up a pile and started to reach into my hip pocket when it dawned on me that I'd spent all my money on my call home. I drew only $20 a month in Korea, feeling I didn't need any more, Kitty having run up a big furniture bill for her apartment, putting half down from an advance pay permitted for cash-short soldiers (lieutenants, too) to settle dependents being left behind on a 'hardship tour.' We had thrown in what furniture we used to have in desperation to sell our house outside Syracuse.

To hell with it, I thought, all this merchandise has been stolen from the US Army. They're openly peddling Army medical supplies, syringes, Lister surgical scissors, and even certain drugs as APCs (GI aspirins). Not only essential military things, but in almost every restaurant bar window in the train station area were displayed empty bottles of such American liquor as Seagram Seven whiskey and Meyers rum, carried in officers' liquor ration, to let buyers know black market full ones were available inside.

I walked away from the display table with a dozen pairs of lightweight cotton socks to the utter surprise of the old vendor who set up a yell, attracting attention. I didn't run or even walk fast or make any effort to shut him up as he followed yelling and waving. Very soon a ROK military policeman approached and after trying to tell me something in broken English, left and came right back with an American MP corporal who saluted me sharply and asked, "Sir, did you forget to pay for those socks?"

"No," I explained, "I need them and haven't any money."

"But sir, that's illegal. You can't do that."

"I'm doing it."

Whereupon the corporal offered to pay for them. By then there was a crowd of agitated Korean civilians all jabbering at once, some apparently explaining to newcomers, pointing at me, the culprit, a combat officer, wearing the dreaded black shield, white star on profiled Indianhead of the Second Infantry Division, gone crazy. None of the bastards seemed worried that some high-placed American might confiscate their stolen merchandise and return it to the US Army.

I was overcome with hatred at the corrupt Army powers that be, whether the Pusan base provost marshal or area commanding general who had to be condoning this blatant crime. I contrasted table after table of stolen American Army merchandise with our guys dying for this crooked country.

"Damn it, corporal, these socks belong to me. I can't get cotton ones up front and now I know why, American officers back here are selling them to the gooks. Look at you protecting them so they can sell them back to us."

"Sir," the corporal said, "let me pay for them."

As he made a move to pull out his wallet from under his holster, I stopped him.

"Damn it, corporal, this is a matter of principle between me and this fucking country we're dying for. I don't care what you rear echelons back here overlook, that's stolen US Army property, and I'm an American infantryman who uses his feet all the time, needs cotton socks and can't get 'em from supply."

I had worked up so much disgust that in my anger I didn't even thank the young MP for his kindness in offering to pay for them.

"Lieutenant," he said politely, pointing, "would you mind coming with me to my headquarters just down the block?"

Fully convinced by then of my justification, I went along, the jabbering papason Korean vendor tagging behind. The corporal knocked on a door at the train station, ushered me and the old man in and saluted an MP major behind his desk.

"What have we here?" the major asked.

"Sir, this lieutenant refuses to pay for these socks," he said, taking them from me and placing them on the major's desk.

"Lieutenant, forget to pay for these?"

The corporal explained to the major that I had spent my last money calling my wife to let her know I was slightly wounded and not to worry. He explained also how wool irritated and worsened my athlete's foot; how I accused their boss, a colonel, district provost marshal, of driving by that black market to and from his office and getting a payoff, which naturally angered the major who then explained that no one in the military sold them—it was the State Department who gave them to the Korean government under a form of Lend Lease and crooked Korean politicians did the underhanded selling instead of issuing the stuff to the ROK Army, Sigmund Rhee being the ultimate benefactor.

We ended up shouting and my calling him a rear echelon to his face, at which he threatened me with a court martial and, completely out of control, I jumped at the chance.

"Go ahead, Goddammit. I'll contact Walter Winchell; he thrives on this sort of exposé.... Better than going back up there."

"Exposé of what?"

"You pricks back here letting gooks sell our equipment."

We glared, red face to red face, the major reminding me that as an officer I could get an Article 15 court martial just for calling South Koreans gooks, and then, conscious of the absurdity of influencing the situation on our level, and the fact that I was yelling at an innocent man (also a superior), I stopped in midsentence and looked around. "I'm sorry, major, I got carried away. I've been awful jumpy lately."

The major replied in his normal voice, "That's all right, lieutenant. I guess anyone would be." He offered to pay for the socks.

All at once I became modest and ashamed for criticizing him just for working back where it was safe. Hell, right then I'd love to change places, even without his rank. The thing that continued to be so damn irritating was that a guy like me had to be made to seem corny complaining that criminals ran the very government we worked so hard to protect.

I reached over the desk for the provost major's hand and we parted friendly.

"By the way," I said, "how do I get to the 1507th Replacement Depot?"

He had his jeep driver run me up to where it stood in an old warehouse on a hill above Pusan. Halfway there I discovered I left the socks on the major's desk.

We rode a dilapidated Korean train to Wonju, pulled by three engines, one still leaking steam from being shot up the preceding winter by gook guerrillas. Although organized guerrilla bands were gone, unmanned flat cars were still attached fore and aft with sand-bagged, heavy water-cooled machine gun positions.

A tall, good-looking captain asked if I minded if he sat beside me, even though there were at least four empty seats, explaining, "I saw your Division patch." He introduced himself as Captain Charles Carleton (pseudonym), First Battalion, 38th.

"I'll be damned," I said, rising to greet him. "I'm Lieutenant Dudley C Gould, Love Company, 38th." Not knowing Conley was a POW, I asked, "You aren't by any chance in Baker? I've got a buddy there, Lieutenant Conley Clarke."

The captain said, "No, I'm Headquarters Company ... at least I was."

"Where did you get hit?" Carleton asked.

I pointed to my neck.

"I don't mean where on your body."

"Oh, Task Force Yoke," which he hadn't heard of. "Where were you hit?" I asked.

He explained that he'd been home on emergency leave.

I learned later from his battalion commander that Captain Carleton had the relatively safe job of headquarters company commander at Hoengsong in January when they were hit by a large enemy force. The captain was accused of hiding out in a bunker, leaving the battalion sergeant major to fight the company. Carleton volunteered as much to me. He said he was not sure but what he was still under arrest awaiting an investigation to ascertain whether or not he would be court martialed. I didn't ask him, but was curious what the emergency leave had been about.

For all his physical attributes and education, Carleton was a frightened, lonely man. In a period of about ten minutes he told me all about himself: his Phi Beta something or other, ROTC commissioned toward the end of WWII, honor graduate student at Princeton, working on a doctoral degree when called to active duty. He might have avoided recall to active duty he explained but was experiencing difficulty with his PhD dissertation anyway and love of the military ran deep in his family. His brother was a light colonel in the Air Force. His congressman father, WWI vet, decided not to interfere with Carleton's being called up, feeling, Carleton offered, it would be good experience for him in his line of study, history, to see a war firsthand as an infantryman.

He volunteered also that his father arranged for an emergency compassionate leave so he could straighten things out and went on to tell me how savage things were when shit hit the fan. It was his first and only action, confusing, unreal, and how different a man can become from the one he thought he knew. He actually started shaking and stuttering telling me about the combat he almost experienced, hiding in a bunker, and continued as though he had to tell me all about it in detail to get rid of it, like a drunk throwing up, I guess.

"Sounds alone make you have to get out of there."

"I know."

I'm not one to sit quietly through someone's battle tattle without chiming in and when he found that I had actually played dead with chinks around me, he shook his head in amazement.

"Really! How could you do that, lieutenant? I'd have wet my pants."

When I told him I did, although not the circumstances, he assumed I was kidding. After about an hour of unnerving self-doubting and apology he got under my skin. When I learned he was studying historiography, whatever that really meant, I tried to tell him I wrote early American military history but he wouldn't cooperate to change the subject and kept on ventilating on me and finally I went to take a piss and eased into the car behind, joining a black master sergeant, 9th Infantry, wearing our division patch.

At the blasted, bombed-out Hoengsong station, the one near where Carleton failed to perform satisfactorily, I was directed to Second Division's replacement center where I learned my platoon was on duty with the Dutch battalion and got a ride in a 2-ton truck to division forward where I grabbed a ride with a captain in an artillery jeep to cannon sites in the middle of the vast Inje Valley ten miles into North Korea, just south of where X Corps was heavily engaged with NKPA (North Korean People's Army) gooks. There were big guns dug in all over the place in circles of batteries and from my distance, little figures fussing with them, whatever artillerymen do to their pieces. A couple, maybe half a battery, of 155 long toms four miles north in the valley were registering impact action for FOs, otherwise it was peaceful.

A sergeant at the battery I chowed down with that night told me of a young replacement getting down from the tailgate of a six-by, caught a stray round in the leg, hitting a major nerve and, with less than a day in the war zone, earned a combat infantry badge, Purple Heart, and trip home. I should be so lucky.

No sooner did darkness fall than demonical fire broke loose in the wide valley full of battalions of artillery pieces, assembled to do the most damage to enemies. As it darkened, the valley became dotted with frightening flames, thunders and separate storms of fires, burping gases, flaring rumbling of fires and burning vapors, a battle-ground of heroes from Hades struggling with smokey giants of blazing cannon all around me in the early dark for miles of valley bottom, released from the snouts of short-barrel howitzers and big long toms which made the sky about them glow red. Simultaneously, huge blasts of flame, bursting points of fire like spark-spewing, tipped and pouring openhearth crucibles booming, lighting the dry river bottoms and empty rice paddies more spectacularly than Public Square at Watertown on Saturday night. Hell, no, Times Square, New York City.

Shells had been stock-piled for days for this powerful event driving hordes of enemy north, this blowout supporting a regiment of the Third Division and the 187th Airborne charging out of Inje on the ground, headed at dusk north on a rare night attack for Americans, pushing, not chinks anymore, North Korean gooks, hated especially since they treated our prisoners so badly.

Piled away from the guns were hundreds of brightly-burning, partly used nylon powder bags. A full charge of powder, capable of throwing a shell maximum range, came in nylon bags with each shell and the unused had to be destroyed. At Inje range was minimal, the enemy so near when the attack began cannon barrels fired almost straight on the level a few miles northward toward foothills less than a mile away. Ka-pow! Ka-pow! Ka-pow! Ka-pow! went our cannon fast as could be loaded. Flash! Flash! Flash! of hell-fire burning unused powder bags.

I borrowed a blanket and found a spot under a small tree and, working room for my lean hips, I curled around on dry grasses to bed down, as familiar with the bosom of mother earth as any Indian fighter out West. It was hours before I could sleep, harkening to our powerful artillery firing, each boom of the 155 battery near me bouncing me on the ground as they let loose, further and further north, indicating the success of the Third Division dogfaces and the 187th Airborne Regiment. Gooks at this maximum range also fired occasionally into the wild circle around us.

My platoon was attached to Second Company, Captain Jan van Rusbroec, on a high ridge, both we and the Dutch patrolling for security behind lines for the French battalion of our sister regiment, the 23rd on the right flank. Before I joined them, the guys had two minor fracases with trapped gooks, the first since I was in the outfit, and a few chink stragglers. As long as they didn't stay to fight, we were content to hurry them along with artillery and Air. According to Holly's platoon sergeant, former Filipino scout, the word gook was from disdainful native dialect *gugu*, slang for westernized Filipinos, used derogatorily for any people considered inferior, as were Americans in the Philippine Islands. Like banzai, it was used loosely and freely by the real gooks, Americans.

At dawn the mountain finger I should climb was pointed out and, well wishes made, I was off to join my platoon. On the way, about daylight, I witnessed a spectacle that sickened me for several days, especially since I flew for a year in WWII in the back of a bomber. Three twin fuselage Flying Boxcar C-119 cargo planes, killing time, flying 360s, waiting for clearance to drop heavy equipment for the 187th, got caught too low into time-on-target artillery firing proximity fuses, hitting one which crashed into another. I heard the awful noise, saw the huge black puffs and felt it in my bones. Ten men in each plane; the last plane hitting debris from the second, fought the stick frantically, pulled up too short and stalled. Field stoves, to be dropped, slid out the rear before the pilot lost all control and the last plane smashed into the side of a ravine. At least thirty sturdy, intelligent, honorable, fearless, well-above national average young men wiped off the face of the earth all because some son-of-a-bitch at Air Fire Control Center back by the guns allowed the big planes to circle too low. Who needs enemy with 'friends' like this?

"Hi, lieutenant," Doc Lynch greeted casually as though I'd never been gone.

"Back so soon?" Sergeant Eppler complained.

"Disappointed?" I asked. "You saw it, a scratch. Wouldn't have got all the way to Pusan unless they thought something was still in my back."

Karl helped me remove my new fatigue jacket while Doc lifted my undershirt to examine the little pink scars with professional interest.

"Beauties," he decided. "In a few years you'll have trouble finding them," remembering how his dad's scars disappeared after World War II.

Ulriche rotate? I asked.

Doc and Karl looked down.

"My god!" I said. "Not Sergeant Ulriche, he was hot-to-trot, number four on battalion rotation. After all he'd been through. Damn it! Goddammit!"

I was several years older than Sergeant Ulriche, still over here he was my father, teacher, role model, guide, and more. He was my inspiration, my protector. Damn it, God, Sergeant Ulriche's our leader. He came from the mountains of Kentucky to save people one crucial day at Guadalcanal, then scored more after the chinks entered the fight at Kunu-ri and then brighten many days of the Banzai Third; teaching me and others to stay alive.

"Didn't you hear?" J J butted in. "Found him right below one of them machine guns on the left out of sight—Lieutenant Hollingsworth and that Filipino scout, his platoon sergeant, out of our sight to the right under one they tried to outflank. All three got it bad."

"He didn't have to die, was supposed to stay back with you, remember? Goddammit! He wouldn't listen to Dud Gould. Where was Lieutenant Gould at Guadalcanal and Kunu-ri?" Tears started to come and I slammed a fist into the palm of my hand, shaking my head, facing away. Goddammit! I gave him an order, stay back with our medic... with you, Doc, and you wouldn't obey either."

"After you left, Lieutenant," Eppler told me, "the whole battalion was called off the hill by our new battalion CO, Major Wilkes. Remember how muggy it was? That night we had the worst thunderstorm I ever saw with lightning all over. The 15th Infantry, Third Division came over behind us overnight to block. The next day they pushed through us and the ROKs and took that hill without a fight and found Ulriche, one of our platoon riflemen, Lieutenant Holly and his sergeant. This other guy, a kid named Alvarez, a PFC replacement I don't think you knew, followed Sergeant Ulriche all the way, evidently blown up by a frag grenade. His guts were bad off and he bled a lot and I heard he quivered a little and gulped trying to talk, but died on a litter at the doorway to the 15th Aid Station."

Damn, they must have crawled up on the far left flank where I couldn't see them. I was too damn self-centered, busy with Burris and Corporal Turner and those daredevils on the right. Memories haunted me for years, not really memories, silent, accusations of neglect of my men. I should have seen Sergeant Ulriche passing by me on the left and stopped him—just how I don't know. Had I been a halfway efficient platoon leader, I'd of made Ulriche stay way back as I ordered him. But, no, I wasn't man enough for that and the Sergeant didn't respect me enough to obey. As time went by, however, I was able to convince myself that it was Ulriche's fault, too, he should have respected my goddamn rank, if not me, personally, and recognized me with the bars as his leader.

The longer you were in combat, the more quietly you expressed regrets; sometimes a mere shrug of the shoulders; sometimes it seemed you didn't care. You found yourself looking forward more and more for the last attack or defense or patrol and there was always more pressing work to do than sit around a campfire and grieve; one more hill—another unknown place to pencil artillery and mortar goose eggs on our 1:50,000 scale maps, just as hard to find, where you had to leave a good man or two.

I had a friend back home, a neighbor on the other side of the Lynchs, who flew Eighth Air Force out of England in the tail of a B-24. He knew from Eighth Air Force Bomber Command he had just twenty-five raids to pull—would've had fifty in the '26s. I sometimes day-dreamed what it would be like in Korea to know beforehand that I had just so many fights, assaults or defenses, to pull and decided I preferred not knowing. My neighbor saw a buddy crack up because he *did* know how many he had yet to pull.

No man knows when he will die.
– The Koran

Beginning June 1951, Communist propaganda in Korea began to show signs of failure. Short of manpower, gooks selected ROK POWs and captured southern Korean civilians they thought could be brainwashed, gave them a two-week dose of it and integrated them into the ranks of their soldiers. The gooks were naturally curious about the foreign devils invading the South and asked little Kims from the South if it was true about wholesale raping and general pillaging their commissars told them went on. Just how bad was the situation in the South? They were amazed to learn the truth and chalked up one more against their lying leaders.

Every few days an Army C-47 flew low over enemy territory within hiking distance from our line working a loudspeaker featuring trained former NK soldiers urging their buddies to give up. Safe conduct surrender pass leaflets were dropped for their convenience.

Early one drizzly morning at Inje a trembling, wide-eyed teenage gook soldier came crawling up on hands and knees, clutching a surrender leaflet. Like a begging dog he flattened his body, all but wagging his tail, desperately showing friendliness and with a big, toothy grin, pleaded with his eyes from one GI to another for acceptance as a POW. For all he'd been told, he'd be shot outright or used for bayonet practice as japs did.

A Korean interpreter for the Dutch Battalion discovered he'd sneaked away from an enemy patrol. Thirty more were trapped in the deep valley over the ridge opposite Inje, starving and without water, waiting for the last of their two badly wounded company officers to die. The Dutch told him to return and lead the rest up when the time came. For three days we were kept posted on the wounded officers' health by escaping gook privates and then on the morning of the fourth day, twenty-six dirty, half-starved very young North Korean men came trembling up on hands and knees through the early morning fog to our barbed wire. Once through, the interpreter talked to them and soon they began laughing and gesticulating as if there was no war at all, looking around at one another from time-to-time self-consciously for assurance, then at each American in turn, smiling broadly in case someone might think they were even a little un-friendly.

Noncoms had their hands full dispersing the crowd of curious.

"Go capture your own," Eppler told them disdainfully, motioning Dutch pros away with his unfurled umbrella.

"Look," a Dutch soldier spoke up in good English. "These youngsters' hair is turning gray."

Chink POWs happy to be out of it. They seem to be pretty intelligent guys, looking the photographer over. As it got hot, they pulled cotton batten from their quilted uniforms.

"Not gray hair," Doc, who'd been looking them over, said. "They're lousy. Take a good look; those are dead or living lice covering their hair." Body lice were allies in other wars, spreading typhus as they did, the plagues of Xerxes and typhus that stopped Napoleon in Russia, to prevent which all UN troops were inoculated. One of the worst trials at the tragic Valley Forge in the winter of 1778-79 was not only lice, to kill which they smeared sulfur in neat's foot oil (from boiled cattle feet), and heated their clothes in farmers' ovens, but dreaded scabies, a form of mange caused by mites smaller than lice, that burrow under the skin to bite and drive you almost crazy with itching. Scabies are rare in the United States but I ran into those little monsters from the straw of a French boxcar crossing France to join the Yankee Division. Some were the same box cars used in WWI; signs still in French: *quarante hommes ou huit chevoux*, forty men or eight horses, forty by eights that Uncle Art remembered well.

Lieutenant Foney made an appearance on the Dutch ridge puffing and panting, bringing up our overdue May pay in a musette bag less than half full, for combat men were encouraged to make large allotments. After signing three copies of the pay form, the majority turned around to the company mail clerk and made out money orders to send home. Some young bachelors simply signed that they refused pay and let it accrue without interest while they were in Korea. At last I had the Korean script equivalent to two ten spots in my wallet again, with nothing to spend it on unless I wanted to gamble.

There were quite a few foreign nationals in the Eighth Army, some drafted, some few true warriors by nature who looked forward to combat and being decorated and advance in rank, which was, I suppose, to many Europeans, an honor worth achieving and many joined the US Army to get their citizenship after a three rather than a five-year wait. I once had two immigrants, Sergeant E-5 Frank Smith of Hamilton, Ontario, a machine gunner, and Poly, Corporal Jerome Polychromus from Cypress, who refused pay and let it accumulate in Finance. Why didn't he sock it into a bank to draw interest? Nobody 'back there' to trust.

John R Folmer, fellow member of the Korean War Alliance, heavy weapons sergeant in the Dutch Battalion, an American citizen since 1958, international systems consultant, Salem, South Carolina, watched as did I the C-119 Flying Boxcars in late morning 3 June knocked out of the sky by our own artillery. He and two

Russian-made gook 76mm self propelled got some of our guys, as JJ and Smitty, with H and I, harrassing and introductory fire at any time night or day, landing where none of us ever knew until too late.

other Netherlanders were part of an investigation team to comb the wreckage. He remembers feeling as good on parade as we did singing our bitter parody of the Colonel Bogy march —*bull shit makes the grass grow green... bull shit makes for greener grass.* His first battalion commander Lieutenant Colonel Eric Van Oden, was killed at Massacre Valley and his replacement, Lieutenant Colonel Christen, like our first battalion commander, Lieutenant Colonel James Skelden, retired a lieutenant general.

Late on the last night with the Dutch battalion through a storm I heard an harassing and interdictory round land down the ridge in the first squad area and, hustling in the rain to see if anyone was hurt found the body of J C Rodriguez on the trail above his position. What he was doing outside his hole we never knew. Speedy Gonzales, murmured in Spanish, which he translated for me, that J C's superstition was typical of immigrants from Mexico, complaining his time was approaching, he was getting tired of it all; Death had bypassed him too often and he felt in his bones it was time to join his buddies on the other side.

Lieutenant Hurtz once told me that Buddha didn't believe in a god, and one of his nuns taught that man himself created God because his mind is too puny to stretch to the absolute. We saw that plainly from our mountain that terrible night of storming when I myself became a rain-soaked God creator, standing brutishly astride my fallen squad leader cursing: "Jesus! Jesus! God! God!" glaring angrily, jabbing my trigger finger accusingly Godward, beyond the height of rain, way past silver-rimmed thunder clouds. I yelled, why I don't know, and repeated over and over, "J C talk to me, tell me hello once more; say hello, J C." Bloody Jesus, half his face gone, had nothing more to say.

I thought hard for an answer until it hurt to think, and in deep despair, utter resignation, offered him the consolation, "Never mind, Jesus, when God finds time to see you crumpled there...." Then I blubbered out of control in front of my men; lowered my head, shaking from side to side: "Shit, Jesus, I can't help you, you knew we're on our own. Nobody can help us, we're all on our own."

Oh carrion thou art no longer man.

I learned unquestionably from Sergeant Jesus Carlos Rodriguez that night this is how worship and prayers got started, terrible cries of hurt from a mountaintop, and that night Jesus got it so savagely I learned for a fact that fear of death is the fundamental cause of all religious activity, no matter how diverting bingo and other colorful rites and ceremonies. This also accounts for my hard yearning for and belief in immortality and as Lucretius the Roman philosopher noted, fear of death is the mother of all gods.

> *And that inverted bowl we call the sky*
> *Where under crawling coop'd we live and die*
> *Lift not your hands to it for help—for it*
> *As impotently moves as you and I.*
> – Omar Khayyam

Sergeant First Class Jesus Carlos Rodriguez, furious foe to foes of Anglos, a buddy, a nice quiet guy who did a good job running the first squad of the Banzai Third; scion of immigrant working Mestizos; at the tender age of nineteen, blue-green-sickly-yellow, all color drained into the wet ground from his half face; blue-black glistening Indian hair, one pale, unwhiskered, smooth, light-olive-brown Aztec cheek, lightning etched, waxen, bloody, already hardening.

Jesus Nobody now dead, one eye wide open upward, forever beseeching empty Catholic promises, staring through impenetrable storm clouds, playing out his utterly insignificant role in the hidden scheme of the vast universe, dead as immediately his life's blood sloughed back to his true home, the earth.

Poor, lonely soldier-boy, dying without absolution, no snow-white Mexican angels in attendance, no sister to recite prayers for the dying, no elevation of the Host; without a woman's tears; no mother nursing nightly, no friends of before to raise a drink to; no relatives sobbing at his bier. No bier lonely guy. Jesus, our good buddy, on whom south Texas suns shown so brightly—J C no longer here.

> *Yet, ah, that spring should vanish with the rose!*
> *That youth's sweet-scented manuscript should close!*
> *The nightingale that in the branches sang,*
> *Ah, whence, and whether flown away, who knows!*
> – Omar Khayyam

Goddamn shitty death made Jesus lose control as his blood drained, to crap on what dignity was left, returned to the past, a barefoot, skinny waif on dusty lanes of Laredo, son of migrant workers; missed all the fun of being twenty-one; messed his pants the wild, hunted-animal way he died; naughty little Indian boy, what will mama say?

Come on, big-mouth, professional patriots under ivory domes, stand up for Jesus! Make like believers! Believe in our Jesus for a change! Face Korea fat-ass, pork-barreling bastards and scream stars-and-stripes forever 'till Jesus comes marchin home.' Long may Jesuses wave and wave and wave o'er the land of the brave, brave, brave and brave, who are not home anymore, slumped lumps of sod in an oriental charnel.

On Korean battlefield abattoirs, now peaceful productive places, rich draft dodgers meet with Korean businessmen to buy and sell; places for lawyers and politicians; Wall Street brokers, elected officials that our brave teenager died for will never have a chance to vote for; entertainers, tall, handsome, strapping 4-Fers, who get big money and applause pretending war, even one day while national morals fade away a dishonorable, draft-dodging President known by cynical reporters as Slick Willlie, sued by a girl employee for exposing himself, and clergymen hiding behind religions, pretentious authorities on dying who really don't know how soldiers die nor give a holy shit, for it's a living and someone's got to preach, profit and not give a goddamn! None of them! Hear? Don't give a living shit! And you, you selfish fuck face, yes, you, you reading this, dirty, lying fink, you never in your stinking life passed one sleepless night in fear of your life nor got dirtied with blood of buddies, nor lost one goddamn drop of yourself for anything, nor ever had a buddy because you could go in peace all your life alone and never need one.

> *Oh beautiful for heroes proved*
> *In liberating strife,*
> *Who more than self their country loved,*
> *And mercy more than life!*
> – Katherine Lee Bates.

> *a god damn lot of*
> *people dont and never*
> *will know*
> *what they dont want*
> *to*
> *know*
> – e e cummings, ambulance driver, WWI.

Jesus was KIA'd by a fragment of a 76 self-propelled high velocity harassing and interdictory artillery projectile on one of the ridges of the mountains of the east-central front in Korea, ten miles north of the 38th Parallel in enemy land west of the Sea of Japan.

We can't all be Agnostic or serve a quantum god and in the spirit of ecumenism let me offer to the memory of our warrior amigo, quiet teen hero Sergeant E-6 Jesus Rodriguez, died in Catholicism unattended—alone—

Requiem aeternam dona eis, Domine, et lux perpetua luiceat eis. Give him eternal rest, O Lord, and let a perpetual light shine upon him.

Envy those whose beliefs, whatever, are easily come by, for as the song goes, they are the luckiest people. Carry on good Catholics and Protestants, all hundreds of quarreling sects of you Christians. Doubters like me have always to learn and learn hard and are never quite taught; must question and question the answer and question that answer to the question and still question some more and remain Agnostic. It is the curse disbelievers face, newer and newer trials until we ourselves return to the quiet lap of Nature lost in cosmoses. Easier yet, fellow space-travelers, relax and harken to our old buddy Omar—

> *Be of good cheer—the sullen month will die*
> *And a young moon requite us by and by;*
> *Look how the old one meager, bent, and wan*
> *With age and fast, is fainting from the sky.*

No concerned Valkyries lifted our tattered heroes to Valhalla; no Greek maidens bathed them and anointed them in sweet-smelling oils and carried them on their shields to Elysium fields. No, they were poor abandoned puppies dumped beside a busy highway, crumpled, black dried blood, discarded lumps of trash; vain, choked off cries to heaven, where art thou father of dogfaces?

My dogfaces, whose only right was to die, died without rites. No preacher taught them dying and there were no important excerpts read over them in ancient Hemitic from the Book of the Dead. Dying is entirely animal, a dogface soldier's ultimate accomplishment, the only completely individual, completely personal event in his life; a thing nobody can do for others, or explain when done, for which there is no adequate preparation. We are born out of mothers, live for a time among others, and die alone. Organized religion is no part of it and in any event ornate catafalques, holy viaticums, extreme unctions, *dormientum eritium* (the sacrament of those who sleep), *corpus Domini, Ave Maria,* are not for dogfaces but bought by well-heeled, murdering Sicilian gangsters and their avid supporters in and out of government.

The bloody body of Jesus our beloved squad leader, an inert lump, was taken away by Dutch morticians in a body bag and life went on and nobody ever saw him again. An E-5, Zigerfoose with grade over Gonzales was sent by company to try to take J C's place as we were detached from the Dutch battalion, released to rejoin Love. No firefight was heard or seen for three more days and our kitchens convoyed cautiously out to meet us in the Inje Valley. The guys, well rested, plucked wild, short-stemmed blue irises and wore them protruding jauntily from the upturned bores of their rifles. Not that they were your run-of-the-mill ostrich-plumed dandy muske-teers of the Court of Louis XIV, low-bowing, sweeping hats, and obsequious soldiers of times gone by, but they'd seen a movie or two and obeyed pleasant impulses. Time to sport a posy, buddy, Death is looking the other way.

Good byes are short in the infantry, bitterly final but life does go on as Buddha's vital changes come faster in the Queen of Battles. Here today and…. One good thing about an army at war, if you don't like someone, wait a while and either he or you'll be gone. No one can wrong you forever and Lieutenant I B Foney, the strong, silent, stupid type with his ill-gotten DSC, made captain and was transferred to X Corps, a junior on Lieutenant General Almond's staff, sure indication he'd make Regular. The publicity-conscious general got another pretty boy John Wayne, tall, decorated, college graduate, if inarticulate.

In a few days, a Sergeant Bill Hanson, E-5 from Fred Hurtz's platoon with the longest time in that grade in the company transferred to take Sergeant Eppler's slot as guide and make SFC, E-6, and Eppler stepped into Sergeant Ulriche's position to make master sergeant.

We learned that the Fifth Phase of the Communist Spring Offensive was over when one soldier, leading up a CTC chogee train of supplies, was stopped by a fat, pale-face rear echelon captain and threatened with the standard $50 fine for not wearing his helmet forward of regimental headquarters. I'd like to know what brought fatty so far forward. The guys bitched at orders like that.

"Why them damn piss pots all the time?"

I sympathized, my steel helmet sometimes gave me a dull headache and the leather sweatband engraved a red mark across my forehead; besides, it strained my neck. You had to have the neck of a pro football lineman to get used to one and you notice even pro football players often go off the field helmets in hand.

Tables were suddenly turned on the over-extended CCF. Their little Mongolian horses streamed north dragging their tails behind them, our beat-up Blue Battalion in close pursuit. The weather heated up and the far north of that broad Inje valley was soon littered with musty gray cotton batten pulled from quilted chink winter uniforms. As the chinks drove their many captured vehicles north, our Operation Tacks scattered 5,706,000 long roofing nails from low level along the road to puncture tires. Changing tires, when they had them, was major mechanics to those rice farmers.

We had a ring seat at the beginning of a grim harvest as a flight of four Saber jets skimmed in over our backs out of the sun down into the mouth of a long narrow valley to our right front. On the dusty road ahead just within sight was a rag-tag column of fleeing yellow men, the first anybody in our outfit ever saw on the roads in daylight, or heard tell of so near in daylight. Some pushed bicycle-wheeled ammunition carts, others had huge bundles of sundry supplies on their backs, while yet others bullied along weary, mangy, overloaded Mongolian ponies. Ten or twelve captured Korean bullocks pulled creaky, ancient, Korean farmer's two-wheeled wagons, drivers walking beside frantically cracking black whips. Some of our animal-loving fighter pilots seemed to avoid this helpless prey, even though they could assume that, because of the obvious heavy weight, the wagons were full of ammunition.

So preoccupied were the chinks that the only warning to many was the insane fury of 50-caliber machine gun bullets tearing through them. Others were alerted only by screams and groans, for the jets were beyond their targets almost before the sound of their guns were heard. Some country guys remarked how it broke them up to hear the heartrending cries of the little horses from the distance, above hysterical shouted commands and curses in Chinese.

Korean civilian forced-labor recovery squads, struggling hopelessly with wounded chink soldiers, panicked and dropped their crude bamboo litters, running headlong into the squirming mass of men caught along the narrow ledge road of a defile between a cliff that towered up on their right and a drop-off 100 feet into a swollen river into which chinks and laborers were continually falling.

The road was cut by a twenty-foot deep 500-pound aerial bomb crater impassable to wheel vehicles and by the time

Is the Christian God proud of napalm? Photo, Charles AcAtee, by permission of Artwork Publications Korean Vigmettes, FACES OF WAR.

138

Napalm, one-sided terror weapon, sticky, greasy-black, oily smoke, being dropped on a minor industrial center.

the airplanes zoomed back for their napalm pass, two companies and more of chinks were bottle-necked at the lip of the crater. Some made half-hearted efforts to raise their rifles but all ended the same, a clawing, screaming, blackened mess as napalm tanks end-over-ended through the air p-u-u-u-W-OOFT! charring flesh, sucking air from lungs; a black puff of greasy smoke rolling skyward after each strike. Was there ever a greater terror weapon? Ancients hurled fire and brimstone (crude mined sulfur) catapults, but burning balls were petty compared to large containers of blazing jellied gasoline hurtling through the air at three hundred miles an hour, sometimes spreading and spilling forward flaming even before impact, covering ten feet wide and forty long. The mere thought sickened us hardened infantrymen.

Later, we walked among cooked meat, some roasted without a mark of violence. Those in the center of every burst were well done, bloated orange or black skin bags, yellowed teeth grinning sickeningly from burned black charcoal skulls. The odor was especially repulsive because, with your eyes closed, it might seem almost edible.

One chink's uniform was burned off except for what he was lying on, his taunt skin a weird bloated dark orange, cooked brown, glistening like a well-roasted Christmas turkey—not a puncture wound anywhere. Four metal buttons surviving the burned cloth rested on his bare chest, around his waist the blackened remnants of a leather belt held pieces of charred cloth. Even the tops of his cheap tennis shoes were flash-burned away. His dinky stood up, baked stiff between his legs, ridiculously small to be so rigid.

"One chink died happy," Funero observed.

Over the years I have had occasion to relate the above to kind people, anti-war people, and just plain sensitive people, mostly friends of Kitty, who assume that man is becoming more cruel, citing napalmed chinks and the Holocaust in WWII. That depends, I tell them, on how well you read history—check what occurred right here in America. The following from my unpublished *LYING A WOUNDED MAN*—

> ... In the mid-1600s at Lachine near Montreal, New France, French women and children were brutally slaughtered by Mohawks, many being slowly tortured to death over fires and 120 carried off to be eaten at other campfire feasts. Mothers were forced to watch their babies being turned on spits and devoured.
>
> ... Just thirty years before the war that was to free white Americans from "tyranny", thirteen Negro slaves were tortured to death at a public spec-

Dragged together for common burial by tank dozers. Photo by Charles McAtee, permission Artwork Publications, KOREAN VIGNETTES, FACES OF WAR.

tacle in New York City for threatening to revolt from their cruel masters. Their guilt was based solely on the hysterical blabbing of a fifteen-year-old barmaid who alleged she overheard them plotting. The Negro she fingered as the ringleader was sentenced "to be burned with a slow fire that he may continue to torment for eight or ten hours and continue burning until he be dead and consumed to ashes."

The most unpleasant work came when battalion commander Wilkes ordered Love company on a burial detail with Graves Registration back up the valley we left. I took the dirty job personally, like he took all of Love just to get at me. My Third Platoon alone covered over sixty-two chink corpses with the aid of a tank with a bulldozer blade, altogether an estimated 3000 to be buried in the Inje Valley. Dead horses, bullocks, and chinks were all the same; bloated stinks I remembered small scale when a rat died in the partition of our old house on Pleasant Street. All dead flesh smells alike, man or beast. More tragic to me was to see a poor innocent dead horse on his back, bloated, four feet straight in the air.

The ground was too hard along the road and it was inconvenient to drag cadavers to rice paddies. A few had been rotting a week. Bending over to push them with the short-handled entrenching tools, we disturbed clouds of large angry buzzing purple blow flies, maggots dropping squirming and wriggling and black carrion beetles darting swiftly away when their rotting banquets were disturbed. Guys announced unusual wounds.

"Hey, look, blew half his ass off."

One little chink wore a cheap pair of wire-rim glasses tumbling into his grave. I, for one, was resentful that his Army hadn't provided a better-looking pair. He was pathetic enough.

"Yeah? Wanna' see something, look at this."

"Here's a sight for you, lieutenant."

When they grabbed some wrists instead of sleeves to move the body, flesh slipped off greasy bones which, of course, without gloves they did only if absolutely necessary.

Rains came during the night and sunk loose dirt and by morning withered yellow-brown feet, hands and heads popped up pleading with us living for another chance, one more chance to live, exposed rotting flesh that shriveled dry and hard in two days under the baking sun. Under dust and under dust to lie—left exposed wasn't enough dust, not in that rocky ground.

The quilted uniforms of the Chinese were tan and uninteresting, the only distinguishing mark of any kind being an occasional small, dull, half-inch, red enameled star centered on the front of a cap. Some intermediate bugouts went ghoulishly into pockets for souvenirs. Rumor had it that an 81 mortar gunner in Mike Company recovered over $500 in American money that way. I wouldn't have done it for a thousand.

For the two days we were kept in that stinking valley of death, poorly buried, over-ripe corpses literally sprang up from their insufficient coverings, sickening, slimy black fluid exuded from uniforms stained around the wounds. Guys soaked handkerchiefs in water and tied them as masks over their noses, but as they were forced to bend close, scraping with short entrenching shovels, panting, stench precipitating on their tongues; in that disgusting way we tasted death.

Why was it, I pondered, the Banzai Third gets all the shitty assignments? It seemed we got hit with every crappy detail that came along. Still, somehow, we seemed also to have too much time to kill—easy to kill enemy, hard to kill time; too damn long to worry about if and when we'd ever make it back. I'd rather keep busy than die so many times of worry.

Staring at the pathetic piles of human flesh, I walked into a deep reverie of the true meaning of life, successful life and death and glory, where the latter fits in, recalling just two years before, 1949, watching the Watertown Memorial Day obser-

Assembled for burial by a US Marine company after Operation Mousetrap, one night's work, 17 May 1951 during the May Massacre, photo by Thomas Preston, by permission of Artwork Publications, KOREAN VIGNETTES, FACES OF WAR.

vance parade, as I did in '34 when my Uncle Art slipped into the passing parade, proud as a peacock, drunk as a skunk, swinging his arms like batons, laughing like a maniac, limping out of step to the drum beats of the Watertown High school band all alone down State Street for, he explained, his buddies who would never return, never have the chance to display themselves to fellow Watertownians.

Everyone along the route repeated his name proudly, "C'mon Art ole boy!" "That a boy, Art!" Cruelly disfigured by a war that none of them knew, they all knew of him, they owed him for the Argonne Forest; laughing and cheering him along, all but my father who embarrassed me by turning his head in embarrassment.

Whatever he did, Uncle Art was one helluva' hunk of a man, six foot two with scarred face and a fifth-of-the-way-down limp given to him by a kraut machine gun. That is, he'd sag one fifth of the way down at every other step, the reason he could no longer march in step.

Except for Uncle Art parading that memorable Memorial Day, there was no glory recognition of the combat dead, no recounting their deeds in the Watertown Times, not even names of individual dead combatants and the count was small for that war of less than a year. Only a couple of dozen of his buddies alive in 1934, one reason Art got lit so much that day of remembrance. None of us or even our elders knew what those guys who never came back with Uncle Art did dying for us. They went singing 'over there, over there, the Yanks are coming over there,' left over there, that's all as if the trip itself was all that was worth remembering, sufficient explanation for it all, civilians agreed. Why is glory always left 'over there?' Does anyone know anymore what glory is or even where?

As I grew up, fewer people congregated each year to watch the parade while the prosperous always shunned the half empty length of the short march, gone partying by themselves. What a pathetic day with its contrived excitement, a chance for no-bodies to show off; the not-so-intelligent ones who chose to be part of it; be herded anywhere, in formation, to line State Street long as it was an occasion to get them out of the house; annual move to display patriotism.

First in line of march color bearers from the always available publicity-hungry Marine recruiting station, followed by caricatures of soldiers, fading personalities from the two veterans organizations; a sprinkling of overweight World War II veterans and two skinny, red-faced, white haired, poorly-attired survivors of the War to End All Wars, proudly, hardly remembering why, too impoverished to afford more than faded blue-and-tan aging wedge overseas caps bearing the insignia of their former organizations; meaningless, forgotten campaign medals, and forgotten campaigns, insignificant, me-too notations of service, on one side, emblem of the VFW on the other, soiled insignia of faded colors, faltering reminders of once glorious regiments that trumpeted loudly and bugled in bloody wars and, drumming and trumpeting ever more quietly, faded now into the mist of history. Hallowed with the heroes of 1776, 1812, 1846, 1861, 1918, 1942, but not the *Forgotten War.*

Al Cummings, lively, mouthy, publicity conscious commander of the Watertown American Legion, which was always more full than the rival Veterans of Foreign Wars because one did not have to have left the States to belong. Cummings, the local foreign car dealer, decked out with unearned combat infantryman's badge, Bronze Star and Purple Heart, even though he was aware that the whole town knew he'd been a supply officer in the ETO, European Theater of Operations, Com Z, Communications Zone, running a small supply

142

depot in Antwerp towards the end. No one ever called Al for being a phoney; indeed, few knew the difference between Com Z and combat or between red, white and blue and sickish yellow.

"Hell, at least he was over *there* wasn't he?" ... *'there'* the mysterious land.

He was a real joker and knew everybody in town by first name and ran the American Legion, helping it out financially from time to time with money, they said— some people said, gotten by doctoring books at his agency. Personally, I never liked the guy. I guess I was too idealistic; never grew up some might say: always for the dead who lost every opportunity to join anything.

I've been unable to understand the necessity for civilians to assume that by donning a uniform one is an authority on the military or has to be believed; everything he says about common Army experiences is true. So and so was a captain in the infantry, therefore he's an expert on hand-to-hand combat; what he says about their shooting POWs is a fact. Fact is, he spent his time in division rear, thirty-five miles from a shot fired in anger or sorted paper as a clerk in the States. It's the nature of would-be he men to be more familiar about combat (notice about, not *with*) and the further away they were the better listeners. Hell, Stephen Crane wrote *Red Badge of Courage* that way, listening to veterans.

There's no longer Armistice Day on 11 November as the one I recalled as a kid in knickers, celebrating the end of the costly first worldwide war, the War to End All Wars; crippled veterans with wedge hats, limping, impoverished in the Great Depression, selling red paper poppies, symbolic of the blood of soldiers fallen on Flanders Fields. Canada was hit much harder than the US for they fought much longer, and then it was always and still is Remembrance Day.

Then too many wholesale tragedies and so Armistice Day was dropped and in its place, supposedly to remember all those who served anywhere, anytime, not just those whose lives were taken away in the Civil War or the first World War, but the cheapened, unfocused variety of a very impersonal commemoration everywhere but Virginia and Oklahoma, called Veterans' Day, conceived by rear echelons. And then there would one day be another declared Armed Forces Day every May to celebrate the living, active-duty military.

In my youth, Memorial Day was Decoration Day when we visited cemeteries and decorated graves of veterans with flowers in bottles or pots and little American flags on thin wooden sticks made in Japan, supposedly for just the one war, our great-great grandfathers' Civil War.

The Nation had to put a stop to accumulating so many days to show gratitude and ease public guilt, or work wouldn't get done, as they would acclaim a Presidents' Day to lump General Washington, Abraham Lincoln and whomever comes along as insignificant as Slick Willie Clinton who typified the decaying morality of the Republic which brave, honest men died defending.

Now so-called moral standards are relative to politics and practicality; reverting to the argument as to whether truth or falsehood is acceptable and morals mean anything, as electing a proven liar to the Presidency twice who, during the Vietnam War, dodged the draft, lying about ROTC service, and paraded in protest against our country in the land of our Cold War enemy, while brave, honest young Americans died assuring the freedom of his despicable breed.

"Oh, but he's so young and glib compared to his predecessor Navy hero of WWII and he promises us everything, including an Army of queers.

At Watertown's Memorial Day parade 1949 there was little grief left in the faces of aged women in the back seats of self-advertising Checker taxis, just weariness due to too much dull living, Gold Star mothers of two world wars looking straight ahead, trying to do their duty by recalling a sorrow which, for one group, was just beginning to harden over after four years.

The local parochial priest, using invocation time to further his pet peeves—

We have gathered here oh heavenly father to pay homage to dearly departed fathers, sons and brothers who have given their lives so cheerfully that we might live....

Want to bet they didn't *give* anything or go to dangerous places cheerfully. Did Jesus give his life cheerfully or did 'they' take it away by force? Does anyone try to depict Jesus smiling on the cross.

...All-knowing Father, help us make this a decent place to raise our children, that those who gave of themselves so gal lantly on the field of valor may not have died in vain. And help our news distributors of the written word do honor to those who so willingly laid down their lives.

A dig at the Congregationalist ownership of the *Watertown Times*.

I looked in vain for professors from the Watertown Junior College, or lawyers, and for a well-to-do banker, instead saw kids climbing trees for better view as part of an overall artificial excitement, complacent housewives in drab finery, fat arms folded, gossiping, and the town halfwit drooling, shaking a frayed miniature American flag upside down.

Mayor Charles Henning stuck to the speech he'd used for several years—

We are gathered here today to thank the brave soldiers of all our wars, may their souls rest in peace.... Are we living up to the solemn promises made to them? Have we, right here in Watertown, for all their sacrifices done our best to make our modest community a really better place to live? We, each of us, must search our souls and make our own decision. Only last week I proposed an ordinance that in my estimation is sorely needed ...

And so another Memorial Day wore down in Watertown in Northern New York, still failing to mention the truth about soldiers—how hard they died.

> *We are the Dead. Short days ago*
> *We lived, felt dawn, saw sunset glow,*
> *Loved and were loved, and now we lie*
> *In Flanders fields.*
> – John McCrae

*   *   *

On the 5th of June, one hectic month after being overrun on the outpost, our company strapped legionnaire rolls wrapped like inverted horseshoes over our packs and, following kitchen trains in their trucks, made a long march into X Corps reserve to the valley at Hongchan just north of Hoengsong, of such bitter winter memory of so many of our men. Here regiment gathered its own again and battalion its own and rifle companies sought small private valleys radiating from a wide former rice-growing drained flatland. Erecting a neat, straight-line pup tent village, we slipped easily into garrison, as armies do, and into the training routine which in the uncertainties of combat we forgot was so boring.

The company fell in and spread out by platoons and squads to lay out a little village as enlisted men in formation took so many paces along his line away from the man behind and, facing right or left, side stepped to their sides marking out streets into pup tent homes away from homes. Once in place, unrolling half a pup tent, the outside of the legionnaire roll, to set up a full tent, two men button together the tops of their overlapping halves, each half with reinforced button holes, and zinc alloy buttons labeled US. Each puts the spike, the top of his tent pole that folds in three sections, into the metal eye at one end of the tent half and runs a white cotton rope down to stake into the ground. The tent is stretched and steadied sideways with five wooden pegs on each side. A foot-deep trench is dug all around to run off rain water. Rice straw or heavy grasses are hunted down to soften the earth under bed rolls, fart sacks, not named for nothing, especially when beans were on the menu, and when lucky, an air mattress that held air.

Right away friends start parting, for one of the least pleasant memories soldiers have are rainy days passed in the close confinement of a pup tent. Begun in the Civil War as dog tents, when made even smaller, circa the first World War, shortened to pup. When one tent with a greater-than-average amount of straw bedding caught fire after lights out, burning a young private slightly, candles were turned in to supply. This ban was also indicated because of the stale air the tiny flames created in a tent completely buttoned down during a rain.

Businesses were quickly reestablished, supply, a pyramid tent, combination clothing store, gun shop, boots and Army surplus store; our large squad tent messhall a thriving restaurant, popularity depending on the ingenuity of the cooks and mess sergeant, or mess steward.

Some among us worried aimlessly or brooded unnecessarily as did untested replacements living outdoors for the first time even this far from danger. For them a few nights were almost as sleepless as those of their platoon leader trying to readjust to the opposite comparison, unfamiliar with being off guard, peace and quiet.

J J Jenkins, runner, radioman and along with Doc my holemate in a tactical situation, was one of those worrywart guys who always had to check things. J J, by the way, stood for, of all things, Jack Jerry, what was probably the basic reason for his nervousness; afraid someone would find out. He blurted it once resentfully and was wary of my power ever since, even though I swore on my mother's memory not to tell.

Mostly it was body chemistry he worried about. He worried about his blood, cerebral and spinal fluids, glands and metabolism which he had read up on a couple times. Also, he warned, never neglect the color of your urine and excrement, "that's, your shit," he explained. "Especially when your urine, number one or piss, seems unusually brown, or gold. All is not gold that glitters said the pirate as he peed in the sea," he joked.

"I always turn around and look over what I did," he once explained, "whether it's okay or not. If I'm ever cut, check to see if my blood's too dark or too thick, or maybe too thin or something, and once last year it was sort of bluish but I didn't get to a doctor and never found out why. Of course, you need a powerful microscope to see what kind of bugs you have.

"Sometimes I get too tired too easy and wonder what's wrong with my metabolism. Usually if there's trouble, it's got to be me for us guys eat the same all the time. Everything you eat has to go somewhere, you know. Sometimes I have an awful craving candy and I know that's wrong; you don't have to tell me, too much sweets makes your teeth rot and you get sugar diabetes from too much too often.

"I wonder a lot about what happens when you die. Does your soul actually go anywhere, like the Bible says, heaven or hell? And what is a soul, how does it live anyway? And Catholics, they also worry about that Purgatory place in between.

"I'm almost on the verge of discovering something real big, but then every time I start getting close, I get tired or something, my mind wanders, and somehow can't seem to follow my thinking through and my thinking just runs out of steam or goes off on a tangent. Lieutenant, suppose I could have a tumor or something in my head and that's why my thoughts seem to just melt away right when I'm on the verge of something big?"

"I know what you're talking about, it happens to me, but I honestly don't know, J J. I honestly don't."

We trained two nights a week until 2200 hours. I was beginning to answer a letter from Alice Wardwell and it took about three days, in between training, to finish it. This was a big surprise, her writing to me. Nights were the worst time for loneliness. I began to dream almost as bad as when very young when I'd walk and talk in my sleep. I'd give almost anything to avoid that type of sad, sometimes miserable and always frightening dreaming. My mother, not Kitty, appeared more and more frequently, always a losing battle to keep her alive like she appeared to me for so short a time; sickening thoughts that sneaked up on me. And coughing. Oh, God, spare me those rags of blood she couldn't hide.

When first in the friendly valley I was claustrophobic and for four nights took my cot out of the officers' arctic tent to sleep under the open sky. Hurtz and I really missed Holly but we didn't have much to say to Captain Shallow, our new company commander. For a week I woke regularly as I did on line, hand on an imaginary carbine; sometimes at reveille it was as though I didn't lie down at all. Fighting alone hopelessly, rolled in a ball in my canvas cot in my corner of the arctic tent trying to hide from melancholy paranoia, doubting my ability to meet fears yet nameless.

Reserve was one big make-believe. Just what were we doing now, fooling around? Training? There's no better training than combat where you learn in a hurry. Death is the real teacher; waiting to explain, explain good and just once before failing you. Death doesn't have to speak loud. Training was a farce, 'position of a soldier at attention,' a one-hour bore; 'interior guard,' three hours in one week. 'Drill and ceremonies' and stupid preparation for parades. Up your ass Benning School for Boys, there's a war to be fought!

"Don't they know we got twelve new guys to get ready?" Eppler complained. "What good's all this crap, this goddamn division training schedule? I had this shit back in basic training."

One afternoon we had off, personal time, it was called, and Sergeant Eppler was a roaring bull all over the company area. "All right, who's the wise guy tired of livin'? C'mon, make it easy on yourself. Who stole my umbrella? Kee-rist! Nobody can have nothing of his own around here."

After the roar subsided, Pop Miller cornered Funaro and demanded he return the umbrella.

"Why to hell you do that? You know Sergeant Eppler's got no patience."

"I know, Pop. Muggsy dared me and things been pretty dull around here. I was going to slide it in his tent tonight and run."

Pop, being no child psychiatrist, couldn't decide whether Funaro was more malevolent, mischievous or malicious, but warned the pain-in-the-ass not to bug Karl anymore. "There's better ways of dying."

We got to debating about Funaro in a rather heated way and Pop blurted out, "Leave me alone, lieutenant. I ain't had no kids of my own."

"Well," I told him, "I got a boy, not very old yet, so there's not much to understand. You just have to slap his fingers and say 'no.' One thing you and I know, Pop, your Funaro will never make a soldier."

"Yeah," Pop confessed, "that's what he keeps telling me."

Sometimes, mindful of the policy not to fraternize with enlisted men, I'd sit with Sergeant Eppler on the fringe of bull sessions at which they amused themselves shooting the breeze, what shrinks call ventilation, and charge outlandish fees; old timers wishing mightily for rotation to hurry up and save them; young ones bragging about broads they'd had or women they wished they'd had, very prestigious jobs they held or high-paying jobs they wanted to have, which were more believable among our draftees, some few of whom were sons of wealthy men patriotic enough to avoid fixing the draft, and college graduates waiting for their work lives to start.

Despite the good percentage of conscripted men in the services, the percentage in dangerous infantry positions was proportionately very small with few exceptions. Millionaire sons, to begin with, managed, with help of their fathers' attorneys to keep out of uniform or at least be assigned safe in the States. Sons of honest, hard-working fathers, the greatest percentage of our RA, Regular Army enlistees, 'RA all the way,' many of whose dads were proud to have fought in the infantry in World War I, disclosed the obvious wide gap between them and sons of the wealthy and influential. Being a real man among men is of high value and not once did I hear one of my dogfaces wish he was a millionaire's son able to dodge the draft. Without saying so, very probably without even knowing so, he accepted manhood's hard-to-obtain value as life's biggest prize; where else could he brag, "I was right there packing a rifle," and be known automatically as a fullgrown man, a real patriot, to enemy a dangerous man?

> And millions in those solitudes, since first
> The flight of years began, have laid them down
> In their last sleep—the dead reign there alone.
> So shalt thou rest; and what if thou withdraw
> In silence from the living, and no friend
> Take note of thy departure? All that breathe
> Will share thy destiny.
> – William Cullan Bryant.

They were attracted to campfires at night like Indians, the center of life, except that American Indians, like orientals, squatted, which whites can't do very long, and, like wild warriors of our past, they bragged about what they did or thought they did in the fury of combat, sometimes inadvertently attributing to themselves the exploits of others, never dishonestly. "No you didn't, Hank. That was me." It continued to amaze me how many true versions there could be about what went on during the hysteria of battle. Even in as small a unit as a rifle platoon, no one could hope to encompass the entire panorama of its fights every minute of every guy.

"Why you was way over by that big rock all the time. How could they be peppering you so bad?"

"You insinuating I'm a liar? That was Johnson over there."

"Didn't say that. Maybe you was getting it bad, too. I don't know, I had them up the ass, myself."

"You should have some of the peppering we got. How about it, Red? Know he was in it, right?"

"Sh-e-e-it! You guys back there was rear echelon, practically back at company. Ask Smitty where we was when them 82's started droppin'."

"Like so much fun! You won't believe me, ask Pop Miller. How about it, Pop?"

Pop, slowly sipping cold coffee from his canteen, was slow to give his version. "We-ell, now, I don't know...." so slow they went on bragging without an answer.

Guys talked about anything and a lot of nothing worth remembering or repeating during breaks in training classes or short rests during work details, or just lying in warm, wild Korean mountain grasses heated by the sun. The main themes were evaluating their future, rumors and wishes. Can I survive? Will I live to rotate? What rotation number do I have? What about peace talks? How far they gone? Will it save us? Why don't they get the lead out?

Draftees vs Regular Army—RA all the way! and 'them stupid bastards' the US serial numbers who had to be dragged in. Regardless, everyone felt he could be promoted given ordinary breaks and enough combat, if he survived, for ranks turned into second lieutenants fast, if they survived. Like Napoleon told his men: "There's a marshal's baton in every knapsack."

And then came weather and women, silly arguments about the latter in which some of the very young men without sisters showed surprising ignorance. One corporal, a self-proclaimed lover tried to wear his hair longer than the regulation rear echelon brushcut and was always getting nailed for it when we were there long enough to get a GI cut by one of our dozen or so Korean houseboys.

"C'mon, no woman's like that. You saying she didn't have no thing!"

"Cross my heart; must've grown together."

"Come on!"

"Sure she didn't have even a little hole?"

"No, damn it, you couldn't get your finger in beyond your knuckle. Hell, I've been around; I've had a few all right."

He then appealed to Sergeant Roundtree who gave one of those real deep, gurgling, infectious Negro laughs no whitey whose laugh was from his mouth, could ever imitate.

"Ha ha ha ha, he he he, ho ho ho, dummy, you got hold one of them whatcha' call 'ems. One of them transtights or something, guys made up like women."

"Oh yeah, smartass, then where'd the prick go? I tell you I got my finger in about two inches and the rest was solid."

"Maybe the way she was sitting."

"Or got it sewed or something."

"Hate to change the subject guys," Sergeant Eppler butted in, "I heard we're pulling all the way back to Pusan."

"Forty-eight ... forty-nine ... fifty, s-o-o-me shit!"

"Laugh, you bastards. We're getting amphibious training so we can land way up to the Yalu and blow bridges to shut off the chinks."

"What's wrong with the Air Force, run out of bombs?"

"Air Force, shit, they overshoot everything."

Another chimed in, "Yah, I heard that one about special training, returning to Fort Lewis for some top secret training that'll can the war for sure."

"Atom bombs?"

"Maybe yes, maybe no. It's classified. I ain't saying."

"You got a clearance?"

"Maybe yes, maybe no. That's classified."

"Sh-e-e-e-it!"

"They changed their minds now about that amphibious deal and we ain't going to the States just yet."

"Sh-e-e-it! They're always screwin' us outa' somethin'."

"First we get to go south of Pusan and guard that Koje-do prison camp we been reading about. Stars and Stripes guesses each regiment will spend two weeks. Anyway, it's better than back on line; look at all the lead you can dodge."

"May be true what you say, but I'll bet fifty bucks it'll all be over in a week or two anyway. According to a guy I met who works in division headquarters and has a top secret clearance, they've decided to drop the old A bomb."

"That's what Pete says."

"Makes sense," his friend reflected. "Won't take many."

No sweat anyway, there were other ways the war could end. Pop Miller went around telling everyone the Ruskies were trying to get all chinks killed so Mao wouldn't be too big for his boots. "What else makes them chinks stick their necks out? Look how the little bastards'll run right at a machine gun. Don't think Mao's no fool, do you? He knows well as we do Stalin's planning to take over China and pull out and let the war fizzle. The chinks are going to revolt anyway. A guy was telling me he was talking to an interpreter back at the prisoner cage that chink POWs are sicker of this war than us. Wait and see."

Peace talks began at a place named Kaesong, above the 38th parallel, ancient capital of all Korea. The positioning of the place itself gave prestige points to the oriental mind. Despite bitter memories of the false negotiation promises with Soviet Communists in 1946, resulting in the necessity for the Berlin Airlift, our gullible State Department and United Nations started out in good faith not knowing, or more probably, we thought, not caring, that the enemy was using the occasion to secure objectives in lieu of using their weakened military.

Right or wrong, there was order again in one's mind and strict regulation of time as the majority tried smiling and relaxing, content to be ordered about from one menial housekeeping or training task to another. Putting in our time, weren't we. Suddenly then one night, end of the third week in reserve, Private Ethan Youngs, one of the first squad's new men, became semi-delirious. His tentmate, PFC Quick, guided him stumbling to the aid station where the duty CQ, charge of quarters, asked what Youngs was complaining of.

"I don't know. Just started talking funny, slurring his words, and finally got like this, out on his feet. When we hit the sack tonight he did say he had a bad headache and his chest hurt some. He took three APCs but he wasn't complaining enough to worry me, nothing real bad until he started mumbling in his sleep. What is it, sarge, suppose it's catchin'?"

The medical sergeant didn't answer but told Quick to put a thermometer in Youngs' mouth, pinch his lips over it but don't touch the thermometer, while he took his blood pressure. Obviously out of it, Youngs was not resisting. Once done, the medic turned quickly to his assistant and told him to run, not walk, and wake a litter jeep driver. "On the right going in the aid squad tent. Hurry, understand. Now!"

Youngs died at Regimental Collecting without awakening just minutes before the arrival of an evacuation helicopter. Choppers didn't usually fly at night in Korea. The surgeon said he wasn't sure what Youngs died from but a medic, a Spec-5, told our Doc that it looked suspiciously like a new sickness called Manchurian fever, the sudden way it came on. It was brushed over in our training.

Tears gather in my eyes today, forty-five years later thinking of the great sacrifice Ethan made, not that I remember the kid personally, for I have no memory of anything physical about him.

"That thin guy Doc Lynch always talked to on breaks," Speedy Gonzales would tell others. "They'd get out of the way and talk serious for hours, great friends in short order like guys often do in the field…. Youngs spent a lot of time talking to the guys in the aid station, remember? Maybe he caught something up there."

"Poor Youngs," he worried. "One year to go in college, then med school. All he was planning to do for everyone, having to die for nothing way over in this damn hole."

"He what?" I asked.

"Didn't you know, sir? He was halfway to being a doctor and got reading about what was going on over here and talked himself into enlisting. His dad, he told us, used to be a medical missionary somewhere in South America when he was a kid. He learned Spanish from his friends, could talk it better than me." Speedy was silent for a minute, a kind, sorrowful stare on his face rare for a sergeant before suddenly exploding with a hateful glare. "God damn fucking world! Don't make guys like Ethan! Take them goddamn draft dodgers in Canada. My uncle died a volunteer fighting with them Princess Pats, fighting for draft-dodging bastards. He'd turn over in his grave to know Canadians are harboring our cowards."

The 2d Princess Patricia's Canadian Light Infantry was fighting a little west of us in the Canadian Brigade of the Commonwealth Division.

I was told Youngs joined 23 May, the day I got it, which explained why I didn't know him so well. He was with us the three weeks I was back but I couldn't recall his training with us. He was not a medic; medics don't train with us except in certain reserve classes. They have their own training at battalion medical company, or division for special classes, but they really belong to us infantrymen; they're with us during combat to save lives.

"No, sir, Youngs wasn't a medic," Doc agreed. "He joined us the day you got hit and heaven knows, rather, hell knows, how busy you've been ever since you returned from the Third Station."

I can't help tearing up even today thinking what a brave young guy; didn't have to come, volunteering against his mother's wishes, dying serving the fuckin' free world. Like his dad only more dangerously. The Goddamn fuckin' world of greedy, selfish bastards. I'd be having a few beers after the war and the subject would come up and I'd wet my eyes thinking about him and so many thousands of American draft dodgers and swear 'Goddammit! Goddamn lousy draft dodgers!' And now as I write we got a draft dodging, immoral President preferred by 72% of the people.

I've had lots of tears roll down putting together this sad story, wetting my eye-lashes and inside my glasses. This comes all too easy when you're jam full of memo-ries. I'm just uncontrollably weak when it comes to those we left behind. At danger-ous times while making memories when young, I could take it in my stride; lately, being all stirred up writing this journal, bad or sad memories won't lie back down. I cry lots of times without making noise and Kitty is no longer here to pat my head and tell me, "Don't worry, honey, everything will be all right."

"Shitty-ass war!" Pop agreed. "Nothing here worth fighting for in the first place."

"Look," Funaro said, pointing expansively to the barren, eroded Korean mountainsides. "One dogface is worth more than this whole goddamn country put together."

It was Manchurian or hemorrhagic fever, the first any of the enlisted medics had heard of the dread disease. PFC Quick was quarantined, whisked to the 11th Evacu-ation field hospital forward of division, checked over ten days. An epidemic was rumored. Their tent was buttoned up without moving anything and fumigated.

"Makes your eyes bulge and turn red," one man said.

"Eyes turn red?" a medic corrected. "Hell, I heard blood leaks out all over, anywhere. Got all the doctors licked; it's a virus, you know, no medicine for it. All we can do is what they call support him, see he gets a lot of rest and liquids and hope his insides can hack it out alone.

"I heard from a guy at division. It's powerful stuff to fool with. That's probably why they got so many new replacements in graves registration."

"Not exactly unknown," the medical sergeant told us, "and there's more than one group of viruses cause hemorrhagic fever; it's an arena virus so far confined to Manchuria, eastern China and the Soviet Union and the central mountains in Korea. They think its carried by vectors, Latin for one that conveys, like humans, insects or rodents, but primarily by chiggers living on rodents. Aren, by the way, as in arenavirus, is for RNA granules which they find in this particular virus."

"Oh."

Colonel F L Wergeland, surgeon of the Eighth Army Forward, recalled that the disease, precisely *virion*, infectious form of a virus, wasn't isolated until war's end. It was often confused with atypical scarlet fever, war nephritis, songo fever, kokku disease and korin disease, none of which can be found in the average dictionary. In its first year, 1951, eighteen of every thousand soldiers were stricken, ten percent of whom died quickly. Lucky for us the disease was most prevalent in the Chorwon Valley miles to our left.

"More graves registration guys than ever before, know why?" someone asked. "The general was going cross country in his chopper and spotted two GIs, one thrown on top the other, somewhere in the wilds where one of our outfits was fighting a month ago and he landed and found them rotted."

A new job called vector control, with special training classes, suddenly became more important than preparing to kill chinks and gooks. And there were Japanese B influenza (Italian, under the influence of a bad star) and soft chancres that Korean men are immune to which rot off your prick, and water flukes from snails whose eggs or whatever get through the skin between your fingers and down to your liver, which blows up and hardens, with no cure, all they could do was ship you home. And there were rumored to be a couple other beauties, such as a sleeping sickness like no other in the world, a bit different from African sleeping sickness.

Normally, unless there's a large attack, on a daily basis nonbattle casualties in a division are double, even triple battle casualties. The actual killed in action, KIA, in the US Army in Korea 1950-53 was 27,700. With 77,596 WIA and 2542 nonbattle deaths. Someone has figured out that early in September, 1951 an anonymous soldier killed in Korea was the 1,000,000 American man to die in combat since eight Minuteman got it on Lexington Common, Massachusetts on the morning of 19 April 1775.

A division's like a city, with all its hazards. There were many sicknesses, even among such healthy guys, and jeep accidents, drownings, stepping on by-passed mines, accidental shootings, and even a few suicides. A careless jerk in King Company killed his best friend while cleaning a forty-five.

I was summoned to Graves Registration's morgue back at regiment the day after Youngs died.

"Have a seat, sir," a private told me. "Sergeant's on his way."

"What's he want?"

"Some mix-up on one of your men, sir."

"Must be Youngs. Someone find out what happened?"

"We're not supposed to tell anyone, but there's more of that Manchurian Fever, Hemorrhagic Fever they call it, and some bad Jap B flu."

"Want to see something good?" the private went on self-importantly. "See what we do back here?"

I didn't say anything so he went all the way.

"Some guys think all we do is sit on our ass and ship bodies to the mortuary. That ain't no picnic. Anyone told me I'd be an assistant to an undertaker, I'd say was nuts."

He handed me a form, a copy of an Army coroner's Preparation Room Report. "Go on, sir, read it, and this is only half what we do back here."

"This for Youngs?" I asked, glancing at the title.

"Not this one; it'll give you an idea. This is that lieutenant crashed in an L-19. We just got this copy back from the mortuary in Japan"—

REMAINS OF (Name, serial number, grade, arm, service)
 Alfred Arnold Johnson, 1st Lt, Inf. 0-2017049, US Army
LENGTH OF ILLNESS OR HOSPITALIZATION PRIOR TO DEATH
 None
OPERATION PRIOR TO DEATH
 None
CAUSE OF DEATH
 Encephaltpathy due to trauma

EVIDENCE OF DECOMPOSITION PRIOR TO EMBALMING
　　None
BISECTED ARTERIES PRIOR TO EMBALMING
　　Yes
JAUNDICE EVIDENT
　　No
DISTENTION OF ABDOMEN
　　No
IF ANSWER IS YES - INTENSE OR MODERATE
　　N/A
CAUSED BY - FLUID OR GAS
　　N/A
RELIEVED - YES OR NO
　　N/A
POINT OF INJECTION - CHECK
　　Iliac
　　Brachial _
　　Femoral
　　Axillary _
　　Carotid
METHODS OF INJECTION - CHECK
　　Pump, hand _
　　Gravity
　　Machine pressure
IF OTHER THAN STANDARD HARDENING FLUID WAS USED ARTERIALLY,
GIVE STRENGTH OR CONCENTRATION OF FLUID (Percent)
　　Each artery noted was injected with 10 oz fluid to one gallon water
NAME PARTS WHICH LACKED PRESERVATION
　　Head
PROBABLE CONDITION OF REMAINS ON ARRIVAL
　　N/A Internment within this command
REASON (If doubtful or poor)
　　Due to mutilation
DRAINAGE
　　Poor
AMOUNT
　　2 quarts
CAVITY TREATMENT AND RESULT (Describe fully)
　　Organs were removed and placed in fluid, replaced and packed in hardening
compound
EXTENT OF MUTILATION OF REMAINS UPON RECEIPT (Describe)
　　His head split from clavicle bone to back. Compound fractures of left leg.
Hands badly lacerated and bruised.
　　Head and face lacerated beyond recognition.
BURNS
　　None
LIST TRAUMATIC AMPUTATIONS
　　Left ear missing and three fingers of left hand

PARTS EMBALMED HYPODERMICALLY
Thoracic walls
PLASTIC SURGERY
None
REASON, IF FEATURES NOT RESTORED
Badly mutilated.

The private retrieved the report hurriedly when he heard the sergeant bid someone hello outside the tent.

"Lieutenant Gould? Sir," the sergeant said. "Sorry to bother you but some tags were switched and we needed his officer to identify these things we think belong to Private Youngs. Would you know of anything that might be missing?"

"Sorry to say, I didn't know him that well. I'll sign it blank and send his buddy, PFC Quick up to check it out. Right now he's quarantined. What happened to Youngs?"

"Well, Special Regulation 600-400-5 states: 'When remains are recovered and individually identified, they will be buried in an overseas cemetery.'"

"In them rubber bags?"

"No, they're just to handle the remains until they can be placed in Army caskets. The SR states that in case of death, a letter of sympathy written by the unit commander or chaplain will be addressed to the emergency address. It will contain condolence, cause and place of death, any religious services administered to the individual before death, an appropriate expression of appreciation of the services rendered to the nation by the deceased, and other information of a personal or sentimental nature which may be comforting. No one but his company commander or the chaplain is authorized to write. No reference will be made to the recovery or identification of remains, date or place of burial."

This visit made me more morbid than I wanted to be. Back home you don't give these guys a thought but in Korea every regiment has to have a Graves Registration officer with assistants.

You could run a small town with the talent and trades in a division. Fred Hurtz of our regiment was an exception, what could Freddy do aside from fight? Philosophize? At least I might do some landscaping or pour a casting. He majored in psychology and minored in oriental philosophy, which I'd kid him about.

"What you going to do with it, Freddy? Open a Chinese laundry?" I got to know Lieutenant Frederick Hurtz in those June reserve evenings when there wasn't a good movie on or night training, although Fred did a lot more letter writing than me. I'll never forget when he told me he studied abnormal psychology.

"I thought all psychology was abnormal," I said, tongue in cheek. "I suppose you minored in strange birds."

"Why sure, Dud, didn't I recognize you?"

"Plan on owning a Chinese restaurant with educated fortune cookies?"

"That's not funny, any more than ending up here in the center of the Orient just because I minored in it. I do have a little more insight than the average; know how these people lived before communism. The 38th has always been a line of demarcation. Mongols stopped along this imaginary line in the 12th Century and natives we find in these mountains live pretty much as they did in those days. They have the world's oldest religion, Animism."

"What's that?"

"They believe that everything has a soul, even rocks if they display character different from other rocks. One's spirit can exist without his body."

We talked more about death and the hereafter than most guys, even in the middle of Frozen Chosen, so-called Land of the Morning Calm where a hell of a lot of it was around—death, I mean. You didn't have to pretend, it's all around. We agreed there's a big difference between a dead civilian and a dead soldier. When I look down at them, it isn't all in their face. I can look at one boot and know how awful dead the cadaver is and get the same feeling of disturbing awe as if I'm looking again at the bronze Christ at my father's church with his faraway pleading stare.

A dead civilian looks like he's just home from work resting; like my mother freshly rouged, had proper care, a decent sendoff. Only dead Hurtz and I saw were those who met it like other hunted animals. Over here you don't have to be lonely and sick to go and you don't lie down for death, it grabs *you* on the move. Civilians look so peaceful in their caskets; we never see soldiers in caskets decorated and perfumed, so terribly wasted and outraged are they and hurt and somehow noble in spite of grim and hateful atmosphere.

Christ was my age when he got his. Dead GIs remind me of statues of Christ, a cross right there telling you his occupational hazard, whereas our guys carry rifles to be dropped beside them. Spikes through his feet and hands to hang from, to die slowly from loss of blood and traumatic shock, or whambo, a hunk of shrapnel through the hearts of GIs dead in bloody mud. They both died hard for what a lot of people say is good cause. Along with Jesus, many were hurt bad before they went away but some never knew what hit them or that they were hit. Some were familiar old dogfaces, hurting you bad to look down at them. Many pained for only the split second they're hit; lying there on the whole belt of pain along the 38th Parallel across Korea.

I could glance at a bent foot and recognize death; Death, you fuckin' bastard! Same hurt feeling I get from an icon of Christ and I'm no Christian, it's just my guys been through so much more physical danger than did Jesus, neither allowed to beget kids or grow older or like him rise to heaven on Easter—not that you know about. I mean, certainly your whole body doesn't go anywhere but in a black rubber body bag.

Civilians have expert, peaceful care and before their proper send-off usually allowed to live some. On the broad scale, however, death is beyond criticism for if you think about it, it's every bit as essential as life; without its steady pressures little conscious effort would be made and to intelligent people life would become an endless bore.

5

INTERLUDE

Death is not an event in your life; you cannot experience
death for as it strikes, you are no longer there.
– Ludwig Wettgenstein German philosopher.

One week in the early June heat before the division training schedule came down included swimming under organized athletics, guys rented inflated inner tubes from the motor pool sergeant and the few air mattresses that didn't leak and like ancient Greek gymnasts (Greek, to exercise naked), sublimely naked, floated down the slow shallow river behind battalion headquarters or played a rough form of above-water water polo.

The crème de la crème of all floaters was Master Sergeant Clarence K Eppler, two mattresses lashed together, using his black umbrella alternating as a sail and sunshade, dozed off once and took half an hour to limp back tender-footed to battalion.

"Hey, Ski," someone yelled, "here comes a nurse!"

"My God!" Ski yelled, bending, turning away cupping his hands over his privates.

They yelled, "here comes a woman" at Funaro another time and he cupped his hands between his legs and held them tightly together, and then, teed off, flipped out his sizeable prick and waved it hello up and down.

"Come and get it baby!"

A behind-the-lines security patrol discovered eleven rotting chinks in the river about two miles above, bloated beyond recognition, covered like fur coats with white hairy filaments of some kind of fungus and the medics put the river off limits because of that and dangerous liver flukes hosted in rice paddy water snails, brought to our attention by a touring preventive medicine team.

Our beloved Doc Lynch, brave young medic (medic, hell, he was our hospital) who, among his miracles saved the Banzai Third gallons of blood and more lives than old timers could recall, got to rotate. Having survived his tour in hell, he was free at last. Karl Eppler, closer to Doc than anyone else, insisted on riding in the back seat of a company jeep as his private shotgun guard the forty kilometers to Division Rotation Center.

"No gook's getting Doc this late in the game. Not while I'm here."

Some folks pooh-pooh Doc Lynch being sixteen and say I lie. I've talked to a medic a year younger. A lot of kids that age made damn good fighters; take President Old Hickory Jackson in 1780, thirteen when his British captor, dragoon Lieutenant Colonel Banastre Tarleton, at Hanging Rock, South Carolina, ordered him to blacken his boots, and Andy told the greatly-feared Britisher to rub salt up his ass (very probably) although historians who copy each other put it politely as if a brawny boy who was a man already would answer such an order like a sissy. "Sir, I decline to do that." He wore scars on his head and fingers the rest of his life warding off a saber blow. Orion P Howe, five feet, four inches, of Streator, Illinois won the Medal of Honor in infantry combat in 1864 when he was 12, endorsed by Major General William Tecumseh Sherman and the only group aside from Waffen SSers to slow down our Yankee Division's rat race across the Sudetenland were Hitler's Jungen Corps, thirteen, even younger, who refused to surrender until a number were killed.

One of Walter Winchell's pet projects, at the insistence of letter-writing mothers, was to get Congress to save their underage sons. An Eighth Army search was made and when I came down the gangplank at Pusan seventy-two boy soldiers were being readied and returned against their will, most with combat infantrymen's badges and more than a few with Bronze or Silver Stars for gallantry—three in Army transfer canisters—all under the legal limit to enlist, even with parents' consent.

When Carl Myles Carlson of Joliet, Illinois was assigned to the Third Battalion to replace Doc Lynch, he was plain Specialist E-4 Carlson until he earned the very respected sobriquet 'Doc.' Carlson, who, like Sergeant Eppler, went by his middle name, unlike Eppler could never be awarded the combat infantryman's badge. Being in the medical branch, he earned one a little bit higher in the esteem of combat riflemen, the hallowed combat medic's badge, bearing in low relief a caduceus, the winged staff of Mercury over an outstretched litter.

"Carlson," I told him, "combat medics are the only guys in the world I'll take my hat off to."

"Sir?"

"You realize you have the most risky job; hotter than mine. I get exposed a lot checking back and forth on sergeants. You, and I feel for you, get to go where some one's just had it. It's zeroed in; not just a possibility you'll get it, too. Guys with field commissions are right along there; have to prove something. From my little experience, it's been, at least in our battalion that I know of, in the order, medics, field commissioned second lieutenant rifle platoon leaders, and then first lieutenant rifle platoon leaders. ROTC officers usually come here as second lieutenants, field commissioned second louies are not only commissioned but usually decorated as well. You'll often see field commissioned guys with Silver Stars. But I'm rambling. Let me ask you a question."

"What's that, sir?"

"What would you do if one or more of our guys was getting it in a mortar barrage?"

"Sir, it's my job to get to them soon as possible."

"Hell no!" I said, raising my voice. "First, size up the situation. That's how we lost two good medics on Hill 442—nobody could talk them out of it. Lieutenant Hurtz saw chink observers on top the hill spotting for the mortars that got them. Two of his men were already down and the bastards made them bait for a medic like you, using wounded as staked-out goats. No one was breathing by the time it was safe enough to get to them, not even the medic. The only trouble I ever had with the guy you replace is that Doc Lynch was too eager to patch someone up. The medic is the last guy we want to lose.

"Yes, sir," Specialist Fourth Class Carlson said crisply.

I examined replacements just as I'd been checked out by the guys a month earlier. You so want Carlson to succeed, he has your life in his little aid kit and ability to use it. Taking him on a little walk, I quizzed, "Myles, y, old spelling? Or Miles, with an i, new? You know, of course, it's Latin for soldier."

"With a y? Where'd you hear that?"

"I read it about Captain Myles Standish, who, by the way, was a closet Catholic, scion of a long line of British Catholic warriors. You know you have to take care of everything from a sliver to an artillery shrapnel hole and a boil on someone's ass; know that, don't you?"

"Yes, sir. I've had the training."

Taking out a list I'd borrowed, I thought, here's where I'll trip him. "Suppose you tell me what's in your aid kit. Technically, Medical Kit, Individual 9-274-960."

"Where you want to start, sir?"

"Anywhere."

"Well, my badge number is same as was Lynch. There's cascara sagrada for laxative, one bottle of 100 tablets and...."

"Wait a minute," looking over my list, "How you spell that?"

"Sagrada, S-A-G-R-"

"Okay, got it."

"Well, there's one bottle of that, a bottle of iodine and a package of fifteen, it's usually fifteen, I think, tartrate of morphine ampules."

"You should get more."

"I'll try, sir." He paused to think. "We have to sign for them and turn in un-used."

"How about that stuff for burns?"

"Oh, yes, and a dozen tubes of tetracaine ophthalmic ointment for the eyes, two rolls three inches by three yards of camouflage compress gauze bandage, some medium-size muslin camouflage first aid dressing and a spool of two-inch wide surgical adhesive tape. One Lister surgery scissors and an elastic tourniquet, and...."

"Doc Lynch usually carried two or three."

"Yes, sir. I already got them, as a matter of fact, they gave me Lynch's old kit."

"What else?"

"There's a package of large safety pins and an oral thermometer, a bottle of 120 APCs [aspirin, phenacetin and caffeine], and a minor surgery instrument kit, sir, with hemostat, scalpels and sutures, and evacuation tags and a Red Cross arm band."

"No one wears them forward of regiment."

"I don't know, sir. I just remember I'm supposed to have one."

"You know your kit pretty well."

"Ought to sir, checked and retrained me at Medical Company coming down."
Doc Lynch and Carlson are typical. I've never heard tell of a bad combat medic,
one incapable or unwilling to risk his life without pausing to save a life.

*   *   *

Aching bodies and disturbed minds recuperated fast with security, friendly
attitudes, hot food, shower and rest. Reserve was our chance to reequip and train
replacements, a relief period of uncertain duration during which the majority of us
relaxed and did our best to keep thoughts of dead out of mind—*train, train* and
retrain for every possible contingency. To me nothing was such a deplorable
waste of time, however, as the handed-down training schedule and formal lay-
out inspections. Shortages were invariably made up before inspections by borrowing from another company before lining our equipment across a graded dry
rice paddy parade ground, grousing and complaining as we did when needlessly
employed.

Each guy displayed the following, standard and uniform on his neatly folded
shelter half, on which was laid in its uniform place, a poncho folded four times over
a twice-folded woolen Army blanket, a coiled tent rope, five wooden tent pegs side-
by-side, a tent pole in three folding sections, a deflated air mattress, insulated sleeping bag with an almost full-length heavy zipper and waterproof cover, a combat pack
with web harnesses that hooked eyeholes for a folding entrenching tool and a thick
web cartridge belt on which were hooked aid kit, canteen, ammo pouch, bayonet in
scabbard. Later in the war bullet-proof vests were issued.

Each soldier also displayed an OD wash cloth, face towel, bath towel and tooth-
brush, toothpaste, comb and/or brush, soap and dish, shaving gear, all in olive-drab
containers; two olive-drab handkerchiefs, six pair of carefully rolled olive-drab socks,
an extra pair of OD underwear, a mess kit in two pieces, bottom meat can with partition in the center to keep liquid from slopping over and a cover capable of containing
solid foods; aluminum cup with folding, locking handle, aluminum knife, fork and
tablespoon. Each man displayed his individually assigned weapon and required load
of ammunition on the folded Army blanket with rifle cleaning rod and materials. An
inspector might stop and demand of a man to real off the serial number of his weapon
being held by the inspector.

Word was out that the first thing to do when issued a new aid kit was to unsnap
it, open the pouch and throw away the two sulfa pills, discontinued since WWII.
One found to cause hives and the other crystallized in the kidneys if insufficient
water was taken. One inspector might check a man at random to see if this had been
done. Each squad was signed out with a hatchet and a small folding pickaxe in
holder for tree roots and an axe to cut camouflage boughs and five-inch thick bunker
roof poles.

I reported: "First Lieutenant Dudley C Gould reporting, sir!" while saluting the
X Corps commander, Edward M 'Ned' Almond, who made his third star in February,
according to his biographer "a very proud man, intolerant and overbearing, with a
driving intensity, dictatorial manner, a brash, brittle human dynamo." A VMI man,
he'd been Douglas MacArthur's Chief of Staff toward the end of WWII, commanded
the troubled black 92d Division from its inception in the deserts at Fort Huachua
near Bisbee south of Tucson and to Italy in 1944 and its disbandment and lost his

son, Edward Jr, West Pointer (Class of 1943) that same year and son-in-law, West Pointer, 1942, in combat. Born in 1892, he was rated in 1948 by General Eisenhower one of half dozen ablest men in the Army.

The original plan of the Inchon landing, Operation Bluehearts, was conducted by Ned Almond, appointed commander of the newly-formed X Corps and placed in charge of the landing in lieu of Washington's preference, Marine General Lemuel C Shepard Jr, the most experienced in combat landing in WWII. Neither Almond nor his staff had amphibious experience. The newly-conceived command and position as leader of a corps was thought by many (see Clay Blair's *THE FORGOTTEN WAR*) to get the third star for Almond, at odds at the time with Eighth Army's Johnnie Walker and J Lawton Collins, Army chief of staff in Washington.

The inspection party consisted of Lieutenant General Almond, Major General Clark 'Nick' Ruffner, ex-cavalryman, native of Buffalo, New York, VMI class of 1924, who once pulled a long tour as Almond's aide-de-camp and chief of staff before being sent to command the Second Division; John 'Bloody Boots' Coughlin, a former New York City orphan whose guardian got him admitted to the 1935 class at West Point. Behind them were the general's aides, a captain and two lieutenants; Major Wallace W Wilkes, pseudonym, of battalion, lately from G-3 section X Corps, whom nobody seemed to know, and the very nervous Captain Shallow, also pseudonym.

I escorted General Almond up and down the short rows of the Banzai Third. The general, very well groomed and pressed by his soldier valet, wore starched, knife-like creases in his fatigues, was in good humor and should be since he was near the top of the Army pecking order.

"Lieutenant," he asked patronizingly, bending to pick up and examine Corporal Ichimura's pistol and then look me over as another *thing* to be inspected. "Do you or your men have any complaints?"

It was customary on high-level inspections for everyone to get scared of those at top who acted toward subordinates as though they hated their guts. No one smiled, inspectees nor inspector. I piped up smartly as I could, "No sir!"

Holding Ich's pistol to the sky, critically examining the bore, the general asked, "Are you short any equipment?"

How could we be? The general had been at this inspection business over thirty years and must have known that when outfits are short of anything before inspection time, they borrow from those not being inspected—jeeps even, and 3.5-inch rocket launchers, and I heard of one inspection they had to loan out personal combs and toothbrushes, although I'll admit it was a rare incident. Ned fooled with the pistol as though a toy and I felt the cold stare of Bloody Boots Coughlin on my neck.

"No, sir, I don't think so."

This gave the three-star general the opening he needed for perennial theatrics. Now he could be his real self.

"Don't *think* so!" he roared. "Dammit, lieutenant this is *war!* You're in no Reserve unit in the States now. Dammit, lieutenant, don't you *know*?"

I thought to myself, when were you shot at last?

Someone up the line for some reason or another must have told him I was a Reserve officer. I wondered if poor New Yorker Hurtz was marked also, as Jewish and ROTC? Captain Shallow beside me shifted his weight slightly while giving me a stare advising me to be on guard.

"Yes, sir, I'm pretty sure," I said.

"Colonel Coughlin!" the corps commander demanded, ignoring his fellow VMI graduate, General Ruffner, "Don't your officers know whether or not their men are properly equipped? 'Don't think so' ... *'pretty* sure'; why in hell don't they know?"

"Sir," Coughlin responded crisply, stiffening to attention. "I'm certain that if the lieutenant had any complaint I'd know it."

"What do you say we ask him," the General snapped. "Lieutenant, how well do you know your men?"

"Pretty good, sir. I've been in this outfit only two months and guys come and go all the time. It's hard to really *know* anyone, sir."

General Almond frowned, I suspected a bit sorry he'd gone this far with me, dragging him down too close to the truth of things.

"What's this 'pretty good' business? Dammit, the Army is built on rifle squads and platoons. If down at this level you don't know for sure what's going on, how can you expect the rest of us to know?"

"Well, sir, ah..." I offered hesitatingly, getting angry, looking away from Captain Shallow, Major Wallace W. Wilkes and Coughlin. "I know damn well when we're short on inspections, but I've been told to borrow what we needed."

Captain Shallow stared in horror, Major Wilkes had a blank look as though he wasn't even there, it was no concern of his, and Colonel Coughlin and General Ruffner exchanged worried glances. Almond caught off guard completely with the naked truth experienced a flush of confused feelings before settling on anger. Ignoring the chain of command behind me, he turned to his aide-de-camp captain and ordered, "Roy, find out about this. Give me a complete list of everything this battalion's short and schedule another inspection right away."

The three-star general and his grim inspection party cut short the inspection and, walking fast to keep up with their boss, took off abruptly kitty-corner across the field.

At 1500 hours that day, Captain Shallow and I were standing tall before the regimental commander. Why Wilkes wasn't there I'll never know. Fortunately the colonel's abuse was centered on the captain instead of me, after all what could be expected of a recalled Reserve?

As if this wasn't dramatic enough, before two weeks were out, I was standing tall before Bloody Boots by myself for another even more unpleasant reason. I got the first month's officers' liquor ration since I was with Love Company, and per custom brought it to a command party at regiment. The beer ration of one six-pack per enlisted man and officers' one bottle of liquor were as free as most of our PX rations, and, of course, none of us had to pay income tax for the period we served in Korea. Big deal for Regulars while the small businesses of recalled officers were going under attempting to be run by wives.

Some of the younger EM got plastered on six cans of beer, or more when extras were bought from a few teetotaler buddies.

I hit it off with Captain Jan van Rusbroec whose Dutch company my platoon was attached to when I returned from Third Station. We hung out near the bar where four former professional bartender enlisted men mixed and poured our rations, nothing fancy, mixed mostly with number ten issue cans of breakfast grapefruit juice and PX ginger ale. There was more than all of us could drink in one night, what with officers' liquor appropriated from dead and evacuated and guys like Hurtz who didn't show up, whose liquor did, and, especially, for me, with plenty of Bols Dutch gin in stone bottles bearing in full color the picture of an ugly dwarf on the side. The Dutch didn't need liquor rations and like the French and other foreign battalions could buy their own liquor at any time. The Dutch gin I got from them that night was really a liqueur, rather sweet, but, being new to me I was somewhat contemptuous of it and really put it away. I had a sack of fun teaching the *Wiffenpoof Song* to the Dutch.

The few times in my life when I was that drunk I recall suddenly seeing and hearing things almost as though I was cold sober and then suddenly black out completely and do things I couldn't remember the day after. I was jailed for two days once for clobbering a cop whose uniform I don't recall even seeing. How I got so black and blue I didn't know.

At about one in the morning I remember hearing someone telling me rather angrily, I thought, "Lieutenant, the last jeep is returning to your battalion, better be on it!"

I took it as an order. Anyway, the next thing I recall I was in the back seat of a jeep moving about five miles an hour in a fine rain on the road back to Third Battalion. There was a cliff beside a drainage ditch on our immediate left and a dangerous drop-off to our right into a deep ravine and raging river. I remember riding that stretch sober and being shown the wreckage, smashed cab and twisted lowboy with a dozer, way down in the river. The engineer driver's body was recovered by volunteers repelling with ropes but so far it was impossible to haul up the wreck.

As we rode along, I suddenly came to again, hearing a voice in the front seat say, "I ought to kick the shit out of you, Gould." It was Major Wilkes. Evidently I'd been baiting the major about hiding out the day we lost Sergeant Ulriche.

I recall clear as a bell saying, "No time like the present," bailing over the side of the jeep from the back seat. If you know the jeep we had in those days, you'll know it's quite a trick to squirm through the braces that hold up the roof and yet it didn't sober me any. I next remember being astride Wilkes, sitting on his stomach holding his lapels, banging his head up and down in a mud puddle, laughing and having a wonderful time. Then the Battalion S-2, his drinking buddy, Captain Jones, slugged me one hell of a wallop from which I still bear a scar over my right eye; he probably hit with something harder than his fist. The next thing I remember was at battalion Aid Station being readied for a ride to the 11th Evacuation Hospital. They stitched my eyebrow and noticed my bad post nasal drip and tight, hurting chest and cleaned me up and kept giving me shots of some sort for three days without a single cigarette. For the same period of time I was in Third Station for a bona fide honorable battle wound, now I was facing a general court martial. Aside from teaching the Dutch to sing the *Wiffen poof Song*, I had only a faint memory of events at the officers' liquor party.

I reprimanded myself, "You asshole, you've gone and done it. Going to be court martialed and sent to Leavenworth. What will Uncle Art and your mother say?"—real mother, not Emma. My initial reaction did not concern my father nor Kitty, only the dead, mother and Uncle Art. I was sorry for staining the memories of my mother and her brother, Arthur Wiedeman, machine-gunned and gassed at the Argonne, gone since 1939. One thing for sure, I committed a general court martial offense, striking a superior officer in a war zone. Technically, I suppose, I could be executed. But no matter what I did, I did it when I didn't know I was doing it; Wilkes, on the other hand, knowingly neglected to do his job, and by doing, or neglecting to do so, murdered our men and was getting clean away.

The day after I returned from the 11th Evac, at the lowest level of self-esteem I've ever been, I was ordered to report immediately to the regimental commander. After knocking on a doorway pole of his private pyramid tent and identifying myself, Colonel Coughlin gave me the old sweat-it-out treatment, his orderly told to tell me, "Wait there, lieutenant, the colonel's busy."

I saw Coughlin through a crack of the door flaps reading a civilian magazine which he continued for a good ten minutes before snapping, "Report!"

Facing him at his table, I saluted, with the expected: "Lieutenant Gould, reporting as ordered sir!"

I was held to that brace longer than I thought I could take, my hands and knees shaking like leaves of a tree. He never gave me at ease and as he raved on with me standing at attention I relaxed my muscles as best I could at attention by shifting weight subtly back and forth.

"Lieutenant Gould," Coughlin sneered, "This your way of getting out of combat? Think you're going to get away with this?"

He continued to badger me for about five minutes, saying nothing about the impropriety of slugging a superior officer. Not once did I hear Wilkes as Coughlin went on insinuating that I'd done whatever nameless thing I'd done to dodge combat, giving me the impression that another officer somewhere to his knowledge, must have done the same to dodge combat. Frankly, it never entered my mind.

On his last charge against me trying to get out of combat, I blew my top as never before nor since. Having been at the very depth of despair four days and nights, scolding myself for disgracing everyone in my family, headed for a Federal prison still a bit fatigued and depleted, secretly proud to have beaten Wilkes and more sad than ever for his killing Sergeant Ulriche, I let everything go. Why not, the book's being thrown at me anyway, there's no way to dodge Leavenworth. What've I got to lose? Slap on the handcuffs but stop lying about me.

"Me dodge combat?" I blurted. "Sonofabitch, dodging combat's what I beat Wilkes for."

Colonel Coughlin ignored the outburst, looking away as I raised my voice to complain loudly about that favored West Point son, Wilkes, who could do no wrong. "Because of his cowardly lack of leadership, Third Battalion's morale is at rock bottom; rear echelons stealing the May beer ration, rifling packs while we risked our lives, and that bastard cringing well down the ridge, not getting us any fire. Dammit, colonel, I'll lead my platoon anywhere in Korea, but long as we have to depend on support from Wilkes, I'll refuse to be responsible. That sonofabitch is a sneaky, gutless drunk."

I went on loudly, saying how little I thought of Wilkes and how he couldn't be trusted; that he was responsible for the deaths of good men and rotten morale in the battalion rear the very short time he was acting battalion commander.

"That's enough, Lieutenant!" Bloody Boots finally snapped. "You're being insubordinate right now!" He paused while I breathed heavily after my emotional outburst, and in a lower voice, "I tell you what, I think your intentions were harmless. I'm no psychiatrist but I saw myself you were stupid drunk, not that it in itself is an excuse. You're damn lucky it happens that Major Wilkes is rotating next week and doesn't want to be held up. He tells me he isn't able to stay and bring charges."

Later that summer the S3 sergeant about to rotate told me not to say anything that might cause him to be held up, but he overheard Captain Jones, before he rotated, advising the major to press charges against me for slugging him and bayonet-ting a young King Company replacement, if Colonel Coughlin failed to do so. Jones, a Regular, passed-over twice for promotion, the operations sergeant told me, called me a 'goddamn punk bugout.'

I walked out of the colonel's tent on air. I didn't really know why but I wasn't going to be court martialed for one of the most serious court martial charges there is, striking a superior officer in a war zone. I remembered then how surprised and more angry the colonel was when I mentioned what happened to Sergeant Ulriche, one of the all-time heroes of the regiment, and why we had no preparation. How ironic that Sergeant Ulriche was forced to resign his commission because of a disgraceful supe-rior, then killed because of the cowardice of another. I suspect the colonel had little use for Wilkes anyway, if only because of the loss of our new Third Battalion execu-tive officer, Captain Tracey, and someone told me that Coughlin wasn't getting along so well with Almond and resented Corps' giving Wilkes a combat command for his career and promotion without consulting him.

Bloody Boots was known to be hard to know, not that I wanted to. Still, I puzzled over the real reason why I wasn't court martialed and I didn't find the right answer for thirty-some years when I happened to read that in June '51 at a low point of the 38th, Senator Magnuson of the State of Washington was in the 38th's area with a committee investigating soldier morale and such leadership failures of the division as the Massacre Valley incident in January 1951 when large elements of the Second Division were held on a long, winding mountain road for a day and a night while chink fire plunged into them from both sides killing, among valuable men, Lieuten-ant Colonel M P A den Derden, paratrooper commander of the Dutch Battalion. Air strikes finally cleared the way, but to this day, Army historians fail to release casualty figures of the Second Division for that abortion, if, indeed, they were tabulated.

Before the war the Second Division was in garrison at Fort Lewis, Washington in the Senator's area prior to embarking for Korea and a rash of loved ones living there sweating out the return of their men complained to the Senator, showing his staff bitter letters from the front. Coughlin would certainly not want me and the Senator to meet.

One day in reserve a young soldier approached me during a break in training and after ascertaining that I was Lieutenant Gould of Love Company, to my surprise dropped his pants to his knees in front of everyone, pulled up the right side of his undershorts and pointed to a two-inch pink scar.

"Sir, I want to thank you for saving my life. I never knew I had the strength."

He was that chubby, pale-faced kid of King Company. I was embarrassed.

"Hell, anyone would have done it."

"I don't think so."

He explained to my replacements what happened that morning and he told me that the battalion surgeon, assuming the bayoneting was a wanton General Patton-like loss of temper, complained to Major Wilkes and Wilkes tried to get him to testify to what they presumed I'd done, but the surgeon declined, himself high on the rota-tion roster. No one wanted to be held back to testify. Before Wilkes left, the surgeon learned from the private when he came for a checkup that without that bayonet jab he couldn't have moved to safety. Nevertheless, Major Asshole Wilkes called me in and tried to get me to confess in front of the sergeant major to what seemed to hap-pen. I told them what the draftsman corporal said on the *Jutlandia* and bluffed that he was willing to make a sworn deposition witnessed by Lieutenant Opoulus, being careful not to remind them they both had been evacuated to the States. I lied that Sandy would swear that on the 15th of May, King Company never received word to withdraw from the battalion outpost patrol base.

Wilkes didn't rotate, I learned, as Colonel Coughlin said he would. A clerk told me that no one knew why, not even Coughlin, not even the sergeant major or adjutant, but Wilkes was becoming irritable and snapped at nothing and could more often be found by himself near a hidden bottle. He simply filled his musette bag one morning and had some things taken to the aid station, announcing to his acting exec that written orders would follow, and never returned. It was assumed he was an emergency medical evacuee. He enjoyed a very high, mysterious clout, moved about independent of any chain of command and it was assumed that he was evacuated to the Tokyo General for an apparently serious reason. A special order on the morning report was not self-explanatory. It was well known, however, how X Corps headquarters took care of its own.

*   *   *

Clay Blair, THE FORGOTTEN WAR, Anchor Books, 1981—

The battered Second Division withdrew from the Inje area into X Corps reserve, in accordance with Ridgway's orders. By that time the division was shattered; it was to remain in reserve for forty days, rebuilding and reorganizing and rating those who had been in combat longest. During that period three regimental commanders, the 9th's Ed Messinger, the 23d's Jack Chiles and the 38th's John Coughlin were rated. Coughlin retired as a colonel in 1954.

The new commanders of the 9th, 23d, and 38th regiments were all young West Pointers. Command of the 38th went to the youngest of the three, Almond's G-3, Frank Mildren (West Point, 1939), who was given another X Corps staffer and Almond confidant, Edward L Rowny (West Point, 1941) to be his exec. The X Corps assistant G-3, Joe Gurfein (West Point, 1941), was named exec of the 23d Infantry. Both Rowny and Gurfein would later rise to command their regiments. The appointments of these X Corps staffers to line positions appeared to confirm the story that Almond was running a 'command nursery,' giving choice jobs to the 'teacher's pets.'

Major David Duncan (pseudonym) shipped over from the 101st Airborne Fort Campbell, Kentucky to become Third Battalion commander. His kind lived for infantry combat; it's what they did, with strong willpower and with years of training he strained hard to sustain it.

He once told me bluntly: "We like war and we're tooled for it." and reminded us at an officers' call when some reference was made of the powerful CCF: "Don't ever forget America's powerful secret weapon, the SAM-51, Soldier American Model-1951."

Duncan, battlefield commissioned early in the fighting in Europe, was about as short as they allow in the Army, hawk nose, perhaps appropriately having been a veteran of 'screaming eagles' in WWII and afterward, which patch he proudly wore on his left shoulder when he arrived in Korea.

By 1951 good aggressive combat company and battalion leaders were not plentiful. Class of 1950 West Point was hit hard the year they graduated and with few exceptions, rifle platoons and companies in the Second Division, were led and would be led in the foreseeable future by recalled Reserve lieutenants, rarely captains. Some few were even ROTC officers who aged and learned fast, earning infantry master degrees in fierce combat; rapidly promoted by attrition, and in a few cases, master sergeants, like John Pater, later to receive a field commission with a limited duty waiver and a waiver on age.

After Lieutenant Foney left, Love was supplied with a captain, I M Shallow. Both Captains Ted Toth of King, already in Korea six months, the recipient of a Bronze Star, and I M Shallow of Love, were to leave their commands within a month in disgrace. Coincidentally, both were somewhat overweight, wore dark-rimmed glasses and had considerable experience in the supply field, which in the peacetime Army isn't such a bad field to be in. Expertise in requisitioning, inventory and supply is a plus in any branch at any time, in any business for that matter. That those particular ones ended up commanding rifle companies speaks of the shortage of that grade.

Neither Toth nor Shallow would be seen in a rifle outfit during better times; you'd find them working efficiently in civilian clothes at office jobs back at some Army supply depot. In fact, Shallow reported to the Second Division from the Delaware Water Gap Army Depot and Toth from a small U S Army support group supplying several classified research projects somewhere in California.

Duncan estimated that even among the most elite troops, eighty-five percent of those killed in action were new men with only a fraction of a second to learn it all, paralyzed by fear or fatigue. Physical fear *is* a fatigue that makes the body and the mind suddenly confront each other by the blood path; never having had the luck to
endure combat to discover how much grit they had and where it was to come from; never in former life having been made to try hard enough, just a little further than straining hard; who were careless and stuck up their noggins too soon at the wrong time and place where an enemy sniper or machine gun was lying patiently in wait; to ignore what their ears warned them of, neglecting to advise them not to expose themselves taking a peek; failed to first let their ears estimate the situation, locate the exact source of danger, or felt sorry for their excessive fatigue and became slow to move, careless and plain self-indulgent.

Duncan was pleased to learn that my reserve training made it mandatory to read Marshall's *MEN AGAINST FIRE* for he was a new second lieutenant in a flank battalion outside Bastogne, Belgium, when Marshall was pinned down in that open field of snow with a 101st battalion commander; where Marshall ascertained that less than twenty-five percent of the best-trained elite soldiers fired their weapons, though the only protection they had. I figured they must have been quite green like I was that day at the Soyang river; a couple brisk actions will snap one out of that kind of thoughtless unsoldierly cringing. Snap control of it by sounding off.

Our division was back in a X Corps reserve at Hongchan north of Hoengsong to fill our ranks again; to prepare new ones for slaughter, you might say if you were bitter like a lot of us; to give ourselves a rest from what we'd been through, assaulting and being assaulted. However, nobody got a lie-down, goof off rest, for training schedules came down and regular Army officer inspectors from the Division G3 (sneaks, they were) popped up everywhere to check us out and get us ready to return to war as soon as possible—they planned we'd be one step ahead of the ambitious chinks with such peacetime training as 'Position of a Soldier at Attention,' 'Rites and Ceremonies,' 'Interior Guard Duty.'

It was June and already sweltering in the afternoons. The deep mountain valleys, however, remained cool, damp and chilly long after the hills and mountain tops were warm and sunny. In those Korean east-central mountains which ran up much of the peninsula, it was always foggy in the morning. In our particular valley cuckoos went coo-coo at the first light, along with lonesome-sounding whippoorwills, and crows or maybe ravens, in the wooded areas that went 'huba huba,' Korean, I guess, for 'caw, caw.' Men in the Seventh Division, the first to occupy Korea at the end of WWII, became deathly ill from eating pheasants purchased from Korean farmers, birds caught with poisoned rice, which over a period Koreans became immune to.

Until I was fully clothed, slipping on my already buttoned fatigue top while keeping my legs and thighs warm in the fartsack, I thought I'd freeze. Even in early July, though we were on the same longitude as, say, Kansas, our elevation, though not great, was such as to keep mornings chilly like mornings in deep valleys back home.

Groping my way out of the officers' tent, stumbling over tent ropes, I'd slip into the back door of the mess tent for coffee and a cigarette. Gasoline fumes from field ranges when I approached too close stung my eyes and my post nasal drip leaked so some mornings I had to go outside several times during the first ten minutes or so to hawk up phlegm. Fred Hurtz once bragged it was easy to give up cigarettes; he did it twice in a single day.

Every morning before chow Field First Sergeant, Sergeant First Class Martin strode up and down the tents rousing everyone with his damned brass whistle until all backed out, crawling, bitching and struggling in various stages of dress and boot lacing, trading early morning grumpiness for a properly servile military decorum. I wondered what happened to the old Army bugle they played for us at CMTC in 1937. I guess good buglers are hard to find. Third Infantry veteran Sam Houston himself blew what few calls they had for his rag-tag, revolutionary Texian Army.

Duncan taught the spirit of the bayonet—bayonets before breakfast, he put it once intimating he might get that copyrighted as a slogan. The guys were ordered to be nasty, get mad at each other.

"Snarl, damn it!" Sergeant Eppler growled. "Call the guy you're sticking dirty names and cut out snickering. This ain't funny. Get mad or I'll give you a hundred pushups; you'll see how funny it is."

All couldn't act ferocious that early and there was lots of snickering.

"All right, knock off the funny stuff!" a sergeant yelled. "Get mad! Snarl like you meant it! For chrissake, my kid sister's meaner'n that in the morning."

My guys were easy going that early, unlike Bloody Boots who was always tense. No one ever saw him smile. I heard there was a young, brown-nosing ROTC second lieutenant, political science major, waiting at regiment for assignment who for three days positioned himself to greet the colonel when he came over to the regimental staff's private mess tent for breakfast in the dark and chill of early mornings. Confronting the colonel, he would click his boot heels a la Hollywood Nazi as dramatically as possible; with a big phoney smile salute him with a loud exaggerated, "Good morning, *sir*!" The third morning, Coughlin, middle-age vet of World War Two, former G3 of the division, ignoring the salute, snapped angrily, "A matter of opinion, lieutenant and I don't need a weather report from you."

It was a good sign when replacements quieted down and asked serious questions about combat.

"What's it like?"

I did my brief best to tell them.

"We've heard that," they'd interrupt impatiently, "Seen the movies, what's combat *really* like?"

"Can't describe that fear, have to find yourselves."

They sat around campfires at night honing bayonets as soldiers have since the War for Independence, hoping they'll never have to use them, as very few did.

"Pity chinks stuck with that."

"Yeah?" another countered. "Run your finger along this, don't cut yourself."

"Sh-e-e-it!" Pop Miller sneered. "Crap your pants that close to a live chink."

"Yeah?" a replacement came back, inflating his hairless chest, "That's what you think."

"Yeah?"

"Yeah!"

The sergeants ran them uphill and across dry rice paddies and back across a ford of the river, holding their rifles at a high ready port, sloshing through, splashing, screaming dire threats ahead of them.

"Git them sonsabitches! . . . Stick the bastards!"

They stabbed to death straw-filled dummies crudely decorated with cartoon slant-eyed yellow faces for chinks and gooks alike — as J aps did live POWs — then ran double-quick back through the water, lifting their feet high as chorus girls.

Hurtz took me to task for repeating the language of sergeants. "You never talked like that, Dud. I don't think you realize how you're changing. It's a bad habit to get hold of."

"She-e-e-it!"

"Somebody cares. Nobody can go through life by himself."

I thought about that a while. Far as language was concerned, who I talked like, my attitude, I guess I've always been in between. Ever since I can remember, it's been my father opposite to mother and Uncle Art, God bless their memories. Somehow, I'd like to live carefree as Uncle Art and end up as respected as my father. I was always between two life styles with a strong affinity for my modest, plain-talking mother who never graduated from high school, and her older brother, Uncle Art, over my father. Art, she used to tell me, should be pitied. He was slated to be a chemist and after graduating from Watertown high school was being trained by the city engineer who took a shine to him. However, when he came home from Walter Reed in 1920, the year I was born, Uncle Art never went back to the water purification plant, instead spent his time with fellow combat veterans, those few in Watertown who actually fought 'over there,' and bottles of cheap wine talking endlessly about what happened 'over there,' talk nobody else could share.

My father, whom Art and his three brothers, George Herbie and Leo, used to embarrass sometimes for sitting out World War I, was a farm boy, as Goulds have been since landing at Topsfield near Boston from England in 1634 on the Bemus. He worked his way through college and in 1915 got into advertising and finally Secretary of the Chamber of Commerce in Watertown, a position he helped establish. My father, who was never dad nor pop, represented intelligence, the religious, straight, politically correct, conservative, conventional life, while Uncle Art Wiedeman and his facial scars from mustard gas and bum knee from a machine gun, was a big German-American guy, son of an immigrant who was an orphan, a nine-year-old indentured servant, water boy for seven years in a limestone quarry in the late 1800s.

Art once went around northern New York state in a medicine show as the Hun with a support made from a truck inner tube over his knee, offering five bucks to out wrestle him. He was glamour and adventure, truly masculine man, consummate soldier, to me. All my life they've warred in me—muscle and freethinking vs brain and discipline; physical animal and simple pleasures vs mind, denial, study and religion. Working guys, day laborers like Art, went with the flow living their lives day to day. My father figured hard how he should handle his life and, worrying a lot, got pretty high up compared to the farm where he started.

All my life I have felt akin to so-called lower animals, cats, dogs, horses and such, or as people call them contemptuously, animals, as though they didn't have hair around their own assholes. I remember clearly on my way to school one January morning when I was about nine, all bundled up with my breath pouring out like steam passing a sled full of heavy canvas bags of coal outside the State Street Diner. It was thirty below and a poor horse was standing shivering. His sorrowful eyes pleaded with me and Gordy to help him, and Gordy agreed what a dirty shame it was and dared me to say something about it, going into the diner behind me as I shouted at the coal man sitting at the counter, "Hey, mister, your poor horse is freezing to death."

He growled something without even turning around, and all we could do was to go back out and try to rub some warmth into the poor guy, slapping his sides, telling him to hang on.

*For that which befalleth the sons of man befalleth beasts; even one thing
befalleth them; as the one dieth, so dieth the other; yes they have all one
breath; so that man hath no preeminence above a beast, for all his
vanity. All go unto one place, all are of the dust, and all return to dust
again.*
– Ecclesiastics

As I grew up I seldom did or said the right things and was always an outsider. I could never understand why I alone lost my mother so painfully. As a family, did we anger God some way? This turned to a smoldering hatred! "Goddamn you, God! You mean bastard!" I never got in team sports, no sports but skiing and wrestling and I was essentially lonely with an inferiority complex, too self-concerned to give myself freely. Each contact with another was an experiment which, by the time I learned to put aside our differences to get along with him, rarely her, the situation was gone.

I've thought back hard and I'm sure now that I dropped out of college after my second year not so much to attend an art school as to rebel against my father who took out an insurance policy when he was a struggling accountant at the peak of the Great Depression and really couldn't afford the payments to see me in college. It's always been Uncle Art, the scarred war veteran and his sister, my mother, for warmth and humor vs Ernest Curtis Gould, my cold father, self-made college graduate who came from a farm to overcome all odds; very respectable, churchgoing, civic-minded leader of the community. I wondered who, if anyone, would ever win me over and the more I went through combat the closer I grew to Uncle Art.

At times in Korea I almost believed in the God most Americans do. Logic, Syracuse University Philosophy 101 class, 1937, convinced me, however, that I really don't believe in the revealed, organized religion Christianity but am an Agnostic who does not either spoof or believe in any God blindly. Agnosticism was coined in the late 1800s by Thomas Henry Huxley, grandfather of Aldous, as the term badly needed by religionists and philosophers and, doubters like me, to apply to not believing in a pro or con of a supreme being. It came from St Paul's *Agnosto Theo,* unknown God, contra to the then contemporary Christian cult called Gnostics claiming mystic knowledge that all matter was evil and Christ was never human.

Shooting the breeze, passing time, I once asked Fred jokingly if he killed anyone yet.

"I've shot my carbine in their direction a few times and directed my men to, but when you come right down to it, I never got the opportunity to deliberately kill anyone... you never ever see them within range."

"Me, too. I don't think I'd like to kill a man point blank, especially a fellow soldier like yourself you're not mad at. I'd sure as hell blast the asshole who put him there. If he threatened my life directly, I'd have to draw down on him to save myself. I guess then for sure I'd have to kill a guy. I know that's funny from a guy who volunteered to be trained to kill but was raised not to kill. I don't mean my parents harped on it, but you hear about it on the radio all the time and newspapers are full of what happens to killers. It's what they built the electric chair for . . . and how about the Christian Bible; it's one of the ten things not to do; how do priests and preachers in the Army get around that?" Fortunately, we get to do the killing by platoons so it's not personal. Like Voltaire said—

It is forbidden to take life and hence all who do so are punished,
unless they kill in large companies to the sound of a trumpet.
– Voltaire

Christians, Agnostics or simple pagans, we were thousands of miles from kindness, hidden from law-and-order and churches, committing thankless, perilous, public crimes of blatant murder, despite loud postulation from self-righteous preachers that Army killing is not against the Christian sixth commandment so long as it's on order *en masse.* In any event, our chaplain told us, Jesus Christ and God Himself were with us at a level a bit higher than generals.

God is with the strongest battalion.
– Frederick the Great and hypocrites ever since.

I thought once I'd like to be a Deist. Getting myself spiritually ready for the brutal end of me, sweating out my orders to go back on active duty, I reviewed the little there is to read on Deism. There's just too damn little written about it to really convince me. Many of our Founding Fathers were Deists, believing there is a God,

Latin *Deos,* but believing that Christ was no one but a very pure believing guy, a great philosopher like Buddha, except Buddha didn't believe in a supreme being people call God. Deists' belief in a God was based purely on the evidence of reason and Nature. No fallible human in betweens, trinities or silly, confusing parlor tricks.

There was never a chaplain in that unclean, bloody place, Korea, where the fighting was done, bragging there are no atheists in foxholes; no spokesmen for any god; no high-priced shrink there to stop our dead from staring accusingly at us, save them from chewing maggots and burping foul gasses from putrefying guts. My men died with no angel of death greeting them, a superstition which transpired in prequantum Biblical days. Nor did anyone report the neighing of a pale horse. If there was any hint of the supernatural, it was the awful fury of a heavy mortar barrage, chilling screams of an excited Satan and mocking capers of the Greek god of tragedy, Dionysus the horned one, jumping gleefully up and down clapping, throwing around parts and pieces of my men.

Nor was there organ music, stained-glass windows, open Bibles or hymnals and that is why I am content to know my riflemen never roasted in anyone's hell nor suffered purgatory. They stood bravely, in total obscurity before me, more noble than man has ever produced, bucked Hell headon and now rest in peace deserved, souls migrated; this poor demonstration their only testament.

*   *   *

In corps reserve, the duration of which was unknown, there was little time to make up for neglect in basic training at such places as Fort Dix. Writing inappropriate division training schedules was all some young West Pointers as assistant operations staffers ever did in Korea, aside from traveling within a quarter of a mile of incoming artillery fire to get combat infantrymen's badges and maybe Bronze or Silver Stars, depending on how well they were connected. They taught such critical things as 'the position of a soldier at attention,' and the 'uniform code of military justice.' Sh-e-e-it! I could have failed it again. They don't have to explain things before throwing the book at a guy.

Our new battalion S3, Captain Arthur Detweiler, agreed with me that training belonged in the hands of those trained in combat, not immaculately attired West Pointers at division rear. I began with my own platoon first and then, by tacit agreement and understanding with Detweiler that I'd take the blame if caught deviating from the schedule, I offered training to other platoons as well and was proud to do so in the short time we had.

One lesson we taught, Lieutenant Hurtz, Master Sergeant Eppler, Lieutenant Capler of Item Company and myself, was how to begin an approach march single file as up a mountain finger to make an assault, and pass information from front to rear or rear to front of our outstretched column man after man. "Send horseshit forward," or something as ridiculous, would be the serious message. After a few minutes the platoon would be stopped and the platoon sergeant walk back along the line until he discovered just who decided it was a silly request and stopped repeating it. Everyone was finally convinced it was not up to him to judge the value of a request from or to the front. This neglectful personal opinion occurred on the 23rd of May when first sergeant, Master Sergeant Pater of King Company tried to pass the word back to get M Company's heavy machine guns up to lay fire for us. The message wasn't relayed all the way to the guns and delayed them for an almost critical time. A common excuse was, "I didn't understand what it meant." Don't have to understand, just repeat what you hear.

Another unorthodox training was how to knock out a machine gun, like Sergeant Ulriche and Holly tried, and untold others in wars to come everywhere as they always do somewhere. The principle consideration was knowing, or realizing, the great difference between cover and concealment. Too often a guy would crawl behind a bush for protection, which concealed him from a chink all right but gave him a false sense of security and was no cover from bullets.

Sergeant Eppler would hide himself in a pocket on the hillside or behind a big boulder with a brass whistle and one at a time the men would be told to banzai his position, which few at first were able to do safely. Every time Karl spotted a vulnerable part of an approaching man he'd give a blast on his whistle denoting a fatal machine gun hit and critique the guy on the spot. "See, should've crawled that open stretch on your stomach!" After a while most knew how low they had to be and covered to make it successfully within grenade range. It was practical training like that, so different from the stiff, bloodless peacetime military classes of rear echelon's G3 that gave our men confidence I'm proud to say, and got me a Bronze Star, meritorious, sponsored by Captain Detweiler and Colonel Duncan, bypassing Shallow who warned me not to deviate from the official training schedule.

It seemed that only me and a couple lonesome privates were absent from the anxious mob at daily mail calls by the company water supply, a hanging Lister bag. Kitty and I were having a little misunderstanding over the claim she kept harping on that I didn't love her anymore; all I really wanted was to be off in the Infantry to be a hero with that O'Brien character I met at summer training. She maintained that I was tired of her and refused to have another kid.

"Crimus!" I wrote, "from way over here and what's wrong with heroes? Some people respect heroes."

Real estate was rough in Watertown what with no building during WWII, shortage of materials and labor, and the apartment Kitty finally found, she complained, turned out to be a rat's nest. She wrote that I had no idea how hard it was to bring up Dickie in a lousy apartment where you froze in the winter and now in the summer was sweltering with no central air-conditioning and her old secondhand Maytag danced all over the kitchen floor, had a leaky hose making a swamp of the linoleum floor, the boards of which were rotting.

I got an especially insulting letter describing her "garden apartment, they have the nerve to call it," she wrote. "It's a pigpen. Someone is always taking the parking spot for my apartment and a couple crazy young men moved in next door that wrestle and pound on the wall and get Dickie crying. And when they're together sometimes I think they make indecent remarks as I pass by. If you were home, they wouldn't dare. The old Maytag wringer-washer is broken again and they have to send to Syracuse for parts and where will I get the money? And the truck's down again— won't even start."

"Should of bought a new washing machine. We had almost a thousand left, where'd it all go?" I wrote back. "What did you spend it all on, plus what I borrowed on my pay? What did it all go on, I'd like to know. Is Bud up on his payments?"

Me? My full-time family was right here in and under the ground with me. I had all I could do to look after them, and where in hell were Kitty's mother and stepfather, Bud, and older sister and brother-in-law; couldn't she get any help from Betty? Bud's a real tough guy, why doesn't he clean their clocks? In a pinch, I think she might even depend a little on my father and Emma . . . if it got bad enough.

Instead of bringing to focus images of Kitty, for some reason when I thought of sex and got horny, it was Holly's bitch, a powerful earthy urge, the looks of her on Holly's couch would raise a hard-on in a second. I could tell she'd put out to near anyone. I jerked off a few times thinking of her. Man, what a piece of ass she'd be, ripe for pluckin,' mighty good fuckin'! I could see from that strip tease nude pictures she needed a real stud to nail her down. I was just the guy. But I was careful every time I put the blocks to her to say something good to the memory of Holly to compensate. Honestly, Holly, you were a damn good fighter.

I was a loner, unfriendly, Kitty'd say, wasn't selling any of my 'stuffy' writing, which pissed her off.

"Who likes to read about colonial wars?" she'd say. "Why don't you learn to write sexy novels, ones that make a pile of dough like Mickey Spillane? I read how he got started making his first million. He was no writer but simply sat down to write a little book to pay for a home he fancied in the suburbs; he never considered himself a professional writer but created a fantasy character called Mike Hammer that everyone respected who didn't fool around but took care of evil Russian undercover agents with all kinds of diplomatic immunities by meeting them in an alley in New York near the UN building and splattering their brains on brick walls with a surplus Army forty-five while CIA and FBI hands were tied. Why can't you write something simple like that?"

I wasn't being hoity-toity when I tried to explain that I couldn't write fiction, hard as I tried; like a fine artist painting signs. They used to ask me since I was an artist to paint them a sign. "Can a sign painter paint you a picture?" I'd tell them.

The first week in Korea I wrote three letters and spent a lot of time composing poetry. I'd show a few here but I never got around to copyright them. One I liked very much began: "Never let them say he cringed when he died/Rather should they say they lied/who would say he faltered in his stride." This will give you some idea how serious they were. Rereading some even today brings a lump to my throat. I dedicated them to Kitty and imagined tears in her eyes when she read them and waited patiently to see what deep effect they had, but our letters deteriorated and there was no room for poetry.

Her mail was scanty. English was never her strong point, she'd say. For a while with me there was little time for letter writing anyway, as I said, and one day after I returned from the Third Station I was surprised to get a letter from an old friend of Kitty and mine, Alice Wardwell. Alice wrote, "It took me some time to get up the nerve, but as you must know, Dud, I was just divorced and that makes you moody. I knew you must be blue, too, and Kitty told me to go ahead and write to you; she knows we go way back together in Watertown High School." Alice said she always admired my standards, riding off like one of King Arthur's knights to join the Royal Canadian Army when they needed real men, and if there ever was a real man in Jefferson County, it was Dud Gould.

I got about a dozen letters in all from Alice like that and if you laid them all out, it was easy to see how she was falling for me. "Laid them all out," a pun maybe, like I used to lay her. She must have reminded me in at least four letters how we were in love, or thought we were, long before Kitty came along, and "remember what we used to do on your couch when Emma was shopping and your father was at the Masonic Lodge?"

She kidding? How she was just sick to think of the four years wasted with Norman Short when she knew deep in her heart it was me she loved all along, even though I went off and married one of her best friends.

For a time I was right there in front of the company Lister water bag like a homesick private even before they announced mail call—like a real waterhole attracts thirsty animals. Do you know there's even a bugle call for mail call? They'd blow it at CMTC and some forty other calls, including even one for swimming in Lake Champlain.

I agreed with Alice about Norman; what a jerk! I had a little fight, shoving match really, with him once when he tried to run down the CMTC. He stayed out of the Services in WWII with a hernia he never got fixed until 1946 and was never afterward the guy we used to go ice skating with on Beaver Meadow.

I even went so far myself to hint to Alice that I might be more than a little interested in her. She was some of the best pieces I ever had, a little on the plump side the way I like them. I reminded her I like something to get my hands on, especially tits, hard nipples to suck and asked for a wallet-size photo of herself, you know, full-length showing things. Know what I mean? Some sex in it.

Frankly, I never fantasized about oriental types; not enough meat, skinny little things with no tits, or even nice legs and plump asses to think much about. A lot I saw were bowlegged. Besides, there were more Western broads than one could shake a stick at.

Reason enough was that the only women I saw, aside from Army nurses after joining my outfit in Korea were refugees, almost always from a distance coming through MLR check points, pushed through by the enemy. From our ridges, they're hard to study even with binoculars. These were all back country women, what you call peasants, who, Fred said, dressed as in the days of Genghis Khan, always in a homespun natural undyed hand-grown spun cotton material with middy blouses they pull tightly over their breasts as though to hide them. They're tough cookies for my money; nothing weak or happy or feminine about them—hard-working, rice paddy workers, no feminine softness to get your teeth into, so to speak.

You used to hear a lot about slipping saltpeter into the food of prisoners and other all-men concentrations to cut down sex drive. Before WWII I remember hearing it about the CCC, Civilian Conservation Corps, and the Army. I doubt if there was any in our C rations for I'll have to admit that I pulled the pudding once in a while. I didn't intend ever to jack off but a few nights, alone in our hole, I had a series of pretty sexy reminiscences and a hard-on came by itself without my so much as touching it. I'd heard you weren't supposed to play with it when you grew up and I only took hold of it to try to quiet it down, and one thing led to another and it refused to lie down so I decided to slap it around and it felt so damn good I kept on pushing it down and pulling it up. You can imagine what happened. I jerked off a few times after I got that string of ten or twelve redhot letters from Alice Wardwell with pictures. Some guys who probably aren't good at it or lack a hormone or two won't even talk about it, don't realize how much concentration it takes to keep pulling steady faster and faster without missing a beat to the climax and how much imagination you need to be good at it—and what a deep thrill and relief it is to pop off after all that day-dreaming, yearning and frustrated desire. Almost drive you mad like the

174

real thing. It was good hand exercise too. Usually I was so calmed down I fell sound asleep for it was always night and so relaxing to get rid of that sex drive. One of the most rewarding things about being over the hump as I am today, that damn sex drive never bothers you.

I jerked off on the QT, I'll admit it, when I was sure J J and Doc were asleep, catching it in a 4x4 Carlisle bandage. After all, I didn't lose my dinky just because I went to war. I hesitate writing about this underhanded thing (pun intended) and you never read about it, for no respectable person admits doing it and there's never been a survey that I know of. It's everyone's best-kept secret, why I don't know. Can't tell me I'm the only guy who slaps the bishop once in a while when he's lonely and his imagination runs away with him. I'll bet even healthy generals—we all got a set of balls, right? I remember back in the late twenties—early thirties, when you couldn't say whore or venereal disease, and there was more syphilis and doses of clap than today.

I've done some reading other than early American military history, my share about sex. Don't kid yourself mister stuffed shirt, sex is the primary function of all living things. Even plants live for sex and nothing else is as important. While you're not looking, they have their own sneaky sex, this thing, male, into that thing, female, just like us slow and quietly. Man has been known to die for and during it. More than rats or rabbits, he overestimates his responsibility to perform. Unlike most animals, except for a few days every month and sometimes not even then, the female, that's your girlfriend, uses sex purely for recreation, simple gregariousness, personal power, monetary gain (well, maybe not *your* girlfriend) and the sheer animal fun of fucking, and I don't believe Lord Chesterfield when he grumbled: "The pleasure is momentary, the position ridiculous, the expense damnable," or T S Eliot—

> *Birth and copulate and death,*
> *That's all the facts when you*
> *Come to brass tacks;*
> *Birth, copulation and death.*
> *I've been born and once is enough.*

Once, when I was a kid and we were jawing about sex, one of the older guys stated authoritatively that doctors can always tell a guy who jacked off too much because hair would begin to grow in the palm of his hand. I almost fell for that and two of the guys did take quick peeks.

It wasn't hard to keep up the jerks with Alice in mind because I actually laid her and she's the hottest screw I ever had, easy to visualize way over in Korea. Man, would she moan and groan and scream; built like a brick shithouse. I confess I also masturbated a few times imagining I had Holly's redhot piece by the ass. But real sex over in Korea was only for rear echelons like MPs. Up in the mountains we didn't have time and energy left over, even if there'd been women; not where we in the Second spent our time, puffing up trails that must have been there for hunters hundreds or thousands of years.

I hinted to Alice if I ever got home we'd have to do something; that Kitty and I weren't getting along so hot any more, always complaining that I didn't love her. Alice wanted me to swear that Kitty and I were getting a divorce when I returned, for she couldn't sleep with me knowing she was cheating her friend. In a letter dated eight days later she told me that, without waiting for me, she point blank called and asked Kitty if it was true that we were separating. Kitty was indignant and wanted to know who told her such a thing. Like poor Holly, out of the blue I got a dear John letter, but not from my wife—

Dudley—One of you is lying and until I learn the truth, I'm steering clear of you both. Forget all those crazy things I told you about what me and you used to do on the couch. Before you get any more crazy ideas, I must inform you that Norm and I are getting back together. Something was wrong with us to break up in the first place. When I received your first letter I thought it a bit irregular but knowing how lonely you guys in Korea must be, somehow I felt it was my patriotic duty to cheer you up, and I gathered that you and Kitty were contemplating a divorce. I've always known you to be a dreamer but how wild can you get. Me and you together again? Never! If you were pulling my leg with those mushy letters, I want you to know I don't find them a bit humorous. Your so-called poetry stinks.

Bitch! Who wrote first I'd like to know!

I guess I did insinuate a little that Kitty and I might be breaking up and now that Alice told Kitty, we'll break up for sure. Perhaps it's just as well the way we're falling apart anyway. One way or anther, everything was falling apart. For some reason I was unaware of, I was a "dirty rat," had "run off to war to be a big hero," leaving her in a dangerous, dirty apartment. Ever since the 1950 Reserve camp, I'd been a different person she said. I ran off to be a big hero, leaving her with the baby, a washing machine that didn't work half the time, cockroaches, and hardly enough money to get along.

"Now that you told Alice we're getting a divorce, we might as well go through with it, but the Army better do it for us because we don't have the money."

Crimus, with the pile of dough she spent on new furniture, why didn't she buy a decent washing machine?

During my entire time in Korea I received one letter from my father; just as well, always criticizing me for not finishing college. "Look where you've landed." I got one from Emma explaining proudly how she signed for the telegram and broke the news gradually to Ernest. Broke what gradually? What, being nicked, in the hospital all of three days? My father's one page letter: "I regret that I didn't order you not to attend CMTC.... You were still under age. It has been military, military ever since. . . . You do such immature, foolish things."

"Happy businessing to you, Mister Gould."

*   *   *

I marvel sometimes in writing this journal how few of us company grade combat officers made it back whole and are still around. Must be just bad luck but so many of my surviving fellow infantry lieutenants have dropped off one way or another in Korea or home from Korea; Carse of cancer in the '80s and Sandy, the most inspiring warrior I've ever known, together in F Company albeit for only several days, had, when I was finally able to contact him, strength enough to give me only two greetings, two days in a row for about ten minutes each. His wife shut me off both times because he was so weak and he died in his bedroom two hours after my last call where they brought him three weeks earlier to pass away. Sandy should never have done that, passed away, he should have died sword in hand.

I tried over a year to locate Sandy, until November 1995, when, through the efforts of our Korean War Veterans Alliance, and the miraculous National Telephone Directories Select Phone Computer, they located nineteen Opoulises with unrestricted phones in the USA. Sandy, Alexander, was the second on the list, in Charleston, South Carolina. I'd been concentrating all along on the Mt Kisko area from where he first joined the Army.

This super-valiant infantry officer held two well-earned Silver Stars, one in Italy before he was eighteen, one in Korea as a platoon leader and two Purple Hearts in Italy, before his final wounding in Korea. At age nineteen veteran second lieutenant of the 34th Iowa National Guard (how he got there, I never found out), he was invalided out of the service with a forty percent disability medical pension. When the Korean War came along, Sandy waived his pension to come back on duty. He shared my disgust of Major Wilkes, although I never got details except that he once gave Sandy an Article 15 for a supposed offense but Sandy had so little time to talk anymore.

Now bedded with fair virgins in the land of his father, sipping wine in the shade of olive trees, tonguing a bunch of grapes, enjoying gentle strumming zithers, far away from the threatening foes we guarded against as terrorizing Chinese moons waned. Sandy, by god, I salute you. Sandy left home at seventeen, his immigrant Greek father signing, applauding and warning: "I hear you run, my son, don't come back, you're not my son"; the father Sandy talked to strangers about with bursting pride. Sandy, the fearless, invalided out as was Sergeant, finally Second Lieutenant, Pater. I'm so damn proud to remember. Sandy, old buddy, you are alive within me long as I go on.

Fred Hurtz and I were quite thick but I was never able to locate the right Fred Hurtz in the New York area. Carse and Sandy dead for sure; I sometimes wondered about Fred, maybe his phone is unlisted.

Close though I was to my guys on line, back in reserve it was more like stateside; you shouldn't fraternize with enlisted men. I didn't have to discover this fact in Korea, I learned it well at the end of WWII in Europe when I got a delayed four-bottle liquor ration. With no officer friends to share it with, my sergeants and I crawled into a hay loft of an old barn outside Budejovice, Czechoslovakia and had a little party. The next morning I was hauled on the carpet, hangover and all, by my battalion commander who chewed me out good for fraternizing with enlisted men. Lieutenant Colonel Gladding once killed a kraut paratrooper with his bare hands in a fair fight after he had dropped behind our lines in a GI uniform at night to knock off generals and other brass. The colonel, a lieutenant in the Yankee Division National Guard unit at Springfield, Massachusetts had earned his living delivering ice on his shoulders house-to-house, so we affectionately called him the *Iceman*.

He also told me I had no right to dismiss my orderly, even though he didn't like the idea either. All officers had enlisted orderlies, privates first class for company grade officers, to care for their sleeping quarters, make their beds, etc. and assist in other servile ways. It went dead against my grain but my orderly never complained for it got him out of a lot worse jobs. The Hoover Commission after WWII did away with these so-called bat men to shine boots and do personal work for officers. Baron de Steuben did the same at Valley Forge, where he found every quartermaster major with three personal soldier servants.

Our regimental 105mm artillery, 38th Field Artillery battalion, had its artillery park in reserve several miles distant from us to preclude straightlegs (infantrymen as opposed to bowlegged cavalrymen and redlegs, artillery mixing it with them, red being the artillery color.) At every reserve period like this, there were plenty in the infantry who wished physical harm to the "Goddamn artillery that lowered on our guys." As far as I can recall, we were short-rounded four times, the last in November, so bad they had to take Love Company off line and lock me up, so to speak. I have little or no memory of that real close one but have had it reconstructed for me by fellow survivors. I understand fifteen were killed outright and fifty wounded there on H 1243, including me in a nonbloody way.

Major General Young, Rufner's replacement, ordered the artillery to set up county fair pieces and for Div Arty Brigadier General Thomas DeShazo to give us a lecture, explain how pieces were laid and sighted and used in general and hopefully sweeten some of the bitterness. But there continued to be bad blood in us who had buddies killed and wounded by the bastards. We had nothing against cannon crews, that would be like blaming the weapon; it was officers at fire direction centers and forward observers who gave wrong information. There were no computers in those days but artillery fire directing under officers and fancy guidance equipment seemed foolproof enough to us to have prevented it when properly used.

"Nobody is more sorry about those fine young men you lost than the artillery, but for reasons we have tried to explain, accidents will happen," DeShazo mouthed.

"Ever consider paying better attention to where you bastards sight those barrels," I wanted to ask him but it would have started a riot.

Muffled cat calls came at the end of the general's talk from the rear of our infantry group and then loudly, "forty-eight! ... forty-nine ... fifty ... so-o-ome shit!" As Shallow ordered Love Company to fall out, I cautioned Sergeant Eppler, "Let's get them out of here before some redleg gets hurt by a short round of our own."

Our greatest enjoyment, aside from most of the movies, some of which we saw before their being released in the States, were hot meals, which was more of a sensual pleasure than it was for civilians. We hated parades and inspections. Organized athletics passed time, which we officers and senior NCOs refereed or monitored or judged in some way. Fortunately, we had a real gung-ho PFC with a PT, physical training, major in college to lead calisthenics.

Freddy and I respected each other, you might even say liked each other, as many do in a battle zone. With sudden death on their minds, buddies are contagious. He was a Jew, religious, but not orthodox, from New York which city I disliked the twice I'd been there looking for my orders, uncomfortable in the rush-rush of the subways and the mobs in the middle of the afternoon on the sidewalks in the middle of the week when folks back home would be working or at home raising the kids.

Fred figured he'd be as out of place in Watertown, so quiet, almost on the Canadian border. When people hear I'm from New York, they immediately think New York City. Hell, Watertown's almost 500 miles away. We don't have any big saltwater harbor to keep us warm in the winter and I've seen it forty degrees below, so cold moisture after a warm humid day freezes out of the air as hoar frost, beautiful paper-thin ice crystals over an inch high, at times so cold you can't get a six cylinder started without pouring boiling water over the head a couple of times and keep your battery well charged.

I got lonely once in a while, or homesick, or sad and sometimes an existence seemed meaningless without friends. I considered it an indictment of my personality that the one person in all the world I called friend didn't even write to me. Gordy Geddings volunteered over the phone as late as the afternoon before my departure. "Don't forget to write." He said it, not me. He certainly had time to answer the card I sent from 'somewhere in Korea' plainly marked with my return address, albeit Fox Company 38th, which would bounce back to APO (Army Post Office) at Division and be relocated to me in L Company, same regiment. Some people might say why didn't you write him another, and I say if one isn't enough for him to answer, to hell with him. I'm the one in Korea. Who needs buddies who won't even write.

Fred had a much better memory for details than me. It was fourteen years since I was in college. Once, when we got into real serious talk about death and dying, and religion, I told him about the book I started about my search for the soul. Kitty thought it was corny, and maybe it is, but I could never really say good–by to my mother. Some day, some way, our souls will meet somewhere. It's a fact that I came out of her, so young when she left, I've always thought we never parted, not my real mother, her soul, that is. Fred quoted Epicures, a Greek philosopher—

Death, the most awful of evils, is nothing to the living. So long as we are alive death has not visited us; once we are dead, we are no longer alive.... What we are, death is not; and when death is, we are not.

You have to run it by a few times to see what he's saying. Think about it; he's got something there.

I figure we don't understand death and afterlife any better than did Adam, who, according to the Christian Bible brought death on every living thing regardless of religious belief. It's not a proven fact but few refute it nor does anyone say the soul can't remain on earth outside the very fragile, accident-prone, microbe-ridden appendage, your body. The real you, the soul, has direct contact with Nature in tune with all that is, always, and that means before and after death of the body which as a hunk of clay doesn't matter. We don't have to stand in awe of the universe, we souls are part of it. One day the body turns to a stink worse than shit, but the soul, an as yet undiscovered form of energy, I believe, goes on living in unstoppable ways; reincarnating probably to make one living thing or another, like butterflies flitting from flower to flower.

Fred said, "the long habit of living indisposes us for dying, which we can't visualize, far less than being able to understand. Life, loaned to us for a short run, early on gets to be an unshakable habit, a necessity, a damned addiction; we can't imagine doing or being without it."

Yeah, since all provable understanding of what we think is reality begins in the input of our sense preceptors, it's inconceivable for us not to continue to perceive that way. How can one live without his perception of what he is? That's all life is, perceptions, animal perceptions. We can live without other humans, lonely as it might be, but lose oneself—our perceptions? What a sure way of becoming nothing, to be at last without oneself. How can my body let death murder me? No one loves me like me, no one outside my body ever could. The loss of myself will be unbearable; shit, I might as well be dead—which I might well be soon. But life is less than half of it, there's the *real you*, what the soul has left to do.

"I say I'm Agnostic," I told Fred, "and we nonbelievers of conventional religions have no place, church or temple or anything in which to record and dispense learning or preach opinions about our religion, or study the lack of it, and we must be Agnostic each by himself, taking the best wherever he finds it; like Agnostic Mark Twain used to say—

"Heaven for climate, Hell for company."

I doubt if Fred and I would have stayed for long side by side on a park bench in normal times or whisper together in a rare book reading room but, thrown together in the Army, submerged in an urgent cause, we were not only stuck together but, relatively speaking, enjoyed being that for it meant I was somebody else. I was rough, no doubt about it, but way down deep I am a frustrated poet and philosopher. Fred could bring it out, the only one around I could play up that side of me. We infantrymen were dogfaces. Me a wild, shaggy one; Fred, a well-groomed city dog who was smart enough to recall whole paragraphs of what impressed him. I'd try but like as not get it wrong like any he-man heretic allowed to dream.

We would naturally seek each other's company when there was time to kill; sit at the movies together, eat together, etc. and when apart store up subjects and things to say the next time. We more than tolerated each other.

With but only two years college, I didn't even get to major, my formal education was nothing compared to his—at twenty-five, working on a PhD. The one thing we really had in common was reading; his philosophy and religion, especially oriental, mine early American military history. I hadn't any money to travel around to hunt down primary sources, like college history professors do to impress other professional historians, or have graduate students help me for nothing, but I had in three years of my free time emptied the Watertown Flower Memorial Public Library of early American military history ideas and used interlibrary loan for many more books, and yes, later, build us a little house in Syracuse. If I did finish a book, there'd be no need for an acknowledgment page. I had to scratch a living landscaping and the past two years at the foundry, but I'll bet a lot of good historians started out small.

Fred tutored at a girls' school part-time and no doubt was sharper than me but I picked up a few choice tidbits myself in the six years more I lived. He was better educated and more recently, whereas I had to search to recall facts which had dwindled down to rough ideas, his were nearer the surface, so to speak and refined as with scholars, and he could quote a lot accurately where I could only cover it roughly without much detail.

If you asked Fred why he joined ROTC, when his avowed interest was academia, he admitted he was also incurably romantic, as I guess I am. Without being able to explain it, we felt a tingle up the spine listening to the Star Spangled Banner and watching the flag going up or down. How corny can you get? That's us.

"It's mostly unexplainable," we agreed.

One afternoon I came right out and told him, "You're the best Jew I ever met."

"Out of how many?" he laughed.

"Oh, I've rubbed elbows with a few."

"Meaning what?" I wanted to know. "What do you mean by that crack?"

"Since you aren't Christian, you can't go to hell like your friends and relatives."

Stephen Crane had the right idea—

Men never have deserved Christ and Buddha because they went to work
and changed the teachings of generosity into teachings of wars and threats.

What difference does it make what you believe and aspire to? Death's pulling
you down one way or anther, which reminds me of a Mesopotamian tale, what they
now call Iraq; let's see if I get it straight—

A merchant's servant is jostled by Death in the marketplace in Baghdad.
The frightened servant begs his master for a horse so that he can flee to
Samarra. Later that day the merchant meets Death and asks him why he
had threatened his servant. "That was not a threatening gesture," Death
says. "It was only a start of surprise. I was astonished to see him in Baghdad
for I have an appointment with him tonight in Samarra."

As I say, I never had much to do with Jews or Hebrews, whichever name they
prefer. I didn't live or work near any. The same with Negroes, never having anything to do with them, hardly ever saw any except in movies. I still don't know
whether they want me to say Negro, black or African-American. Black, small b, is
not just them, it's an adjective, ironically for any object that reflects no color, but I
don't think I'll ever settle on African-American. It's geographical rather than racial
and too long. Negro is Spanish and Portuguese for black; Latin is *nigrum* or *niger,*
bigots' nigger, French, *negre,* which seems to make Negro more plausible. Nigger
isn't bad as it seems. It's the way it's used. If African-American is correct, then
English-American, Canadian-American? English-German-and-a-little Scotch-Ameri-
can every time you to refer to me?

When Fred Hurtz heard about Tree kidding that he was our token nigger, he told
his guys he must be their token kike but the humor fell flat; most guys outside New
York City never heard kike. I remember in WWII soldiers weren't divided by religion but every outfit in the Army had to have a guy from Brooklyn for comic relief
and if you were real lucky, a tall skinny guy called Tex who talked slow and was
philosophical in a homely way. No one was broken down into race and religion. The
lines were drawn naturally in segregated labor units and no white guy even mentioned the differences.

*   *   *

Shallow displayed himself each morning in clean, starched fatigues, spit-shined
boots and a louder than necessary commanding voice. He looked forward as none of
the men did to the first formation when he would have Love Company, his private
property, assembled before his headquarters tent.

"Lieutenant," he once said, calling me aside. "You're a disgrace to the uniform;
those grease spots, what are they? Look at you. You're supposed to be an officer."

"Oil for guns, sir, we get to use it."

We who had been in combat hated awards and decoration parades *they* always put on for *themselves* when in reserve long enough. Captain Shallow and other staff-type officers were in their element. He came alive in reserve and tried to look masculine and militarily important in front of our twelve-man-wide mass company formation, shouting orders. Another opportunity for him to putter with us, bookkeeper came to mind before commander.

"Let's dress it up in there. If you're taller than the man ahead, step in front of him. . . . Left face! Now if you're taller than the man in front of you, step ahead. Steady now! What's the matter with you noncoms, don't you know anything? The eighth man there, no, not you, stupid! Let's see, the one, two, three, four, five—the fifth man there, move up one. Yes, *you,* Goddammit, the fifth man in the one, two, three, fourth row.

"Okay, now, the fourth file there, a hair to the right. Side step; hear me, side step. No! No! No! Goddammit, too far. Short side step! Just a hair now. Noncoms and officers, get your men on the ball. Shape up!"

From some anonymous one safe within the massed men, "Heard the guy, one cunt hair!"

Loud guffaws, Captain Shallow bellowing, "At ease in there!"

Fussing that way on minute details for half an hour in the blazing sun while other companies were resting in place, pacing back and forth, with steamed-up dark-rimmed glasses before the front rank of six-footers, he finally gave us rest.

"Rest! No moving! I said you may rest now, but no smoking and keep one foot in place. If you don't get on the ball, I'll stand you at attention for an hour. We'll be out here every night practicing." As an afterthought, "Keep your right foot in place."

"Why don't they hand out the phoney decorations and be done with it?" Sergeant Eppler muttered in ranks.

Standing first on one foot and then the other, I fumed. The sore on my thumb, about a month old, cracked open again. Seemed every time it was about healed, I whacked it on something. Sucking on it thoughtfully, I fell into an elaborate daydream about the big parade they were having for me in Washington, D C. . . . There was a much larger and fancier band in flashy red, white and blue dress uniforms. The President of the United States of America, Harry Truman, was there, along with Congress and a bunch of beautiful movie stars who stood on the sidelines, awed and terribly impressed after looking me over good. I almost felt sorry for Kitty, but she had her chance.

Although theoretically I was able to will whatever happy ending I wanted in my daydreams, I tried to stumble on a bona fide one that might evolve naturally, believably in my favor. More like the real thing.

What I had done to inspire this fancy parade in Washington was to volunteer to parachute into Moscow, Russia late at night with a black chute and knock off Joseph Stalin. I got the job done without too much trouble, although my pistol misfired and I had to finish him with my bare hands, a couple well delivered karate chops, but when I tried to fight my way back out of the Kremlin, they finished me off and I died with my finger on the trigger of my special-built Tommy gun, 1000 rounds per minute blasting away at the bastards, yelling, "C'mon, you stinking Commies. Come get me!"

The State Department threatened to go to war if the Soviets refused to give my body back, and they were so scared after their leader was killed that personal way, they forked my body over. I was easily the biggest hero in the world. Probably what with our modern communication networks the biggest the world had ever seen. My eyes were swollen shut and my face black and blue from the terrible beating they gave me before I died, but a scientist at the Watertown Junior College was able to bring me back to life and . . . no, I ought to get out alive so I could tell Washington the secrets I learned. Wipe out everything back to the point just before I was killed. Then, because I spoke Russian so fluently and had such an engaging personality, I talked a battalion of the infamous Kremlin Guards into revolting and we shot our way out of Russia and across the Iron Curtain into Western Germany. Quite a few Ruskies were killed. The Luftwaffe flew me directly to Washington to report to the President. They had this big parade in my honor and I had to walk across the wide, impressive parade ground like a smooth golf course, with newsreel cameras, and cops trying to keep back the crowd. That day was proclaimed National Dud Gould Day and is still celebrated in places where real heroes are appreciated.

Jim McKinney from the Watertown Times was in back of a lot of reporters from the big papers. There was a hush when I started across the parade ground all by myself and it took five minutes for the President of the United States to settle down so he could put the Congressional Medal of Honor around my neck.

"Lieutenant Gould," the President said in a solemn voice. "I was, as you know, an artillery captain in the War to End All Wars, but I would far rather have done what you have done than to have been the first President of the United States, George Washington. Because of your extraordinary heroism, never before equaled in history, the Communists are disbanding the world over. I predict there will truly be peace in our time."

A big dance, no, a ball, was thrown in my honor with important movie actresses and dignitaries from all over, including generals Eisenhower and MacArthur. Everyone was cultured, intelligent, and noble looking. The Secretary of the Army insisted I wear a special uniform with more braid, all solid platinum, not gold, a present from Wall Street bankers, better than General MacArthur's that he designed himself, with more gold braid sewed all over, and ten rows of ribbons. Even the Commies gave me one of their red medals which I was applauded by Congress for returning.

I breezed around the floor with beautiful movie actresses and when we danced by, people whispered, "That's him, Great man Gould" and they made me colonel on the spot.

The movie actress, Hedy LaMarr, laughed at a good joke I told her about Truman and we had a perfectly swell time and shacked up that night. What a screw, I'll tell you, she did more than make movies.

No, that's pouring it on too thick. Wipe out the part about Hedy LaMarr. It was actually a very beautiful but unknown Hollywood starlet who was naive and crazy as anything about me. She was real excited to be seen with me and she was stacked. Was she ever hot for me! She kept pushing it tight to me asking for trouble and that night she got it good, better than Hedy LaMarr who was starting to slow down a little.

The President stopped Tommy Dorsey's orchestra and announced that for my extraordinary heroism, Congress, in a special session that afternoon, had voted unanimously to make me a brigadier general, the first time since Custer an ordinary lieutenant jumped up so fast. Bloody Boots Coughlin would be my aide de camp.

I told Mister Truman it was nothing any conscientious American wouldn't have done if he was as courageous and athletic, and went on to tell him how rough the poor guys had it in combat and that they should get more recognition and what hell they had to go through. Truman reminded me again how he was an artillery captain in WWI so I nicknamed him, Short Round With Glasses. I made such a good, unselfish speech and moved them so much everyone had tears in their eyes and my agent had it copyrighted. The President remarked how modest I was, and what a truly great American and everyone clapped and shouted and cheered. Then the band started up—the Second Division band?

"Straighten up, Gould," Captain Shallow hissed. "Look sharp, you're at attention."

The regimental adjutant made his, to me, very funny adjutant's walk all the way across the field, fast little snips, snips, snips, pumping his arms like a walk racer, to the reviewing party and in a high, theatrical voice from across the parade ground, the size of a football field, yelled, "Persons to be decorated, fo'ward' 'arch!" After this was done, "Pass in review!" and in step with the band, we marched by giving our flag a snappy salute with "eyes right!"

Nominated by the division artillery commander, Brigadier Thomas E. DeShazo, and Major General Ruffner, Lieutenant William Baker, artilleryman forward observer, who really was caught on our outpost and killed back on 15 May, was awarded a posthumous Silver Star. His dog tags were used by an American-educated chink to try to lift artillery. No one questioned that award, although some of us who were there also wondered if it wasn't really him on his radio, just a matter of bad luck that he got killed and we survived, and he was given the medal for his bad luck. Some of us endured the same 'heroism.' The inference was made in his favor that he remained behind deliberately to call *in* artillery. Maybe he did, maybe he didn't. If he did, he didn't last very long. But nobody ever questioned a posthumous award to a captain or higher, if only for the sake of his survivors.

Next the adjutant sounded off, "Captain Seymour Green, Headquarters and Headquarters Company, the Bronze Star Meritorious, entered service from New York." No mention made in the powerful regiment grapevine that kept the guys abreast of everything, what the personnel officer was supposed to have done to earn it, although the redhot suspicion was he was one of the rear echelon who endorsed two DSCs and six Silver Stars for Regular Army brass in the rear. These were round robin deals wherein I recommend you for a Silver Star as do the right number of other endorsers, in turn for which they join in to write me up for a medal of lesser rank.

There was no sense that anyone was 'honoring' anything, nor pride felt or reflected in my men drawn up across the dried, bulldozed-leveled rice paddy. No, we who did the fighting bore the monotonous brunt of the parade, despising the rear echelons we faced who held parades for self aggrandizement, stealing combat infantrymen's badges and decorations, making us stand in a hot sun to watch them do it.

The CIB, combat infantryman's badge, was never intended for field grade officers and generals. It was devised toward the end of WWII by General Mark Clark's Continental Army command at Fort Monroe, Virginia originally for enlisted combatants only to lift the sagging morale of overworked footsloggers, small compensation for three long weary, thankless years of suffering on battlefields around the world while the vast majority of soldiers, rear echelon, enjoyed safety, cleanliness, comfort, women and hot meals. Later, along with the blue and silver badge of honor were light blue plastic tabs to wear behind crossed rifle insignia and light blue silk or nylon bibs to cover the throat like gorgets of old.

Cursed be the first dishonest general to assume possession of a wreath-encircled silver rifle on infantry blue of the combat infantryman. Some say it was Van Fleet as soon as they were introduced toward the end of WWII. General officers are not even authorized to wear crossed rifles insignia like infantry officers, instead, their stars allow them as generals to command any branch of service in the Army. The real exclusive pride of wearing the distinctive blue combat infantryman's badge and bib ended soon as every branch came out with its own colored bib and insignia background, maroon, for medics; yellow, signal; red, artillery, etc. After being in combat with the infantry, the Queen of Battles, medics were authorized their own all-silver combat medics badge, which they well deserved.

Field grade and general officers didn't stop there; they wrote one another up for Distinguished Service Crosses, Silver Stars and Purple Hearts. This is no secret and we were bitter about the phoney ribbons professional officers entitled themselves to wear via round robins. 'Fruit salad,' we called it and sometimes 'garbage'; aptly named, since the decoration system stinks to high heaven, inspired because rear echelon brass have to work in such false ways up a ladder to earn stars bestowed by Congress. The more pretty colored ribbons, the better chance of dazzling congressmen and making general, which promotions from there on must be individually approved by the Congressional Armed Forces committees. Valor ribbons belong to us nobodies who earned them on the field of valor, primarily enlisted men by the very nature of their work, numbers and proximity to the enemy, not by big shots far away who stole their decorations.

It was not bad enough that the dishonest recipients remained protected from enemies by us combat infantrymen, they were sneaky, dishonorable thieves, every last major, colonel and general beribboned with what they never earned. Such dishonor occurred while I served the Second Indianhead Division with at least one of Major General Ruffner's Distinguished Service Crosses, handed down by X Corps, Lieutenant General Almond's private club; one to every one of the original 1950 regimental commanders before leaving Korea. I would like to have compared the truth with the shit spelled out in their citations, which are not made public.

Recipients of Bronze Stars were not listed and in our Blue Book rank, names and organizations of the hundreds of Silver Stars winners for the period 1950 through 1951 were given in two pages. A half page was given for the Distinguished Service Cross, ranks and organizations not listed with the names, although there is plenty of room, which would obviously have been a great embarrassment as long as copies of the history lasted, for not only would it be obvious that every regimental commander and Ruffner had one, the majority of other field grade and staff officers also.

Medal of Honor was the one award they found impossible to steal, seventeen of which were awarded to heroes of the Second Division in Korea only three were earned by officers, two rifle platoon leaders and a rifle company commander. Most were posthumous. One of these was a brave young fellow rifle platoon leader of F Company 38th before my time. Not counted was Sergeant Burris in my own Banzai platoon who won the award posthumously for actions at Mundung-ni right after our Blue Book history went to the printer.

Guys like Sergeant Karl Eppler and the likes of Lieutenant Hurtz and I were not even made to feel we were a part of the Army; recalled Reservists who like ROTC were used as seen fit, while Regulars were unselfish professionals who did it because it was their careers which we could pursue only when the war was over. Neither Lieutenant Hurtz nor Sergeant Eppler planned on Korea but simply sought what little financial help we could while pursuing other ways —Fred a PhD in psychology, and me working to establish myself as a writer. Of the three of us, Eppler, bent on soldiering, needed less of the small change we got from Reserve. We all also just happened to have a little of the warrior in us else would we be wearing idiot sticks (crossed rifles infantry branch insignia)? That subtle feeling, seldom mentioned or understood, a hidden passion echoing down the years as loyalty to clan, patriotism or love of country from Neanderthal caves, caused me to look up to my brave Uncle Art above my own very conservative religious and politically correct father.

However, none of the fighting Goulds, Wiedemen or Spicers in my family tree, neither Emiro Spicer who fought with William the Conqueror, Duke of Normandy, in the Battle of Hastings in 1066, nor his namesake remained a soldier. Not Private Emiro Spicer, my grandmother Gould's grand uncle of the 71st New York Volunteers, a drummer boy who died from camp fever in the Andersonville Confederate Prison, nor Private Solomon Gould, my father's ancestor shouldering a borrowed weapon in the Pequot War in the Massachusetts Bay Colony in 1637, three years after landing in America, nor his great grandson Enos, one of Captain Lovewell's men in Lovewell's War Massachusetts bounty hunters a century later. Sergeant Nathan Gould and his cousin Captain John Gould wielded Brown Bess muskets captured from the British in the Battle of Sackett's Harbor, New York in the War of 1812. None of them made a career of the Army, but they were men who harkened to the fifes and promises of recruiters and picked up the shilling from the drumhead.

Populations and armed forces were thin in those days and standing armies did not exist except in Europe. When a part-time wartime American civilian soldier did an especially brave thing, that is, risked his life, it became known to all for whom he did it and was described briefly but proudly in dispatches sent back home and published in local newspapers.

While Congress voted medals of gold or silver in the War for Independence to high-ranking officers, designed and made by Parisian craftsmen with profiles of the recipients in low relief and names of the hero and what he was cited for, such outstanding leaders as Mad Anthony Wayne at Stony Point, taken entirely by bayonets. The first enlisted men of any Army since Caesar's who awarded leather wrist bracelet for bravery were awarded cloth purple hearts, which had nothing to do with wounding— two sergeants for whaleboat raids on Long Island from Connecticut and a Sergeant Brown for heroism at the Siege of Yorktown.

For every soldier not awarded a medal, though richly deserved, there are dozens of high rank phonies who got medals they didn't deserve. A whole regiment of Maine volunteers were given Medals of Honor in the Civil War by the Secretary of War merely for helping to defend Washington by extending their time of enlistment a few days, and many in the 82d Airborne received a Bronze Star Meritorious whether dropped in the afternoon scuffle at Grenada or not.

In the American Army today, valor decorations are so inflated by field grade officers they mean little, handed out freely, acquired by tacit agreement of commanding generals, who, to be promoted by Congressional committee, must have a chest covered with pretty ribbons, few of which can be identified by congressmen but are assumed to speak well of the recipient.

I got my Silver Star supposedly for firing "an enemy light machine gun from the hip leading my inspired men to victory." What a picture of devil-may-care! In the first place, I saw only one enemy light machine gun in Korea unless the imaginative rear echelon awards and decorations author was referring to a burp gun. Actually, after turning the left flank with Edsel arriving on top with my platoon, seeing gooks running north up the ridge, I turned a heavy Maxim around with the help of a couple of gung-ho guys (Maxims had two cast-iron wheels a foot and a half in diameter and a large cast-iron shield), charged it and fired, spraying the ridgeline north as much as one can spray with a weapon that goes chug . . . chug . . . chug . . . chug. I doubt we hit anyone.

I offer for scrutiny the combat fiction authored by a stranger to that action who quizzed no one in my battalion to my knowledge and never left X Corps headquarters, some thirty kilometers to the rear—

HEADQUARTERS
2d Infantry Division
APO 248 c/o Postmaster
San Francisco California

GENERAL ORDERS

28 October 1951
NUMBER   641

Section I

AWARD OF THE SILVER STAR—by direction of the President, under the provisions of the Act of Congress, approved 9 July 1918 (WD Bul 43, 1918), and pursuant to authority in AR600-45, the Silver Star for gallantry in action is awarded to the following named officer:

FIRST LIEUTENANT DUDLEY C GOULD, 02017049, Infantry, Army of the United States, a member of Company L, 38th Infantry Regiment, 2d Infantry Division, distinguished himself by gallantry in action on 29 July 1951 in the vicinity of Taeusan, Korea. On this date, during an assault upon an enemy-held position, Company L's advance was halted by the intense enemy small arms and automatic weapons fire. Lieutenant Gould, with complete disregard for his own safety, deployed his men and, firing an abandoned enemy light machine gun from his hip, led his men in an assault upon enemy positions. Inspired by his display of courage and spirited leadership, the men of his platoon successfully overran and secured the objective, inflicting numerous casualties upon the enemy. The gallantry in action and outstanding leadership displayed by Lieutenant Gould on this occasion reflect great credit upon himself and the military service. Entered the military service from New York.

Gould never did suffer from "complete disregard for his own safety," never, else he'd have perished long ago, nor did he ever find any 'abandoned' machine gun anywhere he could "fire from the hip," although he saw John Wayne do it in a movie, Midway or Wake Island, with a regular Browning 30 caliber (how he kept the belt from kinking wasn't shown), nor did we, the guys and I, "inflict numerous casualties" on any group. I hiked many miles up and down northern South Korea thirty some miles into North Korea, seldom seeing anything to take careful aim at. You pointed your weapon in combat, carefully aimed only when sniping. We ran the little bastards off with preparatory artillery and machine gun fire, our small arms racket and especially yelling and speed and steadiness in going up, but seldom saw them—never face-to-face unless dead or POW. I turned and caved in the left flank with a well-directed fire from about twelve rifles and a BAR as Ziggy led straight through and Corporal Edsel Turner again hustled guys. It was we all the way, never me, and we all went over screaming like eagles.

My award gives some idea how dishonest the American Army awards system can be. To begin with, the award was not initiated by my immediate superior, Captain Shallow or Lieutenant Colonel Duncan. Both would say I did my job well. Nor anyone with knowledge of my movements on the objective, as one would imagine it to have been, or observed in action as it should be with personal knowledge of what I did, but, like all awards initiated at X Corps, a DSC for each company on the outpost on 15 May, written by the Awards and Decorations Section of X Corps, and presented by former X Corps staff man, diplomat Lieutenant Colonel John Rowny, then regimental executive officer who submitted my name for taking Hill 1179, as the only officer there. Rowny retired a lieutenant general, chief of President Reagan's Strategic Arms Negotiation team with the SALT Disarmament Committee with the rank of ambassador.

I received a note of encouragement from Rowny, similar to ones Major General Robert N Young of Division was later to dispatch as personal messages via our battalion mailman. My good buddy, acting King Company commander Master Sergeant John Pater, received one very like mine and a belated field commission from Young.

Despite the fact that I led in taking the three highest knobs on the Punchbowl, 1179, 1181 and 1243, this letter and a Silver Star was all I received, not a DSC mentioned later by my battalion commander. I say with pride, without false humility or fear of contradiction, that I led taking those prominences because, not only was I, in each case, less than a platoon from the point man, but at 1179 the only officer on top of the objective until the following day. Me, the only officer left to Love in the field at the time of 1179. Roy Carse was the executive and remained in the rear.

While discussing awards and decorations let me introduce a strange phenomenon that has never been aired in public—the nameless public deciding that a 'true' hero has to be modest; the more self-

August Ninth,

Dear Lieutenant Gould,

I have heard nothing but good about you during and since the recent action. I shall personally see to it that you are given every possible consideration for an award for your valor in the last action.

You have the makings of a fine officer - a fine leader. I trust you won't let me, and others who like myself are betting on you, down.

Be simple, be energetic, show enthusiasm, take care of your men both by doing for them and by making them do for themselves. Above all know your job (and the other fellow should be given credit for knowing something too.)

I want to wish you sincere good luck and hope that by your attitude and ability you will win popular acclaim as one of the Rock of the Marne's best.

A CERTIFIED TRUE COPY   s/ E. L. Rowny
                                         Lt. Col. Exec 38th Inf.

William C. Haines
1st Lt   Inf
Adjutant

effacing and modest the more heroic he is unjustly assumed to be. What rear echelon self-appointed judge, I'd like to know, led those who definitely are not heroes in deciding that in order for a man to be recognized and accepted as a hero he has to be modest and unassuming, hide his medals and pretend there was nothing to the earning of them? Modest Admiral Borda might fit that hero picture, he and Major General William Dean, simply because it was proven they never did anything, in fact, should have been courtmartialed.

The following medals were presented in the Second Infantry Division in Korea from July 1950 to 15 November 1951—

Congressional Medal of Honor	11
Distinguished Service Cross	81
Silver Star	1538
Bronze Star	2910
Purple Heart	22,880

No braver war was ever fought, under more trying conditions, than that which was fought in Korea. In the Army, for example, 41,835 awards for valor, 117,315 Purple Hearts attest to this. The men were magnificent, and we should remember them so.

Cyrus R Vance, Secretary of the Army
March 15, 1963.

Sergeant Eppler, University of Michigan graduate, was picked up while not active in a Reserve unit. Like Fred, he was scholarly, who, as a history project, being of a warrior bent, traced the weakening of valor expressed in decorations from Pearl Harbor throughout that war, essentially, when left up to the dictates of dishonest, self-centered generals.

Lieutenant Colonel George Patton, in the field of combat in WWI as a tanker, earned a highly-prized Silver Star but this was the last time he was close enough to an enemy to honestly earn a valor decoration. General of the Armies MacArthur, strategist rather than combat soldier, was falsely awarded the Medal of Honor for leadership in the Philippine disaster, not for heroism in individual combat in which he was never engaged, not even in WWI. This is what the DSM, Distinguished Service Medal, was designed for, work generals do behind lines. By the end of WWII decorations had fallen in great disrepute among riflemen in many units because of the flagrant disregard for truth. Very few units led by honest generals allowed only bona fide decorations for valor, especially true in the British forces.

As this is written, abuse in decorations for valor was dramatized in the real life story of the former top US Navy commander, rear echelon Admiral Mike Borda, who proved to be as dishonest as the run-of-the-mill US Army generals only less adept at being dishonest. Unfortunately for Mike, no one wised him up on how to go about safely wearing a V for valor he never earned—get another admiral or two to write him up in a round robin.

The most disgusting thing about his case is the unabashed dishonesty in the quick reaction of top-ranking American officers, officials and the immoral draft-dodging Commander-in-Chief Clinton, rushing in to try to disguise that military crime as an asset; indeed, having appointed Borda to the top rank in the US Navy, make him seem to have done a truly heroic thing by giving up wearing a V for valor he never earned and being sensitive enough when accused by a magazine hack, retired Army colonel, a phoney himself, to commit suicide, which is itself a court martial offense contrary to Judeo-Christian principles.

Since WWII you can no longer tell heroes from ribbons they wear, those that used to signal outstanding valor now too often label a brown-nosing conniver, the higher the rank, the more true it is. In fact, today even staff officers dishonestly without conscience wear unearned Silver Stars, Purple Hearts and combat infantry-men badges, which, in the first place, were created for fighting *men*, not rear echelon high- ranking officers.

The US Army Air Force in the ETO, Eighth Bomber Command, Eighth Air Force, gave an air medal automatically for every five raids of the heavies, B17s and 24s. Medium bombers, Marauders, B26s, and Mitchells, B25s, were awarded the same for double the raids, one for every ten raids because they flew lower and went less deep into enemy territories; less certain to be jumped by fighters and hit by heavy caliber, high level flak and less exposure time. Those in the Eighth Air Force heavies lucky enough to finish twenty-five raids were awarded Distinguished Flying Crosses and shipped home to make bond tours. Such automatic issuing of valor decorations by-the-numbers saved commanders from having to make individual in-vestigations and decisions in each case. Not to worry, however, in fact damn few who survived twenty-five raids in the heavies would not have qualified. It came about also that so dangerous and arduous was the work of men who were in infantry combat in WWII, many on line for a number of months, and who had been awarded the combat infantrymen's badge, could receive an otherwise 'unearned' Bronze Star, meritorious, simply by presenting a copy of their War Department report of separa-tion. The majority never got the medal, for this was not generally known, and post-war demobilization spurred on by Communist propaganda was fast and widespread.

Generals buck for more stars by playing up to Congress, and US Air Force personnel, unless they volunteer to fly combat and show how brave they are, must earn their pretty ribbons for such efforts as good housekeeping, cleanest barracks, etc. Combat veterans in the infantry of the Army and Marines are no longer inspired to risk their lives for the hope of being decorated, if, indeed, they ever did, for today's sham decorations are but tinsel for the chests of cheating generals.

In his term paper in 1947 Sergeant Eppler predicted that the big colored ribbon show will become extinct, done in by dishonest overindulgence, as old-fashioned as the tricorn hats and fancy white lace of British Army officers during the American War for Independence; obsolete as fancy black-booted horse dragoons with their plumed white horsetailed brass caps, or the bearskin crown and dyed cattle tails of the Legion of the United States or the black top hat and coat with tails worn by the Fourth Infantry at Tippecanoe. All that distinguishes those now studying and prepar-ing for the likelihood of meeting death in their military professions are occasional dark blue or red berets and their highly technical killing equipment, otherwise, they're drab compared to knights of old and phoney general officers and colonels in today's American Army.

For our regimental parades, Second Division band played the 38th Infantry's adopted regimental band number, the *Colonel Bogey March,* a British Army tune. From across the leveled rice paddies we, with rifles or carbines at our sides sounded off with our own lyrics manufactured for the occasion, not so loud as to be detected —"Bullshit makes the grass grow green! Bullshit makes for greener grass." Older Americans remember *Colonel Bogey* as the theme song for the award-winning movie, *Bridge Over the River Kwai.*

Some of us cynics taught the jingle to our buddies of the multilingual Dutch Battalion and on our last review in that summer reserve, several Dutch lieutenant friends, enamored as they were with the sarcasm, got carried away and let out a "Bullshit makes the grass grow green" with such enthusiasm it was heard by the regimental staff and distinguished guests, including a visiting Congressman, across the parade ground.

Let me introduce a real hero who was so quietly awarded a posthumous DSC no one knew nor remembers except his siblings if alive; unknown, unapplauded, as are almost every DSC and Medal of Honor awards to enlisted men. The following is to a truly brave young Negro, from our Second Division history, the Blue Book—

> Award of the Distinguished Service Cross to Private First Class Lawrence H. Bater, Infantry, a member of Headquarters Company, 9th Infantry, for action against the enemy in the vicinity of Yongsan on 11 August 1950. Private Bater was a member of a motor patrol which was suddenly ambushed by a strong, determined enemy force. From well concealed positions, the hostile troops directed intense and accurate fire on the patrol, forcing it to withdraw. Private Bater, completely disregarding his personal safety, voluntarily remained behind to cover the withdrawal of the patrol as, under withering enemy fire from three sides, he steadfastly remained in place, fearlessly engaging the enemy with his rifle. Until killed by the intense enemy fire, he defiantly resisted the fanatically charging enemy, inflicting heavy casualties on them with deadly accurate fire. His heroic and selfless action resulted in the successful withdrawal of his comrades. Three days later his remains were recovered in the position he had held, the area around littered with enemy dead.

Contrast this honest, simple-to-relate heroism with the citation never made public, as were most ill-gotten awards, the rambling adventures of Major General William Dean, commander of the 24th Infantry Division. Not only was Dean responsible for having to take an infantry division off line for reorganization, he and his jeep driver, also his pilot, got themselves lost behind enemy lines, such a stupid goof off as should warrant at least a severe reprimand. Dean was not reported to the International Red Cross for months and, per custom, was dropped missing in action, presumed after a year to be dead. His wife was presented his posthumous Medal of Honor, written and ordered by fellow generals, signed by President Truman at a White House ceremony and collected his $10,000 insurance. His poor leadership before losing his way resulted in the wrongful deaths of loyal soldiers and nothing is generally known of the fate of his pilot-driver, Arthur M Clarke.

Dean, unable to get an appointment to West Point, came into the Army via ROTC, University of California Law School at Berkeley. He went on active duty in 1923 and in WWII won a DSC the hard way leading a rifle platoon through an intense kraut artillery barrage. The citation for his Medal of Honor was never made public and with good reason, for it must by necessity be contrived, nor was mention made in public how much more he deserved a court-martial for being responsible by poor judgement for the deaths of thousands of brave young Americans before getting lost in a jeep behind enemy lines.

Major General Dean was quoted by Clay Blair, *FORGOTTEN WAR,* page 139, Anchor edition, 1989—

"There were heroes in Korea but I wasn't one of them.... I was a general who took a wrong turn. In the fighting I made some mistakes.... I lost ground I should not have lost. I lost officers and fine men. I'm not proud of that record, and I'm under no delusions that my weeks of command constituted any masterly campaign." He was 'humbly grateful' for the Medal of Honor. "But I came close to shame when I think about the men who did better jobs—some who died doing them—and did not get recognition. I wouldn't have awarded myself a wooden star for what I did as a commander." ... of all the 'mistakes' Bill Dean had made as commander of the 24th Division, none had been greater than his decision to hold Taejon an extra day. The cost was frightful. Of the 4000 Americans deployed in defending the city with the 34th [Inf], 1150 (30 percent) were dead, wounded or missing and presumed dead, the vast majority (874) in the last category.... For the 24th Infantry Division these two weeks had been a ghastly time, one of the greatest ordeals in Army history.... It's surviving commanders could account for only about half the men committed to Korea: 8660 of 15,965. More than 2400 men—including Bill Dean—were missing and most of them dead.

Following General Dean's repatriation in 1953, one wonders did he offer to return the unearned, 'posthumous' Medal of Honor which almost without exception enlisted men and rifle platoon leaders must die qualifying for, and did his wife return the $10,000 life insurance?

When General MacArthur landed in Korea he gave Eighth Army commander Major General 'Johnnie' Walker and his own G3 operations officer, Major General Almond, a medal. According to Blair, "Rather than the *Distinguished Service Medal* [the generals' good conduct medal] which they might truthfully have qualified for, and he gave each a cherished *Distinguished Service Cross*, envy of every fighting man. Some who won the coveted medal on the battlefield would question if the award was appropriate," to which my guys would say, "sh-e-e-e-it!" And when General Ridgway announced the rotation policy in Korea as he began his tour replacing MacArthur, according to Blair: "Divers commanders and other generals who had completed six months continuous duty in Korea would go home. They were to receive glowing fitness reports and *medals*."

Speaking of medaling, when Van Fleet toured the battlefront one of his aides carried a satchel containing Bronze and Silver Stars and a few DSCs. Blair wrote, "He used them the way a corporate executive passes out bonuses." After the Second Division helped stop the May offensive in 1951, and Van Fleet personally pinned Distinguished Service Crosses on Generals Almond and Ruffner, the Baltimore Sun editorialized: "It was a generous gesture, yet it may be embarrassing to the generals when men of lesser rank sweated it out becoming a bit hard to learn that the superior, closer to the man who gives out decorations than to the enemy, is getting the glory."

Lieutenant Colonel Melvin B Vorhees, former Chief Censor Eighth Army 1950-1951, wrote in *KOREAN TALES,* Simon & Schuster, New York 1952—

> It is pretty safe to say that not five out of one hundred medals awarded US soldiers of the rank of colonel or above have any meaning other than that the man did the job he was trained by the government and paid to do. In addition, he had probably reached that point in his career when recognition via each award was due, according to what has become American military custom.

Most general officers commanding in the Infantry today wear combat infantrymen's badges and Silver Stars they never earned, with citations never made public. Take the citation to the second cluster to the Distinguished Service Cross for Major General Clark Ruffner, Second Division, which rambling account had to be lengthy to disguise the obvious fact that he didn't risk his life any more than any rank of combatant infantryman at the time, much less than those on the firing line. From our Blue Book—

> Award of the Distinguished Service Cross to Major General Clark L Ruffner, United States Army, Commanding General, Second Infantry Division, for action against the enemy in the vicinity of Hangyi and Umyang-ni during the period 16 through 24 May 1951. On 16 May, after an ominous build-up of strength, the Chinese Communist Forces launched a massive offensive against the Second Infantry Division and two Republic of Korea divisions of the United States X Corps with a force of an estimated 96,000 troops. Although the attack was expected and enormous casualties were inflicted on the enemy, the situation became critical on 16 May when Republic of Korea forces, overrun by a numerically preponderant enemy force, collapsed and exposed the right flank of the Second Infantry Division. At this juncture, General Ruffner personally visited the most forward positions [we were "most forward" and he was nowhere near] to rally his troops and reorganize the defense of a new line. Through his coolness, efficiency and indifference to danger, he assisted in extricating several units which had been cut off, narrowly escaping death on one occasion when the helicopter in which he was riding crashed on a mountain peak within sight of the enemy. [No, on an unlevel insecure pad about two miles away.] On 20 and 21 May, General Ruffner moved his division in a difficult lateral maneuver across the battlefront, *then personally led a counter-attack against the enemy.* [This is a blatant lie.] As a result of this brilliantly executed counter-attack, the hostile forces were routed after suffering losses 30 times as great as those sustained by the Second Division. On 24 May, General Ruffner organized and *led* a special task force to seize and secure a bridgehead across the Soyang River and sever enemy escape routes to the north. When the troops were stopped by enemy mortar fire, General Ruffner, *with complete disregard for his per sonal safety,* drove his jeep *near* the head of the tank-infan try column over a road that *had not been swept for*

mines and through the area of the hostile mortar fire. [There was no indication that there were mines.] This fearless action so inspired the officers and men of the task force that they mounted their vehicles and immediately resumed the advance. [As they were ordered.] By his brave and daring leadership, the objective was secured in minimum time, thus putting a force 12 miles deep into the territory held by the enemy force and severing two of its main avenues of escape to the north.

Ninety percent of this citation so-called for valor pertains to descriptions of the terrain, disposition of troops; none to describe anything specifically *heroic,* that is self- sacrificing or risky combat actions by Ruffner.

In no single incident of the lengthy citation is a prerequisite shown for any award higher than the Silver Star normally freely allotted to general officers. Not in any instance where it says he personally led does it mean that he was physically ahead of a platoon leader or even a company commander. In no way are generals ever leaders—they command safely from way behind; lieutenant, or sergeant rifle platoon leaders lead in combat; that's why they're called leaders.

His failure to see that the division's unneeded outpost-patrol base was pulled in, the only one left on the MLR, prior to 15 May 1951 was a costly error, whereas the Marines and other divisions across the left flank pulled in their outposts well before the arrival of the 200,000-man Chinese Fourth Field Army. X Corps, division, regiment, battalion and company left us on our outpost-patrol base thereby killing Sergeant Dorn and six good men, plus a two-man wire team and many others who had no military business on that hopeless hill, useless and very vulnerable, while the general, according to his citation for the DSC—

... personally visited the most forward positions to rally his troops and reorganize the defense of a new line.

Shit! General, we neither heard nor saw you forward of anything. No general officers entered our battalion zone without the grapevine passing around the news beforehand. In fact, one of his aides always radioed ahead of his coming to prepare us to greet and salute him. We, on the other hand, were *forward,* those left three miles ahead of the MLR, with a poor defense, a long nail on a sore thumb.

As to the chopper crash, being a passenger in the chopper when it tipped over, through the grapevine relating the most intimate moves of a commanding general as they happen, we heard the chopper merely tipped over attempting to land on unlevel ground; how else did he and his feckless pilot, who goofed and was awarded a Silver Star, get out without a scratch? Oh, I forgot, he did report a little blood on his right arm, good for another cluster to his phoney Purple Hearts.

No one was allowed to read the citation for months and the only way I know about this miscarriage of justice, this other unearned DSC, was because I was in the vicinity when it happened and our grapevines never lied.

It says that the day after the abortive Task Force Yoke (Joke) General Ruffner "...organized and led a special task force...." Led? The only officer in the Queen of Battles with the title for leading is the platoon leader, not a general nor a colonel, nor a major nor a captain. They command, we lead!

At the outbreak of WWII lieutenants commanded infantry platoons. Like all echelons, from platoon up to general, he was called platoon commander, but combat reality in Africa soon taught the Infantry that when shit hit the fan, rifle platoon lieutenants got nowhere simply commanding and their title was changed permanently to platoon leader whose motto is 'Follow me.' Lieutenants lead; all officers from company commander up direct and command. Ruffner's supposedly physically "…led a tank-infantry column…." No way, oh imaginative writer of valor decorations, chief of the special group of fiction writers at division called Awards and Decorations whose full-time job is to dream up such smoke screens as Ruffner's DSC. In lieu of a lack of heroism of the caliber even approaching the selfless Private Bater, it seemed to them sufficient that piecing together and exaggerating a number of duties he might have performed was equivalent to bravery.

In other words, General Ruffner with his jeep driver did what he was charged to do as an infantry division commander. Not once in this narration for the phoney award did he do a thing that other infantrymen, regardless of rank, would not and in numerous cases did do. The citation states that on 18 May, as we in my platoon were hoofing it in the cold rain, me without a blanket or poncho, General Ruffner "personally *visited* the troops." What a heroic move! "Through his *coolness,* efficiency and indifference to danger, he assisted in extricating several units which had been cut off…." Cool? Not nearly as cool, sir, as I was. When every division from the Marines east withdrew unneeded outpost-patrol bases, why didn't you, our fearless, efficient 'leader,' extricate *us*? As a concerned participant, I say that you and commanders on down made a bloody, deadly error—our blood, our dead, your error.

What PFC Bater did to really earn a DSC is described in one paragraph only because it clearly, obviously was heroic. He lost his life serving others. There can be no questions about it while the truth in Ruffner's long citation is camouflaged in suggestions and unrelated words. He did that which was common sense and very doable, not ventured as a deadly personal sacrifice out of love of his buddies.

War correspondents alone were in any position to expose such fraudulent doing by the brass to my knowledge, but none but Clay Blair ever did.

HEADQUARTERS
2d Infantry Division
APO 248 c/o Postmaster
San Francisco California

GENERAL ORDERS
16 August 1951
NUMBER   173

Section I

AWARD OF THE SILVER STAR — By direction of the President, under the provisions of the Act of Congress, approved 9 July 1918 (WD Bul 43, 1918), and pursuant to authority in AR 600-45, the Silver Star for gallantry in action is awarded to the following named officers and enlisted men:

PRIVATE FIRST CLASS THOMAS M MILLER, ER13204577, Infantry, Army of the United States, a member of Company L, 38th Infantry regiment, 2d Infantry Division, distinguished himself by gallantry in action on 30 May 1951 at Kosari, Korea. On that date Company L was on a patrol and had been ambushed in a narrow mountain valley by a well concealed and camouflaged enemy force. Private Miller voluntarily manned a .50 caliber machine gun mounted on a truck. Without thought for his own safety and completely exposed to a hail of enemy small arms and automatic weapons fire, he engaged the enemy with heavy fire, covering the withdrawal of his comrades. After the wounded had been loaded on the truck under the cover of his fire, Private Miller backed the truck along the slippery, wet mountain road for over two miles to evacuate the wounded. The gallantry displayed by private Miller reflects great credit upon himself and the military service. Entered the military service from Pennsylvania.

Mister Miller is retired today in Oakmont, Pennsylvania, as this is written, still working at a General Mills postal facility.

Typical of our medics is a Silver Star to—

SERGEANT ELOY MADRID, RA38085434, Army Medical Service, United States Army, a member of Medical Company, 38th Infantry Regiment, 2d Infantry Division, distinguished himself by heroic achievement on 18 May 1951 in the vicinity of Kunmul-gol, Korea. On that date, a strong enemy force attacked and overran the 75mm recoilless rifle platoon of Company L to which organization Sergeant Madrid was attached, wounding several members of the platoon. Sergeant Madrid, disregarding his own safety, deliberately exposed himself to heavy enemy artillery, mortar and small arms fire in order to give aid to the wounded. With the enemy within a few feet of him Sergeant Madrid nevertheless continued giving aid to a seriously wounded comrade. When given orders to withdraw Sergeant Madrid rejected the orders and remained with the wounded. It was ultimately learned that Sergeant Madrid remained for 36 hours near the platoon position, aiding the wounded, until he was himself wounded and evacuated. His calm, determined attitude in the face of enemy fire and his refusal to leave wounded comrades were responsible for the saving of many lives. The heroism demonstrated by Sergeant Madrid reflects great credit upon himself and the military service. Entered the military service from Colorado.

While mentioning real combat heroes, I should write of one who only his squad leader, Pop Miller, and I appreciated, PFC, class clown, Kiezlowski, Chicago orphan. It was on one of the last days in our long reserve when the cooks were burning trash in a big pit about thirty yards behind the mess tent. Some of the guys were horsing around not far from there during a training break when a grenade exploded. The flames had subsided and fortunately the pit was about five feet deep so the only fragments to escape sprayed straight into the air.

Someone yelled grenade and as they ran away, Ski ran forward and jumped into the pit. After pawing around desperately, he came up with a hot grenade which he tossed away from the guys. Pop and I knew that in his way of thinking it was a great danger. Why else do so foolish a thing, plus that, he burned his hands.

In 1943 in England, another guy and I dragged three Limies away from a crashed Lancaster bomber that was afire and got Soldier's Medals. I found out later that none of the three crew members were in great danger even from exploding ammunition, .30 caliber machine gun, flying relatively slowly through the air end-over-end, which exploding brass cartridges do when not confined to a gun barrel. It's doubtful that it would kill anyone; maybe bruise a bit. Like me, Ski's only intention was to save his buddies. My citation says that I did save them, which is probably stretching things because all three were thrown clear or managed to crawl outside the ruptured fuselage before I got to them.

I helped the awards and decorations guy at battalion, a PFC clerk college English literature graduate, write Ski for a Soldier's Medal and was feeling pretty good

Brigadier General Hill, Eighth Air Force Bomber Command, pinning on Soldiers Medal. I had just made corporal from sergeant for bringing to the base a displaced blonde from London and renting a spare room in nearby Bury St. Edmunds.

197

about it until the following day when Shallow called me over to say not only Ski was nuts but I must be too; he'd never endorse it.

The thousands of draft boards in the United States usually delivered us men in good enough shape, but at least four times that I know of in our battalion we got guys not quite all enough there to

Widely scatterd wreckage of the Lancaster bomber aborting from night raid.

be in combat. One was night-blind and another, aside from Ski who was marginal, was PFC Warren Woody from Worcester, Massachusetts, who went around with a wasted smile on his face, wasted because no one smiled back, hauling mail to and from regiment, playing on his black plastic flute. Major Duncan, with a mentally impaired son of his own, got along well with Woody, and Woody thought the world of him. In some ways, however, the major felt it might be better if Woody didn't feel so strongly lying in wait to salute him whenever Woody could catch him in the open.

Some of the big brains at battalion headquarters used to get their rocks off hiding Woody's flute and couldn't understand when the major ordered his headquarters company commander to put Woody in for specialist fourth class. You kidding? Woody, corporal?

Woody jeeped our letters back and forth from regiment in regulation locked heavy-duty US Mail sacks. One day, as Colonel Mildren delighted in telling it, a strange little soldier with a brand new SP4 insignia walked right into his private pyramid tent while he was shaving and without a salute proceeded to lay down the law, demanding to know "Why haven't you promoted Major Duncan. Every other battalion commander is a lieutenant colonel. Major Duncan is the best battalion commander we've had; he deserves to be lieutenant colonel."

Once he realized that Woody wasn't all there, Mildren was amused. In the meantime, battalion Headquarters Company's mess steward had been asked by the S3 to plan a party for the major since his well-deserved promotion was on its way. When it arrived, three tables were shoved together for Duncan's staff and guest, Colonel Mildren, with Corporal Woody at the seat of honor in the middle. Major Duncan stood up and asked Woody to pin one of his new silver leaves on him, thanking the little guy, and proposed a toast to Woody. Everyone cheered. Woody was surprisingly candid about it all knowing he deserved every bit of it, and graced the occasion with a new tune he picked up called *America*, with a few interesting asides which Woody explained were improvisations.

6

RELIEVE MARINES

Each departed friend is like a magnet that attracts us to the next world.
– Jean Paul Richter.

At 2200 hours on the 14th of July, 1951, Korean time, company commanders were paged by loudspeaker at the hillside battalion movie. Men peered knowingly at one another. The movie was about a mixed-up drunken playboy in New York City who wore a tux all the time and threatened to jump from a building. The fire department strung nets while a daring priest crawled along the ledge pleading for him to consider how his dear father would feel.

"It's no use; nobody loves me."

"Get your ass back in the room, Father," someone commanded from back on the hill.

"Let the sonofabitch jump!" another sneered.

"Think he's got troubles?"

"Push him!"

Then a chorus of voices began the chant: "Draft him! Draft him! Draft him! ... Forty-eight ... Forty-nine ... Fifty ... So-o-o-me shit!"

Battalion movies were overcrowded and there was no privacy and when I took my seat on the ground it seemed everyone turned to stare at me. It was never quite dark enough until the film was half over and ignorant guys were all the time making smart remarks and cat-calls. Just as I was in the mood for the romance each time, some jealous wisenheimer sounded off, "Hollywood he-e-e-*ro*!"

All kinds of winged bugs were attracted by the brilliantly lit screen, and swift, acrobatic night hawks (night jays or goatsuckers) would dart in and out of our view, winging swiftly right and left between us and the screen, feeding on bugs with shrill peep sounds. We knew them well, heard them up on the lower ridges after bugs as dusk fell, and early mornings as the sky lighted mysteriously before daybreak, familiar calls of whip-poor-wills in ravines below relieved us of tensions drawn taunt in the threatening darkness. Familiar, that is to farm and other country boys who could imitate their unmistakable whistle after dawn—whip poor will, whip poor will.

The film stopped abruptly and flood lights went on.

"Up and at 'em! Roll up! Roll up, you he-e-e-roes!"

"This is it!" guys shouted at one another. "Strike those pup tents, this is it! Let's go! Let's go everyone, let's go!"

"We're at it again, kiss your ass goodbye!"

We ran around like firemen moving to put something out; as though joining a race of some kind, throwing equipment in jeep trailers, shouting, "Load up! Load up! Hurry, you guys, let's go-o-o."

Me? I could never discover why the big hurry, concluding it must be mainly because of being excited by the very idea of what we were slated to do. From our Blue Book—

The Second Division had made good use of the well-earned period in reserve when, on 8 July, it received notice to prepare for relief of the First Marine Division between 15 and 17 July. All units had been reorganized and resupplied. Rotation had gotten into high gear and, as a result, training was speeded up to prepare incoming replacements for the days which lay ahead. Special service shows had been sandwiched in between training problems and the other activities of the period. Many of the officers and men had the opportunity to see Jack Benny for the first time in person when he brought his troupe to the Division Command Post for a show. [Men and officers of division rear ten miles south of any combat bivouac.]

But with the alert order in the hands of the units, all efforts were turned to put the finishing touches on the training program. Reconnaissance parties went out to view the Kansas Line where the active defense would be undertaken. Division engineers, who had been devoting their efforts to improving the roads to the reserve sector, shifted northward on 13 July and began extensive surveys and work on the roads in the new sector.

Onset of the peace talks had, of course, raised the possibility that an armistice might be reached at any hour. Few in Eighth Army wanted to take chances and be the last man killed. Rotation changed the face of the infantry, old hands replaced by thousands of newcomers green to combat. Signs went up: "DRIVE CAREFULLY. THE MAN YOU HIT MIGHT BE YOUR REPLACEMENT."

Some tankers nearby, bivouacking like a carnival, not alerted, pissed off to have the movie unplugged no matter how bad, baited our guys: "You're going to Koje-do! Chinks and gooks down there are rioting again. You guys get to change their diapers."

"Shit!" someone yelled back. "Forty-eight! ... Forty-nine ... Some shit!"

"C'mon, we got hiker boots for you tankers. Earn your living! Can't hide in them cans *all* the time!"

Hum of short conversations; guys running around giving and taking orders, trying to give away things they couldn't carry into battle, unloading on fortunate ones who remained in the kitchen trains. Certain highly nonmilitary objects were pulled out, checked and kissed; silver crosses suspended on more delicate chains than dog tags; a rabbit foot tucked safely in an inner pocket; a creased photograph;

very particular letters from mothers ordering 'boys' to take good care; and a souvenir copper good luck coin originally obtained way over value after a few beers at a county fair.

Personally, I never believed in the power of black cats or good luck charms, although, just to be sure, in the Royal Canadian Army I hung on to a Canadian twenty-five cent paper bill with a large beaver in color I got in my first months pay. The Canucks were the highest paid Army in the world and still are. While I was flying, I always carried a four-inch high blue-gray fuzzy lamb a nice girl gave me after a USO dance; when we were shoving off the next day on a top secret flight from Morrison Field, West Palm Beach for the southern route. "It'll keep you safe and remind you of me," she promised. What a frustrating night that was, my last in the States for three years and after rubbing against her belly for two hours and toward the end her not saying no when I gave her thing a pat and was ready to go for it all, an old geezer with WWI campaign ribbons across his suit coat pocket was sitting on guard by the door making sure innocent volunteers didn't leave with us horny flyers.

Down came neat rows of pup tents and fires blazed with absolutely nonessential letters from home and knickknacks the guys picked up here and there since early June. One GI tried to stuff down an entire can of peanuts in a few minutes. "Futsin damn louthy lut!" he sputtered. After push came to shove, all that was shoved in our packs was topped by a three-meal, thin cardboard box of C rations which had to be disassembled, a can in one pocket, a can there, cigarettes and the remainder under your T shirt, ass wipe in your helmet liner.

While I went to check my platoon in the dark, heavy-duty six-bys arrived from division trucking company, fussing and arguing, machines revving up and down and leveling off, shifting into a long line across the battalion bivouac like a string of high-strung heavy-muscled dragoon horses stomping and snorting, roped on a picket line ready to do battle.

"Okay, you guys," officers and noncoms ordered, "Off with them patches and mount up."

The proud Indianhead shoulder insignia were ripped off and slipped into pockets until the next reserve—if you were that lucky. Doc Carlson and other medics made beelines to the aid station to sign for morphine ampules, kept under lock and key by the medical service corps officer.

Young, prayerful replacements who came on line that reserve time with blue battalion would be dirty, tired old veterans, shaving what whiskers they had when they returned—or they were bagged—and mister, how they'd all like to make their own choice.

It rained lightly.

"'Bout time," Funaro said, pretending to be happy. "For a whole fuckin' minute there I thought we'd make one fuckin' move without gettin' fuckin' soaked."

We stood away from the trucks to piss and while I checked with squad leaders each man's harness, pack and equipment, a replacement motor officer, Lieutenant Von Holtz Werner, strode along the line shouting authoritatively, "Mount your vehicles. Make it snappy now, mount up."

When he reached our Banzai Third with his authoritative 'mount up,' I told him, "Stick to the motor pool. I'll take care of *my* men."

The guys snickered as the motor officer tried briefly to stare me down. "Lieutenant Gould," he said petulantly, "Colonel Duncan was the one who wanted it, not me."

At the next platoon, "Okay, fellows," he said, "the colonel wants us to move out in five minutes."

"You heard him," I ordered, "load up. On the double."

The guys jammed in, twenty-four to a truck, with all their personal fighting paraphernalia and cartridge belts unhooked to be able to sit comfortably. I crawled into one cab beside the driver. Before I could sit, I had to unbuckle my cartridge belt. Hooked to it were two canteens of water, a first aid bandage in a small web case, a carbine bayonet so short we called them knives, in scabbard, two pouches of thirty-round magazines for my carbine, two thirty round curved banana magazines joined upside down by adhesive tape in my carbine and a 38 caliber revolver I was given by a rotating sergeant in an issue 45 caliber revolver holster stuffed with rags to keep it from falling out.

On my left wrist was my issue luminous dial watch and a luminous dial lensatic compass, which, not having much occasion to use, I normally kept in my musette bag. On my body, strapped over my shoulder, across my lap or in my hands, always inches from me every minute once we left the kitchen trains, was my sweetheart, my faithful M2 carbine which Doc Lynch returned to me. Hanging from a strap around my neck was a pair of 10X binoculars.

The heavy six-by troop trucks rolled away slowly, while the four jeeps per company with trailers loaded with chop-chop, jerry cans of water, ammunition and what not, pranced by impatiently on the left shoulder of the road, led by Captain Shallow's number one jeep—flaunting high on an eight-foot varnished oak staff the blue pennant forked guidon with the large white L for Love Company. Captain Shallow, on the front seat, arms folded across his chest, stared grimly ahead, reminded me for a moment of pictures I'd seen of Hitler's storm troopers parading in the early years. Following were weapon carriers with ammo and the real bulky crew-served stuff.

I mouthed just audibly: "When this bloody war is over, we will all enlist again," to the tune of the *Battle Hymn of the Republic,* "like so much shit we will!"

"You must be nuts, lieutenant," the driver said, looking sideways. "First I seen happy going back on line."

"Depends on how you look at it. There's worse things."

I wasn't able to analyze the feeling at the time, but the guy was right. I was actually looking forward to going back to combat. Maybe excited like a high-stakes gambler would fit better. I was becoming hooked on combat; the excitement of anticipation as to which cards you will be dealt next, you never knew what would happen. We had a whole new batch of guys to add to those who joined us at Honchon, replacing those wiped out KIA, WIA or my nine MIA, Dorn's men and the three picked for wire patrol, and a few like Doc Lynch lucky enough to rotate.

What I was anxious to do, like any professional gladiator, was test my mettle again, 'test a man of mettle' which I believe originally referred to jousts of knights of yore in their metal suits. I tell the few people interested I wouldn't volunteer to go through Korea again, but I wouldn't trade the experience for anything. How many guys in this world get the opportunity to 'test their mettle' over and over? I did, as mettlesome as real men are. How many anymore get to don metal? Football players and hockey players don a little, maybe, as hooks and guards of their protective gear for an hour or so flat on ice or an attractive level green field. We packed metal up mountains of hills, pounds of canvas and webbing, metal clasps, snaps, rings, tools for heavy-weight, dirty work; weapons, explosives and ammunition and bayonets, heavy as any armored knight of yore, with no sturdy war horse to help us lug it.

Slow rain kept the air cool even in mid-July in the valleys and the guys in open trucks, helmets and cartridge belts between their feet, undid their blankets from their packs, unfolded them and covered their heads and shoulders before replacing ponchos over them, leaning heavily on the man next in line, heads bobbing with the bumps of the hilly, winding valley road.

Moving north into and along the combat line in darkness we passed other battalions on the move. It didn't matter, Dutchmen, Frenchmen, Canadian, Turk, ROK or American, we were samo-samo in this bloody business and we waved generously at one another, emphasizing we were on the same team; thinking alike regardless of language, doing something tremendously big and important together; we Yanks feeling charitable since, even though it was South Korea, we were the hosts of combat teams, which in battalion or company strengths were from, after those already mentioned: Australia, Belgium, Columbia, Ethiopia, Greece, Luxemburg, Netherlands, New Zealand, Philippines, Thailand, Union of South Africa and United Kingdom. Noncombat aid was provided by India, Norway, Panama, and a Swedish field hospital and the Danish hospital ship *Jutlandia*.

Who cared we were dogfaces? Koreans did. They had an old custom of fattening up little red-nosed pet dogs once a year, putting them into large rice cloth bags, beating them to death and eating them. Dogs? They used to take dogs to war with them, as Shakespeare had Caesar yell: "Let loose the dogs of war!" Dogfaces? Who cared if civilians back home didn't appreciate us; we weren't in their world anymore anyway—three-headed dogs guard the gates of hell. We ought to know, we've been there and beware the dog, *cave canem,* who protected Rome's villas.

We who risked our lives were all respectful and loyal to one another. Expendable? Did congressmen say we were expendable? Goddamn right, expendable in the hottest gladiator arena in the world, setting forth in our caravans ready to die like proud warriors of old, of the tented tribes of Israel, Christian Crusades to defend the faith; evermore swearing to uphold the politics in power.

Men were to be separated from boys again and it was stand up and be counted, warriors, this is it, or bugout weaklings which none of the Banzai Third ever were. Face up, stand tall, time again to deny frailties. We are men, Goddammit! Men! Like you'll never see on TV; we smelled of men in combat. We'll show you and, yes, me too! No matter that I was medium size, an ordinary Joe, a laborer, only two years college. "Fuck 'em all, all those clean, pretty, rear echelons and successful, happy civilian college graduates back home. Fuck 'em all, the long, the short and the tall. Fuck all the draft dodgers and their bastard sons; fuck all headquarters and WO ones." WO, warrant officer, administrators. Were there weak willies or women among us? Shit no! Women? Sh-e-e-it, you kiddin'? Women don't exist. Money, home, business, personal ambition, appearances—all stuff like that forgotten. Right down to the core of us, we got a big job, gooks to clobber. Stay out of our way!

No rear echelon could do it. No mister can step into the well-worn boots of an infantryman and be professional like us, not by a long shot. He'd have to be lucky enough to live through a few of our deals even to know the score; no amount of thinking it, theorizing, not even training, can make a combat infantryman. No daydreams, man, you gotta' do it to be it!

Leaving the MSR, trucks crept along a narrow mountain road (weren't they all?) up to the wilderness country of Pia-ri and Satae-ri, using cat-eye, down-shining slit, blackout headlight covers in pitch darkness, lighting no more than a few feet of the road. Rain came and went and returned and for a time eerie fog formed and rolled in mysterious dense clouds silently through blackness of night glimmering reflected starlight on top across drained highland rice paddies as the enemy's harassing and interdictory artillery fire, H and I, came searching for us awakning those sleeping. One shrill menacing whimper way over to the left, s-s-s-s-wampt! A bright quick blink of yellowish-orange flash against the side of a gully. A quarter of a mile closer, e-e-e-e-E-umpt! CRASH! Then, back only a hundred yards on the road we had traveled, S-s-s-s-swampt! on a visible bit of road selected and zeroed in in daylight by gook forward observers for just such an occasion. After five, long worrisome minutes, another, and this time well ahead of us. They were reaching, searching, questing frantically, feeling, wanting us badly. We were being bracketed.

Where would the next one land?

The guys who up to now were dozing mumbled low, peering around nervously. I leaned under the dashboard to light a cigarette and smoked it hiding the glow carefully in the cup of my hand. It was stimulating to be in action again, to be important and useful once more; if it did make you shiver a little.

"Yes, sir, 1179, here we come!"

We knew that no matter where we unloaded tonight, 1179 was in our offing, a little nearer, more real to our fate than that final enemy OP (observation post) 1243 which we didn't seriously consider yet.

I was a real veteran and nobody better forget it. Was I important? Sh-e-e-it, leading those two truckloads I forgot anyone back in Watertown existed. What the fuck does a civilian know? Regiment for that matter; battalion or goddamn company; we were the Banzai Third, proud scion of Onis L Ulriche the Bold who died for us trying to knock out a machine gun.

"To hell with Shallow," I added, "I've taken about all the shit I'm going to from that garrison jerk. Fuck 'em all, anyway, the long, the short and the tall."

This from a song we used to sing route marching in the Royal Canadian Scotch Infantry—a British Army lament. "There's a troop ship that's leaving Bombay bound for the land we adore, heavily laden with time-expired men, bound for ole Blighty's shore."

We unloaded before the hill mass of the Taeusan mountains lining Pia-ri valley on one side and the Punchbowl and while the trucks gunned out fast as cat-eyes would permit, back to the safety and comfort of trucking company, everyone found his place in the dark and organized with whispered confusion into a long single file for chogeeing, or if you prefer, motoring. Those of us in charge spread the word for each guy to take a five-yard interval between himself and the man ahead. But it was cool and wet, dark, lonely and mysterious in our fearful wilderness and the guys naturally bunched up and stuck close to buddies despite threats—humble, very suspicious and apprehensive of what was concealed up ahead in the dripping darkness. "Dammit, one round will get you all!" In leaving sea level passing by one of Love company's jeep trailers, each picked up another cardboard three-meal box of C6s with a grumble as we tried to find places for it. "*Find* room," Field First Sergeant Martin hissed loudly. "Can't tell when you'll get more."

A commo guy handed out four-foot pieces of wire for us to tie the box onto our packs.

"Kee-rist," Ski complained, "some sneak's grabbed our fruit again." He held up everyone pawing through the boxes in an effort to find one.

Captain Shallow hissed loudly, "Let's not hold up the line. What you want, sirloin steak?" He chuckled at what he took for humor and was then suddenly peevish. "Dammit, soldier, I said *move!* Don't be so damn fussy. Grab any box and move along."

Ski lifted his leg and farted.

"Period," someone added.

I never heard of anyone on C rations make so many farts.

"There's another kiss for you!" Ski added.

Everyone knew he was talking back to the captain and snickered at such ancient humor. I wondered at big hairy Neanderthal soldiers threatening to blow out the campfire if they didn't get more to eat, and the whole hairy family laughing. The fart had to have been man's first spontaneous joke. I had a spaniel once who lived to sixteen and was waiting for me when I returned after five years in 1945. His farts would drive you out of the room and I was surprised my prissy father hadn't had him put to sleep while I was gone for he claimed it smarted his eyes.

The rain poured on us as we slipped, slid and crawled, cursing and panting, up the steep zig-zag path that led to our ridge 900 meters (2827 feet) above the valley road. Gloomy, yes, but there was humor to be sure, laughing at some poor guy losing his footing and sliding in wet mountain clay, six to ten feet back down, guys stepping gingerly out of his way. Geezus, that was funny, or did we find humor in his bad luck because our laughs were so far behind?

Many veterans dug out olive drab Army face towels from their packs and wore them tightly around their necks to sponge water dripping from their helmets.

Seven hours after we began to climb half the guys were still trying to make the greasy slides. Sounds in the rain were sharp curses and equipment being dropped or thrown away by fatigued men.

"Sonofa …" "S-h-h-h!" … "Speed it up there." "Don't bunch up." … "S-h-h-h!"

"S-h-h-h yourself; what the hell you take me for," Funaro bitched for all to hear, possibly gooks, "a goddamn machine?"

I will never forget that torturous night. Great lumps of sticky yet slippery clay clung to my boots, the superhuman strength I needed to lift them and plant them forward time after time after time again, and the rain that dripped on me until broad daylight, just enough to make sticky mud slippery, turning the mountain trail to an escalator of churned-up mud moving the wrong way.

Forty-five years later that particular climb of dozens we did was a common ground of memory. "Remember that climb from the Pia-ri Valley?" "Man, *do* I?" Guys on more level places rested for what turned out to be shorter and shorter efforts. One bunch, huddled figures from K company covered with shiny black ponchos, blocked the path where it leveled off a few feet, dozing there in the mud like shrouded dead men under rain-slick, rubberized, dark olive-drab sheets. I was cold and miserable and mad; when I was mad, I plugged along steadily putting my head down near my knees as they upped and downed under the steady load of me, resigned as a bridled ass to quiet slavery.

The lead element reached the high ridgeline about 0830 and found Marines sullen and unfriendly. It was customary when transferring positions for the officer in charge of the relieved unit to run the line with the reliever. I sought out the Marine platoon leader, a bright, young twenty-one-year old Naval Academy graduate. Me?

Why, you know me, a recalled Reservist in his early thirties, quasi-civilian compared to this guy with four years of expensive military schooling."

"Hear there's gooks, been tough?"

No answer. No frivolity, friendliness or even common courtesy as brighteyes snapped, "Where in hell you been?" The Annapolis graduate, almost with tears in his eyes, accused, "You were supposed to be here last night."

"Made it soon as possible."

"Why doesn't nobody relieve on time?" the young man whimpered. "My men got all they can take."

"We was takin' in a movie!" Funaro explained out of order.

Death tainted the air while maggoty eyes of two bloated enemy blinked unceasingly near where we stood.

"I should think so," I chided. "Why haven't you hauled this mess away?"

"Never cleaned their mess," Sergeant Eppler repeated bitterly. "Get some heavy sticks," he ordered. "Roll them gas bags out of here."

"Them's not soldiers," Funaro explained. "Fuckin' bell hops."

"Pipe down," Pop Miller advised. "Don't need more fights."

I found out that one of our replacements was night blind, a nice little draftee from Long Island. He had to be helped find things even though, when rain clouds spread open for stars one could read a newspaper. After two nights of complaining by Sergeant Olsen, his squad leader, at two in the morning his holemate came scurrying into my CP crying.

"Lieutenant, lieutenant, get rid of that guy. Can't see dick in front of him and I ain't had a bit of sleep last two nights, not when he's supposed to be on guard."

I carried the poor guy to battalion the next day in a borrowed jeep, humbly apologizing to me over and over for his shortcoming, telling me several times how he appreciated saving his life and he was sorry it was such a hell of a long heavy climb returning. Duncan, without advising Shallow, whom I gathered he didn't trust, sympathized with me.

"Life's too short to worry," he told me.

"Yeah," I told him. "That's what's worrying us."

I learned later that the night blind kid was dropped from our morning report and ended up a member of X Corps Honor Guard, his spot in our defense not filled for a week.

Colonel Duncan surveyed the line and ordered us to destroy the Marine bunkers and build a new defense down from the skyline ten feet on the enemy side instead of smack on top where they were silhouetted targets for artillery. Later that day, after the first chogee train brought us heavy leather gloves and big cutting pliers, we strung barbed wire down the hill in tangled or concertina rolls, using some of the little laid by the Marines.

That first day I examined old artillery shell holes closely. By the hardness or looseness of the soil, the size and shape of the craters, the direction the spray took leaving the impact spot, the smell of the dirt, and the age or freshness of powder burns, I gauged the extent, direction, approximate time, and effectiveness of enemy artillery even though it happened earlier to Marines.

We watched in awe our first night as darkness was challenged by an eerie light of the mist-screened Chinese moon, mountain glows like weak, shapeless florescent lights, signaling the peak of another moon month of turmoil, lighting the country around except where occasional dimouts occurred from puffs of low clouds drifting northward. Machine gun tracers, straight line, red-orange jewels traveled ordered paths across our world and further than that came the distant underworld rumble of artillery contesting peels of thunder.

We slaved on our bunkers the next few days, Doc Carlson and I helped by J J, who lamented as usual: "Over thee moun-tains! Wa-a-ah-ay o-ver thee seea a-see mah ba-a-abee-ah-ee come back to me-e-e-."

As darkness came over us the first night, I appointed myself first guard. With the three of us, we had two hours longer sleep in between than had the normal two-man holes. It continued to rain lightly as J J relieved me at 2100. An electrical storm moved through the steady monsoon above us delivering separate cloudbursts that filled an inch of our CP hole with ice water. Seated on our hard-rim helmets above the mud, none of us got sleep until it let up, fizzling out about 0200 as puddles sank away. I'll bet Uncle Art knew a lot about that.

We dug communication trenches between bunkers so resupply could reach each safely during a prolonged attack, and our medic could slip from hole to hole without being clipped. Bugout ditches, they're called.

We had just settled into the earth as darkness overcame twilight over the mountain world the second night when a series of sharp single whistles came over the innerplatoon sound-powered telephone circuit—someone raising first squad. Sergeant Eppler held the receiver to his ear, eavesdropping. We did that, whispered and kibitzed on the phone to help pass hours of darkness.

"Wh-e-e-et w-e-e-et, wh-e-e-t!" came the whistle. "Eppler here, who you calling?"

"Wh-e-e-e-t! Wh-e-e-e-t. Second squad here! ... Did I give four whistles? Get off the line, Karl. I'm calling first squad."

Talk on the sound powered and phoning in our situation report to company in low voices every hour during the night on the EE-8, magneto battery operated line, gossiping with other platoons and with company made our perimeter tighter and stronger. It was good to know that in the dark other guys were awake and nervous and, hopefully, as watchful as you. Hero of riflemen, General Patton, once warned his Third Army men to be on guard always, "or some kraut's going to sneak up and hit you over the head with a sockful of shit."

The first night passed without incident except complaints about the night blind guy, and for the next few days we made parapets, walls of sand bags heavy with wet spoil from our diggings. The platoon sergeant and I made the guys string barbed wire until they complained it was coming out their ears. One chronic goof-off bitched that Tree, Pop Miller's assistant, by-passed the squad leader and was chicken for riding him so hard. Only in such ways could one take a cheap shot at Tree for being black. Not that it bothered Tree any. Those were the few eight-balls in the platoon who ate our rations, gave us a hard time, and then bawled bloody murder for somebody, white, purple or black, to save their lives.

"Just nice you don't like me," Tree told him. "Don't want nobody liking me; liking leads to love; love leads to fuckin' and ain't no one fuckin' *me*."

We were paranoid, clinical cases, suffering persecution in varying degrees; doomed men who only occasionally found temporary release from some great anxiety or another. None of us liked it. It was a very unlikeable place. We were sent there against our will to die and would not do it cheerfully. No soldier since the

Christian Crusades ever *gave* his life for any damn 'cause.' For a buddy, certainly, whenever necessary, for a stinking politician, preacher or weird poet who lies about our so-called willingness to die, never. Aside from a fierce combat loyalty to one another as with any group of condemned ones, most work was accomplished under threat. We moved north against the enemy under constant threat of death at the hands of that enemy and to turn our backs without competent orders, military imprisonment and disgrace. The few who did give up resigned themselves immediately to Leavenworth, even though some, like Captains Carleton and Toth, lucked out. This motivation, dire threat, civilians fail to consider when they attribute a certain amount of bravery to us.

> *Death in battle takes place in the greatest and noblest danger. And these are*
> *correspondingly honored in city-states and courts of monarchs. Properly then, he*
> *will be called brave who is fearless in the face of a noble death. Yet while he will*
> *fear, he will face death as he ought and as the rule directs, for honor's sake;*
> *for this is the end of virtue.... Of the five kinds of courage first comes the*
> *courage of the citizen soldier. Citizen soldiers face dangers because of the*
> *penalties imposed by the laws and the reproaches they could otherwise occur.*
> – Ethics Nicomachea, by Aristotle, arbiter of public morals.

Not to run the Marines down, they're good, average, untidy infantry, but under Mighty Mouse Duncan we toiled without breaks to clear fields of fire, cutting down every concealment for forty yards downhill, chopping and hacking with bayonets and entrenching tools so a gook would stand out. Less appreciative of camouflage than the enemy, we put off replacing tell-tale wilted leaves covering the spoil around our holes, thus pointed to our positions rather than conceal them.

Contrary to James Fenimore Cooper who introduced whites to American Indians, it's a fallacy that all Indians were as alert as creatures of the wild. The Loyalist Queen's Rangers, New York town men, on 31 August 1778 surprised and overran an Indian outpost north of them entrusted to the care of Daniel Ninam of the Wappinger tribe, Chief of Stockbridge Indians. In this affair, the Valentine Hill Massacre, or Indian Bridge, only two natives survived, and later British-led Indians of the Six Nations lost a battle at Newtown (Elmira, New York) because, having waited in ambush eight days for General Sullivan's column, their camouflage was so wilted their position was observed a mile away.

We hung empty C ration cans Marines littered the hill with on barbed wire with small stones to rattle, and heaved empty cans way downhill so enemy, moving at night, might accidentally kick them. We made brush piles over three 155mm cardboard shell canisters filled with napalm—planting a white phosphorous hand grenade in each after replacing its friction fuze with an electric percussion cap and manhandled fifty-five gallon steel drums in front of two very likely avenues of approach by attackers, up prominent fingers, one downhill from our machine gun. They contained napalm triggered by a remote controlled electric detonator or a white phosphorus hand grenade with an electric detonator set off by a crank of the magneto of an E-8 phone, in place of the ordinary pull fuse. They were otherwise known as *fougasse*, a French military term, originally a mine (explosives) so placed as to hurl stones in a desired direction. We hadn't enjoyed such security since I joined for we hadn't been on a regular defense, always on the move, attacking, flanking, patrolling or on outpost.

regular defense, always on the move, attacking, flanking, patrolling or on outpost.

Each squad dug a small slit trench latrine on the friendly side of the ridgeline opposite its bunkers leveled off so it could be straddled. An entrenching tool was stuck in the loose spoil and one shoveled in dirt after going. "And you ... yes, you, Funaro," Pop Miller warned, "No pissing outside your hole no more."

One night gooks took over our band on a spare 300 I'd scrounged. I'd just called Item company commander to let him know I read his trouble with fading batteries; he should call me on a 536 and I'd relay his messages until he got new ones.

"Buzzard Five leader ... Buzzard Five leader, this is Seven, save your batteries. We'll relay."

As soon as I released the butterfly switch on my 300, a North Korean monitor took over the classified channel picked for us that day, one of fifty channels on the SCR 300 each normally good for an unobstructed range of three miles.

"Buzzard Buzzard Buzzard," he mimicked in his high, oriental voice. "Want

Stars and Stripes Forever.

lowed by an even higher pitch, certainly higher than the ordinary GI would reach. A senseless "Ondong-ondong-ondong-ondong-ondong," whatever that meant, if anything. It kind of frightened you, as if, by taking over our communications, they knew all our intentions. It made you nervous.

Two could play this jamming game and after waiting intently for a break, as a gook voice momentarily stopped while handing a receiver to another, or to listen if we would try to talk, I pushed the switch fast and yelled: "Ee-dee-waa fuckface, I'll jam that radio up your keister meester; Audi-audi-audi, ondong-ondong-ondong and audi-audi yourself." After that it wasn't so scary to think that they were there all the time listening to our talk.

One afternoon, supposedly to entertain us, the division band trudged all the way up to our ridge (pity the tuba man), a team of about thirty carriers hauling their chairs. It went over like a lead balloon, a turd in the punchbowl, doing for division's publicity what we tried hard not to do—attract enemy fire. Even though the band set up on the friendly side, they were somehow spotted and five minutes after they left with their sun-reflecting instruments encased, we were bombarded along the ridge by about forty long-range artillery shells.

Coincidentally, despite a rumored artillery ammo shortage, two days later it was decreed that every crew-served weapon across X Corps' front would fire a five-round salvo at 1100 hours to salute Lieutenant General Almond finishing his Korean tour, each cautioned to pick a good target. We watched the Marine's rocket battery, returned for the salute, mounted on a truck half way down the finger behind us let off all its rockets at once and then out of there before the dust settled. Seconds later twenty HE (high explosive) shells came crashing in where the truck had been. That those gooks were easily spotting us from 1179 and 1243 was the big reason someone would have to take them out.

Mighty Mouse Duncan, regiment's sarcastic sobriquet for his exceptional aggres siveness and small size, put out an order for every bunker to dig a firing well, unencumbered by a roof, from which we could toss grenades and do individual firing; each bunker to have on hand half a wooden box of forty-eight fragmentation grenades. Replacements long before they were committed became well acquainted with their weapons and in the combat zone all the way back to regimental forward went nowhere without them. Like Pilgrim forefathers facing the threat of hostile Indians. "This baby here," they affectionately referred to M1s and carbines. Some were seen kissing them in the small of the stock, hugging them and purring lovingly, "Old sweetheart, don't let me down." The closer to combat, the more they realized rifles were all that separated them from graves registration.

My carbine and civilian Smith and Wesson .38 caliber revolver were my constant companions. I oiled my weapons and rubbed them and polished and sharpened my bayonet knife, patted my carbine, always in my hands or on my right hip or slung over my right shoulder. With nothing else to do, I'd remove rounds from the magazines, wipe them and put them back. The creases of my hands remained dark with particles of dirt dissolved in gun oil like carbon during my foundry days and my guys and I smelled of gun oil blended with stale wood smoke and sweat.

Korean laborers were assigned to help construct an elaborate sand-bagged company command post half way down the long winding trail to the jeep dismount point. On the occasion of Shallow's first inspection trip of our positions, he complained,

"Lieutenant, the colonel's order was very clear. There'll be a roof of three feet to withstand a direct hit by 120mm mortars."

"Yeah," I answered, "and we're supposed to have carriers get the stuff up here; you've got them tied up."

A sister regiment, the 9th Infantry, designated the Manchus in 1908 after the regiment's involvement in the China Relief Expedition, the Boxer Rebellion at Tiebtsin, Yang-tsun and Peking against the Manchu Dynasty of China, whose regimental insignia is a gold, coiled, five-toed dragon, had a battalion and a half of segregated Negroes, one platoon of which tied into my left flank at a wide patrol path leading to gookland.

Presidential Executive Order 9981 by Harry Truman 26 July 1948, one of the very politically brave decisions he made, was to free blacks from segregation in the US military services—"It is the declared policy of the President that there shall be equality of treatment and opportunity for all persons in the armed services without regard to race, color, religion or national origin." However, we were segregated in the 38th until August 1951 with the exception of Sergeant Roundtree who was slipped through a few months early.

X Corps commander Almond, major general with MacArthur in Tokyo when the Korean War began, born and raised in Luray, Virginia, commanded the all-black 92d Infantry Division a year and a half at Fort Huachuca, Arizona, before taking it to Italy late in 1944 where it was decided the division failed in combat because Negroes were, in so many words, cowards. The division was broken up. Almond, who of all bigots was given command of blacks, opposed integration, holding the widespread erroneous belief: "Negroes won't fight," knowing which could have been a good reason not to fight—for him.

White platoon leaders of the black companies of the Ninth were allowed to bunk at company well down the friendly side of the ridge, a good twenty-minute climb to the fighting line. One of the greatest problems of the ROK Army in the early days was that officers were not with the troops during darkness, and the men easily spooked in night attacks at which, being forced to move only at night, made the enemy far superior to us. Topping the disgrace to Negroes were officers in the regiment using the well-known threat among white lieutenants: "If you goof up, you'll get a platoon of the Ninth," meaning, of course, a black platoon. Negroes were well aware of this.

Returning on a goodwill visit to America in 1824, and to collect $40,000 owed by the Congress, Lafayette was struck by the changes, the increase in racial prejudice he observed on every hand. He fondly recalled the days when black and white soldiers messed, fraternized, tramped, battled and died side-by-side, rolled together naked after battles into mass graves, and now found that whites were rarely seen with blacks unless blacks walked behind as menials. Lafayette complained sorrowfully that he came to aid America in its fight for freedom of *all* mankind and when he pleaded with Jefferson, then in the last two years of his life, that manumission should begin by education, Jefferson agreed only in part. Blacks could learn to read print, he allowed, but not to write, for that would enable them to forge papers, making it impossible to keep them subjugated.

I doubt if any soldier or officer, black or white, in the 38th Infantry knew that a unit in the War of 1812 designated 38th Infantry was mustered 29 January 1813 in the Baltimore area, later absorbed by the 4th Infantry. The second to be designated the Baltimore area, later absorbed by the 4th Infantry. The second to be designated 38th Infantry was all Negro, constituted 28 July 1866; consolidated 15 March 1869 with the 41st Infantry, all Negro, and redesignated the 24th Infantry Negro Regiment that fought as late as Korea in the Negro 25th Division of IX Corps. As most infantry divisions in Korea, the US Second Infantry Division's 23d and 38th Infantry commanders managed to exclude blacks and a battalion and a half force-issued only to the 9th Infantry.

Most labor units of quartermaster, ordnance, signal, transportation and engineers remained segregated and there was, as mentioned, buffalo soldier – the all-black 25th Infantry Division, the 92d in Italy, WWII, the famous 9th and 10th Cavalries. The 24th Regiment in Korea was not only all black, it was ten percent overstrength from assimilating many who back in the States were intended for white units. There were many Negroes in the 65th Puerto Rican with the Third Division and, of course, the 450th AAA, antiaircraft battalion in the ETO, and tank destroyers in the battle of the Bulge where Captain Jesse Purnell of the 98th Army reserve division, whom I met in Syracuse, earned his DSC. Blacks fought in all our wars.

In Korea, two blacks killed May 1951 won posthumous Medals of Honor, the latter field commissioned second lieutenant Cornelius H 'Connie' Charleton, one of seventeen children, son of a West Virginian coal miner who migrated with his large family to New York City

I was raised in northern New York, much closer to Ottawa than New York City, and the first Negroes I ever saw were roustabouts raising the huge canvas of Ringling Brothers Circus. I was struck by their large black muscles reflecting ebony in sunlight and their musical jabbering and spontaneous songs they'd break right out with. One thing about those of the 9th Infantry, however, that bothered the hell out of me—their repulsive use of the term, 'motherfucking.' The first I ever heard the distasteful adverb I threatened a court martial, a bluff when given had them yell over: "motherfuckin' whitey lieutenant." Consequently, on occasion when I neared their positions during the day revisiting our machine gunner Ich, I'd hear hidden catcalls, "motherfucking lieutenant." How can one accuse me of being a prejudging racist or Negro hater when they force on my sensitive ears such choice material.

I used the word 'fuck' (Middle Dutch *fokken,* to thrust) in all its forms in Korea whereas I never did working alongside the most crude landscaper or foundryman back home. Sexual meaning was never intended, only as an intensifier of something, any violent thing I had to say or complain about multiplied. Leading my men I usually had no reason to use the word but when there was an emergency or something had to be moved in a fuckin' hurry, or something hit fuckin' hard, the word popped out naturally instead of a polite insufficient word like 'awful,' or maybe I wanted to sound like a real tough guy. I can't explain this; anything actually sexual you think, having to do with that kind of intercourse?

The platoon of Blacks that tied into my machine gun bunker sent two men every other day to haul up a box of forty-eight frag grenades expended in two nights of evenly spaced throwing. I had a sound-powered phone strung to them from my machine gun emplacement and having gone down twice in the middle of night to warn them, got their platoon guide on the line about 0300. After a lot of whistling,

"This is Lieutenant Gould. Gould, g-o-u-l-d, Gould. You all asleep? We're the platoon of the 38th tied into you at the patrol path. I had this line strung to you guys. Yes, that extra line, the one you're talking on, to Sergeant O'Neill ... right across the saddle. Now listen good, I'm tired of warning. Cut out those grenades. We've got to get some sleep around here. We have the patrol path covered and no gooks climbing that steep hill in front of you, it's too steep and wild. We got concertina wire and trip flares and fugasse in drums and primer cord around a dozen trees as well as two tank sirens ready to go off if they trip them. You guys have a bad case of nerves.... I know you don't have any officers with you. If you want one, give Ich a call here on the phone and he'll raise me. I'm up running the line half the night anyway. You understand now? What's your name? ... Washington? Okay, Sergeant Washington, we're all together in this thing. Now buck up and hang on to those grenades until you might really need them, but as I tell you, nobody's climbing that hill in front of you guys. Okay? Well, all right, Sergeant Washington, get your guys on the ball ... calm them down. You hear? You get some sleep."

"No suh, we're awake. Yes suh, yes suh, you right, you right. I knows you right. Yes suh, good you call and talk to us. Okay, suh, glad you call."

The sound-powered phone was near my ear when I heard Washington explain to someone in his bunker.

"Fuck dat lieutenant! He not here. He here, he'd know what's what. Suppose he knows about us way over here? No, he don't know. You know, man, if you was a gook, would you go after someone better than you? I mean it. I mean here's you sneaking up on us and wambo a grenade goes off. Man! Man, youse getting the out of dat place. Youse hitting some place else. Right, man? Dis ain't de onliest place to hit. Right, man?"

I yelled over the phone: "You black sonofabitch, Washington, keep tossing them grenades and Ich is turning his machine gun on you. Understand?"

Picking up the receiver beside him, Sergeant Washington replied, "Suh, Suh? Dat youse, suh? Youse right. I knows youse right. Youse the onliest officer we got. 'Course youse right."

The same rifle platoon sergeant, Washington, had hauled up to his position from the company a .50 caliber machine gun and its tripod mount, the one weapon infantry companies in the 38th I contend were sadly neglected. Three mounts were provided for it; a post mount welded into the center of a jeep, a ring mount for over the cab of the 2-_-ton or six-by supply truck, and the tripod for ground mounting. Our Air Force used fifties or twenties on all our bombers, whereas the RAF mounted thirty caliber.

It was almost the same caliber (inside diameter of a circular section) in millimeters as the chink 'elephant' gun, a single shot .55mm, same as the .50 caliber machine gun plus .05 of a millimeter to prevent using their ammo in our weapons, although they used ours in theirs. Large as this caliber seems, as much as we dreaded it, it was nowhere near as large as the Charleville musket the French provided to our Continentals in the War for Independence which fired .75mm lead balls

We cut what necessary-size logs we could with our little hatchets, and small axes, the few trees in Korea that recovered from Jap excesses during their thirty-five- year exploitation but no one in our battalion had formal instruction in bunker building. While we were exposed on the bare May Massacre outpost patrol base in open holes, the other outfits on the main line had been instructed by Second Division engineers and greatly aided by Korean carriers to build mortar proof bunkers.

Engineers sent up by General Ruffner after a fatal bunker cave-in to inspect ours in our new location were appalled by the mistakes we made in supporting and laying bunkers. They told us how hydrostatic pressure works in those mountains and we were also able to thank the engineers for their primer cords, putty-like shape changes of C4, ignition caps, pickets and fugasse to prepare us for the first time since I'd been in Korea for attacks on the several plausible approaches in front of our zone of responsibility. We were so confident we wished gooks would step into our fields of fire. We'd blow the hill down on them.

Beginning with our third night on line, we would hardly know a quiet one for weeks. Gooks were aggressive, so much more harassing than chinks, battalion established an all-out alert at 0400 every morning just prior to false dawn, favorite hour of attack by both chinks and gooks. False dawn is generally known only by sailors on watch at sea, outdoor night watchmen, others who work late at night in the open and soldiers in trouble and they thrill silently to that strange, weak zodiacal glow, that faint nebulous effusion in the sky seen as a promise in the east before true dawn. Both men in every hole had to stand guard together and catch what sleep they could during the day. No hardships for Sergeant Eppler or I for even before the general alert order, either of us was up taking turns roving the 400-yard front.

Come what may, guys did sleep on guard. Eppler and I tried to keep our platoon reasonably honest and woe unto the jerks like Privates Funaro and Sizemore, his buddy, if we caught the two sleeping. Once I beaned Funaro on the noggin with a golfball-size rock. I hadn't intended to hit him quite so hard or hit him for that matter. I guess I'd been waiting too long to catch someone at it, but it didn't do Funaro a bit of good to complain to our battalion surgeon. He refused to believe PFC Funaro that his platoon leader beaned him on purpose, "Not Lieutenant Gould; he'd never do that," and warned Funaro about horsing around so roughly with his buddies. One thing about a known goof-off, his word is worse than anyone's.

Hardest job for Sergeant Eppler and me and the squad leaders, was the first week on line keeping guys like Washington and our own men from tossing grenades promiscuously. After the first probe the third night jittery guys tossed grenades off and on for hours, as guys up and down the line thought they heard something.

We analyzed night sounds. Stuff thrown by nervous GIs was hesitant and widely spaced.

Even old timers were skittish for a few nights back on line and gave jumpy nerves benefit of the doubt. In their case, it was rotationitis. Invariably, when I demanded to know what was going on, they'd say, "Lieutenant, we heard something down there," or "something moved." I don't care how sharp you think you are, you stare at any bush in the weak light of a starlit night at a distance and you're facing enemy that moves. Many times a bunch of them move. Not stand up and move fast, but sort of slide stealthily along like a gook sneaking or something.

The night has a thousand eyes,
And the day but one;
Yet the light of the bright world dies
With the dying sun.
 – Frances William Bourdillon.

One night Freddy Hurtz caught a small grenade fragment in the shoulder, thrown by his own men—just barely broke the skin. A field grade officer or general would've gotten a Purple Heart. Believe it or not, like a baseball in the bleachers I once caught a hot piece of artillery shrapnel in my right hand holding it up to wave back a guy prone to spend too much time out of his hole after dark gossiping. It didn't really burn me, having cooled off after cutting small tree limbs. That happened often, shrapnel and bullets zinging overhead snipping off leaves and small branches.

Because of the threat of infiltrators probing behind our line at night, the wounded not considered dangerously so were set down by the company CP to sleep if they could until there would be light to evacuate them with Korean carriers.

Two or three times every night, quiet or not, at different hours platoon Sergeant Eppler and I split, taking separate flanks to check. On the worst night we got a real probe, they tried to penetrate your defenses with no intention of following through. Doc Carlson took three slightly wounded down to company. Sometimes, when there was heavier activity one way or the other, we went together to investigate, but most times sat outside our bunkers listening, keen to hear what, if anything, would develop. I thanked my experience in reading with my ears. Twice during the third night I called for mortar fire in front of our hill; concentration number seven for the eighty-ones of Mike, Heavy Weapons Company.

"What you think, J J?" I asked, listening intently. "Any more?"

We were scared a good many times and made awkward jokes to cover our anxiety and embarrassment, but only after broad daylight did guys laugh outright at their fidgety nerves, kidding one another with catcalls back and forth from hole to hole.

"Who's the brave guy threw a grenade without pulling the pin? One landed—no explosion."

"Sh-e-e-it!" Tree answered, "Never seed such a bunch of women."

No one came out immediately to admit his fear, but each accused others jokingly of being scared and kidded any guy known to have done something foolish; forget to pull the pin from his grenade, or yelled that the enemy were right on top of us.

"Say I didn't toss one? Stay right here, I'll find out."

"Wouldn't do that if I was you."

"Oh yeah, why?"

"Pulled the pin, it had to be a dud. Tired of living? Pin stuck, got to be a dud. I wouldn't step four feet of it."

Sometimes in early morning, warming C rations over tiny smokeless fires, a civilian type camp stove run with canned heat guys ordered from the PX, or a rare sometimes issued squad burner on gasoline you pumped like a Coleman camper's stove, or if you had a buddy in the engineers, lighting marble-size composition C4 plastic explosive, like balls of putty pinched off from a larger brick, that burned fiercely for a short while, tensions of the night were released inadvertently by a man too honest, or too naive, to carry on a pretense. Ski was like that—couldn't disguise his true feelings. He was comic relief for us and if he wasn't there, he'd have had to be issued by Special Services for morale.

"Yeah, for a whole minute there I didn't know whether to wipe my ass or wind a watch."

"You mean shit or wind my watch," Pop corrected.

"Yeah, that, too."

Immediately the tension was relieved, everyone blabbed excitedly how scary it was, as though each discovered it independently. Light humor without tension was lacking as was literate expression or serious discussion of any length. The laughs came not from healthy fun or playfulness but sudden releases of animal anxiety and wisecracks they snickered at went with bitter expressions as "Fuck 'em!" ... "Trigger-happy bastards!" ... "Scared? Man, I was shittin' and gittin'." "Sh-e-e-eit!"

*　　*　　*

The Korean monsoon was on and around us night and day, days that usually were free of fear. Early one evening before rounds J J, Doc and I sat in our mildewed tomb, our command post bunker, the most secure position I enjoyed in all my days on the line on any objective, listening to erratic gunfire move slowly in our direction. Awfully slow, I fretted, coming at us too damn awfully slow. I lit one cigarette from another.

"How may gooks you figure?" I asked.

But they backed off their probe about 1800 and firing cooled. After listening intently, Sergeant Eppler scurried from his hole.

"You guys hear anything suspicious out there?" he bellowed.

"Loud mouth!" I swore under my breath. "Yelling away our position like that; every gook within five miles knows exactly where we're at."

Then I recalled my stupid, seemingly cowardly silence the night of the outpost and I myself yelled, "Yeah, you guys, get on the ball." Shit, they know exactly where we are all the time so don't be bashful.

"Lieutenant," Sergeant Eppler asked, crawling head first into the CP firing well grenade pit, "you really think them Peace Talks are on the level?"

"Do you think they're going to hit us?" I asked.

"S-h-h-h!" he said anxiously. "King's tangling with them."

"Yeah, listen, they're at King. Listen to those Russian 120s."

We donned our helmets. Was it night already or a very dark monsoon afternoon? Little difference. We lay in our hole watching lightning silhouette the far away northern mountain tops well into gook land with uncanny, startling blue light against a deep purple sky, and heard random rifles—a hundred angry dogs barking up and down a line across the low mountain ridge. Ski slid in, splashing muddy water from the grenade pit, whispering excitedly that four white-clothed men walked slowly past his bunker almost floating across the path that led to King Company.

"Regular zombies."

"Let them get away with it?" J J Jenkins scoffed.

"They took me by surprise, I was stunned."

"That's buck fever, where's your rifle?" I demanded.

"Goddamn!" Ski swore. "In my hole."

"Get back, tell Pop and the guys," I told him, as Sergeant Eppler and I left in opposite directions to alert the other squads. Gooks were very professional at line crossing; seldom seen and less often shot at. They wanted no trouble crossing through us, usually in Korean peasant white and one at a time, and would rendezvous in the rear to kill higher ranks if possible, prepare maps for future actions, or whatever mischief they could find.

Brilliant heat lightning flashed three or four times beyond where the most monsoon rain was falling, then stopped without apparent reason as though by a celestial signal; or went away fast angrily chasing black clouds scudding off to the Sea of Japan. A faint, frightened voice cried out pathetically way back on the trail, maybe from King.

"They're comin' all fours."

No one heard from the mysterious zombies in front of Love until my midnight tour when something rustled bushes a hundred yards downhill. A hideous sound made hair rise on the nape of my neck. Coming from several directions at the same time, at first I was convinced it was inhuman, bringing to mind zombies—living dead.

"J-o-o-e!" it whimpered, a very sick woman pleading in a soft, but loud, wavering lament. "You g-o-o-o-o n-o-o-ow!"

Few of these gook demons followed easy-going, marked and possibly mined trails, but made their athletic way up through bushes, scrub trees, steep fingers leading from western valleys. They'd sit behind a boulder a hundred yards down a finger and whistle or taunt us with a smattering of expressions they'd overheard. "Hi, Joe, Ko ka mo. You go Kokamo, Joe. Go now, Joe," and map our fire plan from jittery guys throwing fear at them. They were especially after machine guns and BARs and mapping artillery and mortar concentrations.

You never got artillery or heavy mortar merely by calling for it unless you were field grade. They quizzed you at battalion, those who had to relay to Fire Direction Center, the S3 wanted to know how many you thought there were out there and what you thought their intentions were. This applied to the next several weeks and as far as I know the gooks never were strong enough to hope to break through and follow up. They probed. And back in the valley they asked how much incoming artillery and/or mortar you were getting and could you locate them. They were much more detached back at battalion than we were and they were right, most of the time gooks were fooling with you simply to waste our mortar and artillery ammo. How many are there?

"Keep asking and you can count them going by."

While an apprehensive dawn spread light slowly throughout the scene on my last watch, it was whispered in awe over the platoon phones to be alert for a powerful gook capture team that dragged off two from their holes on a Charlie Company listening post, like probably happened to Dorn and his men. You were terrified by the cold nerve of the enemy and at the same time shuddered at the fate of those men. It was known from escapees that they were interrogated without letup less than a mile away and sent north to starve to death for failing to give them choice information Gooks were usually merciless like japs or kraut SSers, whereas chinks are more on our scale of humanity. I was thankful many times that chinks took Sergeant Dorn and his guys.

The following night, frightened by a silly giggling downhill, I made the mistake of throwing a grenade. Guys along the ridge tossed grenades for an hour, encouraging the probing gooks to increase their harassment, and on my last tour when they whistled disconnected bits of what I imagined were popular Asiatic tunes to attract fire, our platoon machine gun disclosed its position.

"Doesn't sound like Ich," J J grumbled. "Should know better." But then, so should I.

Item struggled on the far side of King from us and the main pressure of gook's probe was strung out generally in a long column along the ridge. Our regiment, weakened by untested men from civilization who had to be taken by the hand, stretched out along our defenses until, even during fair weather, its elements were lost to view. Occasionally, from his lofty observation post on the MLR, Colonel Mildren was able to point out to a visiting congressman, news photographer, or war correspondent, the tiny spectacle of a bent-over figure hurrying point to point. The lieutenant or a platoon sergeant would drop away from time to time, and Colonel Mildren would explain to his visitor, "Now he's briefing his men one hole at a time; or maybe distributing food. They're hard to supply."

A civilian photographer peered into his view finder and cursed the distance.

Settling down for a long grind, it wasn't enough that our enemy came to test us, we had to take turns patrolling from the main battle line to test him and platoons were dispatched piecemeal to assist Red Battalion in maintaining a precarious toehold on the steep approaches to H 1100 across the Pia-ri valley.

Love Company's command post alone was impregnable, a sand-bag fortress located as it was at the end of a short path backed by a cave. Company runners armed with tanker's grease guns stood twenty-four-hour guard over the entrance and a squad leader of weapons platoon was carefully briefed to allow no one to pass without signaling the company commander, especially Colonels Mildren and Duncan.

Reconnaissance patrols worked nightly from both sides to ensure contact and grab prisoners if possible for Intelligence, to keep tab on gook outfits facing us, and so limited were traversable pathways of the wild terrain that on one of our patrols we lay flat to the ground off to one side, almost suffocating as a larger enemy patrol passed dangerously near. We heard gooks argue in low voices, strange, oriental voices growing steadily louder and more excited as the argument deteriorated. I thought sadly of Dorn and his guys. It was funny the following day—we were starved for humor.

Insomnia overcame me again. "What you have to do around here for some shuteye?" a voice in me demanded. My brain raced against nothing full speed without arriving anywhere as I went down a familiar road over and over and, as each succeeding fear and its peculiar threat arrived, multiplied by the deaths I in some way participated, reviewed and closely examined by my conscience, the sum total a gnawing guilt which, in the best of nights pressed me awake, shaking my ears like any startled wild animal. I indicted myself—

You lost Sergeant Dorn and his men, Sergeant Miller and his wireman and a three-man guard. It's no real consolation that every commander from Lieutenant General Almond to Major General Ruffner to Colonel Coughlin to asshole Major Wallace Wilkes to Lieutenant Foney was wrong for not withdrawing you from the outpost a day earlier or the latest before dark that terrible night. And you added more men to the slaughter by taking them out of their secure holes....Goddammit, Gould, you murderer.

"Go after them!" voices urged. "Help them, help them! ... Never mind now, they're dead. Oh my God, all dead! ... Why did you let them down?"

"Damn," a voice nagged, "why did you have to be so military? Why let Foney send those wiremen to certain death? Why didn't you keep them safe with your platoon on the ridge for just those few hours and make up a story to Foney?" That would have been the right thing to do and none would have been the wiser. Discipline, it's called, wouldn't allow it; damn obedience killed them. Learn again how to think free like a civilian.

I catnapped as I could and the following night enemy sneaked up in the stealthy manner of wild Indians from Satan's Valley to hit us with a vicious probing attack, a series of short, rugged jabs starting a mile or two to the right and bouncing along four miles of front line. I was terribly nervous over a three-hour period, waiting, listening and wondering when they'd get to testing our platoon and what was their strength.

Our artillery flares came over every ten minutes. We avoided looking at the flare itself and placed our hands over our eyes to shield them from the intense glare as we carefully followed the powerful light down, scrutinizing dense shrubbery at the bottom of the hill, full of 'enemy' movements caused by swinging flares. "Crimus, look at them bushes move!"

My nerves were highly pitched, waiting and listening, when suddenly b-r-r-r-r-rupt! 900 bullets a minute each from several guns poured at us. A deliberate action of my own was necessary to counteract the stunning effects of the flood tide of blood and adrenalin surging all through my being and it was a whole minute before I was able to snap control over my thinking and yell, "Up and at 'em!," crawling from the bunker.

I had to shit. There was no avoiding it. My asshole muscles didn't have patience or strength to stay shut. I stumbled to our latrine and squatted there fearfully, pants down around my knees, carbine across my lap, paper between my lips, peeking around nervously, both ears strained to the utmost for incoming mortar. No time for wiping, I dropped the folded paper, yanked up my pants and ran stumbling bent over to the rear of a large boulder on the ridge top, holding my unhooked belt together with one hand, carbine in the other.

"All together, men!" I yelled, setting down my carbine, zipping my fly with my left hand, anxiously threading the end of my belt through the buckle. "Play it cool! Check and make sure safety's off."

The guys liked my yelling. It was as important to them as our flares and the powerful searchlights with which our engineers on several occasions lit the ridgeline. They wanted to be led and liked to hear from their platoon leader and sergeants during a fight and know we were up working for them. Soon as I yelled down my own fear, I visited replacements in bunkers near the CP and found one new man cringing, lying sideways on the bunker floor, legs pulled underneath him in the passive pose of a fetus, as though fated to leave the world in the position in which he entered.

"Please, Mister Gook, shoot at anyone but don't hurt me."

When I spoke to some replacements, two in particular, they ignored me completely or motioned anxiously for me to be quiet and hunker down, afraid I'd attract attention. Man, did I understand the fear that numbed them. They wished to play possum, those badly frightened guys, whispering and begging me to get down in the safe, dark hole so the horrible monsters wouldn't know where we were.

"If we're awfully quiet," they'd think (as I did on the outpost) "and don't make no noise, or threatening moves, the gooks will go for someone bothering them."

"That's wrong! Wrong!" I scolded. "You can't cringe like that and lose initiative." Damn it, hadn't Sergeant Eppler and I drummed that into them?

I heard of men found gunned in their holes playing make-believe. I thought of Marshall's MEN AGAINST FIRE, 101st airborne battalion guys at Bastogne, Belgium cringing in the snow of an exposed field, hoping the bad krauts would tire of killing them.

"Listen to me!" I shouted. "Stand up, face 'em, and sound big, or you'll wish you had only gooks to put up with."

"Yes, sir," they promised, relieved and bolstered by my shouted aggressiveness.

I slipped back into the CP bunker, put on my wrinkled fatigue cap and pulled my civilian revolver. It gave me more confidence at night than the unwieldy carbine, and out checking the line the steel hat was an amplifier, making false echoes of each warning sound, lying about where it came from. You needed something soft that wouldn't make or reflect noises.

I ran at a half crouch to the assistant weapon squad leader's hole from where shots had just come.

"Brown?" I called out. No answer. "Brown? Brown?" I questioned, louder and louder as I approached, thoroughly apprehensive. "Goddammit, boy, it's me, Lieutenant Gould."

Something clicked. I went flat as wet paper.

"Who's there?" a voice hissed.

"Lieutenant Gould," I answered, relieved and at the same time angry, slithering head first into his grenade pit. "You deaf or something?"

"Why? What's the matter, lieutenant?"

"Matter? Who fired the shots? You scared the hell out of me. Gooks are somewhere downhill from your squad, now clean out your ears and shape up."

Poking my head slowly over Sergeant E-5 Brown's parapet, I turned my face toward him. "Hear anything?"

"Me and Wheeler heard some funny jabbering before you came along," Brown said. "Just now we thought you might be gooks."

Suddenly a burp gun tattooed the darkness, a 220-volt shock! Thump! Thump! Thump! Thump! grenades showered from nearby bunkers to the sharp staccato bark of rifles and there was a fierce one-sided firefight for five minutes. Firing slackened and Brown started to whisper. I slipped my hand over his mouth and pulled him forward. Cocking our heads over the sandbag wall of his firing pit, we listened to noises quiet as raindrops; faint rustle-rustle of cloth downhill rubbing branches and the indistinct snapping as they returned to place. When a tin can rattled, I pulled the cotter pin from an illuminating grenade, holding the handle down.

"Take off your helmet," I whispered. "Watch carefully where I heave this grenade and get ready to blast them."

The grenade sailed far downhill, the handle landing ten feet from the bunker with a thin, tin noise. The fuse popped in flight and we heard the snakelike sizz of its fuse and soft tennis shoes running for cover. Two shadows scurried as the grenade blossomed, a sputtering magnesium flower spraying shards of light on the wet branches.

Sergeant Brown and I blasted our frustration with an Army forty-five pistol and my civilian thirty-eight revolver throwing bullets into the bushes where the enemy had been.

The probers moved left hoping to draw fire and map fire plans and defenses of the Negro battalion of the 9th. Our company continued to fire sporadically and toss grenades half an hour. Sergeant Washington's guys showed better discipline holding fire while the gooks retreated all the way down to the valley bottom as I predicted, so steep and entangled was their front.

Enemy 76mm, SP, self-propelled, high velocity artillery paid a screaming visit, landing greedily back and forth along the ridge top. "Where you, Gould?" Death shouting for me in that heavy traffic of shells. Avowing my complete innocence, I crouched against the enemy side of my hole and explained that I really wasn't harmful, cringed waiting for heavy broken hunks of metal to come crashing down, thankful they were weak at making air bursts.

"Why, me?" I whispered. "What've I done to you?"

We knew from the peculiar loud screech when a shell would be especially close. Immediately afterward we were speechless. Looking across the hole to one another, we could express only sickish smiles of relief until someone said, "Wow! That was close!" Or, simply, "My Gawd!" Anyone attempting a conversation was hushed so we could track everything incoming. None of us could carry a thought further than a short sentence; and if we were very quiet, sometimes we heard the initial warning sounds of mortar shells leaving the tubes—pw-w-oooop! their range very short compared to artillery.

There is no accurate way to describe that rushing-at-you, howling, death-on-the-way sound of incoming artillery, except perhaps that of a heavy express train bearing down with you tied to the tracks, or slightly less than a tornado although I've never heard either first hand. Quietly and carefully, oh so carefully, we breathed our last, never knowing so satisfying a delicacy as what might be a final draught, that wonderful, clean taste of mountain air. We treasured this great luxury, the air we breathed, particularly the ability to breathe in succession, and, gazing quickly along the small perimeter, experiencing a feeling of deep brotherly love, as danger molded us tight; all of us there that night felt the very same, at the same moment—fear.

"Now I lay me down…." I began unconsciously, interrupted then by another sudden scream of hell fire.

"Medic! Doc!" came from the left in the Second Platoon and I had to order Doc Carlson to stay put.

"Cisco'll patch his own; he'll yell if he needs help."

In the First Platoon, one burst opened the ground and flung shattered rock over and into two riflemen in their hole. Neither knew it. We preferred a dirt hole, for shards of rocks could finish the job the shell set out to do. First and Second Platoons were hit. A Second Platoon man, Hurtz's, had a leg blown off and as the fifty-round barrage lifted, I watched the sad spectacle of two guys struggling awkwardly, slipping and sliding back down the ridge past our CP with their buddy, a little man on a litter, his neatly severed leg beside him tied on with commo wire.

"Hurry! Hurry!" they urged one another. "He's bleeding bad."

"Put him down," I yelled after them. "Stop the bleeding; press something on the wound, feel for an artery … Medic! Medic! Myles!"

Myles scampered over too late to save the guy as his head dropped beside his shoulder on the litter. If only Cisco'd tried first to stop the blood, but Cisco couldn't, he was patching a head wound and Hurtz another man when the guy was rushed away by fellow riflemen replacements who should have known better. First, stop the bleeding.

When he discovered that one of the dead of the First Platoon was an old-timer, J J swore under his breath. Had he been a new man, he would've said politely, "That's too bad." Learning a familiar old-timer was killed was like hearing prematurely of your own death; you lived in violence so long your memories are all the same. Time was closing in. If we live too long, are hit too hard by too many attacks, we get the fixation that since all our buddies have died, we must go soon, it's only a matter of time, and watch out for guys carelessly standing straight up; one might be you.

"Hey," I asked, "who'd they say?"

"Lederman. Remember Lederman? Came with us at Inje."

"Lederman? Lederman? Must've been a pretty quiet guy. I can't remember his face. Tough, all right. That's the way it goes."

Working on our hole later, busily discarding rock loosened by hacking or picking at it with my locked down entrenching tool, Lederman returned to mind and I suddenly remembered exactly what he looked like. I could see the guy standing before me.

"Oh, sure, Lederman, Indiana farm boy; blond kid about eighteen. Always in the front row at battalion movies.... Sonofabitch! Dirty, lousy luck! Now Lederman."

We were moody and silent, each paying his last farewell to PFC Leo Lederman, another of us nobodies gone forever from his buddies and his mother who bore him, gone into a cold military grave in a foreign boneyard.

"Remember?" I said. "Always first at the movies; he'd go sit there to get the best seat an hour before dark reading a pocket book while we were still at chow, having another coffee and a smoke."

"I don't know 'bout that so much," J J said, "but man, sure had a good-looking sister."

"Goofed up on parade, remember?"

"I know one thing, he was dicked out of a Bronze Star once; they went and lost the paperwork at regiment.... He wasn't the only one."

"Lost it, yeah. They write 'em for their own that never gets lost."

One of our most cherished surprises in combat was after dreading death all the dark hours, finding yourself at first light alive again, an infantryman's Easter Sunday. You've risen again, revived, allowed to hope to live through another day.

Late the next night there was more H and I than usual for so late and promiscuous rifle fire on our part as though someone actually saw a gook, until machine guns opened up almost playfully, each signing off his own way. B-r-r————upt. Lewis of the Second Platoon, Love. A long, drawn-out burst ending with a sharp tap! tap! tap!, a showoff gunner from King Company down the way, heard from other nights when he shouldn't be. It took finesse to knock off separate rounds from a machine gun, tap and tap. You have to acquire a light touch, snap your thumb down and off the trigger fast for rounds to be separate and individual. Gunners would brag with it, as I used to show off on the big .50 caliber Air Force guns shooting aluminum powder sticks we'd drop out on the Gulf.

One night after I returned from checking the bunkers as a light rain all evening became quite heavy, more typical monsoon, I heard low voices approaching commiserating and crawled out to find two men carrying a litter. Another walked slowly behind with bowed head. My Army watch read 0315.

"Look where you're going," someone complained.

"Won't hurt him none."

Seeing me, they set it down.

Him, I discovered, was a little man on a mud slimy litter, soaking wet, covered with mud-thickened rags, jet black hair under slurpy mud. Bending closer, I recognized corporal, soon-to-have-been sergeant E-5, Tommy Ichimura, ears and eye sockets packed with mud, right hand dragging limply along the trail over a side of the litter.

"What happened?"

"Bunker cave-in," Doc Carlson said, shaking his head sadly. "Roof crushed him on his machine gun."

"Oh, no!" I blurted, overcome by a compelling urge to make Ich live again. First

J C, now Ich. I couldn't understand our guys going their lonely ways, especially little Ich; not pleasant, alert little Ich. Damn!

"You," I snarled at our new medic, uncontrollably savaged by the tragic event, "Used artificial respiration—everything? Can't let him go like that."

Carlson was silent as I impatiently rolled Ich on his stomach and pulled out his tongue, a long, unresisting, dead man's tongue. "Out goes the bad air," I said aloud, pushing in on Ich's rib cage, the old-fashioned resuscitation way. "In comes the good air. Out goes the bad air. In comes the good air."

"I wouldn't," Doc advised humbly.

"That's the difference," I snapped. "Doc Lynch would've tried everything. Out goes the bad air … God's sake, try it all!"

A crackling, juicy, popping noise came from Ich's mouth, followed by a bloody froth slowly bubbling from his nostrils. I stopped, motioning for Carlson to look at what I heard and saw in the predawn glow and turned to look up at him.

"I know," he said without moving. "Broken ribs; pushed them into his lungs."

"Oh God! God!" was all I could say and stood up glaring at the hands that mutilated Ich. No blood visible on his small muddy body and to me where there might have been some little hope, now these hands of mine, which continued to feel the smallness of our Neisi's broken chest, the soft, still warm, damp limpness of his body, had killed him. I should have known how dead he was after seeing the awkward angle of his head.

"You pushed in Ich's ribs," one of the litter bearers accused.

"I know! I know it!" I snapped.

Tears fell from my eyes as Myles placed his hand on my sleeve. "Sir, Ich's neck was broken anyway."

I yanked my arm away. "Shit! Shit!" I cried. "I hurt him bad…. Oh, shit! Shit! What've I done!"

I ordered them to leave Ich's remains and crawled into my bunker for my blanket.

"Nobody can help him now," Doc said.

"Shut up!" I shouted. "Shut up!" He was right, of course, but I thought the least we can do is see he's covered. You always see that in the movies. Much later I pondered the meaning of covering the dead, especially always their faces. Because you can't stand their stares accusing you? Even with their eyes closed they haunt us and we cover to hide our guilt, our mistakes and omissions with them.

Picking up Ich's litter, the bearers, buddies of his from the weapons squad, moved with their light load. To think he'll always be light now, hidden, poorly embalmed skeleton, never a potbelly Neisi, esteemed member of his Japanese-American community. Tommy Ichimura, tough little guy's gone, feisty little boxer never use fat gloves again on any opponent. Ich is gone. Goddammit, now Ich, too.

Crawling into my bunker, our platoon command post, J J asked, "What's up, lieutenant? Where's Doc?" When I told him, he hung his head and said softly, "Oh God, Oh my God," and he really meant it for he was a devout Christian. With us there were more "my Gods" than the average church on Sunday. But when I said 'Oh God,' it was purely a handy, violent expletive, an automatic expression hardened in me many years ago, what any Agnostic would say in lieu of knowing anything as powerful. A very sick old man, I fell into a fitful sleep where a scolding nightmare lay in wait—

I should have listened to you, Myles. It's just I go to pieces losing one of you. What kind of a platoon leader am I? Jesus H Christ, Doc, why do I always have to be so close to everyone, in charge of dying? That young commo guy, Sergeant Miller's assistant—"You and asshole divvy up my Medal of Honor." That was before you arrived, Myles. A damn nice guy, the minutes I knew him. He knew he was walking to his death straight down the saddle. Heard the chinks waiting for him; knew it was his last. Instead of turning and bugging out, like cowardly bastards going to Canada, he marched like one helluva' big man right to his bloody end. Knew it . . . knew it. . . . Knew what was facing him and never wavered. Why Sergeant Miller and his young assistant, noncombatants? Did they ever harm anyone— anything? What could they do anyway with those little pea shooters?

Myles, I heard you say, 'I wouldn't do that, sir,' and got the impression you didn't want to do anything, or you didn't know what you should do, and I swore at you. I'm sorry Doc, I don't deserve you. Myles, you're Doc now.

Passing Tree's position on my way home from my 0400 tour, I paused to listen to him coming off guard promise softly to himself, singing himself to sleep in a strange, musing, retrogressive talk-song in a strangely old voice—
Swing low, swing low, sweet chair-e-e-et, come for to carry me home. Hear de man say he be resurrection and de life. Believe in him, man, you'se all right. Sweet chair-e-e-t, you'se ain't ever goin' to die. Man, I believes in Jesus. I'se comin' Lord! I'll be there! I'se comin' with ole black Joe. We's ready.

Early that July morning it steamed. While I slept the sleep of tormented, our guide, Bill Hansen, carrying the 536 walkie-talkie, worked carefully down the enemy side of the hill in front of our positions, setting out four additional flares with almost invisible steel trip wires, checking the wet ground closely for broken weed stalks and footprints. Our hard rubber heel combat boot footprints were obvious but those little guys with their soft tennis shoes left no prints in the hard soil. We found trip flares hadn't gone off because gooks bent cotter pins back on the pull fuses and stuck cotter pins they must have brought with them in the release ones and cut the wire, feeling for the tautness or slackness of the wire and tracing it down. From the signs of broken weeds, Bill concluded there'd been a reinforced squad; half a platoon at the most.

That day the sun came clean and dry two hours. Back home rain clouds were occasional, in the Korean monsoon the sun was. No one but us goof-offs, no-good dogfaces, flop and snore almost before hitting the ground. But then no one but us and insomniacs are up half every night. Others lolled about relaxing, puttering infantrywise —noses buried in pocket books. I was too tired and grieved to sleep, a quiet gentle man, albeit aggressive, dependable machine gunner, gone in another terrible nightmarish night. J J carefully cleaned the glasses of our binoculars, using ass wipe, stopping every once in a while to focus on distant objects, never quite satisfied with the adjustment.

Sergeant O'Neill recovered Ich's machine gun from the mud and sent it to company for a trade. Everyone spread his equipment on his blanket to dry in the hot air. What a filthy lot; greasy, flat, matted hair; dirty beards and dirty worn-down fingernails; dirt-caked, horny cracked hands. Our soggy rags and blankets steamed as we scraped mud and removed boots from dirty, wet socks. Fatigue uniforms were stiff from a mixture of dust, mud, rain and sweat and more than occasionally blood— someone you tried to help.

We poured rainwater collected in staked out ponchos into the steel hull of our bare helmets and in rare sunshine used face soap to shave, wash our dirty underwear, socks and handkerchiefs. Water was lugged up the torturous trail in five-gallon jerry cans, forty-pounds each, two cans per Korean carrier on a shoulder yoke, so we dabbed at our faces and shaved, when bullied into it, with a single cup for a rinse without trying to really clean anything.

Without rain it rose to eighty-five in the shade. Through the clear mountain air of our high land, we watched a peaceful convoy crawling slowly along on the MSR behind the MLR. A truck brake screeched, handing up a little piece of America to our lofty wilderness. Some smart guy told us the truck was thirty-five straight air miles away.

"Sure?"

"Course, simple mathematics."

A college boy draftee we got in the last bunch.

Monsoon rains held off two days in a row, midsummer Korea, sixteen hours of light from 0500 to 2100 and the damp earth stewed. A pretty little mountain bird warbled rippling stanzas, starting low, climbing up over ten complicated music scales ending in shrill beauty. What a little sweetheart. I'd love to take him home with me. Home? Home?

Six riflemen worked in relays to fell the largest of the knotty pines up to five inches in girth for bunker roofs with sharp engineer saws delivered at noon by Korean laborers. Chain saws? Not invented. All afternoon Ski lay under Sergeant Eppler's large black umbrella in undershorts and unlaced boots, reading a lurid pocket book, *Machine Guns Through Hell.*

"Where'd you get that?" Pop demanded.

"Traded with Funaro for *Sex in the Alley.*"

"Damn it," Sergeant Eppler demanded from behind, "he means my umbrella. Ought to beat the shit out of you."

"Funaro told me the sergeant wouldn't mind," Ski said. "No one asked for it, he just handed it over."

"Hold up a sec, Karl," Pop interceded. "You have Funaro to thank for this."

"Sh-e-e-it!" Ski said, and, finishing the page, laid the pocket book down hard, his bookmark a dirty finger. "The lying bastard. Sh-e-e-it!"

Sergeant Eppler, realizing there was no bad blood, retrieved his umbrella and left toward a heated argument taking place down the ridgeline.

"You promised me the fruit cocktail this time, you know you did."

"Think I'm crazy? That's all that's good."

"You did so! Ask anybody."

"You're full of shit!"

"I ought to kick the shit out of you!"

"Want to try?"

"Keep it up and I'll kick the shit out of both of you," Sergeant Eppler threatened.

Way off to the left someone fired a lazy old machine gun in short bursts; sounded like a housewife on a sunny morning beating a rug. Does anyone beat rugs anymore? From where I was up the trail I heard Sergeant O'Neill, weapons squad leader, yell angrily to the distant gunner, "Check your headspace!" knowing from the sound there was a need. Overly tired, becoming irritably tired, avoiding our damp hole for the rare sunlight, I tried dozing against a tree, back to a large rock, and then propped up against the same tree again. Lying nearby on their sides, facing each other, Sergeant Olsen and Sergeant Tree were playing whiskey poker, neither much ahead.

"How're the squads?" I asked, tired right out, feeling mean spirited, lighting another cigarette.

"All right, lieutenant, we just this minute checked. Pop's with them."

When I remained silent, feeling threatened, Sergeant Avery Olsen looked up from his cards. "Lieutenant, what if something bad should happen to me? I should get it, or rotate, or something? My assistant's got to learn, doesn't he?"

"I just asked how's your squad, Olsen. I know you guys are tired, someone has to finish the bunker roofs."

"There aren't logs enough, sir," Olsen said, working up an indignation. "And the guys are picking them up fast as they're ready." A pause. "Those guys better get on the ball or I'm going to start turning them in."

Laying down his hand, he added, "Hold these cards down, Tree; don't cheat. Lieutenant's watching you. I'll be right back."

While Sergeant Olsen was satisfying his conscience, heavy artillery opened suddenly against the hill we knew of as 1179, swishing close above us. Usually we listened to our artillery only when we wanted to, but on this day the big eight-inchers jarred my nerves. Proximity fused, so sensitive a drop of dew or a fleck of dust in the air could set them off. Sure enough, black cotton smoke puffed suddenly high overhead and showered the ground widely with jagged fragments. We pretended not to worry, but when falling shrapnel thudded and crashed especially close in the bushes, we buried our heads in our helmets just in case. Friendly fire premature? Sh-e-e-eit! "Set them damn fuses right," someone yelled. "Learn to elevate them big bastards!"

Each infantry division in 1951 was authorized three artillery battalions of about 500 men each, one per regiment, manning eighteen 105mm howitzers in batteries A, B and C, which included the Dutch. Each division had two battalions in support, 155mm tractor-drawn or self-propelled, also batteries A, B and C. The relatively few

8-inchers belonged to Corps or Eighth Army. Two years later 240mm and 280mm 'atomic cannons' were sent over by President Eisenhower and an armistice was quickly signed.

Ideally, each infantry battalion had a train of fifty semimilitary Korean KSC, Korean Service Corps, formerly CTC (Civilian Transportation Corps) carriers issued like pack mules, signed for, fed, handled roughly as property, and given such unpleasant nicknames as 'Old Fuzzballs,' 'Charlie the Creep,' and 'Greasy-Ass' by surly, goof-off soldier handler guards happy to stay out of combat.

The first train before daylight left daily in a strung-out column of climbers from the new company forward supply point with food, ammo, water, and if the riflemen shot up their basic load the night before, the chogee train was instructed by radio to pack nothing but ammunition and water. Up where we operated springs were few and far between and water hard to come by.

KSCs wore brilliant blue uniforms easily detected from the top of 1179 and when a chogee train arrived late in the afternoon gooks greeted them with self-propelled seventy-six shells. Somewhere across the valley and up on that ominous mountain a particularly personal enemy, a gook forward observer, was trying his best to wipe them out. Later, at 1179, climbing the more difficult protected route, we lost two to precipitous falls.

One day back at the kitchen trains to sign a MIA certificate, Sergeant Louie LaPlace, our mess sergeant, told me Captain Shallow's houseboy, known as Billy, turned up missing while Shallow was up with us. The mess sergeant was puzzled. "Hell, he treated that kid better'n us guys; the Captain was teaching him English and to write a little. Kim told the captain he was an orphan, his folks killed during the last shelling of Seoul and he was going to adopt the kid. The captain's plenty shook. Billy didn't say boo; left his Korean-English dictionary and especially tailored American clothes and bugged."

"Why would he do that?"

"Beats me. Him and the captain was lovey dovey."

"What do you mean lovey-dovey?"

"An expression. Maybe Billy got tired running errand," the mess sergeant suggested. "Polishing his boots, starching and ironing his fatigues, bringing the captain his hot coffee at 0600. He's no good for anything else and I hear they'd a big argument of some kind.... Wouldn't be the first time but he felt he owed Captain Shallow something. You should've seen him."

Sergeant Luther was there when Shallow first spotted the kid, half starved and almost naked. "Good riddance. If the kid can't take a little ribbing what would he have done in the States?"

"What ribbing?" I asked.

"You know, because he wasn't really a kid any longer and big for his age, some thought he was playing up to the Captain too much. And the Captain ain't the most he-man you know. Know what I mean, lieutenant? Well, I guess we can trust you, sir. Some of the guys call him a fairy. How in hell do you say that in Korean? It wouldn't be in the Captain's English-Korean dictionary.

"No need," the mess sergeant said. "Everyone knows about them."

"Do you think Billy'll be back?" Captain Shallow asked me later. "He was such a good little kid, such a good kid for his age. He'd do anything I asked." He went on, not recognizing my thoughts were elsewhere. "I think he liked me for myself. I'm resigning my commission anyway—and after all I've done for this Army … I'd adopt Billy and get him away from all this crap."

Sergeant LaPlace ran herd on a gang of lost or runaway Korean boys, ages eight to probably twelve. Where they came from no one knew; they just staked out Frenchy's warm mess tent last winter at Hoengsong for temporary room and board purporting to be his essential helpers. Taking turns, all they did was wash pots and open cans. Potato peeling was passé in the Army and everything came in cans or waxed boxes. All you did was open them. Every time we got wind of an inspection, the entourage, at times as many as twelve youngsters, was shooed away.

Every once in a while, Captain Shallow had a mean spell and told Frenchy to get rid of at least half of them. The interlopers would lie low for a day to humor him. Occasionally, Frenchy's GI cooks complained that the 'little bastards' got in their way and on their nerves and didn't do anything told to do. Especially the many rainy days the whole jabbering bunch would be in a corner of the large company mess tent squatting on the ground, completely wrapped up in some kind of a gambling game they played wherein they shouted at each other, held up cards with strange figures, and exchanged paper money, sometimes shouting like on the floor of a stock exchange.

There were always problems and arguments as the babble would rise to an irritating degree and when it got too noisy out would come Frenchy in his white mess coat and apron, sleeves rolled up, swinging a meat cleaver, yelling in Korean to get out cudda cudda, bali bali, and they'd hightail it in mock terror. During our long reserve he periodically chased them down to the main road that ran past our camp, swearing at them in a mixture of Korean and English colored with French-Canadian.

"Catch a bus or something … take a tank, *alle sortir!* and don't come back begging no more. Chogee! I like a daddy you boys."

They would leave in a bunch bawling like babies and each time, before dusk, infiltrate back under the broad canvas where it was dry and warm, where unlimited food, which they grew to prefer to rice, could be had.

The usually accurate grapevine had it that Marines would have to take Death Valley and we would cross the Pia-ri Valley to capture the western rim of the Punchbowl, remains of an ancient, long-extinct volcano. Everyone buzzed about a place called Taeusan, which the gooks referred to, according to prisoners, as the Gateway to the Orient. To us it was plain Hill 1179, the third highest knob on the rim, what the Press nicknamed from many miles away Fools Mountain, later Five Million Dollar Hill. We were fools to risk our lives on so dangerous a hill with the Peace Talks going on. Sergeant Eppler told us he heard a hundred ROK Marines attached to the US First Marine Division were killed there in two days of unsuccessful assaults. While the guys kicked that around, Tree observed, "They're all like that."

PFC Kiezlowski lifted a leg and farted, explaining, "A kiss for them all," which basic crudity reminded me of Geoffrey Chaucer's *Canterbury Tales*, English I, describing a pilgrim who "lifteth his legge and ferted," which permissible public vulgarity at seventeen in my college classroom awakened a love for poetry.

7

H 1100

He who fears death either fears the loss of sensation or a different kind of sensation. But if you feel no sensation, neither will you feel harm, and if you acquire another kind of sensation, you will be a different kind of living thing and you will not cease to live.... Nature, which governs the whole, will soon change all things and again other things from the substance of them in order that the world may ever be new.
– Marcus Aurelius Antonius, Mark Anthony, soldier, buddy.

From the Blue Book—official history, Second, Indianhead, Division—

Later in July Van Fleet ordered a northward advance in the X Corps zone to shorten the line, prevent the enemy from freely observing the Kansas Line, and force the enemy to pull back his mortars and artillery. The specific objective was a 3878-foot mountain, Hill 1179 designated Taeusan, Gateway to the Orient, at the southwest edge of the Punch bowl, known to the American press as Fools Mountain, which ROK marines had unsuccessfully attacked. It was defended by an estimated two regiments (3400 men) of North Koreans. Elements of the US Second Division were directed against the objectives. Air and artillery pounded enemy positions on the 25th in preparation for the assault; 7000 rounds of artillery hurled into the well-bunkered positions and H and I on the approach behind it.

The attack was scheduled for 26 July and the 38th Infantry named as the attacking element. The 23rd infantry was to launch diversionary attacks to seize three objectives on the Punchbowl from which it could cut off escape of enemy elements from 1179 and also provide fire support for the 38th.

At 0415 hours, 26 July, I Co of the 38th Infantry moved out in a dense fog to take Hill 1100 forward position of the elements defending 1179.

Although hampered by poor visibility, supporting fire were all the weapons of the 38th Regiment plus the Heavy Mortar Company of the 9th Infantry. Attacking through the haze and streams of tracers, I Company became exhausted by 1245 hours, with its forward elements giving ground. K and L Company immediately inched upward. Suddenly the sun broke through clouds giving artillery and mortar observers a clear view of the enemy and immediately crashing salvos of exploding shells were called on the defenders. The infantry surged forward, following the artillery bursts within 75 yards, firing every available weapon. By night fall the inspired foot soldiers had battled to within 50 yards of the crest of Hill 1100 and there they halted, digging in to wait until daylight for the final assault.

Five days earlier, Third Battalion, 38th, was relieved in place by elements of the 13th ROKs and we bivouacked back where we dismounted trucks several weeks earlier. At 0400 hours on the drizzly, misty morning of 25 July 1951, 30 km north of the mountain wilderness of that 38th parallel border between North and South Korea, the order went out to blue battalion's rifle companies K and L to move out, which arrived rudely early one morning as we slept—

"Off your cocks! on your socks! Hands where we can see 'em! Move dogfaces! Let's go-o-o! This is it!" Chogee!

By the time blankets and pup tent halves were rolled tightly together into legionnaire rolls and strapped to knapsacks it was pouring rain and sitting under little pyramid tents of ponchos bloused over our knees and weapons—hurry up and wait—a half-hour wait for the trucks. No doubt at all something big was up but as yet none of us were in the know. The most prevalent rumor, introduced by a corporal who worked for battalion operations and was sworn to secrecy, was that we were going after 1179 all right to whip two crack regiments, 'Hero' and 'Tiger,' toughest outfits in North Korea.

To the more imaginative, the very few of us steeped in early American military history, this portended a most forlorn hope, such an upcoming "glorious" military thrill as few Americans ever experienced: Freeman's Farm at Saratoga, the pivotal battle of the American Revolution, led by the soldiers' super hero Benedict Arnold; and other decisive battles of our glorious past: bloody Antietam, Civil War; Buena Vista, Mexican War; Belleau Wood, WWI; Battle of the Bulge, WWII, come to mind, in which we risked our lives for our country in deadly combat against an armed enemy who threatened our homeland. Of course the Korean threat wasn't nearly as immediate as the advance of the London playwright, Gentleman Johnny Burgoyne and his krauts (including Hessian). No one but we few history buffs thought in this round-about way of our past that ugly morning. To the guys it was another goddamn personal harassment 'they' thought up for us. Frankly, nobody, not even history lovers, conjured up a comforting taste of glory that wet, dismal morning. All was noise, blood, incoming artillery and fear.

We trucked over in dripping blackness to the Pia-ri Valley using cateye headlight covers and dismounted, falling in our accustomed company groups, answering roll call in low voices. I remember roll calls well from World War II, roll calls and long queues and every time ordinary GIs, sergeants excluded, were transferred from one unit to another or one place to another, we underwent short arm inspections for venereal diseases, pausing before a seated doctor, taking it out, our short arm, skinning it back for a look-see, what British Land Army girls called the monthly flip the lip.

By companies we turned our faces toward the always-inhospitable north and marched away in the normal column of twos from the retreating trucks up the road for several miles until we turned right, broke ranks into a single file and started to struggle up a steep, wandering finger of land, zig-zagging back and forth in the dark, slipping and sliding as usual on a mountain mud trail.

Just before daybreak we were ordered to rest in place; the low-voiced order, "Rest! Keep it down! Don't light up!" traveled a ghostly voice from the rear upward. I dozed off and awoke abruptly a number of times sliding slowly downhill. All that was kept dry that memorable monsoon morning were what we wrapped double in plastic C ration accessory bags—wallets, handkerchiefs and cigarettes tucked inside our fatigue jackets. Many of us that long gray morning caught sniffles, noses that ran, as the palms of our hands got blue-white and wrinkled from stabilizing upward movement, pawing under heavy packs at the steep, wet trail.

At 1100 hours we reached the top juncture of our trail and a wider mountain path leading down another steep finger into the huge Punchbowl where Captain Shallow ordered Ich's replacement, our new machine gunner, to set up; Sergeant E-5 Frank Smith, RA12370526, Hamilton, Ontario. I was pissed off and knew then how much Pop Miller must have felt; the next time he took one of my guys without my permission, I'd complain to Colonel Duncan.

I laid down the rest of the platoon up the high trail atop the Punchbowl running northward toward H 1100, 1179, 1180 and 1243. Hill 1100 fought over initially by ROK Marines and, more recently, the First Battalion, avoided the name-labeling Press; no correspondent ever made the difficult climbs to find out what went on up there and we were above and beyond long-range photographs.

We were a mixture of disgusted, cursing draftees and Regular Army facing our first GIs trial, Hill 1100, many wishing they'd never enlisted, discouraged recalled Reservists and federalized National Guardsmen under a few career officers and sergeants, painstakingly crawling, often on all fours, grabbing at finger holds, holding the rifle or carbine or helmet straps with one hand while edging slightly off the trail for traction, one long torturous mudslide. Damn this! Damn that! Why can't we bypass this bastard?

Someone leaked the big picture that King Company would man the rear ridge of the Punchbowl behind us while Item and then Love pushed through to take H 1100. H and I fire from several 76mm SPs and old US Army 75mm mountain pack howitzers captured from Chiang Kai-shek's Nationals rustled low above us, overshooting but, I worried, dangerously near Smitty's dominate trail-crossing position, apparently zeroed in.

As Charlie Company passed through us I heard one-sided arguing; a loud authoritative voice whose adversary made an apologetic whine. I left our position to see what the trouble was and about 100 yards up the trail came upon a stubby lieutenant colonel, black nonreflecting leaf rank on his helmet, who, I later learned, was George W Kimbrell, intrepid commander of the First Battalion, one of few field grade officers I knew to actually earn a DSC, killed in a car accident in September 1952. He was glaring at a tall guy trying his best to worm into a shallow gook hole who I was surprised to see was Captain Carleton, fellow historian.

"Move, dammit, move!"

"I can't, sir," Captain Carleton whined.

"You mean you won't. You refuse!"

"No, sir, I can't."

The colonel tried to get the captain to admit that he refused to go, which, of course, was a general court martial. Each time Carleton replied in a meek voice that he didn't refuse to go, he just couldn't.

"All right, you're under arrest for not leading your men in combat when ordered to do so. I've talked and pleaded with you like a father, Captain, and you will not obey my order. Give me your .45 and report to regiment."

"Yes, sir. I'm awfully sorry," came the reply in a submissive voice.

If you take a look at the official Second Division, blue cover, history, *SECOND TO NONE*, Korea 1950-51, halfway down the foreword, you will see Carleton's real name as one of the division assistant historians. This is where this intelligent, sociable man ended up, having begun his career in ROTC toward the end of WWII because that's what red-blooded sons of congressmen did and for that reason quickly became captain and stayed in the reserves after the war through pride of association with the victorious American Army, also a certain amount of inertia and a little pocket change for attending meetings. Besides, in those days it didn't hurt his father's bids for reelection to be photographed with two sons in the uniforms of their country, a reserve infantry captain and a lieutenant colonel of the US Air Force, even if war was most unlikely. Unexpectedly, like me the captain was recalled in July 1950 for being out of a training unit.

Weeks after the incident, I met Colonel Kimbrell through Colonel Duncan while visiting battalion forward and after telling him of meeting Captain Carleton on the train from Pusan and of course tying in to the episode on the Punchbowl, asked what happened to him. The colonel frowned and seemed disturbed.

I asked again.

"What about what?" he demanded irritably. In short, I didn't know what I was talking about. "Every man has a limit, you know, lieutenant.... His father's a congressman, you know, and he's been to Princeton. He was malassigned and is now at division where we can use his talents doing good work."

I could tell from the tone of Kimbrell's voice it wasn't his idea, nor did he, he told me, feel it necessary to explain everything to a lieutenant, but, like it or not, although he didn't say so, he had to cover up when told to. Some time later, by chance, returning on the troopship, I heard from a sergeant of headquarters and headquarters company, First Battalion, that the sergeant major who led headquarters in combat at Hoengsong, an old Regular Army man, refused a direct order to forget the entire incident and this sergeant major, not Kimbrell, was attempting to charge Captain Carleton with running and hiding at Hoengsong and refusing to face an armed enemy on the Punchbowl which Colonel Kimbrell clammed up about. As a career soldier, the sergeant major showed another form of courage for he knew how dangerous it was to buck the brass. Not only did 'they' protect Carleton, first by approving emergency leave without Red Cross confirmation, and then with an unjustified transfer to division, 'they' also transferred the sergeant major to X Corps as an operations sergeant, at which, having come over from Fort Lewis with the division in July 1950, he was immediately rotated whether he wanted to or not.

It takes both hands to count the officers who had been in combat in the 38th and somehow misbehaved and were given safe rear-echelon work, kicked upstairs to the rear so as not to stain the combat leadership record of field grade officers, such as Captain Carleton, rewarded for failure to perform not once, but twice, by becoming an assistant division historian

Coverups were true of other divisions in Eighth Army, there being one outstanding exception I know of, company commander of A Company, 2d Battalion, 24th Infantry, early in the Police Action charged under Article of War 75 who, like Carleton, refused a direct order to engage the enemy. He was sentenced to die but President Truman commuted his sentence to twenty years of hard labor—Captain Leon A Gilbert, who according to Clay Blair's *THE FORGOTTEN WAR,* page 162, Anchor edition, was black.

I, myself, could understand Carleton being saved from Leavenworth, but for a different reason. What I do resent is the fact that from early the first day on the Punchbowl and including taking 1100, the dismal period when we lost Sergeant Ralph Smith to H and I, one of my most promising replacements taking Ich's job, has been omitted by division historians. Smitty and I had one thing in common; I joined his Army when they needed me and here he was fighting for us. At least they should have mentioned the critical rear guard position our machine gunner held if not his name, so some of us who bought our history book could point it out to friends in black and white and fill in his name "our token Canuck." It would mean more than just our word for it that he died right there fighting for you and me and make his folks right proud.

Must this episode in our unit history remain blank because of Carleton's guilt consciousness, I wondered? One does not expect the Division to expose its dirty linen in its official history, but we who went through the costly, backbreaking assault of 1100 deserve some mention somewhere. Pity our assistant division historian didn't forgo his guilt consciousness and write it for us.

Another disappointment was an overly-touted lieutenant colonel written up in stateside infantry publications as an outstanding heroic leader during the May Massacre. He was never unmasked. He was an erstwhile commander of a sister battalion in the 38th who failed to entice a Reserve rifle platoon leader acquaintance of mine into signing a round robin for a phoney DSC. He had already finagled a Silver Star and was soon, although he didn't realize it then, to make it home early because of a serious allergic reaction to penicillin for which he was awarded another Purple Heart. Men *and* officers returning from R&R were encouraged to routinely receive a massive shot against venereal disease, just in case.

An incident was created by coconspirators for this battalion commander to 'earn' a DSC, whereby a rifle company would supposedly be cut off by the enemy down a valley road and the 'brave' colonel, "without thought of the great danger to himself," would command a tank and take C rations, ammo and water to it. Lieutenant Colonel Wallace Paynes (not real name) would be written up in the round robin for a DSC and the main endorsers, his commo officer, and a captain tank commander, would receive Silver Stars endorsed by the colonel and Lieutenant John Logan, lay preacher, a Bronze Star with V for valor. Logan refused to sign because, he told me, it was dishonest.

One day Logan turned back his reconnaissance patrol without permission when mortared from a distance. Army law is that as long as a leader has communication, radio or otherwise, with his superior, he must receive permission to withdraw. The same would be true of altering his instructions in any important way. John explained to me that in all conscience, he could not stand to lose another man. In lieu of a court martial, Colonel Paynes ordered him transferred to the battalion motor pool and must certainly have concluded he was *his* man from then on. No colonel of the 38th wanted a junior officer court martial staining his leadership record, for Regular Amy colonels were expected to so inspire and lead junior officers they could do no wrong.

Another phoney, Lieutenant James F. Faster (pseudonym), with whom I served briefly because he was briefly in Korea, former member of the airborne X Corps Raiders under Colonel Paynes, was an opportunist, managing a Purple Heart from a barbed wire scratch, signed by a friendly battalion surgeon, and with help of a mistress employed by Department of Army at MacArthur's old headquarters in the Dai Ichi building, Tokyo, managed after a month in Korea to be transferred to Japan from Love Company with a phoney mortician's MOS. He was as fast a talker as Paynes, a hero by mouth.

All the proof I need personally that it was impossible for an officer of the 38th to be court martialed was the fact that I punched out my battalion commander, a West Pointer, with impunity.

Another failure was Captain Theodore 'Teddy' Toth (pseudonym) who, when he refused point-blank to go any further, there being no other experienced officer in King Company, was replaced summarily by first sergeant, Master Sergeant John Pater, who one day was called on the SCR 300 from battalion headquarters in the Pia-ri Valley. John related to me that Toth, like so many sensitive ones in that godforsaken war had enough—reached his limit. He earned a Silver Star during the winter at the Twin Tunnels which proved he could be courageous.

Duncan told Pater that he was in command of King Company, noting that Pater was a real pro; his leadership and example common knowledge on at least four occasions. Sergeant Pater was too old for a commission, but Duncan didn't think it would be very long before an officer would be assigned.

"What's wrong with the captain?" Pater asked.

The colonel, on the defensive, told Sergeant Pater not to worry, the Captain was being transferred to regiment.

"I don't understand," Pater said.

"You'll know some time, Sergeant, right now I'm not at liberty to say."

"We got two ROTC lieutenants."

"I know, sarge, and despite you being thirty-six, I'm putting you in for bars with an age waiver."

The next time Pater or I had dealings with Captain Toth was while he was Regimental Graves Registration Officer. Both Pater and I had occasions to raise our voices to him, the careless job being done. One never did see or hear of him climbing up on the Punchbowl checking his work, looking for bodies and his assistants were equally incompetent. After all, it was the least choice job in the infantry, cleaning up after battles.

Master Sergeant Pater and myself received Silver Stars for taking two high objectives in a row, both decorations initiated by Lieutenant Colonel Rowny at the request, I was to find, of X Corps, generous giver of pretty ribbons.

I last saw John in July, 1995 when he stopped at my house following delicate surgery at the Audy Murphy VA Hospital here in San Antonio. As this is written, John, eighty-three and in bad shape, who gets lonely sometimes, lives at Weslaco, Texas.

The Blue Book said—

Meanwhile, on 26 July the Third Battalion of the 38th began moving forward to join the First Battalion. Eastward, I Company was struggling to take Hill 1100 and by nightfall its every attempt had been repulsed for the enemy, hanging onto it to keep open his supply route to Hill 1179, was determined to stay. Item pulled back for a renewed attempt the following day.

Throughout the night, the big guns laid a protective screen of steel around the weary infantry clinging to their slim foothold just short of the crest of H 1100. At first light on 27 Jul the Third Battalion, L Company of the 38th moved forward to take the peak guarding the natural, south approach to 1179. Braving a rage of machine gun, mortar and small arms fire, they were repulsed and K Co pushed through L Co, returning to the attack and by evening the hill was secure.

Item pushed past Love on through the mist but was soon hit with a strong counterattack and knocked back, taking ten casualties, two from our own fighter-bombers. Because of this, Item fell back twice the very day it attacked and because of its additional weakened effort along that ridge and finger, gooks didn't slow their protective fire, keeping Item's men properly frightened. By the sounds we knew much of the fire was from captured weapons.

Driven off the enemy saddle by heavy fire, Item was forced to leave dead where they fell as we side-stepped the trail to let the parade of wounded hobble back down, ambulatory slowly, those on litters, usually bounced up and down hauled tied down by worried buddies or carriers when available, on a hunched over run and down steep descents backing slowly with great care of those wounded who couldn't hold on, down to where carriers could take over safely.

The mountain breezes exhaled on us as Item, engaging in its third effort, fought valiantly upward, replacements climbing up white-faced at the end of the supply train, bound for the open trail of a dangerous kangaroo court; hell of a bad time to be tested. Pure pandemonium (the poet John Milton's capital of hell), presided over the continuous fighting, a ruthless judge exonerating only dead and wounded. One GI, big smirk on his face, fatigues scissor-slashed in a jagged line across his chest, flapping over large Vaseline Carlisle bandages, with yards of heavy gauze, under strips of adhesive tape, on the left shoulder to under the armpit, that arm in a sling, came triumphantly down the bloody hill from the firing where two platoons of Item were still exposed to the bluntest of human cruelties. I knew well why he smiled but flinched for him for when all that body tape would be pulled off.

While we were supposedly resting in place, Sergeant Eppler and my gang carried ammo to Item, bandoliers of M1 clips and 1000-round metal cans, four belts of 250 each, of machine gun ammo, either web belts or newer metal links. Crossing a beaten zone exposed saddle path, they crouched low and made quick dashes, zigzagging to reach Item digging in desperately under the noses of gooks. Sergeant

Eppler was asked by Item's commander if he minded taking the ammo around to the men. Minded? Anyone preferred being pinned down to visiting guys who are, but being a warrior, my brave platoon sergeant complied.

One of Item's reluctant replacement riflemen coming past us up the trail kept spinning his wheels, falling down twice trying to crawl back to the top of the short, slippery incline. While we all were laughing, I heard powerful hissing and saw white smoke coming out from under the poncho that covered him and his rifle slung upside down.

"Grenade! Grenade!" I yelled, scrambling sideways as far away as the brushy terrain would allow, burying myself under my helmet. As I scrambled, from the corner of my eye I saw the man's poncho blow into the air like a lady's skirt over an air register. My God, I thought, the guy's had it for sure and immediately rummaged about my own body for a possible wound.

An Item Company medic was over him in a flash and, hard to believe though it is, the guy was the only one hurt, a nasty blood-gushing gash on the inside of his right thigh. The medic scissored off his trouser leg and applied a tourniquet above the gash and sterile Carlisle 4x4-inch Vaseline bandage over the wound, tying as tightly as he could. I understand that the man, a replacement, survived and with large damage to a nerve was returned to the States. So much for attaching grenades to one's shoulder straps by their pull rings, al la General Ridgway, which it was rumored were dummies or had their handles taped down.

As the war went on I was continually amazed at how a wounding could be so considerate of some like me, so deadly to others. How a new company commander of King Company was dead on arrival at the aid station with a minor leg wound and how Lieutenant Colonel Payne, the blowhard, made it home, with a stop-over at the Tokyo General, before his tour was over, shortened by a reaction to penicillin because he laid a whore.

Colonel Duncan caught me on my 536, pissed off for not being able to contact Shallow on either the 536 or the company 300. It's unheard of for an infantry unit to be out of contact, usually indicative of a tragedy, as with Sergeant Dorn's listening post.

"Gould, I can't raise Captain Shallow; take Love Company through Item. King will back you. Toth's no longer with them; a Sergeant Pater is in command. Don't bother telling me they have two second lieutenants; Sergeant Pater's the man for the job. I want you to work with him and when he gets bogged down, work your men through his."

"Okay," I replied, "Don't know half the guys in Love Company, all I can say is I'll try."

"All anyone can do."

The Banzai Third was already first in line and we chogeed along almost within touching distance of the last engaged platoon of Item. Our guide talked up the spirits from the rear, telling the guys how tough they were, threatening any man wanting to give in to the boy within him, checking on everything. In wars with horses, the job was performed by hussars, dragoons, who, foot soldiers knew, were ordered to shoot anyone skulking, hiding or sneaking away.

Captain Shallow, paleface and reluctant to move, cowered snug to a big rock formation as all three rifle platoons passed by obediently to meet fate head on. As I prepared to lead Love through the rear of Item, I came to a particularly advantageous hole for safe observation off an open trail to my left. I needed its protection to have time to study the immediate dangers but it was occupied by a wounded guy of Item Company, his pants undone, a tag tied through a belt loop and a large blood-stained bandage on an inner thigh.

"Hit any other place?" I demanded, lying flat on the open trail. When he failed to respond, edging closer I saw he was going into shock, black pupils dilated wide open, staring straight ahead, sweat all over his face of a pale greenish-yellow pallor. My God! I got an ugly sinking feeling in my stomach like I always had as with the sight of Ich; what a terrible, useless way to go. I'd seen guys go off the deep end this dreamy damn way and knew it as a failure of blood to circulate, either because of excessive loss of blood and therefore no pump pressure to get what's left to the brain, or an overall contraction of small blood vessels pulled taunt from fear, also preventing free flow of blood and instinctively I reached down and gave his face a hard back-and-forth slap as though to force him to return, whereupon he shook his head, color returning immediately, his eyes focusing as he grunted "Huh? Huh? What?"

Sticks in my craw to watch a poor bastard slip away as he was doing and nobody do anything to help him. I simply reacted to a strong instinctive need to express my anger at what was killing him and slap the fatal shock out of him—the crazy idea they have to die of their own fear. No! Man, how I hated them sliding away like that! No! That's what happened to the King Company replacement captain I mentioned earlier, dead on arrival at battalion aid station from an overdose of self-concern and pity, mere flesh wound on a leg.

Kitty told me later it sounded like the reasoning behind giving newborn babies an upside-down whack to jump-start their circulation and breathing. The same general principle, maybe? Of course, I'm no doctor.

"Not hurt bad!" I yelled at the wounded man then recirculating his blood. "Stop selling yourself a bill of goods and get the fuck out of here!"

I had no thought he was a coward, except that it was weak to give in like that. I couldn't see how he'd lost any great amount of blood. I grabbed his sleeve, guiding him to slide sideways out of the hole and as he started to stand I brought him down fast and warned him to keep his ass and head low or he'd get it again. The wounded man went clawing with his hands, dragging his leg, kicking with the good one, bent over up the red-hot trail toward safety.

After we got moving up 1100, PFC Funaro slipped and fell in front of Pop Miller and remained on the protected side of the trail complaining of a broken ankle. Pop took him by an elbow and pulled him up. Funaro slipped again, obviously on purpose. Pop yanked him roughly to his feet.

"Like I said, Philip," pretending concern, "nothing beats exercise for a broken ankle. Now exercise!"

The line dragged even more slowly than forced to on that slippery trail until word passed from the rear for the lead man to move out smartly and Captain Shallow came rudely elbowing his way up, sliding on his feet, turning all the way around two or three times as he skied back down the slick mud, hanging to bushes.

"Sonofabitch, Gould," he hissed fearfully. "Battalion's on my ass. Why don't you keep it moving?"

"Who's on your ass?" I quizzed. "Duncan tell you that?"

"Not exactly, but I know he'd want to."

"Duncan's trying to get hold of you."

No answer and Shallow settled into a safe hollow as I took off pushing the men.

Better an Army of stags led by a lion than an Army of lions led by a stag.
            – Napoleon Bonaparte.

Master Sergeant Juan Maldanado was my Love Company point man that morning physically leading his First Platoon smoothly with as proven expertise as any efficient tradesman on any job. Juan earned his first two stripes as a rifleman in B Company of the Second Division's 23rd Infantry at the Battle of the Bulge in WWII, helping in the cruel cold and snow to relieve the 101st Airborne at Bastogne, Belgium. By coincidence, the veteran sergeant who had the platoon I joined in the Sudetenland was a Maldanado, also Juan, who used the English John. I have been unable to get either home address or phone number and if one of the real sergeant Maldanados is still alive and reads this, John or Juan, Second or the Yankee Division, please write to me for the publisher to forward.

We approached the violent staccato of machine guns dueling in close as, stooping, I motioned overhead with my carbine to deliver the guys with momentum into the forward-moving column and was sucked into Item's fracas without being technically committed by our company commander, who didn't realize until it was over that I was in command. By then it was obvious to the observations of those who passed him that Captain Shallow was no longer combative; in fact, in spirit no longer with us.

To have enough men up to bolster the attack, I had Fred Hurtz's platoon, Master Sergeant Red Rose leading, pushed on either side through thin brush off the trail and my platoon along the broken, rough Taeusan, dangerous, side of the ridge trail.

We finished chogeeing through Item half way up H 1100 from the depths of the saddle where Corporal Turner took over the right flank. I read SLAM Marshall's book, *THE RIVER AND THE GAUNTLET,* along with his article in April 1953 in the *Saturday Evening Post* which mentioned several soldiers I knew, particularly a Corporal Edsel Turner whom I inherited in the Banzai Third and watched in attack while we and King were taking 1100 on the Punchbowl. Marshall, a brigadier general in WWII, Chief Historian in the ETO, was recalled to Korea and afterward wrote *THE RIVER AND THE GAUNTLET* about his personal experiences in the massacre at Kunu-ri, North Korea in November 1950, cut off with the Second Division as the CCF entered the war, even as he had been cut off with the 101st Airborne by krauts in the open field of snow at Bastogne. Both bitter cold.

As remnants of two shattered battalions of the frostbitten 38th sought to escape to the south that late November, Corporal Edsel Turner volunteered to take a BAR with as much extra ammo and grenades as he could handle and hold back the chinks on a defile road as long as he could. His company commander, killed in an ensuing action, saluted him and enthused that he would write Edsel up, possibly for a Medal of Honor—at least a DSC. Everyone present said good bye to Edsel, what a selfless, brave little guy, never expecting to see him again. From about five miles away, as they reached safety and daylight failed, they heard his BAR peppering from way up the valley. Turner was dropped MIA two days later on the morning report, which would routinely change to KIA after a year, but he came in several days later, yelling for food and water, dragging a foot through the lines of the 23d Infantry shouldering an empty BAR, having survived, wounded and a little frostbitten. Flying Edsel to a general hospital, the surgeon told him he was lucky it had been so cold or he would have bled to death.

The same Corporal Turner first came to my attention when we banzaied 1100. I knew then by his reputation he was a damn good man when shit was hitting the fan. No officer knew he had successfully protested being evacuated to the States. He was a maverick, a rebel who, like me, wasn't overwhelmed by authority. In reserve, like Funaro, he went looking for trouble and excitement and having been out of sight, out of mind in hospitals for months, had not been promoted since the past November, nor had anyone behaved generously toward him since the whole regiment had all but turned over, with no mention of his heroic exploits at Kunu-ri. Fact was, the Banzai Third platoon got hit good at Kunu-ri and aside from close-mouthed Sergeant Ulriche in a different platoon at the time, there were not more than three originals left. Tony Burris was one, the strong, silent cowboy type, half-breed from Oklahoma. Edsel was in Korea longer than anyone in the regiment except for rear echelon Regulars furthering their safe careers.

I worked my way, urging guys from my platoon especially, up through the brush from large rock to large rock, yelling my lungs out, as Sergeant Eppler and I taught each other to do, when, checking the extreme right flank about fifty yards toward the Punchbowl drop-off, I saw, not Eppler nor any sergeant, but little tornado Corporal Turner. Right away I found what a beauty of a terrorist Turner could be shouting orders like a combat veteran rifle platoon leader, bossing sergeants around who hopped to at the sound of him.

"Come on! Get firing! … FIRE! Dammit, fire! Get your asses up and chogee! C'mon, you bastards! Let's go! Get up there! Nobody lives forever. Chogee!"

With his strong loud-mouth inspiration, the guys moved and after that day I found myself paying attention to the little guy. I say little for at 5'7" he was an inch and a half shorter than me.

Incidentally, General Marshall must have assumed that I was at Kunu-ri with the 38th, when I was an unhappy civilian. He asked me to call him Slam, after his initials SLA. In *THE RIVER AND THE GAUNTLET*, William Morrow and Company, 1953, pages 138-42 and 281-87, and mentioned several officers I became acquainted with briefly in the Second battalion. Lieutenant John N Knight, San Jose, California, Lieutenant John E Fox of Trenton, now working on his own book, and Lieutenant Charley Heath, Secretary/Treasurer of the Korean War Veterans Alliance, Olympia, Washington, also previously mentioned, all three retired lieutenant colonels.

Nine pages in *THE RIVER AND THE GAUNTLET* are devoted to Lieutenant Hollingsworth. As soon as I read Marshall's book I wrote to him at *The Detroit News* and began a short correspondence, including several phone calls. I told him that he had been vindicated for neglecting to initiate an award for Edsel for on the night we took 1179, just as soon as a wire was brought up, I got a call from regiment.

"Lieutenant Gould? Captain Inglesby; have one man down at 38th CP by noon tomorrow for a decoration from X Corps."

"What if no one deserved one? Nobody can make it that fast anyway, even starting tonight."

A long pause and … "Colonel Mildren here, Lieutenant Gould?"

"Yes."

A long pause as he awaited a sir, then with emphasis on sir telling me how he should be addressed, "Yes, *sir!*"

"Sure," I said to irritate him.

"Is it understood, lieutenant? My CP by noon tomorrow."

"Wilco," I told him using the WWII Army Air Force term. Of course Turner couldn't make it on time for the ceremony and was handed his DSC in its dark blue box unceremoniously the day after as was befitting his antisocial ways, along with a fabricated citation which, like Foney's, I never got to read.

My first thought had been that, like all company commanders of the 15 May outpost disaster, except Captain Posten and Sandy, I should present myself for the award, which I knew would be a coveted DSC. After all, I was the only officer on that knob until the following day. This selfish thought was dissipated after an inward struggle in which several grandiose ideas were squashed, but I got the platoon sergeants together and, with Master Sergeant Robert 'Red' Rose seconding, it took all of five minutes to nominate the bundle of fury, Corporal Edsel Turner, great wartime soldier.

Except for extended hospital time, since the worrisome days on the Naktong river in July 1950, Edsel, had he not been so hard to get along with off the line or so embarrassingly heroic, might have made it to the rotation center a master sergeant a month earlier, or even a battlefield second louie a month or so earlier.

I never mentioned rotation to Turner, but I'll bet anything he would've insinuated for me to go pound salt, he'd rather stay with his buddies. Or maybe it was the outfit he loved, like street kids loyal to gangs, the nameless thing with deep mysterious spiritual continuity some willingly sacrifice for; in this cruel world, a home away from home. He wasn't happy to leave the area of combat even for a DSC but the regimental powers there allowed him no alternative.

"I'll be seeing you guys," he waved in our general direction, but none of us ever did for he was handed his once-hard-earned DSC and rotated to civilization, which I doubt he preferred. His days of bullying gooks and chinks were over. I was saddened to learn years later after finally obtaining his phone number that bad boy Turner died alone in a VA hospital in 1993 from a heart that no longer wanted to live, so dull had life become.

With far less resistance, I reached the trail above on the left before Turner that day where I shot the first of two men I personally know of—a young gook so busily tossing potato mashers down toward where Turner and his guys were yelling up a storm he didn't know what hit him. I watched him falter and fall with one hand outstretched as though to break his fall, and in the hot flush of the occasion I pumped several more rounds into where I thought he ended up in the low bushes. We all heard tales of guys killed by enemy after they hit the ground.

Finding what cover we could along the trail the guys and I crouched expectantly, blocking behind a loaded King Company which pushed off through us in the discouraging mist to consolidate the attack. Master Sergeant John Pater climbed behind his first platoon up toward the bunker-studded top of Hill 1100, against emplacements that covered each

Pictured here with his wife, John Pater, underwater demolition chief US Navy WWII. Joined US Army for Korea, acting company commander for three months, badly wounded on the Punchbowl.

other with automatic weapon fire against approach from the south. The steep sides of all but the north-south trail precluded us attacking from any other direction, unless, most unlikely, air-dropped to the north. We called them suicide bunkers because the only way to get in or out was through firing apertures facing us.

"Follow me you bastards! Let's get 'em!" roared Pater as he held his carbine high to the sky for emphasis facing the final objective. "Big Time, we're going over. E-e-e-e d-e-e-wa-wa. You yellow cunts, here we come. King Company! King Company! Show 'em who's King!"

The way Pater said bastards was a compliment as well as a curse.

There wasn't time to repeat himself, for the enemy stopped his spirited attack on the grenade line; one arm in particular lobbing many from behind a dead tree in the very middle of the trench. King Company was able to heave its heavy frag grenades half as far. I worked up on elbows and knees to survey the threat.

"What now?" a King rifleman asked, turning on his side, smiling nervously. "What do we do now, Lieutenant?"

It was a fierce battle, a noisy hot bloody engagement as Item buttoned up in place and Love and King, or King and Love, got mired in a series of hot firefights, but the only explanation anywhere in the world in writing for the deadly period from one minute after midnight on 27 July 1951, Korean time, was a terse mimeographed paragraph of the activities in the Division's periodic operations report, seen only by a handful of business-as-usual professional Army staff officers and their unemotional sergeants.

The firing up ahead was anxious, at times frightening to hear. Wounded stumbled by dull eyed, scurried down past us holding to the terrible red marks made in them, ran past hunkered down, white faced, slipped or limped by us waiting our turn, silent; staggered along half blind with hands out thrust dripping blood through fresh bandages, feeling bushes going by, led by less wounded ambulatory; and undulating passively on litters.

"Good going man," we murmured at brave men passing.

First one and then another fired along the stalled line of King. There were no fusillades. Everyone else was a sightseer, lying on his belly or his side watching the battle ebbing away, yelling occasionally to correct another's aim, a few detached and careless enough to light up. The longer they stayed cringing in that awkward position, the more brave the enemy became. Suddenly a terrified bunch of five GIs turned, stood up, and ran pell-mell, slipping, sliding and stumbling down the hill from the left flank, their backs to the enemy.

"Here they come! . . . They're coming down!" they cried.

I scrambled sideways like a crab across the ground, yelling, "What're you doin'?"

"Orders to withdraw," one of them yelled.

"Whose orders?" I demanded, working into them. "Who are you guys?"

I threatened them with my mounted carbine bayonet, stopping them with the help of two sergeants. They were some of Item's people—what I called intermediate bugouts—who, remaining hidden behind boulders, mixed somehow with Pater's holdbacks, not knowing of their company's silent withdrawal.

"Somebody said better withdraw."

"Get back before my men let loose on you goddamn cowards!" I yelled.

"Yes, sir!" they said, ashamed, realizing their panic; Item men along with King as though they belonged now to King. The silent rains, lifting, hung poised in a heavy gray sky in what seemed the most pitiless day of the war. Apertures of enemy bunkers staring coldly from the very top of 1179, unblinking reptile eyes fixed upon us, winking death, 'seeing' us dead, with outgoing flashes of aimed rifle fire. As our demoralized men returned the stare with nervous upward glances, someone near me observed sadly, "Our last go-round."

Leaving the stymied protected riflemen, I crawled into an abandoned gook hole, mind and body, every bit of me, aching so it seemed I had to squeeze my chest with my hands to breathe. I needed at least a half hour rest. "Take over. Give me a few minutes," I told Sergeant Eppler.

"King'll get livin' shit kicked out for sure," J J said, glancing anxiously over his shoulder. "Nobody, brother, I mean *nobody* getting over that hill alive."

Little Kims are anxious to get off the ridge and every once in a while they'd hear a cry in Korean and dart from cover in two-man teams to hurry back with a wounded man on a litter—their ticket to safety. Sometimes they'd be so rattled and scared they'd put a corpse on a litter and head for the safety of the valley for kimchee and a big black pot of rice.

Four KSC came down past me hauling a litter high on their shoulders, bouncing a large man strapped on with commo wire. Sergeant Eppler saw at a glance that the man was dead and ordered the carriers to set him down, indicating for them to take him off the litter. He called Smiley, our company interpreter, and told him to give the carriers hell and even though they belonged to King, remind them that they were not to pick up soldiers on their own; the decision whom and when to evacuate being left to medics, certainly not to take dead until all wounded were off. Smiley jabbered away, as was their custom, it seemed five minutes, and by his weak inflections and volume, we knew he didn't have the guts to bawl anyone out.

"What they say, Smiley?"

"They say they make mistake. Man look living."

Another litter came by carried hip high and I could see that the man still lived. I motioned the two carriers to set him down to check his tag and make certain bleeding was stopped and he was properly bandaged and given a morphine shot, if necessary. He was what gunfighters out West called gut shot, his fly hastily ripped open, exposing olive drab undershorts soaked through with coagulating blood oozing slowly from above. The man, a rugged, dark-bearded sergeant from King Company, opened his eyes slowly with a dreamy, morphined, far-away look, half focusing as I bent over him. I had noticed him leading his platoon in King Company on our June parade, passing by so proud, handsome and virile—a recruiting poster to entice our Nation's manhood to do something patriotic.

"Lieutenant?" he asked feebly, catching sight of my silver bar, almost begging, it seemed but he had not the energy to pursue his thought and ended with a feeble, "Good luck … sir," closing his eyes to dream again.

"Good luck, sarge," I said, patting the man's shoulder. "You did a number one job."

We cherish praise from our own kind, and half unconscious, the wounded man smiled as a reaction to my valuable praise, or perhaps because he was returning to his fantasy world of morphine, hopefully kidding around with his girlfriend. A true warrior, RA all the way, he'd die proud to have it said by one he respected that he did his job well. Save your pity rear echelons, it's his chosen profession, the job only a real man can do.

"He don't look so good, do he?" Tree commented.

We resumed crouching behind a large boulder splitting my can of lima beans and ham chunks.

"Knows somethin'?" Tree said awkwardly, clearing his throat. "Lieutenant's changed."

Still mindful of the brave sergeant, I was taken off guard.

"What's that?"

"Sir, we knows you changed."

"Soldier," I countered irritably, "we all have."

"Never tole a guy he done a good job 'cause he's dying."

Having spent the day standing back of King, we passed through to take our brief turn again and then after two hours on the grenade line, a rejuvenated Pater led King through us, amid the clamors, clashes, shouting, explosions, screaming, swearing and plain battle noises wherein it became obvious to us that neither side was having it easy. We curled up in the most protective positions we could manage under our ponchos.

As darkness fell that violent night, the battle subsided. A temporary cease fire took place not over twenty climbing yards from one another. I begged the average American's God's pardon for leading that wire patrol to oblivion, an entire squad made into dead unsung heroes, gone, especially the young wireman whose blood-full goiter I remembered too easily, and my sacrificing three of Pop Miller's men without clearing with him. While in that God-beseeching mood, I asked Him respectfully to try to take better care of my guys. Should be Your guys first, and pardon me for being Agnostic.

We all dozed off on the battlefield. I was knocked out by fatigue, leaving one ear open, not so much tired muscles but nerves; tension that terrible afternoon and evening sweeping softly over me, lulled again by our amateur gospel singer, Sergeant E-5 Raymond Roundtree, mouthing a muffled musical deep-throated litany—

Is I blue? Is I blue? Tell everyone around de' place I is blue. De' angels tole me dey's comin'. Hear what, man, dey's comin'. Man, angels dark as me, you see, as this night's gonna' be. Hear me ... how dark this night's gonna' be. De' angels tole me. It's gonna' be dark as me.... Is I blue?.... Tell everyone I'se blue.

"Crimus, Tree," I pleaded to myself as its touching tenderness put me under, "It's bad enough without moaning like that."

Rifle shots landing nearby like heavy bees shook me fully awake and Tree went silent as a hooty owl. Moaning like that was no way to lick the problem; it was just another temporary escape. Better we sing '*Battle Hymn of the Republic*' sad but angry tune, loud as we could and get furious and angry and mad. I began mumbling uncertainly, off-key: "Mine *eyes* has *seen* the *glory* of the *comin'* of the *Lord,*" and broke off weakly when I sensed Tree's change of pace, wistfully louder than his usual, from two holes away of the upper class white man's *Whiffenpoff* song, the few introductory words he knew from what little he'd heard me trying to sing.

"From tables down at Duffy's...." large, white eyes staring through the dark fixed in fatigue as he improvised pathetically: "From young squads that were Love, to 'de fresh graves outside Seoul, good men come and go ... down 'de dark ground of 'de soul."

Tree was right, '*Battle Hymn*' wouldn't work. It was theatrical and out of pace with our miserably low life.

"I'm sorry I interrupted you, Tree," I apologized silently. "Go ahead, talk to anyone who'll listen."

Later, as it darkened more, gook terror teams behind cover below on the steep Punchbowl side banged C ration cans and yelled taunts in broken English to draw our fire. "GI, you die." My men were restless and I crouched, scooting sideways checking our positions, spending half an hour with the last young replacement, a machine gun ammo bearer.

"Ain't I glad to see you, Lieutenant Gould. I'm awfully scared, sir. I know'd I shouldn't be; just can't help myself. What'll I do when they're on top of us?"

"Take that M1 and use it. Fire at 'em, that's all you can do. Toss grenades when they're close enough and don't forget to get under your helmet and duck. Make your old M1 part of you. Always lay it down pointed where gooks might be. Have one in the chamber. Soon's you spot one, sound off 'Gooks! Gooks!' and let 'em have it low. Don't forget to take your safety off. Try to sight on them, but at least point directly at 'em and keep firing fast as you can."

"What if I can't sir? What if I get too scared and freeze?"

"Yell and get busy and keep your mind on the killing that's coming—them before you. We all are scared when we're still. Don't forget they're human like you and just as scared. They call us foreign devils, yell like it."

"'*Stars and Stripes*' says they're fanatics, sir; don't know the meaning of fear, and supposin' everyone gets too scared and runs off and leaves me? ... Lieutenant, I'm awful scared to die." He broke down sobbing softly to himself.

"Damn '*Stars and Stripes,*'" I cursed, "better send reporters up here to see *us* banzai; Goddamn rear echelons would learn what yelling fanatics are.

"Goddammit, boy, think we're not fanatics? Wait for daylight, it's our time to lead. Act like you're part of the Banzais. Man, we scare the shit out of them. Should've watched your buddies banzai last May. Shit, man, watch Turner and Burris. They yell a lot louder and if that isn't being fanatic, what is? Don't let any writer or radio announcer, any rear echelon blowhard tell you that chinks, gooks, or Turks was any more fanatic than you.

"Man, I'd walk straight up on any company of chinks before I'd tackle a squad of you guys. ... Know at all times where your buddies are. Look, you can almost see your assistant squad leader over there. Hey, Ed. Ed? Ed? You there, Ed?"

Following a brief questioning silence, a shaky voice hissed from a hole ten yards away, "S-h-h-h! Ed's sleepin'."

Reassured, feeling comfortable again, the replacement wisecracked, "Hell, lieutenant, that's Sergeant Ed Brown. You don't have to see the guy, you can smell him. That old guy'd sleep through an earthquake."

Crimus, I thought. Ed couldn't be more than twenty-eight or nine. Old guy?

"Well, dammit, man, get mad. Get busy and join him. Now get some shuteye."

On the subject of cowardice, I used to have an unsanitized copy of General Patton's speech to the men of his Third Army on the eve of crossing the channel—

> ... And if there are any cowards out there, I hope you get it the first day. We don't want cowards going back to the States breeding more cowards!

Taken from the sweet intimate warmth of their mothers with no understanding of violence, riflemen learned fast in Korea how to stay alive, forgetting what nonsense civilization taught about human rights to perceive evil in flight on their own. Some of our paleface replacements failed to live long enough, succumbing to habitual trust in short, piteous rites of passage. *Imors improvisa,* sudden death, anciently regarded as ignominious.

> *Take this message to the Spartans, passerby;*
> *Obedient to their orders, here we lie.*
> – Somonides of Ceros of Spartan dead at Thermopyle.

Unlike the gray-haired, four-eyed, pot-bellied, boastful bastards in Washington, we were the sinned against, meeting high explosive expletives from the foe head on, silently suffering disgusting sights and odors, falling to the bottom of human despairs, crying again and again within us, some like me openly.

Most of my guys didn't sign up for dirty government jobs overseas to be hurt by all that misery, nor were any of them noticeably bellicose by nature. They were plain GI Jocs, RA all the way, Regular Army, and Reserves and National Guardsmen doing it for excitement and pay, to prove their manliness, or they were draftees with US serial numbers complaining of being drafted and hauled all this way to make violent political protests against fellow draftees of another color. Having been ordered by public law to go out and act tough and be trained to kill, to serve weapons in dangerous ways, they were set up to be presented to history as anonymous, clean-cut, devout, young male American citizens, implying that they volunteered, as in past ages mustered by fife and drums to protect the public. All committed to die so fat shirkers would flourish, and all this whether or not their draft boards interviewed, much less ascertained that they wouldn't mind being dead prematurely. Father Almighty, don't forgive a single draft board; bastards know damn well what they did.

No, most dogfaces didn't volunteer to disappear from their homes lonely and scared, they were swept up in an immoral lottery which decreed that only healthy young males of good character could 'give' their lives for democracy. That is, be taken overseas and ordered to shoot or be shot, proof of the enormous criminal power of politics. Better rid ourselves of shirkers and law breakers we board and feed and clothe and take medical care of for free; take them rather than innocent ones.

We admitted no fear in following orders. Dogfaces die without mentioning fear, supreme sacrifice, cowardice or bravery. Being in the way of duty makes it easier to ignore fear—that fear we never talk about, that possesses us. To be or not to be was *my* question. Fuck Hamlet and his stage prop—when do *I* get it again? It was absurd to believe I wouldn't—only hoped it would be little and stateside, and in any event I had one consolation, my death was the end of it for everyone, final act of Nature.

HEADQUARTERS
2D INFANTRY DIVISION
APO 248 c/o Postmaster
San Francisco California

GENERAL ORDERS
5 September 1951
NUMBER   683

Section II

AWARD OF THE SILVER STAR—by direction of the President, under the provisions of the Act of Congress, approved 9 July 1918 (WD Bul 43, 1918), and pursuant to authority in AR 600-45, the Silver Star for gallantry in action is awarded to the following named enlisted men:

MASTER SERGEANT JOHN M PATER, RA1226680080, Infantry, United States Army, a member of Company K, 38th Infantry Regiment, 2d Infantry Division, distinguished himself by gallantry in action on 20 July 1951 in the vicinity of Taeu-San, Korea. On this date, during an attack on hostile positions, Company K met heavy enemy resistance of small arms, automatic weapons, and grenade fire. Sergeant Pater, with complete disregard for his personal safety, continuously exposed himself to enemy fire while leading his unit in the attack. Throughout this action, he remained with forward elements and directed the fire of his men. When the gunner of a recoilless rifle was wounded, Sergeant Pater unhesitatingly operated the weapon and employed devastating fire upon the enemy. By his undaunted leadership, the men of his unit were inspired to greater heights of daring to successfully overrun hostile positions and secure their objective with a minimum of casualties. The gallantry and outstanding devotion to duty displayed by Sergeant Pater on this occasion reflect great credit upon himself and the military service. Entered the military service from Maryland.

BY COMMAND OF MAJOR GENERAL YOUNG:

E. L. Rowny
Lt Col   GS
Chief of Staff

This citation shows one how little, if anything, the talented valor awards writer knew of what actually transpired. No one on our hill had a word to say in determining the wording of Sergeant Pater's Silver Star, any more than for mine. "Sergeant Pater, with complete disregard for his personal safety, continuously exposed himself to enemy fire while leading his unit in the attack. Throughout this action, he remained with *forward* elements and directed the fire of his men." The rear echelon fiction writer also had him "operating the recoilless rifle," which are never in *forward* ele ments but well to the rear, and as for Pater manning one, the only one he recalls operating was in laying a base of fire for us to take 1179.

I don't know exactly why anyone at X Corps was elected to throw valor medals around when prominent objectives were taken, but I know no one at company or battalion level, where the fighting was done and where it should have originated, knew anything about me firing a captured machine gun from the hip or Pater, a company leader, way back with a 57 recoilless. We are goddamn proud of what leading we did.

For all his services in Korea, John deserves far more than a Silver Star. It would be hard to prove if any of our three rifle companies should get full credit for taking H 1100 midway up the Punchbowl rim from the south, but Master Sergeant Pater got his Silver Star, as I would later for 1179. One can always tell who was in on the final assault for they have trouble breathing. Pater and his field first sergeant were rubber-legged, gasping desperately for breath, bent over, gagging, close to vomiting on the smallest area of the very top of the objective. We let loose with unbottled tension, wild Indian warwhoops, yelling cheers hoarsely, laughing and choking, and he was yelling when able for his sergeants to get the rest of the men up fast when sergeant Eppler and I arrived out of breath.

While Pater and his men gasped for wind, men of both companies dug in around the top where King's sergeants pointed, taking sporadic plunging fire from 1179; despite which, everyone was deliriously happy. What a pumped-up happy feeling; proud, teeming up there in the tight, proud ball with your guys. As a matter of fact, platoon comes from the French, *peloton,* a tight ball, which we did miles and miles above mankind, loving one another in gruff, manly ways, ahead of any mere rear echelon soldier who was, in turn, miles and miles ahead of any damn male civilian. If only our backers everywhere right up to congress could see us taking prime real estate from 'fanatic' gooks. They were tough fighters, sure, but right here we kicked their asses good, ending up yelling back and forth in cracked voices, throats hurting from cool, raw air pumping in too fast.

"Christ's sake, dig defense, they'll counterattack soon's they turn their men around, within the hour," "dammit, man, get your machine gun facing north and charge one in . . . move!"

Combat noises were partially muffled by the thick air as Mike Company's 81mm mortar men set up their own effort in a small gully behind 1100 to chase enemy sliding down from 1179 to muster a counterattack, dropping shells into tubes so fast they ran out of all but the few rounds kept for self-defense. The tubes steamed in the slow, cold fog-rain while strong-smelling, thin, bluish smoke from propellent charges and oil burning from the tubes mingled with mist into a heavy swirling haze over the gully in which they planted their heavy base plates.

Mortar observers made sure bursts stayed well ahead as they called out to their gun crews over 300 radios to correct azimuths and ranges of new targets on the trail just north of 1100. "Drop two-zero," they instructed Double-Bubbles, nickname for their gunner. "Right five-zero. Check your bubbles again." After two more adjustments for range. "Okay? FIRE FOR EFFECT! . . . Let them bastards have it! On the way! On the w-a-a-y! On the way!" mortar forward observers yelled to everyone within earshot.

Everyone ducked just in case the rounds were short which I never saw happen with mortars, and listened intently for the air fluting whisper of indropping enemy mortar rounds, much more apparent and threatening at the receiving end.

"You guys and King better be damn much on your toes tonight, we're out of ammo. More on its way, but you know how few rounds a man can carry in those canvas mortar vests. From the valley a good eight miles at a 30-degree climb.... Poor monkeys, most older'n my dad."

Our platoon casualty report reached me through PFC Wheeler from Sergeant Roundtree. "Thompson and DuBonney got it, sir."

Since both were new men, I concentrated on PFC Bob Cartwright from Farmingdale, Long Island, who took a shell splinter in his thigh. Doc Carlson worked on him.

"Get a bone?" I asked. "You bleed bad there."

"Hell," Doc said, "you bleed bad anywhere."

Company runner, PFC Blum, came all excited looking for me. Private Funaro, Private Sizemore and two privates from King were threatening to finish off a gook. Pooped as I was, I went up the trail to a tight group of about ten Johnny-come-latelies gathered around a wounded gook unmindful of the world around him, trying to crawl away, pulling himself over the ground ever so slowly with outstretched fingers, like an old abandoned dog trying to pull himself off a busy highway by his front paws.

"Let the cocksucker have it," bigmouth Funaro ordered.

"Yeah," another intermediate bugout agreed. "Put him out of his misery!"

Yet another, "Finish him off!"

They dared each other like naughty boys.

"Get the fuck out of here, you yellow bastards!" I yelled, firing a burst of my M2 carbine close over them.

It was hard to imagine being that cold-blooded, even as antisocial. Much later, when I had time, I figured maybe down deep in their beetle brains they were trying to do the guy a favor for he was shot up bad and did die of his own accord before one of our medics got to him. At the time, I hated their guts for not contributing to our banzai and then talking so damn tough to an honorably wounded man when fighting was over. In the real old days an officer could shoot the poltroons on the spot for skulking—turning their backs on an enemy and threatening wounded prisoners.

"Get to your squads, punks!" I yelled.

Somehow, I've thought since, subconsciously PFC Funaro and his buddies must have pitied that poor gook, maybe felt so deeply the pathetic sight of the courageous dying man striving for safety and they not suffering at all by comparison it made them angry or they needed to put him out of his misery like any painfully wounded, incurably sick animal; actually to ease their own conscience because they were helpless to aid them. Or do you suppose they were just hardened, brutal guys like Genghis Khan, who so despised an enemy? I don't know. I wish there was some psychologist smart enough to clear it up for me. Sometimes it worries me to know when will it be right to put a fellow human being out of misery like we do old cats and dogs. When will it be time, compassion used up, time to put us oldies 'to sleep'? Like me, for instance as I write, useless asshole, marking time in place, no erection in fifteen years nor place to put it.

I never studied sociology or psychology but did a lot of reading and drew my own conclusions anyway. As Thomas Caryle said: "A true university is a collection of books" and experiences too. What, for instance, makes a guy like Funaro tick? Fred gave me a good idea of how miserable a slum he came from in South Bronx, but not everyone from there was like Funaro. Look at company runner, PFC Sydney Blum, about as upright a little guy as they come. Some say it's Blum's religion, but I say no, the way he was raised. Blum was religious all right; every time he and Fred and a couple others in battalion got the chance in reserve, they'd take a jeep for services at division. Funaro made faces at Jews behind their backs and what did he have to be thankful for or care about, doped whore of a mother, short-term 'fathers' taking turns with her?

Still, I realized, someone along the line taught him the fundamentals of right and wrong, at least some discipline, else he couldn't have lasted basic training and would've been kicked out of the Army before he got in it, like so many big city know-it-alls. Fellow New Yorker Fred, who must have done a lot more brooding about this subject than me, suggested Funaro's essential strength and learning came in the very early years from grade school and then good and bad from his gang. Where were his mother, father and big brothers? His salvation was pure luck when a kind judge backdated his last misdemeanor charge over six months so he could threaten: "Son, go to jail or join the Army and try to make something of yourself. Have a seat, Philip. In about an hour your father," smiling, pausing to motion toward the unsuspecting bailiff, "will escort you around the corner to the recruiting station and sign for you. I know you don't have a place to sleep tonight."

Funaro was very defensive of his gang trying to convince me that there are bad and there are good ones.

"What's a good gang?" I asked.

"Mine."

"What's so good about it?"

"We're the toughest in the Bronx and. . . ." he broke off, smiling to himself.

"And?" I asked.

"I better not say; you won't believe me anyway."

"Believe what?"

"Believe our name."

"Which is. . . ."

"Okay, lieutenant, we were the Banzais long before this platoon."

I sort of scoffed and watched him start to boil.

"I told you you wouldn't believe me."

"Where would a bunch of kids, excuse me, guys, in the Bronx ever run across a name like Banzai?"

"One of the guy's dad, a Marine, got a Silver Star banzaiing japs."

"With a name like Banzais in New York City you have to be good, but now don't tell me you guys do missionary work."

"Ever hear of Robin Hood?"

"Don't tell me, rob in the hood to pay Paul?"

"If you don't shell out with a donation, sir, we'll get it the hard way. We're appreciated in our neighborhood and our guys got as much moxie as any one here in Love Company."

I wanted to ask him where his moxie was but it wasn't a time to taunt him. I learned a bit about street gangs from Funaro and came away thinking of their good qualities—how they instilled discipline, demanded personal courage and above all, strict loyalty and a strong sense of honor, twisted though it was. Stick by the gang, it sticks by you. That's the best our Queen of Battles can do. Funaro mentioned a litany of heroes in his gang. One even stole a friendly cop's revolver while he was sitting on a stool at a lunch counter with the strap unsnapped. They made him sweat a couple hours before handing it back. Like old-time American Indians, you didn't just talk hero, you did it, "and one of our buddies was killed proving it pushing a little girl from the path of a bus. And lieutenant, she was a nigger of a rival gang, our worst enemy."

The few of King and Love who did the dangerous in-fighting were dehydrated and could do little more than cough and spit sticky saliva. Johnny-come-latelies were busy souvenir hunters, running about searching enemy pockets, poking through dank supply bunkers for loot, shouting impractical threats toward the top of 1179.

"Had your chance right here," Eppler yelled. "Next time keep up with us."

King Company, first to overrun the very top and the bunkers, passed around bright red North Korean paper currency and inspected rusted pieces of our own heavy artillery shells and 500 pound aerial bomb shells, jagged hunks of steel several inches thick. Abandoned by the fleeing enemy were two partially disassembled American-made WWII 75mm mountain pack howitzers; twenty or thirty Russian-made carbines with unstained and unvarnished, poorly finished pine wood stocks and, in one supply bunker, open rice straw bags half full of millet and barley crawling with white grubs.

Pop Miller explained to Ski that gooks fattened the grubs to eat rather than the millet which they hated.

"Aw, you're kiddin'."

Captain Shallow, arriving cautiously about an hour later, talked the battalion S3, Detweiler, out of Love remaining on the scene; that Item and King could hold without trouble. I didn't give the captain a hard time even though, technically, until Duncan said otherwise, I believed I was still in command. Pater declared it plain crazy "expecting a half-strength company to out-fight burp guns at night." And, indeed, at night one Communist with a burp gun was worth ten GIs confused and fearful of the dark.

"Let me clear with Captain Shallow," I told Pater.

"What's the matter?" Shallow, already halfway back down the finger, stammered in his 536 radio. "Afraid to run his own company?"

"He's in a jam, morale's sinking; they lost *takusan* guys."

"We all got troubles."

"You don't understand, Captain; we shouldn't leave a beatup company like King without a backup."

"Duncan's in charge, not me, and how about Item?"

"I was only asking."

Colonel Duncan *was* in charge and after I radioed him of the situation he made arrangements for Item Company to set up on the western side of the newly captured hill and for us, Love, to marry with them at the center to the north running east and north where King Company, facing 1179, the greatest threat, closed the tight defense circle.

Lieutenant Rawn, artillery observer attached to Love, came up to register defensive fires, relaying through the artillery liaison officer at battalion CP. From Fire Direction Center Rawn would order a marker round of william peter safely away from us on a preregistered map coordinate so many range clicks up from existing goose eggs (concentration or circled impact areas drawn on map overlays) and from visible willie peter smoke markers make quick corrections—typically, say, 50 meters north, further out, or 60 south, nearer to us, or left or right, further away or west so many increments. When he had the burst exactly where he knew or thought gooks were or might be later, he radioed back, "Give us that one." Fire Direction Center in the friendly valley five miles to the south radioed back through battalion what number to label the new concentration. Lieutenant Rawn and I, acting company commander on the spot, made ovals on our maps where each concentration landed or should land and wrote the number given to it in the middle. Concentration number fifteen, for instance, which we never asked for, put fire below and behind us smack on what the Press would label Bloody Ridge.

Not until Love was settling in after the battle, digging new holes facing north, did we learn that Ski was missing again. For some reason, his boss, Pop Miller, had a feeling that this time he was killed, asking members of his squad when they last saw the wanderer.

"Feeling?" I accused. "Where'd *you* last see him?"

"You know Ski."

"Damn right I know Ski. You and your assistant, Tree, were supposed to keep an eye on him."

"Christ, we got our own war to fight."

"Too busy? I've known you a long time now, Pop, and you've never been too busy to watch after any of your men, much less Ski. What's the matter?"

"Lieutenant, he volunteered to help distribute ammo to Item Company. I told him I'd rather he didn't, but he went anyway. I'll bet he decided to get into the fight himself. You know how mad Ski can get seeing just one man hurt. . . . I've had to tell that guy when to shit and how to wipe his ass. He gives me a worse time than everyone put together; expects me to be his father."

"He's also a damn good fighter once you point things out."

"Geezus, Dud, none of us live forever...." He paused and then, choking up a little, "I'm going to miss that kid. God, wasn't he funny, and nobody didn't like him, even if it was pity." Then, glaring at me, he practically shouted, "You accusing me of something?:"

"I'm not accusing nobody of nothing, and don't yell at *me*."

"Who you think I am, everybody's old man?" Pop shouted.

"Who *you* yellin' at?" I shouted back.

"*You*, lieutenant, dammit! You should've taken my request to send Ski to the rear, like that kid who was night blind. Ski was every bit as bad off."

We stood toe-to-toe, both of us flushed with dread at losing Ski. A second later, confused and ashamed, we looked away. I doubt if either of us thirty-one-year-olds was aware at the time of Pop calling me Dud. When I did recall it, it made me even closer to Pop. He was one guy, he and Sergeant Eppler, I couldn't get along without. They inspired me to stay alive, like I used to depend on Sergeant Ulriche.

"All I can say, lieutenant, is I'm going to miss the kid. He and Dorn and Ich, we all got hit the same day late in February in Operation Killer and frostbitten a little while pinned down and Ich limped some until the day he died. We hitchhiked from the hospital back to the front together and went on R&R to Osako together. We all could rotate together; now I'll have to go it alone. It's going to be awful lonely. We even planned on what we'd do on the boat together." Pop stopped, starting to tear up and stammer, then, looking away, continued in a low monotone to himself. "He was never bright, wiseass like the average. He was good and honest; good as they come— too good—and big-hearted? Do anything I'd ask . . . give you his beer if you asked. At least to me. Poor guy all alone up there. . . . Didn't have nobody to talk to but me. Guys ribbed him to get him going; didn't have nobody anywhere but me. Boys Town, or whatever he was in, head man signed him up in the Army at seventeen to get rid of him a year before this mess started over here. Had trouble being accepted, even as a category S4 IQ, who, they tell me, recruiting stations can take only two each month.

"Don't know, lately I'm getting so I don't care if school keeps; me, only one's left . . . around too long.... After Pearl Harbor ever think there'd be another sneak attack? More Goddamn yellow slant eyes, all of them—japs, chinks and gooks! Why should anyone care about life if they have to go on and on and on like this?" He stopped, looking at me through sparkling eyes.

"Sir, I'm going up there at daylight and find my buddy and bring him down so we can say good bye and give him a proper sendoff.... With your permission, sir, I'm goin' to take him down the mountain and find a Catholic chaplain. Ain't goin' to throw him on no old truck without a proper good bye.... Sir, he was as comfortable to be around as a dog. I don't mean it bad about Ski, I mean that good, sir, no dog you love will ever question you or make you unhappy, or growl at you unless you hurt him, and then you have no right to live with him. He should give you the boot. Ski would run right down that path and step on a mine if I asked him to. I want to thank you again, sir, for trying to get Ski a Soldier's Medal; me and you know how coura-geous it was of him in his mind to grab that hot grenade."

After a long pause, Pop jabbed the back of his fingers at his tears and swiped them off. "Probably better he's dead. Most people won't have nothing to do with him, and he'll never have to be teased no more…. What could he do in civilian life? they won't let him back in Boys' Town or any other place. Maybe better he got it good. Ski's got no place to go where he could do the job right; no other one to live with and keep him straight."

He paused again before airing more sad thoughts. "Almost everyone I used to know, even back home, is dead one way or another. I don't know. I just don't know why any of us want to put it off."

"I'm sorry," I said softly, patting Pop's shoulder. "Awfully sorry. I know about you and Ski and I've always admired you for it. We all know how much he was to you. You always did your best and everyone praised you even if nobody said so."

Pop Miller grinned sheepishly, swiping clumsily at his eyes.

"C'mon, now," I said, trying to get him to smile, "buck up; this war can't last forever."

"Far as my buddies, Ich and Dorn and now Ski are concerned the war's over already. I'm no good to no one no more," Pop said, tearing up again, his voice husky, lowering his head.

"Cut it out, you're just imagining things."

"No I ain't." He bit his quivering lower lip. "I ain't no good to no one no more. I had two women, couldn't keep either. Both quit each time I was transferred. Didn't want to go on with me. Said I couldn't provide a home and both judges agreed. I just ain't somebody a woman can want." He paused, then blurted out, turning away with tears flooding, uncontrollably. "I can't help no one no more. I'm losing 'em all, one after 'nother."

"C'mon, Pop, get hold of yourself."

Pop shook his head. "None of us deserves to live no more. All we're good for is killing. Here I am my squad to the left and the right; suddenly Death is more immediate than anytime. Lieutenant, Death is getting close for all of us. World War Two was easy; I was never in charge. I'll never allow myself to get this close no more without Ski. A terrible thing, death, so final, gone, gone, always gone; unnatural to postpone it. I'm not religious. I'm not sure I'd even want to rejoin my family; all gone but a sister, but still, if, in only a negative way, there's comfort in knowing I'd be gone and my personal struggle over. I know it's finally going to happen. At long last it's going to happen to me and, although I never go to church, maybe I can find Ski, and Dorn and Ich and we can go home together, somewhere together, like we planned."

As Pop armed himself at dawn to go look for Ski's remains, the object came wandering in with two full boxes of machine gun ammo, stewing and fretting.

"Fine buddies, where'd you guys get to? One of these days you'll want something from me. Fat chance! I won't give you the sweat off my balls…. Fine buddies, sneak off and leave a guy alone.'

"You for real?" Pop demanded, feigning anger, wrapping his arms around the big befuddled Pole. "I'll shit you not, Ski, you're too ignorant to get yourself killed."

He pulled Ski tight to himself, causing Ski to lose his footing and Pop held him steady for a minute, as his voice cracked with emotion, blurting, "Goddamn you, you homely bastard, you damn Polock, you! Next time you gotta' shit, let someone else wipe your ass." He reached out and gave Ski a couple slugs on his arm.

Late the next afternoon Captain Shallow called on the 536 from down the saddle ordering me to report. When I arrived, I was told I'd have to spread my men to back up Master Sergeant 'Red' Rose and his Second Platoon in the hottest part of the perimeter.

"Give him a hand, Gould. I don't know about Hurtz anymore. I'm thinking of taking a little rest myself back in the kitchen trains or maybe R&R and I need someone I can trust. I'll see you get a Commendation Ribbon and maybe another Bronze Star Meritorious."

Green hornet? I thought, commendation ribbons are for rear echelons, and who wants another Bronze Star? Colored ribbons mean so much to careerists like the captain.

"And if you write it up for Sergeant Dorn again, Bronze Star for Valor, and Soldier's Medal for Kiezlowski, I'll sign them this time and push them through, only you got to know your Sergeant Dorn's dead as a doornail. He's MIA and can't qualify for posthumous for a year. By the way, would you mind taking some ammo up to King Company?"

"Captain, we were the last to do that yesterday afternoon to Item and even took it around to the positions, which is more than others do. You know it's someone else's turn."

"Yes, that's the point. It's Hurtz's turn and I don't know about him anymore."

"What do you mean?"

"He's been acting strange."

"Strange?"

"Various things. Made an ass of himself yesterday with those bodies, risking snipers, going around pulling their fatigue tops over their faces, bothered the hell out of me to get up a burial detail. You know we haven't authority to make even a temporary burial and with short rations and everything, the guys are too pooped to do extra digging. Besides, it's all rocks up there and I can't have people moving around the ridge attracting fire."

"What's wrong with Lieutenant Hurtz?"

Captain Shallow laughed uncomfortably. "I never knew Hebs were so religious; said we were sinning, leaving dead unburied. Sergeant Luther stopped him from ordering chogee bearers to haul bodies down. He knows them King carriers don't take orders from us and are due back fast as they can to grab a wink and bring up more critical supplies. Hurtz knows well as any one how used up they are. I can't put my finger on the trouble, but he acts like he's nursing a yellow streak." He stopped abruptly to correct himself. "I mean, he's getting timid and too concerned about guys getting hurt.... I can't do everything. I need officers I can trust."

"He's got a number one sergeant in Rose."

Rabbi chaplain praying at the grave of a Jewish soldier.

"Would you mind awfully taking up ammo again?"

"Don't ask me to volunteer for my men, sir."

"Then I guess it's an order, if you don't mind," he laughed nervously and went on angrily. "It's not our responsibility anyway. Jesus H Christ, I tried my best to talk Mighty Mouse out of it but battalion is way short of carriers. And we're not supposed to expose them like that. Well, I guess you better get at it."

I thought Major Duncan must have reinstated Shallow without relieving me and planned to give him a hunk of my mind next time I talked with him. Or was I good only for combat?

Sergeant Rose himself was worried that something was very wrong. "I got a damn good officer there," he told me. "There wasn't a cooler guy in the Army back there in January on 755 at Hoengsong and everyone freezing their asses off. Lately, however, I think Lieutenant Hurtz has had the course. Simply had enough. Jesus, can't any of us just have our fill all the time and not too much? Couldn't we be relieved sooner?"

Lieutenant Hurtz went about with a bewildered expression. One of the few who reckoned time with any accuracy, he made a point to remind the men when Sabbath came, only it was Jewish Sabbath, Saturday. Even more religious guys never called Sunday Sabbath, that was old fashioned.

"Today's the Sabbath," he told them enthusiastically. "Let's clean up around here."

The men smiled secretly, looking nervously at one another.

"Our Heavenly Father," I stumbled over the words and broke off to begin anew. "Please, dear Lord, protect us." Man, that Ski thing opened me up. My eyes moistened and I blew my nose hard. Why I said that, 'Our Heavenly Father,' I didn't know myself. Hell, I'm not religious.

Later, while visiting Pater on the enemy side of 1100, I overheard a heated argument. Men of King grumbling that a lieutenant of Love Company held up their fire to allow a squad of gooks to escape.

"He's bugs!" one exclaimed. "Instead of shooting, stood right in our line of fire, hands in air, yelling us down."

"Gave me willies," another said.

"Christ!" a squad leader remarked angrily. "Aside from letting those bastards go, somebody could've clipped him accidentally."

"What was he yelling?" I asked.

The sergeant and the riflemen hesitated.

"Well?" I insisted, "what was it?"

"I might've heard wrong, sir, it sounded like 'forgive them,' some screwy thing like that and 'put down your guns.'" He laughed uneasily.

"Yeah," the squad leader agreed. "I heard him plain as day. 'Forgive them, Lord.' He's plain ordinarily had it."

When there was a lot of firing on the ridge, Captain Shallow stayed in his cave, hole, bunker or anywhere he could seat his ass and lower his profile at the moment it began, rousing himself only when it quieted down, or when a carrying party arrived with mail and news and other supplies from the forward ammo supply point behind the MLR.

One time we saw our company commander hunched over, reluctantly escorting Mighty Mouse along the company perimeter and his runner, Blum, heard him ask the colonel for a three-day pass to Seoul.

"You know better than to ask for a VOCO [vocal order from a commanding officer] while we're committed."

"Sir, I *have* to get to Seoul."

"What's so pressing about Seoul?"

"Important business, sir."

"What's more important than this?"

"It's Billy, sir. I've lost Billy and I know something's happened to him. He needs me."

"Billy?" the Colonel asked in a loud voice. "Who's Billy?"

"My houseboy, sir."

Duncan stopped and turned to examine the captain's bloodshot eyes and trembling hands, his glasses with a cracked lens, greasy and finger stained. All riflemen of Love Company were dirty, shaggy-haired, unshaven, fatigues worn wet from sweat and rain, almost beyond endurance, yet every one was somehow cleaner than their captain. Shallow was unkempt as a man possessed; his face ashen, jowls sagging repulsively and unshaven, as were all of us.

"Captain," Duncan said coldly, "clean yourself up!"

"Billy kept care of things," Shallow whined.

"Captain!" the colonel snapped, "Take care of yourself."

"Yes, sir," Captain Shallow answered meekly.

When Colonel Duncan arrived at my platoon, he asked if there was anything we needed and I told him bluntly we needed food. We were down to two twelve-ounce cans of C rations a day and on heavily rainy days the trail was unusable for the little men in low-cut sneakers with heavy loads. Although Army field rations were supposed to contain extra calories and vitamins, judging from awareness of our weakness, it wasn't enough. I told him the dead lying around were a bad morale problem, not only a few guys we used to know, but gooks and ROK Marines from earlier days felled by artillery and Air who, in some cases one had to breathe, others turned halfway to skeletons with blades of grass grown through their rotting fatigues.

"We're well aware of that, lieutenant. We are confident that if anyone told us the truth, it would be you," he said smiling. We both knew he was referring to general Almond's inspection in June. The colonel explained to me as curious sergeants gathered around, that so many things were popping all over the Corps area— Marines on line pushing across Death Valley, Saber Ridge starting up, along with Bloody Ridge and the Second Battalion, all to put pressure on the so-called peace talks—so busy hauling men and ammo and water, supply trucks for soft stuff like food were in short supply.

"How about commo, reconnaissance, P&A and your shotgun guard; how many Cs are they getting?" I suggested to the colonel's obvious displeasure.

"Lieutenant," he sounded off sharply, "I appreciate your concern for your men, but suppose you leave headquarters for me to run." He paused then, mulling over just what he was going to say. "That so-called shotgun guard went to the companies two days after I took over and don't think for a minute I'm Major Wilkes."

"No, sir, I'll give you that. He was somewhat bigger."

"Lieutenant!" he barked.

"Yes, sir."

"I apologize for not telling you you were relieved of command of Love, but I told you how damn busy we've been."

Miles to the rear, Colonel Mildren reflected on the situation of his beleaguered blue battalion—being mildly reprimanded by the new X Corp commander, Lieutenant General Clovis E Byers, going over division commander Major General Young's head asking for relief. Our foreign battalion, the Dutch, had left for Pusan to rotate and exchange time-expired men. Another Second Division Regiment, the 23d, was heavily committed on the right flank in the open Punchbowl and it was rumored that a massive Chinese buildup and movement was crossing in our direction over the North Korean front.

Frank T Mildren, with the nickname Fearless Frank, Coughlin's replacement, with a legitimate DSC in WWII, was a sharp West Pointer (1939), a thirty-seven-year-old officer with long ties to the Second Division. Upon graduating from the academy, he joined the 38th Infantry where he commanded the 1/38, First Battalion, 38th Infantry, at Omaha Beach, D Day two, and in six years rose to be regimental executive.

"They [meaning us] must maintain positions at all costs," Fearless Frank told Mighty Mouse Duncan. "While essentially a holding force, bad off as they are the NKs are not only hurting for food and ammunition, many POWs and dead are found with empty pockets, whereas they were in the habit of carrying rice balls, cooked rice patted into softball-size lumps wrapped tightly in seaweed.

"Two gook divisions facing the 38th were cannibalized to fill one on line. Intelligence tells us that gook soldiers, who hate millet, are down to half a pound per man per day and, as always, no medical attention forward of division."

As early as his May 30 inspection of forces in Korea, Ridgway cabled the Joint Chiefs of Staff from his headquarters in Tokyo of an unusually large bag of POWs and a large stock of abandoned enemy weapons. All three corps commanders reported a noticeable deterioration in the fighting spirit of CCF. In many cases their units were so desperately short of rations the men had to eat grass and roots and the withdrawing CCF abandoned ammo dumps, mortars, machine guns, burp guns and rifles, indicating that disorganization exists among both CCF and NKPA forces.

"The results are already being felt at Kaesong but to complete the pressure we have to take H 1179 and the all-important objective, H 1243 at the north end of the Punchbowl. 1179 may be indefensible afterward, too difficult to supply, but we must show Nam Il and Kim Il Sung, political officer and dictator, supreme CO of the North Korean People's Army, we're capable."

Just as negotiations seemed to be pacifying Kim Il Sung, a misguided plane of the Third Bomber Wing on 10 September 1951 bombed a North Korean camp at Kaesong. Ridgway was compelled to apologize. The error did, however, succeed in getting the enemy to move to a more neutral position, Panmunjom on the border, a tiny unoccupied hamlet just over the 38th parallel of four abandoned huts with mud walls and thatched rice straw roofs, which area the United Nations preferred. Its name translates 'Shop Within the Wooden Gates.' Not shown on the most detailed maps, it was the most neutral spot in Korea, six miles south of the communist-occupied Kaesong.

Three days after we got 1100, I happened to be at Shallow's fortress when Colonel Duncan called. The captain huddled in a corner of his cave, staring at the section on his mapboard featuring 1179.

"Captain, Lieutenant Colonel Duncan calling, sir," Tony Zurlo, Shallow's radioman said, extending the receiver toward him. Captain Shallow remained in an apparent trance, staring at the map.

"Captain Shallow!" First Sergeant Luther said more loudly, "Captain Shallow, the colonel wants you."

Finally Captain Shallow reached for the receiver and pulled it into a corner, facing away from us and the cave opening. He answered in a low voice and when ordered to speak up, began to stutter.

"But, but, sir, that's impossible … ask Lieutenant Morris … Yes…. Yes, sir, I mean … I know, but, but, sir we can't…. But, but, but, sir, there's more than a division up there…. I know, sir, but, but, please, sir, we'll all be killed…. Maybe in a couple days with reinforcements…. It's 1630, do you roger? … What? … Oh, no, sir, what I mean is there isn't time anymore today …. Maybe we could get the Air Force to work it over with bombs a couple more days…. But, sir, I…

Shallow turned, holding his hand over the mouthpiece and smiled sickeningly into the air. Then, turning his wrist, he studied his watch.

"Yes, sir! Sir? … But, sir, they won't go for me. No, sir! I mean, yes I will, sir! … What? … Yes, *sir*! … No, sir, I didn't say I refuse, sir, its just that I…. I just can't make them go for me, sir…. They've had too long to think it over. Yes, sir! … Alright, sir…. Yes sir, he's right here…. Here, Lieutenant Gould, he wants you."

"Lieutenant Gould, you're it now. I'm placing you in command of Love with Item in support for the assault on 1179. Hear me?"

"I hear, Colonel."

"Well, okay, Gould, say something. Give me your ideas on how you'll do it. Might have time to get a little air-ground support."

"We don't want Air now, sir, too much time lag. We can make it tomorrow … bombers today. We'll work better with artillery. But, sir, tell them to lift it when I say to and I'd like to have eight-incher concentration eleven until we're fifty feet from the very top." I paused to catch my breath. "If it's all right with you, Colonel, I'd like to work two platoons forward and one not less than 100 yards in support followed closely by Item Company. I'll have our observer, Lieutenant Rawn, take charge of supporting overhead fire. Sir, I never studied planning. Don't see what's to plan, looks like a clean, nasty, one-way shot, sir. Have any ideas on that, sir?"

"You can estimate the situation better where you are, Gould, but I should think it would be better to try to flank them if at all possible. I'll call back to confirm your attack plans. Put Shallow on."

Listening for a moment, the captain's face turned blank. "I'm sorry, sir," he said in a low voice. "I'll have to take my chances. Here, Dud, he wants you again."

"I've informed Shallow he's under arrest for refusing to go," Duncan said in disgust. "I want you to take his pistol and see he gets back here soon as possible. Over and out."

Shallow busied himself cleaning his glasses with a dirty handkerchief, holding the lenses to the sky examining them and then covered his eyes and sobbed softly.

"Sorry, Captain Shallow, sir," I apologized, "I have to take your pistol."

"But, Dud, might be infiltrators along the trail."

"I can't help it, sir, orders. If you want, you can wait for the next chogee train with guards. Sorry, Captain, I'll have to take your forty-five."

"I know you don't think much of me, lieutenant," Captain Shallow said, drying his eyes and becoming suddenly as if he was in full control, unhooking his pistol belt, removing the canteen and handing the belt with forty-five and holster over to me, "I'll be alive."

"In what prison?"

"It won't be so awful bad; one way or another, I'll be alive and soon it'll all be over for all of us. How about Captain Toth, what did he get? A dirty job at regiment, at least he's alive."

"And maybe Sergeant Pater won't be for long."

The captain had the bad habit when excited of holding on to his subordinate's sleeve. I used to think I had to put up with it, but now I yanked it away abruptly.

"Dud, I'm giving you a good efficiency. I'm not going to stay in the Army after this is over. They're going to RIF me anyway. I wouldn't stay in the Army now if they got down on their knees and begged. Maybe they should beg me anyway after all I've done for them. They should write me up for at least the Legion of Merit after what I've done. I earned a commendation ribbon on my past job in civilian clothes supplying an above top secret research project.

"Bad enough Billy deserted me but I think I'm losing Shirley, too. You think Shirley will get a divorce without letting me know? Dud, think her father would let her do that? Why else would she stop writing and go back to Boston with him? ... I'd resign my commission right here and now but they need good supply experts and maybe won't let me resign. I know too much; never should have been here in the first place, what with my clearances. You have no idea how I worry about us up there.... You have no idea what it's like commanding a company in combat."

"Sorry, Captain," preparing to tell him I'm *Lieutenant* Gould should he use the familiar again, and I'd never heard of Shirley.

I was excited as hell. I'd probably never make captain out of it, and didn't really want to anyway, anymore than I ever wanted a commission. With the acute company grade officer shortage in the 38th, I could understand why me. Shit, they wouldn't think of it otherwise. Still, I was excited; I was going to lead an infantry company in combat, in the assault. Maybe I'd get stuck with it longer; look at Sergeant Pater, in charge for a couple weeks now, and him with two second lieutenants, one of whom was acting exec, while the other was about to get a promotion. Sergeant Pater led his men up 1100 all right and he, like me, no college graduate, we didn't know diddly-dick about supply, running a messhall, administration or military justice. We learned to hand out military justice—to the gooks. We didn't study banzaiing, it's obvious; we just did it our way. I was fortunate to have Roy Carse to take care of the rear, as he did with Shallow, and Duncan promised me I'd soon be relieved by a Regular Army captain.

Peace talks remained in hopeless impasse. Our small, worried, worn end of the Army, unleashed temporarily by the United Nations Command through corps, division and regiment prodded Lieutenant Colonel Duncan and he, in turn, let it be known to Item and Love Companies that we, me in charge, must get together on an attack against the main defenses of 1179, Fools Mountain, Taeusan, or whatever. Here we are. Miseries, here we come!

Protocol was that Lieutenant Morris of Item report to me to work out details of our upcoming assault, but while inspecting Love's positions that crossed fire with his, I went a bit further to Morris's CP, reminding him, since he neglected to mention it, that Colonel Duncan put me in charge. I watched for his reaction. What did Duncan have against him, or maybe he had some better reason to trust me. But crimus, Morris was Regular Army.

"That's quite all right," Morris said, even though we both knew that not only was he Regular Army, rugged and manly, with curly black hair, he had plenty of time in grade. "What happened to Captain Shallow?" he asked.

"I don't rightfully know. The colonel's pissed off at him for something."

"The colonel told me Shallow's being relieved and only certain things can bring that about."

Observed and corrected from the air by a division artillery L-19, heavy salvos of artillery began working the crest of 1179, causing the men to stand and cheer.

"The Colonel just called," Morris said. "Told me about you. Congratulations, Gould. He's nuts, expecting us to take that hill. What did he say to you?"

"Wants the top tomorrow by nightfall."

"Sonofabitch! Easy for him to say. What's he think we're made of? Listen, Gould, let's get him on the line and reason with him."

"Shallow already did his best. Orders are direct from Corps anyway. I'm too damn busy to waste time on it. Let's work out an order of assault and perimeter defense plan. The gooks been ordered, according to S2, to hold at all costs. They're part of two of the top regiments in the gook Army and we're going to have it rough."

I tried to think what a company commander was supposed to do preparing to lead a major assault on one of the most important and best defended positions on the eastern edge of the Hays Line. First, I had to take over the company. Master Sergeant First Sergeant Luther had gone to the rear to rotate and field first sergeant, newly-made Master Sergeant Ray Martin was now first sergeant in charge of headquarters forward in lieu of an officer. Ray Carse technically commanded only the rear CP, appointed to that position. I turned the platoon over to Hanson and took Sergeant Eppler with me as a sort of unofficial enlisted aide de camp. At the company CP, Tony Zurlo raised Captain Arthur Detweiler, battalion S3 operations officer, for me, well back down the ridge at battalion forward.

"Buzzard One Three. Buzzard One Three. Buzzard One Three, come in. This is Buzzard Seven."

"Buzzard Seven go ahead."

I took the mouthpiece and announced myself: "Lieutenant Gould; I'm sending a written battle order for our attack tomorrow. Be on a C ration box, got no paper."

No sooner had I released the butterfly switch than Captain Detweiler radioed angrily, "Buzzard Seven leader, don't transmit in the clear. I repeat, do not send messages in the clear. If there are serious questions, Buzzard One says to report in person ASAP."

Tony Zurlo expressed amazement at my ignorance of such matters. Evidently I had a lot to learn about the niceties of communications and Army procedures.

"Lieutenant," he said, "first you jeopardized yourself by giving your name in the clear. They have captured equipment that allows them to sweep all channels until they identify units facing them so they can listen in. Now they know that Buzzard Seven, leader of Love of the Third Battalion, 38th Infantry, Second Infantry Division is commanded by a Lieutenant Gould rather than an anonymous Buzzard Seven. What they'll do with it, I don't know. Worst of all, you gave away our biggest secret. We're going to attack tomorrow."

Later, face-to-face, Colonel Duncan expressed his disappointment with my lack of communications discipline and marveled at how I got commissioned until I told him that I wasn't even a Ninety-day Wonder; I got my gold bars after sixty days of madness, a special rough and tough combat indoctrination course in Napoleon's old Artillery School at Fontainbleau in the Barbizon Forest. All emphasis was on the purely physical aspect of leading a rifle platoon, and testing to see that we candidates could take it, such cute tricks as blowing the whistle at three in the morning after a day of strenuous physical training, making up our cots so tightly a centime could be bounced six inches from a two-foot drop; making one's pack immaculate, subject to close inspection and within five minutes out into formation, marching. March in pitch blackness a mile in cold rain to a swamp, halt, sidestep left and right off the road and sit, pack and all, in fifteen inches of cold water holding our carbines over our heads until four more guys complained and were returned to their units. One officer marveled openly that I, a flyboy, could take it so well. True, I was an assistant instructor but that was restricted to weapons instruction.

"Buzzard One," I radioed, "when you told me over the radio I was to take over and what support we could get, were we using a scrambler?"

There was a long pause and Duncan said, "Dammit, you're right, that was in the clear, wasn't it? Sometimes one gets so wrapped up with what he's thinking or doing he forgets proper procedure'"

When it came to tactics, the colonel agreed with me there wasn't much choice for there was no room to flank but to go straight up to hit fortifications head on on top up a long finger with dropoffs on either side. All we could do was stick to the old SOP, standard operating procedure, plaster the objective with artillery and Air and work right under it with accurate heavy machine guns and 105 HE ahead of us as we banzaied. Like a football game, you planned on what major maneuver to make and reach alternatives as indicated, and made them on the run fast as possible. Like no other game, however, it is all up a steep hill, moving individually over the terrain, maneuvering from cover to cover with a heavy load of ammo.

Should your yelling lessen or stop and you lose momentum in upward movement, get permission to get the hell off that hill. It's always up a steep incline loaded with combat gear, hot, thirsty, sticky mouth, sucked dry even, packing two canteens. Oh for an attack on the level, but that's tank country where they get to ride to their death.

Very important, as Sergeant Eppler and I discovered by ourselves, yell like demons, get it going loud from man to man to build a momentum of high spirits to motivate your men and overawe the enemy. Old-fashion battle cries, man! Eppler and I didn't discover it, we uncovered it. Hell, lions come on snarling and roaring, as did savages all over the world. Shout your lungs out! Battle cry; just what words no manual recommends. In fact, no manual in the American Army says a thing about charging a hill; at least not when I was in uniform. Probably because no real infantry combat veteran was ever in charge of training. It was left to rear echelon generals with their phoney combat infantrymen's badges, Purple Hearts and DSCs.

Maybe as a result of my booboo over the radio, we were hit by three widely spaced probes that night as I tried to sleep in a hole outside the command post Captain Shallow had built in a cave; as far as I was concerned, a trap. If I got overrun again, I wanted to be able to get up and go, not pinned down from the start.

Twice after I dozed off, PFC Sidney Blum, company runner, woke me.

"Lieutenant, you awake? There's something out in the Punchbowl. Something going on in that big valley."

From our lofty perch we sat in the dark watching the surrealistic firefights of a tank infantry team outpost of the hotly engaged 23d dug in the center of the Punchbowl. Many minutes after watching long lines of slowly moving machine gun tracers lobed gracefully through the air, we heard the reports, individual shots mingling into a continuous gentle eruption many minutes later. Putputputputputputputput, a small motorboat far away; maybe thirty miles as the crow flies.

When Blum awakened me the first time, I thought he must have something, then, seeing what a stupid thing it was, I snapped irritably, "Crimus, I told you a thousand times, that's our tanks down there clobbering gooks. Now listen carefully, you woke me enough for one night; between gook banzais and you, I'm not sleeping at all. We've got a busy day tomorrow."

Blum was paying no attention. "They say some poor guy from King was taken prisoner early tonight. Could hear him yelling."

"I heard him, now shut up and let me sleep."

"Please, please, God, whoever, or whomever, wherever you are, you don't owe me anything, but for the guys' sake let daylight come?" I muttered and I guess prayed bluntly for the best gift of all—tomorrow—an Agnostic's prayer was better than none I figured.

Although I was a bit worried at being a company commander with so little military background, I was grateful for being handed such a prize, as if I passed an important test that seemed easy and natural for me. Now I'll have to show them. I raised Lieutenant Hurtz on the EE-8 and told him I was in charge and I couldn't say what over the phone but get ready for something big. I asked if he was okay and he said "affirmative." I called the sergeant platoon leaders and told them what little I could. After all, what was there to know? Even before leaving the Pia-ri Valley our target was obvious; only a matter of time and who would be the unlucky guys to try it? Certainly there was no flanking available, straight up about four hundred meters, the ridgeline and a left turn over a saddle and straight up to it. Our only shield would be artillery rounds, machine gun bullets going into the apertures of their bunkers and recoilless rifles keeping them from leaning over their ramparts aiming directly at us and, of course, what firepower we carried with us, rifles, carbines, BARs and one light 30 caliber machine gun per platoon..

Fortunately, division called off the attack, postponing it a day ; most probably because of my blabbing our attack time over the open radio. Sorry, I told myself, but we can use a better work- over with several flights of fighter-bombers, and maneuver several batteries of my favorite, eight-inchers, for a few minutes from direct support of the Marines. Even with such additional support, I learned odds at division were ten-to-one we'd fail. Fools Mountain had a very ominous reputation and was extra important to the gooks overall defenses.

8

TAEUSAN

FOOLS MOUNTAIN

Dead, we become the lumber of the world
And to that mass of matter shall be swept
Where things destroyed with things unborn
are kept.
– Lucius Annaeus Seneca.

Fools Mountain, smartass American press called our 1179, never nearer to an angry shot than thirty miles, carefully shepherded by rear-echelon division informa- tion officers and other starched fatigues, explaining grease-pencil marks on a huge plastic overlay in the G-3 operation tent War Room, commenting knowingly—non- combat rear-echelon officers talking to protected civilians for transmission authori- tatively to stateside customers about us getting rubbed into it.

War hath no fury like noncombatants.
– an observation.

Fools Mountain they labeled it from afar. Those dogfaces are fools, they opined, dying for ground returnable in upcoming peace talks. Fools themselves! The talks were used by our enemy to tie up our tactics in protecting our painfully paid-for advantages. Talks began in the first place only because nobodies with scruffy beards and muddy faces were simple, brave, trusting of one another and obedient enough to be on the top of Hill 1100 looking down a long tank-country valley straight to the commie seaport of Wonson.

Gooks called their roost Taeusan, Gateway to the Orient, overseeing vast valleys from three sides. Before we took it away from their bravest, it was ordered held at all cost. Our good soldiers, names, serial numbers, blood type,

Top of the Taeusan mountain, 1179 meters, viewed from the Pia-ri valley. Unseen in the back lies the Punchbowl.

and first letter of their religions stamped in stainless steel tags on chains around their necks, paid their share of the high price so fat, bald-headed old men in Congress and the United Nations could prevail in their petty piques against other peevish bastards.

Captain Shallow placed Fred Hurtz on the northern, hottest spot of the perimeter of 1100 where a lone sniper wounded one of his men and was terrorizing the rest, shooting the entrenching tool out of the hands of one man tossing spoil from his hole. When I called Fred back over the EE-8 there was no answer and when I couldn't get him on the 536 radio either, I sent Blum to see what the trouble was. Soon thereafter company First Sergeant Ray Martin came down the trail.

"Think I know where the sniper is," he told me.

I followed Martin up the trail to within firing distance and followed his finger down to a solitary mountain pine. There was no movement but I planned on dropping a grenade over the most likely spot. Kneeling, I placed the butt of my carbine on the ground with a WP grenade can held by a spring in the grenade adapter, estimated elevation of my carbine for distance, and fired it off. To my dismay it repeated the disastrous grenade the day I was wounded, hitting a sapling down the trail to bounce in front of PFC Blum returning from hunting for Lieutenant Hurtz.

"Oh Geezus," I thought. "You've killed one of your own."

The thing did explode on line with Blum but, fortunately, far enough in front to no more than scare the shit out of us both. As the puff of stark white smoke of burning white phosphorus was cleared by a breeze, Blum, eyes wipe open, stunned at the unexpected threat, was running toward us off the trail to avoid the burning phosphorus, pawing himself all over for a wound.

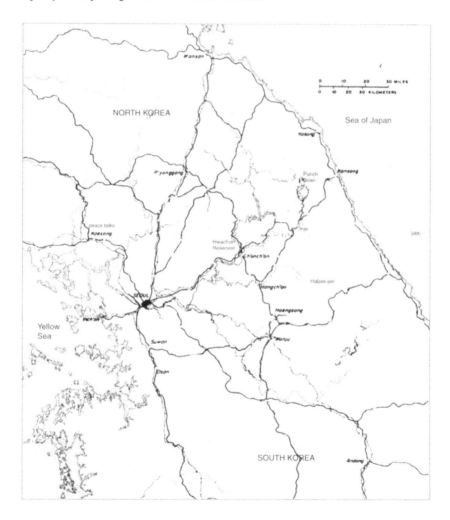

"Medic! Medic!" he cried unnecessarily since Doc Lopez was already in plain sight running toward him. "I'm hit. Doc, I'm hit."

He came to us running, holding up an inch-wide hole in his sleeve that, with frayed, bleached threads, obviously was laundered more than once. Although he tried his damndest to be evacuated, I'll give it to Blum, he stuck it out to his end.

Giving him a good look over, Doc said scornfully, "C'mon, Blum, quit acting. You aren't hit any."

I went back working the company's SCR 300 trying to catch the French Battalion, a bunch of chattering old women, the second they ceased hogging our wavelength. The French, given our working channel by mistake for the day, had not been taught radio discipline. I had a list of things, particularly machine gun ammo and water, which we would badly need to get and keep 1179. My French was very poor, a year in high school, a little French Canadian, but it seemed plain in the pace of their blabbing I'd catch the word *mange*, which I recalled was food or eat.

Sitting on my left talking across me to our company medic, SP5 Ed Lopez, Blum moaned how a terrible headache was going to kill him. Nervous little city boy from the Bronx, PFC Blum was blown to pieces like any brave soldier the following day in a 120mm barrage in the saddle before 1179. Later, Sergeant Eppler and I wrote him up for a posthumous Bronze Star with V for valor for his folks' sake. Like no damn rear echelon ever could, we appreciated what an extra hell Blum suffered being scared practically all the time, with no confidence in his own ability. To have resisted the urge to flee was courageous in itself. Compare him with bugouts Captains Carleton, Toth and Shallow.

Later, I discovered that the reason I hadn't heard from Fred or his platoon guide Collins was that as the sergeant awakened Fred and drew him close to peer over the rim within their CP foxhole, his face lined up almost touching Fred's, pointing out where he'd seen the sniper, Collins was zapped in the forehead by the sniper's bullet, blood and brains exploding over Fred's face and neck, the sergeant's head slumped on to Fred's shoulder. Shit, it can't get worse than that!

Meanwhile, knowing nothing of this, I sent another runner to find Red Rose and have him report but in a little while, Fred Hurtz himself came sliding down to where Blum and I were sitting on the friendly Punchbowl side off the trail. He pulled up unusually close and sat down. Concentrating on slipping in a call on my 300 to battalion, I gave him a brief, impersonal 'hi.' Hurtz said nothing that I recall but made a faint baby-like whimper, a pathetic appeal, I thought later. I was too occupied trying to cut off the French to learn what everyone else seemed to know, the lieutenant was in serious trouble.

I began to sense Fred's presence uncomfortably and looking sideways saw him staring into space, sniffling, a strange, hurt look on his face.

"Shit!" he mumbled, almost incoherently, "shit." I stifled a nervous laugh; Blum and Doc stared at him in disbelief and snickered. Lieutenant Hurtz wouldn't say shit if he had a mouthful.

Blum stared incredulously at Lieutenant Hurtz and watched Lopez out of the corner of his eye, working up nerve to say something. Very shortly he addressed Doc loudly enough that I would be sure to hear, "Doc, got any APCs, a thermometer or something?"

"Thermometer?" I asked. "What you want with a thermometer?"

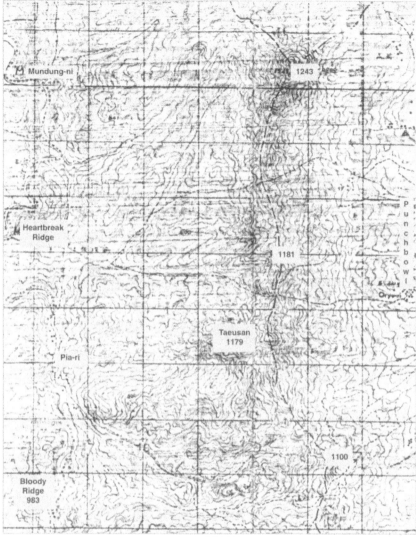

Scale 1:50,000

"Oh, sir," Blum whined. "My head aches. I got an awful feelin' I'm sick. I tell you, I think I'm coming down with something."

His whining and complaining continued until I raised my voice, "We're all coming down with something now. Have your damn headache *after* we take 1179."

Lopez and Eppler snickered.

There was something pretty wrong with Fred. Instinctively, although I had the reputation for being hardass, a quick flash of Kitty protecting me that night in May swept over me and I reached my arm around Fred's shoulder and hugged him to me, telling him, "Buddy, don't worry, everything's all right." This was the worst I could have done for instead of soothing him it was like bursting a boil; he put his head in his hands on his knees and bawled like a baby, convulsively, desperately, shaking, sobbing loudly, trying to catch his breath as though he'd gotten rid of everything, even his breath. I didn't know what to do. Doc did; he started writing a tag.

"Crimus, Fred," I said gently as Lieutenant Hurtz continued to shake, sob and gasp for breath. "You've got it bad, man. Hit the trail."

Controlling deep sobs, gulping, Fred shook his head violently back and forth, at the same time incongruously making crude attempts to clean his fingernails as though nothing was wrong and he was only sitting there passing time. Seems his mind was in two places at once. I was beginning to get mad at what was wrong with him.

"C'mon, now," I said coldly, inching away from him. "Quit feeling sorry for yourself."

"Honestly, Dud, I'm all right. Let me rest a while; I'll get hold of myself."

His bloodshot eyes were so steady then and he spoke so calmly, so matter of factly, I was ready to agree. I wanted to; I couldn't understand what was going on with Fred. Maybe he'd be all right after a little rest. No one was exactly normal anymore.

It was somewhat funny, a veteran platoon leader acting that silly. I was on the verge of laughing again. Blum chuckled uncomfortably to himself, laughing low from embarrassment with no enjoyment. Fred stopped and stared slyly at him, then spoke loudly facing him, but addressing an unseen audience. "You should be ashamed. You aren't so darn smart either, or you could tell it's shit."

"Get hold of yourself," I told him. I'd never heard tell of anything like it. "Doc's writing you a tag to get out of here."

"But, Beth, I can't," Fred mumbled in a monotone, studying Doc. "I can't, honey." He whimpered again, turning to face me to implore: "I can't leave my boys up here alone tonight."

"Fred," I shouted, standing up. "Let Doc tag you. I'm not fussin' any more. Get hold of yourself and that's an order."

Lieutenant Hurtz, momentarily hurt by my sudden anger, sat silent for a second, slyly studying my face. I was tired and irritable, dirty face under whiskers as were all of us. Fred must have seen that I meant it. All of us were weary. Nobody really let loose last night and slept, tight as we were, knowing what an impossible task we faced,

"C'mon, now," I told him, trying to sound normal and pleasant. "Let's chogee out of here."

His face was calm. "I can't. I can't. Dud, I can't leave my boys alone up here tonight."

Boys? Crimus, I thought, what're you, all of twenty-five?

A chogee train came around a bend on the friendly side of the mountain trail, loaded with bandoliers, 60mm mortar ammo, radio batteries, and mail but no water. We'd been having trouble with batteries with short lives made in Japan. Those under sixty today have no idea how junky was everything manufactured in Japan before WWII and up until the 1960s.

"Letter from Alice," the guard said, anticipating my interest, reading the return address before handing it over. "Say, lieutenant, when you see Ski, he's made corporal."

Corporal? For a minute I'd forgot why, although he was a little smarter than Woody. Alice? I thought, that's the furthest from my mind right now. Somehow I never got to open that letter and in the ensuing confusion and material madness of Fools Mountain lost it.

In my several months in Korea and in all WWII I never heard of a guy cracking up like this. I mean in his own world of make believe, going back and forth with phoney names even, like Beth. I'd never heard him mention that name. First he'd be nuts, then tired and acting almost normal. I guess it's to each his own, the way we flip. I wondered how, if it happened to me, perish the thought, I'd act and talk. I felt bad losing my buddy like that, although it beat dying.

Sergeant Eppler and I soaked up what gossip was to be had from the chogee guard; what was going on in the trains. "Lieutenant what's his name was killed the other day."

"Infiltrators? Long-range H and I? No, they don't have anything would reach that far south. Step on a mine? No. Well, how? Who did you say he was? Rear echelon, battalion headquarters? Motor pool?" He repeated names of headquarters officers until he came to Werner. "Von something or other Werner. Lieutenant Werner, that new officer. Right?"

"Yeah, that's him. Lieutenant Werner. Motor pool jeep went off a bank and busted his neck like a carrot stick," the chogee guard said, snapping his fingers.

"$50 fine for officers driving jeeps in the division anyway unless on special assignment as I was."

"He wasn't driving; got thrown. His driver didn't get a scratch. Them jeeps aren't made for over forty and sharp turns—they're top heavy."

Borrowing the filled out evacuation tag and the stub of Doc's pencil, I turned it over and jotted down a list of what we badly needed—grenades, BAR ammo, machine gun ammo, C rations and water, more water. I underlined machine gun and water and scribbled 'very urgent' in large letters. Must have machine gun ammo and water!

"Fred," I said, "if we don't get this stuff, it's curtains. Understand? I'm sending you because we have to have a good officer on it." As I talked, I stood up and pressed the tag into Fred's limp hand, giving him a friendly slap on the shoulder.

Fred, eyes glazing over, absently-mindedly dropped the tag and I picked it up and as he watched me closely like a curious little boy, I tied it around a button on his upper fatigue jacket pocket.

"See that the lieutenant gets this back okay," I said, winking at the chogee guard behind Fred's back, indicating the evacuation tag tied to him. "The lieutenant has a list," I went on in a theatrical voice. "See it stays on; he's got to get it back, understand? Make sure he gets back with that *list*."

Holding the palms of his grimy hands over his eyes, Fred stood up slowly behind the guard. He'd done his mortal best and now must have to admit he was through. He couldn't be forced any more to go on killing innocent men week after week, so conflicting was it with his religious upbringing; his own men he was responsible for, buddies he'd lived among so long. Sobbing softly, Fred mumbled, shaking his head slowly, "Terrible, terrible," and followed the chogee guard back down the ridge like a programed zombie. He was gone, really gone, was Fred.

C Company, in a diversionary attack up a finger down to the left of 1179, encountered unexpectedly savage resistance and was forced to withdraw. The following morning, according to our official history Blue Book, Love, my company, backed by Item in position behind, set out in the attack—

The first day's action sketched the picture of the enemy defenses. He was determined to stay on 1179 at all costs. His elaborate preparations, plentiful supply of ammunition and determined resistance in face of terrific concentrations from all the supporting fire weapons, including nine battalions of artillery, indicated the fight for Taeusan would be more difficult than first anticipated.

The night before, the skies were kept a flaming red as the artillery fire was intensified. Dust from the roads swirled hundreds of feet into the air as trucks rolled around the clock to provide ammunition for the barrage.

At first correspondents gave it the name Five-million Dollar Hill, after someone supposedly figured out the cost of artillery and Air laid on the preparations for four different artillery battalions one after another. It was estimated that more than 115 tons of bombs had supported the attacks on Taeusan. A total of 74,823 rounds of artillery had been hurled onto the hill and added to that were 49,000 rounds of mortar fired in the assaults.

The 38th spent the morning and early afternoon of 28 July in preparation for another attack on 1179. Murderous artillery concentrations were laid on the slopes and at 0600 hours 29 July L and I Companies struck out in face of enemy cross fire. The assault was carried out with such vigor that the crest was reached and Hill 1179 was in the possession of the Second Division by evening. The enemy fortress fell after some of the most intense offensive fighting the Division had undergone in months. The fanatic defenders had to be dug out of their deep entrenchments and it was a slow, bloody, body-tiring job. The enemy was pushed off suffering more than 2000 casualties with the annihilation of one complete regiment and the crushing of another. The decimated North Korean 27th Division withdrew its thin ranks in disorder after the onslaught of the Second Division.

I had to laugh at whoever, maybe Captain Carleton, composed the fanciful prose, "dust from the roads swirling hundreds of feet into the air as trucks rolled around the clock. . . ." Must have been some other day for as far as we could tell, it rained all over on that day of the July monsoon, everywhere at least once a day, so where did "dust from the roads swirling . . ." come from? And where in hell, we'd like to know, were the '2000 casualties'? We might well have run off a thousand altogether but kill or wound 2000? Never happen. Orders be hanged, soldiers everywhere in every war aren't assholes, they know when to get out of the way.

In the terse military manner that follows, our work in the field was described in the S3 and G3 operations sections of regimental and division staffs for record and historical purposes. As this stylized division operations report indicates, Love Company of the 38th Infantry shoved off in the morning of 29 July 1951, Korean time. Not written, what I would like made a matter of record, was that the brave (maybe stupid) asshole, First Lieutenant Dudley C Gould, laborer, college dropout, amateur soldier, was acting commander of the whole shebang—

Period 29 0001K Jul to 29 2400K Jul. L Co relieved K CO at 29 0100K Jul and I Co relieved C Co. One platoon of I Co occupied location DT 204363 at 29 0600K Jul to secure trail junction. I Co placed one plt in vic DT

193346 to observe left flank Third Bn moved to DT 204381 arriving at 29 0500K Jul. From the position at 29 0600K Jul at 0800K the battalion launched an attack to secure hill 1179. Enemy was immediately contacted. L Co was lead Co. At 29 1630K Jul L Co and the Bn secured Hill 1179. Enemy broke contact at 29 1850K Jul.

As soon as Fred departed with the chogee train, I got busy with the coming attack for the following morning at 0600 and called SFC Sigmund Zigerfoose on the EE-8. Ranking Speedy Gonzales, he became leader of the first squad and made sergeant first class. Master Sergeant Robert 'Red' Rose, ER52025249, ER enlisted Reserve, led the Second Platoon, and Master Sergeant Karl Eppler, another recalled Reserve, was then in the position of acting platoon leader of the Banzai Third but was physically with me as an aide. Ziggy would lead the assault with his squad of the Banzai Third. Later on I had to review my conscience as to whether I favored or condemned my own platoon in placing it first in line, but it really was Ziggy's turn.

He gave me one of the most glorious afternoons of my life and if he's still alive and should read this journal, I beg him to contact me through the publisher or the Korean War Veterans Alliance, c/o Charley Heath, 8540 Bight Road NE, Olympia, WA 98516-9537, please. Ziggy is not listed in our survival booklet, *The Morning Report,* nor could he be found via our computer telephone directory among the known telephone-owning Zigerfooses centered in Texas, Ohio and West Virginia. I called them all.

In our pell-mell scramble up the steep slopes of 1179, Ziggy led behind his first squad ahead of me by about forty feet and with five of his men threw grenades into the bunkers of the fanatics defending the top of Fools Mountain, turned left and ran footloose, screaming wild turkey calls, like General Davies' Kentuckians charging Little Turtle's Miami Indians at the Battle of Fallen Timbers, just before he, Davies, in his white coat, was killed by 'friendly' musket fire.

I have never been so powerfully inspired in my life. Truly we gloried in making war. Ziggy, a lanky blond of German descent in his early twenties, would not harken to my cries not to overrun the objective and for he and his men to return to the crest— always dangerous to overrun an objective, overextend, until a single short 'friendly' 105mm round came barreling in in front of him on the trail leading south. Fortunately, it hit a high rock formation and the spray went up. Who to hell's big idea was it to throw that?

Too many are the true tales of guys killed wholesale by our own artillery or Air; so-called friendly fire. Name one thing friendly about it. Such 'accidents' occurred during some air strikes when Air Force liaison jerks at Army/Air Force forward air control centers were lousy at correlating actual landscape azimuth with their maps and in the confusion many Korean names looked alike. I was surprised once to learn that one young fighter-bomber pilot diverting with extra ammo after an attack learned the hard way that our enemies didn't wear helmets, which of course we always did forward of regiment.

Before we shoved off, Colonel Duncan in his OP an eighth of a mile south on the ridgeline at the newly acquired 1100, kept raising his voice over the 300. I have reconstructed his harangue like this—

"Gould, get up there, Gould, they're running. Air reports them bugging out the Pia-ri side! Keep 'em moving, Gould, you'll miss the opportunity!"

"Yeah!" I hollered back over the radio. "Opportunity to be clobbered. Did you say the air strike was called off?"

"Dammit, it is, now move!"

"My guys won't move so long as Mosquito is up there waiting to direct an air strike."

"They'll see your air panel and if they do come in, they'll avoid you."

"Avoid, shit, colonel; there's no air panel where we've got to go!"

That gave me a great idea. I folded and wrapped one section of the two-by-five foot bright red air panel, code of the day, which we carried with us to lay out atop 1179, around my helmet and had it tied with commo wire.

"C'mon," I waved, yelling back at Love Company. "They'll know it's us up there."

"Make it snappy, Gould. Air spots gooks bugging off the objective toward the Pia-ri Valley."

The Air he mentioned was a US Air Force circling AT6, an air target identification plane, code name Mosquito Air. An air strike had been laid on by division for early in the morning, but called off at the last minute due to urgent priority assisting an attack by the First Marines in Death Valley. Apparently Mosquito had not been called off as well.

None of my sergeants was born yesterday, so they balked, yelling or radioing me on 536s to suggest that we either wait up for the air strike or call off the attack.

The colonel kept telling me to get moving, they're bugging off the enemy side.

"Good," I radioed back, "less we'll have to deal with."

"C'mon, Gould, get crackin.'"

"I can't convince my sergeants the strike's called off. Who wants to get hit by that?"

If only that damn AT6 Mosquito would clear the hell out of the picture.

"Gould, get on up there! Air says they're bugging down the Pia-ri side."

"Damn it, colonel, call off Mosquito Air."

"Never mind that, get up there!"

"Fuck you, sir. Not with an air strike pending."

"Never mind, it's being called off."

"Yeah? Mosquito's still flying."

"He's observing for us now. Goddamn it, Gould, get up there while they're still bugging."

"I'd rather do it *after* they're through, but okay colonel can you see the red air panel around my helmet?"

"No. We can just make out a bunch of you guys moving up the finger. Where are you?"

"You blind, colonel? Look up ahead, I'm at the front behind just one bunch of guys, under that red air panel moving up from the saddle."

"Okay, Gould, we see the red. Chogee! Will relay to Mosquito."

NOTE: Today, two of my buddies on the scene at the time have vivid memories of the air panel on my helmet: Kenneth D McConnell of Philipsburg, Kansas and Thomas M Miller, ER13204577, Silver Star, of Oakmont, Pennsylvania.

Fred Hurtz's platoon went up rapidly with him on their minds, Sergeant Red Rose in charge with SFC Phil Overton, their new acting guide, pushing from the rear.

"C'mon, guys, let's go over. At 'em, c'mon!"

Most of Hurtz's platoon had been in a deep slump, as infantrymen do when losing a good leader. They needed strong, immediate revenge. Forget Lieutenant Hurtz? Remember other attacks, him always up there—yelling dire threats—leading fighting fools!

Our attack on H 1179 started as they usually do, walking slowly, carefully, self-consciously. Everyone beginning at the same increasingly dangerous level, as the long file widened to skirmishers for the assault, skirmishing about ten guys wide, as wide as footing on the finger of land permitted before it dropped off, looking sideways each way at who's there and back to see who's coming, assessing one's position in relation to such critical strong points as the BARs and moving machine guns which might set up or engage a few times in the assault but was along mainly to set up a defense. Overhead covering machine guns were the heavy water-cooled guns of Mike, the heavy weapons company, laying down a steady protective fire. Everyone sought to see who else was coming, wanting them to come hurriedly to his aid when need be. They must keep pace with those who inspired them, else the attack would falter. It was usually one man who inspired and maintained upward movement—not always designated leaders, often changing to one born leader or another as Edsel Turner.

"Why us?" was the first question as Love's rifle platoons kept careful tab of what, where and who, and we platoon leaders were never shy to remind one another that they were the first at such-and-such a place, and how badly hurt.

Half way up, Tony Zurlo dropped behind with his 300 and, driven by the banzai spirit, I kept on stumbling, running behind Sergeant Zigerfoose's Banzai First squad, Third platoon of Love, all cursing and the courage that cursing aroused, spreading up the trail like a mountain wildfire with an updraft. Nobody was hit among us up front doing banzaiing, but Item and some stragglers of Love Company suddenly lost twelve killed in seconds in the saddle behind from a well-directed mortar barrage that had been zeroed in long before. PFC Blum got his bad there for not keeping up with me. I glanced back to see Ed Lopez go down holding a dead medic in his arms, and impressions so terribly, terribly vivid. Combat veterans I have talked with who don't remember much of 1179 should have been up with us; no way they could ever forget.

Gook heavy Russian-made 120mm mortars came crashing down upon the saddle bottom without warning, dragging up and throwing tons of rock, shrapnel, wood splinters and parts of soldiers whizzing through choking clouds of powder smoke and dust, well zeroed in, blowing up a hundred square feet of the path, with sharp shards of steel. Men behind us, including two stragglers of my Banzai Third, lurched, suspended three feet in midair like high, wavering dancers, slammed to the ground, or scrambling madly through choking dust, men shrilly screaming like wounded horses, falling, hitting ground, wind knocked out in horrible grunting. Demanding God, as customary, they came face-to-face with Satan.

Others entered endless reality, scared white, left this world forever, quietly toppling over. Enemy 120s continued to land in fast salvoes of three, an awful cutting, smashing machine of widely scattered, razor-sharp shrapnel.

"God!" a helpless dying man ordered and then humbly, weakly, no longer giving orders, "Please?"

"Get out of it!" I shouted loud as I could, facing behind toward the barrage. "Get on the move! Git up here!"

"Where are they?" a man sobbed in the storm of dust. "Nothing to shoot at. Where are they? Somebody, where are they?"

There was barely time between mortar salvos for the guys to hear our yells (and add their own), for them to reopen their eyelids and stumble upward, climbing hands and knees up the steep hill. How those gook FOs on 1179 must have jumped with joy.

Ziggy and other sergeants in the squads above me turned looking back down toward them momentarily in their concern facing away from the enemy, yelling for them to get out and up fast through the barrage for that was all could save them. There, in the pandemonium of exploding shells in the most contained, destructive barrage I've ever seen or heard of was where Corporal Delmar Dyer displayed his heroism.

HEADQUARTERS
2D INFANTRY DIVISION
APO 248 c/o Postmaster
San Francisco California

GENERAL ORDERS
16 Aug 1951
NUMBER   173

Section II

AWARD OF THE SILVER STAR—By direction of the President, under the provisions of the Act of Congress, approved 9 July 1918 (WD Bul 43, 1918), and pursuant to authority in AR600-45, the Silver Star for gallantry in action is awarded to the following named enlisted man:

SERGEANT DELMAR J DYER, RA17170716, (then Corporal), Infantry, United States Army, a member of Company L, 38th Infantry Regiment, 2d Infantry Division, distinguished himself by gallantry in action on 29 Jul 1951 in the vicinity of Tasusan, Korea. Company L was assaulting the enemy on high ground when the company was subjected to small arms fire and an intense mortar barrage by enemy forces entrenched on a high hill, forcing the rear of the company to withdraw hurriedly from the area. Sergeant Dyer, with complete disregard for his own safety and totally indifferent to the heavy mortar barrage falling in the area, remained behind to render first aid to the other members of his squad, all of whom had been wounded. He then dragged his comrades to safety, thus saving them from possible death. The gallantry and loyal devotion to his comrades displayed by Sergeant Dyer reflect great credit upon himself and the military service. Entered the military service from Iowa.

Suffering from severe concussion, what rear echelons call shell shock, with no penetrating wounds, when Delmar Dyer was returned to duty a week later, he refused to leave the kitchen trains.

"Damn," he complained. "I almost got it again. I see everyone no better than me back here sleeping every night in peace. What's wrong with everyone taking a shot at it? How about Captain Shallow refusing to go, flying observer in an L-19? Why can't enlisted men get a break? Look where King Company commander landed, back at regiment. Got a sergeant in his place."

Lieutenant Carse asked me to talk to him and got us together on the 300. I lied that I'd been watching this very hurt, over six foot young man, and knew he would soon be put in for sergeant E-5 and didn't he know that he was being written up for a Silver Star for saving his buddies? When it comes through, Colonel Duncan himself wants to pin it on.

"Delmar, you're a proven hero. Don't go spoiling it."

"I prefer to make it home in one piece, lieutenant. I'm sorry, sir. I'm going back standing, whether at Leavenworth or not."

NOTE: Delmar has been engrossed in locating survivors for our *Morning Report* who served Love Company from July 1950 to war's end. So far, he has recruited eighty members for the Korean War Veterans Alliance, including Karl Eppler, Dudley Gould, and Master Sergeant Pater. Delmar would like to hear from anyone interested in the exploits of Love Company, 38th Infantry. He can be reached as this is written at 1713 Dorcas Street, #3, Omaha, NE 68108.

Battalion S1 preferred charges against Dyer avoiding me, his acting company commander, and the Division JAG officer threatened not only to have Delmar busted and sentenced to prison, but cancel his Silver Star, which Colonel Duncan and I wrote up. None of this uncalled-for rear-echelon hate came about, however, for the Division shrink who observed Delmar for a time within the division stockade, spoke up for him and not only did he not lose his hard-earned Sergeant stripes and sacred Silver Star nomination, he was released from the stockade, promoted to sergeant E5 and, having fourteen months combined service in Korea, with prior service in combat engineers, given a hammock on the *Marine Adder*.

Too much is too much, you hand out hard military law, Mister Judge Advocate General but you don't know combat, which riflemen of the Infantry do. Come up and work with us a few months and find out that strong men wear out their iron as does any machine.

As the guys swept by me assaulting 1179 in their pumped-up enthusiasm, I heard a polite voice, "I'm sorry, sir, I'm hit." Slumping under his own weight, Tony Zurlo, who had caught up to me, repeated, "Sorry, sir," as he stumbled down to stay.

Yelling, "Doc! Doc! Here, doc!" I retrieved the radio, handed it to the first private I could reach, traded Tony's carbine for the private's heavier M1 rifle, and hurried to catch up. Weeks later, Tony wrote to a buddy from the Army Osaka Hospital they were letting him go home to his wife and new baby minus his left arm.

Moving up to where a fellow rifleman ended his life, a leader would usually decide without listening or feeling for a heart beat, just how he lay so impossibly contorted and staring hard at you that he's had it. "Get his ammo and rifle. Let's keep moving." And to young replacements, "Quit rubber-necking and get goin', there's guys paid to take care of him."

"Why don't they? Aren't you going to take his dog tags, or wallet or anything to identify him?"

"That's Grave Registration; we're not allowed to touch them, or even write their women."

Past the grenade line we took little fire due to the accuracy of our artillery, recoilless rifles, heavy machine guns, light machine guns, stopping occasionally to sight on particular targets to keep the defenders down. Climbing was a full-time occupation, especially tough when bent under a load, firing our pea shooters was secondary. It was critical that once begun we must not stop at the grenade line but pour on more energy somehow and shout curses and scream battle cries to display a superior morale. We must make them think we know we're going over until suddenly they agree it sounds like it's true.

Try this at home, run as fast as your fat legs can travel with forty pounds around your waist, plus four-pound hand grenades in your deep fatigue jacket pockets; heavy cartridge belt with aid kit, two canteens of precious water; bayonet scabbard, ammunition pouches and, in my case, a 38 caliber revolver in a forty-five caliber holster stuffed with rags to keep it from flopping out; up an uneven, sometimes mined, thirty-degree slope, stopping from time to time to get off a round or two and straighten your helmet that's almost jiggled off its liner, shouting and screaming, keeping your ass as low as possible and still move forward and up, and always prepared mentally to meet your Maker.

Faces I remembered in the blustery, screaming inferno—Tony's and First Sergeant Ray Martin; a kid from Fred Hurtz's platoon; even Private Funaro yelling and laughing like someone intoxicated, at home in our crazed banzai as incapable of reasoning as in any of his street-rioting affrays. With all that furious yelling and explosion, it's possible, as one propelled in a street riot, to be taken out of oneself, incited to do things he wouldn't normally do; like any riot, mass hysteria gone amuck, people welded into a moving monster, led on by those shouting the loudest for violence.

I'm telling you, all you reading this, we climbed together, side-by-side, sometimes crawling, stumbling through downpouring, sporadic small arms fire, using rifles and carbines for crutches, careful to keep muzzles up out of the dirt, stopping only to get off a choice shot until we closed ready to duel hand-to-hand with the enemy, the majority of whom gave way to sudden panic and fled as we crossed the grenade line, fleeing their bunkers, or, a few, cowering, hiding the badly wounded, through whose firing ports they were grenaded, and drove the panicked survivors from 1179 with the display of yelling and the shining, threatening steel of bayonets.

"Kill the bastards! . . . Stick 'em!" we yelled to one another. "Let the sonsofbitches have it, they're getting away."

I never saw one of us chase after them however, wanting them to get away and stop threatening us.

"Let's go! Get over it!" I yelled, and the classic combat observation, "Nobody lives forever!"

Mass hysteria. Love Company to the front and Item hot behind, guys crawling, stumbling uphill fast, Item belatedly fastening bayonets on the move, Love fanning out to cover the ridgetop. Ziggy and I waving more and more action into them until we were a machine devoid of sensation with momentum carrying us forward and up not needing to be restarted. We were aware of how essential to low casualties was our smooth, unwavering upward momentum for it is a fact that in any war many fewer infantrymen are killed in an aggressive attack than a passive defense. More and more and more on their feet firing from the hip, screaming insults, frolicking among demons of death shaking them like dice, striking fatally here and there. "Dirty bastards!"

Some of our attackers, inconspicuous dogfaces, were suddenly wild, rioting Indians, darting cover to cover, screaming berserkers, suddenly flamboyant actors, photogenic, reckless young heroes aspiring to conquer or die on center stage, playing lead rolls in the greatest drama of the ages, foe against foe, yelling away their dread— "E dee waah! Cuda-cuda! Bali-bali." Come here! Quickly! Hurry!

Oh god! I am passing away in the hand of the wind!
– Nizan-al-Mulk, Persian vizier.

Et moriermur!, and we too shall die.
– Legionnaires of Caesar.

Ad astra per aspera, to the stars through difficulties.
– Roman warlord.

Come and get it yellow cunts!
– my draftees.

We stopped once before the grenade line to get our breath without which we never could have finished the job, thanking the god of war there were no mines, barbed wire or frag grenades. A strange silence above told me that Mosquito Air reported well to Duncan, for panic overcame the gooks and most bugged down the steep trail west to the Pia-ri Valley where pass after pass of triumphant, greedy fighter bombers greeted them without resistance other than popping of puny rifle fire. Being unsure of total victory, as soon as we got half our wind, we climbed quickly, still short of breath, wobbly-legged over the parapet, thrusting our bayonets into bunkers and trenches.

Lieutenant Charles F Kramsvogel of East Grand Rapids, Michigan, rifle platoon leader of Item Company was there that day but tells me he can't recall much of what transpired. "Dud, I've tried all these years to forget," and he was not alone among survivors who "try to forget the whole thing." Right maybe, but a few of us gloried in combat and wanted to remember that great highlight of our lives, and for people to hear us tell them something of all that went on under the flashes of explosions and smoke and fury that was an unparalleled experience.

Behind Zigerfoose's second squad I was among the first to reach the summit. No last-ditch fighting as our history Blue Book says, for the gooks panicked and ran off downhill toward the Pia-ri Valley or, wounded one way or another, cringed in the dark recesses of bunkers, one calling out to us pathetically, "No, no" over and over; most so terrified of us 'devils' they were motionless. An interpreter might have convinced some of them to come out safely to us, but the only interpreters we had were our weapons. We couldn't trust them to be left behind so we tossed in grenades. It was necessary to do this because desperados were known to play dead and shoot well-meaning dogfaces in the back rather than try to escape or surrender. It takes only one treacherous gook to spoil it for all. None of our guys was stupid enough to crawl in to coax them out and our Korean combat interpreter wasn't up with us yet.

"Goddamn it, Gould!" Duncan radioed. "Goddammit! We did it . . . licked the bastards. Buzzard Seven, old man, a terrific job. I'm making you honorary airborne."

"Airborne, shit!" I radioed back. "Better yet, we're Love of the 38th on top of Fools Mountain."

We found the positions from which showers of potato-masher grenades had stopped falling empty but in one bunker ten gooks huddled together, some badly wounded the night before by artillery. They didn't subscribe to the Geneva Convention and I put two men to guard them, alert and watching for tricks. Two of our medics got to them before night fell and the five faces that lived occupied spare litters early the next morning.

Sere, blasted, twisted, tortured trees, hanging forth loose torn branches with brown-paper leaves stuck on; earth crumpled and thrown up, artillery quaked disaster land. "My Argonne, Uncle Art."

"Blown-up cemetery," one man observed, gazing into a 500-pound bomb crater with shredded remains of gook soldiers. Three heads, I saw.

I'll never forget Zigerfoose leading the squad ahead of me, beating me to the top of 1179 and the big bunkers there; skirting bomb and heavy artillery craters, some of which still smoked, burning willie peter all night. In truth, I can't tell you how proud and excited my men were, and being in charge of Love they were now all my men, such disregard for their lives and bodies, derring-do, the proud wild banzai up 1100 and 1179 against the best the gook Hero Regiment had to offer. We all screamed and cursed in unison, and, relieved suddenly of all that strain, with energy we no longer needed for survival, laughed and cheered even choking on sticky saliva, some laughing, hysterically, a few with tears of emotion in their eyes, in all that wild hysteria of victory.

Average American, you, yes you reading this, overweight, weak, dishonest, lazy good-for-nothing, immoral shirker; selfish, lying, cruel to the defenseless, conniving bastard, take off your hat to brave Sandy, son of a proud Greek, and the other real classical hero warriors who volunteered that you might hide at home—Mexican-American fighters, numero uno gunmen in all the world; penniless American Indian featherless braves looking to help white man make coup, with a huge selfpride you'll never even suspect there is and other men of great hearts and manliness from poor families, uneducated, which in your high-finance, involute technological ways you can't even recognize, because you dandies at home will never know what a great warrior is and has done for your family. No greater heroes ever served rear echelons better, more bravely than those of the Forgotten War, dropped from memory half a century ago.

I am proud to count myself in their ranks, we who gloried in infantry combat. For one great, if sad, summer and fall a thirty-one-year-old recalled Reserve infantry rifle platoon leader (MOS 1542) of no mark in civilian life, was the ranking man in Love. Virile men and boys all over the world play king on the mountain each in his own way, as do spirited 'lower' animals. Like proud, aloof mountain goats, we sought to take the high ground by our own strength and courage and win only after a hard struggle to look down upon, not up to. Nothing, not even knocking an opponent down in the prize ring or getting a ball over the net, the goal post, or through the basket, with millions, standing up cheering, paying them billions of dollars to succeed, will dimly approach the deep-felt thrill of mortal combat in a nasty, lonely, unsung, depressingly dangerous, self-contained sport leading to glory for a chosen few who must remain unknown and unsung.

Ironically, we used the very method to take 1179 that precluded me in the closing days of WWII in the Sudetenland from earning a combat infantryman's badge, a headlong attack so shocking as to weaken the resolves of our foe. In Czechoslovakia our recon jeeps and truck-mounted 50-caliber machine guns rat-raced, taking weapons from kraut POWs as they sped along and now, up to the summit of 1179 as fast as our legs under a weapons and ammo load would let us. By speed and battle cries alone, we saved a lot of American lives, while at Bloody and Heartbreak they died weekly and into months attacking piecemeal,

A high point well below and south of us was to be referred to as Bloody Ridge; north down the valley would soon be Heartbreak Ridge, a favorite of war correspondents, made notorious to people back home and in France solely because of cruel repeated tragedies brought on by incompetent colonels who, rather than form and push along a smoothly resupplied juggernaut as did Duncan of the 38th, committed individual rifle platoons of the 9th and 23rd piecemeal without close backup and resupply and officerless ROKs spooked at night.

Colonel Frank Y Adams of the 23rd Infantry of the Second Division, and a Lieutenant Colonel of the 9th, Manchus regiment, visited our vantage point on 1179 with forward observers to sight their entire objective at a glance to the south and below us so lofty and important was our 1179. Fools Mountain? I think not. From our vantage point they directed accurate artillery and air strikes and we watched tracers from disastrous firefights every night as weakly committed guys of the Golden Dragon and then the 23d Infantry with their French Foreign Legion attachments on Bloody Ridge suffered loses in similar struggles up in the daylight, down in panic at night; night attacks by the gooks wiping out our men.

Our sister regiment, the 23rd, was organized July 1861 at Fort Trumbull, Connecticut with the motto, We Serve. Its crest on a wreath of colors is an Alaskan totem pole of an eagle above a dinner plate which is, in turn, above a Russian bear, the old Alaska. The plate represents a feast given to the eagle, new Alaska, by the bear, Russia, as it's soldiers moved out. Part of its regimental shield is a top view of the globe, signifying that the 23rd was the first American regiment to circumnavigate the world.

The unnecessarily violent, unsuccessful escapades of our sister regiments made our men worried and sad—our brave fellow Indianheaders going down so needlessly isolated and unsupplied. The inhouse, combined services, *Far East Stars and Stripes* newspaper and no others worldwide mentioned our smooth success in taking and holding 1179, to that date the highest, most valuable point on the enemy side of the Punchbowl. How quiet we made it early all over our battlefield, as our noisy sister regiments bled daily and every night for pitiful weeks on Bloody and Heartbreak ridges.

> *Only when man shall roll up the sky like a hide, will there be an*
> *end to misery unless God has first been known.*
> – The Upanishads.

Sleeping as though dead in my open dirt grave atop 1179, I expanded with my dead riflemen in a great primordial force, knowing that all things live forever if in some perhaps forgotten or unknown way as electrons move within atoms within molecules; a secret life ever changing, where all is one and one all, as is the massive mountain we clung to, whose flanks we profaned with flesh, scarred with high explosives.

> At those who come to my grave with flowers,
> I can but laugh,
> Those ignorant, unheeding, what you please,
> Who think I bear some relation to this stone
> And do not know I am in those flowers and these.
> – Cahit Sitki Taranci,   One of the Dead Speaks.

Physically and mentally exhausted, after voting to nominate Edsel for a DSC, I slept soundly the night of our great accomplishment. White phosphorus smoked lazily among the artillery-plowed ruins of the enemy fortification. Somehow in the mysterious realm of make-believe, in the swift passage of great fantasies, and, of course, fatigue of a bruised brain, I dreamed I saw bloody waters flow downward from 1179's crumbling granite slopes on Nature's way over the ample bosom of our protector, mother earth, the great earth goddess Gaea, mother of Titans.

I dreamed of green, unharmed trees giving sweet breath to cool mountain night winds; rustling leaves taking on sinister meanings at night to worried riflemen in some country somewhere, in safe, hastily dug holes in the ground everywhere; stars glittered down among clouds of heavens sent awry scudding the vast mountain darknesses seeking to brush us off; empyrean clouds grazing our mountain tops, black clouds formed again and again and reforming, cast away by the breath of giants, racing along with the urgent whisperings of fleeting lives lost in the ground, souls of warriors; rain and shafts of lightning, pale, blue-purple to brilliant yellow-white. Foolish humans fretting in peaceful cities half a world away, fools lying to superiors, kissing butts, bowing low, appraising pieces of matter, unable to realize the short duration of even gold and steel scattered into subatomic particles; making elaborate plans for time they hold no receipt for; talking casually of morrows no need for, for time and truth are known only in dying.

Those lost forever to Love in that campaign of carnage were moths blown into a mountain afire, tender wings singed in the flames of war. As Buddha warned, suddenly all of us meet change; subtle, cruel, savage, heathen change, as parents suddenly lose children, children their parents passing on the essence of all ruination of things; war a rapid compression of change, most abruptly in infantry combat. Nothing stands still. Movement is change and the universe is inconceivably dynamic with change, everything from particles to galaxies, revolving, unceasing motion, change, darting, zipping, zapping, slashing, combining, around going around, slitting around energies living and dying— life and death, becoming and going and soldiers, young soldiers, long before their normal time.

The surface of the earth except where snows lie year-round is strewn below with the bones of exhausted soldiers savaged, ravaged and bled. Gettysburg is the mass grave of my great grandfather's son Corporal Spicer, New York's 71st Infantry, who as they used to say, died in the Glory of the Lord, and it's well-known how the Western front in the first world war turned poppy red each spring from blood of soldiers on the ground—*ne funestentur,* defiled by death. It did anyway back when people cared, when infantry combat was still the Glory of the Lord. Once there was a day set aside for remembrance, limping veterans selling red paper poppies on Armistice Day. Poppy vendors hobbled into the earth long ago and there is no more Armistice Day.

At one time the thought of such squandering of soldiers appalled my father, as Gettysburg did his grandfather, as World War II and Korea did me; as Vietnam would appall my son Richard, combat medic. In what sacred library are the names of soldiers who sleep forever under battlefields—*nomina pausantium.* Now that the saddened mothers of the Korean War dead are gone to their final sleep, we must mourn our buddies ourselves for the few years we have left, and say to our MIAs—

> *The moving hand writes and having writ*
> *Moves on—nor all thy piety nor wit*
> *Shall lure it back to cancel half a line,*
> *Nor all thy tears wash out a word of it.*
> – Omar Khayyam.

Preachers, safe in churches, brag to captive audiences that faith moves mountains, but for months in all that wild mountain world, not a pebble was moved by prayer, prayers supplanted by angry curses where God was only to damn the enemy and save us from violent deaths. We held no real hope for kind intervention, nor could minesweepers aid us, so befouled were our forward paths with shrapnel. Anyway, to what divinity could mass murderers proclaim our evil plans? Mortal combat is pure, basic animal work, gods are for love, peace and intelligence and should remain smiling, placing fingertips together in places of worship at large, impressive conference tables. What we needed was that dreadful god of the Jews, mighty Jehovah, the powerful one, fabled warrior that strode upon mighty winds over the desert, planting footsteps upon storms—whose priests leveled walls with angry blasts.

Standing on Taeusan that first night after midnight, a break in overcast exposed a trillion twinkling stars and I felt belonging, a follower of setting suns behind angry, tossing, distant clouds; some puffing up cliffs to greet me, atoms of all Nature enfolding me with atoms of my mother and Love's many dead, and I was one of and among them. Having lived months intimately with Nature with only fatigue clothes between us, breathing open air on and off 1179, in her when shells arrived, in Korean wilderness as, sleeping coiled within mother earth, hugging her passionately under fire, cowering among tree roots, watching the blood of buddies disappear fast into loose earth, running away on flat rocks, deeply embroiled in symbolic cohesion in dark, damp earth, jagged mountain outcroppings and silvery-gray, brooding skies capping the setting sun, I was home. In the distance were muffled rumbles of thunder challenged by heavy artillery, that world over there by the faint blue-purple mountains going to sleep snoring now, echoing further and further away; then, suddenly, without warning, wild storming from behind, blazing blades of blue lightning flashes flying by an optical illusion straight toward us from a terrible tempest and furious skyquakes.

We were civilizations removed from polite society, locked in deadly combat in a morbid arena of death, ironically in the country called Chosen, Land of the Morning Calm. Few Americans know, especially don't want to know, that their dearly paid-for soldiers' blood fertilizes wildernesses the world over; where in peace greedy money-makers scurry for profit, and there are more battle sites around the globe than peaceful cities today, many grown from campfires of brave young soldiers whose air-thickened blood mortared the foundation of civilizations.

We shared holes in dank earth learning fast together *artes moriendi*, art of dying, a meaning unheard of by noncombatants, through periods of great fear, of what society is like stripped of sanity and what one's self is really worth, which can be truly learned facing death. Living constantly in fresh memory of unforgettable deaths, we, alive, basking in the glow of the amazing selfless acts of our buddies, our mud-stained minds terribly hurt by their bad luck, sharing with other heroes how wonderfully uplifting in death the human spirit can be. Civilians and rear echelon military meet only the lucky survivors of combat; they should be made to feel the great love and homage we combat infantrymen feel for the dead we left behind.

Live whole lifetimes in half an hour's shelling, turn yourself recklessly over to blind fate, forgetting petty worries that beset you stateside—material things, picky personality differences and money worries. Uncommon love, or call it companionship under fatal pressures if you will; mutual, complete trust involving the very soul, unselfishness, camaraderie or single-mindedness facing imminent demise, as people link together their thoughts, objectives and fears facing prolonged tragedy and senseless destruction.

Not in all the United States of America, in all the world in all military establishments thereof, are there such straightforward, humble, hard-run heroes as those who shoulder rifles in Infantry combat.

> *If thou hast a woe, tell it not to a weakling, tell it to thy*
> *saddle bow and ride forth singing.*
> – John Dryden.

In Korea through hundreds of agonizing fears and moments of abject terror on hills red with our blood—1100, 1179, 1181, and 1243—in a strange mental withdrawal from nearby cruelties, there burst forth the revelation that only in combat is there true brotherly love, as *buddy* was reduced from *brother* in the dusty violence of the Mexican War, its older equivalent *matey* derived from Old English *metta*, messmate, from much earlier wars, denoting a close bond among hard-working, self-sacrificing English soldiers.

Death dealt us bitterly in unpleasant ways day after solemn, joyless day, without the mitigating aid of tolling bells or black trappings; still I dreaded it more than gave it hate, for it seemed I was always fated to ask, "Just how bad is it?"

"Sorry. Too early to tell."

"Think he'll make it back okay? Wasn't losing too much blood, was he?"

Bleeding dark red spurts, there's no time to plead, "My god, why hast thou forsaken me?" which would have been immaterial anyway, all combat infantrymen know.

> *Each person is born with one possession which far outvalues*
> *all the others—his last breath.*
> – Mark Twain.

"Limped out all right," Doc reasoned. "Can't say he'll not be crippled, at least he's out of it."

"Too bad about the others," I reflected.

"Yeah," Doc would say time and again. "That's the way we go, shooting craps, winning—losing.

We looked straight at each other in common cause and snickered bitterly.

"Sh-e-e-e-it!"

Item pulled up on a hill tight under us the following morning just in time to be greeted by a furious counterattack from H 1181. I hustled down with my radioman to see how it was going when two sergeants, a corporal, and a private from Item's weapons platoon came stumbling along with a heavily loaded litter, bent over on the run. The way the litter occupant bounced freely on the canvas, not strapped down, made me assume he was dead, at least too far gone for carriers to feel the need for gentleness. His eyes were shut tight—eyeballs puffed terribly, round ping-pong balls of stretched purple skin from the sudden air shock of a nearby exploding shell. His face was a gro tesque mask, pale yellow-green, sweaty, cold-looking skin, irrevers-ible death shock.

"Take him off!" I ordered impatiently. "Save the litter for someone can make it."

The taller sergeant, master sergeant stripes proudly stenciled in black on the front of his helmet, glared fiercely. "Shut your fuckin' face, that's our lieutenant."

"Lieutenant Murray," the corporal said with enormous pride.

It was Murray of Item all right, his face so bloated, bruised and bloodied I hadn't recognized him. He was a big man, too much to fit comfortably in our rocky holes, white matter mixed with the thickening blood where the back of his head rested on the olive-drab canvas. I couldn't understand why they thought him still alive until Murray's mouth gulped slowly wide open and then slowly, very slowly, closed like a tired goldfish.

The corporal supporting the left rear handle had a brilliant florescent Chartreuse air panel strapped to his back.

"Anyway," I told him, "take off that panel. It's a good target."

"Oh, yeah!" the corporal muttered, suddenly remembering. "We feared an air `strike."

"My gawd, that's not Lieutenant Murray!" Sergeant Milligan blurted. "My gawd, what happened? From my hometown; dated his older sister. My gawd, what happened?"

"What happened?" I repeated. "Can't you see his brains?"

"My gawd, sir, that stuff on the outside of his head? My gawd, not Russ Murray." Then quietly, almost wistfully, he mumbled to himself, walking slowly away.

Had I dreamed? As I got deep into the manuscript of YOU TREMBLE BODY, I could sometimes hardly tell. Nightmares of incongruous conflicts that terrified my younger years were actually less disturbing with madeup hor-rors and despairs, more calm, with no lasting horror because they never really happened, and subconsciously you knew you would somehow survive them, but then you did not have to touch how slippery and then sticky drying blood gets, so prevalent are black stains of dead blood everywhere, piles of dirty fa-tigues now stiff, from which a hand or unhelmeted head protrudes.

Whereas I praise the dead which are already dead more
than the living which are yet alive.
— Ecclesiastes.

I praise the dead among whom I scooped C rations and as my admiration grew individual by individual, it dawned on me that the earth is full of soldiers in such numbers as stars in all galaxies; young soldiers gone under the earth to uphold the living, losing their lives that others might prosper unthreatened; quitting life far from home, slipping unthanked, unknown, unhonored into the deep river of time flowing darkly along.

> *Millions of spirits of creatures walk the earth unseen,*
> *both when we wake and when we sleep.*
>   – John Milton.

On Hill 1179 atop the Punchbowl, most days after the first hectic weeks of shellings and intermittent close combat counterattacks, I goofed off with the guys of Love Company's forward headquarters, an Arab tent of ponchos buttoned together. On quiet days that August, on the friendly side of the ridge where it was safe from all but mortar and where it wasn't so steep, we sat on our pisspots to keep our tails dry, huddled together under cold mountain rains around small fires of waterproof, 'fire-resistant' cardboard C ration boxes and splintered wood from grenade boxes; knees-to-knees, soggy, muddy, olive-drab army blankets doubled, wrapped around damp shoulders; straightleg, bewhiskered dogfaces, black crack lines in dirt-packed skin, smelling of stale smoke of many campfires; foot-slogging infantry, kept outdoors like smelly dogs with poor manners, dogfaces chatting idly; fussing aloud about the totally discouraging, cool, gray-black, always disagreeable weather.

And who was the officer on the spot, their acting company commander? Why, that asshole, Lieutenant Gould, who volunteered for such dirty work in an earlier war and now, recalled to another, was being told every day his life wasn't necessary.

> *Indeed the idols I have loved so long*
> *Have done my credit in this world much wrong;*
>   *Have drowned my glory in a shallow cup,*
>   *And sold my reputation for a song.*
>   – Omar Khayyam.

Sometimes we snickered at bitter remarks, punctuated with sharp hissing sh-e-e-e-it!, our carefully protected inner selves secretly nourished by fond memories of sweet, feminine wives, girlfriends and mothers who blossomed into dainty, delicate angels in our absence. Attempts at Hollywood humor stuck in our throats.

Tired by short rations and guarding nights, mostly when uncommitted, we curled like the dogs we were and slept on dirt, face sideways on our paws for pillows, indifferent to light and dark, night and day.

9

DECLINE

*a wind has blown the rain away and blown
the sky away and all the leaves away,
and the trees stand. I think I too have
known autumn too long.*
— e e cummings.

Mountain air told us it was late autumn as Hill 1179 cooled down at night and the loose spoils of our diggings stiffened from a chilly wind blowing down from Manchuria. Some time during the dark silence of our dirt world, Korean winter threatened, leaving a thin layer of frost on the torn-up, battle-scarred land. Frost was rare at this altitude because of lack of humidity but in the waning autumn of my time in Korea it came dark earlier, chilly at night—stern clouds covering the gray-blue northern sky. Back in Watertown in November as it came to hunting season, we'd say, "It's like for snow."

As I assessed the strangely beautiful, deeply lonely mountain wilderness, I found myself for the first time truly in the Land of the Morning Calm, homesick, trembling a lot or jittery, mostly hands and fingers. I grew colder as I grew older for my years; some day real soon I'd have to walk all the way down to the Pia-ri valley and this time tell Colonel Duncan I'm not being a patsy any longer, had all the thrills I can ever use. He promised I'd be relieved soon, well, soon was long past; it's time to send up a career captain who could profit from being where I am. I was learning nothing to use in civilian life.

Night weakened as dawn glowed slowly, faintest gray to a gradual dirty ashen blue—cool, joyless illumination; get set, another day for dying.

"Hear me, man," Tree shivered, "I'se freezen to death; hear me say—freeze, for sure."
Our Blue Book—

The first days of August found the Second Division adjusting its positions and preparing defenses along the Kansas Line. Hill 1179, firmly in control, had eliminated enemy observation of the Kansas Line activities in the east. However, four hills overlooking the western portion of the line—

983, 940, 773 and 1243—were now being used by the enemy as observation posts. Patrols from all three regiments, now on line, ranged out to determine the extent of this new threat. Tanks from the 38th Tank Company, C Company of the Second Division 72d Tanks, kept up continual concentrations on the forward slopes of the hills to prevent the enemy from constructing bunkers and observing our movements.

Reports coming from regimental patrols revealed the enemy planning no offensive action but busily engaged in preparing defenses along the 983-940-773 terrain complex [Bloody Ridge to Heartbreak Ridge]. Greatly increased use of artillery by the enemy covered these preparations and hampered patrol activities of the Division.

Instructions from Eighth Army directed that every effort be made to reduce the number of casualties in the period of the cease-fire negotiations. Offensive operations were to be undertaken only when, in the long run, such operations would ultimately reduce the number of casualties suffered over a given period. Consequently, all operations were conducted with the thought of incurring a minimum num ber of casualties and friendly artillery was utilized to a maximum.

On 12 August, the Division received word that plans for an attack on the enemy hills were being considered. The following day, shortly after midnight, the Division was directed to prepare plans for seizing the hill mass and submit them to X Corps. That same day, a boundary change was received which narrowed the Division front, delegating the portion it had been reduced to the Seventh ROK Division.

Late in the afternoon of 14 August, G3 was notified by X Corps that orders were being cut for the operation to take Hills 983, 940 and 773. The 36th ROK Regiment was attached to the Division for the forthcoming attack.

The 9th Infantry launched its attack the morning of 27 August. Fierce fighting throughout the day failed to net any gain and by nightfall, 983 was still secure in enemy hands. That night, Division artillery unleashed the most intense artillery barrage of the war on the slopes of 983 as more than 22,500 rounds were sent screaming into the hillsides during the hours of darkness.

The Division delegated to the 38th Infantry the sole responsibility of taking Hill 983 and on 28 August, the Second Battalion prepared to pass through the First Battalion to press the attack. The First had been badly battered in the previous day's assault.

Heavy rains turned the roads and trails leading to the battle area into rivers of mud on the 28th and, as a result, it was not until noon that the Second Battalion was in position to move forward. It had no sooner jumped off, however, than at 1300 hours it met with heavy resistance. E and G Companies bore the brunt of the fighting during the afternoon and nightfall revealed them still a few hundred meters short of the crest. There, with darkness upon them, they set up a perimeter defense for the night.

Someone, somewhere coined the inevitable GI nickname for the barren battlefield and it was only a matter of time before 'Bloody Ridge' was known, not only to the weary, wet and miserable attackers, but to all at home who read the news reports of the gallant struggle.

I heard no preacher's plans on our Fools Mountain. Not to say the great majority of dogtags weren't stamped C for Christian. But the cool Caucasian God watched wholesale dying with sublime detachment, day after unhappy day, night upon fearful night, there amid the stench of disappearing buddies, and saith naught, and those marked by the Evil One for the next deaths, trained by rote at home to beseech God, screamed his sacred name in angry goddammits!

I shuddered at the corpses lying about in various stages of decay and occasionally, with unsteady fingertips, carefully traced the outline of my own skull, fingering around the outer rims of my eye sockets and short-lived flesh, reluctantly telling the physical me it's just a matter of time, assuming my features weren't smashed as poor J C's, I'd be left smiling like other guys, teeth protruding, shrinking lips, matted hair intact.

Hell in hereafter for the thoughtless murders we did for hire was always in our offing, but since we already wallowed in one hell, who feared another? Reveling in the clear excitement of being essential for the moment; respected by many good men— and alive! Still alive? Always that pure born-again delight after a firefight, laughing aloud at nothing, grim-joke-time. Imagine, still alive! Really, still alive? Each new breath steady, countable; especially wondrous relief as at the hazy light of false dawn, end of the heaviest of night, we would shout softly from hole to hole like groundhogs checking snouts. Harry? Bill? Funaro? Jones? Andy? Pop? All right? "Hey, Mike, you guys all right? Make it okay? Well, you scared me, you're so quiet." One breath after another until at last it's back on an old familiar rhythm. One breath inspiring another until it's habitual once more. It's not that death is conceived so terrible, only that life in retrospect proved so sweet.

Heroes have always been called upon to die for those who are not heroes and for eons young soldiers fell, as they do somewhere always, serving uncompromising, legal old men. Died from blows of crude clubs, from spear thrusts and flying arrows and, as industry merged with science, musket balls, shrapnel, aerial bombs, poison gas, and even more deadly technologies. Young soldiers have always had to clean up after mediocre old statesmen.

> *He whom the gods love dies young.*
> – Meander.

They died in nothing resembling grace, or gracefully, as the rest of us professional *dramatis personae* cast into a leaden tableau of terror tried desperately to memorize our lines, preparing in unspoken ways for our last earthly bow, that night, or certainly on the morrow. No clarion calls, no fanfares, those bitterly sad evenings, mornings, and afternoons as frightened young men struggled to stay alive. They died as well in gray light as total darkness.

> *I do not know the dignity of their birth but I do know the glory of*
> *their deaths. Their dauntless valor rests, their flags will wave again in*
> *the evenings of our memory.*
> – Douglas MacArthur.

They didn't die clean, white-sheeted deaths and come to rest in flower-covered, pink-satin-lined, polished mahogany caskets; they went twisting into the ground where they got it, some dead before landing, and there was no hushed, hallowed viewing of their cleverly waxed replacement flesh and rouged remains in well-staged funeral parlor dramas; no church-ordained solemnity or respectful calm, but rather the bedlam of hell erupting as they left us, an occasional curse or choked-off plea to save his life, surprise, half angry reaction to pain and terrible power of the hit, a sudden final, pathetic sinking, meeting Death lying down on bare ground.

Dogface soldiers and sad-eyed deer get slammed in their tracks by hunks of hot lead at a ton per square inch, dropped where they stand. Deer get gutted right away and trussed over the right front fender of four-wheelers, proud signs of macho depravity. Hopefully dogfaces are found in a few days, depending on the nearness of the enemy and, already stinking, covered with vicious flies, slid into airtight black rubber body bags, zipped tightly and shoved into the back of crackerbox ambulances or swung unceremoniously onto the beds of six-by supply trucks that are in wait below as far up as trucks can climb.

Dropped KIA by company clerks on the daily morning report to higher headquarters, pathetic little piles of personal belongings mailed home, if mothers were lucky enough, in a cloth bag in a box, a cheap wrist watch, mildewed leather wallet with cracked, worn photos of females and young children—good luck charms that failed.

Shallow and Hurtz left for the rear mumbling and acting 'funny.' I heard someone say I was getting a little weird, too, touchy. Maybe I'm no religious man but one morning I caught myself saying over and over for no reason, "Oh, my God! Oh, my God!" as if I owed Him a few, and that morning without deliberation or taking stock, I told Sergeant Eppler to take over and hiked it down to the jeep dismount point with Master Sergeant Red Rose on his way to division to receive a hot shower, change of fatigues, new underwear and socks, shave and haircut and a good hot meal, decorated with a cluster to his Bronze Star with V for valor and given a little gold bar of minor authority a government commission dangerous to life and limb, a danger even more constant than before, sworn in to take over what was Hurtz's platoon.

Red asked what brought me to the rear and thought I was kidding when I told him I was quitting. When he realized I wasn't fooling around, his first question was who's taken over?

"Karl," I told him.

Right away Red started talking to me like I was one of his disturbed guys. "C'mon, lieutenant ... Dud. C'mon, guy, you don't want to ruin your life after all you been through. It can't last forever. It's going to be over soon. Look at them peace talks. Shit, it could be tomorrow. Think of your family. You got a boy, ain't you, Dud? Think of some day when he learns his dad is in Leavenworth for bugging out?"

"I appreciate what you're trying to do, Red, but I'm losing control and I'm more afraid of what I might do if I went off the deep end and took some guys with me. I've heard what guys have done."

"Things ain't that bad, Dud, let them give you a little rest. You'll be good as new after a couple of days in the rear."

"You're just the opposite from me. I'm going and you're coming. Red," I explained, "you know how long field commissions last in this battalion. Whatever you do, Red, don't try to prove yourself as an officer; you've more than done it as a sergeant. You're not getting that much more pay."

Colonel Duncan and Mildren, regiment commander, together called Karl Eppler from regiment after our banzai up 1179 trying to talk him into accepting a field commission. He turned it down. Two days earlier Eppler and I discussed the great danger of taking a field commission; within a few minutes named seven top-flight platoon sergeants who accepted field commissions and were killed, badly wounded, or MIA in the past months, like long-ago Second Lieutenant Worth H Barber, my predecessor; only four guys in the platoon remember him, how fearless he was. Although the high fatality rate of exceptional courage demonstrated after field commissioning was a well-known curse in infantry combat, the personal pride of being a proven hero and an officer because of it was compelling. These men were highly dedicated and selfless, else they wouldn't have been nominated. Many wore Silver Stars and Purple Hearts.

> In the world's broad field of battle,
> In the bivouac of Life,
> Be not like dumb, driven cattle!
> Be a hero in the strife!
> – Henry Wordsworth Longfellow.

Red's jeep was waiting, headed for division, and dropped me off at battalion. I walked right into Duncan's tent. When I told him point blank I'd had it he was not surprised.

"Dud," he called me, for the first time, "I get your morning report every day and know how you must feel toward those guys. Jesus, Dud, it hurts us as much as it does you, but the peace talks are coming good and…"

"Shit, Colonel," I interrupted, "don't hand me no third-hand grief. I know I'm headed for Leavenworth; I can't take it any more. What am I, somebody's prize executioner, some kind of Judas goat … lead them right to it? Don't you think I got feelings? I should have got it a hundred times myself. I'm what they call cracked up or combat fatigue or something. I never thought this could happen to me, sir, but I can't and won't take it any more; I'm quitting before I blow my cork and really lose guys."

Rather than being pissed off, Colonel Duncan looked worried. Rather than express anger or disappointment, he had his sergeant major, whose name I forget, take me to the headquarters officers' mess (a reserved table in the big headquarters company mess tent) for a sirloin rare and some cold beer. That beer ration was something else the guys sorely missed up on the line fighting week in and month out.

When I returned to Duncan's tent, he introduced me to Captain Sprague, soon to be major, our new battalion surgeon, who said they had some tests that'd make me feel a lot better but we'd have to go back to the 11th Evac about ten miles south where the captain and another doctor, a Lieutenant Colonel Watson, had me put on some hospital pajamas, convincing me that I had to strip down to take a shower anyway and have my fatigues exchanged. I confess I was pretty blood-caked and muddy. Geezus, I thought, holding up my fatigue blouse splattered by someone else's blood—like Mister Jewett, butcher in a blood-spattered full-length white coat at the Mohegan Meat Market back home only mine was dried black.

When I asked what was wrong with me, they said nothing out of the ordinary — whatever was ordinary. I could feel everything wasn't right; as I tried to stop wetting my eyes like an old man as I do now, nor stop quivering. Every once in a while I'd break out quivering or shivering, like shaking only more shallow. After I grabbed a hot shower (did it ever feel good) and clean pajamas, I got a brushcut and shave, one of the smoothest I ever had, from a Korean houseboy barber, with all that nice-smelling stuff they shake on; what is that we used to say, 'shave and a haircut, Bay Rum'?

A warrant officer came to my private room (in a tent hospital yet?), introduced himself as a case worker, near as I remember. He asked me if it was all right if he helped me sleep and I made a little joke, "Hell, you're the doctor," which he wasn't, really. He didn't have sense enough to smile but gave me a shot that seemed to put me to sleep before he got the needle out. I have to say *seemed* because almost from the moment the needle went in I was gone.

They let me sleep into mid-morning the following day and then explained what sodium pentothal (thiopental sodium) was and what it would do and asked me to volunteer to undergo a test. There again I'm a little short on memory, but recall almost everything the warrant officer said. He was a plain, ordinary guy—nothing sneaky like a shrink. I knew there was a psychiatrist or two around somewhere, but they never showed as such unless one was Colonel Watson who left everything to the warrant officer. The warrant officer was real businesslike, not underhanded. Once in a while he'd flip open a looseleaf book and jot something down. He was a cool one who ignored my jokes and comments, I don't think he caught the jokes. Or maybe I only imagined they were jokes. What do you think?

They called pentothal the truth serum, which was supposed to loosen your brain and make you think everything is funny and blab everything you know. I blabbed all right and everything was happy and lighthearted, but I also broke down once and cried like a damn baby someone hurt. I told him lots of things, about the runner the other day from Red Battalion who stopped at our CP. Doc Singleton, our new company medic, and I caught him by his arms as he keeled over in front of us and before he could get a word out tears began rolling down his face making long dirt streaks as he bent to puke green saliva and bile from his guts, straining until the whites of his eyes were blood red and fine capillaries in his cheeks ruptured. When he stopped, tremors shook his entire body.

"One way or another, they're not going to kill me. I'm going home," he choked, gulping, coughing and spitting deep to clear the sticky, bitter taste. "If I have to shoot my foot off, Lieutenant, I'm making it home. Throw the book at me but I can't live with dead men no more." Doc tried to console him, only the guy, duty-bound, canceled it, and left with some important message for our battalion commander.

I told the warrant officer social worker what a big impression this kid had on us and how I'd quiver and sometimes shake so I feared I was probably headed the same way. I could describe it only as falling apart, losing control of my muscles and even thoughts.

"JESUS H CHRIST! man," I yelled, "can't you tell!"

I was like that Biblical Job—my men and I were being tested, except that Job lived comfortably to 140, the Christian Bible states, to own "14,000 sheep, 6000 camels, 1000 yokes of oxen, 1000 she asses; to beget seven sons and three daughters and live to see his sons and his sons' sons, even four generations." Job died in peace; my guys died hard in battle, very young, some still virgins. Job's cries could have come from them word-for-word, except God was too busy to Love—

Lord, let me know my end that I may know how frail I am.... Why died I not from the womb? Why did I not give up the ghost when I came out of the belly?.... They are destroyed from morning to evening; they perish forever without any regarding it. When I lie down, I say, when shall I arise and the night be gone? And I am full of tossing to and fro into the dawning of the day.... My flesh is covered with worms and clods of dust; my skin is broken and become loathsome.... My days are spent without hope. The eyes of him that hath seen me shall see me no more.... As the cloud is consumed and vanisheth away, so he that goeth down to the grave shall come up no more. He shall return no more to his house, neither shall his place know him anymore.... Our days upon earth are shadows. He breaketh me without cause. Man dieth and wasteth away; yea man giveth up the ghost and where is He? So man lieth down and riseth not; 'til the heavens be no more, they shall not wake, nor be raised out of their sleep. My days are past, my purposes are broken off, even the thoughts of my heart.
                                        – Job and Love's riflemen.

Within minutes as the pentothal took effect I was shooting the breeze with Sergeant Dorn. He didn't know what happened any more than me. I knew the guy only two weeks but like Sandy he made such a big impression, a valuable friend within two days. I'll take the memory of him to my grave. Who knows, maybe I'll get religion before I go and meet them all there, something an Agnostic never gets to do.

Then I was talking with Sergeant Eppler and J J about guys we'd known. "Remember the time he ..." I broke off and turned away. "Damn it," I blurted, tears in my eyes, "he was a harmless little kid not out of high school; didn't look as old as Doc Lynch. Poor little guy. You know, Sergeant Eppler, at thirty-one I'm their old man; but after a while it's not so easy to do any more. They're too damn trusting of me, making me responsible. I can't afford being so liable to them so damn beholden."

Sergeant Eppler asked if I knew so-and-so from another platoon who used to visit Funaro and Sizemore and liked to tease Ski until Pop Miller chased them away. Did I remember them? Dorn, Ich, Smitty, all of them, even those whose names I can't recall. I am bound to remember the tragic aura they moved in for I, too, was wrapped in it. Remember where and the way each fell; the hateful parts of hell where they left this world: Sonag-chi, Inje, Soyangang, Habae-chae, Sergeant Ulriche, oh God, that terrific hero, Ulriche, my idol when I was new and so young over here, Habae-chae, Manun-gol. Sapdyo-ri, even Private Youngs while supposedly resting at Hongsong. Now on 1179, Punchbowl, worst of all, so exposed to view from 1243.

A report I sneaked a look at said that all this "came flooding out." The warrant officer wrote and, "he [me] removed an imaginary steel helmet that weighted his head down and wiped his forehead with the back of his right hand," but I don't remember doing anything like that and what would it mean anyway?

Two days later, I was still undergoing a lot of uncontrollable worrying about my guys. At least I was physically rested and clean. I was sent back to battalion aid where the battalion surgeon, Doc Sprague, got a secret report from the shrink that told him I should go on R&R (rest and rehabilitation). I argued that now that I was so rested, I should go back with my guys but he and Duncan convinced me that first I should take off a few days in Japan. "You're overdue for R&R." The rest and recreation list was made for every soldier in Korea after he served a certain minimum time compared to others, whether rear or forward. Guys in combat were supposed to come up for it sooner but it never shows on a roster. It is too bad there wasn't a computer in those days for the list was alive with changes among combatants which the roster had no way of knowing beforehand. I learned that I was instrumental in delaying a rear echelon light colonel's third trip to Japan. That in itself was worthwhile. I had, indeed, been scheduled three weeks earlier and Mighty Mouse never knew it either. One forfeited his time when he failed to show and it was given to someone else—a rear echelon more than likely right there on hand to fill the slot.

They fixed it so I would go and radioed Master Sergeant Eppler and he said he agreed with them, and joked he and the guys were giving me an order to get lost for a few days. What with a lull on 1179, it was the best time in our sector for the Army, as well as me.

"Sure you can run it?" I demanded.

"Shit, duck soup, Dud, Lieutenant Rose has already taken over. Can I run a company? Remember, you didn't even know that Buzzard Seven was you.... You kidding, sir? Look at old Pater, no West Point captain could do better. They don't issue guts."

Incidentally, this change of scenery and relapse of tension called R&R, to some S&S, Sin and Sake, was more than a whim of Special Services. It was the direct result of the six-volume study mentioned earlier, *STUDIES IN SOCIAL PSYCHOL-OGY IN WORLD WAR TWO* by Harvard's Professor Boring. Soldiers, tired of routine combats and constant losses, especially, needed a break from the death scene and it was begun in the ETO toward the end of World WAR II. I was negative about R&R being still deep in the unrecognized, undiagnosed oppressive mental trauma of losing so many of my guys and being on line so long, I wanted to stay and avenge them. I asked Roy Carse to find someone else; I wouldn't know how to enjoy myself anyway. It might be worse away from the guys. Roy called back after an hour to tell me it wasn't up to me anymore to refuse Colonel Duncan's orders. Colonel Mildren had taken a personal interest and grapevine was that Fearless Frank served with Wilkes in peacetime and got a kick out of my clobbering him. I was a hero of a different sort, taking the initiative in what he and others would have liked to do.

I tried the excuse of lack of money which, with my large allowance home, was certainly true, but a short stop at division rear finance got me $100 advance payment as could anyone on R&R regardless of rank. I recall a flight of about six hours to Tokyo with a planeload of Ethiopians, half an hour busing into the R&R Center where a bevy of Japanese seamstresses clothed guys from all divisions and separate units in ODs with Ike jackets, and sewed on division patches and we dropped our fatigues. The next stop was an orientation talk warning of venereal diseases (uncommon compared to US and Europe) and confidence games we might run into, also rare compared to those against soldiers in the States, and a caution not to use certain terms such as 'japs,' even though they called us yanks, or discuss politics of any sort. Japan was to be occupied by American troops for three more years and we were warned seriously against being ugly Americans in our dealings with a proud people. I don't know about jap pride, but to me, they'd always be sneaky, murderous japs, beheading POWs, using them for bayonet practice and starving Jimmy to death like they did.

I made three casual friends on the plane, junior officers of the 38th. No sooner were we properly uniformed than they urged me for the umpteenth time to accompany them to a well-known brothel for celebrated hot baths, massages, dancers and 'other' entertainment, even names of the 'best girls,' which had been handed down. Me? Even though Kitty and I were writing cooler and cooler letters, more formal and further apart, she called me Dudley now, I adhered to habit and kept my sexual desires subdued. I never realized, however, what a lonely thing continence could be until dropped in the center of Tokyo's night life on the fabled Ginza, Broadway of Japan. It was like Picadilly Circus in WWII, only lit up, where British whores grabbed your arm in the dark and told you: "'Ave another go of it luv your mother'll never know." The Ginza was ablaze with lights and excitement, an American soldier unable to walk half a block without being propositioned, either by the real thing or, more seldom, a pimp. The bright colored blaze of neon lights, and mirrors, sushi bars and the smell of other exotic foods, the babble of a strange tongue and sing-song music, loud oriental music and strange activity was exciting, almost unworldly to a guy who lived in a small town and was like a mole the past months.

"Have nice girl?" eyeing my rank on my overseas cap, "Lieutenant? Got number uno sexy girl, Hollywood. You see, you see, numero uno stuff, ichiban."

I had a small list of things to do during my five days and screwing women wasn't on it. Top, and certainly unique, was the name of a former Japanese Secretary of the equivalent of the Chamber of Commerce, or Commerce and Industry, I think it was, with whom my father had exchanged Christmas cards for a number of years before WWII. I forgot and left the letter to one of them in my B-4 bag but recalled his name and planned to look him up first thing the next day. Meanwhile, being late as 2000 hours and me quite hungry, looking for a nice quiet meal, I whistled up a cab— something like a quarter for ten blocks, as I recall—and had him drive me to another item on my list, the British Officers' Club in the Prince Marinuchi Hotel. There I sat alone at a table and took my time devouring a huge, what they called, 'offshore' steak. It was one of the prime items, no pun intended, recommended by fellow officers during lighter moments in Korea. "If you do nothing else, get yourself one of them out-of-this-world Australian steaks at the Prince Marinuchi."

The cabby taking me back to the R&R Center looked me over in his rearview mirror. "You go sleep, lieutenant? You know time? Twelve o'clock. Too damn early. I find you number one girl. Ichiban, you see, dai ichi!"

"I don't think so, papasan. I tired, go sleep-sleep."

"You sleep tomorrow, okay? Ichiban girl, you see." He then switched to what, from the familiar way he enunciated it, had to be a special pleasure. "Suck a hatchi, sore. Number one fuck, suck a hatchi." *Hatchi,* a rather large wooden flute. "Ah so, whore she suck you hatchi."

I never cared much for that, although I've had women, and Kitty, try to get me off that way. It was their idea, not mine. I'd look down at them trying to get me off and roll them over for the right way.

While walking the Ginza the first night, I bought what we called Ginza wings sold by street peddlers. From further than three feet at an ordinary cursory glance one could not see that the supposed silver wings was actually a naked woman's bare legs fanned out on either side from the middle, holding her knockers together with her hands, her face also in the center, smiling. I pinned on a pair to go along with the ribbon of the second highest medal in the North Korean Peoples' Army, which I found hidden under a board in the large OP bunker atop 1179. I was bitter and contemptuous and lonely. Why wear them? Why did I shave off half my handlebar moustache? To protest the chicken shit order for all enlisted men to shave theirs; I'm no psychologist, but to protest the brass I saw making stupid moves, stealing badges and valor ribbons, and causing too many unnecessary deaths. I was a recalled infantry officer whose two applications for extended active duty in response to beseeching letters from 90 Church Street and the Infantry Center were ignored, causing me and my wife much agony, quarrels, money and trouble; selling our home at a loss in between earning a hard living on the second shift of a foundry, the house I built, in a hurry at a loss; being without an income for a time; handed a loyalty certificate to sign on my way to combat; Major Wilkes' negligence to give us the promised preparatory fires on 23 May, neglecting to make us aware that his CP was pulling off the outpost, and for a number of other embittering causes, including Toth safe back at regiment with Shallow who, we learned, ended up flying observer in an artillery L-19. Yeah, I was bitter!

At ten the next day I checked several cabbies standing outside the R&R Center until I found one able to decipher Chamber of Commerce, working back from the word commerce. He deposited me not far from the landmark known to most Americans, Frank Lloyd Wright's earthquake proof Imperial Hotel. Fortunately, the Chamber of Commerce had a very pleasant, pretty bilingual secretary who was, at first, puzzled as to what an American infantry soldier wearing strange wings wanted. When she finally understood what I wanted, she broke out with the most pleasant smile I'd seen in many months.

"Ah, so! Watertown, New York. Not New York City. Smaller one, Watertown? No?" She commented at length on size comparison of the two cities and sat me down in a chair, returning in ten minutes with her nice smile and escorted me to a large, well-appointed office to introduce me to a gentleman who left his desk and came forward

rapidly as though pleased to see me, or had been expecting me for some time. Whatever, it was flattering. He bowed from the waist when the interpreter gave him my rank and name. This was my first meeting with a jap other than a cab driver or waiter, and guessing I couldn't lose, and not wanting to be an ugly American I returned his deep bow at a little less of a pitch.

I informed the gentleman how my father had appreciated and bragged about those very ornate Japanese Christmas cards he received at his office before the war, hand painted on an elegant rice paper and that he had paraded them, about five years' worth, up to December 1941, in full view every Christmas time behind a glass trophy case in the foyer of the Asbury Methodist Church. Now, six years after the war, Japan was hungry for American attention and trade. I was only a lieutenant in the Army but one couldn't always tell, I might have an address or reference and at least was one of the rather rare visitors from America to their office and the idea was, after all, quaint; that there had been such a thoughtful exchange in peace time. I caught both he and his charming secretary-interpreter making sly looks at the wings I was wearing.

The Secretary excused himself, I imagine to talk it over with his staff, and returned to ask me if I had lunched. When I said no, after all it was only 1100, he insisted that the interpreter take me to an expensive, wait-to-be-seated, European-type restaurant within easy walking. When we returned, he bowed again and I returned it and he introduced me to everyone in the building, it seemed, as though I was winning the Korean war single-handed. He put a finger on my Purple Heart ribbon and smiled broadly. Unlike the average American, he knew well what it meant; unlike cynical Americans, they knew how to treat a war hero. They promised to write to my father to explain that they met his hero son, and that, unfortunately, the Japanese correspondent was no longer alive. I was curious and brash enough to find out why, and after five minutes of slow English and rapid, at times excited, Japanese, I was informed, apologetically, it seemed, that he died in one of the fire bombings of Tokyo. I noted my pretty interpreter was polite enough not to say American bombing.

At last I peered at my left wrist and they seemed relieved. My lovely interpreter ushered me to the elevator. While waiting, she asked, "You no have girl?"

"You?" I replied incredulously, assuming she was offering herself.

"No, no," she answered, giggling, covering her mouth. "No me, sor!"

I learned later from an Army officer stationed in Tokyo that in those occupation days had I indicated a desire for a female, my guide would have made a present of an expensive geisha.

After leaving the Chamber of Commerce (its Japanese equivalent which might have had the word Industry in it), I caught a cab to the Imperial Hotel, central meeting place and favorite bar for Americans, as Harry's Bar was in Paris after WWI. While tossing a few beers at the long downstairs bar, a young officer came from a table across the room shouting, "Dud! Dud! Am I glad to see you!"

Me? At first I failed to recognize him and it was not until he was about six feet away did I see my old buddy, Freddy Hurtz. Man, we did everything but kiss each other. I've never held a man's hand so long. Fred's field tan was gone in the month indoors and his face had reacted to a string of hot meals. He was taller, all the time Freddy and I were together we humped over making ourselves small as possible.

"Dud, tell the guys I'm coming back. Tell them to hold on; I'll be seeing them."

A glance at the winged wheel insignia on his collar told me that wasn't true.

"Okay, Freddy," I humored him. "We'll be seeing you."

Not being a drinker, even lightly, after my telling him over a gingerale everything I could think of, how proud Red was of his gold bars and since Shallow and I were gone was running the company, sparing the names of those killed unless he pointedly asked me as he did of two, who I could recall by name because they were old-timers. I was curious to ask him what they diagnosed was wrong with him but he looked down and changed the subject. Then looking at his watch, he excused himself to catch a train. As weeks went by, more and more Love Company men on R&R bumped into Lieutenant Hurtz on various troop trains or one of the American hangouts. He was filling the obligation of a recalled reservist infantry officer, in the Transportation Corps in Japan as a train commander in charge of sergeants keeping GIs in line and seeing things run smoothly. A Transportation Corps lieutenant with a combat infantry badge, Purple Heart and Bronze Star with V for valor must have been intimidating to his fellow rear echelons

I was wearing the Ginza wings at the Prince Marinuchi my second night in Tokyo, sitting there waiting for my steak and chips (French-fried potatoes) when a large South African pilot, a Major, in khaki shorts, wearing South African Air Force pilot's wings, and a huge black handlebar mustache, asked if I minded if he sat down We exchanged the usual courtesies, I was a Second Division infantry rifle platoon leader, he an F-51 jockey. During the ten minutes waiting to place his order, as he talked, he made furtive glances at my wings, thinking perhaps, although I mentioned that I was a rifle platoon leader, it must be a new kind of wings for an artillery spotter,

L-19 pilot. Suddenly, he let out a roar that shook the room. Everyone turned to stare at our table. As he stood up from his chair for a better view of the wings, I told him that the yellow and red ribbon below them was for the second highest decoration in the North Korean Peoples' Army, and he let out another guffaw. I handed the wings to him, expecting to get back to the Ginza before leaving, which never happened. I still have the gook ribbon and medal that goes with it. Later, I asked men leaving for R&R to buy me a couple ginza wings but none remembered to do me the favor and since that night in the Prince Marinuchi have met only a few guys who even remember seeing them.

The third night in Tokyo, still alone, thinking how Smitty and everyone we lost would have enjoyed R&Rs, I sat feeling sorry for myself, drinking from a dark brown imperial quart bottle of Nippon beer, *beroo,* in Peter's Restaurant, across from the Imperial Palace grounds, touted as one of the must-visit spots in the Japanese capitol. Two Marine second lieutenants, with fuzz for beards, made a suspicious remark and giggled the first time I passed their table to the men's room. Maybe they snickered. On my second trip, after having given me a couple of evil-eye glances, one of them recited audibly, "Pitter, patter of little feet, the Second Division's in full retreat." This is the ditty we used against the only patch larger than the Indianhead, the First Cavalry, a large yellow shield containing the black profile of a horse's head.

This brought out my smoldering meanness and thinking this a good opportunity to kick a little ass and get over feeling sorry for myself, I continued to my table, picked up a half full bottle, although I hadn't had a brouhaha in years, and went to their table in the best John Wayne manner, holding it by the neck, slamming it down on their table as hard as I could. It was supposed to break; instead, beer sprayed all over me from the neck and the bottle vibrated in my right hand like a heavy tuning fork. Fortunately, the marines didn't catch the misfortune. They jumped up, saluted me, swearing they didn't mean a thing. In fact, one swore they hadn't said anything at all.

"Well, keep it that way, sonny!"

"Gee, sir, there's nothing to get mad about."

"Okay," I said patronizingly. "See it doesn't happen again."

Not used to being so damn Hollywoodish, an obviously heroic figure to strike fear into the hearts of young marines, I had second thoughts about when they had a few more drinks what might happen and decided to leave while I was ahead. On my way out, my hand still seeming to vibrate, shivering, worrying what might happen after they had a few more drinks, I avoided looking in their direction but a sneaky glance back through the front window saw them at their table pointing to one of their bottles and laughing. That would be their first step, laughing at me.

On the next to last night I could think of no diversion better than tying on a load and having another swell dinner at the Prince Maruanchi. I did just that and, around 2300, got into a cab with the intention of returning to my sack at the R&R Center.

"Sore," my cabby said, "you good time?"

The man sounded familiar and looking more closely, I recognized the persuasive driver as the one who propositioned me my first night in Tokyo. He turned around from the front seat and facing me, confided, "You see, ichiban, numero uno virgin."

The promise of a girl being a virgin never appealed to me and I wondered at any man being excited about such a prospect. Pray what psychological reason was there for wanting one? I never screwed a broad under twenty except Alice but we were in school together and I was her age. There was Kitty, at nineteen, but we got married.

"Papasan," I joked, "you know virgin? How many GIs you take to virgin?"

He smiled to be caught in a lie.

"You fuckin' numero uno big liar. No? Comedian ... You comedian?"

"Yes, sore," he answered showing his top front teeth. "Jack Benny funny. Comedian make you laugh ... funny."

Somehow, going on midnight, being still drunk, he began to make sense. I thought for a fleeting second about Kitty and quickly dismissed her with a sneer. But then I couldn't just dismiss her like that. It must make me feel better by making her guilty first. The way our letters had been going, she was probably shacked with someone right now anyway. She did say we were going to divorce if the Army would foot the bill. She came out and wrote that, didn't she? And she called me a dirty rat ... right? For another second, I saw the terrible hurt on Holly's face and what he did because of his wife—bitch!—and actually made myself angry at my own wife. Goddamn Kitty! She has a lot more chances than me and how about those young bucks she complained about making wisecracks.

"Damn her, they're all alike," I scolded, and returned to the business at hand. Damn it all, who better deserves a good time? Good time, I wondered, just good time, nothing else? Did I mean good time merely in opposition to bad time—lonely time I was having, or was it all simply a piece of ass, an orgasm? Hello, slam, bang, thank-you-maam good time not too much more fulfillment than jerking off and you could catch something.

I became completely oblivious of Kitty and settled back in the cab to anticipate. "Okay," I instructed the cabby salesman pimp, "show me."

We ended up on the other side of Tokyo, down and along twisting narrow stone-paved streets, dimly lighted, if at all. I became suspicious, even a little worried, and queried the driver several times, "Where go? When see girl?"

"Okay, don't worry, sore. Pretty soon. You see."

Once I had him stop so I could piss in a benjo ditch and in due time he pulled up to a house that would be considered tiny in Watertown. He got out and pulled a little clacker on the door. An older woman padded up, handed him some yen and waved me in. Certainly no proper move for a protector of virgins. I got the cabby to promise he'd wait for me, although I thought it suspicious that he should insist on being paid for the trip so far, plus tip. I was instructed to remove my boots and was ushered through a translucent paper sliding doorway to a back room with paper walls. All doors were sliding for there was no space for swinging.

My virgin was waiting. The powerful sexual animal craving that I had controlled as well as I could for months suddenly freed itself as I stared down at a living doll but somewhat older, not over five feet, two inches tall, wearing what I later learned was a wedding gown, complete with a big bustle on the back. She kowtowed low several times, making a sweeping gesture for me to come in. For a guy who always preferred big-breasted white women, fat cushioning of a plump ass and love muscles to hang on to, I was surprised that she so aroused my desire. I found myself standing dumbfounded, suddenly almost sober in a doll house, a stiff hard-on pushing out my pants. For a second then I came halfway to my senses. What am I doing here, I berated myself, a married man? It was no longer just a piece of ass. I sensed this little lady was putting me through her paces, going to use me for something on her part—not just seeking to tear off a piece. There's style to this.

"Lieutenant," the lovely Japanese doll told me in good English, "please sit down, have saki."

She poured from a ceramic bottle into a tiny, shallow cup. I had tried the stuff at the Prince Maruanchi and didn't like it, especially after being informed that it was made from fermented rice. I tried a couple of words I thought were Japanese and returned to English.

"No, thanks. No like."

Without waiting, she reached around and came up with what she informed me was plum wine.

"Okay," I told her, though I was not that crazy about plum wine.

It was evident that she was disappointed so, not wanting to embarrass the little doll obviously bent on satisfying me, I gulped down three little cups of the stuff.

A small, low table beside where she slept was outfitted like a little shrine, her bed a straw mat, a tatami she unrolled on the floor and a large rectangular cushion with a wooden pillow. On the 'shrine' were two ornately framed photographs under glass, a stern man in the showy white uniform of an admiral, her father, I found later, lost at sea early in the war, and a virile young man in an aviator's uniform, her fiancé I found, not mere boyfriend, a proud kamikaze pilot wearing a World War I-type leather flying helmet.

I became fascinated with the intimate Japanese bedroom scene, the almost ceremonial sadness apparent in her quite good English. Somehow I found it hard to imagine this little doll to have entertained other men before me. Sure looked like a virgin with her obviously expensive wedding kimono and almost noble bearing. I got the impression she was carefully performing a sacred ritual, the way, for instance, she presented my plum wine with two hands palms up. She began a slow, strongly seductive disrobing; not just take off her clothes, disrobed majestically, ceremoniously, more sexy than any strip teaser I could imagine.

Then she went after my clothes, slowly enticing me to conform to her wishes, running her warm tongue over flesh as she exposed it, slowly pushing down my rod to get off my undershorts, giving it a caressing, gentle squeeze before releasing it, as though to say don't go away, I got plans for you, as though it was something very special, something to worship, maybe.

For a second Kitty emerged to reacquaint me with guilt and I was forced to get rough with her. "Get out of here, bitch! I'm busy! You had plenty of chances and all you did was nag." I'm no ordinary guy now anyway; I'm a friggin' warrior, bled for my country and you pooh-pooh my Silver Star. Better believe it, woman; better learn to appreciate that. Smart people in Japan know already; the spoils of war belong to us and don't forget it. We licked the japs. We're the conquerors the spoils belong to. Only right we fuck their women, if a few years late, and they don't resist like they're supposed to if you raped them. And, I might have added, "you had to pay them."

I thought of Jimmy Lynch and was mad at them all over again but looking down on my little concubine, bad thoughts went away suddenly and I stopped philosophiz ing, or whatever I was doing, and returned to the thrilling, exciting, thoughtless, flesh gratifying business at hand. Crimus!

After all, I could return from R&R and step on a mine, get a sniper's slug. Now bug off, woman, wait your turn. Not you, you little sweetie, my wife.

The little lady's movements were slow and graceful. With the shrine or altar and all, priestess came to mind. No doubt she was in charge; her enticements in serving me seemed a strange, deeply religious experience. Compared to Kitty or Alice's tits, her's were nothing but certainly more than sufficient for the dignified, ceremonial way we were doing it where it would be wrong to dive right in and make a pig of myself.

Like butterfly wings, her tender little fingers explored everywhere and I could feel every nerve ending in my body respond. I groaned when her long fingernails scratched lightly up and down my hardened cock. The pink tip of her tongue circled its head again and again before her rosebud mouth closed over it and she sucked, gently at first, becoming greedier as my groans increased. It was the only time I ever came that way, never realizing there was so much hot white juice.

After my first orgasm, I wanted it in her as she thumped her small, perfect breasts with my cock, then placed it between them, pushing them together to form a warm sheath. I wanted to rush inside her, but she held me off gently. My trigger finger worked into her hot, moist interior and I could feel her tightness pulsating, wanting, awaiting me. I wondered how she could ever accommodate me, but need not have worried as she applied a sweet-scented oil of some sort, her hands moving up and down my erect length with slow, rhythmic strokes. I felt close to bursting and had trouble holding back to prevent coming in the air as the thrill and excitement mounted.

When I finally entered her, I understood the necessity for the fragrant oil as it eased the tight fit. That little survivor of fire bombing and loss of the two important men in her life was one acrobatic, squirming, pumping hot screw. She caused me to lead her into two more organisms before daylight. Her exquisite little body, knowing fingers, coaxing mouth and tongue aroused me again and again. In between insertions, as I rested, she licked and sucked my neck, nibbled on my ear lobes, massaged my back and poured me more plum wine. I lavished on her all the pent-up sexual drive dormant since leaving home in that blizzard except the comparatively little I wasted in sneaky masturbations.

While I rested after our second climax, quite sure I was unable to achieve another erection, she dribbled some of the plum wine over my chest and lapped up the pale pink liquid, seeking and sucking up the drops as she moved lower and lower down my body until she reached my hard cock. With a groan I grasped her hips and guided her onto me. She writhed and plunged, taking me deep inside and I feared I would hurt but her soft little cries and moans were certainly not those of pain.

After resting yet again, she enticed me into a fourth entry, after wrapping her legs around my neck. Her head thrown back in the throes of our last orgasm, she cried out in Japanese what I learned from the cabbie was "Daddy, Daddy," and the name of her fiancé. Ah, I thought, riding away in the cab, her game was using me for both roles, daddy and fiancé; a virgin every time, and what about me, big, bad enemy warrior, enjoying the spoils of war as I should?

It was daylight when she called a cab and I returned to the R&R Center and had a pro (prophylactic), a completely exhausted, guilty husband. I went to bed at nine my last night on R&R and the following morning we traded OD for fatigues with patches and we who had flown to Tokyo so eagerly chatting and anticipating, returned sound asleep.

299

Back home on 1179 I learned that SFC, soon to have been master sergeant, Bill Hanson, slated to be my third platoon sergeant, was killed by a sniper as he walked defiantly upright, exposing himself to a ridge leading to Bloody; bled to death before anyone could close his artery.

"Not Bill! Shit, not Bill! I kept saying, keep your butt down!"

And as the war was waged with underdogs, the many self-righteous quarrelsome sects of American Christian society went on quoting gratuitously from their black books—

> *He shall redeem their souls from deceit and violence; and*
> *precious shall their blood be in His sight.*
> – promised the Psalms.

Shit saith dead soldiers, we'd settle for light.

I'd known Bill since he took over a squad for Fred Hurtz, counting, in outpost time, five dreary months, and was on the verge of talking Doc Singleton, Ed Lopez's replacement at Company, into tagging him. We kept eyes peeled for oldtimers defying death with which they grew too familiar; strolling skylines, not crouching and dashing cover to cover, standing still in an exposed position staring blankly, out on their feet, sudden mood changes, depression, then to rage, startled and pissed off when addressed from the rear. I understood it to be an advanced stage of guilt consciousness, overpowering, depleting, dislike of self at so dirty, demeaning a job so long; combat fatigue, guilty for being still alive with so many buddies dead, indication that the guy is no longer entirely alive himself; in his badly mauled heart, beaten spirit, and benumbed brain marching off with the dead he must somehow always follow and be responsible for.

Looking back, I realized that, although twenty-eight-year-old SFC William Hanson, professional infantryman, did make the Army his career, something I thought I'd never do, he confessed he didn't remember exactly when he made that choice. At first it was a decision to be made every three years, and once he enlisted for six to get the more generous reenlistment bonus. His wife at the time helped him make that decision when she went down a week before reenlistment and bought expensive new furniture. He planned on a new car.

After his second marriage failed, he was ordered on a year's hardship tour, that is, unaccompanied by wife or family, and he had fewer and fewer American civilian friends; more and more Germans as he returned there twice. He brought home an expensive German sports car he never could have afforded in the States. Another big inducement was the topnotch stage acts booked at overseas NCO Clubs, two bits for any drink in the house. And it was so easy playing the slots, visiting whorehouses and working with other single guys who spoke his language and knew where he came from. 'Overseas tramps' they were called. "Hell, I ain't no millionaire, I'm a damn efficient sergeant. As for movin', the more the better. Newer friends all the time." By friends, Bill meant acquaintances, none of whom thought of him after he was gone, so there really weren't any old friends.

Aside from the beginnings of two short marriages, Bill's happiest times, he told me, were working as a deck hand aboard a fishing boat out of Miami, Florida.

"Like to fish, Lieutenant?"

"Never did much," I told him. "Funny, I lived near a lake and never did much."

I recalled my father's abnormal fears of the water because my brother drowned; my mother's extreme fear, and after she died, Emma and my father arguing about it.

"I can't be responsible, Ernest, if I'm not right there to watch your son."

"But I'll be with Gordy and some of the guys who go fishing all the time."

"Realize how many people drown every year fishing?"

It was an irony when my only and older brother drowned, his body lost in a sudden squall on Lake Ontario. One of my brother's friends died, too, along with the stupid bastard, his grandfather, visiting from Virginia who took them out that day. Everyone in the area was well aware of the dangerous weather on northern Lake Ontario beginning in September, sudden squalls from nowhere.

Hanson and I hit it off so-so. We respected each other's expertise but he didn't think deep enough. One thing in common we both had was in and out of jobs waiting to find something suited to us. The US Army had to do until a better job came along, which never did and then with my valor medals to wear at work, especially the Silver Star, all the proof of accomplishment I needed, and twenty years passed by, Kitty and I retired.

When Bill subconsciously decided to join his guys, looking back I realized it was after he had already left our Love, slipping away gradually into sweet-scented nights of Nebraska summer, warmed and fed by women of his family, laughing and loving again, cared for safely at the home he avoided so long.

Hanson began acting strangely before I left on R&R. He had, for a time, been nervous with frequent irritable outbursts and unpredictable headaches. Coffee seemed to calm him at first, but toward the end he grew morose. I worried, worried especially after I came upon him one night and heard him mumbling in his hole. His holemate was asleep.

"Who you talking to, Bill?" I joked in a low voice.

"Oh! Didn't see you."

"What you mumbling about, Bill?"

"Nothin' important," he answered sullenly.

It was apparent that he was embarrassed, or ashamed, or angry to have been surprised or maybe he'd gotten some bad news.

"Something troubling you, Bill?"

"Saying his prayers," his holemate informed me.

Bill jumped to his feet, threateningly. "Goddammit, Gould, get off my ass. It's none of your fuckin' business, hear? I was saying prayers, if you gotta' know. Any harm in that?"

We were placed on that mountain chess board without spiritual guidance. Chaplains stayed back at regiment, nor did any ask where they were; no one wanting to go out sad-faced and scared of anything else. No death certificates were issued, as I recall, but each of us enlisted and commissioned wore the official badge of legal murder, crossed rifles, and packed a loaded license from Congress to shoot anything facing us. Nor was there on H 1100, 1179, 1180, or 1243 any of the big-mouth statesmen who by failing to do their jobs got us into that mess. Those elected decision makers, savages in tailored suits, fierce ordainers of the rear who dispatched us to die on our mountains of sorrow.

No one asked our political opinions for we were patently inaccessible, legally muzzled, by law designated silent killers; represented in absentia by Congress, those professional mouths who make gratis boasts that they damned well could lick anyone in the world, having no sense to apply that pressure before a war, instead of after it got started.

If any question why we died
Tell them, because our fathers lied.
– Rudyard Kipling.

Dying was declared our trade by universal conscription law; for unlucky ones shortened military careers, retired medically and put up free in US Army caskets; sacrificed as expeditiously as soldier ants, only those tiny guys were bred to die, not made over for it. Our guys were preparing for much less violent careers when summarily ordered to strap on a pack. Society disguised as 'friends and neighbors' imposed on them unfamiliar altruistic attitudes flattering the average bitching draftee in order to clear society's conscience long enough to boldly lie, "they gave their lives for God and their country." More likely the other way around; isn't it God that gives away sons?

Riflemen don't resent appearing to die for rear echelons; aren't we supposed to strive for glory? It is undramatic to Hollywood and unpatriotic in American schools for men in our predicament to resent having to die, being so much of that dieable age, gender and all and it's good for the safety of the country that strong motivation based on logic and love is not essential for morale in combat. In battle we are conscious only of protecting ourselves and our buddies and avenging their deaths, not giving anything away for strangers back in the states, especially when it is cover-up for incompetent legislators, miserably failed statesmen, and the goddamn weak, selfish, immoral majority of citizens. Yes, asshole, you right there in your easy chair being entertained by gladiators armed with revolvers, applauding television's daily slaughters.

Oh, for the days when wars were truly democratic, when patriotic leaders were more than big-mouth politicians and led by strapping on armor, brandishing shields and wielding swords like the famous leaders under Pericles of Athens—

With life and limb stood stoutly to their task, and the brief instant ordained
by fate, at the crowning moment, not of fear but glory, they passed away.

At times I could've given it all up, slump to the ground and sob. It was no longer a secret dependency, their making it so obvious I was there for them to lean on and talk to and it was a long tedious wait for peace, interrupted negotiations from 8 July 1951 to the cease fire on 27 July 1953. The only sure things were death and rotation; at least you knew where you stood. In our time on 1179 we waited for the peace talks to reconvene, as Love passed an Army-wide record line time, 103 days on line facing enemy, exposure to every type of fire except Russian Migs; especially to snipers and unpredictable H and I.

Supplies were haphazard, depending on monsoon rain that washed out footholds on the mountain trails as our physical conditions grew sad waiting for some outfit to relieve us so we could attend to bunker sores and exchange rotting fatigues, and me, the bloody mess of athletes foot, skin sloughing off when I tried to itch it. Damn lucky it didn't get infected.

We missed our secure, mortar-proof roofed bunkers on the Marine hill, for 1179 was very difficult and dangerous to supply with building materials, no light soil to fill our sandbags, carriers so few the best we could do was build deeper holes in rocks and depend on fields of fire.

Having waited nearly two weeks for Graves Registration, both Pater back on 1100 and I got Colonel Duncan on the horn about Captain Toth and after explaining to us that the other two battalions were also committed, he had body bags sent up to zip in all but two of our dead to get them down from 1179; two had landed in inaccessible places over dropoffs too dangerous for retrieval. *Requiescit in isto tumulo*, here he lies forever in his grave.

> *Unwept, unhonored, unintered they lie.*
> – Alexander Pope.

We had to blast rock to make high-priority machine gun emplacements and the mountain ground elsewhere with our little folding entrenching shovels was too rocky for graves, the ridge too narrow and burial being contrary to Army regulations anyway, no one suggested we lay bare hands on our buddies while we waited vainly for Graves Registration from regiment to do its job or disturb them in any way as guys we kidded around with and exchanged short biographies with and gave orders to receded into soggy lumps of rotting fatigues beside ridge paths, exposing their sunken eye sockets and triangular nose holes. Teeth minus gums and lips grew longer, like snarling dogs, protruding ominously, faces no longer with macabre death smiles. We had not wanted this terrible thing to happen. By our brotherly love, I swear we had not intended it. We felt very bad about it but could do nothing.

Although not as harassed as during the first two weeks and more rested, the bearers balked with well-demonstrated anguish at handling our decaying buddies, cadavers, carrion; grotesque fetid monstermen; bloated until exploding; stinking, rotting protein; dark fluids draining from their injuries, oozing stinking blackness that once was the pulsating blood of a young man's life; swarming, squirming maggots, black carrion beetles and sickening mephitic stench of putrefying flesh.

Our Korean interpreter, Smiley, explained apologetically, patiently, yet obviously perturbed, that little Kims (our sobriquet for all South Korean males) were afraid that darkness would overtake them going down 1179 with unburied dead on their backs, and being devout animists, they were far more frightened than any American could ever be of evil spirits hovering over those who have not been buried early enough with proper rites. Spirits of men who die violently, especially warriors, not properly buried, are condemned to wander forever, harassing and terrifying the living as they seek expiation, he explained. Oh how sensitively we knew our unburied were disgraced; what a prolonged, dirty, pitiful association, the crying out from diminishing, flesh-dissolving heaps for decent burial in consecrated earth.

"Men who do not bury their dead suffer eternal damnation," Smiley warned—as if our consciences didn't nag us.

> *But oh! more horrible than that*
> *is the curse in a dead man's eye*
> – Samuel Coleridge.

I remember a long conversation one night when the Chinese moon was just beginning to fill, a seventeen-year-old replacement asked me to stop at his hole; lonely to talk to someone more mature than his scary hole buddy. I could sense their relief when we began to chat a bit. I squatted and rested a hand on the rifleman's shoulder. "Nobody's letting you down, don't forget it for a minute."

In the pale light of the moon I saw him gulp and try to smile.

"Sir," he said, "you know this is my first week. Can't you do anything about those poor dead guys; can't you get them away from us somehow? At least cover them; after what they've done, the Army should take care of them."

"I'm sorry," I told him. "It bothers me as much as you. We've asked repeatedly for Graves Registration to come up for them or send more body bags but they won't respond. Kims, those little blue chogee guys, are way understrength and most are hauling priority ammo, chop chop and water one way and for emergencies regiment's got working other places. We haven't been engaged for some time and are the hardest to supply, easiest to slight.

"Can you imagine packing an A-frame up and down those steep slippery trails loaded with a hundred pounds when you're over forty and they call you papasan, and young Koreans who can hardly understand orders, transferred as misfits from ROK infantry units. We haven't been able to bring up litters for some time now; the few we have are held for badly wounded. After that ballbreaking zig-zag climb up here by the protected trail, you can't expect them to haul down a 200-pound rotting body. Besides, they're terrified of unburied soldiers."

"But, sir, after all they've done...."

"I know."

I started to stand and he added quickly, "How about food? I'm half starved."

"There's plenty of Cs in those yellow ones." I told him, pointing over the sand bags in the moon glow down to where colored nylon supply chutes were hanging from branches on the Pia-ri side of our ridge. "Want to try for one?"

"Where do they come from?"

"They're made up by Air Force Japan Logistical Command and dropped here at first light, damn hard to judge the drop angle and speed with unknown mountain winds and this ridge so damn narrow, hard enough to hit square even with L-19s zooming in with boxes of Cs."

We fortified rocky 1179 as best we could, skyland of grief and great peril, sacred to Korean mountain dwellers not known to American fighting men until early in July when daring L-19 reconnaissance pilots, skimming low above the quiet, secret land in their little tin-covered kites to scan for us, drew occasional angry flecks of fire. What lurked in those dark ravines we would climb up and over, behind jagged rocks and slides of crumbled, decomposing granite over small bodies of Korean Marines, we did not know until we reached taunting, high-pitched voices headon?

When we finally surmounted the bloody summit of 1179, we were struck by an infinity of skyscapes; how finite we were in comparison. Beyond great distances we perceived greater distances; mountain hills, valleys submerged in soft blue-pink haze, and mountaintops visible like misty stepping stones of a vast ford extending beyond the limits of our most powerful magnifier, the BC scope, all defended by squatting soldiers as ruthless as any who served the Khans.

Our avenue of attack in taking 1179 had been relatively simple but dangerously exposed to 1243 and sniper fire and we were often at least partially surrounded,

One tough mountain climb after another was the route of the US Second Infantry Division in Korea, right back into North Korea during late summer and early winter of 1951. The most burdening supply was not ammo but water.

easily watched from the gook OP on 1243 north of us, the highest ground on the Punchbowl. At the same time we were very difficult to supply. The relatively safe, roundabout way took nine hours of tough climbing, some places, especially when wet, only hand-over-hand steadied by heavy, knotted ropes, for battalion supply trains of KTC to reach us by the only route possible unobserved from 1243; slippery, sloping slides of mud-slime and loose rock, some beside drop-offs hundreds of feet to oblivion.

By the time fatigued carriers reached our aerie the first two weeks, unloading 100-pound rice-straw bags of loose supplies, cardboard boxes of C rations and green-painted wooden boxes of grenades, OD-colored cans of machine gun ammo, OD cloth bandoliers of eight-round M1 rifle clips and five-gallon jerry cans of water from yokes or A frames, they were too pooped to haul down the dead—only the strongest able to assist our few walking wounded, stumbling, hanging to empty A frames from the rear; others hauling crippled or weakened wounded strapped down with empty machine gun web belts, when we had litters.

After a day's rest, those carriers who hadn't deserted or been removed for medical reasons, were sent up again with ammo, water, grenades and Cs, but there were times, as many as three days in a row, when the rains were too heavy for them to use the mud-slide trail, and we lost two of those little guys and their precious loads to falls from which they were never seen again, and one to sniping infiltrators.

Other than the flight from Japan, the Air Force tried several times during short breaks in overcast to supply us from above at low level, cardboard boxes of C's, jerry cans of water, precious water, pickets (triangular steel stakes six feet high for stringing barbed wire), barbed wire, flame throwers, axes, picks, etc. Each time only nine parachute packs in twenty hit the ridgeline high enough to retrieve. What gooks were unable to reach hung in bright, multicolored nylon chutes from scrubby trees down the steep slopes—each color a type of supply. Soon, the gooks wore jaunty red, blue, green or yellow nylon scarves. Chutes were returnable and we were warned of a $100 fine for tearing one.

For a month and a half we lived on short C rations, two cans a day each of wet ration (that is, containing 'meat'); one twelve-ounce can of beef (gristle), spaghetti and meat balls (gristle in thin tomato sauce), sausage, lima beans and ham, hash (too salty, gristle), which at one time our starving prisoners refused, and an anemic pasty chicken something-or-other. Killers of little girls enjoyed wide news coverage, years of appeals and favorite hot meals before execution (the few that are), while the last suppers of us professionals out to kill strangers on sight were cold, paltry, picky picnics in the rain with little clear plastic spoons.

We ate as-is, never dressed for dinner, only occasionally built a small, ration cardboard or wooden grenade box fire, or were lucky enough to have a so-called squad stove, one for canned heat or heat the tiny cans over pinches of burn-

At times knotted ropes.

ing composition C4 plastic explosive we bartered for with engineer buddies making a solemn ritual of scooping out the unsatisfying rations, holding cat-food-size cans over the lower lip carefully so as not to lose any—stingy *fêtes des fous.*

After meals, we lit smokes, 'those that got 'em,' an old Army saying, harkening to the Great Depression when it had meaning.

There was a greatly reduced need for pre-folded C-ration asswipe, and to our surprise we thrived, growing alert and lean as hunting hounds; napping any hour night or day when not on watch or being fired upon, snarling when rudely awakened; fatigues rotted in the slime we wallowed in during the monsoon rain which ended 15 September as our houseboy predicted, costing me a ten dollar bet which I didn't have while deducting to pay back my R&R loan. Roy Carse covered me with a loan.

> *If I should tell of our labors, our hard lodging, sleeping on crowded decks, the scanty blankets. Tossing and groaning, rations that never reached us, continuous drizzle from the sky, dews from the marshes, rotting our clothes.*
> – Agamemnon, king of Myceanae, the lucky guy.

Reason floundered on those mountains and hills in the unpredictability of random and frequent killings gone amok, a deadly game of madman's bluff, sorry scheme of unbridled hate, rotten tales gasped by vicious idiots, mouths oozing blood.

Combat infantrymen are warriors to whom the closely-shared thrills of fierce infighting are many times more exhilarating than the games of the Olympiad. Not only is it more strenuous and longer-lasting, the loser's prize is death. Freud told us we all are trying to commit suicide; trying harder to die than to live, believing death the only cure for our madness.

Threatening sights, sounds and smells of combat quickened our interest in basic differences between life and death so deep to disturb our very souls, as opposed to normal concerns over money, sex and other material things. The difference, say, between cheering on a gaily bedecked Easter parade on a clear, sunny Sunday, and being forced in soft purple overcast to harken the sobbing of the faithful before the tortured, blood-scabbed, fly-covered body of Jesus, six long hours dying.

After two weeks on 1179, serious counterattacks slowed to night probes and an occasional suicide assault, usually in the gloaming, right after false dawn or under the diffused light of a dreaded Chinese moon that filtered down through rain clouds to expose us. Those courageous, athletic, mountain-climbing gooks, who on several occasions reached our perimeter to die, were swung by their wrists and ankles, bags of oriental garbage, out and over, down the precipitous way they came.

> *There is an evil among all things that are done under the sun. . . .*
> *Yea, also the heart of the sons of man is full of evil, and madness is in*
> *their hearts while they live and after that they go to the dead.*
> – Ecclesiastes.

As days came to nights, often blended in that monsoon malaise, the hostile atmosphere gave rise to an equally universal fear. Who among so many dangers is ever safe from snipers as the one who got Hanson and H and I night and day as that which killed Frank Smith and J C Rodriguez, and several men in King Company along the ridge, by unpredictable, random rounds? We learned that fear is as accumulative as carbon monoxide—sensing full well that the longer threatened, the more remote our chances of surviving.

> *And he who died with the light of yesterday shall be no briefer in*
> *Death's no-more than he who perished months and years before.*
> – Titus Lucretius Carus.

There, at the height of manifest bravery, youth's greatest test, we were dying prematurely, as we sank down in our minds with the moldering corpses of comrades whose flesh shrank as they tried to ebb into the rocks to avoid embarrassing us.

> *He sinks into the depths with bubbling*
> *groan*
> *Without a grave, unknell'd, uncoffin'd*
> *and unknown.*
> – Lord Byron.

Corporal E-4 Hector Alvarez, our new company radioman unknowingly named after the great Trojan hero, cursed the evil wind that blew from Tetzatilipoca, black spirit of the night, vanquished by the wind god, the feathered serpent Quetzalcoatl, chief of the gods, from whom Hector's mother's Mixtec relatives descended. I respectfully disagreed. It could be none other than the great Thoth, Egyptian wind god, carrier of souls, bearer of rains, as well as judge of evil.

The steady rains came over us in mid-July before we began our perilous climb from the floor of Pia-ri and now fall winds harried us with cold, wet, swirling blasts, as mountain specters screamed like tortured soldiers. Toward our last days on 1179, we feared it was raining blood as spirits of Taeusan, mighty hunters of old, we were solemnly informed, hidden in contorted clouds whistled for us like devils their hounds, shouted in welkin-shattering voices, "GI, you die!," shooting forth great darts of aimed lightning, jagged sparks from hell.

Other tormenting belials, keeping out of sight, sent cold rain to deluge us in our shallow havens, in our *miserere personne* up at the source of clouds; home of rain, pain and damnation. Were St Paul with us, he would not have to cry: "Death, where is thy sting?" or the Black Night of the Soul, St John of the Cross, lament, "I die because I cannot die!" Ours was the ideal spot for both.

Men died unaided by experts, others saved by the strangest luck. Our ranking savior was Sergeant E-5 Doc Singleton, followed closely by Banzai platoon's specialist fourth class E-4 field medic, Doc Carlson, he of a charmed life. Doc Singleton was Love Company's own supervisor of brain surgeons, receiving-ward triage experts and specialists in closing puckered, sucking and gaping wounds. Often by their devotion to fellow dogfaces, by uncanny abilities that many times exceeded their brief training and little canvas bags, we lived or died.

Occasionally my life ebbs low these lonely late septuagenarian years, I return in spirit to visit dead riflemen on the bloody summits of North Korean mountains, knowing that all things alive still live if in some unknown way as electrons within atoms within molecules; a secret life always changing, commingling electronically soul with soul, soul, an undiscovered energy form, in the vast universe where all is one and one all, as the massive mountains we clung to and scarred with high explosives.

Sometimes in growing weakness, dread of solitude and supernatural disabilities, in loneliness that hurts, in the gray dampness of late nights along quiet threatening paths between holes, I sensed my soul bleeding internally, hungering for relief, striving silently to be free from the miserable unreliable physical me—waiting, waiting, at times impatiently, for the appointed time for its cosmic call, inside the physical me waiting for the final litter ride, I'd ask—

What ghost is this that walks with me; always in darkness walks with me?
    – Conrad Aiken.

The heavy Korean monsoon sat on us and rained sporadically through August and almost into the first thin mountain snow flurries of fall. We slowly sagged in sadness as damp as the air of our earthen holes, reduced to bones pushed outward at the filthy skin that bound our blood and tissues; hunting and hunted animals; stark, eyes sore of thousand-yard stares, black balls of grime rolled by sweat in their corners. But who of us carried mirrors; we grew to complain less, fatigued, some from mild malnutrition, others from constant attention to nagging worry; knowing that the ultimate price of relaxation was death. Our hiding in dampness of our holes was unsatisfying, constantly alert for H and I and snipers, in muddy slime so close to an ever-menacing enemy. We were as tame animals gone wild quivering nervously, when exposed rapid glances around, crouched alert, peeking over the rims of our holes like prairie dogs, catching naps whenever rather than a good nights sleep. We grew short-answered, snapping, ugly men, childishly resentful of one another's real or imagined comforts, eyes wilted when unstimulated by fear, earning well our name dogface.

Time passed unregulated, escaping our attention for days, knowing dark and light only, one after the other, yearning for something until someone, seeking order in chaos, might ask, "Hey, what day is it?" and like as not receive a wrong answer.

Time was discussed haphazardly, without routine, counting, say, to the terrible sudden second when Corporal Brossard was killed by a sniping elephant gun, or a week or so ago when, to our surprise, hot chow came up in insulated marmite cans.

"What day of the week was that?" one asked.

"The day Garcia got it, and the cook, what's his name."

Guys with whom we'd shared everything were alive one moment and delivered to us dead, badly wounded by incoming fire, mutilated by random artillery or splattered with blood by expert snipers, and, as all too often, left for days in positions from where or near where they left us, on a long-forgotten mountain warrior path, along which are tatters of weathered US Army fatigues and hanks of blankets in a skyland junkyard of battered helmets and broken liners, cardboard recoilless-rifle-shell tubes, snarls of insulated copper communication wires and rusting tactical steel barbed wires, empty wooden grenade boxes splintered for firewood, moldering cardboard C ration boxes, empty, rusting away C ration cans and broken M2 rifles and carbines with burned-off stocks, burned to heat rations and warm hands; among thick pressed cardboard mortar shell tubes, aerial bomb and artillery craters, way above the real world in a thunderland of clouds, beneath violent electrical discharges that wrench open the sky to shake the earth and peal thunders up and down forbidding ravines that in Korean summers are huge furies, under unrelenting monsoon rains, far above and beyond scarred, fire-blackened hulks of war tanks in distant valley voids miles and miles away and down below, down through clouds, mists and ominous shadows of the vast Punchbowl.

Some few were felled by shrapnel from exploding shells; hot, jagged sirens, sharp chunks of steel whirring every way from point of impact or worse yet from an airburst, Soviet-tracked SPs (self-propelled) artillery dug in and hulled up for high trajectory, and hollow whooompt!, deep-throated 120mm mortars. Others, replacements, as they prepared to leave the floor of the valley to climb and greet us old warriors, died crossing abandoned rice paddies, where they were forced to run splashing, hunched over, from unseeable zip-zips of snipers, and we had to leave our buddies floating and bloating and in short time noisily blowing out their gas before sinking from sight. We seldom returned to land we fought over and there were many places in those wild landscapes of death for MIAs to hide from the living, where no American ever climbed again, where sense-deadened soldiers of graves registration preferred not to be; ground unvisited even by curious Korean woodsmen or rice farmers for another planting season as our dogfaces sank slowly, flesh bloating, worm eaten, cloth and webbing rotting.

> *I sometimes think that never grows so red*
> *The rose as where some buried Caesar bled;*
> *That every hyacinth the garden wears,*
> *Dropt in her lap from some once lovely head.*
> – Omar Khayyam.

Death meets you early in combat in some guise but those who get to know him never tell what it's all about—indescribable in terms of the life we know so well. They dropped pawing at death wounds, bled short whiles, died without a word to buddies, stiffened in a few hours, bloated, and in two days erupted swarms of squirming maggots—bright, living young men suddenly very disgusting, spoiled meat rotting fast, sinking to disjointed pieces of flesh held in place by rotting fatigues or tendons. In lighted hours we observed their deterioration and smelled them between rains throughout dark nights, much more closely than we liked; sadly, but without expressed sympathy, knowing that sentimentality has no place in infantry combat and is a feeling untrue to that most profound subject; replaced by an indescribably terrible feeling of utter hopelessness.

The real drama finished when the bullet or shrapnel slammed into them with finality, THUD!, a long-handled sledge hammer well-muscled into a bag of wet sand, and since society already passed judgement on their relative worthlessness, determined by draftability, of what count was the final act in the short, tragic tale of the young condemned ones? Rather than display sympathy for our pathetic dead, in mute ways we died with them, in modes of respectful solicitude—

Watch Thou, dear Lord, with those who wake, or watch or weep tonight.
       – St. Augustine.

I spent too many times for the well-being of my mind meditating on the weird disappearance of Sergeant Chuck Dorn and his entire squad, the deaths of Youngs, who I never got to know, J C Rodriguez, the silent one, and Smitty, my short-term Canadian buddy, Ich and Holly and Sergeant Ulriche and, goddamn it anyway, all the others, some like Lieutenant Werner who I spoke crossly to and hadn't even met. I was being relentlessly crushed under a load of compounded guilt. I wasn't exactly to blame for the death of Werner what's-his-name, but I was inexcusably unkind— didn't have to embarrass him like I did.

Although I was becoming every day more capable a combat leader, I was also a weakened guilty old man with no future to contemplate. At thirty-one, believe me, I was old, old, worrying from thirty-one to sixty-one in a few months.

The greatest crime was that I let myself down, considering me too often a victim out of control neglecting the positive. How does that song go? Accentuate the positive? Worry was ruling and ruining me. My death was made certain, as with all guilty ones. One day on the ridge H and I artillery would land with me in the open and I'd go down like Jesus did at my age or his namesake, J C, a decade younger 1951 years later, or Hanson's assassin would focus on me all the way from an approach to Bloody in a moment of my carelessness. No one lives forever in this business.

Yet for me likewise there is a strong destiny and my own death and there
shall be a dawn or an afternoon or a noontime when one man in a craft of war
shall take my life also by a stroke of a spear cast or the arrow flown from a
bowstring. [Or a burp gun fired, a 120 mortar dropped, a 76 SP artillery shell,
a Chinese mauser or a .51-caliber elephant gun].
   – Achilles to Lycaon [Lieutenant Gould to himself many times]

The future became more far away and elusive and every little daydream, controlled or otherwise, began with "if I get down from here alive" and ended with "I'll really be some easy-going guy, never worry about anything the rest of my life." Money? Sh-e-e-eit!

I sat in my hole gasping for air, apparently I'd never recover my normal breathing, a cigarette between my lips constantly, at night carefully covering the glow. Something was awfully wrong with me. I'd never been this terribly run down and utterly fatigued before. My heart seemed sometimes to flutter and leave me vibrating weak. If I ever find safety, I'll sob myself to sleep and see a cardiologist.

In the quiet periods between probing, we picked at ourselves, joked miserably about bushy hair, and with Doc Singleton's surgical scissors snipped and hacked out clumsy haircuts for each other. You could tell those most recently returned from Japan, relatively clean, smelling like women, and could smile some.

We scraped mud and worked out rocks and made what improvements we could to our homes. Alternating with my 'aide,' Sergeant Eppler, I checked the platoons of Love. Creeping along between widely-spaced holes at night, I stopped frequently to listen, startled at a twig seeming to snap or when wind scraped together the few dry, brown leaves of shrapnel-shattered branches of a maimed tree. As routine wore us down, I found myself longer and longer at each hole, crouching, talking to guys of their home and families, keeping it low so as not to waken their hole mates; studying snapshots by hand-covered flashlight of love at home of one form or another, kids, wives girlfriends and dogs, which occupied their minds so much of the painfully wasted time away from them. Within weeks I knew many nicknames of friends back home—"This one's Jesse."

"I know … sister's boyfriend."

Without realizing it, a few oldtimers, enlisted Reserve, or drafted college graduates who hadn't lost their all to the US Army, called me Dud which, me not being lost to the Army either, I took as a compliment and no disrespect. I was flattered and actually embarrassed that a kid I led should come right out and want me for a real father. I figured the only valid respect on late night visits was our dead guys, whom regardless of lack of rank we salute and loving respect. General, in your rigid war room don't tell me I can't be friendly with my buddies when I am separate from brother officers? There's no damn wall between us after dark, no room in serious, man-to-man conversations in the middle of the night to begin or end with titles, not when we're sharing family secrets. To hell with the title private, sergeant, lieutenant, we're all wed by fear and night, buddies cast away. Shit, general, we down here at our low level have stepped deep enough in it together to make us familiar, like one youngster confiding in me that his dad deserted them, his mother would like me.

One young RA replacement told me his brother wanted to know if I was the Lieutenant Gould who commanded one platoon in the 29th Infantry Division at St Lo although he thought not; should be captain or major by now.

"I'm old enough," I told him. "commissioned at a jerrymade OCS in France long after St Lo and joined the Yankee Division in the field and was a second lieutenant a month before the war was over but nowhere near your brother's outfit."

"Seems you're old enough to be my dad.... Sir, can you get us something to eat?"

"I'm as hungry as you guys."

"Sir," he mumbled, head down, obviously embarrassing himself.

"Well?" I asked. "You were saying?"

"Dunno, sir, maybe I'd better not."

"Not what?"

"I mean, I don't know how to put it."

"Put what? What's bugging you, Bob?"

"Well, lieutenant, I've wondered a long time and I don't mean just here in Korea."

"Wondered what?"

"Well, how I'd react when it comes right down to it. I mean, if it's me or them. Do you think I'm a coward?"

I laughed and he returned a contrived smile.

"Listen, young man, it's your right to know and your duty to get it straight now; you don't have to be a hero or a coward but based on your rifleman brother, you're a hero automatically. Aside from certain set character cases, a normal man can be a hero or a coward on different days and different times of day, in different places, under different circumstances. One thing you know for damn sure, however, the way a man reacts to fear-of-death stimulus is not a matter of whim nor always permanent, it's in one of three ways: growl and attack, as the king of beasts; cringe and try to hide to be neutral as most animals do in Nature, or bug out for safety like a big bird. Any way might happen to surprise you. Even a lion hauls ass when really scared. I'll never forget a granary rat that Gordy and I cornered when out of 22 shells. When I tried to kick it to death it bit through my sneaker and chased us out of the building.

"Being scared doesn't belong to you alone. Fear of immediate danger to self affects everyone the same, all animals for that matter; how you handle it determines whether you are called a hero or a coward, and that depends on two things, the extent of the fear stimulus, your anxiety level, and how you were brought up. If you were brought up to be selfish, weak, babied and overly protected and have high anxiety too you might well take off running away on your own, which is cowardice. If your mom and dad taught you to stand up to trouble and think of the other guy and support an average anxiety, you'll stick with the rest of the guys and fire as long as you can, but if you have a good character like that and a high enough anxiety, chances are also good you'll take the danger just so long and make moves toward eliminating it— knock out that damn machine gun that's scaring everyone. You're called a hero.

"If you have any choice, best be average, be alert but keep covered up, and sweat it out with your buddies."

"How about guys who bug out?"

"Ever heard of one in Love Company? Never will, not when you're well led. I've never heard tell of a coward in this whole battalion since Colonel Duncan's the boss. A coward's like a hero—neither have tolerance for anxiety, neither can stand to be afraid very long. If he has a low tolerance for anxiety and a weak character, he stays clear of the Armed Services to begin with because he knows damn well what's expected of him there. Cowards are very rare in our Army. If threatened by the draft, he'll like as not cross the border, or go to Sweden and have his momie mail him money.

"Depending on the intensity of the fear stimulus and how it's conceived, there's such a thing as intermediate bugouts; about one-fifth in any attack. We all start moving together, hunched over, walking slowly together up toward the objective firing our rifles when alerted to a target, each in his regulation position, but some behind the lead elements soon slow down, duck behind boulders or trees and stay there. They're not really outright cowards. I don't begrudge them that so long as they hang on to their weapons and ammunition and my BAR men or machine gunners don't join them. Don't be afraid of being afraid but no matter what, try to stick to your buddies as close to us as you can.

"My first attack, the day I got hit, I cursed them all as cowards and thought to have one or more court-martialed. On 1100 I saw how it worked to our advantage to have them skulking bastards safe back down behind us as reserves. Beat-up as we are, panting, gagging at the top of the objective, we need those johnny-come-latelies with their unspent energy and ammo to help set up a quick defense. While they're running up looking for loot, reveling in the great general pride of the sergeants and I, we grab them for perimeter defense."

"But sir, how about worry, doting on getting killed. How to get fear out of your mind? Me and Art worry ourselves sick about all the things can go wrong."

"You never get rid of fear. If you did, they'd get you off guard sooner or later. I go through it all myself all the time. Doesn't everyone? Shit, man, don't think you're Lone Ranger. Everyone in combat knows fear, it's natural; it's how to react that's a big secret, nobody has all the answers, not officially. The Army pretends fear doesn't exist, like your parents don't explain sex to you, only they know about sex for they've been through it, but the rear echelons in the Army in charge of training don't know anything about fear. They've never been exposed. If you live long enough you'll teach yourself about controlling fear reactions but pretty soon Sergeant Eppler will explain it all.

"Believe it or not, man, the minute hot blood starts double-timing through you there suddenly isn't room in your flooded brain to manufacture more fear fantasies. Once you start moving you are back to reality, under control of facts and movement, mostly movement, are all you can think and plan on. Plan how and where to use that rifle, when to squeeze the trigger. Once you move in combat, keep your eyes constantly on where enemy fire is coming from. Fear and fantasy got no room, unless, of course, you're stupid enough to let mental fantasy fear take over your natural animal fear from the beginning completely before you can start movement. When you freeze, you're a mess of a lower animal. I've seen guys collapsed, cringing in the bottom of their holes or behind a boulder. They weren't being shot at personally but thought they were. Instead of throwing the book at them, since they were willing and able to help us when they got control and associating with us closely again, we worked it out, not saying a word.

"Remember, obvious heroes and cowards are exceptional, both have low tolerances for anxiety—neither can stand to be afraid—depending on the character developed in them by parents and role models they run or fight. The average, about ninety-eight percent of you, can control your anxiety enough to stay put and do what you're trained to do—fire and duck but never turn your back. Because of such variances as exceptional hunger, lack of confidence, physical weakness, lack of ammo, weariness, etc., your low tolerance guy may one day be a hero, the next day a coward despite his upbringing. I've seen good men, officers perform for a time in combat and leave in disgrace, like self-inflicted wounds, deciding they had all they can take. They're not cowards! We all wear down a little day after day; engines, run long enough, weaken and wear down at their breaking points."

*   *   *

I missed Fred Hurtz. We had some damn interesting discussions. I never talked with anyone else about death, religion and immortality and, in fact, the universe. It felt good trying to keep up with him, all he knew; at least a lot of the time. Fred and I shot the breeze by the hour back in reserve or while some other unit did the patrolling. He taught me a lot; how if you were a Buddhist you find it much easier to die, not associating all the time with stinking failure, rotting flesh, weird and ghoulish, skull and cross bones or an old man with a scythe and hourglass, something to be terrified of joining; how that potbellied, almost naked little oriental with legs crossed was a teacher like Christ and he and Christ were a lot alike in many ways. According to Fred, all great religions are basically alike, only the personal opinions of dishonest egotistic followers vary and if you pay close attention to what Christ and Buddha said rather than the jerks who followed, you'd find they all make dying seem more like a blessing, a release from misery.

If immortality be untrue, it matters little whether anything else be true or not.
        – Henry T Buckle.

While we clung to our North Korean gateway to the Orient, Peking radio broadcast that the 38th Infantry had been completely surrounded and all officers killed or surrendered. Hard hit by the chink breakthrough in November 1950, at Kunu-ri and bearing the brunt of another in February at Hoengsong, the May Massacre and elsewhere from February to June 1951, the chinks already held 1252 POWs from the Indianhead Division.

Several magazines printed the false boast verbatim without an effort to qualify or even to state that it was a boast, cruelly giving wives, mothers and girlfriends the belief that the chink lie was true. It made exciting copy, the bastards that kept it going. In a week or so guys came to me with letters beginning with such statements as "This letter probably won't reach you..." or "I pray God you have escaped" or "I hope you were not up there with the 38th Regiment when it was captured." Somehow, I guess Kitty didn't read that yellow journalism; she never mentioned it.

Like 'friendly' artillery and Air, greedy sales-hungry editors did more damage to our morale and efficiency than a division of chinks or gooks just to sell their damn papers and magazines or draw listeners to their radios.

"They have us surrounded, the poor bastards."
    – a tough old infantry rifle platoon sergeant at Bastogne.

A new rumor circulated every day. We are going to be relieved soon, look how beat-up we are. We broke an all-time US Army record for time on line without relief and every rumor made sense because we wanted relief from the Punchbowl and considered each unit in the corps which conceivably could be used to effect our relief.

Later we learned of poor guys in the western sector down the Pia-ri valley on what the Press called Heartbreak Ridge, also badly clobbered almost nightly, committed piecemeal and overrun. Our King and Item companies were to be involved on Heartbreak before it was taken as was Love on Mundung-ri even further into North Korea. Those regimental commanders of the 9th and 23rd should have taken lessons from our paratrooper Lieutenant Colonel Duncan who ran his companies steady ahead, bolstered, well-supplied from behind. Hit, take a few casualties, run low on ammo, fall back, let another company through, as we juggernauted up 1100 and 1179 like an obstinate rhinoceros head down and heavy, ready to gore, being continually resupplied and reassured of direct support and relief as Love and Item were on 1179.

Those poor guys were slaughtered by the dozens almost daily on Bloody, well below, behind us, and Heartbreak north and below us. We could have pulled up a chair and watched the one-sided firefights as gooks ran them off piecemeal at night from the top of Bloody, platoon after platoon.

Fighting bogged down across the front at about thirty kilometers above the 38th parallel where we were dug in, positional warfare in which neither side could force a military or diplomatic decision. Nevertheless, hours and days and weeks passed in killings at or around us. We followed the long, tedious, peace talks from the first word, with every new issue of the *Stars and Stripes* delivered by our chogee train, one copy per ten men, read on the friendly side of the ridge or down in our holes out of sight of the enemy, each copy, baring ominous interruptions, beginning a new daydream for me.

One short daydream, repeated for reasons unknown was a Hollywood movie I saw before WWII about a kraut lance corporal, one stripe, former school teacher who got himself clobbered crawling in front of his trench after a butterfly on the day the WWI Armistice was signed. I told Sergeant Eppler about *ALL QUIET ON THE WESTERN FRONT;* its hero in the movie actor Lew Ayers, conscientious objector, served in our infantry in WWII as a medic and died as I write this.

This tale about an infantryman in combat is touted by 'experts' as the truest account of what it is really like, no holds bared; written by a German soldier who survived trench warfare in WWI and wrote such bullshit as, "One soldier ran by with his head blown off, blood spurting from his neck like a fountain," and "He was blown clean out of his clothes, landing naked in a tree." As far as I know, although we threw more lead, it never happened in Korea.

What other real authorities ever tried to explain infantry combat? Ernest Hemingway, a blowhard whose total claim to combat was as a short-term ambulance driver on the quiet Italian front in WWI where evidently he was nicked by longrange artillery shrapnel; rear echelon clerk Norman Mailer, whose only combat was knifing his wife?

Eppler agreed the guy should've kept his ass down at all times. You can't depend on peace talks. Gooks and chinks used peace talks to stall while they restocked their caches of ammo and stuff. Our generals knew this and that's why we fell back for five days and went after them on the sixth in the May Massacre.

Peace talks, shut down since 23 August, began anew in November. Especially applauded by the guys was the Communists' insistence that all foreign troops be withdrawn from the peninsula.

"Hey, gooks, we're foreign as hell. Let's go!"

But this demand was dropped after nine sessions, for the UN Command insisted that cease-fire was only an agreement to stop shooting, not a settlement of territorial rights. An original settlement on the 38th parallel as agreed upon temporarily in 1952 would mean that all the land our buddies so dearly paid for since June would be returned.

Ridgway, MacArthur's replacement, once ordered a boycott of meetings after one UN convoy to Kaesong was fired on. It was time for more UN military pressure. With the deterioration and suspension of peace talks, we felt our leaders in Washington let us down, leaving us with more and more dying time. We've done the dirty work, how's about you guys doing something worthwhile?

Fool's Mountain would be followed by other named objectives as Heartbreak, Bloody, Porkchop, Baldy, etc. Taking limited objectives was a steady diplomatic pressure applied to the hesitant Korean Peace Talks, a despairing stalemate on our painfully moving, sometimes dying, battalion-size outpost on 1179.

Weeks passed reckoned by failed negotiations and as the blood of young men sank into Korean soil through July, August and September of the year 1951, from short, jabbing, probing enemy attacks and our combat and reconnaissance patrols went deep into noman lands without letup, I caught myself sighing often, complaining to myself I died too slowly. I knew then how fatalistic Gonzales felt about J C. "Come get me, you bastards, get it over with!" It was a monotony that was not dull because it was always threatening, quiet, a violent, threatening sameness. Time was oppressive while the monsoon hung low upon us; yet, because time now was all there was to our lives, we looked forward sadly to our own sudden death, or, less certain, to that healthy day when we rotated.

When not engaging persistent enemy, who wanted very badly to regain Taeusan, the men rested and worked on their rocky holes and went, hunched over, calling on buddies up and down the line. Unfortunately, being an officer I had no kindred spirit now that Fred Hurtz was safe in Tokyo, no longer wearing idiot sticks. Sergeant Eppler? College man, yes, but all business; aside from his military bent, he'd make my father the conventionally correct son he always wanted.

I heard promises from battalion via Lieutenant Carse, who I knew was pulling for me, that a replacement captain was on his way. It was a scandal for the high and mighty West-Point-owned Regular Army to depend so much on a poorly trained recalled-Reserve lieutenant and, I might add, master sergeant Pater doing a regular captain's job? Me? Sunday soldier, they called us, who didn't know how to play the Regular Army game. I was a sometimes rather nasty, outspoken thirty-one-year-old, questioning one at that. Fortunately, the act of commanding a rifle company in combat was itself direct and earthy, rather exhilarating to this warrior's psyche to remain in combat, weary though I was.

At Lieutenant Carse's suggestion, Sergeant Eppler was moved to a platoon leader's slot pending my return from company, so he could more easily be field commissioned even though he had turned it down twice. Master Sergeant Warren Milligan became the Third's active platoon sergeant. He was a Regular, vet of the mountains of Italy in WWII, a real pro. We went inspecting the Banzai Third together and when not checking firing positions, ammo reserves, and equipment (I was espe cially fussy about cleaning gas ports on BARs), weather permitting, lolling about the CP gabbing. Carbon builds up after a lot of firing in the BAR port hole for escape of gases not needed to eject the bullet, slows the rate of fire of the weapon and in the midst of a fatal battle freezing solid so the BAR won't fire at all. I've seen this happen and heard about it in other cases.

There was constant sniping from 1181 as well as 1243 for three weeks after taking 1179, and both sides took cover, then seemingly by tacit understanding allowed a certain amount of untroubled daytime housekeeping. But there was no written agreement and at least one notable exception—Bill Hanson—was enough to keep us from ever relaxing. On cold days of light blowing rain, normal for those mountains, the new first sergeant, Martin, and I sat huddled together in the Company CP hole, olive-drab blankets around our shoulders, playing cards, of necessity close to the chest, squirming for warmth on the Korean mountainside as summer fled from cruel Manchurian winds.

We scratched ourselves nervously like caged monkeys; bunker sores with serum leakage on our thighs and asses. Some picked up a maddening fungus crotch itch appropriately called Chinese crud by our sister regiment, the Ninth Infantry, following the Boxer Rebellion. Unbrushed teeth contaminated our mouths; the excuse, hard-to-get water after the monsoon, not toothpaste. When it rained solidly, we rigged spare ponchos to collect water and store it in empty five-gallon jerry cans. Steadily, relentlessly it dripped on us and when there was a dry hour, me of the bloody toes ordered the guys to remove their boots and socks to massage their feet while the sergeants, after checking their own, inspected them for potentially dangerous sores.

Rosters turned over, while replacements grew old in a few days, and veterans lucky enough became ancient and rotated. I'll swear some died up there

Waiting feet inspection by platoon leader and sergeant before donning dry socks.

whose names had never been mentioned, most likely replacements. Time was on hand to recall old complaints and suddenly discover new ones, time to evaluate whether replacements were men or boys, as ranks gave way slowly to questionable illnesses with which the weaker made poor, but unbegrudged exits. A squad leader from the First Platoon limped down to the rear one day without a tag groaning about his appendix to those who'd listen, an attack which in the comfortable rear cured itself in several days, allowing his unprejudiced return to duty showered, fed, with clean fatigues. He wasn't any deserter, just an honorable overtired dogface who needed a respite. No one could begrudge him. Hell, I brooded, he might have stayed back there with Captain Carleton or Shallow or be Toth's assistant.

Another miserable man evacuated himself with hemorrhoids grown suddenly unbearable in the unfriendly climate of the mountain outpost. Some thoughtful surgeon back down the line harkened to his many woes and shipped him all the way to Pusan for an operation—and return to duty. Dammit, my own piles were well behaved;, since twenty-mile forced route marches in the Royal Canadian Scotch Infantry under heavy packs, wearing thousand milers, ankle-high boots with double-thick soles with metal horseshoes and cleats. Mine rarely protruded; the medics told me how to push them back in. They were itchy and at times painful, but stayed inside most of the time.

Coming down the mountain trail into the busy peaceful valley behind the MLR, the wounded were often asked, "*Where* you been?"

"Shows that much?"

Because of the greater area covered as they moved through space, most wounds occurred to extremities, arms and legs, but mingled with the flow of legitimately wounded from the battalion, one or two SIWs every week or so, self-inflicted wounds, most always in a foot, rarely a hand. Most of us combat veterans were so rubbed into it we probably considered it once or twice but not seriously. We old timers didn't despise them, they'd been brought up with less self-respect, less sticktoitiveness than we who would, we told one another, rather die than flinch this way. I've never seen statistics but I doubt if ever a Mexican-American or native Indian was SIW. Ones I saw were city boys of soft lives from well-to-do families.

One that stands out for utter stupidity, was a hospital returnee early one morning evacuated originally not for a wound, but to cure a nervous tic, a likeable humorous guy, twenty-two-year-old draftee from Washington, D C, who, I heard, was grabbed by his draft board for flunking out of college. Not only do tics come to nervous ones after too much line time, a battalion surgeon told me they usually need only a week's rest, same as those with regressed fear reactions, fear paralysis, actually had immobilized hands, arms or feet, a subconscious effort to protect the whole body from annihilation. Authenticity of the symptom is tested by a surgeon sticking a pin into the 'dead' arm or leg while watching the man's pupils for involuntary reaction. Should they react, he is threatened with a court martial for faking, which usually is enough for a confession and return to duty with no punishment other than shame.

When filling the squad's canteens at a spring a quarter of the way down from 1179, as punishment for goofing off, the hospital returnee yelled loudly for a medic saying that a sniper hit him in the foot. By the time the medic got there, he was going into shock, which I'm sure he hadn't planned on. The medic gave him morphine, checked his blood loss, massaged circulation back into his arms and head, noting that both his boot and sock were off the injured foot when hit. How come, his platoon sergeant asked, for though he received nasty damage to a major bone that would leave him a life-long cripple, there wasn't a mark on his boot or the sock tucked neatly within it?

"I took them off so my blood wouldn't be contaminated by wool or leather," he confessed naively.

"What made you think of that?"

"Doc told me once about someone he knew got hit in his foot and got blood poisoning."

"You and the sniper in cahoots?"

This young man limped from the 10th Station in Pusan straight home after a dishonorable discharge; alive, he felt he was a winner, even though flunking his two greatest life's efforts, college and combat.

Of the proud Red and Blue Battalions, including the Korean Marine regiment, in two months on 1100 and 1179, 200 were killed and 500 wounded of 9400 engaged. On Bloody and Heartbreak, the 9th and 23d infantries lost that many in a week, very embarrassing to generals and politicians, what with bold talk of peace. It took 103 days and savage nights to take Heartbreak. It might have been so with us on 1179 if Item and King, not mere platoons, weren't close behind us to play musical chairs. Knowing you got all that more power backing you up close by makes for morale and a damn powerful machine.

Our Blue Book—

In due course X Corps succeeded in slaughtering uncounted thousands of the NKPA and advancing to its 'limited objective,' a new line north of the Punchbowl. But the cost to make these minor improvements in the X Corps line was shocking. The Second Division and attached ROKs incurred 2700 casualties in capturing Bloody Ridge and 3700 American casualties in capturing Heartbreak Ridge. Concluding it was 'unprofitable to continue the bitter operation,' Van Fleet told corps commander Clovis Byers to 'firm up his line' and 'plan no further offensives.'

Several times I was a fraction away from knowing the secret of afterlife and even   kidded myself that a true religion was being formulated in my mind and there evolved in me a dim but direct understanding, almost primitive Nature worship, a form of animism, that of man, brought to or wrought on this lonely little planet, sustains his living by products of the earth until his body returns automatically to rejoin that from which he was made; the food his mother ate became his first physical self, to be disintegrated back into mother earth from which other foods would spring anew, nonliving back to living, one form to another—

The sword of Charlemagne the Just
Is ferric oxide, known as rust.
– Arthur Geuterman.

Thrashed mountain plants, would, in turn, be nurtured by our blood and their own fallen leaves. All physical life becomes earth and springs from the earth and, used temporarily by one or other forms of life, returns for the abode of yet another soul. The souls of everything living, prerequisites for being alive, are, it dawned on me, as yet undiscovered forms of energy, even as was electricity until the spark phenomenon was recorded by the Greek philosopher Thales in 400 B C, when amber was rubbed with wool, the second most important energy form after gravity not even named until Sir William Gilbert, physician to Queen Elizabeth I, in 1584 coined the word electricity, from *elektron*, Greek for amber. Like electricity, which hauls water up 200-foot Sequoia trees, allows man to think and without which life could not exist, souls—of every living thing—are a latent as yet undiscovered forms of energy, and therefore indestructible.

Religious leaders teach that our souls are eternal. They can be that indestructible only as energy, never matter, attuned to the cosmoses of universes and eternity, that so long as our universe exists loans life (soul) to one temporary chemical mass after another. What matters that we 'give up the ghost' suddenly as we do in Korea without ceremony on the bloody trails between holes, as our flesh returns permanently to the earth? The forlorn souls of dogfaces are an as yet unsensed form of everlasting energy. All this my good buddy, friend Freddy Hurtz, and I decided during our hectic sojourn in the southern mountains of North Korea.

10

KACH'IL-BONG
H 1232, MAGPIE MOUNTAIN

One short sleep past; we wake eternally And death shall be no more;
death, thou shalt die!
– John Donne, Mystic.

From the Blue Book—

Plans were drawn up on 29 September for a new limited offensive for all X
Corps. Scheduled for 0600 hours, 3 October, it called for an attack to the
newly designated 'Hays Line.' The principle objective of the Second Division was a north-south hill mass extending 3000 meters in length in the
eastern portion of the Division zone, dominated by a rocky crag-covered
peak, honeycombed with enemy bunkers, one of the most rugged, inaccessible peaks it had encountered in Korea. Towering high in the distance, its
top shrouded in clouds and mist, the objective was the northernmost crest
of a string of hills jutting northeast from Taeusan. Like an arrow, it penetrated into the heart of the enemy defenses, 1243, Kach'il-Bong.

Between H 1179 and H 1243 was a well-dug-in outpost on H 1181, command
responsibility for taking which was split between myself and Master Sergeant John
Pater. Three officers were with Love, myself, leader of the Third Platoon on duty as
temporary commander of Love Company, Roy Carse, and newly-commissioned Second Lieutenant Robert 'Red' Rose. Blue Book—

Supporting fires, including eight-inchers, directed from Battalion OP, were
registered and effected into known positions on 1181. [The larger the caliber, the less affected by atmospheric conditions on the way, the more accu-

rate.] At the same time, a lieutenant from Mike's Heavy Weapons company aimed rounds from a 75mm recoilless along with a 57mm recoilless of L Company's weapons platoon with excellent results at ragged North Koreans seen many times in and about the bunkers, bobbing up and down along the trenches.

Pater, acting CO with one ROTC lieutenant up with him, the other made first lieutenant and remained below as company executive, would support the attack this time rather than lead, which, as the ranking man, was my privilege. Because of the acute officer shortage, Colonel Duncan ordered company commanders, me and Morris of Item Company and Pater, to direct our attacks "from maximum protective positions," which made Pater and me sneer, "she-e-it, man, move troops against fire that far behind? Never."

On the morning of 3 October, Third Battalion was five days ahead of X Corps schedule. The First Marine Division, 5th Infantry, was that day still in general attack two-thirds of the way along the northeastern rim of the Punchbowl, their registering phosphorus clearly visible from the towering real estate of 1243.

Following is the S 3 Third battalion's official operations report from 0101, 03K to 2400 04 K, Korean time, September, in other words, from one minute after one Korean time on 3 September, to midnight the next day—

1st Bn remained in previously reported positions providing fire support for 3rd Bn attack on Hill 1181, two platoons of L Company, forward elements of 3rd Bn in vicinity DT 199380 at 0100 03K Sep engaged by an estimated two (2) enemy companies. At 0155 03K Sep the 3rd plat of L Co was dispatched to reinforce the 1st and 2d plats at the forward positions. K Co was dispatched from its positions to join L Co for the assault on Hill 1181 and the objective was secured by 1600 03K Sep. Battalion (-) broke contact with the enemy at 1930 04K Sep and consolidated its position vic DT200340T by 2400 04K Oct.

I went forward from 1179 to brief the attacking rifle platoons of Love and on the following morning, minus a forward observer who failed to show, I proceeded with the assistance of King's acting commander, Sergeant Pater, to call in and adjust preparatory artillery fire. We used my SCR 300 to battalion, who relayed to Fire Direction Center on a SCR 609, who then fired the batteries. The summit of 1181 was defended from long irregular ditches and several heavily constructed log bunkers.

Initially, two light machine guns positioned by Pater give overhead support fire and I added two light thirties from Love Company which continued to maintain in bursts a good accurate fire; then, with minimum delay, replaced light thirties one at a time with the sustained fires of heavies from Mike, Heavy Weapons Company. These 30 calibers, whose barrels are water-cooled, maintained direct, almost continuous overhead fire on all targets known, raking the rims of the ditch tops, correcting by tracer sighting plunging streams of bullets into bunker apertures.

As leader, I worked from a rock hole facing enemy down the northern forward slope of 1179 about ten feet from the silhouetting crest. The communications between Colonel Duncan, Pater and myself were at all times excellent. Nevertheless, there were occasions when the situation became confusing to the man in charge, for Duncan had poor visibility of the forward, enemy-facing portion of 1179 and the saddle leading up to 1181. From his OP on 1179 he couldn't see concealed elements of Love Company for his OP was slightly to the left of the line of sight along the north-south ridge mass.

Machine guns attempted to conserve ammunition by lifting whenever salvoes of artillery arrived. Once they were slow in starting again and during the lull when neither artillery nor machine gun fire landed on 1181 we observed five enemy slip out of the apertures of suicide bunkers in panic and disappear over the hill behind them. Germ of an idea, turning to the heavy machine gun sergeants: "When artillery lifts next time, button up your guns; give them a chance to bug. Remember 1179 how easy we made it? Let's synchronize."

An estimated twenty to thirty enemy vacated in this manner, reducing our occupational hazards considerably. Our FO, an artillery lieutenant independent of our command, was supposed to join us sometime in the night well before our attack but failed to show in time and I called Pater to tell him how we were synchronizing with the machine guns only to discover that the ROTC officer was acting FO. Pater was hit and evacuated. The young lieutenant, then acting company commander of King, was pleased when I relieved him. What a thrill dishing out so much HE, what power! I never realized FOs had so much fun. I almost didn't know when to stop; imagine throwing whole batteries of three-gun salvos at them. The regular FO then appeared and took over.

As we watched enemy chogee between bursts, a little bareheaded gook, about fourteen, in a dirty, sloppy uniform, slid through a bunker aperture near the top of the objective to come running hell-bent on surrendering down the open saddle path. When some of my men fired at him, I yelled: "Can it! Let the kid surrender!" By the time he started up from the bottom of the saddle, a gook was whittling away at him with a burp gun. The kid finally made it, running sixty miles an hour right up over the rocks and onto my lap. The machine gunners and riflemen within sight laughed, clapped and cheered. "Who's your new friend?" someone yelled. Still on my lap, the visitor wiped sweat from his forehead with a sweeping movement of his hand and, face-to-face, went: "Whew!" saying in North Korean what I imagined was 'what a relief,' then beamed like any happy little boy and grabbed my left hand to shake it, an uncommon gesture for a gook.

Remembering my training, I opened a C ration can and, setting him up in full view on my lap, gave him a plastic spoon. There, in front of everyone, he sniffed the can suspiciously while ducking as much as he could and, though our intelligence told us that they were starving, made a face and handed it back. No reflection on Army dietitians, we couldn't interest the hungry little gook in a C ration hash either.

I stood him up in the hole to let gooks see us good from 1181 and stuck a cigarette in his mouth. The kid was impossible to light up, refusing to suck in, turning for frightened looks at 1181, trying to crouch. I wanted his buddies to see how well he was treated. Then the youngster and I nearly got our fuckin' heads blown off by a sniping elephant gun. You can't mistake that big bastard. Evidently the lad never smoked, for Corporal Alverez saw him throw the unlit butt away with a look of disgust.

Meanwhile, Colonel Duncan kept pestering me like on H 1179. "C'mon, Gould, get up there. We can see them crawling out of their bunkers and bugging."

"Who do you think's giving them that opportunity? The fewer we have to fight."

He called every five minutes asking what in hell we were up to and for us to get the lead out of our pants.

"What makes you think it's lead?" I asked.

There came a time, however, when no gook crawled out during the lulls and I had to move. I figured out the fields of fire of enemy bunkers and two machine guns and then checked with the lieutenant in charge of Mike's heavies, also noting where was the opposition, the greatest threat. We agreed that most faced the Punchbowl side of the enemy hill and the finger that led down into the bowl, most likely avenue of approach from where they had the greatest fear of attack.

Love's platoon leaders and a few eager sergeants of King were in a ten-foot-deep ravine to left rear.

"Lieutenant Rose," I yelled, "take your men on the trail along those supply bunkers on the left. Keep well off the saddle trail. I'll be behind you. Third Platoon, follow in right behind Rose. Ziggy, good luck. Weapons platoon, give us all the machine gun and mortar you can. Don't forget to keep it high when we near the top."

"Ready, everyone ... let's banzai!"

It's not necessary to tell each and every soldier exactly where to go and what to do; that's where hours of training went teaching him, his squad leader's job. As a lieutenant rifle platoon leader, theoretically the only ones I order are my platoon guide and platoon sergeant, who in turn has four squad leaders and they, each with an assistant take care of directing each individual soldier, eleven when up to TO&E, table of organization and equipment. That's why any major general who's been in the infantry will tell you a rifle squad leader has the toughest job in the Army, more men to command directly than a four-star general.

I called the colonel to tell him to raise all preparatory fire when I asked; we were finally shoving off and for him to tell Fire Direction Center I'd personally call off artillery when we were ready and to make sure battalion relayed immediately and correctly. King Company and the machine gun sergeants would support us with their own fire from the northern ridge of 1179 to keep gooks above us from poking their heads up and lowering rifles.

I turned to my new radioman, Corporal Andy Hill. "C'mon, we're taking off."

"I can't," he pleaded, pointing to the stripped-down carbine lying beside him. "The thing won't fire right. I have to clean it."

No one could pull a Funaro on me again. "Damn it, come along with the 300, you'll find someone's soon enough."

Several replacement riflemen who needed to be broken in thought the trail on the saddle looked easier going but Lieutenant Rose hustled them off just before a swarm of bullets drilled in. I took up toward the end of Rose's platoon. The men stopped near the bottom of the saddle, going through a thick clump of tangled bushes.

I worked my way forward, yelling, "What's the matter? What's the holdup?"

The lead man was getting high fire from unexpected enemy on a finger leading east-west toward Heartbreak. We directed our combined machine guns to take them out and before we got out of the bushes just off the deep saddle path, King Company's water-cooled guns and two 57mm recoilless rifles were on to the unexpecting enemy. King's overhead made it so hot gooks abandoned their machine guns and bugged.

When they heard me hard by them, Lieutenant Rose, Pop Miller, and two or three other noncoms got the men to scream war whoops and "E-e-e-e-e D-e-e-e W-a-a-a-a! Cuda, cuda!" Corporal Boggs, a Louisiana swamp boy, let out a stream of ear-piercing wild-turkey calls, that in an early American war were 'rebel' yells. We moved right along then and I got hoarse keeping the yelling up to pitch. Scattered along one section of the vague supply bunker path we passed a dismembered 75mm mountain pack howitzer, ten pieces or carries altogether; two spoked wheels here, the heavy breech there, and so on for about fifty yards. The only thing missing was the hard-working mules that packed them up mountain trails under Colonel Bull Boatner's chinks. By one supply bunker there was a neat pile of what must have been about 500 rounds of 82mm Russian mortar ammo—82 so they could use our 81 ammo but its ammo too large to fit 81mm.

A rifleman behind me let off a round by my ear. I whipped around shouting: "Goddamn sonofabitch! Watch where you're shooting. I know you can't *see* gooks, but fire up where they *might* be."

Lots of guys whammed into the ground a few yards ahead, subconsciously not wanting to attract gooks' attention and make them retaliate.

I ducked behind large rocks to answer Duncan on the radio. Friendly fire was tight over our heads. I felt so safe there I had to work up a lot of willpower to make myself move again. About ten riflemen bunched up behind the big rock formation with me and I had to move out first before I could expect them to chogee. I was stopped a couple more times when the battalion commander called. It burned me up every time I was handed the radio receiver; the guys thought I was quitting them and lagged and stopped yelling. Finally, half way up, I told Duncan my radioman would continue to receive but I was too busy to reply. As I handed back the receiver, I heard him say something about a direct order. "Fuck you," I muttered, "want to run things get your ass up here."

After a while, when we started over the bald, dangerous top of 1181 through the grenade line, I shoved Ziggy's and Pop Miller's squads through Lieutenant Rose's platoon. They balked just as the tail end cleared Rose's men. "Lift the damn artillery," Pop yelled back. I had planned to work in about twenty-five yards closer to it, but it worked out just as well. I learned not to argue with fate.

"This is Buzzard Seven. Lift the artillery, it's holding us up." Then I yelled to the men ahead of me, "Okay, it's lifted."

Unfortunately, one three-gun salvo, in flight as I talked, bansheed in close above. The men stopped, dropped to their knees, turned and glared at me. One shook his fist.

"See," I yelled, hoping to calm their fears. "Just the one salvo already loaded. They're through until I call for more."

A few minutes later, as the first half of the lead platoon and I were in an irregular circle, panting and puffing, stumbling through artillery-plowed earth just below the enemy position without warning a single red-hot 105, as had threatened Ziggy on 1179, tore the air apart, crashing like a meteor into the middle of our group. When the black smoke and dust settled, all I saw were white-eyed Tree and white faces, stunned, questioning, angry.

"Where the fuck did that come from?" someone yelled.

I bellowed into the radio, disregarding procedure. "You dirty cocksuckers, have them lift that fuckin' stuff or we're gettin' the fuck off here and hunt you bastards down." Hopefully the right guy heard it.

As with Ziggy on 1179, we were lucky the round hit a huge rock formation above us and the spray went up. No one was nicked and it was observed from 1179 that it helped to break up a ten-man counter attack beginning to form near the summit.

By 1600, when we reached the very top by the large OP bunker, one old Maxim gun to a flank was still chuggin'. It took a few grenades. We rousted out altogether twenty unarmed and pretty tame-looking gooks, one of whom kow-towed to me when riflemen brought them over. I figured he was a *honcho* (Jap, important person), so I told the sergeant in charge of a guard detail to tell S2, intelligence, about his kow-towing. He was older than me— festering, draining burns on his right forearm and shoulder. It had been about three and a half weeks since Marine Corsairs worked this ridge with napalm for the ROK Marine Regiment attack.

The Johnny-come-latelies scrambled over the rocks and into bunkers looking for loot, trouble or victims, checking everything carefully for booby traps and throwing around what loose junk there was. They found about eight Russian carbines, several long rifles, two elephant guns, beauty of a well-machined WWII kraut machine pistol with a skeleton stock and a brown, Bakelite hand grip.

It was a job getting the men back to their squads and calmed down after that exciting victory. The NCOs and I were so pooped and hoarse we could hardly talk. I had to stumble around, gasping, to get us into a perimeter defense and then drank dry the last of my two canteens of water.

Half an hour later, as Sergeant Martin, the ROK interpreter, and the late-arriving artillery FO were moving up the saddle path to join us, we got a very aggressive counterattack; it sounded like a hundred jabbering monkeys firing and throwing grenades. Hashing it over, however, we agreed it was only about a reinforced squad, nevertheless, athletic, armed with burp guns.

A private named Miller was killed in this attack (no relation to Pop or Tom). To our rear, Corporal Robert Davis, Love Company's 57mm recoilless gunner, did a terrific job until killed by a sniper. Sergeant Richard 'Nick' Nicholson of Beaver Falls, Pennsylvania, his squad leader, told me on the phone what a terrific young man Bob was and what a good shot. Also KIA was Corporal Salvador Bourbon, National Guardsman. Bourbon had just returned from the 10th Station two days before with a draining head wound and was ordered by the battalion surgeon to remain near the aid station to have his dressing changed. King Company found him the next day off in the bushes on the right of the trail, apparently trying to outflank one of the gook guns by himself, how Master Sergeant Ulriche died. Bourbon was one more heroic Mexican-American, as I knew them all to be potentially.

The taking of 1181 was nothing like the grand conscript armies of Napoleon sweeping across the plains of Europe, flags thrust aloft by mounted noblemen cornets, or George Patton's snarling, clod-throwing Sherman tanks, guidons and antennas fluttering aloft, sweeping across open fields of France with truck-speeding infantry regiments of flankers outmaneuvering the enemy; the static mass tragedy of muddy WWI trench warfare or the horrible mass suicide stumbling up twice to die on Cemetery Ridge in our Civil War. After all, we were engaged in a Police Action never accounted for. Forgotten, unworthy of American civilian concern.

What we had to do on mountain hopping (loaded with equipment) was crawl up wooded fingers to ridgelines and slip-slide up or down narrow trails and footpaths, sometimes with scary dropoffs on both sides. And we lost good men who turned wrong in the dark or misjudged foot- or handholds and the enemy had a pretty good idea of where we were at all times.

The most memorable power, best of big drama for reporters, most appealing combat that could be applied, was chronicled at higher headquarters calling air strikes, artillery salvoes of heavy artillery from the batteries and making diversionary raids to the flanks of particular objectives on the plastic situation maps at division headquarters.

By far the worst casualty to Third Battalion in that assault was the loss of Master Sergeant John Pater. I particularly felt terrible and worried since his company medic told me he got it in the back, the vertebrae with their important conduit of nerves. I came as close to prayer as an Agnostic is permitted. Instead I hoped hard, conscious of how much important scientific work was being done in the spine field. He did return several weeks later but was wounded worse on his way back to King. Following are some notes he jotted down about his efforts to rejoin us after release from an Army hospital in Japan. He intended to write his own story about all he went through in WWII and Korea, but grew too old in constant pain. Many deeply moved infantry combat veterans yearn to record their experiences, as John and other buddies are very interested in my efforts—

Back to Drake [Camp Drake, north of Tokyo after partially recovering from wounds] for transport to Korea and the 38th, where returning to company area, a medic and I were given a verbal inaccurate briefing of company location and got lost, wound up in a hill position of 23rd Infantry [in foothills of Bloody] where we spent the night under light sniping action. Off next morning—I was in lead, coming around a steep turn, came under machine gun fire; doubling back, yelled at medic to take cover and stepped on land mine. Could see my legs over my head, surrounded by shattered fatigues before I landed. Medic tried to come forward and was turned back by machine gun fire. I yelled for him to stay back and the machine gunner kept a line of fire between me and medic who kept trying to get to me. I lost blood and passed out.

Next remembered lying on rock shelf with several other wounded attended by two medics and medical officer. Could not move but could see tiny medics very clearly and could hear them very clearly. One medic called to doctor while standing over me, "This one next?" Doctor replied, "No, he's too far gone. Get the others first." Irrationally, I felt I was giggling because I believed that I was OK.

Back to 121st Evac where red-headed surgical nurse had me on a gurney naked except for a cloth over my genitals, started to clean me up and to remove fragments from legs, arms, face and back, and asked, "Haven't I seen you before, Sarge?" and I told her, "Yes, you've done this same job on me several moths ago." After debriding arms, legs and face, she asked, "Is that all?" When I said, "No," she lifted the modesty cloth and examining my appendage, said, "This will never do, Sarge. You'll have to learn to play the flute."

Japan again, a hospital on a beach after an hour-long bus trip. Full cast on left leg., half cast on right leg, full cast left arm, half cast on right arm to immobilize pulped muscle. Severed nerve on left large toe and they splinted shattered toe and metatarsal arch. Evacuated to Air Force Hospital Nagoya, casts replaced, tissue removed. Wrote to company and asked if someone would secure eight rolls of exposed film from company clerk's desk and my old .45 revolver and S&W 357, but never received either.

Colonel Rowney managed me a field commission with limited duty in absentia, gave me a Silver Star and General Young endorsed a Silver Star and commission and wrote him a nice letter.

This was the end of his very active duty for, despite his threatening protest, Second Lieutenant Pater was flown in traction to the zone of interior, handed over to the Veterans Administration and systematically forgotten by everyone but me and his wife.

He once told me the VA made him feel like a spent shell casing covered by weeds up in those mountains of North Korea for that's where usable life left him.

"Damn dirty rear-echelon sonsofbitches. I could wipe out the whole fuckin' congress with a shopping bag of grenades. Dirty, sneaky bastards! I ain't begun to fight; they'll see ... boot me out will they!"

"Sorry," a fair man would tell John. "Awful sorry. You would have been beautiful posing as the underwater demolition man you were in a World War Two in a war bond drive surrounded by beautiful young starlets and music like *Stars and Stripes Forever* making you feel like they'd hail John Pater, the war hero, forever. To think you began your great odyssey a cocky underwater demolition man in our Pacific Navy before Pearl Harbor who dove to help raise some of those pathetic wrecks. How vital and picturesque in your hard-earned medals and your six-foot-two, eyes of blue, blue steel, that is. I hear you lashing out at the rear echelon. "Man, don't fuck with me no more! Ladies, you're something else."

We spent the rest of the day and most of that night on 1181 making emplacements facing enemy, with overlapping fields of fire, watching beautiful greenish-blue lace lightning (St Elmo's fire) play up and down our commo wire in a late autumn electric storm. About seven the next day, I was awakened and ordered by Duncan to report back to 1179. What the hell now? I thought. My poor radio procedure? I turned the company over to Lieutenant Rose. Knowing the great odds against field commissioned guys, before leaving, I went over everything I could think of bad that might happen to him until he stopped me. "Don't try to prove anything," I told him.

"Geezus, Gould, who you talking to? I've been over here a few more months than you, right?"

"It's just I'm superstitious."

Lieutenant Colonel Duncan returned my salute, took me aside and without beating around the bush told me point blank I was picked to lead an assault on 1243, which didn't surprise me; I was on a roll. What got me, however, was there wouldn't be a lot of time to get ready, it would take place on the morrow, hardly time to get resupplied. Seems it was the bright idea of our newly arrived division exec, General Boatner and I was cautioned that he would question me to check out my self assurance and how I'd take the prominence. "No secret about it," I told my colonel. "The same with the others; you approach it up a finger, the only way, get as much preparatory fire and Air as you can, move up as close to the artillery as you dare, lift it, and banzai the sonsofbitches."

With Lieutenant Colonel Duncan was Fearless Frank Mildren, and to my surprise the new assistant division commander, Brigadier General Haydon L Boatner, chief of staff of the Chinese Army in India during WWII. After brief introductions, I told him in short order my simple plan. He was not enthusiastic, as I learned generals and colonels never are, but had nothing to say against it; get as much preparatory fire as possible, a good air strike that afternoon if possible before dark, and charge up there as close behind our artillery as we did at 1179 and 1181.

"Stick to those plans; you ought to come out all right, lieutenant," the general said as a benediction of the highest order.

"I'm *sure* I will," I said and was handed an angry glance from Duncan. Later, at my request, he told me why.

"Getting in the last word, as you often do, Gould, you appeared trying to up the general."

By this time, Lieutenant Colonel Duncan, paratrooper, and I had been through a couple battles, and so long as no one else was listening, I knew, if I felt it important, I could say what I pleased. After Mildren left with Boatner and his aide, I let Duncan know how tired I was becoming. I told him I was very proud of what I found like a game, natural to me if dangerous, but it's gotta' stop sometime. I was fatigued and weary and as he well knew, no one lives forever and why push my luck. Besides, it's not my job, not at my rank; it belongs to a Regular Army captain.

"Colonel, I don't give a shit anymore, if I ever did. I'm awfully tired of sticking my neck out for your Regular Army. I'd like a crack at my own career; instead, on every hill I get further and further away, closer and closer to getting knocked off; I'm tired of doing some Regular Army captain's work, wherever he is."

"Gould," Duncan said, seriously. "Right now your career is leading men in combat for your country. I don't have to tell you what patriotism is and nobody has said anything to you, but ever since you took over from Captain Shallow, you've exhibited those magic qualities that cannot be learned; not taught at the Point. Some things can't be taught and you've got the men with you. There's something about you that makes the men want to follow and please you. Maybe it's because you're not professional, a relief worker like so many of them; one with more enlisted time on your record than officer. They seem to realize that you have a naturally aggressive attitude and generally disrespectful and it's a good thing you're in a rough and tough rifle outfit in the field, you'd have been court martialed long ago in a quiet unit in the rear. You started out, far as I can learn, with that moustache bit, a cheap trick that caught their fancy, becoming a hero to the men as far away as division rear and went on to assault a field grade officer with close ties to X Corps, and why Colonel Coughlin let you get away with it, we'll never know. Apparently you've become a soldier's Jesse James.

"I'm talking out of turn and could get my ass in a sling if you tell anyone, but personally I'm trying to say I wouldn't want you around in a peaceful situation junking the division training schedule, for instance, made up by Army pros, but for your valuable service at 1100, 1179 and now 1181, General Boatner and General Young are putting you in for a DSC and a captaincy and as soon as he prepares a suitable slot transferring you to division. Boatner said he was thankful for a few leaders like you in WWII."

The few times someone is kind or speaks well of me I tend to get belligerent.

"Shit," I blurted, "I wouldn't last back there a day. I'd be calling them rear echelons to their faces. I worked back there with Regulars for a week when I landed in Korea and its prissy-prissy military careerists who hang together and have their own jokes and do things their way and look down their noses on Reservists like me. I made the mistake once of pissing down the wrong tube."

Colonel Duncan, who wouldn't know about that one, probably took it as an idiom; pissed down the wrong tube?

"Well, the general could make other arrangements for you as a captain. Damn it, man, you certainly earned it, but don't push your luck."

"Thanks, Colonel, I'll believe it when I see it. I'm proud though that it comes from an old combat man like 'Bull' Boatner."

Man oh man, I told myself, after quietening down some; that's the best compliment I ever had; shit, that's the only compliment aside from Colonel Rowney's. Captain? DSC? Wait 'til Watertown hears this. Nobody thinks that well of me.

Division called in a good FEAF (Far East Air Force) four-plane rocketing, strafing and napalm attack on 1243 that afternoon and that night an extensive bombardment by ten batteries of 105s and 155s, FO'd by a captain from division.

I returned to where they were still digging in a defense facing the gooks and called in Lieutenant Morris and the ROTC officer of King named Wadsworth as acting commander, telling him here was his big chance and the platoon leaders and I all agreed it was too bad losing Master Sergeant Pater and after reminding them all to move fast from cover-to-cover and keep together and the machine gunners and mortarmen give us good cover and for Christ sake, stop when they see us taking the hill, and, damn it all, good luck. Nothing fancy about it, here we are and there's the friggin' hill and each has his job. Let's do it again. Love, King and Item in that order. We'll shove off in the attack at 0600. Oh, yeah, let's synchronize watches.

"Sh-e-e-it!" someone complained in good infantry style. "Here we go again."

Another man, discouraged and pessimistic, yet plainly duty-bound, said, "Guess this is it," which is less lyrical but roughly the same as the ancient saying in the former Japanese Imperial Army—

> *Duty is heavier than a mountain*
> *and so to be much regarded;*
> *Death is lighter than a feather,*
> *and therefore to be despised.*

At 0530, before the sun was up, I worked through King to a safe hole on the enemy side of 1181 where I could observe, I radioed for two of Mike Company's heavy machine guns and as preparations began with our FO registering rounds on 1243, soon to be in better view, I noticed a tall blond guy on the trail behind me, Pater's company radioman, Ken Johnson, I learned, lying on his side, radio beside him, rubbernecking, watching the stuff land on 1243. King was well behind and Johnson came forward for the sideshow. When he first came over to the enemy side I told him to take cover. "Dammit," I yelled. "Get off the trail, it's zeroed in!" I threw myself off that trail after a bee's nest of bullets came zinging in on either side of me. "Get your ass out of here!"

Instantly, SWAAP! smack in his heart. I'd never witnessed so direct a shot before so closely. I was yelling right at the guy. He died as blood poured freely out of his chest through his undershirt and fatigues over his tight belt collecting in a puddle down by his feet, his face turning rapidly yellowish, pale and blank, like pulling down a shade.

Someone behind him yelled, "Medic!" and I turned and yelled

Guys displaying themselves to an elephant gun sharpshooter.

back, "Get away, zeroed in! He's gone!"

So strong was his instinct to save guys, Love Company's second platoon medic disregarded my warning, and as he continued to slide low down the ridge, I yelled again to get back over the hill and fired a burst of automatic carbine over his head into the trail behind him. He stopped, wide-eyed, finally got the gist of what I was yelling and crawled his way back over the ridgetop. Plain luck he wasn't hit.

Pater remembers the dead radioman well to this day. "A real beaut, Dud, one hell of a nice kid. I was evacuated by then, I never knew it until you just told me."

It's my belief, although I have no proof, a fifth to a fourth of men killed or wounded in rifle platoon combat become casualties because of their own carelessness, curiosity, laziness, or utter stupidity. They somehow detach themselves from the action to be neutral observers. I'd warned Johnson twice that he wasn't needed on the forward slope and to get back to the friendly side where it was safe.

My new runner brought Love up and we began to move down to the saddle. I was the only officer aside from Lieutenant Rose along the ridge from the enemy side of 1181 to the approaches to 1243. Our new FO, a young lieutenant named Blackwell, wasn't aggressive, but there was one heroic 57mm recoilless rifle gunner back down the trail from us, Corporal Davis's replacement, who fired canister on his own, doing a terrific job.

Swatches of low morning clouds pushed slowly through the broken trees and bushes on the steep southern slope of 1243 and draped over to blank out the depth of ravines along the fingers. Fuzzy white holes of varying depths formed mysterious tunnels in the clouds through which we occasionally spied the top of 1243, desolate and as forbidding as Count Dracula's castle in a thunder storm.

"Good day for murder," Sergeant Milligan told us.

"We will!" someone promised.

Shoving off that cheerless dark morning, Love Company was relieved in starting positions by Item so we could pass through King's defense of 1181 over a line of departure in the fog and drizzle. As we moved out for 1243, guys bitched, demanding to know how come Love did it all.

"Because we're Love," I told them proudly.

But then, I brooded, who gets really hip to this job?

Since H 1100, we were indeed the preferred point company, which I took as a big compliment, especially to the guys. Shit, no company, no goddamn rifle company in the world was more aggressive, worked so smoothly together. But, as I explained to Sergeant Milligan, much credit goes to Mighty Mouse committing companies like steam rollers in train. We hit, got hit, passed our wounded back, stepped to the sides of the trail, and let King through. King was hit, and stepped aside for Item, and just as important to the juggernaut was supply, back down the trail near enough for all of us, resupply of everything we needed, ammo to an armament specialist and extra weapons, to chop chop and, particularly important in those dry mountains now the monsoon was over, water. Above all was our terrific morale. We'd been through a few things together and trusted one another and like the colonel said, I was at heart one of them. I never wanted to be an officer and turned down an OCS at Brockville, Ontario in 1941. I even learned to be comfortable about intermediate bugouts like Funaro for I knew they'd come rushing up at the end, good and fresh for loot and we'd grab them to dig in for a counterattack. It was almost like I planned those bugouts for that job and, to give him some credit, Funaro never actually bolted and ran; there below us all the time, hungry for loot, quick to join with us.

The first peek of the rising sun was enough to run off mists and low clouds as I hissed back from the front to be relayed to the rear to be sure bayonets were fixed. "One in the chamber, safeties off." Our column moved slowly as delays up front became longer.

Group intuition told us it had to be about time for something to pop. It did; someone accidentally tripped a taunt wire stretched by King Company across the trail about six inches above the ground, pulling a cotter pin from a flare fuse that released a striker to ignite an explosion that popped up to ignite 500 feet above—colorless, brilliantly burning in the weak daylight, swaying back and forth, splattering burning, spitting magnesium dripping fire streaking toward earth, blown slowly along by an early morning high-flying breeze up above as it descended slowly on parachute, sizzling and crackling. It was strange, no, ridiculous, to see a flare in daylight. Our mountain world knew someone goofed.

"Damn fool!" a sergeant hissed, "watch your step. Pass that back."

Each man said goodbye to the world as he passed King's hasty, scanty barbed wire. That damn flare was more than a bad omen; certainly destroyed any surprise we might have had. Or, I hoped, might actually reassure the gooks that it must have been one of their returning night patrols; no enemy on the attack was dumb enough to throw up a flare over himself in daylight. Slipping and sliding on wet ground leading down the saddle and up toward 1243 in the light of early morning in that strangely luminous environment, Private Funaro landed on his ass the third time, no record for that miserable morning, but a good average. He remained down, refusing to budge.

"Damn sonofabitchin' Army!" he swore out loud. Always damn Army; never dirty statesmen or even bad enemy; always a hard-on for the US Army.

"The Army ain't ours, it belongs to taxpayers; blame them," someone hissed nearby. "Keep it down!" another hissed more loudly than Funaro.

"You keep it down," his sergeant said in a low voice.

Pop waited patiently until Funaro, sensing him standing above, looked up.

"Can't make it sarge," he whined. "Ankle's broken."

Pop reached under Funaro's arms and yanked him up face-to-face talking softly as a trainer to a recalcitrant animal.

"Damn it all, boy, we'd be mighty lonesome without your old M1. Step along best you can, all our ankles are broken."

"I ain't no RA," Funaro shot back. "I didn't sign up for this shit."

"Shut your fuckin' mouth," someone ordered.

Funaro was lucky to have been permitted to join, to find square meals after his stepfather or one of the men he sometimes called that, ran him off. Lucky he'd not been convicted of a felony for then he could never be accepted in the US Army, and felonies were just where Funaro and his street corner gang, the Banzais, were headed.

Who *is* hep to this job each man brooded? Looking back, I realize I was becoming pretty much on the shaky side again. My right trigger and middle finger were dark mahogany from cigarette tar, smoking up to three and a half packages a day depending on the supply. I was once put in my place by the platoon sergeant of the Second Platoon (who took Red Rose's place) for snapping at him over the EE-8 and warned by Colonel Duncan on the radio to watch the way I talked to my superiors.

R&R maybe saved me once but it worked against me now for it reminded me of the contrasting world I'd recently visited. I could hold out my hand and stretch my fingers and they'd quiver. I mean move up and down by themselves. Nights I was often wide awake reminiscing in a low voice with myself about guys we'd lost, talking in the middle of the night imagining I was about to be awakened for my two-hour tour, and sometimes when I did get to sleep, I'd be awakened by a violent dream. "God! Oh God! Watch out!" I'm no doctor but I'd have to say I was falling to pieces. Falling, why yes, that was one of my worst nightmares, everything falling away below me as I told myself I had a parachute somewhere, if only I could find it.

One man in the approach column, for good reason more skittery than Funaro, was the lead man, point man or first scout. Stalking forty yards ahead of everyone, bent from the waist with rifle at high ready port, finger within the trigger guard, safety off, one in the chamber, the ready pose of a tense grouse hunter, moving his head from side to side to widen his view, listening intently through the silently drying mist, taking furtive glances at the ground ahead for trip wires or sunken ground, signs of personnel mines. Now and then he stopped abruptly, cocking his head like a robin listening for movements of an earthworm, to catch in the antenna bucket of his steel helmet any noise at all that might warn him in time. Somebody or bodies up there ahead wanted to shoot him down like *he* was the game. Meanwhile, drip and drizzle of slow rain was a disruptive waterfall to ears searching only for certain guarded, most sinister sounds.

We relieved our point men frequently. One of the stories rear echelon soldiers tell at Veterans of Foreign Wars bars is how they put goofoffs on point to punish them. Liars, that spot is held by men with whom you must trust your lives.

Suddenly the mysterious mist went from ominous to dangerous to horror as early morning came awake abruptly with the ugly canvas-ripping sounds of deadly burp guns blazing. Corporal Brand of the Banzai Third was point at the time and as the file of us anxious men stopped, I ran hunching, scooting, zig-zagging, charging up to assistant squad leader, Sergeant Tree, to find Brand laying on his back in a small depression behind a tree, his shoulders pulled up under his helmet. As Tree began to crawl toward him, Brand rolled over on his stomach and got cautiously to his knees, pointing to where the sudden fire came from.

"About ten gooks dug in right there, sar...."

S-s-s-zlapt! blood splattered from Brand's right shoulder and shuddering, weakened by the powerful hit, trembling from the powerful physical shock, he rolled over and over into a shell hole away from the point of contact. "Thousand to one he's finished," went through my mind; then quickly modified, "for a week, anyway, and if he got a stateside wound, a bone or a nerve, say good bye, Brand'll never be back, the lucky bum."

"Lead man right of the trail," Tree yelled. "Get us moving. Off the trail, José, now; chogee."

Private Joseph ran past, bent double, zig-zagging from boulder to another, tree to tree, scrub pine to scrub pine, as someone yelled for the company Doc to clear out. Third Platoon medic Myles came scurrying up and I stopped him with urgent hand signals.

"That's suicide. For the love'a Christ, Doc, wait. Brand's red-hot. See if he can't stop bleeding himself."

Disregarding our yells, Doc Singleton, company medic, reached the wounded buddy and tugged open the stiff snap of Brand's first aid pouch. Brand attempting to sit, pushing up with the hand of his good arm, like a drunken man in a forward slump, still shaking, rocked half unconscious from the shock and slumped back.

"You'll both be killed!" someone shouted. "Get back! Get back! Grab his feet, pull him to cover!"

"What's the situation up there?" I yelled.

After a silence of two or three minutes, "All right here," Brand said, scarcely heard above the angry barking of rifles.

"Except for Brand, my squad's under cover," Sergeant Tree responded.

"Anyone else hit?" I asked.

"None of mine," Sergeant Zigerfoose said.

"We're all right," Pop Miller sounded.

"Okay here," came from Sergeant Olsen.

"All okay?" I yelled. "We're going after them now. Who's leading point?"

"Brand's up moving, sir," Pop shouted with evident joy.

"Brand? Brand?" I yelled. "Hear me, Brand? Can you move us out?"

There was no answer.

"Brand, get us moving," I repeated, getting a little teed off, assuming from Brand's "All right here," and "Brand's up moving," he was only nicked.

Still no answer.

"What's the matter, Brand?" I shouted, crawling up on my belly past Pop Miller.

Doc Singleton, ignoring the warning to pull Brand by his feet to safety, worked quietly and efficiently, hunkered low as he could, had cut off Brand's fatigue jacket, working a bandage over a low, badly bleeding shoulder wound. Myles crawled up then to help Singleton drag Brand back behind cover and when the company medic scampered back for his aid kit, preoccupied with his job, he made the mistake of standing part way and a bullet went sh-u-u-umft! straight through his helmet, throwing it off its liner and through the air. Flopping from momentum down a steep slope, Doc's quivering body turned over twice in a rapidly decreasing motion, limp arms and legs flopping down a two-foot dropoff through the air like a ragdoll. Ski, near where he landed, went crazy, standing in full view, yelling his lungs out at the gooks, screaming for them to show themselves. It took three soldiers to get him down and hold him and two slid with him down the slippery trail to a slight hollow where bullets couldn't reach, where Pop sat on the gangly Pole and held him with one of the men, like talking to calm a frenzied horse; "C'mon, buddy, get hold of yourself. Calm down, Ski, or get killed. Steady, steady, boy. There, there take a deep breath.

We'll get them bastards, don't worry…. C'mon there, that's my buddy, take a deep breath."

Ski, not as bright as most guys, never tried to hide his feelings and although he calmed his body so Pop didn't have to worry any more, he started sobbing like a little kid, growing softer and softer until, as Pop scooted up the trail to the rest of his squad, he sat there staring with a little whimper. Ski felt things deeper.

The platoon cursed savagely reverberating pure hate throughout Love company, spreading from cover to cover, with the bad news that one of our Christ-like medics, sainted savior, chief of company medics, was gone. An enemy machine gunner became active and immediately the battle was rejoined. Doc Singleton had not had time to give Brand morphine and evidently the slug hit a bone, probably the collar bone for it was observed from a distance from Brand's face he was in great pain. After Doc's sudden death, we were too occupied with the enemy to check Brand and, indeed, most of us having witnessed Doc working on him assumed he was taken care of medically. No one got to Brand for an hour and when one did, Brand's blood was gone. One glance in his face could have warned me of shock. Damn sonofabitch anyway, where were you, Gould, when Brand died? Where was his God?

We were in the flurry and the din of furious battle, each sergeant thinking he led the attacking squad, platoon size though it grew. As for lead thrown through the air each way, it was greater and much more dangerous and dramatic than Crysler's Farm on the St Lawrence in a sleet storm on 10 November 1813 as American militia turned back the British 49th Foot; much less than an average assault on Vicksburg in our Civil War but greater than the battle of Santiago in the Spanish-American War which taffeta the Army proudly flaunts.

Dying was all around and with many fewer involved than at Crysler's Farm, engulfing us with lead and jagged steel, biggest battle in all American history. To us it was all we could withstand and no way to get it commemorated, even by the Queen of Battles herself. All our dead put down from National memory in black bags with no one or method to applaud their supreme sacrifice, or remember it even in that Forgotten War, not even their mothers gone today with them knew how their loved sons died, no one save a handful of old guys like me all alone at a typewriter trying to commemorate. God and a very few of us know how they were wasted. I don't suppose there are more than five of us in this world anymore even can talk firsthand about that battle for Hill 1243. Goodbye forever and ever Corporal Brand. Excuse me, I do not remember your first name. And Specialist E-5 Doc Singleton, your first name escapes me too for which I apologize. After all these forgotten lonely years, only the God of War remembers it, thrown away young warriors, brave as any who have been discarded, ever lived in whatever age, used up, unidentified. Like our buddy, Private Fisk of the Battle of Tippecanoe, eighty-one in 1851—

Everyone of Captain Harding's company is in heaven except Solomon Westbrook and me; all passed from the earth. There's nothing left of us old soldiers but memories, recollections so strange and unsharable.

Above the wamp wamp and woompt woompt of grenade and mortar explosions, the snappy individual bark of rifles, were my frantic calls of encouragement as I estimated and directed changing situations: "Over there; c'mon, you! … yes, YOU! … Sergeant Roundtree. *Tree,* don't look at me, look up! Watch it! Christ, watch it!

"... WATCH IT! WATCH IT, I SAID! ... Goddamn gook there! ... Can't you see him by the tree? ... Get the sonofabitch! SKI! ... WHERE ARE YOU, SKI? ... All right, watch that side over there! ... WAKE UP! ... WAKE UP! ... HERE THEY ARE AGAIN! ... UP AND AT 'EM ... Funaro, good boy, another Edsel Turner! ... YOU, YES YOU! GET SOME HEAVY FIRE IN THERE FAST cover that BAR! ... ON THE DOUBLE! ... NOW LET 'EM HAVE IT AGAIN! ... ATTA' BOY, KARL. LET 'EM HAVE IT! ... Rose, Lieutenant Rose, work your men through. That's the way! ... Hey, you. What's your name, boy? ... Well, put that guy behind rocks and get your ass back up ... We can't spare anyone ... He's hit in the arm? Call your platoon medic! He isn't going to die ... HEAR ME? I SAID STOP HIS BLEED-ING AND DROP THAT GUY AND GET BACK FIRING ... Catch up, WE'RE GOIN' OVER! ... Hey, *you*, get your BAR over here ... WATCH IT, MILLER! ... HEY, POP, WATCH IT! THERE'S TWO BEHIND THAT LITTLE PINE TREE ... NOW GET 'EM. GET 'EM BOTH ... THAT LITTLE ONE THERE! ... TOSS 'EM A GRENADE! ... GO AHEAD, GIVE 'EM ANOTHER."

And leading in all outbursts of E-e-e de-e wa-a and other desperate battle cries, were the sergeants and Red Rose and I yelling our lungs out. We drove the enemy before us so close we clearly heard the hollow-tube CHOOOMP of their mortar rounds leaving tubes from a ravine hidden to the north of us. We drove an advanced enemy back up to their permanent position. This, mixed with sharp, bark-ing rifles; metallic sounds, tinny peeee-w-w-wink! of empty M1 clips flying from the automatically-locked-back ready to be reloaded actions of rifles; the resounding metal-plate-clattering of empty burp gun ammo drums dropping on rocks; and the frantic jingle-jangle of war materiel hanging from cartridge belts or loose in fatigue pockets of men running through fire that blue-smoked morning.

"Aim low," came a calm but loud voice. "Keep your ass down and fire up and we'll have 'em on the run." Warren Milligan, baptized at the Abbey at Casino in Italy in 1945, Master Sergeant volunteer replacement from Division for Sergeant Eppler's spot.

When the brief commotion was over, King and Item closed and blended in be-hind us to help beat back a stiff gook counterattack. The enemy was stubborn, how-ever, fell back orderly across a saddle and dug in swiftly before the permanent instal-lations atop 1243, concentrating small arms fire, forcing Lieutenant Rose to slide back, abandoning three dead.

When the yelling subsided and all were under cover and silent again, in clear English came the order shouted from a gook bunker further up the hill for Red to "Throw it in! GI, quit now! Go way!" Red took it for a while and then responded, without realizing it, with Zachery Taylor's noble answer at the Mexican surrender ultimatum as the furious Battle of Buena Vista turned against the Fourth Infantry: "My wounded are behind me and I'll never pass them alive," except Red prefaced his with "fuck you, yellow bastards!" as old ZT might well have done with quaint profanities of his own times, prissy Ivy League historians notwithstanding.

Nearing the critical grenade line, guys in front bogged down under a sustained burst from an enemy machine gun which, with unappreciated flippancy, closed with braggadocio a short burst of 'shave and a hair cut, Bay Rum.' Horsing around like that was momentarily confusing. Plain gooks, of rice fields, weren't supposed to know that diverting jingle nor have a sense of humor, or maybe he knew only that it was a tune coming from an American gunner somewhere and thought it daring to reproduce.

Braving a rage of machine gun, mortar and burp gun fire, I tossed my head, motioning upward, making the ancient challenge of warrior leaders, a flourish to the sky with my carbine in lieu of a sword as active combat leaders do—me, chief brave leading braves, those wonderful warriors. C'mon, Indianheaders. Damn, not just brave, I was somebody worthy of any history, as far back as military history goes. They should compare me with Israel Putnam, Old Put, on Bunker Hill; with Uncle Art floundering in mud at the Argonne; or the hill at San Juan, Cuba taken not by bigmouth unmounted Teddy Roosevelt as newspaperman Hearst lied, but by hard riding, mounted black Buffalo Soldiers of the unsung Ninth and Tenth Cavalries. "Yipeee, give way, white boys!"

In my mind, as the looks of approval I got right and left assured me, I was some man among men. Dammit, guys, together we'll protect the faith and the Nation, womanhood, too, when we get our hands on them. I've never been so important and needed before or since. I was Mad Anthony Wayne at Fallen Timbers telling his guys they had his permission to pray for themselves and practice physic, and General Benjamin Harrison in his fancy top hat with the dyed green ostrich plume at Tippecanoe; Sam the Raven Houston at Horseshoe Bend, Alabama slaughtering Creeks; Ulysses Simpson Grant, the 'Little Beauty,' lieutenant of commissary of the Old Fourth Infantry at Churubusco, Mexico, where he observed: "Peons could be firing at you all day without you ever finding it out." Hell, I wouldn't be cheating if I told you that to my guys for a few minutes there that beautiful, successful day I was Audy Murphy, except not so pretty and a little taller. At least I had followed him in his three times through the portals of the 15th Infantry's medical collecting tent.

Tragic as war is to humanity as a whole, to we initiated into the warrior class it's the opportunity to savor deep thrills, proving our manhood over and over, if only to ourselves. In peaceful times warriors are unemployable except to train new soldiers to be warriors; while we who have gloried intentionally wait in vain for recognition and recall to colors. Being long neglected in peace, we disappear inside to pin fading colored ribbons on the walls of our fast disappearing memories of that great turmoil long ago.

Those who have been men above men at war, in peace recall in the long silence brought about by our useless early attempts to relate or explain, locked up tremendous secret thrills of accomplishment; remembering well panting, hard-run dogs atop objectives, kings of mountains, raw thrill of achieving physical victory, rapid flush of pride hearing the division commander radio: "Damn good job, lieutenant!" Would that we could hold all that praise to the ears of our friends like a seashell, in our hearts forever, to be applauded by noncombatants if only briefly, silently by mere know-all looks as from a band of fellow combatants, reward of rewards for a man once so admired among men, a swelling lifelong pride. It's a great personal treasure you cannot spend nor even give away; no, nor explain to others as your hair turns gray and then white and you fade away back into a war as forgotten as that hellacious day at Tippecanoe..

There is much pretense in civilian life, concerning the manifestated core of the worth of a man. In the very opposite of civil life, violent infantry combat, sharing great life-and-death crises close together, failures are starkly revealed, the very, very few, as are the common great unsung virtues of the men. Heroes of ages joined by the particular fears they lived a while that can never be conveyed to noncombatants; even to those drawn to violent athletics. But forever high on the plus side, I tell you, there's no more thrilling, soul-fulfilling game for true warriors than putting your life up for grabs, lunging forward sweating, upward; primal gut-wrenching, lung-aching, raw-throated, body-tingling scion of ageless warriors, conquering fierce enemy, and Fear and Death themselves; assaulting, screaming savage battle cries, rifles and hot carbines blazing, feeling the air about you full of freshly liberated souls—to work and possibly die among men you're so damn proud of.

> *The neighing troops, the flashing blade,*
> *The bugle's stirring blast.*
> *The charge, the dreadful cannonade,*
> *The din and shout are past. . . .*
>
> *On Fame's eternal camping ground*
> *Their silent tents are spread*
> *And glory guards with solemn round*
> *The bivouac of the dead.*

– Lieutenant Theodore O'Hara. Written at Monterey, Mexico after the battle, mourning a bloody stack of fellow Kentuckians.

As I turned to cheer on my men, several coordinated burp guns opened up from a hitherto unknown suicide emplacement down the hill from the large bunkers on the very crest of 1243. Out of the corner of my eye, behind me, I watched horrified as Tree, forward of his squad, slumped to the ground, then stood halfway unsteadily and began to fall the second time, pawing air with his right arm for support. Eppler, M1 in one hand by the small of the stock, turned back to grab at that arm to ease his fall but missed and while falling hard this time, Tree's face drained of blood turning ashen gray-brown, his constant hateful symbol of comparison, color, nearly gone; that token black we in Love learned to respect and, yes, love in a masculine way.

"God! God! What a sight. No, God, NO!"

Those who watched the swift drama stopped, shook and shocked, their faces pallid too, stricken with abject disgust, hate and remorse.

"My God," someone said. "Look how white Tree is."

There went our buddy, self-proclaimed 'token nigger' who sang and hummed us to sleep, lying face up, smiling as usual—like he always did and dead often do.

I stumbled forward, completely out of myself, upward in blind fury standing tall, screaming: "Bastards! ... sonsofbitches!" and choked out uncontrolled ineffective words. There suddenly weren't any in infantry jargon strong enough to fit the occasion and from my throat came meaningless animal growling sounds and aggressive curses used in mortal anger since caveman days. Moving ahead and upward, waving my carbine, temporarily out of ammo and my mind as blank, I yelled: "Get 'em! Ee-dee-waa, yellow cunts!"

At the bitter end it was always yellow cunts! Never evil North Korean soldiers, or dirty enemy, but something down below in a woman every man who is a man cherishes and vies for in perpetual heat. Why? Why not yell: "Lousy shot!" or "Murderer, you"? Why at the hottest point did we always call those we would kill cunts? Don't tell us we were simply sex-crazed. Women were furthest from our thoughts.

Heavy Weapons let loose behind us with a steady tirade of water-cooled machine guns, recoilless rifles and salvoes of 81mm mortars as I swung around waving my empty carbine over my head with one hand.

"Get it over with! Get over it! Kill the bastards! You can't live forever! ... Let's go! Let's go! They got Tree! Blow 'em up! Bayonets! "

We crawled and ran stumbling up the last steep grade through soft artillery churned soil, every man yelling like a banshee, welded into a mobile foray of fury, forlorn hope of screaming madmen running enemy off with the shear blast of voices, Jericho trumpets of our own, inspired to commit suicide over the death of an outstanding buddy; assaulting with the spirit, crying for vengeance of the brave heroes of all wars; Continentals and militia whose bones are long forgotten dust, storming British redoubt in mad furry with bayonets only. We followed in their heroic steps, unknown compared to such illustrious names there at Yorktown as Alexander Hamilton and the Marquis de Lafayette to glorify the assault and register in the mind of the new Republic. No never we of the Forgotten War.

An historical comparison: one Russian burp gun burst we faced would blow the fancy hats off Hamilton and his whole concentrated New York militia battalion.

Dudley C Gould? Clarence K Eppler? Pop Miller? Who they? Nobodies but to each other; everything locally for a day or two; combat buddies, next to the marriage of men and women life's tightest bond. We're simply us, us guys who did the Nation's dirtiest job, never to be immortalized in history books. Had we not sacrificed there as soldiers of yore, we would have been immortalized in the negative, for, marching over Korea, the Communists would have taken Japan in a year or two and Africa, and, strengthened, taken West Germany to seal our economic fate for all time, included us in their dictatorship. Taking advantage of the widespread political rot, the fashionable demoralization takes place among the majority of Americans today who don't even know how to salute the flag, much less rise to defend it, whose children burn it in contempt, who so easily forgot the Korean War because they never wanted to know.

Hell, man, neither we nor our dead were known outside battalion to those who served behind us; actions not even mentioned after a single day anywhere but to fill space in the Far East edition of *Stars & Stripes*. Our heroics were so expected they were usually unknown even to regiment except unique tragedies traveling on the grapevine. We struggled and died anonymously, unsung, unknown to all but our immediate buddies, only our true, transient brothers in blood knew and applauded our efforts, respected and loved us the manly way.

King moved into our immediate rear and warriors of both companies within earshot stopped briefly, stared disbelievingly as they passed Tree's tumbled body where, after a glance, in an electrifying second, they took up our angry cries, "Get 'em! Get 'em! Kill the cocksuckers!" "Them bastards got Tree!" Sergeant E-5 Tree, known to every man and officer in the battalion just for being black. In those days he was, indeed, our token black, humorously declared by himself in mock slave jargon, "Yeah, man, I'se yo' token nigger."

"You heard the lieutenant!" Sergeant Burris yelled. "They got Tree. Let's go!"

If one cares to dig for the truth about the likes of our 'token' blues singer, our proud, stand-alone Negro, he can be seen at every battle everywhere in America's military history. He was first brought to America in chains on a Dutch slaver to Virginia in 1619, torn cruelly from his loving home and family in West Africa, foisted on the Jamestown English by threatening to throw him overboard if not paid for and he became slave Peter Salem on Bunker Hill, so deadly a natural marksman loaded muskets were handed up to him by trained white militiamen and he killed among others Major John Pitcairn, leader of the British Marines. Colonel Christopher Greene, a cousin of Nathaniel, led a whole regiment of blacks, Rhode Island's First Infantry Regiment of Foot in '79, half freed, half slaves who volunteered to die for two freedoms, their's from slavery and from the British if they survived, along with whites promised a $50 Congressional bonus should they survive, which was never paid.

The black 54th Infantry, Massachusetts Volunteer Guard, was led to their and his deaths in the Civil War by a proud ancestor of mine, Colonel Robert Gould Shaw. Thousands of black soldiers lie in military graves unsung in all our wars, many after desperate acts of bravery, many led poorly by white officers down-graded to the job and written down thereafter.

It will sound corny to readers sitting in easy chairs at home unaware of any strife in Korea and there's no direct correlation physically and certainly Tree would never have let himself be so obviously abused, but he was unavoidably blackened in every sense of the word, *denigrated* every day he lived among whites, accidentally by the very skin color of him and I can't help but apply Kipling's sad lament to Love's own Gunga Din—

> *So we'll meet him later on*
> *at the place where 'e is gone —*
> *where it's always double drill and*
> *no canteen.*

> *Though we've pelted you and flayed you*
> *by the livin' God that made you*
> *you're a better man than we*
> *Raymond Tree.*

Yes, my valiant buddy, through ages whites have flayed you—'token nigger,' now be pleased to rest forever with all our buddies of one color, brave, in peace forever.

> *Yet not to thine eternal resting place*
> *Shalt thou retire alone, nor couldst thou wish*
> *Couch more magnificent. Thou shalt lie down*
> *With patriarchs of the infant world—with kings,*
> *The powerful of the earth—the wise, the good,*
> *Fair forms and hoary seers of ages past.*
> – William Cullan Bryant.

The word 'soul,' given lip service only for two millennia by Christian whites, one day came alive to become uniquely Negro, describing objects and ideas Negroes love and respect. I'm very prejudiced and will always associate soul with Raymond Roundtree, an outstanding sergeant in my platoon and company. The morning of this combat infantryman's dying, his ascension was way above the battle we fought on the mountain of magpies and I thought hard as I could to praise Tree, my mother and Jesus Rodriguez and Ich and Dorn and our token Canuck, Smitty, and assail the very brevity of life; shaky, poorly lighted span of anything that lives, and what time is hereafter which to us living is always thereafter? My living soul and Tree's freed, must they be punished so severely before we go? Is our life all purgatory? And why us lined up to be slaughtered in far off Korea rather than phoney preachers, long-lived criminals, cowardly, dishonest pork barreling politicians and all the increasingly immoral, dishonest people of the United States? Is it just to mock us to die for them? Why must plain dogfaces, nobodies, be cast out of our country by absentee draft lotteries to die, why must we, most innocent, bleed the way of Jesus in scorn, while fat, selfish slackers be eased whole into caskets after a full, selfish life, lied about in lavish funerals?

"Dear Heavenly Father...." I began. No, not cut-and-dried like that and not without an introduction and explanation—

> The revelations of devout and learn'd
> Who rose before us, and as prophets burn'd
> Are all but stories, which, awoke from sleep;
> They told their comrades, and to sleep return'd.
> – Omar Khayyam.

I tried and tried harder to think what socially I wanted to believe and it was the most difficult thinking I'd ever tried, but though it was done on a high mountainside under great stress like with Moses, but it was not enough and tired questions kept slipping back into my worried, barren mind to sidetrack me. I could not force myself to embrace a revealed, organized religion as long as it makes man central, as for many years Christian leaders have made our insignificant earth, that grain of sand in a vast Sahara, central to the universe. They lied that everything circled around us, we of such import as a damp plop of mosquito shit.

Surmounting 1243, I yelled myself hoarse. This was my most successful assault, I, with the largest number of guys up with us, attributable greatly to revenging Tree. Usually only a handful go all the way over the grenade line—the critical moment that spells success or failure. The number swells as soon as intermediate bugouts see you've taken the hill. They want to be seen with heroes and you got to have them for a quick defense,.

We smashed across the grenade line and stumbled on and took the summit about 1430 in the afternoon and beat back the first counterassault half an hour later, eight or ten suicidal enemy emptying burp gun drums, running up as close as they could to die. We dug holes to protect our bodies until our strength was gone and laid on our arms for hours as we answered radio queries from the rear. By 1700 we could no longer transmit to battalion over our dying batteries, although sitting in the setting sun worrying we continued to faintly receive and made out a weak, wavering voice. Surrealistic over the air—

Buzzard Seven? Buzzard seven? ... Buzzard Five? Buzzard Six? Anyone up there? Report your situation ... This is the Buzzard One, Buzzard One ... Buzzard Seven? Buzzard Seven?

My second known-for-sure victim, came suddenly in front of me in the second counter attack against 1243 just at dusk, balanced on the outside of his right foot suddenly about twenty feet away, right shoulder and arm stretching his body back to throw a grenade at me, an easy target. I squeezed my carbine trigger in two short bursts. His grenade dropped and blew up two or three feet behind him.

As we crested, five or six badly scared gooks ran silently, unburdened, through tree stumps down the saddle path leading north from 1243. All ten or fifteen of us out or almost out of ammo were too pooped to bother the runaways, good targets though they were. Sand gritting my teeth, sweat from my scalp smarting my eyes, and my throat and mouth were parched by hot, rasping breath. I yelled, "We made it. Sonofabitch, made it!"

Soon Pop Miller came over to my portable company command post with a proud look as he urged along four bloody prisoners. "Al's got more," he told me.

The wet, spongy ground at the top was barren of debris of battle comparable to 1181—empty cloth bandoliers, a bullet-punctured helmet, empty burp gun drums, clumsily soldered cans of grenade fuzes and sacks of gunpowder with which to assemble their frag grenades on location, empty cardboard mortar tubes of 60mm rounds captured from ROKs, pieces of personal equipment, and bloody cloth dropped by a wounded. A rifleman stooped to recover a meaningful item beside a square yard of blood-soaked earth.

"Ain't this Pete's old harmonica?"

It sure was, his name scratched on it. Pete Simpson of King, who entertained us some evenings with a buddy playing a banjo before a movie, dropped MIA, taken off with a capture team several weeks back from an ambushed night patrol.

Everywhere, always after every battle, debris scattered in the ruins from pilfered pockets of looted enemy. Whoever so much as touched a downed buddy could expect a beating by more than one of his friends including even Philip Funaro, the double

banzaier. In trampled mud—a small, gay Japanese doll good luck charm, brought from R&R, a jackknife with a broken plastic handle, an unexplained blood-splattered legionnaire roll, and a yo-yo, all taken from Americans. One of Pop Miller's men picked up a rain-soaked booklet of instructions in English on how to take successful pictures with a German camera. Having tried to thumb apart the wet pages, he flung it into the bushes.

There was little enemy loot, nothing personal. Two or three large canvas bags of frag grenade hulks with leather carrying straps, rolls of gook Army-issue tobacco leaves, and twenty or thirty white cloth bags of Communist Army issue unroasted peanuts. Why they hadn't assembled the grenades we'll never know, unless they were newly arrived. One guy recovered a US Army-issue forty-five caliber pistol.

Dropped here and there in that litter, twisted bodies of gooks killed mostly by artillery.

While the chogee train which slaved for our battalion took a break, the shivering, wrinkled old carriers scrambled about to salvage what they could from the wreckage. One papasan slipped, with guilty glances about him, into the blood-stained fatigue jacket a medic had peeled from a man, and tied to his crude rope belt a cloth toilet kit someone had foolishly brought along. The old gentlemen pawed eagerly for rare scraps of rations and poked through broken litters, empty machine gun ammo metal boxes, spent assault wire reels, and other junk of battle.

As soon as new batteries reached us, Buzzard One wanted our casualty report. In addition to one MIA, I was surprised to learn we had only four killed aside from Corporal Brand, Doc Singleton, and Sergeant Roundtree and nine wounded, three seriously, already well on their happy ride down, one, unconscious from an ominous head wound. Being gone, we seldom understood how MIAs were missing, although in those wild mountain ways there were plenty of half-hidden gorges and precarious dropoffs.

A young King Company Korean interpreter interrogated the prisoners in an intimate circle squatting on their haunches safe from gook fire behind a rock formation. Shaggy conqueror Sergeant Eppler stood over them. One, obviously an officer, was the most disappointed man I'd ever seen. Noticing the silver bar on my collar, he faced me, straightened smartly to attention, slapped his moldy tennis shoes together, bowed low from the waist, and then proceeded with surprising candor to tell me in good English his "American foe" were pretty good fighters, but their firing didn't scare his men half as much as the sudden yelling at the very end. Using third person, he gave no inkling he was describing us directly in case it was taken wrong.

"Americans, you had? ... has? ... cigarette?" he asked, searching for the correct tense, at the same time making a motion of pulling a cigarette from his mouth and coolly blowing smoke into the interpreter's face.

The interpreter scolded the captive's boldness and as the POW grinned broadly in turn, I lit him up.

"Hey, Kim," I said, "Ask this cocky guy how come they never wear officer insignia?"

Side-stepping a direct answer in English, the honcho jabbered back and forth with our interpreter for five minutes before an answer was produced.

"He say North Korean People's Army real democratic and he say...."

"Shit," Eppler scolded the King Company Korean interpreter, "tell him he's full of shit."

"No shit!" the POW spoke up defensively.

"Yeah," came from someone in back of us, "if bullshit was music, he'd be a brass band."

Enemy bunkers, the usual suicide apertures facing south, were of no use to us and we had to hurriedly dig foxholes facing the threat from the north side of the pinnacle. First, we took care to hunt down booby traps, duds and all-wood, shoebox mines. Many a soldier was maimed or killed by merely touching a dud or jostling it with his toe. Dud is, of course, a word I'm sensitive to. What usually causes a dud is an activated firing pin released to strike a primer to set off a charge hanging in its shaft part way to the primer, with its spring energy held back. The pin is bound or caught or hung up, to one degree or another, to one side of the shaft in which it rides and may take only a slight jar to dislodge it to complete its strike, stepping heavily on the ground beside it, picking it up.

A special, impressed carrying party approached us late in the afternoon from down the trail, pale-face, pussy-footing men of the Second Division Band and sundry regimental headquarters personnel under a Graves Registration master sergeant, with twenty unhappy Korean civilians and their recently emptied A frames and litters ready for hauling down wounded and dead, had they litters enough. Clearly the brass counted on many more casualties.

"We've been waiting back down the trail since yesterday afternoon to see how it went up here," the bandmaster admitted.

I warned him about becoming their own casualties and demonstrated to his musicians how to creep bent over. I asked him if he remembered playing for us back in mid-July. No, he heard of it but most of the band, having come over with the Division, had rotated.

"I know it wasn't your idea to haul all them instruments up that ass-breaker. Lucky to leave before your welcome committee arrived."

"I know, lieutenant, we heard about it. Sorry if we caused trouble, but like you say, it sure wasn't our idea."

"Had to be at least a general, right?"

"They took a lot of pictures up there; made newsreels in the States. Folks back home must have thought we had the war knocked."

"That's the idea."

I found myself thinking that since Brand and Funaro were in the same squad, why couldn't it have been Funaro, immediately apologizing to the delinquent Italian-American street boy. Shit, it's fate that's all, and Funaro's got every right to live. He's better than any ass-kissing rear echelon. He's no prize, but he's earned his right just by surviving this far and is part of a fire team, riflemen and BAR, whether always up with us or not. He's one of our banzai gang for sure.

Light of a slowly setting sun spread over the badly-maimed trees below as I scurried along the perimeter of 1243, checking the guys of Love Company, encouraging them, pulling them as tightly together as I dared, covering the contested ground mindful of the age-old threat of infantrymen: "One round will get you all." Early fall chill was everywhere, arriving with gray darkness. Digging like woodchucks turning over freshly plowed dirt, some brought white phosphorous to air that caught fire again and, burning quietly, stunk like skunks.

I wished Uncle Art was alive; I'd tell him, "Move over, old buddy. We can talk about it now. I've been through your Argonne, minus mustard gas. I know now why mother insisted you could never tell me painlessly. I couldn't really listen. Now we're real buddies and don't have to talk. We've been through it."

The band carriers and the regular bearers gone, while settling down for the night, a heavy fire opened on us. We dove for cover and I bellied behind a large rock waiting to hear what would transpire. Burp gun racket would mean they were attacking in force but there was no small arm fire and as the second terrible air-rush-screech came in, we realized it was coming from the south where our friends were, so-called 'friendly fire'; on the wrong elevation, one wrong digit, failed to understand his forward observer, or trouble reading elevation on his own map, a simple, mistake at Fire Direction Center way down the valley behind us. We could never call our own artillery but it had to go through several stages and then we had no control over it and they could not be corrected until radioed back by their own forward observer, wherever he was. A dastardly crime never atoned by the observer who called for it across the valley with the Marines, or the guilty air control man who misjudged elevations. Fear in me equaled the night in May playing dead in that impact area, except that few of my guys were in a protecting declivity. This artillery, long tom 155's, I learned much later as I was writing my journal, was intended to sail high above us on its way to support the Marines attacking from Death Valley.

I knew that *amicide*, killed by friends, as Cain and Able, Caesar by Brutus et al, was older than artillery. Somehow bad things would always happen to us unless targets could be on a line of sight to him who pulls the lanyard. Among its victims in WWII was Major General Lesley J McNair on the front inland from Normandy when marker smoke dropped as a forward line of advance from Air Force Pathfinders was blown behind friendly troops, and in every war, as early as 1672, when General Jean Martinet, the rigid disciplinarian of Louis XIV, was killed by a short cannon round, although in his case it might not have been an accident.

While most rounds pass on over, some, notably proximity fuses set to explode so many feet from an object as determined by returning radar waves, will sometimes prove to be shorter than they should be, and at times difficult for gunners dependent on their maps and the accuracy of forward observers to calculate the correct clearance of their shells passing over terrain features such as a newly conquered mountain top. Our tactical maps were hurried US Army Engineer copies of old Japanese civilian maps of Korea, sometimes with faulty or no elevation markers.

"Third squad! Pop! Hey, Pop Miller," I heard Sergeant Eppler yell. "You guys all right?"

"Okay over here!" Pop replied.

There was still confusion as to whose fire it was and I shouted, "Brown? Keep the machine gun where you can get it out from under. That goes for all three platoons."

Those around me on the enemy side of 1243, down from the ridgeline digging a defense were untouched.

"Short of us, sir; on friendly side."

"Ziggy? Speedy? … You guys all right?"

"Okay," Ziggy yelled and Gonzales's affirmative was relayed up to me. Suddenly it was landing behind us again, on the friendly side, a short TOT, time on target, barrage of angry salvoes. One minute they were living, upright, warmed by their blood, talking animals, human beings, shouting warnings and encouragements, closely bonded to face any danger, a second later human parts strewn about the ridgetop were torn, unrecognizable broken, bloody remnants of fury as salvo after salvo, screeching 155 shells from one of our own artillery battalions, no longer angel kisses but flying packages of magma. My forward portion of the crest was spared and as soon as the rounds stopped crashing in, giving a five-minute safety wait as was customary, I ran up and over the crest to where many of my Banzai Third platoon used to be.

As I neared, a private volunteered matter-of-factly, "Mostly dead, sir."

"Doc!" I shouted, "where are you? Pop?"

"Sergeant Miller's over here!" a voice croaked and I found my old buddy, old timer, fellow WWII vet, like me, fellow dogface, lightweight, pale, sickish, bloodless yellow face of him, suddenly transformed by raging pieces of jagged hot steel into a terribly hurt, broken up, prone, blood-covered man doll. When you're a real live human and hit as hard as Pop was, you don't think of heroic gestures; if able, you make a weak supplicant gesture toward your punctured chest pumping cherry-red spurts soaking your fatigues and the blood-soaked glimpses of an exposed shiny white shattered bone, the shredded stump of an arm. Fast as blood flows you quickly lose all hold of yourself, all contact with dying parts. Say goodbye to yourself, search your personal history fast as you can, if you can, and goodbye to everything living.

In writing this, I could discover only one sergeant who claims to have survived that disaster and it is not strange that I do not recall him; I have talked to some who though we have proof we served together do not remember me. This is normal I've discovered, as the most engaged in combat have to forget or learn to sleep less at night.

Exactly when my buddy Pop Miller left us I do not know, I only know I ended up holding him.

"Medic! Medic! Hurry," I yelled as I slid off my sweater, wadded it up, pulled Pop onto my lap and pressed it into the unbandaged chest puncture that was sucking air, hoping to slow some of the bleeding long enough to clot. Pop's face was yellowish-green, his eyes closed and he was limp as Ich when I tried to revive him.

"Doc! Damn you! Doc! Singleton, Singleton! Hurry!"

"Doc?" a voice demanded. "Dead, remember? Gone. Doc's gone, remember?"

"Get an aid kit, hurry!"

"Lieutenant Rose got hit trying to fix one of his men and his medic's using it."

The awful short time it took Pop to die, most probably instantly, the terribly short while anything could have been of help, drowning in so much blood as I held him in my arms, keeping his head up by his hair, pushing in on the chest puncture, trying to stop the still pump from leaking, assuring him all the while that he was doing well, when I knew it was over. "Okay, old buddy, don't worry." I knew he was gone but I so wanted him to stay alive. I could do no more than push in over his chest wound, that had been, I thought, pumping erratically or convulsing, pulling in bloody air from outside his chest straight into his lungs in spasms, only seconds, eventually drowning in blood. And his half-severed arm? Oh God, fix it, someone hurry. Put it back together.

"Someone help! Get bandages, hurry! A tourniquet! … Stop bleeding! My God, he's all blood, bleeding everywhere." His blood was all gone but I thought still bleeding; some chance of saving him if only I tried hard enough.

The hysterical pleading of a nearby rifleman, "I'm hit? Doc! Please, Doc! Running down my leg."

"Blood? That's piss!"

Pop and I were together on our own and as his blood drained killing him on my lap or maybe before, vomit from a short C ration supper and bitter bile rose in my throat. I was beyond short-winded; suffocating from stomach bitterness, my throat burning from acid, searing stomach acid sucking cold air. My chest pained as it sagged on my aching lungs and expanded slowly, painfully as well. It seemed I breathed a weak eighth inch in, eighth inch out, spitting stringy, sticky, bitter slime from my mouth, gagging, choking on bitter bile and coughing, rasping desperately for air. I could drown in my own puke with no air in me, as I was just sitting there, Pop on my lap, giving me his blood.

Time, still in death, passed Pop and me and it grew very dark so we could barely see. I remember dimly two men from Item Company, I believe, one an officer, bending down taking Pop off me, their hands slippery with his blood—God, he's bled gallons— and I watched him slip out of their grasp crossing the large, smooth rock ledge formation we were lying on, to lay his bloodless body on a litter soon painted red. Without sense of time or where I was, I lost normal feelings and reactions and entered a world wherein myself was referred to as 'him' and only occasionally. I could never recall exactly when Pop's heart and breathing stopped in those seconds that were one. When my breathing returned to a livable rhythm and depth and I rose from where I had been with Pop, a small coagulating pool of his blood ran slowly off my lap down the outside of my pant leg, disappearing in the porous cloth of my fatigues. I remembered scolding as we would kid each other, "Old fart. Yes, you, Pop, you know me and you are too damn old for this sort of thing. Let's get to the rear before something bad happens."

One man, a medic or an officer, wanted to know what I was saying, talking patiently to me as with a drunk, finally seizing my chin in one hand, raising my head back, forcing me to swallow from his canteen and I coughed up more bitter bile to my mouth and spit it out with sticky stuff.

My waist, right side of my fatigues and right sleeve were soaked, black, where blood dried, making my fatigues stiff, my hands sticky while tears flowed like rain of salt water down my cheeks for the terrible thing I was part of, holding that poor butchered animal, old buddy Pop.

"How about that lieutenant?" a distant voice asked as another man stood towering over me. "Must be hurt bad. Look at the blood."

"I checked; someone else's."

"Someone else's blood; again, someone else's blood; someone else's blood," I repeated over and over. "Someone else's blood. You had your chance to bleed, now Pop's made up for us both."

We were in that slaughterhouse, that red abattoir, forever before Item Company finished passing through, relieving what was left to Love. Firing, some far away it seemed, and unimportant, as Item beat back a small probing counterattack. Still later that night, a strange language was talking about me as the Dutch, back from Pusan with green replacements, climbed from the Pia-ri Valley to relieve Item up the ridge from 1100, passing me by, all staring at someone else's blood drying black on me.

During a long, moonless, starless night, the remnants of Love were withdrawn carefully back down the ridge, ushering me tied by commo wire around the waist of a soldier of Item down to the broad valley from where we started two months, or was it a year or so ago? Aside from dozens of litter cases were forty stumbling wounded, including a very rattled me with what I thought was a broken arm, in single file, eight to be triaged hopeless, mute, riding before us, solid lumps of bloody Army fatigues tied to litters.

I sat more forlorn than I've ever been under the perpetual scream of a bad dream in an old beat-up cane bottom chair by the entrance to the Dutch aid station, unnoticed in the general low-toned medical urgency and bustle, favoring my arm carefully, watching a grim parade of ambulatory passing with bowed heads and litter-borne and unwounded in shock, heads bowed, shuffling zombies—quiet and grim.

A medic, doctor or aid man, I was unable to differentiate, asked me routinely, "How're you, lieutenant? Hit? Hurt? Where's your tag?"

"Hurt, not hit," pointing to my unmoveable right arm.

It seemed he knew me or of me and then one of our men gave a Dutch medic my first and last name and helped him write me a tag, for what I couldn't decipher, and I remember trying to be normal, joking that even doctors' assistants wrote so they couldn't be read. "Broken or fractured arm." I thought it should read. A Dutch chaplain came by, a Catholic. Our eyes met briefly and he looked away quickly and passed me quietly in search of needy believers.

From there for many months, or years—time lost to me—my life was weak; its sick residue badly out of tune, or, you might say, discombobulated, if you know what I mean. Months or maybe even years, or could have been just many hours, was a big blank in which I shot the breeze with Dorn and Tree and Bill Hanson and now with Pop, and less with J C Rodriguez who, you recall, was a quiet guy, and, yes, especially that heroic, cocky, little commo guy, with the wire reel forever on his back, Sergeant Miller's young assistant wireman—"you and asshole divvy up my Medal of Honor"— whose terrible dying ended convulsing with an inside bleeding, fast-growing goiter, which memory hurts so I try consciously never to remember and try to skip right by that painful part of my sorry life without thought, blank when I try hard to recall, come unexpectedly in nightmares at times well organized by a mysterious self that dwells inside just to blame me. "I've done my best, dammit, I've tried. I didn't kill them, now for the last time, get out of my head!"

The medic, doctor or aidman, whomever, went by me before I could tell him how I felt. When he came back I could say things and told him my arm was broken. He picked it up and moved it about carefully and said, I think he said, he'd seen such cases, not to worry, it's mental . . . will heal itself. What is mental, a broken arm is mental?

I was in the center of deathly concern for hours or maybe nights and as morning, or even days or an afternoon, as an old horned war devil chased me around and around mountain tops and tripped me and broke my right arm and sat on me so I couldn't escape. His awful stinking self like shit, is again waiting by me, I sense less patiently, another cannon sounded somehow, perhaps with off-center sights, a big mortar with unmatched bubbles. Shit! Understand? Plain shit. Fred said it—shit. In fact, the stink I smelled came from me—shit my pants and sat in it.

My dead lay on that cold Kach'il-Bong, Mountain of the Magpies, all night and I was still at the Dutch forward aid station with other ambulatory waiting my turn when early in the morning they brought down the rest of the cold bodies. How carelessly Dutch mortician helpers loaded them as I'd seen done so many times; two men swinging each rigid body by head and feet alternating slabs of wood, skin-covered meat, onto the hard bed of a truck, one man climbing inside to pull the bodies forward. Like we disposed of those courageous young gooks who penetrated our line, flying them back down the steep hill.

"Where's their bags?" I yelled at a sergeant. "Don't throw them away. They don't breathe doesn't mean they're nothing."

"No say English," the Dutchman apologized.

Together in death they stiffened, Pop's right hand, the good one, pointed skyward in the pile over Ski's tattered bloody knee. Ski's blood-caked head flopped back over someone's torn boot, and Ski, who out of combat wouldn't hurt a flea, glared, eyes frozen wide open in terror to the pitiless sky at what they did to him. At last lost soul, you've found a home equal to any—no more orphan place—as intelligent and worldly-wise as any piled above or below you. You have truly arrived at the common goal, equal to any man.

Forever out of combat, the last day for so many wonderful guys who loved life but were killed in Love in return. And Sergeant Ray Martin, old dogface First Sergent now and forever, didn't have to be there that late afternoon. Stand your last retreat, real pro, Old Glory salutes and weeps for you; joking as usual how you came along because someone had to show us how to do it right, a violent battle curse set forever on your lips. And Funaro, too, poor useless misfit, most reluctant soldier ever denied signing RA. Back in South Bronx they used to say he'd succumb to a zip gun the way he was headed, but already belonging to a dangerous street corner, we killed him legally in our large-scale gang war?

"Good guys, oh so good guys, all so good guys," I sobbed inside. "I'm so awfully, awfully sorry, so tired of dying and being sorry."

I'd been losing energy, mental and otherwise since 1179 and sitting there in the sad sunrise of that day, so terribly alone, so deeply hurt and depleted, stinking in my shit, consciously, unconsciously, subconsciously guilty. You're right, Fred, shit is all over. Jesus H Christ! Guilty! Hear? Guilty. Put me down for all of it. Then slowly, with no one proposing it or realizing what I did, my fingertips went together on my tired, cracked lips, ready for a Buddhist or a Christian prayer? And for the first time since mother left me in 1925, I was uncritical enough to finish—

and if I die before I wake, I pray
the Lord my soul to take.

After a long pause with no answer, slouched to earth again, I guessed I really wasn't Christian. After all, everyone around me, but for a few Jews, everywhere I went in the Army was Christian, all trained to *talk* correct Christian and bow heads on cue. I tried again: "Dear God, bless mommy's soul and bless Uncle Art and Jimmy Lynch and Gordon Barr and Pop, and Ski who has never sinned, and God bless me, their boss, and J J and Tree—all us nobodies not wanted around anymore." Crimus to Crimus, I'm falling to pieces right here. I rubbed my blood-caked beard, sighing hopelessly: "Shit, what's happened to our Banzai Third and everybody?

11

THE CASUALTY

*"The Lord watch between thee and me,
when we are absent one from another."*
– Genesis: 31:49.

My mind returned reluctantly to that night of many deaths so long ago and I was visited by all my dead, beginning with Sergeant Dorn and his squad, standing around me patiently, helmets in hand like a weary football team while a downed lineman is tended to, in some kind of hospital or morgue, dead or barely alive, in rough burlap sand bag hospital gowns, as though risen from and full of the ground where they used to hide where now they must forever remain. "All my brave men I salute," I told them, "crawl forever from your demeaning holes and ride you, lend faces to the sun in America my country is of thee, where it's always shining to which you will never return; your labor, your sorrow and deaths are done. You strained under lethal loads in the warrior year, nineteen fifty-one; fought hard, groaned at death and contained your fears. Lost buddies to whom we never had time to say goodbye now it's done. It's all over. It was "Chuck, nail that bastard over there" and then they got you and you went down never saying good bye. Go heroes tell each other good bye buddy, at last we're free but America will never more see. Good bye buddies, shake hands and resume your silent way."

Man rises to the sun, and to the planets of the night. He touches the remotest pole, and in the center weeps, that he should labor and sorrow, and learn and forget, and return to the dark valley whence he came, and begin his labor anew. In pain he sighs, in pain he labors in his universe. And in the cries of birth and in the groans of death his voice is heard throughout the universe wherever a grass grows or a leaf buds, the eternal man is seen, is heard, is felt and all his sorrows, 'till he reassumes his ancient bliss.

– William Blake, Four Vallas.

I awoke clawing my way out of a sticky cocoon on a cot in the familiar mental hygiene tent ward of the 11th Evacuation Hospital feeling I should be angry at some one or some thing, yet anger was a debilitating luxury; instead, I collapsed on the floor at the foot of my cot and cried again that our own artillery killed us. I sobbed and shook uncontrollably and tried to get it all out of me. Yes, I was hurt enough to die but instead I cried, reaching for my death. When I most needed a philosophy, a belief instead of a doubt, it wasn't there, no pity or promise in Agnosticism, nothing soft, mysterious or at all comforting; nowhere to go just when you're all ready. It's easy to live an Agnostic if you're hard, so lonely and hard, to die alone, for fellow Agnostics, unproclaimed, are never there when you need them.

There at the 11th Evac they convinced me my arm wasn't hurt, a trick of my mind to force the rest of me out of danger. There's a name for it. I was, all of me, a lost one, off by myself again and found me cleaned of my shit, talking to the same warrant officer case worker that prepared me for R&R; another hot shower, clean fatigues, shave, haircut and warm spicy food, plus another shot of pentothal. There, them, we, maybe just me, planned revenge, threatening to press manslaughter, court-martial charges. But first off, there was no recognizable guilty ones. Early on it would have been 'my friend' Walter Winchell, but just who, asked the warrant officer, could I finger? Who's to blame, give me a name, 'They,' whomever those guys might be. He suggested I let it pass as officialdom does, a horrible accident. Nothing could or would be done at my level anyway, for I was a soldier, bound over without rights of citizens, who could I complain to, some rear-echelon sonofabitch colonel who'd white-wash?

I thought a lot—too much—and stretched and yawned and sucked on one weed after another, slept early and up late, accepting the peaceful promises of the day, but days brought no mitigation to my wicked night dreams. Eyes red-rimmed and watery, I arose unwillingly, stooped over to lace my muddy old combat boots and found soft hospital slippers instead and straightened up only part way to face another ordeal called day and they kept me in the 11th Evac as though they owned me for days it seemed, against my understanding.

Why, for Christ sake ... what's happening now? They put me under, again with my permission, to see what they could find and if they ever found anything I was never told. Sleep was so illusive I dreamed without it. I'd sometimes be up in the still of a late hour, in my robe and over through the damp, thick darkness of the open ward to chat with second shift cooks. Once I dreamed I hoofed the five miles alone at night down a dark, winding footpath of a wild hill I recall marching down to an eerie valley of dead civilians and once bivouacked where we slept in rain in the July monsoon, ancient Korean mounds where their ancestors were buried sitting up on the hillside where rice could not be grown. Could it have been another dream? It was so rocky we couldn't dig in either, and I rested against a grave feeling at home, to think deep, solemn thoughts of life and death and eternity. Silently, in half light, one by one my dead walked before me in burlap bathrobes out in a circle around me. I was surrounded by my dead; yes, *my* dead, I ordered it. It was all my fault; they had every right to stare at me; I let them down ... and down, down. "Lieutenant," they seemed to say, "why don't you join us?"

I might have died too had I stayed in the 11th Evac had not someone somewhere exclaimed: "Why, Lieutenant Gould, where've you been?" and they jeeped me to battalion headquarters, fated never to return to the mountains along the Punchbowl except in flashbacks that came when I closed my eyes, times when I saw or heard something to remind me.

A replacement captain took over Love, former rifle platoon sergeant field commissioned in the First Division during their retreat in 1943 in Algeria. This same division, its 26th Infantry, sought to train me in CMTC at Plattsburg fourteen years earlier. Just think, only five years of peace from that war until our forgotten one in Korea. I bumped into the captain a couple times on battalion officers call, which were held sporadically in the field when the old man had something special to let us know. He was incredulous when I bet him I was in the 26th Infantry before he was. "And I don't mean the 26th Yankee Division, because I was in that, too."

"Oh?"

Good thing he didn't take me up on a bet for I not only didn't have the money but I learned he joined the Bloody One right after high school let out in Cheshire, Connecticut in 1936 and if it wasn't for the fact that he was assigned to the horse stables at Plattsburg that summer, he might have met me, but he told me his company ran the post and had nothing to do with CMTC.

For one unhappy late summer, early fall, a recalled Reserve infantry rifle platoon leader with only two years college had been the ranking man to Love; one company of rifles back down the ridge was led by a first sergeant and as this corner of the war was being waged by underpaid few, society went on sucking chocolates, proclaiming gratuitously through its unquestionable authorities, war correspondents, "Our boys like to die for us. It's glory." Boys? Why do we let those furthest from danger call our warriors boys? Boys they may have arrived in tow, punctured dead or hardened killers they fast became, boy wiped off their faces forever. Politicians, newsmen and even generals a generation later would have the ignorance to refer to riflemen as boys in harm's way. We should've been so lucky to go through harm's way. Harm, shit, life and death!

You tell me that the fifty-three lost in Love while I served it are not many of the 54,000 taken down in that forgotten war. To me who loved them the manly way they were the very heart to Love and to many there was never love again without those courageous, chosen few. Daughters, sons and sweethearts, aged wives, drawn and gray, do not grieve; they are blessed to lie in Nature hallowed in the proud annals of bravery by their dying. This I understand religiously, humbly, not merely believe, regardless of any subjugation of words.

Love's new commander and I didn't hit it off at all. He neglected to say anything friendly like my guys were proud of me or anything, or that he knew I got a Silver Star leading and a Bronze Star training them. I think he was probably jealous and probably said things about me behind my back for trying to lead a rifle company in combat as an untrained Sunday soldier. I wouldn't put it past him. No, we had nothing in common except by the coincidence that we were privates at Plattsburg Barracks in the summer of 1937 and commanded L Company of the 38th Infantry Regiment in Korea in 1951. Of course I was no longer up in the mountains.

What to do with Gould was Mighty Mouse's big worry, compounded by Lieutenant Colonel Watson, the 11th Evac's head shrink, telling him it would take time for me to recover from the 'unusual' trauma suffered on Magpie Mountain, that probably would always be a nightmare. Guided by Watson's insistence that I be kept out of combat, Duncan interviewed me and after reminding me that Roy Carse filled the only slot in battalion that because of the provision in his records positively couldn't involve combat, and my little respect for an assignment in the rear echelon anyway, my sharp tongue and predisposition for a court martial, asked me what training I had as a sapper the short while I was in the Royal Canadian Engineers before transferring to the Stormont, Dundas Glengerries.

"Not much," I told him.

"Well," the colonel said, "I don't know how much demolition you learned, but I'm sending you to a ten-day refresher course at X Corps E0D, explosive ordnance demolition, and since you did heavy lifting on your foundry job and have a lot of experience with hard-working guys, I'm giving you P&A Platoon [pioneer, meaning in advance of the main body, and ammunition]. I understand you're still a little shook, but Doctor Watson's keeping an eye on you."

"And I'll keep an eye on him."

"Smart talk again, Gould."

"Speaking of smart talk, colonel, where's my captaincy and DSC?"

"I was waiting for you to mention that. Sorry I went out of my way. As I told you at the time, stuck my neck out to let you know what I heard. If you really want to know, I did it to let you feel proud of yourself because odds were damn high you wouldn't survive. Don't hold me to it, it was talk I heard from Colonel Mildren."

He looked away a second and went on: "It might still be coming, after all, it's less than two weeks. Give him time. Boatner's on TDY [temporary duty] to UN to straighten out that POW mess at Koje-do. He took the 23rd with him."

I was given a cot in the crowded officers' tent at Headquarters and Headquarters Company and settled my pack with what little stuff I had, and I was introduced to master sergeant, platoon sergeant, Bill Hipp, and the P&A bunch. When I got back from a ten-day X Corps demolition crash course, Woody brought me a letter from Kitty and one from Gordy, my so-called best friend, who asked me how it was going and how many I nailed, how sorry he was for not having time to answer my letter from Fox Company. "I've had a new job, Dud, busy as hell." Shirley, his wife, had been sick a lot. "They don't seem to know what's wrong with her; know how aggravating those things are. I bumped into Kitty the other day on the Square; she doesn't look so hot either. I got to go, Dud, drop me a line. Them chinks on your ass all the time? Watch it. If anyone can handle them, it's you."

Woody, who kept close track of our correspondence, wanted to know who was *Catherine* Gould, my daughter?

Kitty's letter was the first since right after 1179 and of course I hadn't written either. I was afraid to open it for fear it was another dear john. "Dudley," she began, seriously. Not Dud or stud, shitpot or any other affectionate nickname. "This is hard to write and you know I'm no whizz at English. You should be right here to talk to face-to-face. I worry about us, but enough about us, Dickie has had a chronic cough and knowing how bad it was with your mother, I took him to Doctor Montgomery who gave our Dick a skin test and x-ray. Nothing like TB he said. The test was negative but he's having his tonsils out Thursday and he's got mastoiditis and where are we getting the money? I don't know, but is it possible to borrow more on your pay? It would be nice."

She began Dudley and signed Catherine which she never called me and I never called her. It was always Kitty or honey, or sweetheart or something funny but nice. At least she didn't call me dirty rat again, but no more I love you honey. It didn't matter to her if I got killed tomorrow afternoon. What does she know or want to know about what I have to do? Later, I learned from her sister she worried all the time about me, days and lonely nights she worried. "You could be dead now, this afternoon, she would worry," Betty said, "all the times you know you're in no trouble; with her you're in trouble all the time."

I never realized that.

After that I got just one letter, in which she did call me honey. "Honey," she wrote, "Why do this to us, hurt me and make me cry? Dickie starts crying when he hears his mother cry. Don't you love us anymore and you hardly ever ask about Dickie. My mother thinks he takes after you. Honey, what's the matter? Don't you love us anymore?"

I didn't know just how to answer that and I didn't have time.

After I took the ten-day demolition course, a Captain Benson, supply officer, and I took

Cold weather gear.

a jeep back to quartermaster depot for a three-day cold weather school to be outfitted with sets of cold-weather gear, heavy zipper lined parka with wolverine fur around the face under a hood, heavy lined mittens with separate soft leather trigger fingers, a long, heavy cord inside the parka around your shoulders like with little kids' mittens fixed to each other so you couldn't lose one; thermal underwear with a large buttoned flap when you have to take a crap and a long fly with buttons instead of zipper so you won't have to worry about them freezing; two pairs of arctic socks and thermal-lined snow boots and wool overalls with suspenders, without a belt so as not to cut off circulation. Back in January at Hoengsong in thin cotton fatigue jackets, some wounded froze to death, just as sometime after I left they issued bulletproof vests, which all of us could have used.

We visited the companies, the captain talking up the benefits while one by one I demonstrated what they would soon be issued. As I took it off and showed each piece, some guys would yell from the rear: "Take it off, take it all off," like I was a strip teaser. Too bad we didn't have a real stripper. With no sense of humor, the captain then had me do it the other way, put the cold weather gear on one by one.

One thing none of us ever heard before was anyone sounding off how dangerous smoking is in cold weather. "Lieutenant Gould, take notice," our physician instructor at Pusan QM Depot said, seeing me light one from another. I told him I was from up north and never heard such a thing. "No serious study has been made before," he told me, "and now the tobacco industry is fighting us tooth and nail. We now know for certain that nicotine, formerly used as an insecticide in Black Flag, causes small blood vessels to collapse in your extremities and without circulation, arms and legs grow colder and colder and easily frost bitten and even death from hypothermia."

Psychologists will probably understand when I say I began to lose self-respect. I mean without my proud dangerous job up there what am I, a rear echelon P&A platoon leader? Plain labor again far from combat. I'll go to pieces in the rear all the time while guys keep dying up there. Up where you don't dare stand up. Nobody back here understands just what I can do, my potential—how valuable and what I can do, and what I've done to prove already. Back here they have a different way of judging guys— how polite and modest you are, how prompt, how servile, how clean and uniform and 'military,' like West Pointers. Only once did I feel good back here, when an E-5 hospital returnee on limited duty came up after a class to ask if I wasn't *the* Lieutenant Gould who took Fools Mountain and 1243.

"Sure am," I told him without any damn apology.

Our P&A platoon was three squads, most important being what all gung-ho guys wanted to be assigned to, demolition men led by SFC Tim Regis. The EOD people at division did the same damn thing as P&A demolition squads with no fear of enemy fire and drew 50% more in hazardous duty pay.

But then, I worried, who else anywhere has heard of my specialty on mountains.

We took our jeeps with trailers and weapons carrier loaded with supplies and equipment over to the Mundung-ni Valley northwest of Heartbreak Ridge past Satae-ri to help demolition platoons of the Second Division Engineer Battalion C, for combat, lay long lines or chains of blocks of explosives at twenty-foot intervals to blow mines. We wired them together with primer cord and fuzes and blew them in long lines where each track of a tank would run approaching Mundung-ni to lay preparatory fires.

Most trouble were chink wooden box mines held together by dove-tailing and glue. With existing shell fragments, the area having been fought over before, our sweeps, mine sweeper SCR 625, would be singing all the time, and because of the time element, probing was out of the question. We simply blew tracks all the way up. Of course we had to be especially observant probing with a long steel rod where we went laying primer cord and charges.

I was surprised to learn that the old juggernaught companies, Item, Love and King, were in harness again at Mundung-ni, Love leading with that professional captain of the Regular Army. Much later, after I got back to the States, former medic, Bill Maddox of North Little Rock, Arkansas, told me that our Sergeant Tony Burris won a Congressional Medal of Honor at Mundung-ni the hard way. Grapevine told me the very day when Tony was among those who got it but the citation wasn't written while I was still in Korea. Colonel Duncan authored it and it was endorsed up the line to the Armed Forces Committee of Congress—

Rank and organization: Sergeant First Class [promoted after he died], US Army, Company L, 38th Infantry Regiment, second Infantry Division. Place and date: Mundung-ni, Korea, 9 November 1951. Entered service at: Blanchard, Oklahoma. G.O. No. 84, 5 December 1951.

Citation:

SFC Tony K Burris, a member of Company L, distinguished himself by conspicuous gallantry and outstanding courage above and beyond the call to duty. On 9 November when his company encountered intense fire from an entrenched hostile force, SFC Burris charged forward alone, throwing grenades into the position and destroying approximately fifteen of the enemy. Spearheading a renewed assault on enemy positions, he was wounded by machine-gun fire but continued the assault, reaching the crest of the ridge ahead of his unit and sustaining a second wound. Calling for a 57mm recoilless rifle team, he deliberately exposed himself to draw hostile fire and reveal the enemy position. The enemy machine-gun emplacement was destroyed. The company then moved forward and prepared to assault other positions on the ridgeline. SFC Burris, refusing evacuation and submitting only to emergency treatment, joined the unit in its renewed attack but fire from hostile emplacement halted the advance. SFC Burris rose to his feet, charged forward and destroyed the first emplacement with its heavy machine-gun and crew of six men. Moving out to the next emplacement, and throwing his last grenade which destroyed this position, he fell mortally wounded by enemy fire. Inspired by his consummate gallantry, his comrades renewed a spirited assault which overran enemy positions and secured a strategic position in the battle. SFC Burris' indomitable fighting spirit, outstanding heroism, and gallant self-sacrifice reflect the highest glory upon himself, the infantry and the US Army.

That was Tony Burris for you. I heard that Doc Carlson patched up Tony's thigh, shot him with morphine and began to write his tag when they heard a particularly nagging gook machine gun let loose. It was like a command to Tony; he brushed Doc aside saying it was only a nick and went limping half upright in a crazy one-man banzai, pulling the ring of a grenade. Then someone in the platoon up above yelled: "Medic! Medic!" Not long after that a voice yelled: "Never mind."

Burris told his assistant squad leader, Avery Olsen, on the eve of that singular ferocity, that, like J C, he had just about had it. He enumerated his weariness: Wonju, Hoengsong, Twin Tunnels, Operation Killer, Massacre Valley, May Massacre, Task Force Joke, Inje and lately Hills 1100, 1179, 1181 and greatest catastrophe of all, Magpie Mountain, 1243, where he lost the last of his old buddies, and he was good and tired of it day after day, losing buddies, being scared. He was sick of battles and constant mourning for dead guys he knew when they were happy and kidded around, and being half starved with death strewn all around him. And Tony, half Cherokee, no man's boss every man's buddy, was a fierce Okie to his last battle, a goddamned heathen berserker (Scandinavian *berserker, ber, bear, serke,* shirt, wearing bearskin only, disdaining armor), a fierce individual, friend to all brother Indianheaders, fiend to enemies; to his mom and dad when he left to join the Army, a polite, modest, gangly eighteen-year-old Southern Baptist boy.

"Now you be careful, Tony, and write and God will look after you and we all will pray."

The day before under sporadic sniping we finished clearing several approaches for our tanks to lay preparatory fire on the high hill trail on which Tony died.

The chinks were using their own 82mm mortar shells for mines because American mortar shells had as a safety device a throw-out pin that had to spin loose out the side of the shell as it swirled beyond the tube to arm by centrifugal force only upon leaving the tube. Because of it, it could not explode in the tube or within short distance from the firing. Russian mortar shells, with no such safety blow-out pin necessary to arm them, were planted in groups of three about two feet apart, either with a nose fuze sensitive to the weight of a foot or tire pressure, or armed with trip wire to pull fuzes.

Being of metal they were easily detected by minesweepers; impossible to detect with the sweeper were wooden box mines. All they required to activate a fuze was for an unsuspecting soldier to step down on a hidden light piece of wood and break it to arm the fuze. Anti-vehicle box mines had larger charges and thicker wood requiring a jeep or other vehicle to break the piece of trigger wood.

One of my demolition guys found a mine with his prod in a dry rut on an access road, alerted by the fact that the area above the box was sunk by repeated rains. Here was my chance to show I had what it takes. I wouldn't have any of them do something I was scared to do so I came up to the guy clearing it and motioned him aside, which he did gladly enough. Platoon Sergeant Hipp stepped between us: "That's all right, lieutenant, it's his job."

"It's mine too, anything you guys do I'm supposed to do better."

He smiled and stepped aside. "Be our guest, sir; be careful, we ain't had no officer since the ground thawed last April."

I drew my carbine knife and dug carefully, flipping the soil up and throwing it out of the way with my left hand until I finished clearing the box all around to the bottom and then reached two finger joints underneath all around the foot-square box.

ROKs laying a 57mm M1 tank mine, which they did haphazardly without a written plan. A pressure fuze screws in center hole. Note helmet liners with string to attach camouflage. Often steel helmets were heavier than their little necks could bear.

US Army engineer stands by with a SCR 625 sweep while man with probe tries to uncover fuze.

"Careful to clear all around the sides, sir. There's wires to pull fuzes. What you got there is a big one planted for jeeps or small trucks."

"I know, sarge, I know, they taught me at Corps."

"In a week?"

"It was ten days and we worked some nights and it was thorough."

I took a deep breath and went at it again. Certain that there were no trip wires to the box from the sides, I grabbed hold of its upper sides and proceeded to lift about ten pounds of explosive out of the rut when there was a sickening tug and a dull snap sound, resistance that warned me in a second that there was a trip wire connected to something below the box in hand. Evidently it broke as I pulled. I held the box, not knowing, as the saying goes, whether to shit or wind my watch. My knees quivered like jelly as I fought to keep my legs in the same position, the box suspended at the same level and turned my torso to face Sergeant Hipp who kept a safe distance as they all did, telling him in what I was embarrassed to say was a cracked, almost whimpering little voice: "Sarge, I think there's something underneath."

"I noticed the tug when you lifted. Now don't panic, gently set the box down and step away and back up to me."

I turned back slowly, and as Hipp said, slowly set the mine down and backed away. He went forward, knelt beside the hole where the box mine was and pushing down with a steel prod found two more mines, one on top of the other. By placing three anti-vehicle mines together they hoped to blow up a six-by or tread off a tank. By the time Sergeant Hipp was through setting a charge to blow them in place, a small crowd had gathered a safe distance and when he told them what I did they cheered. One told me that's how they'd lost their last lieutenant, a guy named Roderick. All that saved me, Sergeant Hipp explained, was the fact that the mines had been planted months ago and the cotter pin of that top mine was not squeezed close enough together to allow an easy pull out and gave resistance enough to break the rusted iron wire to the box mine fuze immediately below.

For the short remainder of my assignment with P&A they were careful to dig under mines far enough to loosen them for easy pulling and rig gin poles, a pyramid of three heavy crossed sticks and commo wire run back about thirty feet and either lifting them out or blowing them in place. The story of my narrow escape got around battalion headquarters and Lieutenant Colonel Duncan chided me for barnstorming. "To begin with, as an officer, you had no business doing the work." His attitude toward me had for some reason cooled. I wondered if that wasn't because he no longer had to depend on me to take objectives now he had an orthodox Regular Army captain.

On that Mundung-ni deal we remained over several nights in hastily dug foxholes down below in noman's land. We and demolition squads of the division's Second Engineer Battalion C stayed until we were through blowing tracks but the powerful tanks which offered protection in daylight and for whom we were clearing the track were helpless after dark without a full perimeter of riflemen and then rumbled behind the MLR back up the Satae-ri Valley before sunset. Otherwise, enemy could sneak in, plant satchel charges or take direct shots with captured 3.5 rockets that would drill and burn over a foot through armor to explode molten metal within. Tankers were justifiably afraid of tank hunters.

Leading a P&A platoon wasn't counted as combat but like other engineer projects, combat or not, has dangerous moments with its demolition squad. Generally, however, we were a labor group, working like division engineers getting heavy rolls of barbed wire, tactical wire, it's called, pickets to snap it onto, burlap bags; all kinds of ammo from an ordnance dump where big ordnance trucks unloaded it; build and maintain secondary roads as best as possible, construct small bridges and fords and clear pads for helicopters. Primarily, of course, we kept ammo stockpiled, including mortar flares and willie peter and delivered it to company supply points.

It was especially dangerous clearing areas occupied by UN or ROK forces, especially ROKs, who failed to map fields to keep track of the mines or laid mines up the ass, and planted deadly booby traps all over the place. Anyone could and did do it. Take a frag grenade, set it in an empty C ration can resting on the spring handle with the cotter pin and the ring to arm it pulled, the handle under spring tension would remain in the can and not fly off to set off the grenade until someone kicked the can or pulled a trip wire to dislodge the handle. It was said that ROKs killed more friendly troops relieving them than they did enemy.

Even with all that, which the guys did without me, I had too much time on my hands— way too much for peace of mind from a very active infantry company commander in combat to a platoon that needed no guidance from me. I couldn't stifle a lot of random, unhealthy thinking. Not so much real thinking like applying my brain to solve problems, but brooding, random and weird, stray thoughts coming to me as disgusting day dreams, not being shoved out of the way as you do when your mind is healthy and preoccupied outside yourself, but dirty thoughts remaining without my permission with even more sordid embellishment of my own nasty day dreams. I wondered, as Doctor Watson once suggested, if my unhealthy, uncontrolled thoughts, which I confessed to, might not have been a subconscious way of getting me not just out of combat as I did subconsciously with my fake broken arm but by deluding me to believe Kitty was fooling around or being raped or other terribly morbid things so I'd have to try to get sent home. Don't tell me Holly's bitch was any figment of my imagination; if it happened to a clean-minded farm boy like Holly, it could happen to anyone. It was no coincidence either that Kitty didn't have very far to walk for sex, what with those two bastards pounding on her wall.

Dirty thoughts not only landed in my brain in the clear; I'd nourish and provide dialogue for them, not only what the two young bucks in the next door apartment said as they forced her to have sex with them both, time and time again, night after night, until it got so they'd get drunk and call my Kitty on the phone and order her to come to them—"and don't be so stupid as to bring that little brat of yours along." They once caught her trying to phone for help and beat the shit out of her; slugged her in the pit of her stomach, telling her not to try to have no more kids. "Goddammit!" I'd wake myself up and write a letter accusing her of asking for it, leading them on. It sickens me now to look back on how nasty and cruel I was. I must have been someone else.

Finally, my Kitty got to like being raped and even got the apartment owner, a vice president of the Jefferson County Bank she called a slum landlord, to waive a month's rent for a hot piece of ass. You know what a good fuck my wife is. "JESUS H CHRIST! MAN, I GOTTA' GET HOME! I'm going crazy," I'd say to me. Don't you see, I'm beginning to believe what I think all the time. DAMN IT, DAMN IT, worms crawling in my brain. My thoughts are sick! Psycho! I can't fight anything from here. I don't even have my guys to worry me anymore—what's left? Combat kept me busy. I'm blowing my top without it and I begged Duncan for King Company, my rifle platoon again— anything.

Brooding thoughts took over, runaway, out-of-control thinking, wondering what Kitty was doing and without waiting for an honest answer, assume she was fooling around or planning a divorce. I wished there was some way to report those young neighbor guys for molesting a married woman. I should have something substantial on them, and I almost came to writing to the Watertown chief of police, veteran of WWII of the 28th Pennsylvania National Guard Division, the Bucket of Blood after its red Keystone emblem, who knew first hand, it was rumored, about guys having their women fool around while they are overseas.

Whatever bad thing I imagined Kitty was doing behind my back the same time my mind entertained it as happening, however, I reasoned it had to be wrong simply because I never accounted for the fact that I was a whole day and hours away on the other side of the 180th meridian, it's an hour earlier for every fifteen minutes of the time zones. Here Kitty and I were not only many miles away but over a day of time apart as well. But the goddamn dirty thoughts remained all the time and to hell with what time it was. It still was happening.

I probably was the only guy in the battalion with no family photos in my wallet, only two nudes of Alice, and I wondered a lot and tried to remember how Kitty looked and sometimes Dickie too, although, as I think I said before, babies all look the same. I was away in Syracuse building us a house when he was born and for months after that, and I never was much on kids and especially tiny babies; that's for women, who get a head start on sex playing with dolls, learning early how to get a live baby. Us guys usually don't have a hint about babies even after hair starts growing down there. I forgot in one letter to ask how Dickie was and Kitty not only took it as living proof that not only did I not want any more kids, I didn't even love the one we had. "And don't forget, buster," she always called me that, emphasizing the *bus* when she was mad, "it's *we* not you. What *we* want, not what *you* want."

Kitty's folks were all right, good drinkers, but nothing to brag on. What can you say, she had a stepfather she wasn't crazy about like I had Emma, who was always Emma, never mother. My mom died long, long ago. Kitty's real father was still in town, remarried and busy with a new family. Before I bumped into her, Kitty had been kicked out once by her stepfather to stay with her married sister despite a lot of crying by her mother, for sneaking out to go roller skating at Sugarland which had a bad reputation among parents for staying open too late and letting kids under age smoke and drink, and do anything, parents thought, older guys, including ones in their twenties there after unsuspecting young girls. At least some said they were unsuspecting.

Kitty had her feelings hurt her share of the time, but never so bad as by my own so-called parents. My father and Emma ignored without any reason our invitation to attend our civil marriage with Bud and Gus (Augusta, her mother), and Bill and Betty, my brother-in-law and sister-in-law-to-be. My father simply said maybe over the phone and had a church thing to attend and never showed. They didn't ever come right out and say so, but we knew they didn't think Kitty was good enough for me. After all, I was a Gould who went back in Jefferson County before the War of 1812 and back to 1634 in Topsfield, Massachusetts. Gus told me once they didn't know how long the Thompsons had been around, or about anyone further back than her great-grandfather when she was very little who, she remembered, had a long white beard with tobacco stains around his mouth. They had a picture.

Three months after we got married Emma invited us to dinner. Kitty didn't want to go. She'd never met them and we were never invited before and why go when they wouldn't even come to our wedding? What kind of in-laws was that? Me? I actually felt a little sorry for them, all the life they were missing. Especially my father who wouldn't say shit if he had a mouthful. I figured they regretted at last not coming to their only child's wedding. Of course Emma had no kids and her line was about extinct, dried up as she was. My father and Emma weren't wealthy but made every effort to appear to be. Emma, back in the late twenties, made a mahogany furniture display room out of what my mother called the parlor, where her casket once was; even had a red velvet-covered chain across its doorway to keep out who I never knew, unless just me. Shit, who wanted to go into the spooky room?

Kitty and I asked each other why they would have us for dinner unless to beg our pardon. Maybe they had learned what love is. Not likely. My father was a cold cucumber, who, except for a few days right after my mother died never told me he loved me or touched me or kissed me, and Emma, a spinster, when she went to pick me up and kiss me right before my father married her, I stiffened and she almost dropped me. She didn't know what love meant.

Right after dinner, which couldn't compare in warmth and goodness with Kitty's, sitting in the fancy parlor sipping little cups of coffee, Emma said she apologized in advance for having to say so. At last, Kitty and I thought, here it comes.

"And your father-in-law agrees with me. As a matter of fact, he is the one who suggested it, but I used to be not only a teacher but the first guidance counselor in the Carthage school system and know what I am talking about. You must realize, Catherine, although apparently a nice enough young lady, you are holding our son back from finishing his education, without which he will never amount to anything."

Kitty looked down at her shoes and made a funny little sound like a gasp.

"Don't get me wrong, young lady. It's for your good too; you'll never forgive yourself later on for holding him back. Dudley is our only son and we feel we have to protect him by pointing him in the right direction. He needs two more years for a degree and now with the Government paying his way on the GI bill, it would be plain foolish not to return to Syracuse and graduate. Especially after his father sacrificed so to give him the little education he has."

Kitty, hands covering her face, broke out sobbing and excused herself to go to the bathroom. I was shaking mad, shaking because I wanted so much to use my muscles to finish this nasty attack now. I stood and so did my father as though to protect Emma and I motioned him down and yelled at Emma: "You bitch! What right have you to make my wife cry? You aren't even related to us."

Emma was thoroughly frightened by my voice and attitude and cowered and covered her face with her raised left arm. My father, embarrassed by any display of anger, started to open his mouth and I told him to shut up, the first and last time I ever raised my voice to him. After what seemed a long time, the two of us glaring at each other, Emma's face in her hands, Kitty came back to the parlor blotting her eyes and in the meekest voice I ever heard from her, apologized: "I'm sorry, Mrs. Gould. I didn't realize I was holding Dud back. He never said anything about wanting to go to college and if he does, ain't there a special law giving veterans more money so they can support their wives or families in college? And he still can draw his 52/20 Club money," referring to the federal program wherein a veteran received $20 a week for a year if out of work, or 52/25 if self-employed.

"Yes," my father spoke up, "and Syracuse University with government money has built on-campus bungalows for married couples, but the wife has to attend as well. Now I don't suppose you'd be doing that, would you young lady?"

"You know damn well I couldn't, Mister Gould. You people just don't want me for a daughter-in-law. I'm from the wrong side of Black river; my mom's only a waitress, my stepfather a laborer. You people live on Pleasant Street and us on Factory."

She put her hands over her face again and cried softly.

I reached over and hugged her. "Never mind, honey, you'll never hear me say anything about college. I've been to war and I've been around enough now. I'm no college boy. I do my own reading. It's my father's idea and if he's so hot about it, let him go back for a masters degree and leave me alone. Did anyone ever ask me what I wanted out of life? C'mon, Kitty, we're leaving."

Matter of fact, neither Kitty nor I, that I can remember, ever asked ourselves what we wanted out of life beyond maybe a year, a new car or something big like that; we just went ahead and lived, which reminds me of a favorite poem—

> *while you and I have lips which*
> *are for kissing and to sing with*
> *who cares if some one-eyed sonofabitch*
> *invents an instrument to measure spring with.*
> – e e cummings.

This was the last I was in my father's house, a place I once called home. Neither he nor Emma called us ever again, or sent a card at Christmas or any other time, and the last I had any business with him, if you can call it that, was when, learning I was headed for Korea and might stop in Japan, he gave Kitty's mother a message to the Tokyo Chamber of Commerce. He never acknowledged the Japanese secretary's presents I mailed home to him and died in 1965 when I was miles away in the Army. In fact, I wasn't advised he was that sick until Emma asked Gus to let me know several days before his funeral. We learned that Emma passed away in her early eighties. Kitty and I wondered a little who they left their things to. A hundred dollar check in a business letter from a law firm in Carthage concerning closing her estate instructed me to cash it, our share of her estate, which I understand was a sort of quit-claim so we couldn't sue for more. Someone once told me that most of their combined estate, whatever, went to the Watertown Asbury Methodist Church.

Kitty never mentioned divorce again in her letters and I certainly never did. Underneath the dirty thoughts I knew I loved her very much. My men were gone every which way and she was all I had left in the world, although I didn't appreciate it then. Of course, there was Dick. I loved her every bit as much as always and could never forget her coming to comfort me, risking her life, I feel, in the most terrifying time of my life, 15th of May; forget any of her for that matter. How "don't worry, honey," patting my head, "everything will be all right," instantly put me in a deep sleep that saved my life.

I never was able to understand my crazy thinking that doubted her unless it was just plain war weariness with paranoia, which I have been accused before of having sometimes. You know what I mean, things and circumstances are out to get you. I know that once early-on she called me a dirty rat, which I referred to as her dirty rat letter, but after I did what I did on R&R I tried to stop inferring she was fooling around. What's good for the gander you know. Maybe I was a dirty rat but how did she know? How could I be held responsible for everything that happened while I was miles and miles away, like her washing machine? We had to give away a brand new Sears and Roebuck one with our Heartbreak House in Syracuse. Fuck the damn Army for that and what happened to not one, but two applications before the bastards insulted me by recalling me involuntarily, shoving a loyalty certificate at me?

It finally sank in that to Kitty I was responsible for everything simply because I volunteered for Korea. I guess I might be at fault; I had no right being married when I felt such a deep urge to have my mettle tested. It's not wrong to go off fighting for your country, just don't be married and have other responsibilities. It was that way always in the Army before WWII; no private or PFC could get hitched without his company commander's written permission. He couldn't afford it.

How ironic can you get? In World War II I stuck my neck out for every dangerous job that came long and for five years, counting two in Canada, I was available for anything. Why couldn't I have seen combat the way Roy Carse did, in the big war? People remember that one and gave you credit. I often wondered what might have happened if the Eighth Bomber Command had let me transfer into the Infantry when I first applied. I'd have had my mettle tried for sure—maybe be dead. Very possible.

Kitty once wrote several reasons she was so unhappy; first she had no reason to feel good or be proud; was she part of a great national effort as I was? Did she have a lot of comrades to pass time with? No! She was all alone in a strange apartment in an old made-over mansion in the snobby part of town with no friendly neighbors and her mother and Bud worked all day and I never talked it over with her about my volunteering to run off to be a big hero. Hero? Certainly not to she and Dickie. "Run off by your lonesome, right out of our lives to be a big hero and leave us all alone. Your buddy, the bigshot paratrooper, what did he do? You're darn right, he talked big and backed out the last minute and that Silver Star and Bronze Star you sent home, stick them up your you know what."

After all I'd been through, my Silver Star means nothing?

I stewed a lot about whether our bad letters, our misunderstandings, were more the result of her miseries or mine. Who was the more miserable? Wasn't it mostly circumstance because of the housing shortage in Watertown following WWII that she couldn't find a decent apartment we could afford, then she had to move in without my help and find and buy furniture from Epstein's Secondhand Furniture Store what with less than $1000 we got left for selling our Heartbreak House and the little payment each month from Bud on the 4% loan. Look at the beatup Maytag Epstein gave her such a big deal on. "Oh yes, Mrs. Gould," they told her, "you have our word. It won't cost a red cent to run, trust us. Would we lie to you with your husband off in Korea fighting for democracy?"

Or was it mostly time and distance that tore us apart; no warm kisses anymore, no touching or even looking or accidentally touching that used to get us back in love in a flash. Love Torn Asunder, we called it, to go along with the Heartbreak House on the hill I built with my own hands in the Syracuse suburb, we so planned and dreamed about, right down the same side of the street from a grammar school and a place they were beginning what some called a shopping center, the first I'd heard of. No shopping center in Watertown, and my '38 Ford pickup on the bum again with costly repairs, and Bud having to haul her Saturdays to the A&P for groceries.

I say I built it with my own hands and that's true, except I had to hire three of my former landscape guys to help level and smooth the concrete base of the house as it was poured; a union licensed electrician on the QT to do my entrance wiring to the fuse box at $20 cash; and a union plumber $50 to install the hidden plumbing before the cement was poured. That's the way his union ordered it and I didn't have oakum or a lead pot anyway. It was the wrong way to go about building a house, pay for materials and whatnot as you go along. You couldn't get a mortgage those days in Syracuse for a place without a cellar and I'd have to have a cosigner for a loan because I hadn't built up any credit during the war. My father? Forget it, he'd charge as much interest as a bank and give me a big lecture about savings.

I know that frustrated sex had a say-so in our long-distance quarrel and don't tell me that Japanese doll, the horny photo of Holly's bitch and Alice's sizzler didn't have something to do by way of my guilt conscience, wanting me to match my suspicions about Kitty and the two guys she complained about in the apartment next to her. Another logical assumption was to accuse them, being right there in the next apart ment. And that hot piece Alice, picking a bad time to get me horny all over again. I couldn't help being a sex-starved sitting duck.

Did I think of Kitty more for sex than being the mother of my child? No doubt that sex was what Kitty and I thought mostly about when together. I'll never deny that. Could I sit down with her and talk more than four minutes about foundry work, combat, religion, philosophy, life and death, eternity, the universe, even hunting, football, or any other important thing? Of course not. One of the few things I got out of college was how to think straight which broads never do. In *Philosophy I*, you begin with a course on logic and the fallacies, wrong ways of thinking, as the fallacy of assumed authority; just because a man's a preacher doesn't mean he knows God. No woman knows what fallacies are and sooner or later they end with the lowest argument, getting personal, using *argumentum ad baculum,* slapping and shoving, argu ment by force.

What Kitty and I did was talk, yakity yak if you will, not discuss; that was too much work. We spent a lot of time man to woman, wonderfully satisfying times flat on our king-size bed. Who can knock that? And talked mostly about the near future and physical things, our flower garden outside the Heartbreak House and what we'd like to grow in it and how we'd grow a lot of our own food. It sure was pretty the little time I had to work on planting that first year. First year? Only year. We liked good food and what a terrific cook she was. She cooked for her mother, stepfather Bud, and sister Betty since she was twelve. And going out Saturday nights when we had money for something special that was hard to mess with at home, as Chinese and Mexican food, which wasn't even in her little cook book. Syracuse's Mexican restaurant opened less than a year before I left. And 11:30 Friday night, pay day, I'd come home from the second shift at the foundry to our half-finished house in Syracuse with raw two-by-fours before I nailed up sheet rock walls, with four green quarts of Schmidt's Cream Ale with the silver tiger label, and we'd sit at a bare table in the kitchen listening to late Friday night music on the radio, the big bands, Tommy Dorsey in particular, getting mellow, ending up insulting each others' relatives and when the ale was gone, hop in bed and screw. Tear off a piece the saying was, or put the blocks to her.

I missed Kitty even when I was paranoid about her fooling around, the unrea-sonable, angry, jealous bane of love. She was the only person aside from my real mother ever loved me and said so many times. Peaceful times on the line I could sit still a while, late on a quiet night missing having her around, chatting about nothing serious, petting, baiting each other, me and Kitty fondling and kidding around, espe-cially lying with her before, and then after a smoke. My father was probably right inferring our marriage was animal, just for sex. He should have added, "red-blooded animals and red-hot sex." What's wrong with that? That's what you need for good baby-making. I don't remember my father in bed with my mother, of course I was very small and remember nothing that went on in their squeaky brass bed, but I'm sure I would have resented it, nor he and Emma who was such a cold cucumber I couldn't picture her even lying down waiting for it.

Kitty cooked a knockout dinner every Sunday and I'd kibitz and get pie-eyed as she did while cooking, and we'd sit and stuff ourselves, especially her spaghetti and meat balls with plenty of garlic, oregano, hot buttered garlic toast and cold beer. Then she'd yawn, pat her belly, and say how full and sleepy she was and I'd say me, too, and be right behind her down the hall. We'd qualify for medals in the speed of throwing off our clothes and we'd rub our hot bare bellies together and go right to the best, most active healthy fucking you've ever heard of. She'd be first and I'd crawl in beside her, roll her over and without using my hands stick it straight between her smooth, hot thighs and give it to her many times; hump away, fuck, screw, put the blocks to her, fuck, and lay her, put it to her, and we'd clue each other when to come together, "Hurry up, Kitty, I can't wait," groaning, and Kitty yelling: "FUCK ME! Harder! HARDER!" I'd grab and squeeze her love muscles and try to shove my tight, swollen, vibrating cock in further and further and thrill to hear her in serious trouble: "Oh my God! My God! Oh my God!" and we'd come together as I'd shoot a big, glob of hot white, creamy life way into her.

Strange, even weird, but I somehow compare this great intensity of feeling with being hit fatally in combat; when guys yell for God. One is out of one's self also at the pitch of an orgasm, as one is out of himself when hit bad in combat. "My God! Oh, my God!" taken suddenly out of oneself. Medic! when just hit; God! when about to be fatal, last cry I heard guys yell before going away for good, and Kitty's orgasms.

No, we never got into deep, serious discussions like I did with Fred. Sometimes, as a matter of fact, even our sex was fiction. Believe it or not, we'd get a trifle bored sometimes and she confessed once she'd pretend I was her Uncle Joe. "Oh yeah? Me too, pretend you was your sister Betty, who has the ass and tits to be a good one." I might have gotten suspicious of Joe but he was a jerk.

Right after our savage climax in powerful body quakes, we fell silent as I slid sideways out of bed and dressed. Kitty, those happy Sunday afternoons, rolled over and fell asleep with a little smile on her face. Then I'd bend down and kiss her and she'd pull down my lips for another and I'd light a cigarette and go out and do the dishes. I always did the dishes. Anybody could cook like her shouldn't ever have to.

We weren't all sex; we were buddies, too. We were tender and I'd hold her hand or she would mine and kiss on the cheek and walk swinging hands like queers. We took in romantic movies. We did such things together as go nutting in the fall, try to beat the deer to delicious nuts from huge, gray, beautiful beech trees and hazel nuts on bushes and hickory nuts hidden by leaves beneath the trees. In winter, when Beaver Meadows was frozen over, we went skating with the crowd and built bonfires on the ice and toasted hot dogs and marshmallows on sticks and sang and laughed, all of us. Another war? Hell no, one's enough! "Korea? Sh-e-eit, who knows where it's at?"

Freddy and I discussed things, what we really are, our souls, the hereafter after our bodies rot, and what is our soul up to while we're still alive. To be fair with Kitty, Fred and I never had hard-ons to distract us. When you got good healthy sex like Kitty and me, you don't need discussions, don't want diversions, and when it's all feelings no room for thinking anyway. I believe we had our long-distance fallout mainly because we were unable to jump in bed and work it out. Some of the best sex we ever had was after she was mad and wouldn't speak to me for a day or two and we'd accidentally bump into one another in the hall. Pow, hop to it!

I didn't mind being P&A leader. Not that the work wasn't too much rear echelon, which it was, although compensated for by being real physical. I always liked muscle work in the sun and open air; you feel like a goddamn man. I took turns with thick leather gloves hauling coils of barbed wire off tail gates, helping build a log bridge over a stream near headquarters and a rock ford down the way in what should have been engineer battalion territory but Duncan asked me to do it without work orders and the lot of stalling you got from division. "C'mon guys," I said, "we'll show 'em how to do it" and almost caught my death of cold, being wet all one chilly December afternoon winching huge flat rocks in place with our weapons carrier.

That was when I got my third liquor ration which I was due every month. The guys tossed down their six-pack of beer and my sergeants and I disappeared the next night to finish my two bottles of hard stuff. It reminded me one night in a barn in the Sudetenland and the ass chewing I got for fraternizing with my sergeants but this time I didn't give a shit. Besides, it was a lot different now, a combat veteran and damn close to my new guys, having just worked our asses off doing someone else's job. That's what morale is, the feeling of satisfaction and communal strength doing real dangerous or choice jobs at great odds and succeeding. The harder the jobs, more dangerous, the more together, the higher the morale, combat buddies the closest of all.

While delivering a load of ammo, I bumped into the Banzai Third resting in the Satae-ri valley; like visiting a haunted house, in a matter of weeks, all my sergeants gone, casualties or rotated, and there was a new guy they told me was missing already. How, nobody knew, dropped on the morning report MIA; something you hate to hear about, leaving his poor wife or mother to wonder forever.

I don't know exactly when my 'personality problems' began again, slowly sliding off the deep end again, ornery with the guys for instance, finding it hard to get to sleep, awakening often, startled sometimes even though we were a good ten miles from gooks. At times I woke up past midnight thinking it my time to pull guard as I did in the platoon, or run the line, checking holes to be sure somebody was awake and once woke officers in our tent talking in my sleep and once, they complained, I even shouted like when I was a little boy, this time banzaiing. The rear echelon officers didn't say boo to me but bitched to Colonel Duncan and I was asked to take my cot to a spare supply tent, "Nothing personal, Lieutenant Gould, we know you can't help it." Never Dud anymore.

One night Master Sergeant Ulriche and I were sitting in the rain under parkas laughing at something Ski said the wrong way. He was noted for mispronouncing and putting common sayings ass-end backwards. "Get off the pot, dummy, if you want to shit." As the guys mocked him he'd snicker to himself trying to believe he was funny on purpose and that's why they laughed and was therefore socially acceptable; looking for an approval he normally got only from Pop and me. Damn, he was the most innocent guy I ever met, the least harmful of any and it was good he didn't slug anyone when he was mad. He was only eighteen but could just hold a guy in his arms and squeeze him until he recanted and he embarrassed guys because he, alone, was so lacking in guile.

I'd wake up at times sobbing softly to myself thinking or dreaming of Pop and Ski together. Pop was much closer to Ski than my father ever was to me, with manly love to give. What a pair they were, Pop disdained by women, feeling helpless about it; Ski who never had anyone to love, a father, a mother, a girl, anything. Ironical that Pop worried so about Ski being on his own after Korea, no orphanage to return to at his age to help him forget his terrible experiences. And Pop trying to impress Ski with the simple fact that he had to keep reenlisting in the same company, and take as long an enlistment as possible until he got his twenty in, if they'd let him, and he hoped Ski could find some sergeant like himself for a new friend. Now, worry and helplessness were of no account, thrown together to eternity onto the bed of a six-by for their last ride in fresh air before being lonely eternally in brown Army coffins, buried deep, white tombstone crosses apart.

Hard to believe, but though I ate three meals a day of warm B rations I lost more weight. I guess because I picked at it and had a fag in my mouth most of the time. My right middle finger and trigger finger were black again with tobacco tar, bad as it got before R&R, for a different anxiety, no longer combat but fretting over my wife, a different kind of no-win war. Free of constant physical fear, with a sharper sense of hopelessness, a paranoia, set in a fantastic, sickening series of dirty thoughts, horrible doubts transferred from worry about my men to bad things happening to my wife to her doing bad things that generated bad letters to her, never asking to find out what reason she could give me or what excuse she had, if any. In lieu of incoming rounds a sense of distance separating me from my love for my men, a cold, gnawing aloofness teeming with sickening doubts and I no longer felt the love of my men. Always sharp, hurtful memories of poor Holly and his cruel bitch. Assuming, never proving, always assuming Kitty was being wronged, or wronging me. Me? What they call cuckolder, a cuckoo laying eggs in another birds nest.

Neither Kitty nor I mentioned divorce again after the brief blowout over Alice and the washing machine, but we both seemed to get our kicks taking pot shots at each other, me much more than her, more vicious accusations, devoid even of common sense. According to her I actually enjoyed Korea, "acting important, being a big hero must be lots of fun. Bud asked me to show that Silver Star and Bronze Star citations to the *Times*, but that would just make you more anxious to stick your neck out and Dickie— remember him?—needs you home."

"Don't tell me you're not fooling around with those neighbor guys you complained about, living so close, and tell them bastards not to bother with Dick, buying him toys, weaseling to get in with you. Tell them they're draft dodgers; I'm kicking the shit out of them when I get home. They better not be around."

I learned after I got home that the characters got kicked all right, out of their apartment after she complained to me about them; couldn't pay the eighty-five a month and went back to live with their folks. I wouldn't believe Kitty.

"Oh yeah," she wrote, "who's fooling with who? I read in *Look* magazine about them Korean soft chancres you guys are catching that can eat your thing until it drops off. Catch anything like that, buster, don't come crying back."

"Fair enough if I lose it, sister, because kissing it is all you're good for anyway. Sure, all those movie actresses you read about falling all over us in those USO shows let us screw them. That's the main reason they come way over here; I already laid Anne Southern and Irene Dunne."

Although I accompanied Sergeant Hipp and the guys on four major mine-clearing jobs after Mundung-ni, most of the time was spent delivering ammo, burlap bags, tactical wire, pickets and other heavy equipment, sweeping and probing for land mines, etc. The guys really didn't need me, they worked together for at least six months without an officer and one good thing about the rear, you didn't go losing buddies all the time. As for an officer, most couldn't remember having one and Bill Hipp was probably better than most officers, certainly knew his business better than I did. Who needed me anymore?

I passed too much free time smoking and fretting about what Kitty might be doing while I was stuck in that asshole of the world. With more time on my hands I wrote more often, but her letters didn't increase. She inferred a lot but never complained she was having a hard time with Dickie. Her letters weren't as hateful as at the beginning but I tried to find them that way. I was as nervous as an old hen, as we used to say; crazy thoughts and weird daydreams I fed along with bad ideas took over and I felt myself slipping away as I did when Love was ended for me by short rounds. Who, I sometimes thought, was I fighting now? Back at cold-weather training, Captain Benson once had to tell me to shape up, demanding: "Who do you think you're talking to?" Being rear echelon as he was, I suppose I had been a little contemptuous. I had to apologize.

As I worried more and more about her infidelity, I regretted screwing that little jap. I was real sorry I let it happen, or, rather, it was me who took the cab. I used to think, that's water over the dam, just because I couldn't help myself. Even though a proven hero and being lonely doesn't give me permission to cheat on my wife.

*   *   *

Some religious guys sent home for Christmas decorations for the mess hall tent and our cold weather issue was doled out. It began to get real cold and one morning as we were about to go to the ordnance depot for a load of ammo, Colonel Duncan sent for me and excused his runner and sergeant major and told me to take a seat and instead of chewing me out for going unshaven and sometimes, I'll confess, without washing every day as I figured he would, he told be bluntly: "Dud, you're going home!"

Crimus, I thought, just like that! I knew something was wrong. That's just what I need, that'd suit me fine. Everyone knows I've done more than my share over here; soft-pedaling it with this P&A job. No one deserves it more than me after all I've been through.

"You don't seem surprised, Lieutenant."

"It's only fair," I told him. "I've done a lot more than my share."

"Modest, aren't you."

"That depends on what others have done. Modesty becomes most people, no reason to be otherwise."

He wouldn't let it go but kept pounding away at my attitude until I was raising my voice to him and had to be warned to control myself, like I heard him talk to Captain Shallow. He made me suspicious and I studied his face and suddenly figured he wasn't any more understanding than Wilkes, trying to get something out of me he could humiliate me with. I cautioned myself to watch out, be careful what I said anymore. Sure enough, soon he was trying to talk me into seeing Colonel Watson again.

"Never mind me," I told him. "Goddammit, colonel, where's all that stuff you promised to get me to stick my neck out on 1243? The promotion and DSC?"

Suddenly no longer nice, he snapped. "Gould, I don't have to kiss your ass to get you to do anything. I order you, understand? You're still a lieutenant and I happen to be a lieutenant colonel!" He paused to settle a flash of anger and continued, "Now something's terribly wrong, lieutenant, and we want to find out so we can help you."

"Everything's bugging me, sir. I'd like to get back to combat, at least you know who your friends are. At least you're with real men."

"Master Sergeant Hipp and the platoon aren't men? Cut the crap, lieutenant. Shape up!"

"Where's the DSC and captaincy you promised?"

Duncan raised his voice: "Damn it, Gould, I didn't promise you anything and what sort of captain do you think you'd be? Look at you, forget where the shower point is? I told you I was taking a big chance telling you what Colonel Mildren told me General Boatner said. In the first place, it's too early for anything. Bull has been on Koje Island since we got 1243, straightening out rioting POWs. And you haven't a right to demand anything."

The way I figured it, Duncan no longer needed me with that First Division combat veteran captain over Love Company. I told him this point blank and made him mad again and we talked angrily for a few minutes, then suddenly calmed down and sounded friendly almost and in a lower voice called me Dud again and told me he had no choice but send me back to the 11th Evac where "they have your case history."

I might've been pissed off that he was trying to pull a fast one but suddenly it seemed just the right thing. I didn't argue. I was actually relieved of a heavy burden realizing I could use some help with controlling my sick thinking and it was the only place to get it. Suddenly what had sarcastically always been *shrinks* were badly needed mind doctors. I could tell I could use one of those shots again and some understanding and if my painful, evil, sickening mental condition, which I was beginning to recognize as such, wasn't enough there's my damn athlete's foot acting up again, reason enough to go back for a visit.

I was more than a little suspicious, however, when they had me turn in my combat equipment and my old buddy, my carbine and all the new cold-weather stuff.

In the first three days at 11th Evac, I got shots to make me sleep which I was happy to do all the way to the next noon. Man, I didn't even realize how I'd been missing a good night's sleep. I snuck a peek at the WO's paperwork—

Subject officer underwent the traumatic sudden loss of eighteen of his men to friendly artillery which he is unable to resolve satisfactorily. He has so far avoided a complete breakdown but his personality has suffered. Subject evinces an adult situational maladjustment to the death of his mother twenty-six years ago. He seems to be suffering from a marginal identity premorbid personality, an inability to adjust to a father/son hostility permitting him to exist only in the role of wrongdoer. He deludes himself that his wife is unfaithful, based upon a lack of affection in their correspondence. He has nothing to support this belief. For unstated reasons, he scorns rear echelon personnel.

Crimus, why drag my parents into this!

I was held in the 11th Evac for over a week and put on a pound or two until I got really loud about getting back so I could go home. "That aggressive attitude, lieutenant, is why we can't release you just yet. Have you been taking your medicine regularly or do we have to give you something stronger to calm you down? Lieutenant Gould, you are going to end up in serious depression if you don't learn to relax. Now take in some deep breaths and unwind." When they did release me with warnings about mental hygiene, unhealthy thinking, and a prescription for what I believed were antidepression pills, I reported to Colonel Duncan as ordered. Before he could say anything, I demanded: "I thought you said I was going home, sir."

"I told you, Dud, but you were skating too close to the edge again, and we had to get you under control. Now's the time," and he held up a message from Division so I could see the Red Cross letterhead. "The Watertown, New York Red Cross has been in contact with the Second Division Red Cross representative. Don't worry, Dud; it's not serious, only potentially, and they recommend you be returned to your family before it is serious. Chaplain Johnson and I agree you have earned a long rest

```
                        HEADQUARTERS
                     2d Infantry Division
                  APO 248 c/o Postmaster
                  San Francisco California

SPECIAL ORDERS                                    1 December 1951
NUMBER     331            E X T R A C T

        5.  1ST LT DUDLEY C GOULD, 02017049 Inf MOS 1542 (Cau) rel asg 38th
   Inf Regt, APO 248 and asg Repl Bn 8068th AU APO 27 to await further trans
   and reasgmt to ZI and subsequent asgmt to 9th Inf Div Ft Dix NJ for
   compassionate reasons.  Off auth 30 days DDALV.  Pers Records MPR allied
   papers and 2 copies immunization register will   accompany Off.  DD Form
   415 will be utilized by pers to inform corres and pub to discontinue
   mail and pub until further advised as to new address.  EDCSA:  8 Dec 51.
   WP PCS TDN TBGAA tvl by RW auth 2122010 1-11-21. P1410,02,03,07, 399-999.
   . .. DA msg 46671 dtd 24 Nov 51.

        BY COMMAND OF MAJOR GENERAL YOUNG:


OFFICIAL:                            WILBUR WILSON
                                     Colonel   GS
                                     Chief of Staff


   JOE A HESTER
   1st Lt    AGC
   Asst AG

   DISTRIBUTION:
        "O"
        plus
   AG MPD. . . . . . . . . . . . . .2    Co Repl Bn 8068th AU APO 27. . . . .6
   Pers Sec 38th Inf Regt. . . . .8      TAG 'n 25, D.C. ATTN: AGPO-S-. . . .2
   (1st Lt Gould). . . . . . . .30
```

and the situation between you and your wife is apt to become progressively worse. You have only a month to go before rotation anyway; we are requesting your transfer to the zone of interior and after an emergency leave, to be stationed as near as possible to your home town."

"What situation with my wife?" I blurted. "I thought I was going home on my own account. It's me you're worried about; I'm the one taking the beating. What does a damn chaplain know? He hasn't even talked to me, and what's this about my wife? I got a right to read what the Red Cross said."

"Sorry, Dud, it's confidential. Believe me, she's not critical, only that the situation, if allowed to continue, could get out of hand. Major Johnson has seen it happen time and again, the cruel breakup of families during wartime separations. The letter is only one paragraph addressed to battalion commander recommending compliance, which the Division Representative endorses and action we have already decided on. Your orders are being cut at division transferring you to the Ninth Infantry Division at Fort Dix from where you will be processed and transferred to Camp Drum, seven miles from Watertown to the Tennessee National Guard unit now training there."

All I could think was something bad is wrong with Kitty. "What situation could get out of hand?" That's all I could think, and I argued with Duncan but not until I teared up a little did he give in, afraid I'd break up right there.

"Dud, if I tell you what's in this letter I can get my ass in a sling." His decision sounded familiar, "I must swear you to keep it to yourself. I'm making a career in this man's Army."

"They're cutting my orders now; I won't be around to tell anyone. If there was anything wrong with your wife, wouldn't you want to know?"

"All right, not a word to anyone, your wife is suffering from severe depression. Do you know a Doctor Montgomery?"

"Our family doctor; delivered our little boy, but what's *she* depressed about? *I'm* the guy's taking pills."

"Well, he's still taking care of your wife and son. He's not a specialist but says she's worrying herself into some serious mental sickness and strongly recommends your presence."

"She never wrote to me about anything serious."

Another sixteen-day voyage, back to Seattle, where I was bused with other guys from the docks to Fort Lawton and had the steel security bands snipped from my B-4 bag. Another infantry lieutenant, George Easly from Charleston, and I grabbed a taxi to the airport where we learned since it was getting close to Christmas all flights east were booked for the weekend. As we turned away from the last airline, a broker for nonscheduled lines caught up to us. He knew one line, a nonscheduled, the Coast to Coast Special, had four seats available, leaving about seven that night for New York.

In those days, passengers bought $25,000 life insurance policies for specific flights, twenty-five cents at vending machines. When our Coast to Coast clerk told us they didn't have an insurance vendor because the policies would be too expensive, it sank in fast why unscheduled lines had such a bad reputation. The nonscheds had ten fatal crashes from 1945 to 1952, by which time most unscheduled companies had been grounded by federal regulations for safety defects or went into bankruptcy.

"Sure beats the old days!"

The Old Sarge remembers, all right — but a lot
of today's younger military men hardly know
what it's like to travel long distances on the ground.
The speed, comfort and friendly service of the
Scheduled Certificated Airlines do wonders for
morale . . . besides saving 4 out of every 5 hours'
travel-time lost in the best surface transportation!

INSURANCE

Only on SCHEDULED Certificated
Airlines: $5,000 to $50,000 at 25c
to $2.50, covers Stateside and much
foreign travel — personal or official.

10% DISCOUNT

for official travel on TR's . . .
covers full Service.

Saving the Military *MILLIONS* of Vital Man Hours

THE *Scheduled Certificated Airlines* OF THE U.S.A

ALASKA AIRLINES	EASTERN AIR LINES	PIONEER AIR LINES
ALLEGHENY AIRLINES	FRONTIER AIRLINES	RESORT AIRLINES
AMERICAN AIRLINES	LAKE CENTRAL AIRLINES	RIDDLE AVIATION
BONANZA AIR LINES	MOHAWK AIRLINES	SOUTHERN AIRWAYS
BRANIFF AIRWAYS	NATIONAL AIRLINES	SOUTHWEST AIRWAYS
CAPITAL AIRLINES	NORTH CENTRAL AIRLINES	TRANS-TEXAS AIRWAYS
CENTRAL AIRLINES	NORTHEAST AIRLINES	TRANS-WORLD AIRLINES
CHICAGO & SOUTHERN AIR LINES	NORTHWEST AIRLINES	UNITED AIR LINES
COLONIAL AIRLINES	OZARK AIR LINES	U. S. AIRLINES
CONTINENTAL AIR LINES	PAN AMERICAN WORLD AIRWAYS	WEST COAST AIRLINES
DELTA AIR LINES	PIEDMONT AIRLINES	WESTERN AIR LINES

In 1945, veteran pilots of WWII raised money from friends and financiers to buy mothballed Armed Services cargo planes for as little as $25,000, repayable at $4000 a year, refurbished with comfortable seats, arrangements were made for pooling maintenance, sharing ground personnel and airport facilities, supplies and routes. In one year alone WWII veteran military pilots founded 2730 so-called airlines with 5500 planes. In many, the president was the pilot and the vice president the copilot. To make a go of it, they had to wait until seats were full, hence nonscheduled, and their rates were much cheaper, from San Francisco to New York City only $88 opposed to scheduled airlines $157. Not to worry about cost, I was traveling compassionate reassignment on an Army travel voucher.

Waiting for our unknowable takeoff time, which we learned couldn't be too long with only two seats unsold, I got plastered. Easly, assistant personnel officer of the 23rd Infantry, doing the buying had to listen to my battle tattle.

I got worrying about seeing Kitty and talking to her face-to-face, almost too excited and tense to go through with it worrying what our relationship would be after our ugly separation, I mean the nasty things I wrote her, listening in the waiting room to Christmas carols with a good glow on, colored lights blinking, my unfaithfulness and uncontrolled meanness, the unjust things I wrote, I admitted entirely my fault for the first time how cruel and cowardly I'd been and after two more drinks got a bunch of quarters and called her on a pay phone. Naturally she sounded surprised to hear my voice, first, she said, it reminded her of the weird connection we had from Pusan back in May. She was strangely subdued and cool and when I told her I had to take a nonscheduled plane she didn't even sound worried. She might have shown some concern that her husband, after all the combat he went through, was flying nonschedule, the stinking reputation they had. She must have known how one crashed a week earlier right in the center of Brooklyn and a few weeks before that in Buffalo.

Dickie was doing "well as expected" she volunteered and sobbed a little just as the operator told me to drop in more quarters, which I didn't have and I was cut off without a chance to tell Kitty good bye. It was more unsettling than my call from Pusan and I worried when I hung up what she meant "well as expected."

The plane we flew in was an Army surplus C46, its large white star painted over but faintly visible under the light blue. Bucket seats facing the aisle were replaced by comfortable upholstered seats facing front, one row each side. As the pilot came over the loud speaker for us to prepare for takeoff—how to prepare he failed to say—our flight attendant came down the aisle telling us to buckle up because it was a law. She neglected to add what we knew she must have been thinking: "That's an order and don't you forget it!" Who would be brave enough to forget it despite the fact that being brave was a prerequisite for flying nonscheduled. A regular Wagnerian opera singer she was without her steel helmet—tall, chesty and blonde. Lieutenant Easly was astonished: "I just saw her outside handing up the luggage."

He passed me a pony of Seagram Seven for myself and we decided to take our minds off it. I was half in, half out of a drunken stupor in the middle of the night when we dropped down in the blackness of a moderately light snow storm rather suddenly on a ranch in the middle of Montana, a single floodlight guided us in as we landed in a foot of powder snow. "We're lucky," the intercom told us, "a big blizzard's coming close behind us." We taxied up to an old barn sporting Christmas lighting and gassed up at a Shell aviation gas pump. We made it up again blowing a snow screen behind and after another drunken, snoring sleep, landed at LaGuardia where Easly and I parted company. He had an hour wait to board a Pan American south to Atlanta.

There was nothing headed toward Syracuse, the nearest airport to Watertown and no trains until morning. I was lonely as hell in that large almost empty Christmas lighted airport waiting room at 0200, rehearsing over and over what to say to Kitty, until an off duty American Airline flight attendant stopped to tell me I looked lonely. I think she had other plans than I had but we chatted and when she found out my case, a sick little boy, she left and came right back excited, telling me to hurry with my bag, a special plane was leaving Newark for Syracuse with an extra crew to fly out a grounded plane. I was hustled to an American Airline transfer station wagon and got to Newark with the extra crew with fifteen minutes to spare, thanks to deserted streets. I was taken aboard, courtesy of the war effort, with a "Merry, Merry Christmas, you guys sure deserve one," a soldier in uniform returning home in distress, as a nonpaying passen ger (no one asked for my US Army voucher) signing a statement absolving American Airlines of any claims.

We arrived at Syracuse's Hancock Field about 0430, 23 December. I remember blinking, colored Christmas lights and an unlit manger scene. There was no train or bus headed north because of a dangerous blizzard off Lake Ontario. I took a cab to the Greyhound depot and was sitting in the waiting room feeling sorry for myself, trembling off and on with excitement and the thrill of being almost home after all those 'years' (it seemed) in a treacherous wasteland, when two guys in their early twenties came over and asked where I was headed. "Good," they said, "we're trying to get to Ogdensburg and need a little help with the gas since we bought two ten-gallon cans extra; there's no stations open this early in the morning going north. We can use your weight for better traction and might need help pushing out."

Snow was light until Pulaski halfway to Watertown where a sheriff pulled us over to tell us the highway north was closed. One of the guys pleaded: "Sir, we got a hero from Korea back there. He's on emergency leave and it's almost Christmas and his wife's very sick and they've been separated two years. We're trying to make it to Ogdensburg where a cousin's getting married tomorrow."

"Okay, okay, okay," the sheriff, an older man with a pot belly advised, throwing up his hands in mock defense. "There's two plowmen having coffee in the Star Diner up ahead. It's thirty miles to Watertown, they're pushing a big rotary and if you keep close in their wake, up close to their taillights, you got a chance, good luck. Wouldn't pay to lose their taillights; you'd be a snowplow yourself. Now you didn't hear me say nothing. I didn't see you sneak by."

Driving along with tons of snow blown high into the air over our right front reminded me of hugging taillights of the 155mm howitzers with their huge tractors on that liaison job to the Seventh Division. I enjoyed telling the young guys about it. The storm messed up radio reception and we chatted. The youngest, registered for the draft, wanted to know all about the Army and combat, and anything else that might make it easier to understand. He was a big, proud kid and didn't think he could take drill instructors shouting at him very well so I warned him to be prepared, emphasizing there was nothing personal about it; the DI had to do it. "DI, that's drill instructor."

Before I knew it, we were coming down Washington Street, main drag through Watertown ending at Public Square. I counted blocks starting with South Junior High School where I used to go, until Paddock, five blocks, and got my B-4 bag from their trunk and handed over the twenty agreed on and a five spot with the trunk key. They told me to keep the five and buy something for the kid but I refused to take it back. We were already old friends; like guys in a foxhole sweating out gooks, surviving the terror of that blizzard made us buddies. We'd been through one of life's tensest times together, a trip through a dangerous blizzard. Had the driver made a slip off a shoulder, a second's lack of attention losing the taillights, we'd have ended in a ditch and maybe, dressed the way we were, frozen to death before anyone found us. At least I daydreamed that.

"Damn it," I told them, "if it wasn't for you I'd still be on my ass in the waiting room. If there's anything I can ever do for either of you, let me know. You've got my phone number and address."

They swore the same and we waved, parting company in a blizzard which was petering out some. They called me collect the next day as I insisted to let me know they made it. In fact, the blizzard let up entirely about twenty miles north. They had coffee in Watertown at the State Street Diner and met the plowmen who knew we were back there behind them and were pleased we'd made it.

Sinking each step into a three-foot snow bank with snow filling my low-cut shoes and even down my shirt front, I struggled half a block with my bulging B-4 bag banging against my thigh and passed Kitty's apartment and came back two houses. Covered with snow, I entered the cellar vestibule of the garden apartment I'd never seen, thinking about the blizzard we had years ago when I was young and patriotic and left her folks house across Black river. When I tried my key which I wore on my dog tag chain along with my C ration can opener, it wouldn't go all the way. I banged softly and then louder and louder until a weak little voice asked: "Who's there? What do you want?"

"Me," I told her, "remember I called?"

"Me who?"

"Dud. Don't you recognize my voice?"

"What do you want?"

Want? What does that mean, I thought, what do I want? She lost her marbles?

"Let me in. I'm cold."

It didn't sound like my Kitty, so weak and mild, and low, somehow very sick or beaten.

"Is this Mrs Dudley C Gould? Kitty?"

"Yes."

She was there yet so far away, like being slugged in the gut; something terrible happened all right to lose her strong, youthful voice, happy lady of twenty-five. She sounded scared and beaten down like an old woman, or something worse.

"This is your husband, Dud. Please, honey, open up. It's cold and there's a big blizzard and my key won't fit."

The door of the apartment across the hall opened ten inches and a man's face demanded, "Who's there? Her husband's in Korea. Now get out of here. People are sleeping." He closed the door but, I felt, kept an ear to it.

"I *am* her husband," I told him over my shoulder.... "Honey, don't leave me standing here; my key won't fit."

"I know."

She opened the door slowly, and stood way back out of the draft and let me push it all the way as she backed further away, standing barefoot in a long pink flannel nightgown, eyes down, arms crossed tightly, squeezing herself, bent over, covering her breasts, hiding them as she shivered. I realized how cold her … that is, our … apartment was. I set my B-4 bag down on a cold air register by the door to let the snow melt. Kitty was a shock; hardly recognizable, so terribly gaunt, dark shadows under her eyes, her hair unkempt. She'd lost about fifteen pounds—twenty, I found out. Her depression, if that's what it was, was very apparent and how drab the chilly place, spiritless, as places are you dislike immediately. This was no home. There was no warmth or happiness there, not one Christmas decoration; much the opposite, cold and dark like a full body bag lying in the rain; and the thrill and excitement of anticipation and returning home turned suddenly to despair. "My God," I asked myself, "what's happened? How terribly haggard she is."

Dickie coughed and cried, "Mommy," from his small bedroom down the hall. Kitty disappeared and returned reluctantly, it seemed, with him, as though she wasn't sure that she should let me see him. Tucking a blue and white striped child's blanket around him, she hoisted him to her shoulder, his bare belly to her breasts, his face away from me, thumped his back rather vigorously, rhythmically, shaking back and forth, purring in a low monotone: "Honey, honey, honey, your mommy loves you. Mommy loves you, honey. There. There. There."

His coughing ceased; he kept sobbing quietly as he pulled on a little pink thumb with his lips. God, I remembered, how I suffered from mastoiditis when very young and how my poor mother put hot oil in my ear and held a tight warm flannel with Vicks Vaporub against it. Even after mother died, my father was up sometimes with me at night rocking me with bad earaches.

"What's the matter with the boy?" I asked, immediately biting my tongue, realizing how cold and aloof 'boy' was. Tough guys I knew—want someone killed? I just came from fighting a blizzard with two. As an infantry company commander in the throes of combat I knew how to be a tough-love father; how to push and lead them, to comfort them, wounded and dying men, but until trained by my wife I was worthless at home with a sick little boy. I felt awkward. Damn it, it's not the boy, it's our Dickie, two-year-old baby. I needed to redeem myself, say sweety or honey, be a natural father. Instead I was an outdoor lout standing there, a cold utter stranger to Kitty and Dickie, inside their home, a brutal senseless killer in this joyless, rear echelon, somehow feminine place. I had to say something that sounded like I really loved my son and wife but the shock at the signs of her suffering choked me.

Avoiding eye contact or addressing me, Kitty pulled her grandmother's old rocking chair away from the bookcase with one hand and sat down with Dickie, tucking his blanket to her body tightly all around and rocked. Several of our books, including a large, fairly expensive, world atlas, that is to us expensive, I bought after hearing of Korea, and several record albums on the bottom shelf had spines scraped off by her rocker, rocking, rocking rhythmically harder and harder, sliding backward into the bookshelf.

"Mommy loves you, honey. Honey, mommy loves you," and when she rocked harder, she began to cry softly in a patterned little whimper: "There, there, there, honey, mommy loves you. Don't worry, mommy loves you. Just you never mind. Everything will be all right."

Suddenly, she turned to me and I thought, as that night in Korea, I heard her again: "Don't worry, honey, everything will be all right."

"Honey, honey," I blurted. "Honey." My god, I thought, looking at the scraped book spines, how many cold nights like this, lonely, worried hours, did she have to rock that hard to keep her sanity? And it all hit me hard.

"Honey," I sobbed tearfully, "I'm awfully sorry for what I've done. I didn't realize I was killing you, too. What happened to me? I was crazy. Didn't mean anything I wrote sweety. I'm awful sorry," and, eyes full of regret, I collapsed forward on my knees and reached to stop her rocker and bent over to kiss away tears on the back of the hand that held our sick little boy to her bosom.

Printed in the USA
CPSIA information can be obtained
at www.ICGtesting.com
JSHW022204140824
68134JS00018B/862